RICH AND POOR IN RENAISSANCE VENICE

To the memory of
Sabina Ellis, 1898–1969

RICH AND POOR
IN RENAISSANCE VENICE

The Social Institutions of a Catholic State, to 1620

BRIAN PULLAN
Fellow of Queens' College, Cambridge
University Lecturer in History

HARVARD UNIVERSITY PRESS
Cambridge, Massachusetts
1971

© Basil Blackwell 1971

First Printed 1971

Library of Congress Catalog Card Number 70-133217

SBN 674-76940-6

Printed in Great Britain

PREFACE

I owe many thanks to those who have helped me to write this book during the past eleven years. An earlier version of the first of its three parts was presented for the Ph.D. degree of the University of Cambridge in 1962. Dr (now Professor) J. H. Elliott supervised my research in England in its early stages and gave much valuable initial encouragement, whilst Professor Gaetano Cozzi, with his great knowledge and wisdom, guided me into the subject in Venice and has for several years given me the benefit of his friendship and conversation. Professor H. G. Koenigsberger and the late Mr H. O. Evennett made kindly and constructive criticisms of the completed thesis. Professor D. M. Joslin has devoted time to reading and patiently criticizing an earlier draft of the third part of the work, lucidly advising me on several technical points. Professor Frederic C. Lane was kind enough to share with me his knowledge of the processes of recruitment to the Venetian navy, and to read a revised draft of the fifth chapter of Part I of this book.

At all times I have been delighted by the courtesy, cordiality and helpfulness of the archivists and librarians of Venice, where the great bulk of my work was done in the state archives preserved near the Frari, and by the generous hospitality of the Fondazione Giorgio Cini. I am much indebted to Dr Alessandro Mazzucato, Cancelliere of the Scuola Grande di San Rocco, for permission to examine the records preserved on the premises of the Scuola itself.

I am most grateful to those historians who have allowed me to consult their work before its publication—to Dr James C. Davis, Mrs Natalie Zemon Davis, Professor F. C. Lane, Dr O. M. T. Logan and Dr S. J. Woolf.

A State Studentship awarded by the Ministry of Education made the first two years of research possible. During the next two I enjoyed the support of the Master and Fellows of Trinity College, Cambridge, who (on the recommendation of their generous referees) awarded me a Research Fellowship in 1961, free of heavy teaching or administrative duties, and so enabled me to return to Venice for further archival research. The University of Cambridge, and the President and Fellows of Queens' College, always unfailingly kind, granted the sabbatical leave which allowed me to complete the book, whilst the Italian

v

government made a generous financial grant towards the cost of pursuing research at this final stage.

I am deeply grateful to Mr H. L. Schollick and Mrs Jane Montali for their care and patience in seeing the work through the press, and to Mr Alfred Rubens for his help in choosing illustrations for Part III.

My wife has worked with me in the Venetian archives, has allowed me to share the results of her own personal researches on the economy of certain parts of the Venetian mainland, and has at all times given me loyalty and encouragement. My debt to her is very great.

BRIAN PULLAN

CONTENTS

LIST OF ILLUSTRATIONS

MAPS

INTRODUCTION

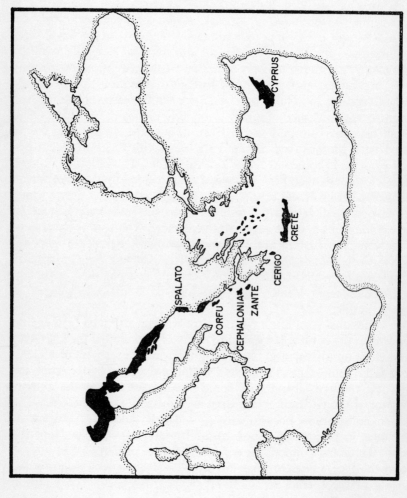

VENICE AND ITS DOMINIONS IN THE MEDITERRANEAN, C. 1550–70

INTRODUCTION

In the eyes of modern historians, the international importance of Venice in the sixteenth and in the early seventeenth century rests—as it once did in the eyes of contemporary observers—on at least three foundations: on her ancient role as an international entrepôt, with her more recently expanded activity as an industrial centre; on the stability of her government, independent of foreign domination in a peninsula overshadowed by the Habsburgs; and on her famous anti-clericalism.

Even in 1600, Venice retained something of her old position as an entrepôt between Europe and the East, despite the shocks long before suffered with the advance of the Turks and with the Portuguese discovery of oceanic routes to India and the Indies. It was left to English and Dutch traders, who both by-passed and invaded the Mediterranean in the first quarter of the seventeenth century, to deal the blows which eventually proved fatal, and to initiate in the economic history of Venice a long phase of at least relative decline. The true successors of Venice were, not Lisbon and Antwerp, but Amsterdam and London. The savage plagues of 1630 brought the decisive recessions in industry and agriculture, which had in the past century compensated at least in part for the losses Venice had sustained in traditional spheres of economic action.[1]

The Venetians' reputation for political wisdom survived further into the seventeenth century. It seemed to many observers that the character of Venice as an aristocratic republic, governed by members of a close-knit, legally defined patriciate, had undergone little change since the fourteenth century—if not, as some maintained, since the remote origins of the city itself more than a thousand years before.[2] The Venetian constitution occasionally provided a model for citizens of other states in periods of doubt, instability and experiment. Venetian organs—the Great Council, the Senate, the office of Doge—had offered hope to the Florentines in their attempts to fill the vacuum left by the expulsion of the Medici in 1494. To them, the Venetian constitution

[1] Cf. especially Domenico Sella, *Commerci e industrie a Venezia nel secolo XVII* (Venice–Rome, 1961), and the volume *Aspetti e cause della decadenza economica veneziana nel secolo XVII: Atti del Convegno 27 giugno—2 luglio 1957, Venezia, Isola di San Giorgio Maggiore* (Venice–Rome, 1961).

[2] On the 'myth of Venice' in general, see Franco Gaeta, 'Alcune considerazioni sul mito di Venezia', *Bibliothèque d'humanisme et Renaissance: travaux et documents*, XXIII (1961).

3

had presented no distant ideal, but had become the foundation of a practical programme—although the times had proved unpropitious for experiments with more open forms of government.[3] A few years later, the Venetian state had successfully resisted the alliance of great powers against it in the League of Cambrai of 1509, and had retained its character and autonomy more firmly than any other Italian state. By the 1530's, the Florentine Republic had given way to the Medicean Duchy of Tuscany and the Kingdom of Naples had become a Spanish Viceroyalty; by the middle of the century the Sforza Duchy of Milan had also succumbed to Spanish rule. Admittedly the Genoese retained their formal political independence, but they became the supreme symbols of Spain's economic influence in Italy—for the warrior nation of Castile, with its ambitious wars and inflated debts, had become their greatest source of profit. In the words of the Englishman, Fynes Moryson, 'if the King of Spayne not paying his debt to the Genoesi, or stopping the payments Course for a tyme, can make all them and their bancks breake and faile in creditt, I may boldly say he hath them fast bound in Fetters of gold'.[4]

The Venetians, however, had kept their 'liberty', in the sense of 'freedom from foreign domination', and claimed to extend 'liberty' to their subjects—in the sense of 'freedom from arbitrary oppression'. The widely circulated writings of Gasparo Contarini, the Venetian philosopher, diplomat and religious reformer, and of Donato Giannotti, who belonged to aristocratic circles in Florence, had elaborated the 'myth of Venice' which already existed embryonically and in unprinted works during the fifteenth century. Both their treatises were started in the 1520's and first published in the 1540's.[5] They portrayed the Venetian constitution as the classic modern instance of a 'mixed constitution' miraculously resistant to change and decay—Contarini

[3] Cf. the recent essays of Renzo Pecchioli, 'Il "mito" di Venezia e la crisi fiorentina intorno al 1500', *Studi Storici*, III (1962), and of Felix Gilbert, 'The Venetian constitution in Florentine political thought', in *Florentine studies: politics and society in Renaissance Florence*, ed. Nicolai Rubinstein (London, 1968). On the actual operation of the adopted constitution, see Nicolai Rubinstein, 'I primi anni del Consiglio Maggiore di Firenze', *Archivio Storico Italiano*, CXII (1954); Nicolai Rubinstein, 'Politics and constitution in Florence at the end of the fifteenth century', in *Italian Renaissance Studies: a tribute to the late Cecilia M. Ady*, ed. E. F. Jacob (London, 1960); Cecil Roth, *The Last Florentine Republic, 1527–1530* (London, 1925), pp. 49 f.

[4] Fynes Moryson, *Shakespeare's Europe*, ed. Charles Hughes (London, 1903), p. 113.

[5] Gasparo Contarini, *De magistratibus et republica Venetorum libri quinque* (Basel, 1547); Donato Giannotti, *Libro de la Republica de Vinitiani* (Rome, 1542). Quotations from Contarini are taken from the English translation by Lewes Lewkenor, *The commonwealth and government of Venice* (London, 1599). Page references will be given to both editions. Cf. Felix Gilbert, 'The date of the composition of Contarini's and Giannotti's books on Venice', *Studies in the Renaissance*, XIV (1967).

writing as if the political structure of Venice had been fully evolved in the first years of the city's existence, though Giannotti showed far greater historical sense.[6] According to this interpretation, the Venetians had found in government the ideal combination of the One, the Few and the Many. The Doge himself provided the monarchical element of the One; the Great Council of all noblemen the democratic element of the Many; the Senate, the Collegio and the Council of Ten the aristocratic element of the Few.[7] Later in the century, Jean Bodin, directly attacking Contarini, had reverted to the view of the Venetian constitution as a pure aristocracy, manned by a very restricted group of noblemen, rather than as a mixed polity.[8] But this reconstruction of the myth did not destroy it. In the early seventeenth century, it flourished in the writings of Giovanni Botero, who still followed in Contarini's tracks, and in those of Traiano Boccalini, who explained the survival and stability of Venice chiefly in terms of the solidarity of the ruling class and of the devotion of Venetian patricians to the service of their state.[9] Later still, Venetian institutions provided a model both for De Witt in the United Provinces and for English parliamentarians during the Civil Wars and the Interregnum—especially during the years 1657–60. The monarchist Robert Filmer might treat the legend with scepticism, but Harrington, in his *Oceana*, wrote of Venice as an 'immortal Common-wealth' 'forever uncapable of corruption'. Years afterwards, those who planned the constitutions of Carolina and Pennsylvania could still look with interest to the Venetian Republic.[10]

Venetian anti-clericalism, a third pillar of the Republic's international reputation, proved more remarkable in the sixteenth and seventeenth centuries than in the late Middle Ages. Most Italian communes

[6] Cf. Z. S. Fink, *The classical republicans: an essay in the recovery of a pattern of thought in seventeenth-century England* (Evanston, Illinois, 1945), p. 38. Giannotti writes of three ages in Venetian history—the first, that of the Doges and tribunes; the second, in which the Great Council existed, but was not closed; the third, when the Great Council was closed—*Libro de la Republica*, f. 19v.

[7] Contarini, *Commonwealth*, English version, pp. 18–19; Latin version, pp. 32–3. Giannotti, *Libro de la Republica*, ff. 21–2.

[8] Cf. Elio Gianturco, 'Bodin's conception of the Venetian constitution and his critical rift with Fabio Albergati', *Revue de littérature comparée*, XVIII (1938). For earlier views of the Venetian state as an aristocracy, see Gilbert, 'The Venetian constitution', pp. 470–1.

[9] Giovanni Botero, *Relatione della Republica Venetiana* (Venice, 1605); Traiano Boccalini, *Ragguagli di Parnaso, con la Pietra del Paragone Politico*, ed. G. Rua and Luigi Firpo (3 vols., Bari, 1910, 1912, 1948). See also Gaeta, 'Alcune considerazioni', p. 72; Brian Pullan, 'Service to the Venetian state: aspects of myth and reality in the early seventeenth century', *Studi Secenteschi*, V (1964).

[10] Cf. Z. S. Fink, 'Venice and English political thought in the seventeenth century', *Modern Philology*, XXXVIII (1940–1); Fink, *The classical republicans*; J. R. Hale, *England and the Italian Renaissance* (London, 1963), pp. 31–4.

had come into existence only through diminishing the temporal authority of local bishops, and in the fourteenth and fifteenth centuries anti-clerical parties, determined to free their states from clerical influence, had certainly flourished, not only in Venice, but also in Florence and Milan.[11] But, in the years of the Counter Reformation, the anti-clericalism of the Venetians shone with a new brilliance—through the activities of the party known as the *giovani* or 'young men', through Paolo Sarpi's political philosophy, and through the successful defiance of Pope Paul V despite the Interdict of 1606–7. In the *giovani* of Venice, whose influence increased after a constitutional crisis in 1582–1583, the great historian Ranke saw an Italian parallel to the Politiques who raised Henry IV to the throne of France. Here, in Venice, it 'happened that the idea of a sacerdotal religion, supreme over all other authority, was encountered by a mighty opposition from that national independence which is the proper expression of the secular element in society'.[12] Generally, Venice had by the early seventeenth century become a symbol of just and peaceful government and of praiseworthy independence—for all who hated Spain and for all who feared the influence of the Papacy and its militant henchmen, the Jesuits. Those who did not share these sentiments fostered a counter-myth: one laying the heaviest emphasis on the tensions which really existed within the Republic, and on the tyrannical nature of patrician government in Venice.[13]

Historical knowledge of Venice in the sixteenth and seventeenth centuries has advanced on several fronts—its economic, political and diplomatic history have become far better known in the past forty years. But historians have still tended to inquire chiefly into the activi-

[11] See below, pp. 60, n., 128.

[12] Leopold von Ranke, *The history of the Popes during the last four centuries*, transl. Foster, revised by G. R. Dennis (London, 1908), II, pp. 13 f. The ideals of the *giovani* and the careers of some of their leaders have recently been studied in the political biographies by Gaetano Cozzi, *Il Doge Nicolò Contarini: ricerche sul patriziato veneziano agli inizi del Seicento* (Venice–Rome, 1958), and by Federico Seneca, *Il Doge Leonardo Donà: la sua vita e la sua preparazione politica prima del Dogado* (Padua, 1959).

[13] Cf. the *Squitinio della libertà veneta, nel quale si adducono anche le ragioni dell' Impero Romano sopra la città e Signoria di Venetia* (Mirandola, 1612); the *Relatione universa delle cose di Venetia fatta da Don Alonso della Cueva, Ambasciadore di Spagna, hoggi Cardinale*, one version of which is contained in British Museum, Additional MSS. 5471, ff. 140–201; Italo Raulich, 'Una relazione del Marchese di Bedmar sui Veneziani', *Nuovo Archivio Veneto*, XVI (1898). For comments see also Juan Beneyto, *Fortuna de Venecia: historia de una fama política* (Madrid, 1947), pp. 79 f.; Gaeta, 'Alcune considerazioni', p. 74.

ties of the patriciate, rather than to examine in much detail its relationship with its subjects, or to discuss the popular institutions of Venice.
The patrician regime of Venice remained mysteriously immune from
any kind of serious disturbance from below—from popular rebellions,
or from attempts by persons on the middle rungs of the social ladder
either to subvert the aristocratic state or to force their way into the
ruling class. This phenomenon cannot be explained in terms of the
flexibility of Venice's social system. For Venetian men, nobility was
equated with membership of the Great Council—or rather, with the
hereditary right to enter it on reaching the age of twenty-five. The right
to participate in the making of policy, to propose and vote upon laws
and decrees, ultimately depended on entry to the Great Council, which,
in theory at least, created and appointed to all magisterial posts.
Between 1381 and 1646, the Venetian nobility remained virtually a
closed caste, admitting to its ranks only a few honorary recruits not
seriously expected to take part in Venetian government. Between the
mid-sixteenth and the mid-seventeenth century, ultimate sovereignty
resided in an order whose numbers varied between some 2,500 in 1550
and about 1,700 soon after the plague of 1630–1. It was confined to
between 1 per cent and $1\frac{1}{2}$ per cent of the population of Venice. This
small, rigorously defined sector of the Venetian people did not replenish
itself with new talent or wealth from below, except through a certain
amount of intermarriage with non-patricians.[14]

Gasparo Contarini himself was fully aware of the need to explain
this mystery of how so exclusive a ruling class had succeeded in maintaining itself in unchallenged authority for so many years. It was

a matter surely strange and scarcely credible, that the people being so
many years deprived of the publique government, did never yet refuse nor
unwillingly support the government of the nobilitie, neither yet did ever
attempt any thing whereby the form of the common-wealth might be
altered, and they received into the fellowshippe of rule, but have always
hetherto faithfully loved and willingly obeyed the Nobilitie.

He himself offered a standard explanation for the immunity of the
Venetian aristocracy from disturbance, which was later repeated and
slightly elaborated both by Bodin and by Botero. The Venetians
showed especial skill in guaranteeing their subjects justice, peace and
plenty—by the impartial administration of justice, by severely punish-
ing the great for molesting the humble, by ensuring that there were
adequate supplies of corn and other victuals, and by the efficient relief

[14] For the general theme, see J. C. Davis, *The decline of the Venetian nobility as a
ruling class* (Baltimore, Maryland, 1962).

B

of the poor: 'especially of such that eyther presently do, or at any time have employed themselves in honest trades of use and service to the commonwealth, and grow at length eyther by age or weaknesse unable to persever therein. . . .' Moreover, the Venetian nobility skilfully contrived to admit its underlings to substitutes for political power. They were allowed to graduate to a measure of honour and authority in certain institutions made peculiarly their own, but which were nevertheless skilfully contained within their proper limits by the patrician regime, and were caused to contribute usefully to the social and political structure of the state. Among these were the guilds, the great religious and charitable fraternities known as the Scuole Grandi, and the permanent civil service (monopolized by a non-patrician élite).[15]

Later analysts of the Venetian constitution proved unable to devise a better explanation for Venetian stability. Bodin remarked on the difficulty of satisfying subjects without admitting them to the estates: but it was 'impossible to concede honourable charges to them without converting the aristocracy into a popular state'. Hence

> in order to preserve their aristocratic form of state, the Venetians threw open certain minor offices to the people, intermarried with them, created a state debt to give them a vested interest in the regime, and totally disarmed them.[16]

Botero, too, asked what compensations were offered to non-noble Venetians for their exclusion from political rights. He, too, suggested that the energies of non-patricians were absorbed by their admission to minor offices, and pointed out that their part in administering Venetian charities, in which they frequently collaborated with noblemen, fostered in them a sense of involvement in the communal life of Venice. The charity itself bred in the poorer Venetians a feeling of security, and the state was careful to take to itself the credit for the charity, so that no individual had the chance to win subversive popular acclaim by his generous acts. On the lower social levels, loyalty was inspired in the people by their opportunities for obtaining honourable posts in the Arsenal or in the police force of the Council of Ten.[17] There was even —or so Botero believed—a certain substitute for democracy in the right of Venetian householders to elect their own parish priests.[18] In short, the genius of Venice lay, not in ability to exclude almost everyone

---

[15] Contarini, *Commonwealth*, English version, pp. 138 f.; Latin version, pp. 190 f.
[16] Jean Bodin, *Six books of the Commonwealth*, Book VI, ch. 4, ch. 6, ed. M. J. Tooley (Oxford, 1955), pp. 194–5, 209.
[17] Botero, *Relatione*, ff. 41, 97, 107–8.
[18] *Ibid.*, f. 98: cf. also Bartolomeo Cecchetti, *La Repubblica di Venezia e la Corte di Roma nei rapporti della religione* (2 vols., Venice, 1874), I, pp. 443–4.

8

from office and authority, but in skill at admitting so many subordinates to places of honour which in no way violated the monopoly of genuine political power enjoyed by the chosen patricians. Venice, indeed, met Botero's stock requirements for survival, which echoed Contarini's: a state must secure for its subjects, 'justice, peace, plenty, and a certain honourable liberty which is in no way licentious or undisciplined'.[19]

In some respects, Contarini exaggerated the stability of the Venetian Republic, and projected it much too far back in time. There was no truth in his suggestion that

> from the first beginning till this time of ours it hath remained safe and free this thousand and two hundred years, not only from the domination of Straungers, but also from all civile and intestine sedition of any moment or weight.[20]

The fourteenth-century conspiracies of Baiamonte Tiepolo and of the Doge Marino Falier were in themselves enough to give the lie to such a contention. But Contarini's treatise could not have become the foundation for a 'myth of Venice' had not the city in fact remained, in the century or so after he wrote, remarkably free of such troubles. There were occasional riots. In the famines of 1569–70, the Venetian people expressed violent resentment against the Doge, Pietro Loredan, in whose name they had been offered loaves made from millet, instead of the usual wheat.[21] Arsenal workers occasionally rioted, as in 1581, for better pay.[22] In 1602, alarming upheavals occurred when the normal coinage system broke down, and when bakers refused to accept the debased coins which the people tendered in payment for their bread.[23] But these disturbances were no more than an immediate and instinctive protest against acute but temporary disorders. In discussing relations between the city of Venice and its subject provinces, Contarini undoubtedly over-estimated the loyalty shown by subordinate cities to the Dominante.[24] In his own time, in 1511, a serious peasant revolt broke out in the province of Friuli—but this was directed against the local feudatories, rather than at the Venetian government. In general, during the prolonged crisis which followed the war of the League of

---

[19] Botero, *Relatione*, f. 74; see also his *The greatness of cities*, Book III, ch. 3, reprint of the English translation by Robert Peterson, 1606 (London, 1956), p. 280.

[20] Contarini, *Commonwealth*, English version, p. 146; Latin version, p. 202.

[21] See below, pp. 288–9, 295.

[22] See Brian Pullan, 'Wage-earners and the Venetian economy, 1550–1630', *Economic History Review*, XVI (1964), p. 420.

[23] Nicolò Contarini, *Historie Venetiane*, published extracts in Cozzi, *Il Doge Nicolò Contarini*, pp. 356 f.

[24] Contarini, *Commonwealth*, English version, pp. 147–8; Latin version, pp. 202–203.

Cambrai, peasants and lesser townspeople showed a high degree of loyalty—whatever their motives—to the Venetians.[25]

Again, despite external appearances, some constitutional crises did occur. They took the form of collisions between groups of men who had based their influence upon different organs in the Venetian government, and who sought to define and exploit the powers of their particular council in the manner most advantageous to them. In 1582–3, a party of relatively 'young' nobles entrenched in the Senate succeeded in curtailing the authority of the gerontocracy centred on the Council of Ten, and in destroying its control of the Mint.[26] Later, in 1627–8, a formidable leader, Renier Zeno, mustered a large following of many poor nobles in the Great Council to protest against the failure of the Council of Ten to exercise impartially the exclusive jurisdiction it claimed over all criminal offences committed by noblemen.[27] But these crises happened on the noble and aristocratic level, with little or no trace of popular intervention. The noble insurgents claimed only to be saving the hallowed constitution from perversion, and nobody wanted to raze its foundations by substituting popular for patrician government.

This book will attempt to increase understanding of Venetian history through a study of government policy towards the poor, and through the examination of certain social institutions which included charity and poor relief among their functions: institutions managed, not only by Venetian patricians, but also by persons recruited from lower social levels. Several of these institutions did not confine their activities to poor relief, but carried out, in addition to this, a variety of other religious, economic and fiscal tasks. Their efforts on behalf of the poor can only be properly understood by placing them in the general context of Venetian history. A study which deals, among other things, with the problem of the poor can, moreover, throw a certain light on a broader historical question not confined to the Venetian

[25] For a useful synthesis of evidence, with many references, see Angelo Ventura, *Nobiltà e popolo nella società veneta del '400 e '500* (Bari, 1964), ch. 4; but cf. the criticisms of C. H. Clough, *Studi Veneziani*, VIII (1966).

[26] On this crisis, see Mauro Macchi, *Istoria del Consiglio dei Dieci* (Turin, 1848–9, 2 vols.), II, pp. 90–3; Enrico Besta, *Il Senato Veneziano* (Venice, 1899), pp. 146 f.; Samuele Romanin, *Storia documentata di Venezia* (10 vols., Venice, 1912–21), VI, pp. 365–7; Aldo Stella, 'La regolazione delle pubbliche entrate e la crisi politica veneziana del 1582', in *Miscellanea in onore di Roberto Cessi*, II (Rome, 1958).

[27] The fullest account of the Zeno movement appears in Cozzi, *Il Doge Nicolò Contarini*, ch. 6; this has replaced the earlier account in Romanin, *Storia di Venezia*, VII, pp. 200–37.

Republic—the question of the treatment of the poor in a Roman Catholic society in the ages of the Reformation and Counter Reformation.

Certain generalizations made in the past about the difference between Catholic and Protestant attitudes to the poor have proved very persistent, although they originated with sociologists rather than with historians, and although they have sometimes been partially discredited by the examination of philanthropy and poor relief as practised in particular European societies.[28] To use Troeltsch's terminology, the Roman Catholic Church is associated with the practice of mere 'charity', and the Protestant churches in general are credited with the formulation of a more far-reaching 'social policy'.[29] In general, Catholicism is made to stand for individual action and for clerical control of the principal endowed charitable institutions, Protestantism for a more scientific form of state intervention designed to promote more vigorously the welfare of the poor themselves, and hence to further the good of society.[30] Far-reaching consequences have been attributed to the Catholic doctrine that good works actually contribute to the salvation of the persons who perform them. Hence, the charitable man in the Roman Catholic society is accused of being concerned chiefly with the acquisition of merit for himself, and of not caring whether the alms he gives have a demoralizing effect on the person who receives them.[31] The Catholic Church is charged with having no

[28] Important recent contributions to the debate include Emmanuel Chill, 'Religion and mendicity in seventeenth-century France', *International Review of Social History*, VII (1962); and Natalie Zemon Davis, 'Poor relief, humanism and heresy—the case of Lyon', *Studies in Medieval and Renaissance History*, V (1968). I am much indebted to Mrs Davis for allowing me to see the typescript of her article before its publication.

[29] See Ernst Troeltsch, *The social teaching of the Christian churches*, transl. Olive Wyon (London–New York, 1931), I, pp. 133–6.

[30] For various expressions of this view, see Albert Emminghaus, *Poor relief in different parts of Europe* (London, 1873), p. 13; F. S. Nitti, 'Poor relief in Italy', *The Economic Review*, II (1892), p. 18; Troeltsch, *Social teaching*, II, pp. 557, 565–567; Shailer Mathews, 'The Protestant churches and charity', in Ellsworth Faris, Ferris Laune and Arthur J. Todd, *Intelligent philanthropy* (Chicago, 1930), p. 121; F. M. Hník, *The philanthropic motive in Christianity*, transl. M. and R. Weatherall (Oxford, 1938), p. 32; R. H. Bremner, 'Modern attitudes towards charity and relief', *Comparative studies in society and history*, I (1958–9), p. 377. It ought to be said that of these writers Emminghaus and Troeltsch confined themselves to suggesting that the Reformation ought to have advanced the rational treatment of poverty, but in practice failed to do so. The others have been somewhat bolder. See also below, pp. 197 f.

[31] Nitti, 'Poor relief in Italy', pp. 4–6; W. J. Ashley, *An introduction to English economic history and theory*, II (London, 1893), pp. 312–16, 340; J. A. Ryan, art. 'Charity', *The Catholic Encyclopedia*, III (New York, 1908), p. 600; Brian Tierney, *Medieval poor law: a sketch of canonical theory and its application in England* (Berkeley–Los Angeles, 1959), pp. 46 f.

desire to eliminate poverty, because of its anxiety to preserve opportunities for the rich to be charitable.[32] Allegedly, if constructive schemes for poor relief were ever devised in Roman Catholic societies of the sixteenth century, they were formulated in spite of the Church and not through its efforts. On the other hand, the Protestant Churches are supposed to have moved towards more rational poor relief, its value determined only by its beneficial effects on the poor and on the society of which giver and receiver form part—not by its profiting the soul of the giver. The willingness of certain Protestant churches to delegate the solution of social problems to the lay magistrate is believed to have contributed to the laicization of poor relief, and to have opened the way to extensive state intervention in that sphere.

The study of Venetian social institutions provides further opportunities for testing the validity of some of these assumptions about the nature of poor relief in a Catholic society. The book is divided into three main sectors. The first deals with the Scuole Grandi of Venice—the Venetian version of a form of religious fraternity, the Scuola dei Battuti or Scuola dei Disciplinati, which was very widespread in Italy. The origins of these Scuole were rooted in the thirteenth century, but this type of association survived and retained its popularity well into the sixteenth and seventeenth centuries, coexisting with the many newer forms of organization introduced from the mid-fifteenth century onwards. The Scuole dei Disciplinati were societies through which the pious combined to do in concert all the things—including poor relief—popularly believed to contribute to the salvation of the souls of those who did them. Their scriptural inspiration was the General Epistle of James—the part of the Gospel on which Luther chose to place the lowest value.[33] They followed some of the principles most repugnant to disciples of Luther and Calvin: for that reason their methods can be regarded as a good test case. In the early sixteenth century, Gasparo Contarini singled them out for special mention: they provided the non-patricians of Venice with excellent opportunities for the fulfilment of their ambitions and for the attainment of an honourable place in Venetian society.[34]

The second and third parts of this work deal with the innovations in poor relief introduced between the mid-fifteenth and the early seventeenth century, and attempt to analyse the new principles introduced at

[32] Cf. Troeltsch, *Social teaching*, I, p. 253; Max Weber, *The Protestant ethic and the spirit of capitalism*, transl. Talcott Parsons (London–New York, 1930), pp. 177–8.

[33] See below, pp. 41–2; for Luther's opinion of James, see his 'Preface to the New Testament' and 'Preface to the Epistle of James', in B. L. Woolf, *Reformation writings of Martin Luther* (2 vols., London, 1954–6), pp. 283, 306–8.

[34] See below, pp. 107–8.

this time. The second part deals chiefly with projects which aimed at the control and alleviation of severe and dangerous poverty through the discipline and education of the poor. It attempts to analyse the religious, intellectual and economic motives which inspired these forms of poor relief. The third and last section of the book deals with another form of highly organized relief which also developed significantly from the mid-fifteenth century onwards—in the attempts made by public authorities to provide cheap credit for the poor and impecunious to tide them over temporary crises or embarrassments, and to control indebtedness by making low-interest loan banks available to them. This purpose was generally achieved either through retaining the services of Jewish bankers, or through the establishment of communally controlled Christian pawnshops known as Monti di Pietà.

The dominating city of Venice was a Catholic society exposed, like many others, to international religious movements which transcended the boundaries of particular nations and states. In some respects, Venice adopted its own highly individual solution to social problems; in others, it proved to be fairly conventional. To see it in perspective, it is necessary to compare Venetian developments with those that occurred in the subject cities of the Republic on the mainland of Italy, and to note certain significant differences between them. In such matters as poor relief, the subject cities were to a large extent left to make their own arrangements, provided these were submitted to Venice for ratification. This book does not pretend to offer an exhaustive survey of social institutions in the cities of the Venetian Terra Ferma: it will discuss them only in outline, and the discussion will be based almost entirely on Venetian sources—on what the Venetians themselves were able to know about the arrangements for poor relief in their own provinces. At the most, one can only hope to prepare the way for further monographs founded on local as well as on Venetian archives, and to sketch some kind of general perspective in which these may be set. It will, unfortunately, be impossible to relate these institutions fully enough to the societies in which they were established—although some hints can be offered to throw light on the matter.

As yet, one important potential source of information about Venetian philanthropy has had to be largely neglected. Professor Jordan's studies of English philanthropy have demonstrated the possibilities inherent in the systematic study of wills.[35] It would, however, be impossible to interpret the material contained in Venetian wills without first under-

---

[35] For the general principles, see the first volume in the series, W. K. Jordan, *Philanthropy in England, 1480–1660* (London, 1959).

13

standing the nature of the institutional machinery available to testators who chose to make bequests to charitable uses, and without examining the relationship between public poor relief and private charity. Wills can never tell the whole story. The study of institutions can complement the study of wills by conveying some impression of how Venetians bestowed charity in their own lifetimes, of how they devoted themselves to the service of the poor, of how faithfully bequests were administered, and of how the 'aspirations' of testators and donors were actually realized. Moreover, there were clearly some forms of poor relief which in no way depended on the gifts or legacies of charitable Christians: surely Christians did not make bequests out of charitable motives to Jewish bankers, and yet Jewish bankers relieved the poor by providing a cheap loan service under state supervision. This book may, perhaps, succeed in outlining some of the considerations to be borne in mind before the evidence of wills can be properly interpreted.

To present the history of these social institutions in its Venetian context, and to make the discussion easier to follow, the next few pages will briefly examine some of the principal features of the political and economic structure of the Venetian Republic from the late fifteenth to the early seventeenth century. Certain economic and political developments will be more closely discussed at a later stage, where they seem especially relevant to the story of particular institutions or governmental measures.

At the close of the fifteenth century, Venice was a powerful, aristocratically governed city state, which had built up immense wealth primarily through entrepôt trade, and had acquired two empires: one, a string of colonies and naval bases extended down the east coast of the Adriatic round the Balkan peninsula and into the eastern Mediterranean; the other, a substantial dominion stretching westwards across the Lombard plain to the borders of the Duchy of Milan. The foundations of the maritime empire had been laid with the dismemberment of Byzantine possessions at the Fourth Crusade in the early thirteenth century. The westward advance of the Turks, especially in the years 1463 to 1479, had caused Venice heavy losses in the east, and these losses were to continue during the sixteenth century—though the acquisition, in 1489, of formal sovereignty over Cyprus partially compensated for them, until Cyprus, too, fell to the Turks in 1571. The Italian empire of the Venetians was the fruit of a policy of more active intervention in the peninsular power struggle, undertaken from the early fifteenth century onwards: partly, but perhaps not wholly, out of a desire to protect vital trade routes into Europe from the threats of potentially hostile Italian princes.

In the late fifteenth century, oriental trade was the most spectacular and profitable of Venetian enterprises, and the one most deeply characteristic of Venice—though it did not account for most of the movement of the port, in which such relatively mundane commodities as salt, grain and timber occupied a larger place.[36] Venice dealt in spices, cotton, silk, drugs and jewels, and also in the fruit, wine and other produce of her own colonies. She supplied eastern raw materials to European industries, and exported European metals and manufactures to the Levant in exchange. In the early sixteenth century, however, the news that Portuguese navigators had discovered oceanic routes round the Cape of Good Hope to India and the Indies caused profound pessimism in Venice itself: for this threatened to destroy the position of the Mediterranean as the great channel of intercontinental trade, and hence to replace the Venetians as the principal intermediaries between Europe and the East. Portuguese competition undoubtedly contributed to a very prolonged depression in the Venetian spice trade, lasting until the early 1530's. However, towards the middle of the century, there were signs of a significant revival in the Egyptian spice route exploited by the Venetians, and the Syrian route was also re-established by the end of the sixteenth century.[37] In the later sixteenth century, the Mediterranean and oceanic routes appear to have competed on reasonably even terms, each suffering its bad years, often as a result of changes in the political situation, and of outbreaks of war or piracy on either route.[38] Despite severe competition from within the

[36] Cf. Gino Luzzatto, 'Le vicende del Porto di Venezia dal primo Medio Evo allo scoppio della guerra 1914–1918', in his *Studi di storia economica veneziana* (Padua, 1954), pp. 7–8. The question of the economic fortunes of Venice at this time is more fully discussed in the Introduction to *Crisis and change in the Venetian economy*, ed. Brian Pullan (London, 1968). Several essays on the subject are reproduced there, some in revised versions.

[37] The classic essays of Professor Lane on this subject, 'Venetian shipping during the commercial revolution' and 'The Mediterranean spice trade: its revival in the sixteenth century', first appeared in *American Historical Review*, XXXVIII (1933) and XLV (1940), and are reproduced in *Venice and history: the collected papers of Frederic C. Lane* (Baltimore, Maryland, 1966) and in Pullan, *Crisis and change*. For details of the depression in the first third of the century, see Vetorino Magalhães-Godinho, 'Le repli vénitien et la route du Cap, 1496–1533', *Éventail de l'histoire vivante: hommage à Lucien Febvre*, II (Paris, 1953). On the Syrian route, see Ugo Tucci, *Lettres d'un marchand vénitien: Andrea Berengo (1553–1556)* (Paris, 1957), pp. 9–18; Fernand Braudel, *La Méditerranée et le monde méditerranéen à l'époque de Philippe II* (2nd, enlarged edition, Paris, 1966), I, pp. 512–14.

[38] See Hermann Kellenbenz, 'Autour de 1600: le commerce du poivre des Fugger et le marché international du poivre', *Annales: Économies, Sociétés, Civilisations*, XI (1956); Braudel, *La Méditerranée*, I, pp. 493–516.

Mediterranean, and especially from Ragusa and Marseilles,[39] the Venetians were still able to continue some of the traditional activities on which they had long relied to bring wealth into Venice. In the late sixteenth century, Venetian merchants were firmly established in Constantinople, Alexandria and Aleppo, with some concerns pressing further eastwards.[40]

Nevertheless, during the sixteenth century, significant changes occurred in Venetian economic activity—in all probability, the Venetian people came to derive a higher proportion of their wealth from textile industries producing for the export market and not merely to meet local needs, and also from more intensive landed investment in the provinces immediately to the west of Venice on the Italian mainland. Before the sixteenth century, shipbuilding had been Venice's chief industrial activity, supporting her function as a maritime power. But private shipbuilding, catering for the merchant marine, began to suffer heavily in the last thirty years of the sixteenth century, when the shortage of timber in regions accessible to Venice prevented the Venetians from easily replacing losses inflicted during the war with the Turks in 1570–3 and later by English and Dutch pirates in the Mediterranean. The Arsenal, where warships were constructed, competed with private shipbuilding enterprises for limited supplies of labour and materials, and in all probability the Arsenal gained at the expense of the merchant marine. The Venetian navy, nonetheless, failed to provide adequate protection to merchant shipping against the ravages of pirates. Although, up to the decade 1560–70, the absolute number of Arsenal employees increased, and so did the proportion they bore to the total population of Venice, they began to fall off over the period 1591–1641.[41]

[39] See N. Mirkovich, 'Ragusa and the Portuguese spice trade', *The Slavonic and East European Review*, XXI (1943); Jorjo Tadić, 'Le port de Raguse et sa flotte au XVIe siècle', in *Le navire et l'économie maritime du Moyen-Âge au XVIIIe siècle, principalement en Méditerranée: Travaux du Deuxième Colloque d'Histoire Maritime*, ed. Michel Mollat (Paris, 1958); René Gascon, 'Un siècle du commerce des épices à Lyon: fin XVe—fin XVIe siècles', *Annales: Économies, Sociétés, Civilisations*, XV (1960); Sella, *Commerci e industrie*, pp. 5–6.

[40] Mirkovich, 'Ragusa and the spice trade', pp. 185–6; Ugo Tucci, 'Mercanti veneziani in India alla fine del secolo XVI', *Studi in onore di Armando Sapori*, II (Milan, 1957); Braudel, *La Méditerranée*, I, p. 514.

[41] See Lane, 'Venetian shipping'; F. C. Lane, *Venetian ships and shipbuilders of the Renaissance* (Baltimore, Maryland, 1934), pp. 217 f.; Ruggiero Romano, 'La marine marchande vénitienne au XVIe siècle', in *Les sources de l'histoire maritime en Europe, du Moyen Âge au XVIIIe siècle: Actes du Quatrième Colloque International d'Histoire Maritime*, ed. Michel Mollat (Paris, 1962); Alberto Tenenti, *Naufrages, corsaires et assurances maritimes à Venise, 1592–1609* (Paris, 1959), Introduction; Alberto Tenenti, *Piracy and the decline of Venice, 1580–1615*, transl. Janet and Brian Pullan (London, 1967); Ruggiero Romano, 'Economic aspects of the construction of warships in Venice in the sixteenth century', in Pullan, *Crisis and change*.

However, for the decline of shipbuilding and for the temporary misfortunes of Venetian commerce there were ample compensations in the expansion of a woollen industry producing broadcloth for markets in the Levant. Even in the 1430's, the Venetians had exported cloth, but their own output had been dwarfed by the much larger quantities of woollen textiles passing through Venice to the East from Flanders, France, England and even Catalonia.[42] Between 1520 and 1570, however, the Venetian textile industry profited from the misfortunes of established centres in Lombardy and Tuscany, and, together with the expanding Arsenal, helped to employ the growing population of the city, which increased from about 115,000 in 1509 to nearly 170,000 in 1563. The growth of the textile industry did not continue after 1570, but, apart from temporary recessions caused by the Turkish war of 1570–3 and by the plague of 1575–7, output remained on a high level until the early seventeenth century. Marked decline set in only after 1620, and seems to have become inevitable only after the plague of 1630 reduced the labour force and increased wage-costs at a time when the industry was facing exceptionally stiff foreign competition.[43] In the fifteenth century, the Venetians had possessed other promising industries—the manufacture of glass, both for utilitarian ends and for the luxury market; the weaving of silks, brocades and damasks; leatherwork; sugar refining; the preparation of soap and candle-wax.[44] But the vicissitudes of these trades are harder to plot. It seems clear, however, that especially through the developed woollen industry Venetian manufacturing was beginning to sustain the city's commerce with the Levant, rather than merely be incidental to it.

The increasing population of Venice, which had fed manpower into the woollen industry, also demanded, especially between about 1540 and 1570, the heavier investment of capital in agricultural enterprises on the mainland, encouraged by public policy, and designed to increase the cultivated area. Extensive Venetian investment in land continued even when, after the mid-1570's and their widespread plague visitations, population pressure had become somewhat lighter. It may have been inspired by the fact that grain prices remained buoyant for some years afterwards, as a result of foul weather and of increased difficulty in procuring grain from abroad; by the desire to take money out of

[42] See Gino Luzzatto, *Storia economica di Venezia dall'XI al XVI secolo* (Venice, 1961), pp. 190–2, 257.

[43] See Pierre Sardella, 'L'épanouissement industriel de Venise au XVIe siècle', *Annales: Économies, Sociétés, Civilisations*, II (1947); Domenico Sella, 'The rise and fall of the Venetian woollen industry', revised English version in Pullan, *Crisis and change*; C. M. Cipolla, 'The economic decline of Italy', *ibid.*

[44] Cf. Luzzatto, *Storia economica di Venezia*, pp. 192–203.

banks and bonds and invest it in a security, such as land, which would not lose value in a period of inflation; or by a certain eagerness to pursue the prestige which clings to landownership and the accompanying sense of having occupied a social position independent of the hazards of commercial, industrial or financial speculation.[45]

Despite these changes of direction, and this alteration in Venetian investment habits, the activity of Venice as a port remained very considerable, at least during the last twenty years of the sixteenth century. During this time, however, it is probable that a lower proportion of Venetian trade was in the hands of native Venetians or of persons long domiciled in Venice. Venice proved to be something of an 'open' society, prepared to discriminate less against foreign traders, and this attitude enabled the economy to benefit from the migration of refugees from the Netherlands and of Jewish exiles from Ferrara. Although the Venetians were sending fewer ships of their own to northern Europe, they were able, through aliens, to maintain commercial links with that area.[46] The presence of the Jews stimulated commerce with the Ottoman Empire through the Dalmatian ports, especially that of Spalato.[47] The growing activity of the port of Venice was reflected in the upward movement of the 6 per cent tax in 1584–1602, and in that of the anchorage tax from 1591–1603: dues which bore witness to the presence of foreigners in the city.[48] The outbreak of war between Spain and the Netherlands had tended to stimulate Italian economies indirectly, by diverting towards Italy much of the trade, treasure and wool and many of the troops formerly despatched via the Atlantic from Spain to the Low Countries.[49] The Venetians met the crisis in shipbuilding both through the purchase of boats constructed abroad but subsequently naturalized as Venetian, and through the relaxation of discriminatory laws aimed against foreign vessels hired by Venetians.[50]

[45] See especially Aldo Stella, 'La crisi economica veneziana nella seconda metà del secolo XVI', *Archivio Veneto*, 5th series, LVIII–LIX (1956); Daniele Beltrami, *La penetrazione economica dei veneziani in Terraferma: forze di lavoro e proprietà fondiaria nelle campagne venete dei secoli XVII e XVIII* (Venice–Rome, 1961), and the extensive review article by S. J. Woolf, 'Venice and the Terraferma: problems of the change from commercial to landed activities', reprinted in Pullan, *Crisis and change*.

[46] Wilfrid Brulez, 'La navigation flamande vers la Méditerranée à la fin du XVIe siècle', *Revue belge de philologie et d'histoire*, XXXVI (1958); Wilfrid Brulez, *Marchands flamands à Venise, I (1568–1605)* (Brussels, 1965), pp. xii f.

[47] See below, pp. 568–73.

[48] See F. C. Lane, 'The merchant marine of the Venetian Republic', in *Venice and history*, pp. 150 f.

[49] Cf. Braudel, *La Méditerranée*, I, pp. 443 f.; also Hermann Kellenbenz, 'Le déclin de Venise et les relations économiques de Venise avec les marchés au nord des Alpes', *Aspetti e cause della decadenza*, p. 113.

[50] See Romano, 'La marine marchande', pp. 47–50; Tenenti, *Naufrages*, pp. 13 f.

The crucial period in the decline of Venice both as an international emporium and as a manufacturing centre lay across the first thirty years of the seventeenth century. It depended partly on the intensification of northern competition from English and Dutch traders both in the Far East and within the Mediterranean itself; partly on an increasingly inept economic policy which tended to discourage these foreigners from using Venice as a base; partly on the collapse of the German market for goods shipped through Venice; partly on the severe population losses caused by plague in 1630–1. After 1602, Venice became more of a 'closed' society, discriminating against the use of superior foreign shipping by Venetian merchants in their Levantine trade. The English and Dutch cut off spice supplies from the routes which terminated in the Mediterranean, establishing far more effective and long-lasting control over them than the Portuguese had ever done. At the same time, the English and Dutch established supremacy within the Mediterranean itself, both in the carrying-trade and in the textile markets. Venetian economic policy did not encourage the northerners to use the city as a base for Levantine trade, and this diverted them towards the free port of Leghorn in Tuscany, which was more accessible, and where they paid no specially heavy dues as foreigners. The German market collapsed for Venetians because Levantine products filtered through to Frankfurt and elsewhere from Marseilles, Flanders and England. To some extent it folded up for everybody because of the heavy losses of population inflicted on Germany during the Thirty Years' War. But the blockage of the overland routes by military operations gave a strong advantage to sea-traffic from the north by way of Leghorn. If, by the end of the seventeenth century, Venetian commerce had somewhat recovered, it had still greatly altered its character: Venice had become essentially a regional port, serving the needs and exporting the produce of its own mainland territories. As a manufacturer of woollen cloth, Venice did not recover.[51] If, in the early eighteenth century, the port of Venice was handling a volume of trade somewhat greater than in 1607–10 (after the first slumps had occurred) there is still no proof that it ever re-attained the heights of the late sixteenth century.[52] In any case, Venetian trade had certainly declined in relation to that of other European countries—whatever its position in absolute terms.

[51] See Domenico Sella, 'Crisis and transformation in Venetian trade', revised English version in Pullan, *Crisis and change*; Sella, *Commerci e industrie*; Ralph Davis, 'Influences de l'Angleterre sur le déclin de Venise au XVIIe siècle', *Aspetti e cause della decadenza*; Ralph Davis, 'England and the Mediterranean, 1570–1670', in *Essays in the economic and social history of Tudor and Stuart England in honour of R. H. Tawney*, ed. F. J. Fisher (Cambridge, 1961).
[52] *Pace* Braudel, *La Méditerranée*, I, p. 267.

In a study dealing with poor relief, it is natural to ask what effect these changes and fluctuations in the Venetian economy are likely to have produced on ordinary people. Plainly, it is impossible to speak of any steady or inexorable contraction in employment opportunities taking place throughout the sixteenth century—whatever may have happened in the early seventeenth, especially in and after the decade 1620–30. Almost certainly, however, a prolonged depression spanned the first third of the sixteenth century, when the diminution in the profits drawn from oriental trade would presumably impair the ability of Venetian merchant entrepreneurs to invest and consume and thereby provide employment in Venice itself. At this time, heavy taxation, designed to support Venetian military and naval operations in the course of the Italian wars, was also taking a substantial toll of Venetian wealth. The textile industry, although it began to grow, had not done so very greatly by the early 1530's. In the second and third quarters of the century, the problems were those associated with an economy expanding partly in response to population pressure, and therefore subject to increasingly frequent outbreaks of severe famine. These famines counterbalanced the beneficial effects of growth in the Arsenal and of development in the textile industry. Some relief came with the impact of an event in itself catastrophic and causing great distress and human suffering—the plague of 1575–7. Although the activity of the port and the production of textiles were both at a high level in the last twenty years or so of the sixteenth century, famine again struck heavily in the 1590's, when foul weather temporarily put the Venetians at the mercy of other countries increasingly reluctant to export grain—on which they had imposed tighter controls. In the early seventeenth century, after 1602, the activity of the port slumped very badly, and recovery was only partial—though food prices probably fell, and in at least one industry, building, real wages may well have improved.[53] Hence, at least in the sixteenth century, there is no impression of a constant increase in the problem of poverty: but there is one of continual uncertainty and precariousness, with no freedom from the menace of famine even in phases of economic expansion. In addition, it is necessary to bear in mind the extent to which poverty is a personal problem rather than one which can be related to the general state of the economy or to the absence of opportunities for employment; and the extent to which grave poverty can survive even in the midst of a highly prosperous society which has failed to develop efficient charities or welfare services. Even in a flourishing economy, some poverty is bound to exist, as a result of the low wages paid to labourers in

[53] Cf. Pullan, 'Wage-earners and the Venetian economy'.

certain forms of employment, overlarge families of young children, or the illness, old age or death of the chief wage-earners in many families.[54]

Some account must now be given of the structure of Venetian government, and of the relationship between Venice and its mainland territories. The structure of Venice's government was usually described by its analysts as pyramidal, with the Great Council at the base of the pyramid, and the Doge at the apex. The Great Council was the sovereign body of all adult patricians, whose functions were to elect to magistracies, to choose members of the smaller councils on which the day to day government of the Republic depended, and to ratify laws of especial moment. Membership of the Great Council was an indispensable qualification for entry to magistracies in the city itself, to the chief naval commands, to governorships in the subject dominions to the east or west of Venice, and to ambassadorial posts abroad. In the second half of the thirteenth century, both the numbers and the composition of the Great Council had fluctuated considerably from one year to another, but the turn of the century had seen the beginning of a series of measures which resulted in the 'closing' of the Great Council. Its size was greatly enlarged, from a maximum of 400–500 members in the 1260's to a total complement of 1,017 in 1311.[55] But membership developed into a hereditary right, and the Great Council ceased regularly admitting new recruits. It showed itself, however, prepared to do so on exceptional occasions—opening its doors to fifteen new families to reward their loyalty to the regime after the Tiepolo conspiracy of 1310, and, at the time of the Genoese war of 1381, admitting another thirty families prepared to pay liberally for the privilege.[56]

[54] See especially the famous survey of B. Seebohm Rowntree, *Poverty: a study of town life* (new edition, London, 1922).

[55] See Giorgio Cracco, *Società e stato nel Medioevo Veneziano (secoli XII–XIV)* (Florence, 1967), pp. 202, 217, 229–30, 237, 254–5, 324–5, 347–9, 371. For conflicting interpretations of the closing of the Great Council, see F. C. Lane, 'Medieval political ideas and the Venetian constitution', *Venice and history*, pp. 306–7: 'Was the reform of 1297 a move by an aristocratic party deliberately designed to exclude lower classes from any share in the government? Or was it an adjustment in the governmental machinery which made no change and intended no change in the location of political power?' Professor Lane himself inclines to the second of these interpretations; Dr Cracco—see especially pp. 348–9—to the first.

[56] See Cracco, *Società e stato*, p. 371; for a list of the thirty families raised to noble rank in 1381, see Daniele di Chinazzo, *Cronica de la guerra da Veniciani a Zenovesi*, ed. Vittorio Lazzarini (Venice, 1958), pp. 206–8. Cf. also Vittorio Lazzarini, 'Le offerte per la guerra di Chioggia e un falsario del Quattrocento', *Nuovo Archivio Veneto, nuova serie*, IV (1902).

After that date, the Venetians occasionally granted membership of the Great Council as a mark of recognition to persons who had deserved well of the Republic: but these concessions were evidently designed only to be grants of honorary dignity. Some scandal arose when Giro-lamo Savorgnan, one of a provincial family which had greatly furthered Venetian influence in Friuli, was elected from the Great Council to the Senate in October 1509, and a pretext for sending him away on military business was soon devised.[57] To all intents, the Great Council—and hence the 'political nation' within Venice—remained effectively closed between 1381 and 1646, when a number of other families entered the nobility during the prolonged siege of Venetian Crete by the Turks.[58] Newcomers and men newly rich could aspire only to membership of a secondary aristocracy of *cittadini originarii*, whose privileges included a monopoly of office in the Ducal Chancery, or permanent civil service. Members of this estate could acquire a good deal of unacknowledged influence, but they held no formal place in the deliberations of legislative councils or on the boards of magistrates who formulated proposals for their consideration.[59]

Above the Great Council, two smaller and more manœuvrable Councils had developed into the real makers of decisions and formulators of policy: for the Great Council was too unwieldy and insufficiently secretive for this purpose. In 1550, the number of noblemen aged over 25 and therefore automatically entitled to a seat in the Great Council was over 2,500, in 1594 1,970, in 1609 2,090, in 1620 2,000, in 1631 1,660, in 1637 1,675 and in 1652 1,540.[60] The Senate, otherwise known as the Pregadi, had between two and three hundred members. It consisted first of sixty Senators proper, elected at ten sessions of the Great Council in August and September of every year. In addition, it comprised a further body known as the Zonta, which had grown in size from the fourteenth century onwards and had reached its full complement of sixty members under Doge Francesco Foscari in 1450. Members of the Zonta were elected by the Senators and by all who enjoyed a right of entry into the Senate, and were subsequently confirmed by the Great Council. The numbers of the Senate were then further swelled by persons whose offices conferred the right of entry. This raised the full complement of the Senate to between two and three hundred—Gasparo Contarini, writing in the 1520's, estimated it at 220. In Contarini's words,

[57] See Ventura, *Nobiltà e popolo*, pp. 172–3.
[58] Cf. Davis, *Decline of the Venetian nobility*, pp. 106 f.
[59] See below, pp. 103 f.
[60] See Davis, *Decline of the Venetian nobility*, pp. 58, 137.

The whole manner of the commonwealths government belongeth to the senate. That which the senate determineth is held for ratified and inviolable. By their authority and advise is peace confirmed and war denounced. The whole rents and receipts of the commonwealth are at their appointment collected and gathered in, and likewise laid out againe and defrayed. If there be any new taxations or subsidies to be laid upon the citizens, they are imposed, and likewise levied by the Senates decree. And if at any time it shall seeme necessary for the good of the commonwealth, to create a new officer or magistrate upon any sodaine urgent occasion, he is by the senate elected. Besides, the senate by a perpetuall prerogative, hath authority to chuse such Embassadors as are to be sent to forraine princes, and likewise to create the colledge of those, whose office is to assemble the senate, and to report unto them.[61]

The college, or Collegio, to which he referred was a highly influential cabinet, responsible for preparing agenda for the Senate and for making proposals to it. It included sixteen Savii or 'Sages' who held office for periods of six months at a time, and were headed by six officers known as Savii Grandi, whose

office principally is, that in waighty and important causes concerning the state of the commonwealth as well in matters of warres, as in thinges of peace, they are first among themselves to hold a long and deliberate consultation, and then to give over their councell and opinion to the senate.

Five other Savii, known as Savii di Terra Ferma, dealt with matters relating to the Republic's land forces, whilst the five Savii agli Ordini were concerned with maritime affairs. In practice, the office of Savio agli Ordini was usually reserved to young men embarking on a political career, affording them opportunities for learning the business. 'In this age of ours', wrote Contarini, 'young men and some in a manner beardlesse are admitted thereunto'. The Collegio was then completed by the addition of the Doge himself, with his six Ducal Councillors, and of the three Chiefs or Heads of the Quarantia al Criminale, the supreme criminal court.[62] The Quarantia was a body exercising both judicial and political functions, since its members enjoyed an *ex officio* right of entry to the Senate, and since its chiefs (chosen in rotation)

---

[61] See Contarini, *Commonwealth*, English version, pp. 66 f., Latin version, pp. 96 f.; Giannotti, *Libro de la Republica*, f. 50v. f.; Besta, *Il Senato Veneziano*, pp. 45–70, 92 f.; Andrea Da Mosto, *L'Archivio di Stato di Venezia* (2 vols., Rome, 1937–40), I, pp. 34–8. Da Mosto's volumes, which are used as a general index to the Venetian archive, are perhaps the most convenient work of reference to the Venetian constitution and to the powers of the various magistracies.

[62] Contarini, *Commonwealth*, English version, pp. 70–1, Latin version, pp. 103–4; Giannotti, *Libro de la Republica*, ff. 53 f.

23

C

formed part of the Collegio and thereby enjoyed the right of making proposals to the Senate. By the 1520's, the Quarantia—in which posts carried a modest salary—was usually regarded as suitable for relatively poor noblemen: a means whereby they could support themselves and make their voices heard in councils of state.[63] Individual magistrates submitted proposals on matters which fell within their competence first to the Collegio and then, with its approval, to the Senate. The function of the Doge, who held office for life, was—as Contarini expressed it—to act as the principal co-ordinator and regulator, keeping the organs of Venetian government in their proper balance.[64] He could also, with his Councillors, act as a bridge between the Senate and Collegio and the Council of Ten.

The Council of Ten fitted somewhat imperfectly into the pyramidal structure, and duplicated many of the functions of the Senate. Giannotti, whilst admitting that its authority was 'equal to that of the Senate', refused to acknowledge that it was part of the main organism of the state: it was 'annexed' to it. It was, in fact, a permanent extraordinary magistracy, a standing committee of public safety, whose duty was to guarantee the security of the state, to track down or forestall all conspiracies against the regime, and to deal with matters requiring special secrecy. It had originated at the time of the Tiepolo-Querini conspiracy of 1310, and had become a permanent feature of the constitution in the mid-fourteenth century. It soon extended its competence, for there were few issues of importance which could not be treated as ultimately affecting public security. The fact that its authority was exercised in secret made it especially difficult to control. It even dealt with the making of war and peace, which Contarini had described as being the Senate's prerogative, and there was ample room for jurisdictional conflict between the two bodies. Hence the occasional constitutional crises, already described, which resulted in a more rigid definition of the Ten's authority. The Council was composed of ten members in ordinary chosen from the Senate by the Great Council—all must be over 40 years of age and chosen from different families. From 1427 onwards, the Ducal Councillors were obliged to participate in deliberations of the Ten, whilst the Doge was entitled to do so if he wished. For a time, the Council of Ten also possessed a Zonta or additional body composed of Senators over the age of 30, but in 1582–1583 the Council was deprived of its Zonta—as a means of reducing its

---

[63] Contarini, *Commonwealth*, English version, pp. 94–5; Latin version, pp. 134–6. Cf. also Brian Pullan, 'Poverty, charity and the reason of state: some Venetian examples', *Bollettino dell'Istituto di Storia della Società e dello Stato Veneziano*, II (1960), pp. 31–2, 37, 48–9.

[64] Contarini, *Commonwealth*, English version, pp. 40–1; Latin version, pp. 63–4.

weight in the constitution, and of forcibly limiting the amount of business it could in practice undertake.[65]

The Venetian patriciate, the narrow sovereign people at the heart of the Republic, supplied governors to hold key positions in the principal cities and towns of the Venetian dominions—on the mainland of Italy, in Istria, on the Dalmatian coast, here and there in Albania, in the Ionian islands, in Cyprus and in Crete. The greater part of Venice's mainland dominion had been acquired in the first half of the fifteenth century. The Venetians first determined to exploit the opportunities created by the death, in 1402, of Gian Galeazzo Visconti, lord of the expanding state of Milan. Later, in the 1420's, they chose to carry the war against the revived duchy of Filippo Maria Visconti westwards into the provinces surrounding the Lombard cities of Brescia and Bergamo. This was not Venice's first mainland adventure;[66] she had previously conducted her diplomacy in such a way as to retain Friuli as a Venetian sphere of influence and protect trade-routes into Germany and Austria; and she had for a time in the fourteenth century— from 1338 to 1381—held direct dominion over such cities as Treviso and Conegliano. But the enterprises of the fifteenth century were the most ambitious, and produced the most enduring results. In 1405, the Venetian Republic absorbed the territories of two once-formidable Lombard principates—those of the Carrara lords of Padua and of the Scaligeri of Verona, which had already been diminished or wholly overthrown by the conquests and intrigues of Gian Galeazzo. By 1420, Venice had acquired direct authority over most of the province of Friuli, doing so at the expense of the territorial possessions of the Patriarch of Aquileia, and holding the region with the collaboration of the Savorgnan, a powerful feudal family based on Udine. Soon afterwards, the Venetians—after much controversy—committed themselves to a policy of further expansion across the mainland, responding to the appeals of the Florentines to join them in containing the renewed Visconti threat. Through the acquisition of Brescia in 1426 and of Bergamo in 1428, the Venetians extended their territory to the banks of the Adda. All serious prospects of further westward conquest, contemplated at least after Filippo Maria Visconti's death without heirs in 1447, ended for the time being with the Peace of Lodi in 1454, which initiated a period of relative equilibrium between the five great territorial states of the peninsula: the Venetian Republic, the Medicean

[65] See Da Mosto, *Archivio di Stato*, I, pp. 52–4; the monograph, *Istoria del Consiglio dei Dieci*, by Macchi; and above, pp. 6, 10.

[66] On the growth, in the thirteenth century, of a 'party' favouring greater Venetian involvement in the affairs of the Terra Ferma, see Cracco, *Società e Stato*, especially pp. 148–9.

Republic of Florence, the new Sforza Duchy of Milan, the Papal States and the Kingdom of Naples. The southward drive towards Ferrara and the Po mouth in the 1480's proved unsuccessful, though Venetian dominion was secured in the Polesine. The Venetians made further temporary gains in the Romagna, in Lombardy, and down the western shores of the Adriatic—but these they failed to retain beyond the conclusion of the Peace of Bologna in 1529.

In the most important mainland cities, the Venetians appointed members of their own patriciate to fill the offices of Podestà and Capitano, adding to these their own Treasurers or Camerlenghi, and sometimes their own castellans. In theory at least, the Podestà (whose office had originated in the era of the independent communes) was fundamentally a supreme judge, dealing both with civil and with criminal cases. But he shared with the Capitano control over the revenues of the city, the Camerlengo was responsible to both officers, and the Podestà's office opened out into broader administrative functions. The Capitano's special responsibility was the care of the troops and fortifications in the area. In the smaller centres, the offices of Podestà and Capitano were usually combined in the person of one man.[67] However, in many purely local matters, the citizenry of the subject towns in practice enjoyed a high degree of virtual independence, and the short periods—seldom more than eighteen months to two years—for which Venetian governors held office sometimes prevented their achieving a very full grasp of the complexities of local affairs. The Venetians lacked the bureaucratic man power to carry through a more extensive policy of centralization, penetrating more deeply into local organs. They did not seriously consider admitting local patricians to the central councils of the Republic in Venice itself, and they reserved the right to rescind or modify the resolutions of municipal councils and to revise communal statutes. In several of the chief cities, the principal consultative body, recruited from the local potentates, was the Deputati ad Utilia—a small advisory board nominated by the Podestà. This organ had existed in Verona under Cangrande II della Scala in 1350, and also in fourteenth-century Vicenza; it was introduced into Padua in 1408. Broadly speaking, under Venetian rule, there was a tendency in the greater centres for the communal councils to close their ranks, and to become the preserve of oligarchs who treated their seats as hereditary and sometimes even as alienable property. Families already prominent under the Carraresi and Scaligeri continued to rule the affairs of their cities under Venetian gover-

[67] Contarini, *Commonwealth*, English version, pp. 126–7; Latin version, pp. 174–6. Ventura, *Nobiltà e popolo*, pp. 45–7.

nors. By the late fifteenth century, the conciliar families had become landowners and rentiers rather than active merchants or industrialists, and in the course of the sixteenth and early seventeenth century they tended to formalize their position by legally excluding persons whose families had—even several generations back—actively engaged in, rather than passively invested in, some form of trade or industry. Guilds and other popular organs took relatively little part in the local government of the bigger centres, though there were certain communal institutions, such as the Monti di Pietà, over which they could sometimes exert a modicum of control. During the fifteenth century, the Venetians were compelled to govern the highly feudalized province of Friuli by somewhat different methods—and especially, between the early fifteenth and the early sixteenth century, by granting extensive privileges to the family of Savorgnan, leaders of the 'zamberlana' or Guelf faction, which had attracted formidable peasant and popular support against the castellans who did not belong to it. The treason of Antonio Savorgnan, who defected to the Emperor in 1511, did, however, force the Venetians to reconsider their traditional policy in Friuli.[68]

The total population of Venice and of the mainland provinces of the Republic stood at about 1·6 million in the mid-sixteenth century, when the population of Venice itself was in the region of 150,000. Just over one-fifth of this population, according to a general census taken in 1548, lived in centres of over 10,000 inhabitants. Of the provincial capitals, Verona had a population of about 52,000, Brescia of about 43,000, Padua of about 32,000, Vicenza of some 21,000, Bergamo of about 17,000, Treviso of nearly 12,000, and Crema of between 10,000 and 11,000.[69] These large cities were frequently markets for the exchange of cattle and agricultural produce—grain, fruit and vegetables; several manufactured woollen cloths or silks in some form, Vicenza and the Vicentino being conspicuous for silk production and mulberry-growing; and Brescia and the Bresciano were especially famous for their metallurgical industries.[70] Some of the larger cities—perhaps

---

[68] This passage is mainly a summary of the very wide-ranging synthesis of evidence about government and society in the Terra Ferma, contained in Ventura, *Nobiltà e popolo*. Also of outstanding importance is the specialized study of A. Pino-Branca, 'Il comune di Padova sotto la Dominante nel secolo XV (rapporti amministrativi e finanziari)', *Atti del Reale Istituto Veneto di Scienze, Lettere ed Arti*, XCIII (1933–1934), XCVI (1936–7), XCVII (1937–8).

[69] See Daniele Beltrami, *Storia della popolazione di Venezia dalla fine del secolo XVI alla caduta della Repubblica* (Padua, 1954), pp. 69–70.

[70] For this, and for most of the information which follows, I rely on the unpublished researches of my wife, Janet Pullan, which concentrate mainly on the provinces of Verona, Brescia, Bergamo and Crema, and are based on the reports of Venetian governors or Rettori.

most of them—were residential centres for landed proprietors who owned a large proportion of the surrounding *contado*, the ancient jurisdictional area of the city. Around Brescia in 1442, inhabitants of the *contado* had owned some two-thirds of its surface, but by 1591 the proportion had dropped to barely a quarter. Similarly, in Padua in 1418, property owned by inhabitants of the Padovano had equalled 80 per cent of the area owned by Paduan citizens (not counting ecclesiastical property)—but by 1548 it had fallen to less than a third, and had sunk to a quarter by 1585.[71] Both Verona and Padua were the capitals of prosperous agricultural provinces. The Padovano, heavily penetrated by Venetian landbuyers, was forced to shoulder the heavy task of providing Venice with a substantial proportion of its grain supplies.[72] The Veronese, on which the Venetians made heavy demands for meat consignments in the first half of the sixteenth century,[73] greatly increased its proportion of arable land to pasture in the course of the century, and experimented with the new cultures of rice and maize, partly in response to increasing population. Both Verona and Padua enjoyed a certain international importance in their own right—Padua as a university town, and Verona as a station through which there passed a considerable transit-trade between Italy and Germany. The plains and lowlands of the Veneto and Friuli produced substantial quantities of grain and wine, with rye, beans, millet, sorghum, buckwheat, and later maize and rice supplementing the diet of the poor and serving as reserve crops in emergencies.[74] The Riviera di Salò, on the

---

[71] See Ventura, *Nobiltà e popolo*, p. 337.

[72] See below, pp. 291–2.

[73] Michele Lecce, 'Le condizioni zootecnico-agricole del territorio veronese nella prima metà del '500', *Economia e Storia*, V (1958).

[74] This information comes mainly from the late sixteenth and early seventeenth century. In 1590, *sarasin*, probably buckwheat, was described as the principal foodstuff of peasants in Friuli (by the Luogotenente Nicolò Donà, A.S.V., *Senato, Terra, filza* 115, 11 August 1590). In the region of Treviso, at the same time, beans and rye (*segalle et fave*) were the normal diet of peasants, and millet and sorghum were possible reserve crops—as they also were at Uderzo and Monfalcone (*ibid., filza* 115, 18 August 1590; *filza* 116, 15 September 1590; *filza* 117, 20 October 1590). In the following year, Francesco Sagredo, governor of Feltre, described how he had established deposits of rye, beans, millet, sorghum and *formentone* for the benefit of the poor, and said that when the town imported supplies from the Trevigiano millet was the normal alternative to wheat (see his report of 14 November 1591, A.S.V., *Collegio, Relazioni, busta* 41). Maize or *sorgo turco* was used to feed the poor in the area of Belluno from about 1622 onwards—see the reports of Federico Cornaro, 20 July 1622, of Angelo Giustinian, 20 November 1622, of Alvise Sanuto, 9 March 1628, and of Ermolao Tiepolo, 18 July 1640, *ibid., busta* 34. According to Maurice Aymard, *Venise, Raguse et le commerce du blé dans la seconde moitié du XVIe siècle* (Paris, 1966), pp. 36–7, maize cultivation was found near Rovigo and in the Basso Veronese in 1554. In the mountainous regions of the Bergamasco, chestnuts were regularly used to eke out the diet of the poor.

western shores of Lake Garda, grew comparatively little grain, but exported much fruit—especially citrus fruits, destined for Germany.

In addition to its fertile plains, the Veneto comprised mountainous regions whose inhabitants solved their economic problems in part by lumbering and quarrying, in part by the manufacture of woollen cloth, in part by the exploitation of iron ores found in the mountains, and in part by emigration—especially in the Bergamasco, whose people sent or brought home money made in Venice or abroad, and sometimes founded charities for the relief of poverty at home.[75] Extensive rural iron industries, closely tied to the sources of the raw materials, had developed in parts of the Veneto, especially in the valleys of the Bresciano, where the mines, ovens and forges were sited. The industries of the Bresciano produced pots, pans and kettles, agricultural implements, nails, hoops for carts and carriage wheels, and armaments. Craftsmen in the city of Brescia 'finished' weapons and armour, whilst firearms—especially arquebuses—were made in Gardone and in Brescia itself.

In the present state of knowledge, it is difficult to say very much about the fortunes of the mainland industries. It seems, however, that Venetian fiscal policy, designed to secure supplies of fine wool for the broadcloth industry of Venice itself, failed to encourage the development of industries on the Terra Ferma that might compete with Venice's own. Coarser cloths, or *panni bassi*, had a better chance of prospering—but they, too, could run into difficulties, sometimes, as in the Veronese, caused by the contraction of sheepfarming as a result of expanded cultivation. The mainland peoples therefore frequently explored other spheres of activity, and showed an especial tendency to develop the manufacture of silk (as in the provinces of Vicenza, Verona and Bergamo, Verona producing haberdashery rather than silken cloth) and of linen (as in the Bresciano, the Riviera di Salò and the Cremasco).

Against this rough sketch of some of the most conspicuous features of the political and economic structure of Venice and her mainland territories, the history of some of the Republic's urban social institutions will now be outlined.

[75] Cf. below, pp. 310 f.

PART I: THE SCUOLE GRANDI

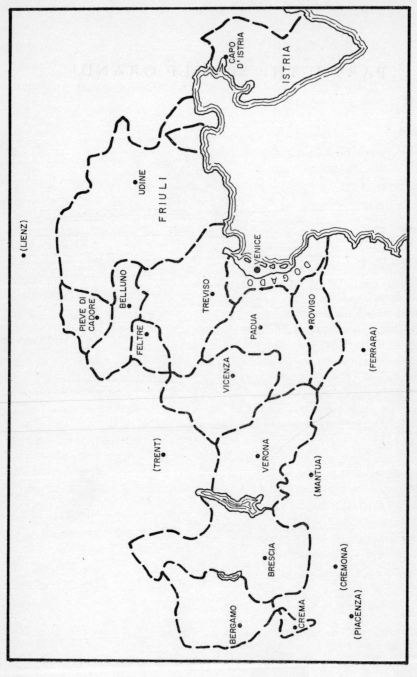

THE MAINLAND DOMINIONS OF THE REPUBLIC, C. 1550–1620

1

THE SCUOLE GRANDI: THE FIRST PRINCIPLES AND THEIR LATER DEVELOPMENT

From the high Middle Ages to the fall of the Republic, Venetians used the term Scuola to denote several forms of religious society among the laity, many of which were professional associations designed to encourage piety and mutual aid. Venetian artisans were normally members of an Arte, consisting of persons who practised the same trade or craft, and of a Scuola—a corporation consisting of members of a given Arte who, meeting on the premises of a particular monastery, placed themselves under the protection of a chosen saint, and undertook to perform certain services for their own poor, sick and dead.[1] Besides these, there were many other Scuole not connected with any particular trade or profession—though sometimes their members were united by other bonds before joining. Exiles or expatriates grouped themselves in Scuole, and the term was sometimes officially used in the late sixteenth or early seventeenth century to describe Jewish fraternities or academies.[2] The blind and the lame had their own devotional communities, the Scuola degli Orbi and the Scuola dei Zotti, founded during the fourteenth century in the parish of San Samuele.[3] Scuole were further distinguished by devotion to particular saints or special cults, like that of the Eucharist; by their performing some characteristic act of devotion or of personal asceticism; or, occasionally, by their dedication to some highly specialized form of charity—as the Scuola di San Fantin accompanied criminals to execution, and administered spiritual consolation on the last journey.[4]

In Venice, about 1500, five Scuole bore the name Scuole Grandi—those dedicated to Santa Maria della Carità, San Giovanni Evangelista, Santa Maria Valverde della Misericordia, San Marco and San Rocco—

---

[1] See Giovanni Monticolo, *I Capitolari delle Arti veneziane sottoposte alla Giustizia e poi alla Giustizia Vecchia dalle origini al MCCCXXX*, II (Rome, 1905), pp. lxxvi f.

[2] E.g. A.S.V., *Ufficiali al Cattaver*, busta 244, registro 5, f. 104v., 9 March 1594 (which speaks of a 'scola di Spagnioli, cioè talmutora'); f. 182, 31 July 1596.

[3] See Giuseppe Tassini, *Curiosità veneziane, ovvero Origini delle denominazioni stradali* (new edition, ed. Lino Moretti, Venice, no date), pp. 474–5, 744; and below, p. 297.

[4] E.g. D.M.S., XL, col. 349, 24 November 1525; LVIII, col. 238, 31 May 1533.

and were officially entitled each to admit between 500 and 600 full members. Their number rose to six in 1552, when the Council of Ten promoted to their ranks the ancient Scuola di San Teodoro, which claimed to have been founded in 1258.[5] Early in the sixteenth century, the number of lesser societies described as Scuole Piccole certainly exceeded a hundred, for in June 1521 about 120 small Scuole paraded with their banners at a Doge's funeral.[6] The Scuola lost none of its popularity in later years, new foundations continued to arise, and an official statistic compiled in 1732 alluded to 357 recognized religious associations, classified as Scuole, *suffraggii*, *sovegni*, and confraternities.[7]

All the Scuole Grandi (on whom this study will concentrate) were known as Scuole dei Battuti, 'of the beaten', because their members publicly scourged themselves on ceremonial occasions. Their ritual flagellation was an attempt to atone for the sins of the world and to placate the wrath of God by re-enacting the sufferings of Christ, and had spread widely throughout Italy since the great flagellant movement of 1260. In that year, a hermit, Ranieri Fasani, had moved to Perugia after leading a solitary life for ten years. He was not an official preacher, but was probably a Brother of the Penitence—a canonical state already recognized for several centuries by the Church. Followers of this rule adopted the way of life enjoined upon all public penitents— fasting, attending Mass daily, observing the canonical hours, absenting themselves from worldly festivals and public amusements, refusing to bear arms or to perform administrative duties. The unmarried renounced matrimony, whilst married persons abstained from sexual

[5] A.S.V., *Consiglio dei Dieci, Parti Comuni, filza* 56, *fascicolo* 28; *ibid.*, *Registro Comune 1552*, f. 95, 98v. See also Rodolfo Gallo, 'La Scuola Grande di San Teodoro di Venezia', *Atti dell'Istituto Veneto di Scienze, Lettere ed Arti*, CXX (Classe di scienze morali e lettere), 1961–2.

[6] D.M.S., XXX, coll. 399, 401, 25 June 1521. On several occasions, Sanuto recorded the number of small Scuole whose standards appeared at the funerals of celebrities: 64 at that of the Pope's representative, the Conte Cavaliere Pietro di Bibiena, in 1514; 82 at that of the Republic's Captain-General, Bartolomeo Alviano, in 1515; 111 at the funeral of Cardinal Cornaro in 1525—*ibid.*, XVII, coll. 547–9; XXI, coll. 274–5; XXXIX, col. 242.

[7] On 11 June 1732 the magistracy of the Provveditori di Comun reported to the Heads of the Council of Ten on the number of religious societies to be found in Venice. They made the following statement:

'Le Scole del Venerabile sono al numero di	67
Le scole di Devozion sono al numero di	176
Li suffraggii sono al numero di	21
Li sovegni sono al numero di	84
Le confraternite sono al numero di	9
Che sono in tutto al numero di	357'

See M.C.V., MSS. *Provenienze Diverse*, *busta* 506c., *fascicolo* 16, f. 5.

intercourse at least for certain periods of the year. All wore plain and simple dress. Self-flagellation in private was no new concept—it had been recommended to laymen during the eleventh century by Pietro Damiani. But Ranieri Fasani now began, in May 1260, to exhort the people at large to the use of the discipline, in public and on an unprecedented scale.[8]

Some months later, the movement spread beyond Perugia. The pessimistic atmosphere in northern and central Italy, after years of famine, plague and civil strife, created a mood of repentance and an unusually vivid sense of standing on the frontiers of eternity, as if the whole world must prepare for death or judgment, and set its affairs in order. Much of Italy seemed enslaved by the enemies of the Roman Church, with the triumph of Manfred, King of Sicily, the bastard son of the late, excommunicate Emperor Frederick II of Staufen. On 4 September 1260, Manfred's partisans and the Ghibellines of Florence and Siena defeated their Guelf opponents at the battle of Monte Aperti.[9] A few weeks later, the flagellant movement began to spread beyond Perugia into Emilia, the Romagna and Lombardy, and in the new year it invaded the Marches of Treviso, crossed the Alps and entered Germany and France.[10] Manfred's henchmen in Lombardy, especially the Marchese Uberto Pelavicino, recognized the movement as highly subversive to their own authority and strove to suppress it or to divert it from the cities, such as Cremona, Brescia and Milan, where they held sway.[11] As well as witnessing the ominous victory of the Ghibellines, the year 1260 also carried a mystical significance for followers of the Abbot Joachim of Fiore. Simplified and popularized versions of his prophecies suggested that this was the year, 42 generations of 30 years from the birth of Christ, in which the Age of the Spirit was due to begin. Some Joachites regarded the flagellant movements as evidence that this Age was indeed dawning—but the

[8] See G. G. Meersseman, 'Disciplinati e penitenti nel Duecento' in the volume *Il movimento dei Disciplinati nel settimo centenario dal suo inizio (Perugia—1260)*, Appendice 9 to *Bollettino della Deputazione di Storia Patria per l'Umbria* (Spoleto, 1962), pp. 44–50.

[9] On the connexion between the Ghibelline victory and the flagellant movements, see Raffaello Morghen, 'Ranieri Fasani e il movimento dei Disciplinati del 1260', *ibid.*, pp. 35 f.

[10] Meersseman, 'Disciplinati e penitenti', p. 58.

[11] *Annales Sanctae Iustinae Patavini*, ed. Philippe Jaffé, M.G.H., Ss., XIX, ed. G. H. Pertz (Hanover, 1866), p. 179; also edited, under its alternative title of *Chronicon Marchiae Tarvisinae et Lombardiae*, by L. A. Botteghi in Muratori, R.I.S., VIII/ii (Città di Castello, 1916)—see pp. 44–5; *Annales Placentini Gibellini*, ed. G. H. Pertz, M.G.H., Ss., XIX (Hanover, 1866), p. 512; Salimbene de Adam, *Chronica*, ed. Oswald Holder-Egger, M.G.H., Ss., XXXII (Hanover–Leipzig, 1905–1913), pp. 465–6.

inspiration of the movement probably owed little to Joachim, and the Franciscan cult of the passion of Christ may have been far more directly relevant. According to a Paduan chronicler, men, women and children of every social class 'shed floods of tears, as if they saw before their own eyes the very passion of the Saviour himself'.[12]

The Paduan wrote that this was essentially a movement of laymen— 'it started among the simple, in whose footsteps both learned and ignorant instantly followed'.[13] Bishops and clergy, however, recognized it to the extent of walking in front of the flagellant processions. Friar Salimbene de Adam, who was by popular request borne off from his friary near Modena to follow the processions as far as Reggio and Parma, described how with the coming of the flagellants men resolved their differences, restored misappropriated property, and confessed their sins with such fervour 'that the priests scarcely had time to snatch a meal'.[14] The movement died down in 1261, but it provided lasting inspiration for the establishment of permanent fraternities, which threw the same emphasis on penance, on self-flagellation, and on the composition of disputes. Many of these devotional societies were erected on the premises of Dominican or Franciscan convents, though others remained independent. These Disciplinati, outside the Ghibelline cities, proved more popular with the civil authorities than did the Brothers of the Penitence, because they did not refuse to bear arms. Their 'penitential asceticism' was confined to the use of the discipline.[15] Otherwise, the Venetian fraternities at any rate merely strove to condemn such obvious excesses as drunkenness, gambling and blaspheming, and to encourage attendance at Mass.

In general, the foundation of these and other lay fraternities formed part of a wide-ranging process, a medieval Counter Reformation, through which the laity were gradually reabsorbed into the Catholic Church and reclaimed from the heretical creeds which had spread so widely throughout the peninsula. Since the twelfth century, the official policy of the Church had tended to disenfranchise the laity and to alienate them by its worldly preoccupations, its acquisition of wealth, and its excessive use of spiritual penalties to gain terrestrial ends. Hence they were often driven into movements which first dreamed of renewing the Church through a return to its primitive condition of apostolic poverty, with a fresh emphasis on the Bible, but were later

[12] See Norman Cohn, *The pursuit of the Millennium* (London, 1957), pp. 125–7— but cf. Raoul Manselli, 'L'anno 1260 fu anno gioachimitico?', *Il movimento dei Disciplinati*, pp. 99–108.

[13] *Annales Sanctae Iustinae Patavini*, p. 179.

[14] Salimbene de Adam, *Chronica*, pp. 465–6.

[15] Meersseman, 'Disciplinati e penitenti', pp. 49–50, 61–2.

forced by the attitude of the hierarchy to form break-away sects. In the thirteenth century, the evangelism of the Franciscans and Dominicans and the assaults of the Inquisition began to cut into the ranks of the Cathar and Waldensian heretics, and laymen were more gently reclaimed and newly involved in the Catholic Church through the foundation of Third Orders and the establishment of confraternities on a much larger scale.[16] Some of these brotherhoods, such as the foundations of Dominican inquisitors and the famous lay militia of Bologna, known as the Cavalieri Gaudenti, were obviously designed for the specific purpose of combating heresy.[17] Almost certainly, the flagellant movement of 1260 was also a popular movement in defence of orthodoxy—its enemy, Uberto Pelavicino, was not only a partisan of Manfred but also a notorious protector of heretics.[18] Moreover, the Venetian Scuole Grandi were clearly devoted both to the sacrament of the Mass and to practices designed to speed the passage of the soul through Purgatory, whose existence was denied by Cathars and Waldensians.[19] It may also be significant that two of the early Scuole were devoted to the cult of the Virgin Mary—which seems to have been designed by the Dominicans and Franciscans to deflect the faithful from a too exclusive concentration on Christ himself (which savoured of heresy), or, on the other hand, from a polytheistic tendency towards diversified worship of the saints.[20]

In a study concentrated on the sixteenth century, it is impossible to discuss in detail the origins of the Scuole Grandi, or to establish their precise connexion with the movement of 1260. However, there is little reason to doubt that this did inspire them, if only by popularizing the use of the discipline as a devotional act. According to a tradition repeated in the sixteenth century by the Venetian publicist Francesco Sansovino, the senior Scuola Grande was that of Santa Maria della Carità, whose buildings and constitutions the other Scuole had copied. This is plausible enough—its foundation statues bore the date Decem-

[16] For the general theme, see Gioacchino Volpe, *Movimenti religiosi e sette eretical nella società medievale italiana (secoli XI–XIV)* (Florence, 1961: reprint of the original edition of 1922).

[17] Cf. *ibid.*, pp. 170–1; Jean Guiraud, *Histoire de l'Inquisition au Moyen Âge* (2 vols., Paris, 1938), II, pp. 438, 476–7, 488–9, 550–1; Edouard Jordan, *Les origines de la domination angevine en Italie* (Paris, 1909), pp. 365–6.

[18] See H. C. Lea, *A history of the Inquisition of the Middle Ages* (3 vols., New York, 1888), II, pp. 229–30; Volpe, *Movimenti religiosi*, pp. 111–12.

[19] Cf. Volpe, *Movimenti religiosi*, pp. 73–4; Gordon Leff, *Heresy in the later Middle Ages: the relation of heterodoxy to dissent, c.1250–c.1450* (2 vols., Manchester, 1967), II, pp. 456, 465–6.

[20] On the cult of the Virgin Mary in general, and particularly in Venice, see Galienne Francastel, 'Une peinture anti-hérétique à Venise?', *Annales: Économies, Sociétés, Civilisations*, XX (1965).

ber 1260, and its rule could well have served as the model for the statutes of San Giovanni Evangelista and of the Misericordia.[21] Lists of brothers of the Scuola di San Giovanni Evangelista, compiled during the fourteenth and fifteenth centuries, contained notes to the effect that the Scuola was descended from a company of flagellants (*fraternità di frari battudi*, or *fraternitade de disiplina*) which had first assembled in the church of Sant' Apponal in March 1261. In 1301, it had moved to the monastery of San Giovanni Evangelista, and there had established its permanent premises.[22] The early career of the Misericordia may have been similar, for it probably descended from a Scuola dedicated to the Virgin Mary and to St Francis, founded in 1261. Here, the use of the discipline was normally compulsory, until 1272, when (owing to declining enthusiasm for this ascetic practice) it became optional. At first the Scuola celebrated Masses and buried its dead at the Frari, headquarters of the Franciscans; in 1272, its chapter was meeting in the church of San Giovanni di Rialto; in 1290, the Scuola had 320 living members.[23] However, it seems probable that in 1308 its statutes were revised and brought into line with those of the Carità, when a new Scuola della Misericordia was formed at the abbey of the Misericordia in Cannaregio.[24] This convent of Augustinian friars had been erected on a grassy plot called the Val Verde, and from this the Scuola took its alternative name of Santa Maria della Val Verde.[25] The Scuola di San Rocco followed, after a long interval, during the epidemic of plague which struck Venice in 1478, and attained the rank of a Scuola Grande after about eleven years.[26]

Permanent Scuole dei Battuti, also known as Disciplinati, existed in most of the large subject cities of the Venetian Republic in the sixteenth century. The Venetian Scuole can therefore be studied in the know-

[21] Francesco Sansovino and Giustiniano Martinioni, *Venetia, citta nobilissima et singolare* (Venice, 1663), p. 281; A.S.V., *Scuola Grande di Santa Maria della Carità*, vol. 233.

[22] A.S.V., *Scuola Grande di San Giovanni Evangelista*, vols. 5 and 6.

[23] A.S.V., *Scuola Grande di Santa Maria della Misericordia o della Val Verde*, vol. 2; cf. also Monticolo, *Capitolari delle Arti*, II, pp. xx–xxi. I have not as yet seen any conclusive proof of continuity between the fraternity of 1261 and that of 1308.

[24] A.S.V., *Sala Diplomatica Regina Margherita*, LXXVI–11; *ibid.*, LXXVI–3. LXXVI–3 is an earlier version of the fourteenth-century statutes, but does not contain the whole of the preamble, which is dated 18 August 1308. For the agreement with the abbey of the Misericordia, see LXXVI–3, ch. 50; LXXVI–11, ch. 3.

[25] Tassini, *Curiosità veneziane*, p. 4.

[26] In 1478 membership of the Scuola di San Rocco was limited by decree of the Council of Ten to a total of 100. Another hundred were added in 1485, and in March 1486 the permitted maximum was raised to 300. On petition by the Scuola in September 1489 the Ten granted it permission to increase the numbers gradually to the full 500 permitted to most of the Scuole Grandi. See A.S.R., *Mariegola*, ff. 11, 12v.–13, 15, 16.

ledge that they were no isolated phenomenon. One historian of the lay fraternities of medieval Italy succeeded in identifying 27 companies of flagellants founded in Tuscany and Central and Northern Italy in the thirteenth century, 98 established in the fourteenth, and 32 dating from the fifteenth.[27] These, however, probably constituted only a fraction of the total number. During the sixteenth century the city, suburbs and territory of Bergamo alone maintained about seventy such fraternities, formed into a single comprehensive organization.[28] The senior Bergamese Scuola dei Disciplinati, that of the Maddalena, recognized its debt to the movement of 1260 by attaching to a version of its statutes drawn up in 1470 a copy of the legend of Ranieri Fasani, describing the miraculous visions which had inspired him to preach the use of the discipline.[29] In 1575, there were fourteen Scuole dei Disciplinati in Bergamo itself.[30] A few years earlier, Domenico Priuli, Capitano of Brescia, had reported that the 'discipline' of Brescia resembled in principle the Scuole Grandi of Venice—over 700 persons walked barefoot and beat themselves, following the cross, every week.[31] A systematic survey conducted by one of his successors in 1611 revealed the existence of fifteen *discipline*, with an average membership of twenty to thirty persons. Evidently, they could hardly compete with the great Venetian Scuole in size, wealth or prestige—for only six enjoyed a substantial income, and the rest had very little.[32] But their aims, principles and devotional activities were probably similar to the Venetian. Ghibelline opposition in the thirteenth century had not succeeded in permanently excluding the flagellants from Brescia.

Verona, like Brescia and Bergamo, had several comparatively small companies. At least thirteen Scuole dei Battuti attended the funeral of Gian Matteo Giberti, the great Bishop of Verona, in 1544, mustering

---

[27] See G. M. Monti, *Le confraternite medievali dell' alta e media Italia* (2 vols., Venice, 1927), I, pp. 223, 265, 285. Monti was unaware that the Scuole Grandi of Venice were Scuole dei Battuti.

[28] According to an unsigned and undated document submitted to Carlo Borromeo, Archbishop of Milan, during his visitation of Bergamo in 1575—see A. G. Roncalli and Pietro Forno, *Gli atti della visita apostolica di San Carlo Borromeo a Bergamo, 1575* (2 vols. in 5, Florence, 1936–57), I/ii, pp. 213–14.

[29] *Ibid.*, I/ii, pp. 198–200. On the legend of Raniero Fasani, see also G. Mazzatinti, 'La Lezenda de Fra Rainero Faxano', *Bollettino della Società Umbra di Storia Patria*, II (1896), pp. 561–3; Emilio Ardu, 'Frater Raynerius Faxanus de Perusio', *Il movimento dei Disciplinati*, pp. 84–98.

[30] Roncalli and Forno, *Atti di Borromeo*, I/i, p. 320, I/ii, pp. 5–6, 16, 63, 76–7, 81, 131–41, 197 f., 272, 308–10, 327.

[31] See Carlo Pasero, *Relazioni di rettori veneti a Brescia durante il secolo XVI* (Toscolano, 1939), p. 122.

[32] A.S.V., *Sindici Inquisitori in Terra Ferma*, busta 64, ff. 24, 27v., 30, 37v., 41, 41v., 45v., 47v., 48v., 54.

D

between them 920 flagellants.[33] But further east, in the towns of Friuli and the Trevigiano, the pattern had become rather different by the seventeenth century. Here—in Treviso,[34] Conegliano,[35] Pordenone[36] and Cividale[37]—each town appeared to have one large Scuola di Santa Maria dei Battuti, sometimes disposing of substantial endowments, and administering (or, as at Cividale, mismanaging) some large permanent charitable institution. The movement of 1260 had penetrated to Friuli, when 'all quarrels were settled, even that between the lord Patriarch of Aquileia and the Count of Gorizia, and the innocent and blameless did penance together with the guilty'.[38] A further movement had begun in Friuli in 1290, when a number of citizens of Cividale had begun to beat themselves privately in a local church. Many others had joined in, whipping themselves by night, and had formed processions which visited Gemona and Udine. 'Then they began to flog themselves throughout the whole of Friuli. Women beat themselves by night'.[39] The Scuole di Santa Maria dei Battuti in Cividale and Pordenone may have been permanent monuments to these penitential movements of the thirteenth century.

The prologues to the statutes or Mother Rules (Mariegole) of the Scuola di San Giovanni Evangelista and of the Scuola della Misericordia in Venice seemed to reflect the deeply pessimistic atmosphere in which the great flagellant movement had spread—the sense of uncertainty, the conviction that the present life was only a prologue to the life to come, the consciousness of sin and of human unworthiness. All these sentiments were appropriate to an order vowed to penance and humility. In the early fourteenth century (if no earlier) the brothers of San Giovanni Evangelista declared their purpose as follows:

> Human frailty itself clearly teaches and shows us how profound are the uncertainties of this present life. For every day man, in his wretchedness, is oppressed with care, overwhelmed by toil, and imprisoned in bondage to the Devil. He is always immersed and enmeshed in sin. Hence, as Scripture tells us, even a child one day old is not without sin; and, as

[33] Described in Girolamo Dalla Corte, *Istorie della città di Verona* (3 vols., Venice, 1744), III, p. 314.

[34] See the reports of the governors of Treviso, beginning with that of Pietro Pizzamano (6 June 1564), in A.S.V., *Collegio, Relazioni, busta* 48.

[35] Reports of Zaccaria Morosini, 19 September 1606, and Giovanni Alvise Salamon, 5 October 1611, *ibid., busta* 40.

[36] A.S.V., *Senato, Terra, filza* 160, 17 and 28 October 1601.

[37] *Ibid., filza* 184, 28 September 1607; *filza* 190, 27 April 1609.

[38] *Annales Foroiulienses*, ed. W. Arndt, M.G.H., Ss., XIX (Hanover, 1866), p. 196.

[39] *Ibid.*, p. 205.

St John the Evangelist says, 'If we say that we have not sinned, we deceive ourselves'. Since, as St Augustine says, every mortal man living out this temporal life is dwelling in a foreign country, he should always keep before his eyes the end of this fleeting and transitory life, and must always think about receiving in future the rewards of good and evil. Our Lord and Redeemer himself admonishes us in his Holy Gospel, saying 'Watch and pray, for you know not the day nor the hour'. Hence, inspired by the grace of God, we have discussed and considered how to acquire salvation for our souls through love of brotherhood and with the aid of prayer, recalling the words of St James the Apostle—'Pray for one another, that you may be saved, for the diligent prayer of the just man carries great weight'. Therefore we, all the brothers whose names are inscribed below, with an eager and joyful mind, with sincere good will and in one single spirit, have established this congregation to the honour of Almighty God and of his son Our Lord Jesus Christ and of the Blessed Virgin Mary and of St John the Apostle, ruler and governor of all our men: so that, under the protection of these and all the other saints, we may prove able to return to our own heavenly country.[40]

The congregation of the Misericordia adopted similar terms in 1308.[41] Although the Venetian Scuole were never, like those of Bergamo, united in a single comprehensive organization,[42] they nevertheless developed on parallel lines, subscribing to the same ideals and enacting similar constitutions. In 1478, a year of plague, devotees of the healer San Rocco returned to the formulas of the early Scuole dei Battuti, and repeated them with only slight variations. Then, as if recalling the words of the founders of the Scuola della Carità,[43] they introduced their rule by speaking of the charity, or supreme love of God and of men, in which they had been drafted, and which they strove to promote. The presence in the brothers of the love of God and of man would cause them to concentrate on the enterprise of saving their souls.

All these things written below have been prescribed and ordained by us in no spirit of arrogance, but inspired by the grace and mercy of God, and they have been undertaken for the salvation of our souls and of those of all our brothers with the utmost devotion and simplicity of heart and soul, and in a spirit of love: so that we may follow the doctrine of Holy Scripture, that love shall cover a multitude of sins. For God is love, and whoever perseveres in love remains with God, and God never leaves him. And since we are gathered here in love, each of us must, in peace and tranquillity, take care not to utter empty words, nor to contend or be

[40] A.S.V., *Scuola Grande di San Giovanni Evangelista*, vol. 7, ch. 2, f. 2r.–v.
[41] A.S.V., *Sala Diplomatica Regina Margherita*, LXXVI–11, Prologue.
[42] Cf. Roncalli and Forno, *Atti di Borromeo*, I/ii, pp. 195–7.
[43] A.S.V., *Scuola Grande di Santa Maria della Carità*, vol. 233.

angry one with another. Everyone, rather, must say only things which pertain to the salvation of our souls.

The mercy of Christ was so great that miracles could always be accomplished by prayer, and the brothers quoted his words to the dying thief, 'Today you shall be with me in paradise.'[44]

Although human life was only a period of exile in a foreign land, it was a time of trial—for a man would be judged in the eternal on his conduct in the mortal world. Life on earth was seen in terms of its end —of the day of judgment, when the soul would hang in the balance. Therefore, the Scuole existed to prepare for death and to maintain a bond with the dead: to commemorate them and, through the celebration of Mass for the souls of the living and of the dead, to speed their passage through Purgatory. The founders of the Scuole set themselves to do, as a congregation or fraternity, things which contributed to the salvation of the soul, to correct sin, to make peace, and to accumulate a fund of merit on which all could draw. Much of their inspiration came, in theory, from the fifth chapter of the General Epistle of James, which greatly valued the prayer of the just man and spoke of the miracles to be wrought by the faith of any sincere believer of any condition. The Scuole retained some of the character of the movement of 1260 as an enterprise started by laymen, in which priests subsequently took part. They included a small body of priests whose duty was to offer the sacrifice of the Mass on behalf of the brothers. The vast majority of members, however, were laymen aspiring to be the just men whose prayer would be heard by God in his infinite mercy. The government of the Scuole Grandi and the management of their property were entirely the responsibility of the laity.

The medieval Scuole Grandi stressed the importance of prayer and of the celebration of Mass, rather than the sacraments of communion and confession—the peculiar concern of some devotional societies founded in the sixteenth century.[45] At first, the Scuola di San Giovanni Evangelista required its members to attend confession and take communion twice a year, at Christmas and Easter: but later—probably before the end of the fourteenth century—made it compulsory only at Easter, as if to comply with the minimum requirements of the Fourth Lateran Council, of 1215.[46] However, the celebration of Mass by

44 A.S.R., *Mariegola*, ff. 1v.–2.

45 See below, pp. 232–3.

46 A.S.V., *Scuola Grande di San Giovanni Evangelista*, vol. 3, ch. 46, f. 15; *Sala Diplomatica Regina Margherita*, LXXVI–22, ch. 14, f. 8v. Cf. the regulations of the Scuola della Misericordia (fourteenth century), which insisted on communion either at Easter or at Christmas: A.S.V., *Sala Diplomatica Regina Margherita*, LXXVI–3, ch. 13; LXXVI–11, ch. 40.

priests attached to the Scuola bulked very large. The rule of the Misericordia required all brothers to attend Mass on the first Sunday of every month. Later legislation provided that the officers known as Degani should attend Mass every Monday 'for the souls of all the brothers of the congregation'. Finally, between 1352 and 1354, the brothers introduced the practice of celebrating Mass daily, and paying priests to perform this duty out of the property of the Scuola.[47] In the mid-fourteenth century, the officers of the Scuola di San Giovanni Evangelista clearly felt some scruples about admitting priests to the Scuola, on the grounds of the many technical difficulties this practice created.

> It is not lawful for any lay or secular person to admonish, correct or demand obedience of any priest or clerk. The Mariegola cannot be observed properly for the further reason that no priest or clerk can on his death be washed and laid out by our brothers as our Mariegola stipulates. Moreover, the said priests and clerks, on account of their churches and offices, cannot attend on dead bodies as they promise and are bound to do.

In 1345, they expressly provided that priests were not to be admitted to the fraternity, and that the flagellants of the Scuola would not henceforth be obliged to attend their funerals. However, priests could be received into the prayers of the Scuola—in which case they would be inscribed on the Mariegola. They would then be informed by the Degano of the death of any brother, and each priest must say a Mass for the repose of his soul. On the death of a priest or clerk, the brothers of the Scuola would each recite fifty Paternosters.[48] But the Scuola did not find it worthwhile to maintain this fine distinction, or to insist that priests were not within the Scuola. Some time later—perhaps before the end of the fourteenth century—the Scuola resolved to admit thirty priests 'of good rank and reputation' to celebrate Mass (in shifts of six, turn and turn about) on the appointed days. Each priest would celebrate a Mass for the soul of every brother of the Scuola who died. Respect for the status of the priest and for his immunity from lay authority seemed to have diminished—'if any of these priests fails to lead a good and reputable life or to carry out his obligations properly, the Guardian and his fellow-officers shall be entitled to expel him and to receive another to make up the aforesaid number.'[49]

In theory, priests and clergy did not account for more than 5–6 per cent of the total membership of each Scuola—with thirty priests to 550

---

[47] *Ibid.*, LXXVI–3, ch. 16, 29, 83; LXXVI–11, ch. 20, 26.
[48] A.S.V., *Scuola Grande di San Giovanni Evangelista*, vol. 3, ch. 58, f. 20v.
[49] A.S.V., *Sala Diplomatica Regina Margherita*, LXXVI–22, ch. 46, f. 19.

laymen.[50] During the sixteenth century, the proportion became still lower in the Scuole di San Rocco and San Marco. Between the 1490's and 1538, the Scuola di San Rocco enrolled only one priestly entrant for every 70 laymen, and the Scuola di San Marco admitted 30 laymen to every priest.[51] However, the Scuole did not invariably succeed in limiting the numbers of the clergy in accordance with their own statutes. The Carità in 1517 and the Misericordia in 1533 had to reduce the number of priestly members.[52] In the Carità they now numbered 80 and exceeded their usefulness: no more clergy (other than parish priests, who were treated with greater respect) were to be admitted until the numbers had fallen to a mere 50.

The clergy took no part in the government of the Scuole Grandi and did not discharge clearly defined functions as confessors or spiritual advisers. Nor, apparently, were the Scuole Grandi of Venice subjected to any form of control or surveillance by the Patriarch: ultimate authority over them belonged to the Council of Ten, which occasionally appointed special commissions to examine their affairs. The Council of Ten had legislated on the Scuole in 1312, two years after its own foundation.[53] As a committee of public safety, charged to examine the affairs of all associations in Venice and to ensure that they did not conspire against the state, it had established in 1360 the principle that no new religious fraternity or Scola could be founded unless it was approved by three-quarters of the votes of the Council of Ten, in full session, and in the presence of the Doge and his six councillors.[54] When, in 1468, the Great Council precisely defined the competence of the Council of Ten, matters concerning the Scuole (both great and small) were expressly included within its authority.[55] The Venetian

[50] In 1431, the Scuola della Misericordia obtained permission to increase the number of priestly members from 25 to 30, to bring it into line with the other Scuole—see A.S.V., *Compilazione delle Leggi*, busta 344, f. 101. For the number of laymen in the Scuole, see below, pp. 86 f.

[51] The Scuola di San Rocco admitted 23 clergymen to some 1,800 lay entrants (excluding nobles, who were only honorary members). See A.S.R., *Mariegola*, where the clergy are listed at f. 54r.–v. In 1538, the Scuola di San Rocco fixed the quota of priests at only 24 (A.S.V., *Scuola Grande di San Rocco, seconda consegna*, vol. 46, f. 58). The Scuola di San Marco admitted 131 clergymen to some 3,800 laymen— A.S.V., *Scuola Grande di San Marco*, vol. 6.

[52] A.S.V., *Scuola Grande di Santa Maria della Carità*, vol. 236, f. 39r.–v.; *Consiglio dei Dieci, Registro Comune 1533*, f. 145v.

[53] A.S.V., *Inquisitori et Revisori sopra le Scuole Grandi, Capitolare I*, f. 1—note of a decree which forbade Scuole dei Battuti and others to assemble or process by night.

[54] A.S.V., *Compilazione delle Leggi*, busta 344, f. 78.

[55] A.S.V., *Inquisitori et Revisori sopra le Scuole Grandi, Capitolare I*, f. 13v. In 1508, the Ten delegated their authority over all routine matters involving the smaller Scuole to the magistracy of the Provveditori di Commun, which also exercised authority over some of the guilds; but the Ten retained control over licences to erect new Scuole (*ibid.*, ff. 23v.–24).

government, at least from the late fifteenth to the early seventeenth century, attempted to exclude the clergy from governmental or administrative responsibility at all levels. The clergy—though they did not normally live in latent conflict with the civil authorities—were always men who might own to a higher allegiance outside the Venetian state. The Pope was not only the spiritual head of the Catholic Church, but also a neighbour prince, with whose territorial ambitions those of the Republic occasionally collided. It was undesirable that the clergy should obtain control of rich lay institutions, lest their wealth elude the Venetian tax-collector. The encroachments of the clergy on lay jurisdiction were best restrained by preventive measures. In 1475 and 1498, the clergy were legally excluded first from serving as notaries or secretaries to government departments, and then—even if nobly born—from participating in the sovereign Great Council.[56] Paolo Sarpi, at the start of his history of the Interdict imposed in 1606, ascribed Paul V's peculiar hatred of the Venetian Republic partly to its practice of excluding churchmen from any rôle in its government.[57] This principle clearly applied, not only to state departments, but also to religious associations under government surveillance.

It was unnecessary to pass express legislation against intervention by the clergy in the government of the Scuole Grandi. However, the principle was specifically affirmed in a case which, at the beginning of the seventeenth century, involved the smaller devotional society of San Giacinto. This Scuola was founded in 1595 in a Dominican church, without obtaining the necessary licence either from the Council of Ten or from the Provveditori di Commun. The authorities discovered its existence only after a period of twenty years, when the Heads of the Ten were informed that the Dominicans had secured undue influence over the management of the Scuola. Indeed, the Dominican Prior was its official president or Cappo. He appointed a deputy to control admissions to the Scuola, and to attend meetings of the Syndics, auditors to whom the officials accounted for the management of the Scuola's finances. Should legacies be made to the altar of San Giacinto with no explicit mention of the Scuola, the Dominicans claimed them for their convent. The Provveditori di Commun suggested that the Scuola, having been so long established, should be allowed to continue: but only with 'an express proviso that the Fathers cannot and must not on any account interfere with any matter concerning this Scuola'. The

---

[56] Bartolomeo Cecchetti, *La Republica di Venezia e la Corte di Roma nei rapporti della religione* (Venice, 1874, 2 vols.), I, p. 133.

[57] Paolo Sarpi, *Istoria dell' Interdetto (e altri scritti editi e inediti)*, ed. M. D. Busnelli and Giulio Gambarin (3 vols., Bari, 1940), I, p. 4.

Scuola must henceforth be governed by lay officials, like all the other *scuole piccole* in the city, and must be subjected to regulations imposed by the Provveditori. All statutes and constitutions hitherto issued should be declared null and void.[58]

The Venetians maintained this principle in their own city, but some distinction must be made between the Dominante and its dominions, where it obviously proved more difficult to check ecclesiastical control over lay fraternities. Decrees of the Council of Trent, widely enforced on the Venetian mainland and in the overlapping ecclesiastical province of Milan, demanded that the bishop should review the accounts and administration of lay fraternities, together with those of hospitals and Monti di Pietà. Before the accession of Lorenzo Priuli to the Patriarchate in 1592, episcopal initiative was far more vigorous on the mainland than in Venice itself.[59] The city and some of the territory of Bergamo formed part of the province of Milan. Here, Carlo Borromeo, in his synods of 1569 and 1573, obliged the bishop to visit the sodalities and confraternities of the Disciplinati, and to examine their accounts, constitutions and devotional literature.[60] During his own visitations of Bergamo in 1575, he obtained access to much information about the conduct of the fraternities of the Disciplinati and other Bergamese Scuole, and himself issued regulations for their reform.[61] Again, in the early seventeenth century, not long after the Interdict, some Venetian governors expressed uneasiness about clerical intervention in the administration of the Scuole under their sway. Admittedly, Tommaso Lippomano, formerly Provveditore in Cividale di Friuli, praised the local Scuola di Santa Maria dei Battuti because

> they make no attempt to withdraw from obedience to representatives of the state, and subject themselves to their jurisdiction, always allowing them to examine their accounts and administration.[62]

But, in 1618, the area of Rovigo gave cause for serious concern. Here, the governor Girolamo Correr spoke of 'many Scuole or lay congregations' which met in churches or elsewhere without the knowledge of the Venetian authorities; 'and', he added, 'I have noticed that the

---

[58] A.S.V., *Consiglio dei Dieci, Parti Comuni, filza* 307, 25 May 1616.
[59] Cf. below, pp. 335 f.
[60] *Acta Ecclesiae Mediolanensis,* f. 34v., 46v. (Milan, 1583). The fifth synod, of 1579, also instructed the bishop to ensure that members of lay Scuole did not discuss matters of faith and doctrine, but confined themselves to matters appropriate to the laity. (*Ibid.,* f. 129.)
[61] Roncalli and Forno, *Atti di Borromeo,* I/i, I/ii.
[62] A.S.V., *Senato, Terra, filza* 190, 27 April 1609.

Vicar of the diocese is assuming rights over them, with some ill-consequences for the secular authority'.[63] Likewise, Andrea Boldu, Podestà of Castelfranco, reported that he had tried to compel the officials of Scuole and other similar institutions in his territory to produce accounts; but they had told him either that they did not keep accounts, or that they had handed the task over to their own parish priests. The parish priest of Sant' Andrea rendered account to the Vicar-General of the diocese of Treviso. Here, the Senate acted on the advice of its Consultori in Iure, one of whom was Paolo Sarpi himself. He and his colleague asserted that

> there is no room for doubt that the revenues of confraternities, Scuole and other lay establishments must be administered by laymen; and it is certain that ecclesiastics have no right to intervene therein or to audit their accounts.[64]

The most tactful method of eliminating priestly influence over the Scuole would be to forget the past and not to force officials to account. But in future the lay officials of the Scuole must either keep the accounts themselves, or—should they be illiterate—delegate the duty to another layman, and not to a priest.

As far as possible, the Venetian government enforced the principle that the clergy must be excluded from the government of lay fraternities and from the management of their finances. In the Scuole Grandi, under the close surveillance of the Ten and officered by Venetian citizens, they undoubtedly succeeded in their aim. Priests became subordinate to the officers of the Scuola, and even developed into their employees. The chaplain's position of subjection to the governors of the Scuola di San Rocco appears from an order regulating his office in 1536. The first article obliged him 'To obey the worshipful Guardian for the time being in all matters ordained by the Bench concerning the government of our church and the processions and devotions held throughout the whole year both within this church and outside it'.[65] In 1543 the Scuola prescribed fees for two groups of *mansonarii*, lesser chaplains or Mass-priests, who earned according to the number of Masses celebrated or corpses buried. In addition to their fees they enjoyed some insurance against sickness. They were liable to be fined if the chaplain reported them to the lay officers for doing

[63] A.S.V., *Collegio, Relazioni, busta* 46, report dated 5 July 1618.
[64] A.S.V., *Senato, Terra, filza* 230, 29 September 1618.
[65] A.S.V., *Scuola Grande di San Rocco, seconda consegna*, vol. 46, f. 38.

their duty inefficiently.[66] The Scuola di San Marco made roughly similar arrangements in the 1540's.[67]

The Scuole Grandi employed more clergy when testators began to request them to choose priests to say Masses specially designed for their own salvation, where they were not content with the statutory Masses offered for the souls of all the brothers and financed by the Scuola. In the early seventeenth century, for which a few figures are available, the Scuola di San Giovanni was especially generous to the clergy: nearly 15 per cent of its net expenditure of some 4,800 ducats a year was devoted to them. The principal chaplain or Cappo, two lesser chaplains, a sacristan and two acolytes, received 260 ducats between them, whilst a sum of over 400 ducats was dispensed to Mass-priests functioning under the provisions of various trusts. Their annual salaries ranged from as much as 72 ducats to as little as 12.[68] In 1648 the Cappo received a salary of 80 ducats, the minor chaplains 60 ducats each and the sacristan 48, though these salaries were then reduced by 25–33 per cent to enable the Scuola to meet its heavy fiscal obligations during the war of Crete.[69] San Marco and the Misericordia were less generous to the clergy, but similar payments still absorbed 7–8 per cent of the net expenditure of these Scuole.[70]

Other bonds united the Scuole and the clergy. Two of the early Scuole took their names from the priories of San Giovanni Evangelista and of the Misericordia. They met on their premises, buried dead brothers in their vaults, and called upon their priests to say Masses for them.[71] Moreover, at least from the thirteenth century onwards it was

[66] *Mansonarii* of the first group were paid 8 soldi for every day on which they celebrated Mass and 4 soldi for every corpse buried in the dependent church of the Scuola, together with certain perquisites in the form of candles at processions, palms on Palm Sunday, and so forth. A second group of *mansonarii*, with lighter obligations, received 5 soldi for each Mass. Fees were still paid to *mansonarii* of both groups for a period of up to twenty days if they fell sick. Fees were withheld if the *mansonarii* arrived late or improperly dressed at vespers or Mass, and they were fined double for defaulting on a festival day. A.S.V., *Scuola Grande di S. Rocco, seconda consegna*, vol. 47, ff. 15–16.

[67] A.S.V., *Scuola Grande di S. Marco*, vol. 8 (a late seventeenth-century summary of the decisions made by the governors of the Scuola), f. 333r.–v.: note of a decree of 28 June 1545.

[68] From a statement submitted by the governors of the Scuola to the Collegio della Milizia da Mar, the magistracy concerned with naval recruiting and hence with the assessment of war taxation, in 1614—analysed below, Appendix, pp. 190–1.

[69] A.S.V., *Scuola Grande di S. Giovanni Evangelista*, vol. 2, f. 170v.: decree of the Council of Ten of 24 January 1648.

[70] See below, Appendix, pp. 189–90, 192–3—statements for the Scuola di San Marco in 1590 and 1611 and for the Misericordia in 1614 and 1627.

[71] A.S.V., *Scuola Grande di San Giovanni Evangelista*, vol. 3, ch. 3, f. 5v.; vol. 7, ch. 17, 19, f. 5v., 6. See also the agreement of the Scuola della Misericordia with the

a common practice for lay fraternities to form spiritual bonds, for the purpose of accumulating and pooling merit, with convents, with whole religious orders, or occasionally with individual churchmen of great eminence or sanctity.[72] Mariegole of the fourteenth century contain extensive lists of the spiritual brothers of the Scuole. Those of the Scuola della Carità were headed by the Dominicans, the Franciscans and (from 1295) the Augustinian Eremites, who received the Scuola collectively through their generals. Later, the Carmelites and the Order of Camaldoli were added. So were numerous local communities of monks and nuns.[73] Lay women were not admitted to the Scuola (the Scuola di San Giovanni Evangelista ceased to receive them in 1327).[74] In one of the Mariegole of the Carità the list of honorary members began with the Patriarch of Grado, the Archbishops of Ragusa and Zara, the Bishops of Castello and Caorle, and other prelates. Good works were pooled—Masses, prayers, fasts, vigils, flagellations, distributions of alms—and each of the contracting parties became 'participants and partners' in the merits hereby accumulated by the other. Similar arrangements were still made in the late fifteenth and in the sixteenth century. In 1489, the brothers of San Rocco entered into a complex agreement with their landlords the Franciscans of the adjoining convent of the Frari or Frati Minori, whereby the Franciscans were to attend the funerals of brothers of the Scuola di San Rocco, carrying their cross, and to receive small payments in exchange. The Franciscans had the right to supply the Scuola with preachers twelve times a year, and the Scuola was bound to employ three Franciscans to say Mass daily as *mansonarii*, and to include them in all distributions of alms during Lent. Courtesy visits were exchanged on the festivals of St Francis and of San Rocco. So much litigation, however, arose from this agreement that in 1540 money payments had to be substituted for the smaller obligations of the Scuola towards the Franciscans.[75] The concept of the spiritual bond was far from obsolete in the mid-sixteenth century, for the Scuola di San Marco formed a 'loving and Christian brotherhood' and 'spiritual and charitable union' with the nuns of San Daniele in 1553 and with those of Santa Marta in 1557.[76]

Laity and clergy within the Scuole collected spiritual treasure through the recitation of prayers, the celebration of Mass and the

priory of the Misericordia, 14 March 1310, A.S.V., *Sala Diplomatica Regina Margherita*, LXXVI–3, ch. 50; LXXVI–11, ch. 3.

[72] Cf. Monti, *Le confraternite medievali*, I, p. 215.

[73] A.S.V., *Scuola Grande di Santa Maria della Carità*, vols. 233, 233 *bis*.

[74] A.S.V., *Scuola Grande di San Giovanni Evangelista*, vol. 7, ch. 61, f. 17r.–v.

[75] A.S.R., *Mariegola*, ff. 37–9, 46v.–48v.

[76] A.S.V., *Scuola Grande di S. Marco*, vol. 21 (*Notatorio VI*), f. 15r.–v., 139.

giving of alms. They supplemented this by attempting to prevent the commission of sin, through the correction of faults. The sins most sternly condemned were blasphemy, adultery and wrath, together with any misdemeanours, such as gambling, frequenting taverns and keeping lewd company, which might lead to blasphemy. Gambling was condemned by the Scuola di San Rocco partly because it might be 'the ruin and destruction' of the gambler's house, but mainly because the Guardian could not 'tolerate so horrible a sin, which is the root of blasphemy; and blasphemy is like a wound to our Saviour'.[77] Adultery was severely reproved,[78] and wrath deemed contrary to the spirit of mutual love or 'charity' on which the Scuole were founded. The Scuole did not, however, expressly mention usury, which was condemned by some other Italian fraternities very similar to the Venetian in their view of sin and misconduct.[79] At first, procedures for the correction of serious offences were very cumbersome, but later a more expeditious system of fining blasphemers was introduced—the officers of San Rocco devised one in 1493, acting, they said, on the example of the four senior Scuole. Any brother who swore by the body and blood of Christ, by God the Father or by the Virgin, was to be fined 10 soldi— blaspheming against any of these would be punished by a fine of double that amount.[80] The laymen of the Scuole Grandi thus imposed their own discipline, adding their own sanctions to the more momentous penalties of the Church. The vetoes imposed by the Scuole had some incidental social value, though social improvement was not their professed object, for they were formally designed to rescue souls from mortal sin.

There remained the public display of repentance in the flagellant processions. Early statutes of the Scuola di San Giovanni listed about

[77] A.S.R., *Mariegola*, ff. 6–7. Prohibitions of blasphemy alternate with prohibitions of frequenting taverns or 'altri luoghi inhonesti e vituperosi se non per qualche caxone de inportunita e necessitade'. Cf. A.S.V., *Scuola Grande di S.ta Maria della Carità*, vol. 234 (*Mariegola*), *capitolo* lii of August 1353, which ordains 'ke nesun nostro frar no osa ne debia andar in taverna in venesia per bere'.

[78] A.S.V., *Scuola Grande di S. Giovanni Evangelista*, vol. 3, ch. 14–16, f. 8r.–v.; *Sala Diplomatica Regina Margherita*, LXXVI–3, ch. 25, 33, 58; LXXVI–11, ch. 37, 38.

[79] E.g. the eleventh-century fraternity of S. Appiano in the County of Florence or the early fourteenth-century Neapolitan fraternity of the Disciplinati di Maddaloni (their statutes are printed as Appendici III and V to Monti, *Le confraternite medievali*, II, pp. 139–43, 159–66). The Maddaloni provided that 'si alcuno fratello fosse bestematore de santi o ausuro publico o 'nprestasse ad usura o fosse judicatore azar(d)o, o fosse siscematico che ponesse la casa in discordia, o latrone; non lasseno intrare a lu luoco persine che non se menda de lu suo peccato'. *Ibid.*, p. 165. The statutes of the Scuola dei Disciplinati della Maddalena in Bergamo also expressly barred usurers from membership—see Roncalli and Forno, *Atti di Borromeo*, I/ii, p. 201.

[80] A.S.V., *Scuola Grande di San Rocco, seconda consegna*, vol. 44, ff. 29–30v.

a dozen days in every year on which the brothers would be summoned to hear Mass, to give alms, and then to follow a cross and lighted candles through the city, 'with the use of the discipline, in a spirit of peace and humility, and without complaint (*cum verberation et dessepina, cum pace et humilità senza murmuration alguna*)'. These were the greater festivals of the Scuola. Similar expeditions were made on the first Sunday of every month, and at all funerals of dead brothers.[81] The rule of the Scuola della Misericordia exempted all brothers aged over sixty from the obligation to wield the scourge, and bound them to stay in the church reciting prayers whilst the procession trod the streets of Venice.[82] In the late fifteenth century, the founders of the Scuola di San Rocco prescribed a habit or *capa* for the brothers who performed the discipline—

let them go dressed in a sack with sleeves and with their hoods on their heads and with the face covered; with grey stockings, white shoes, and the shoulders naked at the back to permit them to use the discipline. And those who wish to go with the habit covering their naked flesh, but with their feet bare, may swell the numbers of the holy discipline.[83]

During the sixteenth century, the Scuole Grandi still practised self-flagellation in public processions. Sanuto described how, on Holy Thursday 1530, they came to St Mark's to see the traditional display of the blood of Christ in its reliquary, and how the Scuola di San Rocco brought with it 90 flagellants.[84] Sansovino, fifty years later, remarked that the Scuola di San Rocco was always accompanied by many flagellants on the processions for Holy Thursday, and added that the other Scuole, inspired by its example, had 'introduced a similar custom a few years ago'.[85] But flagellation had become a special ceremony, a traditional custom and an 'ancient devotion', rather than a regular or important activity of the Scuole. Entries made on the registers of San Rocco in 1576, 1591 and 1615 suggest that these flagellants were not members of the Scuola, but men hired for particularly momentous festivals.[86] Admittedly, Carlo Borromeo, Cardinal-Archbishop of

---

[81] A.S.V., *Scuola Grande di San Giovanni Evangelista*, vol. 3, ch. 10, f. 7r.–v.

[82] A.S.V., *Sala Diplomatica Regina Margherita*, LXXVI–3, ch. 5, 14; LXXVI–11, ch. 22.

[83] A.S.R., *Mariegola*, f. 8.

[84] D.M.S., LIII, col. 144, 14 April 1530.

[85] Sansovino and Martinioni, *Venetia*, p. 288.

[86] In March 1576 the governors of the Scuola anticipated that in the Jubilee year many flagellants would come to the city, and they ordered 50 new sacks and scourges to be made for the occasion (A.S.R., *Registro delle Terminazioni* 2, f. 363). In 1591 the governors reduced to 16 soldi the fee payable to each of 'the flagellants who go with our Scuola on the night of Holy Thursday' (*ibid.*, 3, ff. 199v.–200). In May 1615,

Milan, had attempted to revive this act of asceticism and to regulate the companies of the discipline in his province—which included the Venetian territory of Bergamo. He restated the principle that the use of the scourge was an important form of the imitation of Christ, a means of recalling and repeating his physical sufferings and of atoning for the sins of the world. He ordered the confraternities of his province to gird their habits with a cord tied in seven knots,

> in memory of the precious blood which our Saviour shed at his circumcision, in the garden, when he was flogged at the column, when he was crowned with thorns, when his hands were pierced, when his feet were pierced, and when his side was opened.[87]

In 1575, Borromeo insisted that the united fraternities of the discipline in Bergamo should all adopt the rules he had formulated for the province.[88] But there is no evidence of any comparable effort to revive the use of the discipline in Venice itself.

Throughout the sixteenth and early seventeenth century, the Venetian Scuole took part in many elaborate processions—in public ceremonies designed to flaunt the wealth and piety of the Venetians, and to disseminate political propaganda in a form comprehensible to ordinary people. The emphasis now lay on pomp and splendour, not on suffering and humility. The Council of Ten controlled these processions, and attempted, as in 1513,[89] to settle the bitter quarrels over precedence which frequently disturbed public order—even on solemn occasions such as the exhibition of relics during Holy Week.[90] Later, in 1565, they delegated this task to the Maestro di Choro of St Mark's.[91] In 1576, the Heads of the Ten enforced on the officers and men of the Scuole Grandi attendance at all processions which involved passing through St Mark's and at which the Doge and Signoria intended to be present. 'It is fitting that if the Most Serene Prince and the Illustrious Signoria attend these solemnities the principal members of these Scuole shall also do so.' They repeated this provision in 1596, 1597 and

the governors approved the expenditure of about 35 ducats on 24 shirts or sacks 'to preserve the ancient devotion of the flagellants who are accustomed to come and honour our Scuola on the evening of Holy Thursday' (*ibid.*, 4, f. 225v.).

[87] 'Regola della Confraternità de i disciplinati, per decreto del Concilio provinciale secondo di Milano', in *Acta Ecclesiae Mediolanensis*, ff. 329–34v. Cf. also Giuseppe Alberigo, 'Contributi alla storia delle confraternite dei Disciplinati e della spiritualità laicale nei secoli XV e XVI', in *Il movimento dei Disciplinati*, pp. 205 f.

[88] Roncalli and Forno, *Atti di Borromeo*, I/ii, pp. 131–3, 155 f.

[89] A.S.V., *Inquisitori et Revisori sopra le Scuole Grandi, Capitolare I*, ff. 25–7v.

[90] D.M.S., XXVII, col. 93, 22 April 1519.

[91] A.S.V., *Inquisitori et Revisori sopra le Scuole Grandi, Capitolare I*, ff. 78v.–79v.

1615.[92] Despite the existence of these legal sanctions, there is no reason to assume that such duties were irksome. Participation in these ceremonies may have acted as a bond between rulers and subjects, for they offered a means by which men of many social ranks could assemble under religious banners to express collectively the official sentiments of the Venetian government. They also provided a medium for publishing news of important political events, such as the conclusion of alliances between states. During the wars of the early sixteenth century, these were symbolically acted out in gorgeous processions on the Piazza San Marco, when the Scuole Grandi, the friars and other Venetian clergy exhibited their relics and precious vessels, and produced elaborate tableaux vivants for the delight of the people.

The Leagues which Venice joined in 1511, 1513, 1526 and 1530 were certainly celebrated in this way. In October 1511, the Scuola della Misericordia headed the procession, with '27 little boys dressed like little angels, all carrying vessels of silver in their hands, whilst others bore the arms of the League—of the Pope, of the King of Spain, of the King of England, and of St Mark or of our own Signoria'. The Scuola di San Rocco, fourth in this procession, presented a tableau with the figures of Venice and her patron saint, followed by actors representing the Kings of England and Spain, the discomfited King of France against whom the League was directed, and finally the Pope. Each Scuola proudly paraded its relics—a hand of St Theodosia, a foot of St Martin, the entire body of San Rocco, the ring of St Mark, and the red hats of the late cardinals Bessarion and Zeno.[93] The other ceremonies followed very similar lines.[94] Great festivals like those of Corpus Christi and the Madonna called forth comparable, non-political displays of piety. Persons described as Battuti certainly walked in the processions, but they carried silver reliquaries and precious vessels, not whips for their own backs, and their bearing was scarcely penitential. Sanuto once criticized the Misericordia for appearing in disorder, but the Scuola di San Rocco never failed to earn his praise for its ingenious biblical scenes. At the festival of the Madonna in 1515, the Scuola presented

> a great wooden San Rocco dressed in gold, with a live boy as an angel showing him the plague. Above was the prophet St Zacharias. . . On another float were the twelve tribes and the wand of Aaron, and Moses kneeling before it was giving incense from a thurible. Another showed

[92] *Ibid.*, ff. 84r.–v., 116v., 127r.–v.
[93] D.M.S., XIII, coll. 132–41, 20 October 1511.
[94] D.M.S., XVI, coll. 287–8, 22 May 1513; XLII, coll. 62–78, 8 July 1526; LII, coll. 435–6, 1 January 1530.

how Christ went into limbo to release the holy fathers, and the limbo was complete with devils, etc.[95]

Perhaps these ephemeral creations foreshadowed the great series of biblical paintings with which, some seventy years later, Giacomo Tintoretto covered the walls and ceilings of the Scuola's hall.

Later in the century the Venetian Republic retreated, in peninsular politics, into cautious neutrality. But the government still ordained that processions be organized for diplomatic purposes and for the entertainment of distinguished visitors. In 1587, the Guardians of the Scuole Grandi, protesting in unison against the imposition of heavy fiscal burdens, reminded the Heads of the Ten of the various forms of service they were already expected to render to the Venetian state: for example, 'in many honourable processions for the arrival of many Princes, and most recently in the procession ordered by mandate of Your Most Illustrious Lordships for the visit of the Prince Ambassadors of Japan'.[96] The Republic saw fit to celebrate the peace concluded between France and Spain in 1559 and again in 1598.[97] Since Venetian security depended on a balance of power being maintained between Habsburg and Valois or Habsburg and Bourbon, she strove to conciliate both when there was no urgent reason to incline decisively to one side. The festivities which marked the treaty of 1598 were designed very similarly to those of the early sixteenth century, lit by candles and flaming torches which consumed vast quantities 'of the whitest wax'. By this time, the Scuole were celebrating with music, captivating the ear whilst they dazzled the eye: each brought up a trained choir of children to sing hymns and verses in praise of peace, and moved many of the crowd to tears.[98] Some years later, in 1608, the Scuole Grandi were called upon at short notice to provide entertainment for the sons of a potentially valuable ally, the Duke of Savoy.[99]

Of religious, rather than political, significance were the celebrations of the victory of French Catholics over Condé in 1569.[100] So were other

[95] D.M.S., XXI, coll. 46–7, 8 September 1515. Cf. also XVI, coll. 303–4, 26 May 1513; XX, coll. 274–5, 7 June 1515; XXIV, coll. 347–8, 11 June 1517.

[96] A.S.V., *Inquisitori et Revisori sopra le Scuole Grandi, Capitolare I*, f. 92.

[97] *Cronaca Agostini*, M.C.V., Cicogna MSS. 2853, f. 110; *Cronaca Agostini over Savina*, B.M.V., MSS. Italiani, Cl. VII, 134 (8035), f. 371.

[98] See the very extensive description of these ceremonies in *Compendio di me Francesco da Molino de Missier Marco delle cose, che reputerò degne di venerne particolar memoria, et che sucederanno in mio tempo si della Republica Venetiana e di Venetia mia Patria come anco della special mia persona*, B.M.V., MSS. Italiani, Cl. VII, 153 (8812), pp. 177–82.

[99] Gian Carlo Sivos, *Delle vite dei Dosi di Venezia, Libro Terzo*, B.M.V., MSS. Italiani, Cl. VII, 1818 (9436), f. 154r.–v.

[100] *Cronaca Agostini*, f. 151v.

solemn processions to mark the foundation of a new seminary behind St Mark's in 1581,[101] or the return, transfer or display of spectacular relics.[102] Thanksgiving ceremonies followed the Christian victory at Lepanto[103] and the passing of the plague of 1575–7: then, for the first time, a bridge of boats spanned the water between the *canton della becharia* at San Marco and the site of Palladio's church of the Redentore on the Giudecca.[104] The Venetians also tried to exorcize the plague in Genoa, when in 1579, on the feast of St Thomas the Apostle, the Doge with many noblemen and clergy and the Scuole Grandi solemnly processed round the Piazza San Marco, at the request of the Genoese nation.[105]

During the Interdict of 1606–7, the Scuole Grandi proved especially useful to the Venetian state. They disseminated propaganda designed to maintain the unity of the people of Venice, and to express through comprehensible symbols and slogans the theories favoured by the government. On behalf of the Catholic rulers of Europe, Venice, by defending her right to punish criminous clerks, to tax resident clergy, and to pass laws restricting the bequeathal of real property into the 'dead hand' of ecclesiastical institutions, asserted the absolute separation of the spheres of action proper to the lay and to the sacerdotal power. In a manner reminiscent of Marsilio of Padua, the Venetian Republic returned to certain selected maxims of primitive Christianity to justify reducing the clergy to comparative impotence. From the Venetian pamphleteers, and especially from the pen of Paolo Sarpi, the official theologian to the Republic, came the most lucid opposition to the extreme claims of priestly authority to ultimate dominion in worldly affairs—as formulated, for example, by Bellarmine.[106] Sarpi himself summed up the Venetian arguments as follows:

> that God has established two governments in the world, one spiritual, the other temporal, each supreme and independent, the one from the other. One is the ministry of the Church, the other political government.

[101] *Cronaca Agostini over Savina*, f. 359.

[102] *Cronaca Agostini*, f. 143v.; *Cronaca Agostini over Savina*, f. 364v.; Gian Carlo Sivos, *Libro Quarto delli Dosi di Venetia*, B.M.V., MSS. Italiani, Cl. VII, 122 (8863), f. 103.

[103] *Cronaca Agostini over Savina*, f. 343v.

[104] *Ibid.*, ff. 353v.–354.

[105] *Ibid.*, f. 357v.

[106] See for example the extract from Bellarmine's *De Romano pontifice* quoted in Leopold von Ranke, *The History of the Popes during the last four centuries* (Mrs Foster's translation, revised by G. R. Dennis, London, 1908), II, p. 8: 'Quantum ad personas, non potest papa ut papa ordinarie temporales principes deponere, etiam justa de causa, eo modo quo deponit episcopos, id est tanquam ordinarius iudex: tamen potest mutare regna et uni auferre atque alteri conferre, tanquam summus princeps spiritualis, si id necessarium sit ad animarum salutem'.

E

Spiritual government God has entrusted to the apostles and their successors, temporal to princes; so that neither can intervene in the province of the other. That the Pope has no power to annul the laws of princes on temporal matters, deprive them of their states, or release their subjects from allegiance; that disqualifying and depriving kings from ruling is a thing attempted in the past five hundred years contrary to the Scriptures and to the example of Christ and the saints; and that teaching that in case of controversy between the Pope and a Prince it shall be lawful to persecute the Prince both with plots and with open force, and that there shall be a remission of sins for subjects who rebel against him, is a seditious and sacrilegious doctrine. That ecclesiastics have not by divine law received any immunity from the secular power, either in their persons or in their property. . . .[107]

A state which claimed absolute power over the persons of the clergy was manifesting itself in the bosom of the Roman Catholic Church in a style which recalled that of Philip the Fair in his contest with Boniface VIII.

The successful defiance of Paul V, which ended in honourable compromise, was made possible by two combinations of circumstances. One was the lack of enthusiasm abroad for the cause of the Pope—Venetians were stating the case for every Catholic Prince. In the words of Sir Henry Wotton, the English Ambassador, 'their controversie with the Pope is the roote of all Soveraignitie and the common cause of Princes', and 'hath a particular conformitie with the liberties and exemptions of the Churche of Fraunce'.[108] Sarpi perceived with subtle accuracy that Spain stood to win something whatever the outcome of the Interdict, so that she had no strong interest in securing the utter humiliation of Venice.[109] Moreover, she was, with her commitments in the Netherlands, unprepared for a costly war in Italy. In February 1606 Fuentes, then Governor of Milan, wrote to warn his sovereign that his own interests would be prejudiced if the Pope were allowed the extensive authority over laymen's property which he was claiming in Venice.[110] An ambassador sent by Spain to Venice proved capable of making very Sarpian speeches in the presence of the Doge and of the Collegio.[111] The Spanish favourite, Lerma himself, upheld the

[107] Sarpi, *Istoria dell' Interdetto*, I, p. 106.

[108] P.R.O., S.P. 99/3, ff. 179v.–180; Wotton to King James I, 26 September/6 October 1606.

[109] Sarpi, *Istoria dell' Interdetto*, I, p. 57.

[110] Enrico Cornet, *Paolo V e la Republica Veneta: giornale dal 22 ottobre 1605–9 giugno 1607* (Vienna, 1859), pp. 31–2.

[111] Sarpi, *Istoria dell' Interdetto*, I, pp. 86–8. Whilst Don Inigo de Cardenas made the distinction between the spiritual and the temporal powers, he insisted that the Republic should perform some act formally recognizing the papal supremacy in things spiritual.

Republic's right to refuse to readmit the Jesuits whom it had expelled for subversive activities,[112] though Henry IV, the hope of the anti-Spanish parties in Italy, was (perversely enough) much more cautious and equivocal in his support of the Republic which had been the first to acknowledge him, in 1589.[113]

But Venice's protest, of such wide significance as a European issue, was based upon one necessary condition—the unshakeable allegiance of the people of Venice to their lay masters and not to their spiritual head. They did not divide when the papal monitorium hung above them;[114] they did not respond to the Pope's proclamation of a Jubilee, of which all inhabitants of the territories under Interdict would be deprived.[115] In the Republic as a whole, the Interdict undoubtedly gave cause for grave anxiety.[116] There was much uncertainty among the clergy as to where their duty lay—especially in regions like Brescia and Bergamo, where they were subject to constant pressure to observe the Interdict from Cardinal Federico Borromeo, Archbishop of Milan, and from his vicars on the frontier between Milanese and Venetian possessions. Venetian governors, reporting on the situation, attributed this unrest to the subversive propaganda of the new religious orders, the Jesuits, Capuchins and Theatines, which insisted on observing the Interdict. The friars of Bergamo and Padua suffered from 'the fear of being removed from their friaries and sent to other provinces, degraded, punished and subordinated to those who obeyed the Pope'. Certain writings of Baronius and Bellarmine appeared in Bergamo and successfully confused the local clergy. Benedetto Moro, Provveditore Generale in Terra Ferma, wrote of pernicious influences filtering from Mantua into Verona, 'the centre and key to all your state on the mainland'.[117] Antonio Lando, Podestà of Padua, complained of confessors

---

[112] Ranke, *The History of the Popes*, I, p. 137.

[113] P.R.O., S.P. 99/3, f. 178 *et seq.* Here Wotton lists the reasons for and against Henry IV intervening in the contest on the Venetian side—suggesting, for example, that Henry was old and his heir a child, the legitimation was in question, he would 'seeke to leave his estates quiet and ritche', a break with the Pope would mean a break with Spain, he was under Jesuit influence, and so on.

[114] On the rebellion and division which the monitorium was intended to produce, Sarpi, *Istoria dell' Interdetto*, pp. 52–3.   [115] *Ibid.*, p. 74.

[116] For what follows, see A.S.V., *Collegio, Relazioni, busta* 35, reports of the Podestà Francesco Diedo (1608) and of the Capitano Andrea Paruta (4 August 1606) on Bergamo; of the Podestà Leonardo Mocenigo (18 May 1607) and of the Capitano Angelo Bragadin (28 June 1608) on Brescia, *ibid.*, *busta* 37; of the Podestà-Capitano Francesco Venier (28 October 1606) on Crema, *ibid.*, *busta* 40; of the Podestà Giulio Contarini (27 July 1606) on Verona, *ibid.*, *busta* 50; of the Podestà Antonio Lando, 21 August 1606, on Padua, *ibid.*, *busta* 43. Cf. also Pastor, *History of the Popes*, XXV, pp. 141–3.

[117] See his report of 14 January 1607 Venetian style, f. 21, in A.S.V., *Collegio, Relazioni, busta* 52.

and chaplains of nuns, who persuaded their flocks to recognize no prince but the Pope, so that in many convents no bells sounded and no Masses were said. However, the Bishops of Bergamo, Crema and Verona held firm, and the governors did not report serious unrest among the laity: though Leonardo Mocenigo, retiring Podestà of Brescia, recalled in May 1607 that 'since the Holy See was involved and this was, as they said, a matter of conscience, I did not see quite the ardour I would have wished'. The city council had made difficulties about raising troops. 'And had things gone further, there would certainly have been disturbances (novità), because the greater part of the nobility and of the leading citizens were not going to church, and were staying outside the city in their villas in order to preserve their freedom of action'.[118] Venice herself had pessimists, and a defeatist Senator reminded his colleagues that the people were 'distracted by diverse opinions, uncertain in their consciences and weary of the present state of affairs'. The people were ready to rebel at any hint of famine or plague, which they would surely attribute to the curses of the Pope and to the Republic's contumely. The city itself, he said, was divided by the mutual hatred of noblemen and citizens.[119]

The situation was undoubtedly precarious, but the government escaped the challenge of rebellion in Venice, despite some seditious activities on the part of the Jesuits.[120] The domesticated clergy of Venice, the parish priests, the older religious orders (with the exception of the Observant Franciscans)[121] and the lay religious institutions obeyed the state and showed remarkable solidarity. They contrasted with the Jesuits, Capuchins and Theatines, the relatively new orders which observed the Interdict and left the state. The Heads of the Ten summoned the clergy of Venice and declared that the issues at stake were matters of positive, not of divine, law. Canon law bound the clergy to obey the Prince, and they could therefore execute with a clear conscience his orders to continue celebrating the divine offices.[122] Of crucial importance was the principle of canon law that obedience to ecclesiastical legislation 'to the grave detriment of oneself (sub gravi

[118] Some of the Rettori may have been less than frank or excessively optimistic about the state of opinion among the laity—the Capitano of Brescia, Angelo Bragadin, seemed far more confident of the loyalty of the Brescians.

[119] Cornet, Paolo V e la Republica Veneta, Appendice XVI, pp. 310, 313.

[120] Cf. Giuseppe Cappelletti, I Gesuiti e la Repubblica di Venezia (Venice, 1873), doc. 93, pp. 190–2; Pietro Pirri, L'Interdetto di Venezia del 1606 e i Gesuiti (Rome, 1959), Part IV, doc. 31, pp. 369 f.

[121] See O. M. T. Logan, Studies in the religious life of Venice in the sixteenth and early seventeenth centuries: the Venetian clergy and religious orders, 1520–1630, Ph.D. thesis, University of Cambridge, 1967, p. 461.

[122] Sivos, Delle vite dei Dosi, f. 90.

incommodo)', though meritorious, was not compulsory. The government had helped to solve the dilemma of the clergy by the Senate's decree of 27 April 1606, which forbade the clergy to publish the Interdict on pain of death—although it was widely accepted that the threat of this penalty was an empty one.[123]

There were a few defaulters, including the Benedictine Abbot of San Giorgio, the parish priests of San Lio, Santa Maria Formosa and San Basegio, and the nuns of San Bernardo di Murano:[124] but for the most part the line held firm. The recitation of legal arguments in learned pamphlets was not enough—the simpler theses had still to be communicated to the Venetian people. There was no better instrument for this purpose than the Scuole Grandi, which had so often been called upon to express the piety of the Republic and the outstanding beauty of Venetian holiness. The Venetian state must demonstrate that it was devoutly pious and Catholic. Its unquestionable piety—in addition to the natural right of the Prince—entitled it to demand obedience from clergy and people. The Pope was being rigorously legalistic: the Republic was unquestionably a Christian state. In the procession to mark the feast of Corpus Christi in the year 1606, the government organized a magnificent parade of devotion. The English Ambassador, Sir Henry Wotton, thus described the ceremony:

> . . . Yesterday was the Feast of Corpus Christi, celebrated by express commandment of the State (which goeth farther than devotion), with the most sumptuous procession that ever had been seen here, wherein the very basins and ewers were valued in common judgement at 200,000 pound sterling, besides many costly and curious pageants, adorned with sentences of Scripture fit for the present, as *Omnis potestas est a Deo, Date Caesari quae Caesaris et Deo quae Dei, Omnis anima subdita sit potestatibus sublimioribus, Regnum meum non est de hoc mundo,* and the like. The reasons of this extraordinary solemnity were two as I conceive it. First, to contain the people in good order with superstition, the foolish band of obedience. Secondly, to let the Pope know (who wanteth not intelligencers) that notwithstanding his interdict, they had friars enough and other clergymen to furnish out the day.[125]

An anonymous history of the Interdict described with more precision the rôle of the Scuole Grandi and of the older orders of friars in the procession.

[123] Logan, *Studies in the religious life of Venice*, p. 438.
[124] P.R.O., S.P. 99/3, f. 143—Wotton to Salisbury, 18/28 July 1606; Sivos, *Delle vite dei Dosi,* ff. 122v.–123v.
[125] Logan Pearsall Smith, *The Life and Letters of Sir Henry Wotton* (Oxford, 1907), I, p. 350.

Upon the day of the festival of Corpus Domini the procession was held at San Marco, but with immense and unaccustomed displays of floats (*solari*) and silver and relics, in a way that eclipsed the memory of all the other processions held on that day, and all the religious orders and the clergy who are accustomed to attend processions were present there, though some of these orders were not so numerous as usual. The Scuole Grandi in particular made many fine floats, with scenes which alluded to the rightful claims of the Republic against the Pope (*alla pretentione ragionevole della Republica con il Papa*), because on one float appeared a Christ and two Pharisees with a motto which said 'Reddite quae sunt Cesaris Cesari et que sunt Dei Deo'. On another float they put Moses and Aaron in front of God with a motto saying 'Segregate mihi tribum Levi etc.'[126] On another they put Christ with all the twelve apostles, 'Reges gentium dominantur earum, vos autem non sic', and all these persons were represented by young men with make-believe clothes and beards, and the floats were carried by brothers of the Scuole. The friars also devised some scenes, and in particular a church collapsing but upheld by the Doge of Venice. Next to this were St Francis and St Dominic, helping the Doge to prop the church up. On another float, dressed as a Doge with a beard similar to that of the present Most Serene Doge, was a young man kneeling before a St Mark, who was giving him his blessing. There was also a Venice who had the figure of Faith in front of her, and was supported by lions with a motto which spoke of her constancy in faith. In short, it was a fitting and a memorable spectacle. . . .[127]

This pageantry reflected the gulf between the older religious institutions which had compromised with the state, and the more recent products of the Counter Reformation. Venice, in opposing the claims of Papacy and priesthood, was still acting in the tradition which she had helped to formulate in the late Middle Ages, and which she had shared with the Milan of the Visconti and even with the Guelf Republic of Florence—at periods in which anti-clerical parties gained the upper hand in those states.[128] The Interdict was no isolated phenomenon in

[126] Deuteronomy 10, viii: 'the Lord separated the tribe of Levi, to bear the ark of the covenant of the Lord, to stand before the Lord to minister unto him, and to bless in his name, unto this day'. This text was probably cited to show that the proper function of the priest was simply to conduct worship.

[127] Printed as doc. VI in the Appendice to Gaetano Cozzi, 'Paolo Sarpi tra il cattolico Philippe Canaye de Fresnes e il calvinista Isaac Casaubon', *Bollettino dell' Istituto di Storia della Società e dello Stato Veneziano*, I (1959). Giacomo Lambertengo, a Jesuit, describing this procession, added the further detail that two friars stood on the float on either side of the falling church, bearing large two-handed swords, with the legend 'Viva il Dose' upon them—see Pirri, *L'Interdetto e i Gesuiti*, Part III, doc. 19, p. 223.

[128] Cf. Francesco Cognasso, 'Istituzioni comunali e signorili di Milano sotto i Visconti', in G. Treccani degli Alfieri, *Storia di Milano*, VI (Milan, 1955), pp. 506–7, 524–6; M. B. Becker, 'Church and state in Florence on the eve of the Renaissance

Venetian history—earlier contests with Sixtus IV and Julius II, neighbour princes who had used the spiritual weapon of excommunication for frankly political ends, had furnished the government with precedents and experience. Opposition to sacerdotalism was no innovation of the early seventeenth century, and Sarpi, for all his fame, owed much to Marsilio of Padua.

The Scuole Grandi formed part of this late medieval tradition. It would be too much to describe them as the vehicles of a state religion. But they were purely local institutions with no loyalties outside the Venetian Republic. They were officered exclusively by Venetian citizens or by residents of long standing. The fourteenth-century statutes of the Scuole di San Giovanni Evangelista and of the Misericordia had clearly stipulated that all their decrees must contribute to the 'honour and state' of the Doge, of the commonwealth, of the fatherland, and of every good and faithful Christian. Any ordinance which did not fulfil this condition would be null and void. The brothers of San Giovanni Evangelista included in the Mariegola clauses expressly forbidding them to enter into any form of conspiracy against the state, or to damage the fortifications set up by the government.[129] The bigger lay institutions of Venice were under the surveillance of the Council of Ten, and disobeyed its orders at their peril. There were strong bonds between the Scuole Grandi and the older religious orders, many of whom remembered the Scuole in their prayers and pious works. Many priests were members of the Scuole, or else were employed by them in the capacity of chaplains or Mass-priests. Their ties were material as well as spiritual. The clergy in no way controlled the Scuole. The Scuole were bound to the Council of Ten, and their 3,000-odd members were bound to them in turn, not only by sharing in the common fund of merit accumulated by the Scuole, but by the hope of sharing in the charitable benefits of which they disposed. The Scuole had become the public expression of Venetian piety, in whose splendours the penitential humility of the early flagellants had become submerged.

Fittingly, one of the few Interdict pamphlets addressed to a popular audience, a dialect tirade against Paul V which purported to be written by one Piffanio di Pizzocari of Burano, upbraided the Pope as a turbu-

---

(1343–82)', *Speculum*, XXXVII (1962); G. A. Brucker, *Florentine politics and society, 1343–1378* (Princeton, 1962); Peter Partner, 'Florence and the Papacy, 1300–1375', in *Europe in the later Middle Ages*, ed. John Hale, Roger Highfield and Beryl Smalley (London, 1965).

[129] A.S.V., *Scuola Grande di San Giovanni Evangelista*, vol. 7, ch. 43, ff. 11v.–12; vol. 3, ch. 2, f. 5, ch. 40, f. 13v.; *Sala Diplomatica Regina Margherita*, LXXVI–22, ch. 3, 4, f. 2r.–v.; *ibid.*, LXXVI–11, placed at the end of the Mariegola, after decrees of 1390.

lent Guardian who had subverted the constitution of the Scuola and misappropriated its funds. 'What authority had you, although they made you Guardian of the Scuola and you hold the keys of the church, to give orders in the house of the brothers and strike a relative off the roll for no offence?' The Pope was obliged to observe the Mariegola and to summon the Chapter-General every ten years[130]—perhaps an allusion to the conciliar theories mooted at the time of the Interdict. The Scuole Grandi embodied and symbolized the comprehensible people's religion in Venice. At a time of crisis, like that of the Interdict, the Scuole could be called upon by the state to express, in acceptable terminology, and in tableaux that everybody could understand, the separation of the spiritual and temporal powers on which the Republic's arguments against the Pope were based. It was of great value to the Republic that the devotions which meant most to the Venetian people were practised by well-tamed fraternities whose supreme governor was the Council of Ten.

[130] The pamphlet is copied by Gian Carlo Sivos in his chronicle—Biblioteca Marciana, MSS. Italiani, Classe VII, 1818 (9436), ff. 118–20.

2

THE ORDERS OF RICH AND POOR

During the fourteenth century, the older Scuole Grandi of Venice became, not only devotional societies, but also philanthropic institutions. Charity and almsgiving not only helped to accumulate merit, but also expressed the sense of brotherhood and mutual responsibility essential to the Scuole. By the sixteenth century, important changes had occurred in their inner structure. The brothers, at first men of equal status with identical obligations, had formed two distinctive groups of rich and poor. The rich were potential governors and benefactors of the Scuole, the poor their subjects and beneficiaries. Although the Scuole distributed some of their wealth to paupers and unfortunates outside their own ranks, members of the Scuole enjoyed preferential treatment and monopolized certain benefits. Hence, the Scuole Grandi were not only confraternities of rich men dispensing charity to outsiders: they also provided the framework within which most of the relief was administered.

The early rules of the Scuola di San Giovanni Evangelista and the Scuola della Misericordia present some evidence about the early development of charity within the Scuole—though, in an inquiry focused on later centuries, it is impossible to analyse this in much depth. In the first quarter of the fourteenth century, members of the Scuola di San Giovanni Evangelista met annually on the fourth Sunday in Lent for a 'love-feast' or *prandium caritatis*, at which the greatest permissible delicacy was fish cooked in herbs. Before sitting down to this banquet, the Guardian and other officials were expected to prepare a meal for a number of paupers, one for each brother of the Scuola; and when the Scuola's own feast ended, the remains were swept up and distributed to other poor men.[1] The brothers of the Misericordia evidently distributed a 'charitade' to the poor every year, and contributions to this 'charitade' were made compulsory.[2] However, more sophisticated arrangements developed for the maintenance of members of the Scuola who were themselves impoverished. The primitive rules ordered members of the Scuole to visit colleagues who fell sick, as if to help them prepare for death.[3] This duty naturally extended into some

[1] A.S.V., *Scuola Grande di San Giovanni Evangelista*, vol. 7, ch. 17, f. 5v.–6.
[2] A.S.V., *Sala Diplomatica Regina Margherita*, LXXVI–11, ch. 13, ch. 60.
[3] *Ibid.*, LXXVI–3, ch. 18; LXXVI–11, ch. 27; A.S.V., *Scuola Grande di San Giovanni Evangelista*, vol. 7, ch. 37, f. 13.

concern for the material welfare of the sick, and the officers therefore received instructions to provide for their maintenance, either from the resources of the Scuola, or, if necessary, by levying a subscription on all the other members. The rules assumed that one of the Guardian's chief responsibilities would be the dispensation of charity to sick or needy brothers, and the statutes of San Giovanni Evangelista gave him absolute discretion in this matter.[4] The Chapter of the Misericordia, however, passed a resolution in 1382 whereby the officials were not to give alms amounting to more than 15 gold ducats to any single member of the congregation—unless he was in very grave need, in which case the matter must be judged by a council of forty 'good men'.[5] The constitutions of the Scuole, moreover, gave them the opportunity to inquire systematically into the needs of their members. To enforce attendance at their principal functions and ceremonies, they had to know something of the private lives and circumstances of their members. Each Scuola annually appointed officers known as Degani, eventually choosing two for each of the six *sestieri* into which Venice was divided, and made them responsible for ensuring that all the brothers in their districts attended processions at the appointed times. By the mid-fifteenth century, the Degani were carrying out visitations one of whose objects was 'to see if any of their brothers are ill and need their alms, so that they do not die of hunger and sickness, and so that they can tell their Degani of their needs'.[6] Later, the Degani were charged with other inquiries—in the Scuola di San Marco, by 1542, Degani were responsible for touring the city and informing themselves of the reputation of the daughters of members of the Scuola who were candidates for dowries to be dispensed that year by the Scuola's trusts.[7]

During the fourteenth century, the Scuole also erected small hospitals or almshouses for the relief of the poor and sick. At the Chapter-General of August 1330, the brothers of San Giovanni Evangelista resolved on the establishment of a tiny hospital with four beds for the reception of poor and sick brothers in extreme destitution. Their motive, as they explained, was that 'all our aims and desires are concentrated on the love of our brothers' (*tuta la nostra intention et lo*

---

[4] A.S.V., *Sala Diplomatica Regina Margherita*, LXXVI–22, ch. 32, f. 15. A marginal note written in a later hand suggests that this law was introduced in August 1320.

[5] *Ibid.*, LXXVI–11, ch. 71, 21 December 1382.

[6] A.S.V., *Inquisitori et Revisori sopra le Scuole Grandi, Capitolare I*, f. 8r.–v., a decree issued by the Council of Ten in 1451. Its purpose was to ensure that the Degani carried out their duties personally and did not delegate them to men of low condition, to whom the wives of poor brothers might be ashamed to confess their poverty.

[7] A.S.V., *Scuola Grande di San Marco*, vol. 8, f. 100v.

nostro dexiderio spetialmente se destende in la dilection de fraternita).
They dedicated the hospital 'to the honour of Our Lord Jesus Christ,
who is full of all love and charity, and of the Glorious Virgin Mary his
mother, and to the honour and veneration of the blessed St John the
Apostle and Evangelist, our leader and governor in all our works of
mercy, and to the repose of all the souls of the brothers of this blessed
congregation, both living and dead'.[8] The practice of charity harmonized with the general enterprise of saving souls through the accumulation of merit. Rather later, the Scuola della Misericordia also established
a poorhouse or *chasa di puoveri*, in the parish of San Marcilian. In
1390, they described it as 'newly erected'.[9] These were very modest
establishments, but the age of large general hospitals, at least in Venice
and the Veneto, had not yet arrived; and the small hospitals of the
medieval Scuole foreshadowed the large blocks of almshouses which
they owned during the sixteenth century.[10]

By the mid-fourteenth century, the Misericordia was already visualiz-
ing the possibility that the officers would be called upon to execute
many last wills and testaments, and hinting that these would contain
bequests to the poor. The Chapter of the Scuola decreed that 'for the
honour of Madonna Santa Maria Valverde, Mother of Mercy, for the
benefit of the poor and for the repose of the souls of our brothers' no
officials might henceforth refuse to carry out the last wishes of any
brother of the Scuola—they must accept 'alguna comesaria de anema'.
The Guardian and his colleagues were not to accept legacies made to
them personally. These 'must always be assigned to the poor of
Madonna Santa Maria de Valverde, Mother of Mercy. And this shall
be done to acquire merit for our souls and salvation for our brothers.'[11]
A few years later, in 1355, the Scuola first resolved to admit four
physicians, who would have no obligations other than to visit sick
brothers. This they must do without receiving any payment, either
from the patient or from the Scuola.[12] Physicians, like priests, rendered
a professional service, and were rewarded by the hope of salvation
through sharing in the merits of the Scuola. The chronology tempts

[8] A.S.V., *Scuola Grande di San Giovanni Evangelista*, vol. 7, ch. 65, ff. 18–20;
vol. 3, ch. 53, ff. 17–18.
[9] A.S.V., *Sala Diplomatica Regina Margherita*, LXXVI–11, decree dated 21 August
1390.
[10] See below, p. 185.
[11] A.S.V., *Sala Diplomatica Regina Margherita*, LXXVI–3, ch. 78; LXXVI–11,
ch. 66.
[12] A.S.V., *Sala Diplomatica Regina Margherita*, LXXVI–3, ch. 85; LXXVI–11,
ch. 8. A further decree of December 1369 increased the number of doctors to six.
See *ibid.*, LXXVI–22, ch. 38, f. 16, for a similar arrangement in the Scuola di San
Giovanni Evangelista.

one to associate these innovations with the Black Death of 1348 (disseminated to Italy through the ports of Venice, Genoa and Pisa) or with the series of plagues which began to afflict Venice every few years in the century and a half which followed.[13] But there is no specific evidence of any such connexion.

By the end of the fourteenth century, philanthropy was clearly an important activity of the Scuole of Venice. Distributions of charity were no longer merely seasonal, or confined to special ceremonies performed for the benefit of outsiders. With the foundation of small hospitals or poorhouses, and with the provision of free medical aid, the Scuole progressed beyond mere almsgiving. By accepting responsibility for testamentary bequests, they ceased to confine themselves to donations passing between living persons. Scuole or fraternities in other cities which later became Venetian may have followed a similar course. In Bergamo, four Scuole della Disciplina, those of Santi Barnabà e Lorenzo, Sant' Erasmo, Santa Maria Maddalena and San Tommaso, combined to administer the Hospital of the Maddalena for the sick and insane, and later recruited six other such Scuole to help with the task.[14]

Moreover, between the early fourteenth and the early sixteenth century, members of the Scuola began to divide into separate orders of rich and poor. The primitive statutes of San Giovanni Evangelista imposed similar obligations on all lay brothers, and committed final decisions on the government of the Scuola to a Chapter-General which consisted of all its full members assembled together. But the statutes of San Rocco (of the late fifteenth century) clearly distinguished between 'any brother of our discipline' (*alcuno nostro fratello de la nostra disciplina*) and, on the other hand, 'those who have taken part in the government of our Scuola and are exempt from the discipline (*queli li quali fosseno stadi al governo de la nostra scuola exenti de la disciplina*)'. Should a decree apply equally to both these orders, it was often thought necessary to mention them both separately.[15] Some of the older Scuole were followed by groups of sixty men, required to attend processions as probationers until vacancies occurred in the Scuola proper.[16] Occasionally, the sixty probationers (as in a decree issued by the Ten in 1536) were described as being 'of the discipline' in contrast

---

[13] Cf. Élisabeth Carpentier, *Une ville devant la peste: Orvieto et la peste noire de 1348* (Paris, 1962), pp. 99–100, and below, p. 219.

[14] Roncalli and Forno, *Atti di Borromeo*, I/ii, pp. 213–14.

[15] A.S.R., *Mariegola*, ff. 4v.–5, 8v.–9, 9v.

[16] Cf. A.S.V., *Scuola Grande di San Giovanni Evangelista*, vol. 3, ch. 65, ff. 23v.–25, decree of 1 March 1361.

with the 'ordinary members' of the Scuole,[17] but this was never the normal use of the term, and brothers 'of the discipline' were commonly contrasted with potential governors. They were the poor of the Scuola —perhaps they were the only people sufficiently humble or sufficiently enthusiastic to use the scourge on themselves in public.

The statutes of San Giovanni provided that a Chapter should be summoned three times every year: on the Sunday immediately before Christmas, on the third Sunday in Lent, and on the second Sunday in August. All the brothers must then assemble and hear a report from the Guardian, the chief officer of the Scuola. Any brother who had anything to say 'for the good and profit of the Scuola' must do so, after first obtaining permission from the Guardian. A sermon should be preached by a priest from the Scuola, and the statutes be read so that nobody could plead ignorance to excuse offences against the rule. Officers were to be elected by this body at the Lenten sessions.[18] But such a Chapter-General had no equivalent in the Scuola di San Rocco —which provided that the officers of the Scuola could add to the foundation statutes (so long as these new decrees were compatible with the old) in company with a body of 'at least 50 of the principal followers of our holy rule'. This body was officially termed a 'Chapter'—'el capitolo congregadi siano al manco persone cinquanta di principali de la nostra sancta regola'.[19] The government of the Scuola had, in the intervening centuries, passed into the hands of many fewer people. This was partly due to the inevitable process whereby a small group of persons—more intelligent, more enthusiastic, more wealthy and influential, or with greater leisure for intrigue and for administration— becomes the real power in any cumbersome assembly. Power at first spread thinly over a wide area soon began to concentrate in the hands of a few.

Until 1521, the government of each Scuola, in all routine matters and during the intervals between meetings of the Chapter, was vested in a board of sixteen officers, known collectively as the Bench (*Banca*) or as the Guardian and Fellows (*Guardian et Compagni*). The main principle was stated as follows in a statute of San Giovanni: 'that all the property and moneys of this our Scuola shall be entrusted to the vigilance and care of our Guardian and of his fellow-officers for their year

[17] On 8 March 1536, the lists of new entrants to the Scuole della Carità, San Giovanni and San Marco were approved 'usque ad numerum deputatum per hoc consilium que sunt 550 ordinarij et 60 ad disciplinam' (A.S.V., *Consiglio dei Dieci, Registro Comune* 1536, f. 101v.).

[18] A.S.V., *Scuola Grande di S. Giovanni Evangelista*, vol. 3, ch. 20, ff. 9v.–10; cf. *Sala Diplomatica Regina Margherita*, LXXVI–3, ch. 6, LXXVI–11, ch. 13, for similar arrangements in the Scuola della Misericordia. [19] A.S.R., *Mariegola*, f. 10.

of office'.[20] In the early fourteenth century, the Guardian kept one record of the Scuola's income and expenditure, the Degani another, and they compared their respective registers every month.[21] At some time between 1366 and 1392, the legislators of San Giovanni specified that the Guardian must visit the property of the Scuola, inside and outside Venice, at least once a year, and thoroughly inform himself, by a close scrutiny of wills made in favour of the Scuola, of the property it was supposed to possess and of the revenue expected therefrom.[22] The Guardian and his fellow-officers were allowed only a very slight discretionary power in managing the funds 'without the word and permission of the brothers of our Scuola, congregated always in Chapter or upon one of the appointed days', except in two important matters: the relief of sick and needy brothers, and expenditure on wax for the candles borne in procession.[23] These subsequently became the most important items on the accounts of the sixteenth-century Scuole, when the authority of the Chapter was rarely invoked. It was necessary, for example, when a decree was proposed which was thought to be adding to the content of the Mariegola. The Mariegola was regarded in theory as an irrepealable fundamental statute, not subject to review by any subsequent body of legislators. It could, however, undergo accretions. Again, the authority of the Chapter was sometimes considered essential for the sale, alienation or transfer of the property of the Scuole, or for borrowing money on the security of it:[24] though in the Scuola di San Giovanni it was necessary only to summon a body of 30–40 advisers to authorize such dues.[25]

Apart from this, the small and manoeuvrable executive committee was free to act as it chose throughout its year of office. Legislation could be initiated only by the Guardian himself or with his approval. In 1494, the Ten censured one of the Degani in the Scuola della Carità, who had dared to make suggestions contrary to the wishes of the Guardian. To advance proposals in the Chapter was the exclusive right of the Guardian himself, or, in his absence, of his Vicar.[26] In

[20] A.S.V., *Sala Diplomatica Regina Margherita*, LXXVI–22, ch. 35, f. 15v.

[21] A.S.V., *Scuola Grande di San Giovanni Evangelista*, vol. 3, ch. 43, f. 14r.–v.

[22] A.S.V., *Sala Diplomatica Regina Margherita*, LXXVI–22, ch. 48, f. 20r.–v.

[23] *Ibid.*, ch. 48, f. 20r.–v.: possibly a decree of 1320 (see above, p. 64).

[24] In 1427 the Council of Ten restrained the officers of the Scuola di S. Marco from making decisions of this nature on their own authority (A.S.V., *Compilazione delle Leggi*, busta 344, f. 99r.–v.). In 1552 the Scuola di S. Marco provided that no 'alienations' of property were to be authorized without five-sixths of the votes of the Chapter-General, assembled to the number of 80 or more (A.S.V., *Scuola Grande di San Marco*, vol. 20, f. 165; *Consiglio dei Dieci, Registro Comune* 1552, f. 148).

[25] A.S.V., *Sala Diplomatica Regina Margherita*, LXXVI–22, ch. 49, f. 20v.–21v.

[26] A.S.V., *Inquisitori e Revisori sopra le Scuole Grandi, Capitolare I*, f. 21r.–v.

1554, the Scuola di San Rocco ordered that no proposal should be debated by the Chapter unless it had first been discussed by the Bench and by an additional body called the Zonta. This had been grafted on to the Bench of every Scuola by the Council of Ten in 1521, for the purpose of somewhat increasing the number of persons who made the ordinary decisions. The Bench could not, however, finally veto any proposal which they discussed; the Chapter-General could still consider it even if the Bench had turned it down. But, to judge by the minute books of the Scuola di San Rocco, the Chapter seldom did so.[27]

The other members of the Bench, in addition to the powerful Guardian, were the Vicar, the Guardian da Mattin, the Scrivener (Scrivan) and the twelve Degani. From the beginning, the Guardian was always assisted by a number of Degani. In the Scuola di San Giovanni the Vicar was appointed in 1392 to act when necessary as the Guardian's deputy, and assumed a special responsibility for the small hospital attached to the Scuola.[28] The Guardian da Mattin was originally appointed 'for the relief of our Guardian Grande' and was charged with organizing and marshalling the Scuola at processions.[29] The flagellant processions originally took place in the morning—hence his name. In the sixteenth century he was also responsible for the distributions of alms which accompanied processions. The importance of the Scrivan's functions probably diminished with the introduction of a professional clerical staff to keep the books with greater consistency. The Scuola di San Rocco appointed a permanent book-keeper in 1514, saying that this was also the practice in the four Scuole senior to itself.[30] But the Scrivan was still apparently responsible, later in the sixteenth century, for the custody of deeds and other documents establishing the Scuola's titles to its property.[31] Otherwise the individual duties of each officer were of slight importance compared with his function as a committee-man. The committee absorbed him, and he had little chance to do good or evil on his own.

In 1521, this Bench or board of sixteen governors was forcibly widened by decree of the Council of Ten. Too many unworthy persons were being chosen to administer the property of the Scuole—'those who elect to these offices hand them on to their own relatives and

[27] A.S.R., Registro delle Terminazioni 2, f. 144.
[28] A.S.V., Sala Diplomatica Regina Margherita, LXXVI–22, ch. 52, ff. 22–3. See ibid., LXXVI–11, ch. 73, for the appointment of a Vicar in the Scuola della Misericordia, evidently made between 1382 and 1390.
[29] Ibid., LXXVI–22, ch. 10, f. 6r.–v.
[30] A.S.V., Scuola Grande di S. Rocco, seconda consegna, vol. 45, f. 1.
[31] A.S.R., Registro delle Terminazioni 3, ff. 9v.–10, a decree of 16 February 1577 Venetian style.

friends, with practices that are not to be tolerated'. When elections
were held, almshouses allotted, dowries distributed, or any other
important business transacted, other members of the Scuola must be
summoned to form an additional body or Zonta to deliberate with the
Bench. The Zonta, numbering twelve in all (though eight made a
quorum), were to be elected by the Bench and the Chapter in concert,
and should have no close ties of kinship—either by blood or by marriage—with members of the Bench.[32] At the same time two Syndics
were appointed to guard against irregularities. Their original duty was
to audit the accounts every year, and in 1537 they were further instructed by the Ten to proceed against any infraction of the fundamental
laws of the Scuola.[33] They could suspend the execution of decrees of
the Banca and Zonta, and refer them to the Chapter to be voted on
afresh. If necessary they could hail a Guardian before the Council of
Ten to answer for irregularities committed in the administration of the
property of the Scuola.[34] In 1534 the Ten even empowered the Syndics
of the Scuola di San Giovanni to make proposals in the Chapter-
General concerning the finances of the Scuola and the matters which
the decree of 1521 had entrusted to them.[35]

All the right of initiative in the Scuola, much of the power of curbing irregularities, and most of the decisions concerning the distribution
of charity and expenditure on display had thus, by the mid-sixteenth
century, become concentrated in a committee consisting at the most of
thirty members. By the last quarter of the fifteenth century, the election
of new officers lay in the hands of only 16 members of the Scuola—
probably of the retiring Bench.[36] The Chapter-General was, however,
required to participate in the election of the Zonta from 1521 onwards.

Meanwhile, the Chapter-General had also contracted. The statutes
of San Giovanni provided—in or about 1330—that if the officers
wished to take action in excess of the powers granted them by the
constitution, they should have full authority to

---

[32] A.S.V., *Inquisitori e Revisori sopra le Scuole Grandi, Capitolare I*, ff. 28v.–30.
[33] A.S.V., *Consiglio dei Dieci, Registro Comune 1537*, f. 14.
[34] A.S.V., *Scuola Grande di S. Giovanni Evangelista*, vol. 8, ch. 108, f. 59; ch. 138,
ff. 76v.–77. In 1546 the Syndic Agostino Malipiero of the Scuola di S. Giovanni
reported to the Ten that several members of the present Zonta had not received the
statutory proportion of votes necessary in order to elect them under the Ten's decree
of 1521, and most of their acts were accordingly declared void (*ibid.*, vol. 8, ch. 113,
f. 62r.–v.).
[35] *Ibid.*, ch. 98, f. 33v.
[36] This appears from a decree for the control of canvassing, passed by the Council
of Ten on 18 December 1477, where there are references to there being only 16
electors (A.S.V., *Inquisitori e Revisori sopre le Scuole Grandi, Capitolare I*, ff. 15v.–
16).

elect and summon thirty to forty of the best and most sufficient men of
the Scuola and of those who seem to them most expert and wise, to give
them good and wise counsel. When they have been summoned and
assembled the Guardian must expound and declare among them what he
and his Fellows have resolved to do for the good and profit of the Scuola
and of our souls, and each of them may speak for or against it as his
conscience tells him.[37]

Only if this small Capitolo approved the decree could it then be put
to an assembly of all the brothers 'on the first appointed day' to be
ratified or rejected by a majority of them. Apparently there was no
discussion at this final stage. Similarly, in 1359, the Scuola della
Misericordia stipulated that whenever the officers contemplated adding
any decree to the Mariegola they must summon a body of fifty 'good
men' to discuss the proposal, and that it could be put to the Chapter-
General only if a majority of the fifty supported it.[38] It is possible that
this intermediate Chapter became the effective sovereign body within
the Scuola, and that the practice of conducting plebiscites among all
the brothers died out altogether.

Certainly a small and restricted Chapter was envisaged by the
founders of the Scuola di San Rocco, who were modelling their constitution on those of the four older Scuole di Battuti. In January 1519,
however, the Scuola di San Rocco complained to the Council of Ten
that its Chapter had swollen to an unmanageable size, and that there
were so many different opinions about every proposal that it proved
impossible to transact business with proper dispatch. The officers
therefore suggested that full powers to deal with any situation should
be accorded to a body consisting of the Bench and of an additional 31
men who had formerly held office on the Bench: 'they shall be sufficient
and shall represent the entire Chapter-General', and what a majority of
them decided should be law within the Scuola. The Ten responded by
ordaining that

by the authority of this Council it shall be granted to the Guardian and
Fellows of this Scuola that at the deliberations which have to take place
in the Chapter-General there must be present exactly the same number as
usually enters there in the other Scuole Grandi, consisting, that is, of those
who have held office; so that this Scuola shall come for the time being to
be governed according to the same rules as the others.[39]

[37] A.S.V., *Scuola Grande di San Giovanni Evangelista*, vol. 7, ch. 66, ff. 20–1;
vol. 3, ch. 55, ff. 18v.–19v.; LXXVI–22, ch. 40, ff. 17–18. For evidence of a similar
chapter in the Scuola di San Marco, see *Compilazioni delle Leggi, busta* 344, f. 99r.–
v., *Scuola Grande di San Marco*, vol. 8, f. 9v., 205, 220.
[38] A.S.V., *Sala Diplomatica Regina Margherita*, LXXVI–11, ch. 70.
[39] A.S.V., *Compilazione delle Leggi, busta* 344, f. 178r.–v. On 7 December 1488 the

71

This law clearly implies that in all the Scuole the Chapters-General consisted at this time only of men who had already held office. In this way the distinct order of persons qualified by wealth and other attributes to participate in the government of the Scuola was created, and was finally substituted for the primitive democracy—if that was ever more than a figment. In June 1530 the Council of Ten denied office in the Scuole to men whose affairs were before the bankruptcy court of the Sopraconsoli, and to anyone receiving charity in any form at the hands of the Scuola.[40] In 1537 such people were excluded from the Chapter-General also.[41]

The division of the Scuola into orders of rich and poor was a symptom of its growing social importance in combining men of different economic circumstances into an association which helped to transfer excess wealth, and which enabled the rich to perform specific services to the poor. This internal division accompanied the transformation of the Scuola from a primarily religious into a religious and philanthropic institution.

The foundation statutes of San Rocco contrast an 'exempt' order of members with those more lowly brothers who were subject to the discipline, and equate the exempt with the governing order. 'Exempt' orders appeared in the older Scuole during the first half of the fourteenth century, though exemption then implied a dispensation, not only from the need to perform the discipline, but also from the obligation to accept office. From an early date in the history of the Scuole, acceptance of office was compulsory for all ordinary members.[42] A statute of the Misericordia—possibly prior to 1310—prescribed that the Scuola should receive noblemen 'who shall not beat themselves' at an annual subscription of 20 soldi. Nobles were required to attend the Scuola's functions, or, should they fail to do so, to have a Mass celebrated instead.[43] Perhaps they joined the body of men over sixty years of age who stayed to pray in the church of the Misericordia whilst the flagellant processions took place.[44] Likewise, in 1322, Ser Tommasino, a silk-weaver, Guardian of the Scuola di San Giovanni Evangelista, resolved with his colleagues to admit a number of entrants (probably

Bench had already resolved to petition the Council of Ten to be allowed 'when the Chapter is summoned, to call all the good men who have been on the Bench in the past according to the constitutions of the other Scuole'—A.S.V., *Scuola Grande di S. Rocco, seconda consegna*, vol. 44, f. 3v.

[40] A.S.V., *Consiglio dei Dieci, Registro Comune 1530*, ff. 43–4.

[41] A.S.V., *Consiglio dei Dieci, Registro Comune 1537*, f. 14.

[42] See A.S.V., *Scuola Grande di San Giovanni Evangelista*, vol. 3, ch. 21, f. 10; *Sala Diplomatica Regina Margherita*, LXXVI–3, ch. 9, LXXVI–11, ch. 17.

[43] *Ibid.*, LXXVI–3, ch. 39; LXXVI–11, ch. 7.

[44] *Ibid.*, LXXVI–3, ch. 5, 14; LXXVI–11, ch. 22.

all nobles) on the understanding that 'they shall be exempt from all obligations in the Scuola, save that they must pay for the annual banquet and say the Pater Noster's for the souls of any of our brothers who pass out of this life'.[45] In 1344, the Scuola della Carità and the Scuola di San Giovanni decided to define the obligations of the nobility and other exempt persons more precisely. San Giovanni required an entrance fee of 25 gold ducats, earmarked for the assistance of poor and sick brothers, the Carità one of 20 gold ducats. The decree of San Giovanni Evangelista prescribed that its exempt members should pay an annual subscription or *lumenaria*, and that on the death of a brother each should recite fifty Pater Noster's, 'give four alms', or have a Mass celebrated. The Carità expressly stated that its nobles must be exempt from the obligation to accept office, and that the Scuola must attend the funerals of noblemen, as of ordinary members.[46] All three Scuole limited the number of exempt persons who could be admitted—the Misericordia putting the maximum at sixty, whilst the Carità was prepared to accept only twelve. In 1359, the Scuola di San Giovanni Evangelista limited the quota of exempt persons to a total of fifty. It was then conceding exemption not only to 'noblemen of the Great Council' but also to 'great merchants of the city of Venice'. All exempt members must be at least thirty years of age.[47]

However, the Council of Ten, a few years later, evidently considered it unseemly that a citizen institution should legislate for noblemen or dictate the terms on which they could enter it. In 1366 and again in 1409 the Ten issued orders to the effect that, since such measures brought dishonour both on the Signoria and on the Chapters which had presumed to pass them, it should in future be understood that any nobleman who so wished might enter the Scuole, that there should be no limitation on the numbers of noblemen accepted, and that the sums they paid as entrance fees should be left to their discretion.[48] But the citizens retained their monopoly of office within the Scuola, and nobles were allowed to seek honorary membership only. The Ten would not allow the Scuole to deal with noblemen on their own terms—but neither did they want their service aristocracy, destined for magisterial office, to incur the heavy responsibility of administering the property of the Scuole Grandi. No attempt was apparently made to alter the rules, issued both by the Scuole and by the state itself, which reserved

[45] A.S.V., *Scuola Grande di San Giovanni Evangelista*, vol. 7, f. 31.
[46] *Ibid.*, vol. 3, ch. 57, f. 20; *Scuola Grande di Santa Maria della Carità*, vol. 233 *bis*, ch. 49, vol. 234, ch. 43.
[47] A.S.V., *Scuola Grande di San Giovanni Evangelista*, vol. 3, ch. 61, ff. 22v.–23.
[48] A.S.V., *Inquisitori e Revisori sopra le Scuole Grandi, Capitolare I*, ff. 1v., 2v.–3.

the chief posts in the government of the Scuole to representatives of the citizen class. Noblemen were clearly eager to share in the fund of merit accumulated by the Scuole, to improve their prospects of salvation, and to guarantee a large following to the grave. Indeed, the Scuole were often called upon to receive them on the point of death or even after it, in spite of a rule that they ought only to be admitted at the high altar. In 1457 the Council of Ten issued orders supporting these rules of the Scuole,[49] but the following year the Ten instructed the officers of the Scuola della Misericordia to go to the house of the dying Ser Lorenzo da Molin, and there receive him into membership. The officers respectfully protested, saying that they had 'sworn to observe their Mariegola, which was established for the honour and good of the poor'. They condemned this practice of receiving sick men on the point of death as 'diminishing the religion and piety of this and the other Scuole, because everybody else will now wait until the end of his life to enter them, and will not do so out of religion and piety, which can be of little profit at such a time, but only for the sake of his funeral. The alms and other good works which the poor now receive will cease.' The Ten, informed of these possible consequences, gave way and confirmed the orders of the Scuole.[50] In 1482 the Ten finally provided that under no circumstances could anyone be received posthumously into a Scuola, and that a sick nobleman could only be admitted from his own house on the unanimous vote of the Council of Ten in session with the Doge and his six Councillors present.[51] Such dispensations were occasionally granted in the early sixteenth century —in favour of Ser Lorenzo di Bernardo Giustinian in 1514; or to Ser Francesco di Piero Contarini dai Crosechieri, admitted *in extremis* to the Scuola della Misericordia in 1532.[52]

These restrictions did not destroy the popularity of the Scuole with the noblemen, as the Mariegole of San Rocco and San Marco testify. The Mariegola of San Rocco records the entry of 418 noblemen between the early 1490's and 1556, including nearly 300 between 1536 and 1556. For San Marco, between 1530 and 1590, the figure is less impressive, but still considerable—298 noble entrants.[53] In the Scuola di San Rocco noblemen did not escape the obligation to attend Mass on all appointed festival days, or to pay an annual subscription of one ducat, instead of one lira like the ordinary brothers. They shared this

---

[49] A.S.V., *Inquisitori e Revisori sopra le Scuole Grandi, Capitolare I*, f. 11.
[50] A.S.V., *Compilazione delle Leggi, busta 344*, f. 124r.–v.
[51] A.S.V., *Inquisitori e Revisori sopra le Scuole Grandi, Capitolare I*, f. 19; cf. *ibid.*, f. 15r.–v.
[52] D.M.S., XIX, col. 25, 7 September 1514; D.M.S., LV, col. 629, 14 March 1532.
[53] A.S.V., *Scuola Grande di S. Marco*, vols. 4 and 6.

special obligation with 'all who have served on the Bench, governing this our most honourable fraternity'.[54] Evidently some nobles enjoyed their part in the more spectacular processions of the Scuola, since in 1526 a small group of nobles was granted permission to carry the canopy or '*ombrella*' over the relics in the ceremony on Holy Thursday.[55] Botero was later to list the Scuole Grandi among the Venetian institutions which modified the caste system by drawing noblemen and citizens into a closer relationship, and by allocating responsibility and honour to those excluded from political rights.[56] In this he may have been correct—although noblemen were never admitted to the Scuole on the same footing as citizens. Nobles and citizens shared administrative responsibility in the governing congregations of the sixteenth-century hospitals, or served together as parish deputies in the enforcement of the poor law.[57] But they did not meet in the councils of the Scuole.

At intervals during the fifteenth century the Council of Ten or the Scuole themselves tried to prohibit grants to non-noble members which released them, not only from the obligation to use the discipline, but also from the duty to accept office: for it was becoming increasingly difficult to find enough persons to hold office in the Scuole. Although, in the early fifteenth century, the Scuola di San Giovanni continued its former practice of conceding 'exempt' status to substantial plebeians, it confined this to persons over fifty years of age. In 1414, the officials had decided to allow exemptions to men over twenty-five, but abandoned the experiment four years later.[58] Then, in 1433, all further grants to commoners of exemption from the obligation to accept office were prohibited.[59]

The foundation statutes of the Scuola di San Rocco appear to assume inevitable differences in the condition of the Scuola's members, and are permeated with the idea of there being two orders of men within it. In 1498, however, a last stand was made against this tendency in the Scuola—the officers for the time being rebelled against the Mariegola itself on the score that they were acting in accordance with the spirit behind it. The Guardian Francesco Trevisan and his supporters praised the equality which ought ideally to prevail among all

---

[54] A.S.R., *Mariegola*, f. 10v.

[55] A.S.V., *Scuola Grande di S. Rocco, seconda consegna*, vol. 45, f. 41v. Cf. vol. 44, f. 55, for other evidence of noblemen participating in solemn processions, dated 5 August 1503.

[56] Botero, *Relatione della Republica Venetiana*, ff. 42, 97–8.

[57] See below, pp. 253, 298, 368.

[58] A.S.V., *Scuola Grande di San Giovanni Evangelista*, vol. 8, ch. 62, ff. 27v.–28v.

[59] *Ibid.*, vol. 8, ch. 65, ff. 29v.–30.

the brothers of the Scuola, who should be 'of one and the same rank' (*ad una medesma condizion*) and 'under the same obligations' (*a le graveze tenuti universalmente*). A hundred and more brothers of the Scuola di San Rocco had been exempted from the obligations of the Scuola on condition that they paid an annual subscription of one ducat —six times as large as normal. A certain laxity was infecting all the members, when they saw such distinctions of rank being made. 'This is a thing contrary to charity and to equal brotherhood, and has furthermore provoked scandal and mutiny among the brothers by making one a son and another a stepson of San Rocco, when all should be equal sons (*fazendo di uno fiol e l'altro fiastro de missier san rocho essendo tamen tuti fioli equali*).' The reformers then proposed that in future the penalty of expulsion should be visited on any official who suggested the creation of 'exempt' members. Everybody other than noblemen must observe the Mariegola in full, without the slightest distinction of persons. But the Guardian was fighting a losing battle against the division within the Scuola.[60] Within nine months it was passing a decree granting exemption to a citizen who offered an entrance fee of 25 ducats, and volunteered to pay a subscription of one ducat annually thereafter.[61] Having as yet no permanent endowments, the Scuola could not ignore opportunities to attract members who would pay generously, even if they would not do the work which ought to be required of them. But arguably the acknowledgement of inequality, and the division of functions within each Scuola, was a symptom of its development into an important charitable institution.

Whether out of pure rhetoric or because they really believed it, the Guardian and his supporters, in drafting this resolution, had stated that the other Scuole treated all their brothers equally. Contemporary evidence does not support them, for during the last quarter of the fifteenth century there were several complaints from other Scuole of waning piety among their members. To deal with this situation they did not re-impose equal obligations upon everybody, but instead assigned the drabber devotional functions—especially that of accompanying paupers to the grave—to the poor people who had most to gain financially from the Scuola and who could not afford to lose their eligibility for charitable benefits. The Scuola, having a stronger hold on them than on the well-to-do, could impose its will on them more effectively. Hence, a socially inferior order of 'brothers of the discipline' arose in the Scuole. Attending funerals became, not an act of piety performed by all members of the Scuola indifferently, but a means

[60] A.S.V., *Scuola Grande di S. Rocco, seconda consegna*, vol. 44, ff. 43–44v.
[61] *Ibid.*, f. 48.

76

whereby the poorer brothers obtained alms, either from the testator himself or from the Scuola, if the Scuola buried the dead man for charity—'Amore Dei'. In 1566, for example, four of the Guardians of the Scuole were to tell the Heads of the Ten that for them a major item of expenditure was 'alms given, every first Sunday of the month, to the brothers who accompany corpses to the grave, where no alms are bequeathed by the dead man—otherwise no one would be found who wanted to go'.[62]

In 1476 the Scuola della Carità complained that most processions and funerals were now very poorly attended, adding that 'in this Scuola there are many who enjoy its property but do not appreciate this benefit, and who are ungrateful because they are only concerned with drawing alms, and lazy because they never put off their clothes to accompany the Scuola. Things should be quite the other way about.' In future six unjustifiable absences from the devotional activities of the Scuola were to disqualify a man from receiving alms.[63] Similarly, in 1490, the Scuola di San Giovanni, later securing the approval of the Council of Ten, determined to remedy the dearth of mourners by calling upon the inhabitants of the 42 almshouses of the Scuola, on the 30 men who received regular distributions of alms every month, and on the 60 probationers to attend funerals on pain of deprivation of the benefits they enjoyed, or of the possibility of entering the Scuola.[64] In 1530 the Ten extended this arrangement to all the Scuole, most of which had probably adopted it of their own accord.[65]

This implies that by the end of the fifteenth century it was usual in the Scuole to dispense charity according to the recipient's punctiliousness in performing external acts of piety. Charity should pass chiefly to those who, in the manner most open to humble people, showed themselves to be good Christians. The Scuole Grandi enabled them to perform pious acts and to receive in exchange an *elemosina*, like that handed to a priest for saying Mass, or to an acolyte for assisting him. A small payment for a pious service was not regarded as a wage, but as alms, and the Scuole created large groups of laymen who received alms in this way. Ornate processions and pompous funerals have often been censured as a distraction from almsgiving and from other forms of charity. But they did create casual employment, often specially

[62] A.S.V., *Inquisitori e Revisori sopra le Scuole Grandi, Capitolare I*, f. 80v.
[63] A.S.V., *Scuola Grande di S. ta Maria della Carità*, vol. 236, ff. 10v.–11.
[64] A.S.V., *Scuola Grande di S. Giovanni Evangelista*, vol. 8, ch. 82, ff. 40–1.
[65] A.S.V., *Inquisitori e Revisori sopra le Scuole Grandi, Capitolare I*, f. 33v. Cf. A.S.V., *Scuola Grande di S. Marco*, vol. 8, ff. 262v., 295, 175, 264v. (notes of decrees dated 1501, 1518, 1534, 1546); A.S.V., *Scuola Grande di S. Rocco, seconda consegna*, vol. 46, f. 37v. (dated 1536).

designed for poor persons. Of course, by demanding evidence of conscientiousness in devotions, the Scuole were distributing charity partly according to non-economic criteria. But the poor of Venice could at least know that if they obtained admission to a Scuola Grande and complied with its well-known rules, then they could gain a small measure of social security. As Christian societies, the Scuole proposed to distribute charity only to those who were demonstrably pious.

This attitude to the poor is epitomized in two resolutions of the Scuola della Carità. The first was passed in July 1492, the second, which renewed and extended it, in 1560. Both opened by lamenting the perfidy and the mercenary character of a high proportion of the entrants to the Scuola.

> 'There are many men who enter this our Scuola', declared the resolution of 1492, 'neither from devotion nor to serve our Holy Lady Mary: they wish to live off the property of our Scuola. So it happens that only a few days after they enter they come to the Hall (albergo), some to obtain almshouses, some alms by the month, some alms by the day, when they are men in good health and have good trades, so that they can live according to their estate. By their machinations they gain their request. Then they abandon their trades and crafts, and come only with an importunate wish to be a burden on our Scuola, and there are many of them who have almshouses and alms by the month who do not fail to come every day for alms by the day, and in this way such people devour everything, so that many other brothers of ours of good family and modest character (vergognosi), left without any trade, cannot be assisted according to their needs. Many have almshouses, and when a house they think would suit them falls vacant they try by every means to change it. These are all things contrary to charity, and to the intentions of our forbears and of those who have left property to our Scuola, and in a short time it will be the ruin of this our fraternity.'

It was therefore provided that no alms or almshouses could be granted to anyone who had not served five years in the Scuola, save in a case of extreme need (to be adjudicated by a majority of the officers); and that nobody could enjoy more than one of the three main types of charity. Exchanging almshouses as if they were the pauper's own property was prohibited. The decree of 1476, which ordered everybody in receipt of charity to attend every procession, was re-enforced.[66] The decree of 1492 shows an uneasy suspicion that the Scuola was losing its character as a religious foundation, and becoming a charitable institution which encouraged the most shiftless type of poor, allowing them to engross its property without limit.

[66] A.S.V., Scuola Grande di S.ta Maria della Carità, vol. 236, f. 24r.–v.

The decree of 1560 repeated the complaint about the decay of a 'charitable' into a mercenary mentality, in a fraternity which had originated 'in great love and infinite affection towards one's neighbour'. The rules introduced in 1492 were modified so as to allow the payment of 'daily alms' to any brother who had spent one year in the Scuola. The system could be made workable by reviving the old practice of issuing *tolele* (literally 'tablets') to the brothers—presumably to the poorer brothers only. Each 'tablet' was to consist of a small book of twelve pages, on which were entered the brother's name and surname, and the year in which he entered the Scuola. The Guardian da Mattin, or whoever was leading each funeral procession, would mark the book of every man attending. Hence, when the officers were due to distribute charity, they would be able to see from the books who were the diligent brothers who loyally obeyed the rules of the Scuola.[67]

Probably, towards the end of the sixteenth century, and in the richer Scuole, this criterion became less important. The accumulation of bequests made it possible to benefit all the brothers of the Scuola, and some outsiders also, without exercising such strict discrimination. The brothers who walked in the processions of San Rocco in 1615, to judge by a tariff of payments agreed upon in that year, were mainly men who had been assigned certain menial tasks, and who were known as *fadigenti* or 'fatigue men': the bearers who took up the corpse itself, those who carried the figure of Christ, and so on. In addition to these there were only twelve brothers paid to accompany the Scuola on Sundays in Lent and at charity burials. Each charity burial then cost the Scuola 26 lire, just over 4 ducats.[68] The other brothers who came to accompany the dead may not, however, have been included in these tariffs, but may have qualified for benefits distributed at another time. Be this as it may, satellite trusts grafted on to the Scuola di San Rocco came, by the beginning of the seventeenth century, to distribute more alms to the poor of the Scuola than the Scuola did itself. These alms were destined for all or most of the poor brothers of the Scuola, without necessarily taking account of their attendance at its principal devotional activities. In the decade 1551–60, two-thirds of all alms distributed by the Scuola di San Rocco and its trusts were dispensed by the Scuola itself; but between 1601 and 1610 the bigger trusts accounted for one-sixth as much again as the Scuola.[69] One of these, the Zucca trust, initially provided that all the poor brothers of the

[67] *Ibid.*, ff. 70r.–v.; A.S.V., *Consiglio dei Dieci, Registro Comune 1561*, ff. 1v.–2.
[68] A.S.R., *Registro delle Terminazioni 4*, ff. 220–1.
[69] This calculation is made from the sources discussed below, pp. 162 f.

Scuola should be registered as eligible for its charity—without reference to their record in the service of the Scuola.[70]

The division of the brethren into distinct orders of rich and poor was eventually marked by the compilation of separate rolls of brothers, one for each order, to enable the officers to distinguish between them and to balance them against one another. The Misericordia appears to have taken this step as early as 1533, 'separating those who come to the Chapter from those of the discipline'.[71] But the Scuola di San Marco continued, at least until 1590, to lump all its lay members together—with the exception of nobles and medical men.[72] Likewise, the Scuole di San Giovanni and San Rocco made no move in this direction before 1590. In February 1591, a resolution of the Scuola di San Rocco announced that it had suffered because many of its entrants

'were introduced on the understanding that they should cause the Scuola no loss, saying that they were merchants and men fit to form part of the Bench. But as soon as they are entered we see them coming at the first opportunity with the other poor to collect alms and, if they fall ill, to get doctors and medicines, so that our Scuola has by this means been much defrauded. . . .'

Henceforth two Mariegole should be compiled, the first to bear the names of all the noblemen, citizens and others 'who are in the Scuola and enter it out of devotion alone, with no intention of applying to it for benefits'. On the other should appear the names 'of all the brothers of the discipline who have enjoyed, do enjoy and expect to enjoy benefits from the Scuola'. A standing committee of Regolatori, recently appointed to recommend improvements in the legislation of the Scuola and to reduce its growing expenditure, was now charged with investigating the financial state of any candidate for entry, and with deciding on which Mariegola he ought to be placed. However, if anybody wished to be transferred from the first Mariegola to the second, this could be done on his request alone, because it was incredible that a man really of 'civil' condition should so degrade himself unless he was genuinely in distress. A decree of the Bench and its Zonta was, however, required to transfer a man from the inferior to the more exalted Mariegola.[73] The decree of the Scuola di San Giovanni, in June 1590, somewhat more ambiguously phrased, contemplated the establishment of a third order of men who entered out of pure devotion, paying an entrance fee of three ducats each, and who would not normally be

[70] See below, p. 85.
[71] A.S.V., *Consiglio dei Dieci, Registro Comune 1533*, f. 144v.
[72] A.S.V., *Scuola Grande di S. Marco*, vols. 4 and 6.
[73] A.S.R., *Registro delle Terminazioni 3*, ff. 196v.–197.

eligible for charitable benefits unless they suffered some disaster—in which case a special decree of the Chapter-General could make them eligible.[74]

Thus, there was no absolutely rigid distinction between the rich who gave and the poor who received charity. The Scuole were prepared to confront the problem of poor persons of civil condition, the rich brought low by sudden reversals of fortune for which they were in no way personally responsible. As a trading and speculating nation, the Venetians were well acquainted with the vagaries of fortune. It was no coincidence that in the decade 1550–60 the Scuola di San Marco should make its largest single grant of charity to a certain Sebastiano Bonaldi, who received 40 ducats to furnish his daughter with a dowry. In a petition to the Scuola, he said that his family had, fifteen years before, in 1537, suffered grievous loss. A brother, who was a Knight of Rhodes and enjoyed an income of 600 ducats, had been drowned off Liesena, with a ship of 1,000 butts' capacity belonging to the family, and a cargo worth 15,000 ducats. The following year, another family ship, bound for Flanders, had been wrecked off Sicily. As a result of these far-off misfortunes, Bonaldi was still in poverty, and responsible for a family of seven daughters and two sons. Lucretia, the eldest daughter, was now twenty-one and ready to be married.[75]

Among the virtues of the Scuole Grandi was their capacity to act as an insurance society for the rich as well as for the poor. Those who had served on the Bench and had contributed money and energy to the running of the Scuola were treated with special generosity. In 1509, the Scuola di San Rocco granted former members of the Bench who sank into poverty the right to be buried free of charge in the tombs in the church of San Rocco, because 'in their time they exerted themselves personally and spent of their own for the benefit of the Scuola, especially at the time when they were on the Bench, for we well know that nobody can enter there without incurring expense, because there is no capital'.[76] In the 1550's, the Scuola di San Marco dealt with several petitions submitted by former members of the Bench in debt and distress.[77] Bortolamio dal Calice, a mercer known for his generosity and a member of the Bench of San Rocco, rescued from misery Filomena, widow of Paolo d'Anna, a former Guardian Grande, in June 1593.[78] In 1609 a capital sum of 6,000 ducats, the bequest of the

[74] A.S.V., *Scuola Grande di S. Giovanni Evangelista*, vol. 8, ch. 145, ff. 81–2.
[75] A.S.V., *Scuola Grande di S. Marco*, vol. 20, f. 172: entry for 17 July 1552.
[76] A.S.R., *Mariegola*, f. 19.
[77] A.S.V., *Scuola Grande di S. Marco*, vol. 21, ff. 35, 83v.–84, 134r.–v., 140v., 158.
[78] A.S.R., *Registro delle Terminazioni 3*, ff. 230v.–231. Bortolamio dal Calice, who sold silks and cloth of gold in the Merceria at San Salvador, was described by the

late Maria d'Anna, widow of Beneto Marucini, passed into the hands of the Scuola di San Rocco with instructions that it be used to provide dowries for young women as the officers of the Scuola thought best. They decided that the income could be best employed in helping impoverished fathers who had once been members of the Bench to provide marriage portions for their daughters—taking into account the 'gran rivolutione delle persone', the rapid and apparently senseless turns of fortune's wheel that reduced a man from riches to poverty. Members of the Bench who had suffered misfortune could claim unusually substantial dowries, of 50 ducats each, for their girls. The daughters of other unfortunate citizens, so long as they had never in their father's lifetime exercised any 'mechanical trade' but had respected the demands of their social position, were entitled to a dowry of 25 ducats each.[79] The rich man, too, welcomed some means of personal insurance against disaster. If it came, he could turn to the Scuola to extricate him temporarily from the grasp of his creditors. He could also apply to it when he was morally obliged to produce a dowry to marry his daughter to God or man—always an embarrassing moment for a bankrupt living from hand to mouth.

This chapter has discussed some of the signs of the process by which the Scuole were transformed from devotional societies into charitable institutions. Their material aspect, the thought of what benefits could be extracted from them, had come to bulk disquietingly large in the minds of some entrants to the Scuole by the end of the fifteenth century. The Scuole used the material resources which they commanded—almshouses, alms, dowries for the daughters of brothers—for the purpose of ensuring that the appearance of devotion was maintained. They rewarded only the punctilious. To meet this situation they evolved their selective mechanism and created the order of 'brothers of the discipline' separate and distinct from those 'capable of forming part of the Banca and Zonta'. The primitive ideal, of the religious fraternity uniting all men of different ranks as 'equal sons' of the patron saint, had found defenders in the recently established Scuola di San Rocco as late as 1498. But it was doomed. The constitutional enactments of the Scuole, however arid and taciturn, nevertheless furnish sufficient evidence of the division of the Scuola into two distinct orders. The

chronicler Gian Carlo Sivos as 'a great almsgiver, who gives many thousands of ducats every year. We see that the Lord God gives a hundred to one to his devoted almsgivers.' Biblioteca Marciana, Venice, MSS. Italiani, Classe VII, 1818 (9436), f. 129. Bortolamio dal Calice became Guardian Grande of the Scuola di San Rocco in 1599. See also below, pp. 102, 368.

[79] A.S.R., *Registro delle Terminazioni 4*, ff. 154v.–155. For examples of grants made under this trust, *ibid.*, ff. 176, 179v., 180v., 182v., 195r.–v., 213.

Scuole Grandi were not, by the sixteenth century, democratic or level-
ling institutions. They formed, rather, a transmission system whereby
the rich passed a limited proportion of their wealth down to the poor—
doing so formally in the name of brotherhood. But the name of brother
concealed a sharp division of functions.

3

BROTHERS AND OUTSIDERS:
THE SCUOLE GRANDI AND THE
VENETIAN PEOPLE

The Scuole Grandi were institutions which administered charity primarily for the benefit of their own brothers, but to a certain extent for the relief of other Venetians. Brothers undoubtedly enjoyed priority over outsiders. Indeed, for a brief space, after 1466, the Council of Ten attempted to forbid the giving of alms to anyone who was not a brother. However, in 1477, the Council relented so far as to permit the Scuole to dispense alms to prisoners, to the foundling hospital of the Pietà, and to monasteries or convents if they so wished.[1] These provisions may have been attempts to control indiscriminate almsgiving of the type liable to encourage professional paupers. The legislation ought in theory to have ensured that the officers gave alms only to those whose needs were known to them, or confined their charity to persons enclosed in institutions, instead of scattering alms to vagrants. Perhaps, in this, the Council of Ten shared the objectives of many of the legislators who formulated the poor laws of the period 1520–60.[2] However, in the sixteenth century, the Scuola di San Rocco, at least, came to administer several trusts founded to benefit outsiders as well as brothers of the Scuola. It is now necessary to give some indication (though precision is unattainable here) of the extent to which charity passed to brothers and to outsiders in the sixteenth century; to arrive at some estimate of the total membership of the Scuole, and hence of the number of persons with prior claims to their benefits; and, finally, to examine the social origins of their members.

During the sixteenth century testators charged the governors of the Scuola di San Rocco with the administration of four large trusts, like satellites round the Scuola itself. These were not designed merely to benefit members of the Scuola. In 1528, Maffeo di Bernardo Donà founded a comprehensive trust in which the main objects of charity,

---

[1] A.S.V., *Inquisitori et Revisori sopra le Scuole Grandi, Capitolare I*, f. 13r.–v., 15v. The decree of 1466 permitted certain customary payments to government offices (apparently classifiable as alms) and also the payment of 'the Regalia of the Most Serene Prince'.

[2] See below, pp. 239 f.

apart from bequests made to hospitals, prisoners, friars and nuns, were poor noblemen and citizens of Venice (without further qualification); and 'poor men and women of middling or base rank'. Between 1545 and 1589, 185 noblemen received alms from Donà's charity. Between 1536 and 1556, nearly 300 noblemen had been admitted to the Scuola: but of these only five received alms. The vast majority of Donà's noble beneficiaries were clearly outsiders.[3] Again, in 1552, Nicolò di Antonio Moro, establishing a trust for the distribution of dowries to poor maidens, specified that 'one third of the maidens that the officers elect shall not have relatives in the Scuola, so that every kind of maiden can enjoy this benefit, to the praise and glory of Our Lord Jesus Christ'.[4] The records of the trust itself suggest that his directions were fairly faithfully carried out.[5] Again, in 1563, the officers faced the task of distributing a sum of over 1,000 ducats every other year 'to all the unfortunate poor of the city—to good people', in accordance with the last wishes of a mercer, Piero di Giovanni dalla Zucca.[6] They eventually decided to note 'all the miserable poor of our Scuola, and then the remainder of the unfortunate poor of the city, up to the number of 1,300, and without any further ballotting they shall be approved' by the officers of the Scuola.[7] The will of Pietro Cornovi, called 'dalla Vecchia', of 1585, resulted in alms being distributed in certain proportions in the various *sestieri* of the city.[8] Generally, the bigger and more prosperous the Scuola, the more likely it was to go outside its own membership. The Scuola della Misericordia, for example, which rivalled San Rocco in the extent of its wealth and possessions, and sometimes incurred still heavier fiscal obligations,[9] seems to have paid out large sums under trust to paupers not necessarily members of it—especially to prisoners. However, the Scuole di San Marco and San

---

[3] A.S.V., *Scuola Grande di San Rocco, prima consegna, busta* 438, *Libro de Testamenti*, ff. 28–30; *ibid.*, vols. 607–11, *Giornali della Commissaria Donà*; Brian Pullan, 'Poverty, charity and the reason of state: some Venetian examples', *Bollettino dell' Istituto di Storia della Società e dello Stato Veneziano*, II (1960), pp. 37–40.

[4] A.S.V., *Scuola Grande di San Rocco, prima consegna, busta* 438, *Libro de Testamenti*, f. 124.

[5] A.S.V., *Scuola Grande di S. Rocco, seconda consegna, pacco X, fascicolo* 650/III, a balance sheet of the Commissaria Moro, compiled during the eighteenth century from the books of the trust (for which see *prima consegna*, vols. 545, 546, 547). This shows that between 1562 and 1622 just over 60 per cent of the sum actually distributed in dowries by this trust found its way to young women who were relatives of brothers—duc. 5,470 out of a total of 9,130.

[6] A.S.V., *Scuola Grande di S. Rocco, prima consegna, busta* 438, *Libro de Testamenti*, f. 182r.–v.

[7] A.S.R., *Registro delle Terminazioni* 2, f. 263.

[8] A.S.V., *Scuola Grande di San Rocco, prima consegna, busta* 438, *Libro de Testamenti*, f. 246v.

[9] See below, pp. 147, 149, 153, 155, 175.

Giovanni Evangelista concentrated more on their own brothers and on such employees as Mass-priests.[10]

The Scuole Grandi were occasionally called upon by the state to provide assistance for outsiders. But in the course of the sixteenth century they seem to have done so substantially on only two occasions,[11] during the famines of 1527–8 and 1569–70. In December 1527, the five Scuole Grandi were called upon to contribute 300 ducats each to a scheme of the Council of Ten to provide quantities of coarse bread, to a total value of 6,000 ducats, to be distributed to the poor in the parishes.[12] In the autumn of 1570 the Ten ordered that for a period of five months all moneys normally devoted to charitable uses by the Procuracies of St Mark's, by the Scuole Grandi and by the smaller Scuole, should be diverted to the 'miserable poor' of the city without regard to whether they belonged to the Scuole or not.[13] This included sums destined for the provision of dowries (a matter of less urgency in time of famine). The Scuola di San Rocco paid monthly instalments of 150 ducats into the Procuracies, which evidently acted as a channel of distribution.[14] After 1571 this type of levy seems to have disappeared altogether. Thereafter, the financial obligations of the Scuola to the whole community were of a different kind.

The Scuole Grandi were freemasonries in that they preferred to assist brothers rather than outsiders. But they were not exclusive freemasonries. Initially, membership of each Scuola Grande was confined to between 500 and 600 brothers, with a certain number of probationers who were not full members of the Scuola. In 1318, the Scuola di San Giovanni Evangelista was limited to 550 full members, but was

[10] See below, Appendix, pp. 188–93.

[11] In 1541 the committee responsible for the welfare of the Naupliots, refugees from the Venetian island surrendered to the advancing Turks, asked the five Guardians of the Scuole for a contribution and, having been refused, asked the Ten to back them up. The Scuola di San Rocco at first advanced only 50 ducats and had to be persuaded somewhat ungracefully to increase this sum to 70 (A.S.V., Consiglio dei Dieci, Registro Comune 1541, ff. 14v.–15; Scuola Grande di S. Rocco, seconda consegna, vol. 46, f. 83r.–v.). Between 1545 and 1560 or thereabouts the Scuola di San Rocco advanced only small sums to the Magistrato alla Sanità, which was charged with controlling and reducing the number of beggars—at this time there was much rural–urban immigration (A.S.V., Scuola Grande di San Rocco, seconda consegna, vol. 47, f. 36; vol. 387, Libro di Dare e Havere, under the years 1555, 1556 and 1559; A.S.R., Registro delle Terminazioni 2, f. 215).

[12] D.M.S., XLVI, col. 413.

[13] A.S.V., Consiglio dei Dieci, Registro Comune 1570, f. 184. There were nine Procurators or churchwardens of St Mark's, noblemen of age and distinction: Doges were normally chosen from among the Procurators. As men of exceptional reputation and integrity, they were often called upon to act as charitable trustees.

[14] A.S.V., Scuola Grande di San Rocco, seconda consegna, busta 423 (Ricevute), the volume covering the period from 1565 to 1623, ff. 35v.–36v.

authorized to admit 60 probationers in 1361.[15] From its early days, the Misericordia was entitled to 500 members,[16] and this was also the maximum prescribed for the Scuola di San Rocco in 1489.[17] The Scuola di San Marco, however, enjoyed a special privilege in the early sixteenth century. Sanuto wrote in 1511 that its numbers had been officially fixed at 600.[18] However, the Scuole Grandi did not in practice observe these official limits, and sometimes overstrained their resources by failure to repel would-be entrants. Already, in 1478, the Scuola di San Giovanni was being reproved for exceeding its legal maximum by 200 members.[19] It did so much more blatantly during the sixteenth century, when there is strong evidence of expansion by the Scuole in the period when the population of Venice itself was most obviously growing: between the early 1530's and the great plague of 1575–7. The Scuola di San Giovanni was theoretically allowed 550 ordinary members and 60 probationers, but in 1544 it was found to have 399 brothers in excess of this quota of 610. The Ten contented themselves with ordering that supernumerary members could remain in the Scuola, but must be entered on a separate book and not be replaced on their death.[20] In January 1576, a few months before the summer in which the plague reached its climax, the officers of the Scuola recorded that its total membership had reached 1,800. 450 men were described as having been admitted *per gratia*, by favour, and 1,350 as being 'of the discipline (*per disciplina*)'.[21]

Population pressure, with a consequent increase in the numbers of the poor, was not the only reason for the expansion of the Scuole. Apart from the inefficiency in keeping the Mariegole discovered by the Heads of the Ten in 1542,[22] it was genuinely difficult to obtain reliable information about the death of a brother. Hence, in December 1533, the Scuola della Misericordia, which was revising its Mariegola, complained that its own officers were giving false or erroneous information that certain brothers had died or gone to live outside Venice,

[15] A.S.V., *Scuola Grande di San Giovanni Evangelista*, vol. 3, ch. 19, f. 9r.–v.; ch. 65, ff. 23v.–25.

[16] A.S.V., *Sala Diplomatica Regina Margherita*, LXXVI–3, ch. 24; LXXVI–11, ch. 4.

[17] See above, p. 38.

[18] D.M.S., XIII, col. 136, 20 October 1511.

[19] A.S.V., *Inquisitori e Revisori sopra le Scuole Grandi, Capitolare I*, ff. 16v.–17v.

[20] A.S.V., *Scuola Grande di San Giovanni Evangelista*, vol. 8, ch. 114, ff. 62v.–63; *Consiglio dei Dieci, Registro Comune 1544*, f. 109v. In January 1547 others were still drifting in and claiming that they were members of the Scuola who had been unable to register themselves at the proper time when the Scuola took its census, owing to illness or to absence from Venice.

[21] A.S.V., *Scuola Grande di S. Giovanni Evangelista*, vol. 2, f. 118; *Consiglio dei Dieci, Registro Comune 1575*, f. 108v.

[22] A.S.V., *Inquisitori et Revisori sopra le Scuole Grandi, Capitolare I*, f. 48r.–v.

G

in order to introduce protégés of their own in their places. The Scuola passed a decree forbidding the officers to elect anybody in the place of somebody who was still alive, no matter where he was living. Before a dead man was replaced, especially if he had died outside Venice, a certificate would have to be produced showing the place of his death.[23]

However, in the next sixty years, the Scuola della Misericordia proved the most persistent in asking the Council of Ten for permission to admit additional quotas of brothers who were not simply replacements of the dead, and who would cause the Scuola to exceed its official maximum. Between 1533 and 1589, the Council of Ten passed numerous decrees authorizing the Scuole to admit, between them, over 4,800 additional members. The new men can be divided, very approximately, into two main groups, the richer and the poorer, and were admitted to the Scuole as follows:

Scuola	Rich	Poor	Unspecified
Misericordia[24]	over 700	nearly 1,100	—
San Giovanni Evangelista[25]	705	245	60
San Marco[26]	300	550	50
Carità[27]	191	370	—
San Rocco[28]	201	300	50
	2,097	2,565	160

Among the rich have been counted those described in the decrees as 'men of Rialto', 'citizens', or 'men fit to be elected to the Bench'; as men 'of good rank and reputation', 'honourable persons', or 'men of

[23] A.S.V., *Consiglio dei Dieci, Registro Comune 1533*, f. 145.

[24] A.S.V., *Consiglio dei Dieci, Registri Comuni*: 1535, f. 3v.; 1536, f. 206; 1537, f. 42; 1539, f. 38; 1550, f. 162; 1553, f. 3v.; 1554, f. 124v.; *Parti Comuni, filza 67, fascicolo* 110; *Registri Comuni*: 1561, f. 1v., 49, 65; 1562, f. 142v.; 1564, f. 94; 1565, f. 10; 1566, f. 97v., 185v.–186; 1569, f. 6v.; 1570, f. 120v.; 1575, f. 60; 1577, f. 5v.; 1579, f. 86v.; 1583, f. 6; 1588, f. 67.

[25] A.S.V., *Consiglio dei Dieci, Registri Comuni*: 1533, f. 83; 1536, f. 101v.; 1537, f. 41r.–v.; 1539, ff. 9v., 12, 40; 1545, f. 61; 1548, f. 176v.; 1549, f. 10v.; 1550, f. 183v.; 1551, ff. 4v.–5, 93; 1554, f. 124v.; *Parti Comuni, filza 67, fascicolo* 87; *filza 68, fascicolo* 45; *Registri Comuni*: 1557, f. 33; 1558, f. 190v.; 1560, f. 172; 1561, f. 84; 1565, f. 42v.; 1568, f. 135; 1572, f. 96; 1574, f. 116; 1580, f. 11v., 88, 139.

[26] A.S.V., *Consiglio dei Dieci, Registri Comuni*: 1535, f. 5v.; 1537, f. 14v., 40–1; 1539, f. 12; 1552, f. 104; 1554, f. 92, 124v.; *Parti Comuni, filza 68, fascicolo* 32; 1562, f. 131v.; 1565, f. 10; 1568, f. 164; 1578, f. 145.

[27] A.S.V., *Consiglio dei Dieci, Registri Comuni*: 1535, f. 3v.; 1537, f. 2; *Scuola Grande di S.ta Maria della Carità*, vol. 236, f. 51v., 53; 1539, f. 38v.; 1560, f. 172; 1561, f. 84v.

[28] A.S.V., *Consiglio dei Dieci, Registri Comuni*, 1534, f. 109; 1536, f. 201v.; *Scuola Grande di S. Rocco, seconda consegna*, vol. 46, f. 49v.; *Consiglio dei Dieci, Registri Comuni*: 1539, f. 39; 1562, f. 97; 1577, f. 5v.

such a nature and character that they will not come for alms'. They were normally required to pay an entrance fee of at least 3 ducats, very often of 4, and occasionally of as much as 5.[29] Anyone paying an entrance fee of more than 3 ducats has been counted as probably belonging to the richer order.

The art of good management lay in establishing the right proportions of rich and poor within the Scuola. The mechanical device for regulating these was the entrance fee. In 1523, the Scuola di San Rocco had attempted to fix its entrance fee immovably at 3 ducats. But this resolution was described a year later as closing the doors to the poor, who could only be expected to pay one ducat, and as not exacting enough from rich men, who might produce as much as eight or ten.[30] The officers were then allowed discretion to vary the fee according to the circumstances of each entrant. But in 1557 the Scuola returned to the 3-ducat entrance fee, for it wished for the next five years to confine admission to men capable of taking part in its government. The officers spoke of 'the great quantity of poor men in our Scuola, who cannot be assisted in their need by the small resources of the Scuola as they ought. The Scuola continually distributes large sums for their aid, but, because of their large numbers, they profit little from them.'[31] In 1562 the entrance fee was fixed for an indefinite period at 3 ducats,[32] though the real value of this sum declined with the advance of the price rise. In 1558 the Scuola della Carità fixed its ordinary entrance fee at 4 ducats, but three years later found itself embarrassed 'because nobody has since entered our Scuola, for a poor man, especially in famine years, cannot give so much alms, and during this period many of our brothers who act as fatigue men (*fradelli fadigenti*) have died'.[33] Too many poor would overburden the charities of the Scuola; on the other hand, too few would leave nobody to perform the necessary tasks of carrying heavy weights in processions or of

---

[29] In 1561 the Scuola della Misericordia asked the Ten for permission to admit an extra 200 men at an entrance fee of 5 crowns or 6 ducats each; after a two months' delay it was granted 100 extra men only; but on 24 March 1564 the officers of the Scuola petitioned the Ten saying that they had only succeeded in obtaining 16 entrants at this rate—the entrance fee should therefore be reduced to not less than two crowns per person. A.S.V., *Consiglio dei Dieci, Registro Comune 1561*, f. 49, 65; *1564*, f. 94, 45.

[30] A.S.V., *Scuola Grande di S. Rocco, seconda consegna*, vol. 45, f. 3.

[31] A.S.R., *Registro delle Terminazioni 2*, f. 168v.

[32] *Ibid.*, f. 241. On 20 March 1577 the Scuola received permission from the Ten to admit 200 brothers 'of the discipline' at an entrance fee of 2 ducats each, to repair the depletions of the plague: A.S.V., *Consiglio dei Dieci, Registro Comune 1577*, f. 5.

[33] A.S.V., *Scuola Grande di Santa Maria della Carità*, vol. 236, ff. 70v.–71. Entrance fees were sometimes described as 'alms (*elemosine*)', a general term for payments made to pious men or institutions, and sometimes, more precisely, as *benintrade*.

attending the funerals of poor brothers. In fact, over two-fifths of the supernumerary entrants officially admitted between the early 1530's and the late 1580's were not, or were not supposed to be, poor men. They provided a means of drawing more money into the Scuola and of procuring more people to govern it, thus equipping it to cope with graver responsibilities and with the pressure of a larger population.

Entrance fees for the poorer order varied between 1 ducat and 2 crowns. The poor were normally described as 'fatigue men' or 'men of the discipline', very occasionally as 'good artisans' or 'persons of honest character'. After the outbreak of the Turkish war in 1537–40, the Scuole, as rich corporations with large material resources, were called upon to provide galley crews and to furnish inducements to men to serve in the galleys. In March 1537, the Scuole were compelled by decree of the Council of Ten each to accept 100 men who were willing so to serve.[34] Such entrants have been counted as poor men, since the manual labour required of a galleot was harsh and degrading, and it was therefore unlikely that a prosperous artisan would willingly desert his work and family even if inspired with the most ardent patriotism. By these criteria, about 55 per cent of the 4,800 additional entrants to the Scuola may be described as poor men.

Admitting quotas of supernumerary brothers to the Scuola and pocketing their entrance fees was a form of hand-to-mouth finance which the Scuole practised to save themselves from temporary embarrassments or to meet some special need. The Scuola di San Marco, in 1535, obtained permission to admit an extra 50 brothers in order to add a fine new door to Pietro Lombardi's porphyrous, *trompe d'oeil* façade.[35] The persistent demands of the Misericordia were probably the result of its commitment to extensive building operations, raising its massive and barn-like headquarters over the sestiere of Cannaregio.[36] Most of the endowments of the Scuole were tied by conditions imposed by testators, and were not flexible enough to meet additional charges, however slight. One of the obvious expedients, apart from raising special subscriptions from the officers, was to admit more men. This, however, was open to the objection that it incautiously increased the liabilities of the Scuola, and that the entrance fees might have to be

---

[34] A.S.V., *Consiglio dei Dieci, Registro Comune 1537*, f. 6.

[35] A.S.V., *Consiglio dei Dieci, Registro Comune 1535*, f. 5v.

[36] E.g. A.S.V., *Consiglio dei Dieci, Parti Comuni, filza 67, fascicolo* 110 (23 January 1555 m.v.); *Registro Comune 1561*, f. 49; *1565*, f. 10; *1583*, f. 6. On these occasions it was specified in the decrees of the Ten that the money gained from entrance fees should be devoted to the new building. In 1563 and 1570 grants were designed to help the Scuola to meet its obligations to provide galley crews—see the *Registri Comuni, 1562*, f. 142v.; *1570*, f. 120v.

repaid at interest, no matter how carefully the officers inquired into the finances of candidates for entry. Total membership of the Scuole, at a moderate estimate, reached 5–6,000 before the great plague of 1575–1577—there is strong evidence that the Scuole di San Giovanni, San Marco and the Misericordia were expanding far beyond their legal limits, though San Rocco kept the situation better under control. In 1552, awareness of the need for charitable institutions like the Scuole Grandi may have moved the Council of Ten to accede to the proposals of the mercer Sebastiano Boscoloni and his associates, officers of the small but ancient Scuola di San Teodoro, in the church of San Salvador near Rialto. They suggested that it be raised to the status of a Scuola Grande to supply the needs of the sestiere of San Marco (the only Venetian district still without one), and to relieve pressure upon the other Scuole, which were unable to accept further recruits. They reminded the Ten how their ancestors had always been prepared to authorize the foundation of new Scuole Grandi 'according to the needs and the increase of the people (*secondo le occorrentie et cresimento deli populi*)'.[37]

Of the established Scuole Grandi, only San Giovanni Evangelista expressly declared that it wished to admit more recruits in order to relieve the increasing numbers of the city's poor. It did so in February 1552, and in January and March 1556: 1556 was a year of plague and famine. On the first two occasions the Scuola asked for permission to admit men at the high entrance fee of 4 ducats and to devote the proceeds to poor relief, 40 men in 1552 and 50 in 1556.[38] On 23 March 1556, however, the officers were granted permission 'to admit into our Scuola up to 25 poor men with what little entrance fee (*ellimosina*) we can have, so that these poor men can apply for the alms which are given daily to poor brothers and which we are not allowed to give to anyone else, and can also marry their poor daughters here after the orders of this Scuola'.[39]

Even the numerous decrees authorizing special intakes of brothers do not tell the whole story of the expansion of the Scuole during the sixteenth century. So much appears from the Mariegole of the Scuola di San Marco over the period between 1530 and 1590.[40] The normal entrance fee of this Scuola was low—it was fixed in 1552 at 2 ducats

[37] A.S.V., *Consiglio dei Dieci, Parti Comuni, filza* 56, *fascicolo* 28; *Registro Comune*, 1552, f. 95, 98v. The Scuola was described in the petition as having been founded in 1258.

[38] A.S.V., *Consiglio dei Dieci, Registro Comune 1551*, f. 93; *Parti Comuni, filza* 67, *fascicolo* 87 (8 January 1555 Venetian style).

[39] A.S.V., *Consiglio dei Dieci, Parti Comuni, filza* 68, *fascicolo* 45.

[40] A.S.V., *Scuola Grande di S. Marco*, vols. 4 and 6.

only[41]—so that access was comparatively easy. The number of entrants to the Scuola in each year between 1530 and 1590 was as follows:

1530	1	1532	91	1542	40
1531	1	1533	55	1543	55
—		1534	63	1544	80
	2	1535	121	1545	49
—		1536	199	1546	58
		1537	34	1547	45
		1538	76	1548	52
		1539	92	1549	41
		1540	77	1550	46
		1541	118		
			926		466
		Average	93	Average	52

1551	88	1564	1	1577	74
1552	141	1565	51	1578	119
1553	86	1566	42	—	
1554	153	1567	42		193
1555	44	1568	38	—	
1556	93	1569	59		
1557	118	1570	14		
1558	70	1571	30		
1559	58	1572	29		
1560	113	1573	5		
1561	171	1574	26		
1562	88	1575	34		
1563	123	1576	32		
	1,346		403		
Average	104	Average	31		

1579	52
1580	20
1581	27
1582	38
1583	44
1584	58
1585	70
1586	50
1587	23
1588	42
1589	37
1590	30
	491
Average	41

[41] A.S.V., *Scuola Grande di S. Marco*, vol. 20, f. 155v.

The early Mariegola of the Scuola di San Rocco, spanning about fifty years from the early 1490's to the late 1530's or early 1540's, contains 1,796 names under the heading of ordinary entrants, an average of 35–40 in each year. But the Mariegole of San Marco, stretching over a period of sixty years from 1530 to 1590, carry 3,827 names, an average of over 60 inscribed each year. This may imply that by the middle of the century the numbers of the Scuola di San Marco were hovering around the thousand mark. There were two periods in which especially large numbers were admitted. In 1532–41, building was in progress and the Scuola was incurring heavy additional expenditure through its obligations to provide galleots and to help maintain their families. Hence, the Scuola admitted an average of 93 men each year. Again, in 1551–63, the average intake was 104 men a year. In this period there were at least two severe famines and a plague visitation, and the Scuole were complaining with more than usual persistence of an increase in the numbers of poor.[42] To judge by these Mariegole, many extra members must have been admitted without obtaining permission from the Council of Ten. In 1564 and afterwards the Scuola was more careful, and recruiting fell to a low ebb during the war of Cyprus.

The plague of 1575–77 probably solved drastically the problems of overcrowding in the Scuole. Even the devotees of San Rocco, healer of the plague, had to record the deaths of some 400 of their number on a tablet placed opposite their staircase.[43] In 1577, they applied for permission to admit 200 'men of the discipline' en bloc at the low entrance fee of 2 ducats.[44] To judge by the figures for San Marco, once the plague's depletions had been repaired by large intakes in 1577 and 1578, the numbers were better controlled. However, in 1591, the Scuola di San Rocco, which was trying to retrench, complained that its numbers were illegally increasing owing to an abuse whereby the Guardians were allowed to put up as many candidates for admission as they liked. Each of the fifteen officers was entitled to introduce two new members to the Scuola every year, in a manner contrary to the laws of the Council of Ten.[45] Apart from this, however, it looks as though the Scuole had abandoned the practice of trying to solve financial problems by taking in new members who might subsequently become a heavy tax on their resources. They preferred instead to raise

---

[42] Cf. p. 91 above; A.S.R., *Registro delle Terminazioni* 2, f. 132v., a decree of 3 April 1553; *ibid.*, f. 244v., a decree of 15 March 1562.

[43] The text of the inscription is given in Giuseppe Nicoletti, *Illustrazione della Chiesa e Scuola di S. Rocco in Venezia* (Venice, 1885), p. 49.

[44] See above, n. 28, p. 88.

[45] A.S.R., *Registro delle Terminazioni* 3, f. 196v.

money by juggling with trust funds or by *livelli*—loans on the security of real property. One common cause of the expansion of the Scuole was thus removed.

As a result of their expansion, at a time when the population of Venice was (according to the census of 1563) nearly 170,000, the total membership of the six Scuole Grandi can reasonably be estimated at about 5,500, or $3\frac{1}{3}$ per cent of the total population of Venice.[46] They may have comprised nearly 10 per cent of the adult male population: according to the same census, this stood at about 56,000 in 1563. This figure is especially pertinent, because adult males could pass on to their families the benefits for which they qualified. These included almshouses, which were (at least in the Scuola di San Rocco) designed to accommodate large families rather than aged and solitary people.[47] They also included dowries, which were intended to enable fathers to find husbands for daughters or orphaned nieces, or to place them in convents. By the time of the census of 1586, the Scuole had probably returned, approximately, to their legal limits. In 1586, the adult male population, which had fallen in proportion to the whole in the aftermath of the plague, was about 46,000.[48] On the assumption that the membership of the Scuole was then in the region of 3,500, its legal maximum, it is reasonable to suppose that the Scuole comprised between 7 per cent and 8 per cent of the adult male population.

From two lists of entrants to the Scuola di San Rocco and to the Scuola di San Marco, it is possible to form certain very tentative conclusions about the social composition of these two Scuole. The lists for San Rocco span the period from about 1490 to 1540, those for San Marco the years 1550 to 1590. During these years, about 1,800 persons (excluding nobles and clergy) entered the Scuola di San Rocco, and

[46] The principle that no one might be a member of more than one Scuola Grande had been reaffirmed most recently in 1491—A.S.V., *Inquisitori et Revisori sopra le Scuole Grandi, Capitolare I*, f. 20r.–v.

[47] In January 1512 the officers of S. Rocco determined to aid the poor brothers of the Scuola particularly by 'building them small houses or a hospice to give them a dwelling-place so that they do not by their want remain without shelter, like some people who are oppressed both by poverty and by an innumerable family and cannot sustain the expense of house rent, because of which their furniture is sometimes forfeited even down to the bed itself, and sometimes even their own miserable persons are attached'. (A.S.V., *Scuola Grande di S. Rocco, seconda consegna*, vol. 44, f. 78r.–v.). Sons-in-law were not, however, allowed to occupy the same almshouse as their wives' parents (vol. 45, f. 55, decree of 3 August 1527 provoked by the case of Tomaso dal Christo). See the cases of Gerolamo Gritti in 1528, and of Hieronimo, a textile worker, in 1583, who tried to obtain almshouses by fraudulently pretending that they had numerous children (*ibid.*, ff. 65, 66, and A.S.R., *Registro delle Terminazioni* 3, ff. 71–5).

[48] Beltrami, *Storia della popolazione*, pp. 80–2.

some 2,500 the Scuola di San Marco. The gravest difficulty in interpreting these lists stems from the fact that a large proportion of the entrants were placed on the books without any description of their occupation or status being appended to their names. Some 38 per cent of entrants to San Rocco were undescribed, and the proportion rises to 52 per cent on the books of San Marco. It seems most likely that the undescribed were rentiers, property-owners, merchants or entrepreneurs distributing their investments and interests over several different fields. The simple description 'mercadante' or 'negoziante' is not used on the Mariegole of San Marco, though it appears nine times on that of San Rocco. But it is impossible to be certain of this, and failure to describe the profession or status of an entrant may sometimes have resulted from laxity in keeping the records. The available information makes it possible to sort into various professional categories the brothers of the two Scuole whose occupations were entered on the books: about 62 per cent of the intake of San Rocco, and approximately 47·5 per cent of the intake of San Marco. The results of this analysis appear in the accompanying table. To arrange the brothers according to their probable positions in the social and economic hierarchy is largely impossible, since one cannot confidently distinguish between the large wholesale and the small retail tradesmen, or between the master who directed and the craftsman who carried out instructions. For example, the records of a tax imposed on the guilds in 1582 (*Tansa alle arti*) distinguish between retailing mercers (*merciari di minute*) and those who dealt in bulk (*merciari di grosso*),[49] but the Mariegole of the Scuole do not. It would be reasonable to place government secretaries, notaries and advocates near the top of the non-noble hierarchy, and porters and vergers somewhere near the bottom: but in many cases it is impossible to do this.

Comparisons between the two Scuole are complicated by the fact that their Mariegole are not contemporaneous with each other—so that, arguably, differences in the composition of the two Scuole may reflect either changes in the general economic situation, occurring between the first and the second half of the sixteenth century, or the bias of a particular Scuola towards a particular trade. One cannot always tell which.

However, certain differences stand out. The Scuola di San Marco appeared to admit more professional men, higher civil servants and university graduates—3·1 per cent of its total entry fell into this category, where San Rocco could muster only 0·7 per cent. Forty entrants

[49] See *Bilanci generali della Repubblica di Venezia*, I/i, ed. Fabio Besta (Venice, 1912), p. 285.

to the Scuola di San Marco were described as Dottori, university graduates; only one graduate apparently entered the Scuola di San Rocco. This discrepancy could possibly be explained by a difference in the habits of the book-keepers: but the higher proportion of university men in San Marco accords well with the fact that it admitted more lawyers and higher civil servants than San Rocco. San Marco admitted 11 advocates, 14 notaries and 3 solicitors (*solicitadori*), as compared with San Rocco's three advocates and three notaries.[50] San Marco contained five Government Secretaries, whilst San Rocco admitted only one, a Secretary to the Council of Ten.

COMPOSITION OF THE SCUOLA GRANDE DI SAN ROCCO, *c.1490–c.1540*, AND OF THE SCUOLA GRANDE DI SAN MARCO, *1550–90*

	San Rocco	% of entrants	San Marco	% of entrants
Professions and higher civil service	13	0·7	78	3·1
Luxury trades, books, jewellery, art and music	92	5·1	80	3·1
Groceries and drugs	35	1·9	15	0·6
Traders, brokers, unspecified merchants	32	1·7	4	0·2
Arsenal workers, seamen and boatmen	69	3·8	231	9·2
Textiles and clothing	450	25·0	314	12·6
Footwear and leather	38	2·1	63	2·5
Victuals and wine	135	7·5	89	3·6
Building, construction and furnishing	51	2·8	143	5·7
Wood and metal	74	4·1	53	2·1
Household utensils	32	1·8	34	1·4
Barbers, surgeons and dentists	16	0·9	14	0·6
Clerical workers and small managers	20	1·1	5	0·2
Servants, attendants, minor government employees	36	2·0	51	2·0
Porters, warehousemen, heavy labourers	29	1·6	14	0·6
	1,122	62·1	1,188	47·5

Sources: A.S.R., *Mariegola*
A.S.V., *Scuola Grande di San Marco*, vols. 4 and 6

Moreover, the Scuola di San Marco showed a much greater nautical bias than the Scuola di San Rocco, where, on the other hand, textiles and clothing were more strongly represented, as were the victualling trades. San Marco's leanings can partly be explained by topography— by its position in the sestiere of Castello, within easy reach of the government offices and courts of the Piazza San Marco, and also of the Arsenal. The Scuola di San Marco admitted 46 caulkers, 44 carpen-

[50] On the organization of the legal profession, cf. the brief notes in Giulio Gasparella, *Avvocati e procuratori sotto la Repubblica di Venezia* (Venice, 1874).

ters employed at the Arsenal, 7 oarmakers, 1 mast-maker, 4 persons employed in the Tana or rope-factory adjacent to the Arsenal, and 7 other Arsenal employees. These artisans, all concerned in some capacity with the equipment of shipping, accounted for about 4·4 per cent of the total intake. San Rocco enrolled only 2 caulkers and 2 oarmakers, though it had 9 *squeraroli*—shipwrights or boatbuilders employed in private yards—to San Marco's 4. Boatmen in general seemed far more drawn to San Marco than to San Rocco, for San Marco had 92 boatmen (3·7 per cent of the total intake) to a mere 33 in the Scuola di San Rocco (1·8 per cent of total intake).[51] It is also noticeable that San Marco admitted more fishermen or fishmongers—classified in the accompanying table as victuallers—than San Rocco. 35 fishmongers (*pescadori*) joined the Scuola di San Marco, constituting 1·6 per cent of the total intake. San Rocco had admitted only half a dozen.

However, the textile trades were far stronger in San Rocco than in San Marco—despite the fact that the woollen industry developed to its fullest extent in the second half of the sixteenth century,[52] the period covered by the records of the Scuola di San Marco analysed here. 25 per cent of the total intake of San Rocco was engaged, in some capacity, in the manufacture or sale of textiles, and in the preparation, repair or sale of clothing. San Rocco had 50 silk merchants (described as *da la seda*), 45 mercers, 32 drapers, 27 velvet-makers, 20 furriers, 16 hatters and cappers, and so forth: these groups were feebly represented in San Marco. Textile workers and clothiers still formed the largest single identifiable occupational group in the Scuola di San Marco, but they accounted for only 12·6 per cent of the total intake. San Rocco also showed a marked bias towards the victualling trades, accepting more corn merchants and chandlers, more bakers, cheesemakers, butchers, vintners and innkeepers. Victuallers accounted for 7·5 per cent of the intake of San Rocco, but for only 3·6 per cent of that of San Marco.

None of these contrasts can be explained simply by changes in the economic situation. These differences apart, it is clear that both Scuole

[51] On shipbuilding in Venice during the sixteenth century and on the organization of the Arsenal, see especially F. C. Lane, *Venetian ships and shipbuilders of the Renaissance* (Baltimore, 1934); Ruggiero Romano, 'Economic aspects of the construction of warships in Venice in the sixteenth century' in *Crisis and change in the Venetian economy*, ed. Brian Pullan (London, 1968); F. C. Lane, 'The rope factory and hemp trade in the fifteenth and sixteenth centuries', in his *Venice and history: the collected papers of Frederic C. Lane* (Baltimore, 1966).

[52] See Domenico Sella, 'The rise and fall of the Venetian woollen industry', revised English version in Pullan, *Crisis and change in the Venetian economy.*

Grandi drew recruits from within a wide social range, and from a great variety of trades and professions. Whether they penetrated to any great extent below the level of the artisan or small shopkeeper must remain very much in doubt. In both Scuole the proportion of attendants, servants and minor government employees is very small; comparatively few porters and heavy labourers found their way into the Scuole. On the other hand, the Scuole catered to a certain extent for those workers in the textile trades who probably came nearest to forming an industrial proletariat and perhaps to resembling the Ciompi of fourteenth-century Florence.[53] San Rocco accepted 24 clothweavers and San Marco 27; San Rocco 48 dyers and San Marco 17; San Rocco 15 spinners and San Marco 7. Combers and carders figured on both registers. The lack of sufficient studies of Venetian guilds and labour conditions, and of their arrangements for the welfare of their members during this century, make it impossible to formulate any very sure conclusion here.[54] But it seems likely that an important function of the Scuole was to provide additional insurance or security for persons who already enjoyed some form of protection through their membership of guilds. Allusions to guild arrangements occasionally appear in the papers of the Scuole—in 1648, the Scuola di San Giovanni Evangelista received orders to suspend payments to its two physicians, on the grounds that 'this expenditure is superfluous, because the brothers are assisted by their Arti'.[55] It is unlikely that they gave much aid to domestic servants, who, because of their more intimate personal relationship with their employers, could probably hope to be looked after by them if they sank into poverty. It is also unlikely that they admitted the really abjectly poor or sick, even if they distributed alms to them as outsiders. During the sixteenth century, large hospitals were founded to deal with these paupers, and the state, through the Magistrato alla Sanità, dealt increasingly with the problem of begging and vagrancy.[56] The Scuole Grandi dealt, rather, with the respectable, resident poor, and transferred to them some of the wealth of their richer members.

[53] Cf. Niccolò Rodolico, *I Ciompi: una pagina di storia del proletariato operaio* (Florence, 1945).

[54] Cf. the important observations of Armando Sapori, 'I precedenti della previdenza sociale nel medioevo', in his *Studi di storia economica medievale* (Florence, 1946).

[55] A.S.V., *Scuola Grande di San Giovanni Evangelista*, vol. 2, f. 170v.

[56] See below, pp. 219 f., 235 f.

4

POMP AND OFFICE: THE CITIZENS
AND THE SCUOLE GRANDI

Most sections of respectable Venetian society were represented, in some degree, within the Scuole Grandi. However, office in the Scuole was reserved to members of the Venetian citizenry. Observers of Venice and analysts of its political structure sometimes counted the Scuole Grandi among the institutions which helped to compensate the citizenry for its exclusion from political authority—to give the citizens a sense of involvement in the state, to accord them both dignity and honour, and to siphon off some of their latent political ambitions. To understand the role of the Scuole in the patrician republic, it is important to inquire briefly into the position of the citizens in the state and into their relationship with the governing nobility.

During the 1520's, Donato Giannotti, the anti-Medicean exile from Florence, divided Venetian society into three segments, saying

> By *popolari*, I mean those who may also be called plebeians. These are persons who engage in the lowest trades in order to earn a living. They have no rank in the city. By citizens, I mean those who, because they, their fathers and grandfathers were born in our city, and because they have followed more honourable callings, have acquired a certain glory and have risen one step in the scale, so that they too can be called children of this fatherland. The gentry are those who are lords of the city and of all the state, to seaward or to landward.

Giannotti, in making this threefold distinction, consciously differed from Sabellico, author of an authoritative textbook on Venetian government: literary convention normally cut the Venetians into the two blocks of the ruling nobility and of its subjects.[1] Gasparo Contarini, author of the famous treatise on the Venetian state contemporaneous with Giannotti's, preferred the two-fold division. His work confined the use of the term *civis* or 'citizen' strictly to those who formed part of the nobility, and dismissed the other inhabitants of Venice as 'artificers', 'mercenarie people' or 'hired servants'. He spoke with contempt of those entrepreneurs or merchants who would spare no pains to amass wealth, and approved of the exclusion from the government

---

[1] See Donato Giannotti, *Libro de la Republica de Vinitiani* (Rome, 1542), f. 16r.–v.

99

of 'filthy and ill-mannered men favouring of nothing but gaine, wholly ignorant of good artes'. Nevertheless, even Contarini was unable to maintain this simplistic thesis without modifying it at a later point in his book. As a creator of the legend of Venetian stability and freedom from change, it fell to him to explain how Venice succeeded in avoiding popular disturbance. He then admitted that 'the people hath not beene wholly rejected, but received into such offices and charges, as might be committed unto them without detriment or hindrance of the generall good'. In the end, his position approached that of Giannotti: 'The whole people'—by which he meant non-nobles —'are devided into two partes, the one of the honester and best respected sort, the other of the very base common people, as mechanicall, and handicraftes men. . . .'[2]

These arguments were founded on reality. Citizenship, in sixteenth-century Venice, was a legal status conferring specific social and economic rights. In theory at least, it was granted to persons who, though they might be of non-Venetian origin, had chosen to throw in their lot with Venice and to identify themselves completely with the Venetians. The term included persons of merchant rank and men who followed the liberal professions, as civil servants, advocates, notaries or physicians. Giannotti, who showed far more historical sense than Contarini, conjectured that the citizens of Venice were either descended from men excluded from the Great Council when it was finally closed at the end of the fourteenth century, or else from persons who had more recently migrated to Venice and had since acquired wealth or privileges. The *popolari*, as distinct from the citizens, included immigrants who did not choose to identify with the Venetians, but who—as was the habit of many Bergamasques—eventually departed to enjoy elsewhere the riches they had amassed through trade in Venice.[3] During the sixteenth century, the government granted two forms of citizenship by privilege: citizenship *de intus*, and citizenship *de intus et extra*. A law of 1552, eventually ratified by the Great Council (which gave it additional weight), confirmed the general principle, embodied in earlier legislation, that the privileges of citizenship should be extended only to those who

[2] Quotations in the text are taken from the English version of Contarini's treatise, *The Commonwealth and Government of Venice*, transl. Lewes Lewkenor (London, 1599). References are also given to the Latin edition, *De magistratibus et republica Venetorum libri quinque* (Basel, 1547). For the above remarks, see the English version, pp. 16–18, 141–2; the Latin version, pp. 29–31, 195–6. For the 'myth of Venice', see Franco Gaeta, 'Alcune considerazioni sul mito di Venezia', *Bibliothèque d'humanisme et Renaissance: travaux et documents*, XXIII (1961), and above, pp. 4–5, 7–10.

[3] Giannotti, *Libro de la Republica de Vinitiani*, f. 20.

wished to stay in this city and live here continuously with all their descendants, putting off their loyalty to every other city, with a firm intention to die and to perpetuate themselves through their descendants in this land.

Citizenship *de intus* was open to men who had lived in Venice for a period of fifteen years with their families or households (*con tutta la sua famiglia*), and who had throughout that period paid all taxes and dues (*gravezze*). If a candidate married a Venetian wife, he could aspire to citizenship *de intus* after dwelling continuously in Venice for eight years after the marriage, paying *gravezze* meanwhile. The law granted citizenship *de intus et extra* to those who had lived in Venice for twenty-five years, likewise paying all *gravezze*. These forms of citizenship bestowed certain economic privileges, for citizens paid customs duties and excises at a lower rate than foreigners. A citizen *de intus et extra* enjoyed the right to trade abroad as a Venetian subject: indeed, the law of 1552 obliged all such citizens to present themselves as Venetians in every part of the world in which they transacted business.[4]

These rules were evidently still enforced in the early seventeenth century. In 1603, for example, the Senate granted the privileges of citizenship to eight applicants, most of whom described themselves as fairly substantial merchants who had swelled the customs revenues of the Venetian government by their activities. All the petitioners gave information about the length of time they had lived in Venice, and sometimes drew attention to their having married Venetian wives. The eight applicants included two pairs of brothers, all Bergamasques: Donato and Marco, sons of Gregorio Macarelli, and Giovanni Alvise and Antonio di Raspi. The Macarelli, engaged in the wool business, had lived in Venice in their father's house for twenty-four years continuously, and had been married for about sixteen years to Venetian wives. Their father had apparently become a citizen in 1590, but had omitted to follow the normal practice of obtaining a grant of citizenship for his children and descendants also.[5] The Raspi claimed to have been in Venice for over forty years, 'employed in various mercantile activities', and especially in the leather-trade (*di cordoani*). The Cinque Savii alla Mercanzia, who, with the Provveditori di Commun, were called upon to authenticate information given in these petitions, found evidence only that they had lived in Venice for 32 years.[6] Two other applicants hailed from Brescia. Grazioso dal Calice had spent at least

[4] A.S.V., *Maggior Consiglio, Deliberazioni, Liber Rocca,* ff. 4–5.
[5] A.S.V., *Senato, Terra, filza* 169, 3 January 1603 Venetian style. Various precedents were cited to show that citizenship was normally granted to all legitimate descendants of the person asking for it.
[6] *Ibid., filza* 167, 19 August 1603.

101

twenty-six years in the house of his brother Bortolomio[7]—almost certainly Bortolomio Bontempelli dal Calice, a Rialto mercer who became Guardian Grande of the Scuola di San Rocco and subsequently conferred a substantial legacy on the Hospital of the Mendicanti. Bortolomio dal Calice had obtained citizenship *de intus et extra* in 1579, when he claimed to have spent more than thirty years in Venice.[8] The other Brescian, Giambattista Amigone, had by 1603 lived in Venice over thirty years, and married a Venetian wife more than twenty years before. His son had become a 'citizen by right of birth (*cittadino per natività*)'. Amigone himself claimed to have brought great profit to the Republic by bringing 'a great quantity of gold into the Mint' and by acting generally as a merchant. For good measure he added that his father had served for forty years under one of the Republic's military commanders, Sforza Pallavicino—a generous estimate which the Provveditori di Commun saw fit to reduce to fourteen.[9] The seventh applicant for citizenship, Baldissera Zeni, was a native of Vicenza, who had married a Venetian wife.[10] The eighth was Filippo Emanuel, a native of the Venetian colony of Cyprus, who had come to Venice as a refugee in 1570 or 1571, when Cyprus was menaced and eventually conquered by the Turks. Since then he had served as an interpreter on behalf of the Venetian government in Cattaro and Durazzo, and had devoted some of his time to engaging in trade. He claimed to have been importing merchandise to Venice from 1589 onwards.[11]

One form of citizenship was therefore associated with industry or commerce, and was a status conferring economic privileges. In all the examples discussed above, citizenship was conferred upon persons born subjects of the Venetian Republic who had subsequently migrated to Venice itself and kept house there continuously—or else (like Filippo Emanuel) had absented themselves only when engaged, wholly or in part, on the government's affairs. However, these privileges were often conferred on persons born outside the Venetian state. Most of the grants of citizenship made in 1620 went to such persons—to Giovanni Pietro Appiano of Busimpiano in the state of Milan, a manufacturer of cloth;[12] to Giacomo Noseni, a Lugano cloth merchant who had lived thirty-three years in Venice and wished to trade with the Levant;[13] to

[7] *Ibid.*, *filza* 169, 2 December 1603.

[8] For the grant of citizenship to Bortolomio dal Calice, *ibid.*, *filza* 77, 31 March 1579. For his connexions with the Scuola di San Rocco and with the Hospital of the Mendicanti, see above, pp. 81–2, and below, p. 368.

[9] A.S.V., *Senato, Terra, filza* 169, 24 January 1603 Venetian style.

[10] *Ibid.*, *filza* 167, 24 July 1603.

[11] *Ibid.*, *filza* 167, 30 August 1603.

[12] A.S.V., *Senato, Terra, filza* 240, 9 May 1620.

[13] *Ibid.*, *filza* 242, 14 September 1620.

Paolo Giustinian of Genoa;[14] and to Alcibiade Molossi of Cremona. Molossi, unlike the others, was a civil servant: a graduate of the University of Pavia, he had in 1598 'abandoned my friends, my native land and even my parents, contrary to my destiny at birth', and voluntarily chosen Venice as his adopted country. According to the Cinque Savii alla Mercanzia, he had served as notary in various government offices, and especially as Scrivan or Clerk to the Consoli dei Mercadanti.[15] In 1620, only two persons born in subject towns became candidates for citizenship—Santo Tavon of Salò, who had served for many years as agent to the merchant concerns of the Foscarini and Mula, and now wished to engage in the Levant trade on his own account;[16] and Antonio Carboni of Moncelese, a silk manufacturer.[17] The petitions of Noseni and Tavon confirm that at this time it was still necessary to be a Venetian citizen *de intus et extra* to trade legally with the Levant from Venice on one's own account.

Men of this type, together with their children, were the recruits to the Venetian citizenry. Within this was an élite of professional men born of native Venetian families resident for several generations in the city. As Giannotti implied, *cittadini originarii* were men whose fathers and grandfathers had qualified as citizens and who had never engaged in any manual trade or *arte meccanica*. In 1569, posts in the Ducal Chancery were formally reserved to *cittadini originarii*.[18] These, as Gasparo Contarini had written forty to fifty years before, were offices 'of especiall reckoning and account, into which no gentleman may be admitted, though some of them be such that as well for the commoditie, as title of honour thereunto belonging, they might beseeme any Gentleman of *Venice*'. The citizens provided the permanent salaried bureaucracy, both in Venice itself and in diplomatic posts abroad. The Secretaries who served the Senate, the Collegio and the Council of Ten stood at the head of the hierarchy, which culminated in the Cancelliere Grande. The Cancelliere Grande enjoyed precedence over all Venetian magistrates except the Doge himself. He, in Gasparo Contarini's phrase, represented 'the prince of the common people'. The Secretaries were present at all sessions of the councils they served, and compiled their records, handling many state secrets and much confidential matter. In a state which continually rotated office among members of the patriciate, the citizens provided continuity and stability, doubtless instructing noble amateurs in the nature and scope of their office.

[14] *Ibid.*   [15] *Ibid.*, *filza* 244, 22 January 1620 Venetian style.
[16] *Ibid.*, *filza* 241, 22 August 1620.
[17] *Ibid.*, *filza* 244, 9 January 1620 Venetian style.
[18] See the articles 'Cittadinanza' and 'Cancellaria' in Marco Ferro, *Dizionario del diritto comune e veneto*, 2nd edition (Venice, 1845), I, pp. 395–7, 313–18.

H

'Some of these', wrote Contarini (describing the Secretaries), 'are selected and chosen out to attend upon the counsell of ten, whose decrees they register up in bookes, and are privie to all such things as are handled in the colledge, in which honor they remain as long as they live, not by turns, as the gentlemen do in their offices, of which there is not any perpetuall, but that of the Procurators.'[19] Although they took no formal part in shaping policy, and made no proposals to the legislative councils, the power of experienced Secretaries was clearly considerable. During the constitutional crisis of 1627–8, Renier Zeno, the demagogic leader of the poor nobility, flung bitter accusations at the citizen Secretaries of the Council of Ten, for encouraging it to exceed its proper powers and thereby vicariously inflating their own importance.[20]

Citizens also devoted themselves to diplomatic careers. They accompanied noble ambassadors on their missions abroad, occasionally undertook missions of their own, and served as Residents in Viceregal or Ducal courts which did not merit fully-fledged Ambassadors. In 1596, Valerio Antelmi reviewed a career which had opened thirty years before: it had, among other things, taken him to Genoa with the Cavalier Antonio Tiepolo to greet Don John of Austria and the Spanish navy before Lepanto, and thence to Portugal and Castile. He had been in Paris at the time of the massacre of St Bartholomew, and had subsequently served in Constantinople as well as elsewhere in Europe. In 1596, he was about to become Resident in Milan, and this (or so he testified) was his fourteenth tour of duty and his second residency—he had previously acted, during the 1570's, as Resident in Naples.[21] At the turn of the sixteenth century, citizens were occasionally entrusted with delicate missions to northerly countries to which it was inadvisable (for fear of offending the King of Spain and the Pope) to send noblemen. The Secretary Ottoboni negotiated for grain supplies in Danzig in the famine year 1590.[22] The Secretary Scaramelli, who described the last

---

[19] Contarini, *Commonwealth of the Venetians*, English version, pp. 142–4; Latin version, pp. 196–9.

[20] See Gaetano Cozzi, *Il Doge Nicolò Contarini: ricerche sul patriziato veneziano agli inizi del Seicento* (Venice–Rome, 1958), p. 265.

[21] A.S.V., *Senato, Terra, filza* 141, 11 December 1596; *filza* 154, 20 April, 13 May 1600; *filza* 160, 15 September 1601; *filza* 161, 4 January, 21 February 1601 Venetian style; *filza* 164, 23 August 1602; *filza* 169, 31 December filed under 31 January 1603 Venetian style.

[22] Cf. Mario Brunetti, 'Tre ambasciate annonarie veneziane', *Archivio Veneto*, LVIII (1956), pp. 110 f. Cf. also C.S.P.V., IX, doc. 103, Leonardo Donà to the Doge and Senate, 19 September 1592: 'If it were absolutely necessary to send to England, a merchant would do quite well as Agent, instead of a noble whose presence would imply ulterior consequences.' It was rumoured that the Venetians were proposing to send a nobleman to England to purchase grain.

days of Queen Elizabeth, had been sent to England to discuss the return of cargoes plundered from Venetian ships by marauding English pirates in the Mediterranean.[23] Scaramelli had entered the Chancery about 1565, and had served as Resident in Naples a few years previously.[24]

The citizen class included dynasties of state-servitors. Valerio Antelmi the Younger (nephew of the Valerio Antelmi already mentioned) remarked in 1605 that his father and his father's three brothers had served the Signory continuously for 47 years as notaries and secretaries. He had himself entered the Ducal Chancery in 1596.[25] Valerio Antelmi the Elder—grown desperate after fifty months' service in the expensive Residency of Milan—begged for a replacement in 1601, and asked for his nephew Pietro Bartoli, son of a sister and at present secretary to the Ambassador in Rome.[26] More modest was the family of Angelo Padavin, a Notary Extraordinary of the Ducal Chancery in 1601. His grandfather, Sebastiano Padavin, had acted for seventeen years as castellan at Malvasia, commanding a garrison during the Turkish siege, and his father had been an Advocate-Fiscal in Crete. Angelo Padavin himself had graduated from the colonies to the civil service in Venice, and had entered the Ducal Chancery in 1590. Appointed in 1591 to the office of the Avogaria di Commun, he had served there for four years. He subsequently became Notary to the Provveditori all' Artellaria and also Coadjutor to the Provveditori sopra i Monasterii. For a time he attended on Nicolò Lion, commander-in-chief of the naval force directed against the Uskoks, pirates in the Adriatic, and later resumed his post at the Artellaria.[27]

Venetian society, in its citizenry and in its patriciate, comprised two élites which, though legally distinct, discharged analogous economic, social and administrative functions. Patriciate and citizenry cannot be neatly classified as representing the feudal order and the bourgeoisie in early modern Venice. Venice offered no parallel to the social structures of Castile or France, where a 'nobility of the sword' or race of *hidalgos* contrasted with a 'nobility of the robe' or a bureaucratic élite of *letrados*. The Venetian nobility—especially in the course of the sixteenth and early seventeenth century—may have come to invest increasingly in land, whether because it offered substantial gains or because it provided a safe security and conferred social prestige. But

[23] C.S.P.V., IX, doc. 113: Scaramelli's commission, dated 8 January 1603.
[24] A.S.V., *Senato, Terra, filza* 149, 12 December 1598.
[25] *Ibid., filza* 174, 2 April 1605.
[26] *Ibid., filza* 160, 15 September 1601.
[27] *Ibid., filza* 161, 28 February 1601 Venetian style.

they did not form a military caste, living off rentrolls or plunder in foreign warfare. Some nobles, like the Miani alla Carità in the early sixteenth century or the Trevisan dello Scaglion d'Oro a hundred years later, served with distinction as soldiers.[28] But the traditional destiny of the Venetian nobleman lay in the related careers of the merchant and of the naval officer: in commerce and in its protection. To a large extent, the citizens and the patriciate therefore derived their wealth from similar sources: though it is possible that industrial activity in the late sixteenth and the seventeenth century was the province of the citizens rather than of the nobility.[29] Knowledge of the land-buying habits of the Venetians is still notoriously scanty, but it does seem that at least in the fifteenth century non-nobles as well as noblemen were acquiring land in the newly-annexed province of Padua.[30]

To a limited extent, noblemen and citizens did intermarry. The intensity with which they did so probably varied from time to time; certainly it caused some concern in the early seventeenth century, when the patriciate was probably seeking to relieve financial embarrassment by taking in wealth from below by marriage. In 1608, the Council of Ten attempted to frustrate the manoeuvres of certain nobles who, seeking massive dowries, married the daughters of foreign merchants and then tried to get the best of both worlds by fraudulently proving that their fathers-in-law were Venetian citizens. This would enable the children of the marriage to enter the Great Council as Venetian patricians.[31] In 1609, Sir Henry Wotton, the English Ambassador, reported widespread concern in Venice at the inflation on the marriage market and at the phenomenal increase in the size of dowries. This he explained, not only by the greater volume of money in circulation, but also by the fact that

the citizens growing to great wealth, for the purchasing of some credit and strength in the State, or at least for saving of themselves from injuries, were contented among the nobility to buy a son-in-law at a great rate, which induced the corruption of giving so much with daughters.

28 Cf. A.S.V., Marco Barbaro, *Arbori dei patritii veneti*, V, p. 76; Gaetano Cozzi, 'Una vicenda della Venezia barocca: Marco Trevisan e la sua "eroica amicizia"', *Bollettino dell' Istituto di Storia della Società e dello Stato Veneziano*, II (1960), pp. 67, 76. On Girolamo Miani, see below, pp. 259 f.

29 Cf. J. C. Davis, *The decline of the Venetian nobility as a ruling class* (Baltimore, 1962), pp. 41–2; Brian Pullan, 'Service to the Venetian state: aspects of myth and reality in the early seventeenth century', *Studi Secenteschi*, V (1964), pp. 110 f.

30 See A. Pino-Branca, 'Il comune di Padova sotto la Dominante nel secolo XV (rapporti amministrativi e finanziari)', *Atti del Reale Istituto Veneto di Scienze, Lettere ed Arti*, XCVI (1936–7), pp. 750 f.

31 Sivos, *Delle vite dei Dosi*, f. 157v.; A.S.V., *Consiglio dei Dieci, Registro Comune 1608*, f. 44r.–v.

Wotton, indeed, spoke of dowries amounting to at least 25–30,000 crowns, offered to noblemen with plebeian brides.[32] A list compiled by a certain Giovanni Foscarini provides further evidence of intermarriage between nobles and plebeians, whether or not these plebeians were Venetian citizens. Between 1600 and 1634, according to Foscarini, 192 noblemen married wives outside the pale of their own class. His list gave some description either of the fathers or of the former husbands of 104 of these brides. Among these, higher civil servants and professional men were fairly prominent. There were 16 Secretaries, 9 other civil servants (Scrivani, Notaries or Accountants to government offices), and one interpreter who may well have been in government employ. Added to this were 7 advocates and 6 physicians, with one surgeon, one *solicitador* and one graduate of the University of Padua. Among fathers or former husbands were 25 recent immigrants to Venice from other parts of Italy.[33]

Venice in fact possessed a parallel, minor aristocracy with no distinctive culture or outlook of its own. Instead, it had, parallel to those of the governing patriciate, institutions in which office was strictly reserved to the citizenry. Theorists wrote of the compensations enjoyed by the citizens for their exclusion from really effective authority within the state—they tended to see these as gracious concessions made by the aristocracy to pacify the citizens, rather than to praise the services rendered by the citizens to the state. In this light Gasparo Contarini represented the five Scuole Grandi of his own time, saying that

> there is committed to their trust a great quantitie of money, which is to bee bestowed upon the poore: for such and so exceeding in times past, was the estimation of these fellowshippes, that many who by testament had ordained and bequeathed the distribution of their goodes to the use of the poor, would make these to bee their executors, and wholly referre the bestowing thereof to their discretion, insomuch that some of these fellowshippes in greatness of matters committed to their charge do scarcely give place unto the Procurators of that marke, which is one of the most honourable offices belonging to the Patrician, of which none though he be a brother of the fellowship, may attaine to any of the precedentships thereof, that dignitie belonging only to the plebeians, wherein also they imitate the nobility, for these heads of societies doe among the people in a certain manner represent the dignitie of the procurators, but to the end that neither their societies, nor their heads, may

[32] Smith, *Life and letters of Wotton*, I, p. 439.
[33] Zuane Foscarini, *Notta di Gentil'huomini li quali hanno preso per moglie cittadine, o altre persone inferiori dall'anno 1600 fino il giorno presente*, B.M.V., Mss. Italiani, Cl. VII, 90 (8029), ff. 218–21.

any way be daungerous or cumbersome to the common wealth, they are all restrained under the power and authoritie of the Councell of ten, so that they may not in any thing make any alteration, nor assemble together, unless it be at appointed seasons, without their leave and permission, such honours do the plebeians of eyther sort attaine unto in this commonwealth of ours, to the end that they should not altogether thinke themselves deprived of publike authority, and civil offices, but should also in some sort have their ambition satisfied, without having occasion either to hate or perturbe the estate of nobilitie, by which equall temperature of government, our common wealth hath attained that, which none of the former have, though otherwise honorable and famous, for from the first beginning till this time of ours it hath remained safe and free this thousand and two hundred years, not only from the domination of Straungers, but also from all civil and intestine sedition of any moment or weight, which it hath not accomplished by any violent force, armed garrisons or fortified towers, but only by a iust and temperate manner of ruling. . . .[34]

Contarini's suggestion that Venice had remained free from internal sedition for 1,200 years was clearly a fantasy, though it contributed powerfully to the famous 'myth of Venice'. But in other respects his observations were quite plausible—in that for a time office in the Scuole Grandi did bestow honour and glory and was eagerly sought-after; in that the Scuole do seem to have afforded opportunities for playing politics without disturbing the fabric of the patrician state; in that the Council of Ten did successfully contain these associations; and in that they did administer extensive charitable trusts. The rôle of office in the Scuole must now be examined in detail.

In February 1410, the Council of Ten reserved the four principal offices in the Scuole Grandi (those of Guardian Grande, Vicar, Guardian da Mattin and Scrivan) to men who were *cittadini* of Venice by birth and not by special privilege, and to men who were *cittadini* by privilege who had been in the relevant Scuola for twenty years or more.[35] In September 1438, this regulation was extended to all the other officers of the Scuole.[36] In 1550 the case of one Francesco Pasalù confirmed and clarified the rule that citizens by privilege who had served the period of twenty years in the Scuola could be elected officers.[37] In 1489, difficulties arose when the Scuola di San Rocco asked for admission to the full status of a Scuola Grande, for it had been

---

[34] Contarini, *Commonwealth*, English version, pp. 144–6; Latin version, pp. 199–202.
[35] A.S.V., *Inquisitori et Revisori sopra le Scuole Grandi, Capitolare I*, f. 3r.–v.
[36] *Ibid.*, ff. 5v.–6.
[37] *Ibid.*, f. 57r.–v.; A.S.V., *Consiglio dei Dieci, Registro Comune 1550*, f. 96v.

founded by 'merchants and others who have not been born in this city, but live here with their wives and children and all their property'. The Council of Ten was asked to grant a special dispensation to allow them to be elected to the Bench—especially those who had already dwelt fifteen years in the city with their wives and families. The Ten treated the request with caution, saying that such a dispensation could only be granted for the following ten years, and that no more than half the Bench at any given time was to consist of men who did not meet the ordinary requirements specified at the beginning of the century.[38] It was undesirable that the chief posts in the Scuole should be conceded to men who had not been long involved in Venice, identifying themselves with the city and its people.

Theoretically, civil servants were excluded from office in the Scuole. In 1442 and 1462 the first laws were passed forbidding members of the Ducal Chancery to hold office in the Scuole;[39] these laws were renewed in 1504, 1556 and 1638.[40] In 1591, on the basis of some of them, the Heads of the Ten refused to allow Filippo de Garzoni and Angelo Padavin (elected to the Bench of one of the Scuole) and Bonifacio Antelmi and Gasparo Vedoa (elected to the Zonta) to take up their posts.[41] But the enforcement of the laws probably depended on the extent of the opposition to the election, and on whether the opponents were prepared to hail the offenders before the Heads of the Ten; particularly, perhaps, on the feelings of the Syndics. At times when officers were scarce, a Scuola would hardly wish to be reminded of inconvenient restrictions on the number of eligible candidates. Theoretically, office in the Scuole Grandi should have been a field reserved, not only for citizens, but for the landowning, professional and mercantile groups within the citizenry. This was not so in practice.

A nineteenth-century list of Guardians of the Scuola di San Giovanni, in the Cicogna collection in the Museo Correr (doubtless compiled from Mariegole), shows the names and occupations of the Guardians of the Scuola in 84 of the years between 1500 and 1650.[42] Government Secretaries formed almost the largest group represented here—there were 22 of these, including one who became Guardian three times and

---

[38] A.S.R., *Mariegola*, ff. 14v., 15v.–16.

[39] A.S.V., *Inquisitori et Revisori sopra le Scuole Grandi, Capitolare I*, f. 12.

[40] *Ibid.*, ff. 22–3 (the decree of 1504, bent on saving government servants from any kind of distraction, also forbade them to accept trusteeships on behalf of anyone outside their own families); ff. 62v.–63, 156v. The Ten's decree of 27 October 1638 expressed concern that the Scuole should be served by 'subjects with leisure, who can attend to their service diligently and assiduously'.

[41] *Ibid.*, ff. 99v.–100.

[42] M.C.V., *Cicogna MSS.*, busta 3063, fascicolo 10.

another who held the office twice. 26 men of means, mostly land-owners (*possidenti*) or rentiers (*vive d'intrata, vive d'impiego*) held the office of Guardian twenty-eight times between them. Thirteen merchants (*negozianti*, with one *mercante da lana*) formed the third largest group of Guardians. After them came the lawyers, five advocates (*avvocato, forense*) and three notaries. There were three physicians, and four were undescribed. The Scuole di San Rocco and San Teodoro, on the other hand, sometimes referred casually to the fact that they were officered by merchants and traders.[43]

The gravest hindrance to any analysis based on contemporary Mariegole is the fact that, the higher a man rose socially, the less he tended to describe himself specifically—if, for example, he was an investor distributing money among various different enterprises, this reticence is understandable. Guildsmen could easily specify their profession, but it is almost impossible to pin down those who might, in a society using more elastic social terminology, have described themselves as 'gentlemen'. On the Mariegole of San Marco between 1550 and 1590 about 52 per cent of the entrants carry no description;[44] for the earlier Mariegola of San Rocco the proportion of unknowns is about 37 per cent.[45] However, it is possible to discover the occupations of a proportion of the office-holders in the Scuola di San Teodoro in the mid-sixteenth century, from a fragment of a Mariegola covering the year 1547 and the period 1550–62.[46] This contains the names of 232 men, who held between them 378 offices, ranging from Guardian Grande to Degano and including membership of the Zonta. 103 men of identifiable occupation held 197 offices, and 129 undescribed men held 181 offices. It is thus possible to identify 44·4 per cent of the office-holders, who held between them 51·8 per cent of the offices. An analysis of the identifiable office-holders gives the result shown in the table on page 111.

Mercers formed the most prominent single group of tradesmen, since 14 mercers held 41 offices between them, and they were followed, at a distance, by druggists (*spizieri*), and by sergemakers (*sarzeri*).

In the last resort it seems that office in the Scuole Grandi was the

---

[43] E.g., for the Scuola di San Teodoro, A.S.V., *Consiglio dei Dieci, Parti Comuni, filza* 201, 22 March 1594, dealing with a petition for exemption from office from Bonadio, a sausage maker and corn merchant in the parish of San Giovanni in Bragora. 'This is a Scuola of merchants and shopkeepers like him, and similar subjects have always been elected in this Scuola'—counter-petition from the Scuola di San Teodoro. Also A.S.R., *Registro dello Terminazioni 4*, f. 273, a decree of 12 May 1620.

[44] A.S.V., *Scuola Grande di S. Marco*, vol. 6.

[45] A.S.R., *Mariegola*. See above, p. 95.

[46] M.C.V., *Cicogna MSS*. no. 859.

	No. of men	% of office holders	No. of offices	% of offices
Clothiers and men otherwise connected with the textile trades	49	21·12	104	27·51
Men supplying food or groceries	20	8·62	31	8·07
Other highly-skilled tradesmen	8	3·45	13	3·38
Others connected with some form of commerce	13	5·60	17	4·43
Men of 'liberal' or clerical profession	2	0·84	4	1·04
Men of foreign origin	11	4·74	28	7·42
	103	44·37	197	51·85
Undescribed	129	55·63	181	48·15
	232	100·00	378	100·00

preserve of the entire citizen class, from the landowner and rentier to the rich merchant, from the civil servant to the tradesman. It was open to anybody who was not of noble rank, who did not exercise a 'mechanical' trade, and who possessed the public spirit, the money and the taste for pomp. Service in the Scuole Grandi should have been a branch of the public service separated from service in the Ducal Chancery; but with a growing shortage of men for office this almost certainly became impracticable. In the early seventeenth century, special dispensations were evidently necessary to relieve members of the Ducal Chancery from the obligation to serve as Guardians of the Scuole. None of them appeared to think of invoking the laws of the Council of Ten which forbade them to do so.[47]

Venice had solved with unusual success the problem of containing these large religious associations. She had made them a branch of the

[47] Cf. the cases of Giulio Ziliol and Alvise Dominici in 1613 (A.S.V., *Consiglio dei Dieci, Parti Comuni, filza* 291, under the dates 20 and 28 March 1613), and of Ferrando Ghirardi in 1625 (*ibid., filza* 355, under date 21 February 1624, Venetian style). Ziliol had been exempted from serving as Guardian Grande in the Scuola di S. Marco in 1602 on the grounds that he was involved in the labour occasioned by the liquidation of two of the government loan funds, the Monte Novissimo and Sussidio, a debt amounting to about a million and a half in gold. Eleven years later the Ten hesitated to grant him exemption, although he was concerned in the much greater task of liquidating the Monte Vecchio, which had contained some eight millions in gold. Alvise Dominici was refused exemption from the Guardianship of the Carità, although he pleaded that he was bound to act as Advocate Fiscal to three government offices and was frequently sent by one of them, the Magistrato alle Acque, to inspect parts of the Adige. Ghirardi's case was somewhat similar to Dominici's.

public service, and had designated her *cittadini* as the class privileged to serve the state and people in that particular way. Like the rulers of other medieval Italian cities—such as Perugia, Pisa or Florence[48]—the Venetians distrusted large and wealthy organizations potentially capable of developing into an additional estate and of influencing the conduct of the city's affairs. The fears of the Florentines at least had some justification—for during the War of the Eight Saints against the Papacy in 1375–8 young patricians joined companies of *disciplinati* or *battuti* as a means of protesting against the regime, and the government eventually suppressed these fraternities as instruments of the Guelf party.[49] But the Venetians found it unnecessary to go to these lengths—they felt sufficient confidence in the power of the Council of Ten to control these associations. They could therefore allow them to develop more freely. In 1348–9, the great Florentine fraternity of the Madonna di Or San Michele (founded in 1291) was forced to sell the greater part of its goods to the commune, and in 1349 the commune assumed the right to elect its Capitani.[50] But the Venetians did not adopt these methods: they did not limit the acquisition of property by the Scuole Grandi, through mortmain laws or compulsory sales, nor did they insist on themselves appointing the heads of the Scuole. The Council of Ten merely specified the qualifications for office, in the hope of thereby eliminating men of dubious loyalty.

In 1366 and 1410 the Council insisted that the governors of the Scuole should appear before the Heads of the Ten in March of every year and present lists of the new entrants with whom they proposed to replace the dead.[51] In 1401 the Ten declared that no changes in any Mariegola were to be effected without their authority.[52] State control of the Scuole Grandi was based on these simple foundations. The Council of Ten did not openly pack the Scuole with many nominees of its own, and in 1422 even expressly denied its own right to do so, saying that the Guardian and his fellow-officers must have an absolute right to determine the composition of their own Scuole.[53] In the sixteenth century, the Scuole Grandi recognized the rights of the Heads of the Ten to introduce their own nominees, but this may have meant little in practice—between 1550 and 1590 barely a score of entrants was placed

[48] Monti, *Le confraternite medievali*, I, pp. 143–4, 171, 173, 181–2, 202–3; II, pp. 72–3.

[49] Cf. Rodolico, *I Ciompi*, pp. 54–5; Brucker, *Florentine politics and society*, pp. 320–1.

[50] Monti, *Le confraternite medievali*, I, pp. 166, 171, 173.

[51] A.S.V., *Inquisitori et Revisori sopra le Scuole Grandi, Capitolare I*, f. 1r.–v., 2v.–3.

[52] *Ibid.*, f. 2r.–v.

[53] A.S.V., *Compilazione delle Leggi, busta* 344, f. 89.

in the Scuola di San Marco by the Heads of the Council of Ten.[54] In the fourteenth and fifteenth centuries the Ten, in their legislation on the Scuole, were largely concerned with the preservation of public order, and with forestalling any possible opportunities for conspiracy against the state. In the sixteenth, though not above forbidding meetings after midnight and other such excesses,[55] their tendency was rather to see the Scuole as potential sources of revenue in national emergencies, and to cherish them against the day when they might thus prove useful. They were also seen as institutions capable of rendering invaluable services to the city's poor, who must be protected from the malad-ministration of corrupt officers.[56]

In these circumstances, it was hardly surprising that administrative machinery, pursuing the same ideals as the Venetian government itself and adopting similar devices, should be erected by and for the Venetian citizenry in the Scuole Grandi. The ideal was simple and perhaps un-attainable—that responsibility for administering the Scuole should be distributed among the largest possible number of disinterested men, all of whom should vote and act according to their consciences, and not in response to the dictates of material interest or to the pressures of party arrangement. There must be a rapid turnover in office, indeed a com-plete change of officers every year. This presupposed the existence of an inexhaustible fund of versatile men—men who would in no way pursue their own interests, and who would be capable of learning a complicated job in one year and then of vacating the post and return-ing to temporary obscurity. Out of these could be created a Bench and Zonta of such unquestionable integrity that it could act as a magnet for charitable bequests, inspiring unqualified confidence in the testator.

Several constitutional devices were employed to prevent the govern-ing body from degenerating into an oligarchy maladministering goods left to the poor. In 1484 the Council of Ten issued a declaration that 'men who are joined together by any of the following ties of relation-ship cannot hold office at one and the same time, viz. father, son, brother, son-in-law, father's brother, son's son, brother's son, nephew, cousin-german'.[57] In 1521, when the Council of Ten grafted a Zonta on to each existing Bench to widen the governing body, it was pro-vided that members of the Zonta must have no such ties of relation-

---

[54] A.S.V., *Scuola Grande di S. Marco*, vol. 6.

[55] A.S.V., *Consiglio dei Dieci, Parti Comuni*, filza 69, *fascicolo* 252, 26 February 1557.

[56] This is also the general sense of most of the legislation in the capitulary of the *Inquisitori et Revisori sopra le Scuole Grandi*, a permanent magistracy officered by noblemen, established in October 1622.

[57] A.S.V., *Inquisitori et Revisori sopra le Scuole Grandi, Capitolare I*, ff. 19v.–20.

ship with members of the Bench.[58] On the patrician level, Gasparo Contarini acclaimed the principle 'that not onely in the Senate, but also in all other offices there shoulde not bee any more of one kindred or allyance, with the preservation of equalitie required'.[59] This was extended to the citizens. Family connexions could perhaps usually be tracked down, but it was impossible to eliminate collusion based on the subtler ties of friendship or common business interests.

There was also the device known as *contumacia*, whereby one who had completed a term of service in a given office became for a time afterwards ineligible either to re-occupy it or to enter upon certain other offices. In the early statutes of San Giovanni, the period of *contumacia* which must elapse between holding one office and either returning to it or being elected to any other was fixed at two years, with a further proviso that a man who had once served as Guardian Grande could not subsequently fill any inferior post.[60] In 1394, this period was increased to five years by the Council of Ten, 'so that all may share equally in the offices and responsibilities of the Scuole dei Battuti of Venice'.[61] However, after the introduction of the Zonta, it proved impracticable to enforce this regulation—the fund of potential officers available was not large enough, since thirty of them were now required every year. In 1522 the Ten acquiesced in the suggestions of the Carità and Misericordia that the period of *contumacia* should be reduced to three years.[62] The Scuola di San Rocco kept it at two, with a clause to the effect that nobody could be elected to an office inferior to the one in which he had just served.[63] All voting in elections was by secret ballot, and canvassing for office was held to be a disqualification. Any attempt to exert pressure on electors to office was apt to be condemned in Venice as *broglio*, a corrupt practice named after the colonnade of the Ducal Palace by the Piazzetta where obsequious poor noblemen sold their votes illegally to the highest bidder. In the first quarter of the sixteenth century, Censori were appointed to curb the abuse of *broglio* in the Great Council.[64] In the seventeenth, after a series of increases in the rigour of the penalties, the Inquisitori di Stato were eventually authorized to proceed against *broglio*.[65]

[58] *Ibid.*, f. 29.
[59] Contarini, *Commonwealth*, English version, p. 67; Latin version, pp. 98–9.
[60] A.S.V., *Scuola Grande di San Giovanni Evangelista*, vol. 3, f. 10r.–v., ch. 24, 25.
[61] A.S.V., *Inquisitori et Revisori sopra le Scuole Grandi, Capitolare I*, ff. 1v.–2.
[62] *Ibid.*, ff. 31v.–32v.
[63] A.S.R., *Mariegola*, f. 23.
[64] D.M.S., XXIV, coll. 653–4, 656–7, 659–64: entries for 12–13 September 1517.
[65] See *Capitolare del Maggior Consiglio* (Venice, 1740), for the Ten's decree of 12 October 1588; *Capitolar delli Inquisitori di Stato*, printed in Romanin, *Storia di Venezia*, VI, pp. 109–97: at pp. 148–9.

Broglio, intrigue, and *preghiere*, canvassing, were officially forbidden with equal rigour in the Scuole Grandi. In 1477, the Council of Ten was prepared to allow candidates for office to ask for the support of one of the sixteen electors—the retiring Bench; but, four years later, this concession was revoked. In 1477, also, any prior agreement made by electors to put in a particular person was condemned as a conspiracy, a 'setta over conventicola'.[66] In 1521, certain such groups conspired in the Scuola di San Marco, and succeeded in frustrating one another's efforts so thoroughly as to prevent anyone being elected to the Bench at all. The Guardians were ordered by the Heads of the Ten to cause all the electors to swear that they would choose 'those who in conscience appear to them to be the most honourable and sufficient for the Bench, and to vote against all those by whom they have been canvassed'.[67] In 1541, the Scuola della Carità adopted a device known as the *bozzolo delle preghiere*, already introduced into the Great Council in 1533 for use in certain important elections. All the electors to a particular office would be placed on oath, and then be asked whether each candidate for that office had put any pressure on them to elect him. They would answer by placing a voting-slip in one of two boxes, one for Yes and the other for No. Should the candidate be found to have canvassed one-fifth or more of the electors, he would be disqualified from election for one year. The Council of Ten approved the proposals of the Carità and extended them to all the other Scuole—evidently these were welcomed as an alternative to forbidding canvassing altogether.[68]

Furthermore, in theory, nobody with any personal interest in the property of the Scuola was allowed any part in its administration. This rule was expressly extended to all Scuole in 1537.[69] However, the Carità had condemned in 1518 those who exploited their position on the governing boards of the Scuola in order to secure houses at greatly reduced rates, who failed to pay the proper rent, and who even removed the Scuola's emblem from the front of the houses in order to misrepresent them as their own.[70] Exceptions were sometimes made to this rule on the authority of the Council of Ten, from whom Giacomo Manzoni of the Scuola della Misericordia received a special dispensation in 1552.[71]

[66] A.S.V., *Inquisitori et Revisori sopra le Scuole Grandi, Capitolare I*, ff. 15v.–16, 18.   [67] *Ibid.*, f. 30r.–v.

[68] *Ibid.*, ff. 39r.–v., 45v.–46; *Consiglio dei Dieci, Registro Comune 1540*, ff. 244v.–245v.

[69] *Ibid., Registro Comune 1537*, f. 14.

[70] A.S.V., *Scuola Grande di S.ta Maria della Carità*, vol. 236, ff. 38v.–39.

[71] A.S.V., *Consiglio dei Dieci, Registro Comune 1551*, f. 92v.–93.

Also characteristic of the Venetian ideal of government, both on the noble and on the citizen level, was its distrust of youth. Venetian custom allowed few short cuts to political eminence, and the *cursus honorum* trodden to supreme honour was long and tedious. The constitutional crisis of 1582–3 was a reaction, not only against oligarchy, but also against gerontocracy. The Senate, with its wide age-range, reared itself against the cautious, chill-blooded, elderly Council of Ten.[72] A failing of Venice was her reluctance to admit the possibility that brilliance and flair might be reasonable substitutes for experience. But her constitution was designed as a steamroller running on its own impetus, to be manned by successive shifts of magistrates content to adapt to its ways without trying to modify them. The Venetians 'believed tremendously in the significance of age', and much of the official creed was embodied in the preamble to the age regulations adopted by the Scuola della Misericordia in 1544.

> . . . our good forbears always elected worthy men, of good rank and appropriate age, to the various levels of this government, so that the Guardiani Grandi were not less than 60 years of age and usually over 70, and the Vicars correspondingly less (*cosi successive*), and other officers not less than 30 years of age. They strove to serve Our Lord Jesus Christ and Our Lady Mary our advocate for the good and profit of the poor of this blessed Scuola, and as a result of their work it has multiplied in property and in trusts, as we see by the alms which are continually going forth; but many years ago this charitable way of government failed, and hence our Scuola has received no more benefactions as it used to, to the detriment of our poor brothers. Some time ago the government passed to young men, who are carried away by the usual effects of youth (*che sono transportati dalli effetti, che induce la gioventu*), and they fail in those good offices which our good forbears used to perform.[73]

The remedy was to fix the minimum age for a Guardian Grande at 50. During the year 1544, all the Scuole adopted, or accepted at the hands of the Ten, a regulation whereby the minimum age for the Vicar was to be 45, for the Guardian da Mattin 40, for the Scrivan and the principal Degani 36, and for the other Degani 25. All members of the Zonta, that sage committee, must be at least 40.[74]

---

[72] Federico Badoer, speaking on 21 December 1582, pointed out that the advantages of the Senate lay in its being composed of old men, by nature cautious, of ardent young men and of prudent men of middle age; Romanin, *Storia di Venezia*, VI, p. 367.

[73] A.S.V., *Consiglio dei Dieci, Registro Comune 1543*, f. 258r.–v.

[74] *Ibid., Registro Comune 1544*, ff. 10v.–11. The Misericordia, San Giovanni and San Marco adopted these regulations of their own accord, and the Ten extended them to the Carità and San Rocco.

After the mid-sixteenth century, the constitutional structure of the Scuole suffered no fundamental disturbance. The process by which Venice tried to perpetuate the existence of an uncorrupt board of public trustees consisted of reproducing some of the machinery of patrician government on the citizen level, where the citizens were allowed to function within a carefully defined framework. Botero, in one of his discussions of Venetian statecraft, praised the impersonal system by which poor-relief was organized in Venice. It was always entrusted to public or semi-public institutions, and was never left to private individuals, so that the Republic both guaranteed the poor a certain security and obtained the credit for doing so. Subversive institutions are rarer than subversive individuals. The Scuole Grandi, even if their regulations were not obeyed to the letter, absorbed the individual and tied his hands as thoroughly as the Venetian constitution absorbed and restricted the governing class. Botero had no hesitation in identifying the Scuole completely with the state and with the maintenance of the established order.[75]

Some evidence about the actual operation of these constitutions comes from a curious satirical poem, *Il Sogno dil Caravia*, published in Venice in 1541—though the value of its testimony is very difficult to assess. Its author, Alessandro Caravia, born in 1503, dealt in jewellery at Rialto, wrote verse in Venetian dialect, and occasionally came to the attention of Pietro Aretino.[76] His own opinions were probably Erasmian: for his literary writings, and later his will,[77] consistently showed impatience with pomp and ceremony, with distractions from the essentials of the Christian faith, and with superstitious practices of all kinds. A few years after the publication of *Il Sogno dil Caravia*, he had

[75] Botero, *Relatione della Repubblica Venetiana*, ff. 107v.–108.

[76] Alessandro Caravia, *Il Sogno dil Caravia* (Venice, 1541). Caravia was congratulated on this poem by Aretino, who had received a copy from the goldsmith Gasparo del Toso, in a letter written on 12 March 1542. Caravia dedicated his poem on the death of Gnagni and Giurco to Aretino. Aretino thanked him for the gift, which was accompanied by a precious ring, but suggested he should stick to jewellery rather than to versemaking. See Pietro Aretino, *Il secondo libro delle lettere*, ed. Fausto Nicolini (Bari, 1916), pp. 138–9; Vittorio Rossi, 'Un anneddoto della storia della Riforma a Venezia', in *Scritti varii di erudizione e di critica in onore di Rodolfo Renier* (Turin, 1912), pp. 843–4. Some stanzas of the poem have been extensively quoted by Antonio Pilot, 'Del protestantesimo a Venezia e delle poesie religiose di Celio Magno', *L'Ateneo Veneto*, anno XXXII, vol. I (1909); and by Mario Brunetti, 'Un critico della Scuola di S. Rocco nel '500', in the volume *Scuola Grande di S. Rocco, Venezia, nel VIo. centenario dalla morte del patrono* (Venice, 1927), pp. 57–9. I have used the copy of *Il Sogno dil Caravia* in M.C.V., *Opuscoli Cicogna* 435/3, in which the first reference to Aretino is pencilled.

[77] Caravia's will provided for a very simple funeral, preferably to be attended only by the parish priest and one acolyte, with no torches or candles in the orthodox fashion—see Rossi, 'Un anneddoto', p. 860.

certainly acquired some knowledge of Protestant doctrines on justification by faith, on good works and on predestination—though it might be impossible to prove that he quoted these as his own opinions.[78] In 1550, he published another poem entitled *La verra antiga de castellani, canaruoli e gnatti, con la morte di Giurco e Gnagni, in lengua brava.* This described one of the traditional faction-fights between Venetians from different quarters of the city—from Castello, from Cannaregio, and from the parish of San Nicolò dei Mendicoli. It then depicted the deaths of two valiant fighters, Gnagni, who died a good Catholic, and Giurco, who died a Protestant with a heretical Friar in attendance. This work, in 1556, aroused the interest of the Holy Office in Venice.[79] Eventually, in February 1559, the Tribunal of the Inquisition interrogated Caravia not only about this later poem but also on the subject of *Il Sogno dil Caravia.* Caravia then denied that his writings were composed with any heretical intent, saying that they were merely designed to satirize those who, sixteen or eighteen years ago, 'gathered together crowds and argued about purgatory and confession and such-like'. When asked why he had composed the *Sogno* 'in mockery of religion', he denied that this was its purpose, and truthfully recalled that the work had been licensed both by the Heads of the Ten and by the Senate. He mentioned a dispute over the publication of the *Sogno* before the Heads of the Ten,

> and the argument was started by members of the Scuole Grandi, of whom I say a good deal in this work, and who did not want it printed: nonetheless, they were dismissed, and I was given permission to publish it.[80]

The licence issued by the Heads of the Ten in December 1540 had declared:

> Having heard the report of our servant Giovanni Battista Ludovicci to the effect that there is nothing subversive of the faith, of the state or of

[78] During his trial or interrogation in 1559, Caravia's friend Antonio Dalla Vecchia was prepared to testify to certain orthodox habits on the part of Caravia—how in Dalla Vecchia's house, where he ate and drank regularly, he had never eaten meat on 'prohibited' occasions, and how Caravia and Dalla Vecchia had frequently attended Mass and other services together in the churches of San Salvador, of the Madonna dell'Orto, of San Michele di Murano and of Sant'Alvise. 'I have always seen him generous to the poor, although he is poor himself and has a large family.' He could not, however, testify to how Caravia ate in his own house, or to whether he attended communion and confession as prescribed by the laws of the Catholic Church. See his testimony (dated 25 February 1558 Venetian style) in A.S.V., *Santo Uffizio, busta* 13.

[79] The poem is quoted at length in Rossi, 'Un anneddoto'. I am indebted to Dr O. M. T. Logan, of the University of East Anglia, for drawing my attention to this article.

[80] See Caravia's interrogation of 14 February 1558, Venetian style, in A.S.V., *Santo Uffizio, busta* 13.

EMBLEM OF THE SCUOLA DELLA CARITÀ

facing p. 118

BROTHERS OF THE SCUOLA DI SAN GIOVANNI EVANGELISTA

The Guardian and twelve brothers of the Scuola, in the habits of flagellants, kneel before their patron saint (relief in the courtyard of the Scuola).

facing p. 119

good customs in the work called *Il Caravia* (*sic*) composed by Alessandro Caravia, we, the Heads of the Illustrious Council of Ten, grant to the said Alessandro permission to print the said work through whatever printer he may choose.[81]

Possibly the Heads of the Ten regarded Caravia's remarks on the Scuole Grandi as fair criticism on a matter of public interest. In interpreting them, however, one must bear in mind that they were not the products of a Catholic of unchallenged orthodoxy—though Caravia survived his encounter with the Inquisition and lived to publish again.[82] Given Caravia's Erasmian leanings, he may have been easily scandalized by the abuses he described, and have tended to exaggerate their extent. On the other hand, the papers of the Scuole themselves provide some evidence that they needed to legislate against the types of malpractice of which Caravia complained.

Caravia's verses attacked the diversion of the Scuole Grandi from their initial purpose of doing good to the poor, and complained of the hypocrisy and vainglory which had replaced their original simplicity. Caravia criticized the Scuole di San Rocco, San Giovanni Evangelista and the Misericordia for unnecessary extravagance in building, and the Carità and San Marco for their corrupt government. His observations bore witness incidentally to the power of office in the Scuole Grandi to absorb the ambitions of the citizenry, and to provide opportunities for playing politics. He said of the Carità that its regulations for the dispensation of charity and its constitution, though intrinsically the finest in the world, had been corrupted by a system of patronage reminiscent of the Austrian court. The conclaves of the Carità were hives of intrigue. So much, apparently, for the impartiality which the constitutional mechanism of the Scuole was designed to secure.[83]

[81] A.S.V., *Capi del Consiglio dei Dieci, Notatorio 1540/1542*, f. 48, 24 December 1540. For the ten-year copyright granted to Caravia by the Senate, see A.S.V., *Senato, Terra*, reg. 1540/41, f. 81v., 31 December 1540.

[82] A.S.V., *Senato, Terra*, reg. 1564/65, f. 121v.—on 5 May 1565, the Senate granted Caravia a ten-year copyright to print 'il libro volgar in ottava rima titolato Naspo Bizaro per lui composto'. There is a copy of this work, printed by Giovanni Antonio Remondini at Venice and Bassano, in B.M.V., Misc. 2824/3, with the full title: *Calate fantastiche che canta Naspo Bizaro da Veniesia, Castelan, sotto i balconi de Cate Bionda Biriota, per cavarse la bizaria del cervello e'l martelo del cuor.*

[83] 'If the Carità wants to do some charity, to marry maids or give houses out of pity for the poor, those who want them had better have honey in their mouths and a lot of friends there, and say "Gentlemen, I commend myself to so and so." There are several of them who might be Dukes of Austria. When they enter into conclave, people go about forming factions, one showing he's bigger than the next until it's time to vote. They use the poor like slaves. If they'd have a good look at their statutes, they'd hit the nail a bit more on the head and dish things out a bit differently. Their laws were made by the Holy Ghost, and they're as just and holy as any, but these swine have come and trampled over them for pride, of which they've got a lot.

I

In fact, on 25 January 1541, one month after the licensing of Caravia's book, a party within the Scuola della Carità seems to have challenged the Establishment. The Chapter passed a series of decrees designed to prevent canvassing, to widen the government, and to guard against the maladministration of the Scuola's property by its officials. A decree which imposed or reintroduced a very modest period of *contumacia*, one of two years only, passed only by the narrow margin of 28 votes to 23 in the Chapter-General. The object of this decree, as defined in the preamble, was

> to eliminate all ambition and corruption and especially that of canvassing, and to ensure that the government of our Scuola may not be in the hands of fifteen or twenty men only, and that all our brothers who are entitled to come to the Chapter may take part in the government of our Scuola—perhaps forty or fifty of our brothers who are entitled to come to the Chapter have not taken part in the government of our Scuola these past ten years, because they do not canvass for support and are therefore excluded. Let all be equal.

Another decree was designed to prevent anyone under the age of twenty from holding office as a Degano—Degani aged fourteen or fifteen had allegedly been appointed, 'and with the favours which they enjoy they are kept on the Bench'.[84] The oligarchs of the past decade had evidently secured support by introducing the younger members of their families on to the Bench. The records of the Carità itself bear witness to corruption and clientage. This was doubtless endemic in the Scuola, but had become particularly acute in the years just before Caravia wrote.

Caravia also charged the Scuola di San Marco with becoming a hive of intriguing factions, which formed sordid agreements to exchange votes, and which resolutely obstructed the election of officers of whom they disapproved. The purpose of it all was to satisfy the lust for honour, when the newly-created officers donned their scarlet robes.[85]

Go all round east and west and you wouldn't find a better set of rules, but they don't keep to them.' *Il Sogno dil Caravia*, f. D2v.

[84] A.S.V., *Inquisitori et Revisori sopra le Scuole Grandi, Capitolare I*, ff. 45v.–46v. *Consiglio dei dieci, Registro Comune 1541*, ff. 244v.–245v.

[85] 'They want to do their friends and relations good turns. They're only bothered about the contest between them and not about doing justice. One says "If you hold my friendship dear, make me President this year." So they pledge themselves and send the bills to someone who makes poor satisfaction. Three months before the time comes to make Guardian, Vicar and Fellows, you see them mounting the rostrum to prove they're bigger than the next man, canvassing this man or that to keep his vote for them, just so that they can sit on the great daïs dressed in scarlet, to satisfy the hunger of the proud. Few of them do things for charity or for the love of God. There are signs marking the ballots. I think you know what I mean—pride is the root of all evil....' *Il Sogno dil Caravia*, ff. D2v.–D3.

The haughty intriguers of the Scuole Grandi would have nothing to do with the humbler Scuola of the Blessed Sacrament, liable to be dismissed as a thing only fit for smiths and cobblers. This Scuola was probably one of a number of devotional societies widely disseminated throughout northern Italy. A number of Scuole del Santissimo Sacramento owed their inspiration in the late fifteenth century to the Observantine Friar Bernardino da Feltre—their main purpose was to ensure due reverence for the Eucharist.[86] According to Caravia the Venetian Scuola del Sacramento was worth far more than all the pomp of the Scuole Grandi.[87]

In the mid-sixteenth century, according to Caravia—and there is some documentary evidence to support him—the Scuole Grandi suffered from having offered a pretext for playing politics and for pursuing the forms of dignity and honour. Devotion was smothered by intrigue, and the poor were treated by the Magnificoes as slaves, or as pawns in their own system of patronage. But in the last quarter of the century, the nature of the problem dramatically changed, for reasons foreseen by legislators at the time of Caravia's treatise. In 1573, competition for office was sometimes still fierce, for the officers of San Rocco then found it necessary to protect the Guardian from being repeatedly haled before the Heads of the Ten by men who claimed not to be disqualified by *contumacia* from holding office.[88] By 1576, however, the officers of San Giovanni Evangelista were clearly much perturbed at the shortage of men either able or prepared to hold office in the Scuola.[89] Originally, the Scuole had contented themselves with imposing their own penalties—such as temporary expulsion—for the

---

[86] Pope Paul III apparently recognized the value of these societies in repressing the blasphemous campaign of heretics against the Eucharist, and energetic bishops like Giberti of Verona, Borromeo of Milan and Paleotti of Bologna later tried to establish them in every parish of their dioceses. At the close of the sixteenth century 556 of the 763 parishes of the diocese of Milan were apparently equipped with these fraternities —Pietro Tacchi Venturi, *Storia della Compagnia di Gesù in Italia*, I i (Rome, 1938), pp. 219–26.

[87] 'Sometimes it happens that one of these people is made Guardian of the Holy Sacrament, but at once refuses the job, showing his discontent and saying "What have I done to deserve this? I've got my eyes on something better. Go and get a smith or a cobbler, not a good citizen like me." But proud men like that ought to be ashamed to refuse such a holy and worthy office, where there is Christ in flesh, bones and sinews, who died for us on the holy cross. Pride that robs them of their wits, makes them so bitter towards him. Handling treasure is a form of hypocrisy. A man with sorry ambitions comes to a bad end. The Sacrament is a greater treasure than all the rubbish of the Scuole Grandi, even were they made of fine gold and showered with jewels on every side.' *Il Sogno dil Caravia*, f. D3.

[88] A.S.R., *Registro delle Terminazioni 2*, f. 334r.–v.

[89] A.S.V., *Scuola Grande di S. Giovanni Evangelista*, vol. 2, f. 119.

refusal of office.[90] It was the duty of every member of the Scuola to serve it when required to do so. In 1586, however, the Council of Ten had first to be called in to impose money penalties severe enough to discourage potential officers from shirking their tasks. 'For some years past we have seen a great resistance to accepting office among many of those who are elected Guardiani Grandi, Vicars and Guardiani da Mattin of the Scuole Grandi of this city subject to this Council, and many actually refuse to serve these pious institutions, a thing which must in no way be tolerated . . .'. The object of the decree was to provide that if elected officers would not accept the post 'out of their own charity (*dalla propria carità*)', they must be restrained by fear of a money penalty 'from refusing to administer these Scuole Grandi, which are an ornament to the city and a benefit to the poor who live in it'. Anyone who refused an office was to be barred from election to any other office in future. A Guardian who refused must pay 200 ducats, a Vicar 100 and a Guardian da Mattin 50. Legitimate excuses could, however, be approved, though four-fifths of the votes of the Council of Ten were necessary in order that they should be.[91] A few persons were in fact released from their obligations in the next few years, usually on the grounds of ill-health.[92] In 1600, however, four Guardians-elect in the Scuola di San Teodoro, which had few endowments and so depended heavily on the purses of its governors, refused office in succession, and the penalty for the Guardian had to be increased to 300 ducats.[93] In 1605, again as a result of events in San Teodoro, the penalties were increased to 400 ducats for the Guardian, 300 for the Vicar and 200 for the Guardian da Mattin.[94] Another symptom of the same malaise was the necessity of modifying, in 1587, the age requirements adopted by the Scuole or imposed by the Ten in the 1540's. Otherwise they would have disqualified too many of the remaining candidates for office. The age requirement for the Guardian descended from 50 to 40, whilst that for the Vicar was reduced from 45 to 30, and the Guardian da Mattin was required to be only 25 years

[90] *Ibid.*, vol. 3, ch. 21, f. 10; *Sala Diplomatica Regina Margherita*, LXXVI–3, ch. 9, LXXVI–11, ch. 17; A.S.R., *Mariegola*, f. 3r.–v., which decrees expulsion for a period of five years for anyone who refused an office; A.S.V., *Scuola Grande di S. Rocco, seconda consegna*, vol. 44, ff. 40, 40v., decrees which show a bookseller named Luca Antonio Zonta being expelled the Scuola for two years for refusing the office of Degan de mezz' anno. He was actually readmitted after about fourteen months.

[91] A.S.V., *Consiglio dei Dieci, Registro Comune 1586*, f. 99.

[92] E.g. A.S.V., *Consiglio dei Dieci, Parti Comuni, filza* 243 under date 13 March 1603; *ibid., filza* 287, under date 26 March 1612.

[93] *Ibid., filza* 227, under the date 15 March 1600.

[94] A.S.V., *Consiglio dei Dieci, Registro Comune 1605*, ff. 27v.–28.

of age.[95] In May 1600 the Council of Ten reduced the minimum age requirement for members of the Zonta from 40 to 30.[96]

Other regulations which reduced the number of eligible candidates for office had to be waived—including, as already noted, the rule concerning employment in government business. This the Ten contemptuously described in 1588 as one of the most common excuses pleaded before them.[97] Indebtedness to a Scuola merely for the payment of annual subscriptions ceased to disqualify from holding office in 1603, when it had proved impossible to find a Guardian for the Scuola della Carità.[98] In 1613, the Scuola di San Rocco, having suffered a severe crisis in which no Guardians or Degani could be found by the usual means, complained to the Ten that its members were deliberately disqualifying themselves for office by renting small houses belonging to the Scuola, and by taking advantage of the decree of 1537 which forbade any tenant of a Scuola to hold office in it.[99] In 1620 the same Scuola protested against a severe restriction recently introduced by the Ten—whereby nobody who belonged to the chapter of a Scuola should be allowed to rent any of its property under his own name or that of a close relative. Such a provision was hopelessly impracticable,

> for the greater part of the Scuola's property is let to merchants, and from them we draw every year somebody to perform the service of governing this institution. At present this is extremely difficult, but with the exclusion of these men it will become quite impossible in the future.[100]

In 1612, members of the Scuola di San Teodoro, in their search for a Guardian Grande, could only pick on a certain Giacomo Melchiori, an aged invalid who protested that he had been placed on the books of the Scuola twenty years before without his knowledge.[101] Marc' Antonio Magno, Guardian Grande of the Scuola della Misericordia, was held responsible for an error of accounting committed by a government officer with whom the Scuola had official dealings. He then complained,

[95] A.S.V., *Consiglio dei Dieci, Registro Comune 1587*, f. 128–9v.
[96] A.S.V., *Consiglio dei Dieci, Registro Comune 1600*, f. 22v.
[97] A.S.V., *Consiglio dei Dieci, Registro Comune 1588*, ff. 138v.–139.
[98] A.S.V., *Consiglio dei Dieci, Registro Comune 1603*, ff. 16v.–17v.
[99] A.S.R., *Registro delle Terminazioni 4*, ff. 200v., 202. Two Guardians had refused office, forfeiting 800 ducats between them, and only five of the twelve Degani could be found by normal means. The Ten ordained that in future it should be necessary, in order to incur disqualification for office, actually to live in the house 'loco e foco' or rent one of the estates of the Scuola—A.S.V., *Consiglio dei Dieci, Registro Comune 1613*, f. 7v.
[100] A.S.R., *Registro delle Terminazioni 4*, f. 273r.-v.
[101] A.S.V., *Consiglio dei Dieci, Parti Comuni, filza 287*, 26 March 1612.

in September 1617, of being victimized in a manner excessively prejudicial 'to a citizen and a humble servant of yours, and to everybody
who of his own free will or of his own particular misfortune becomes
in future head and administrator of one of your Scuole Grandi, and
suffers the considerable expense and numberless inconveniences which
these offices involve'.[102]

The common attitude to office in the Scuole Grandi had been completely reversed. It had once been a source of satisfaction to those who
held it, and an object of intrigue to men who sought it for the wrong
reasons. As a substitute for real political power, a replica of Great
Council and Senate reserved to the citizens, it had done well enough.
But fifty years after Caravia wrote, office in the Scuole was becoming
merely a tiresome imposition to those liable to be burdened with it,
responsibility was being ingeniously dodged, and, as refusals of office
multiplied, the Ten were compelled to forego one after another of the
special requirements formerly demanded of potential officers in the
Scuole, in the hope of securing disinterested servants. The pomp of
the Scuole no longer appealed, and the expense of sustaining the
grander offices had become intolerable to most men. The distractions
censured by Caravia were threatening to deprive the Scuole of the
voluntary service on which they depended in order to realize their
ideals.

There were other difficulties. The system of rotating office in the
Scuole demanded a very large reservoir of potential office-holders—in
the Scuola di San Teodoro in the mid-sixteenth century, more than 200
men were required that less than 400 offices might be filled in the course
of about 14 years.[103] Any economic forces diminishing the number
of rich men were potentially embarrassing to the Scuole. There was no
reason for the generality of merchants, manufacturers or landowners
to suffer by the price-rise of the sixteenth century—but moneylenders,
makers of long-term loans and holders of government bonds would
probably fare badly. So would civil servants and professional men, if
official salaries and fees failed to respond adequately to the general
increase. The sums spent by the Scuole Grandi on the organization of
their processions were increasing, though not necessarily through
prodigality on their part—for the state itself demanded ostentation of
them.[104] The rising cost of living may have diminished the enthusiasm
of many people for expenditure on inessentials. Heavier investment in
land might well mean a substantial reduction in the liquid capital

---

[102] A.S.V., *Consiglio dei Dieci, Parti Comuni, filza* 312, 16 September 1617.
[103] See above, p. 111.
[104] See above, pp. 52–5, 59–60.

available for participation in the Scuole, especially if this came to be regarded as an amusement and not as a public duty. A further hazard lay in the state's use of the Scuole Grandi to provide both men and money for galley crews, a heavy responsibility which could again be regarded as a deflection of the Scuole from their original purpose. One genuinely anxious to help the poor might well entertain doubts about the wisdom of doing so through the Scuole. In the wars of 1537–40 and 1570–3, the Scuole Grandi had been called upon to provide galleots when the need was obvious, and they had done so with sonorous proclamations of patriotic enthusiasm and with only an undertone of misgiving. But in the 1580's their contribution to the state was placed on a different footing, and they were required to deposit in the Mint funds to raise galleots in anticipation of the need. Peacetime contributions were understandably regarded as more oner-ous than those exacted in a national emergency, and the cost of a galley crew to a Scuola was increasing very substantially.[105] The bright veneer of office in the Scuole concealed expense and tedium.

As religious institutions with no iconoclastic leanings, the Scuole Grandi were faced with one of the central dilemmas of Christian conduct—with the problem confronting those who did not see the beauty of holiness as a dangerous distraction from the essentials of worship. They had to decide how far to praise God through splendid architecture and elaborate ceremony, and how far to minister to Christ in his own image, the poor man: 'In as much as you have done this to one of the least of these my brothers, you have done it to me'. The Protestant Reformation can, in some of its manifestations, be associated with iconoclasm. The English Reformation has received credit from Professor Jordan for reclaiming moneys hitherto devoted to superstitious uses and for applying them to socially valuable ends.[106] On the other hand, as Professor Mâle has shown, some pioneers of the Counter Reformation, such as the Dutch Jesuit Peter Canisius or Jan van der Meulen of Louvain, set a high value on the visible and tangible beauty of holiness, extolling the power of solid and finite objects and of richly adorned churches to conjure up the infinite in the mind of the worshipper.[107] Certainly, the officers of the Scuola di San Rocco were capable of expressing sentiments akin to these. In 1597, they planned a magnificent altar of the finest marble 'upon which is to be consecrated and offered in sacrifice to the Majesty of God the body and blood of

---

[105] See below, pp. 146–156.
[106] Cf. W. K. Jordan, *Philanthropy in England, 1480–1660* (London, 1959).
[107] See Émile Mâle, *L'art réligieux de la fin du XVIe siècle, du XVIIe siècle et du XVIIIe siècle* (Paris, 1951), pp. 22, 29.

his only son'. The re-enactment of the sacrifice of Christ himself should be accompanied by a fitting sacrifice on the part of members of the Scuola, who must give of their best and not of their vilest possessions.[108] By February 1602 the contributions of the pious amounted to 4,825 ducats, destined to build this altar as the supreme glory of the Scuola.[109] The sum was approximately equivalent to the total amount dispensed by the Scuola and its trusts in various forms of charity to the poor in any typical year between 1590 and 1614.[110] The officers determined to borrow a further sum of 1,457 ducats to meet the cost of quarrying the marble and transporting it from Carrara.

The officers of the Scuole were aware of the temptations which faced them—some of them harder to excuse on religious grounds. Spasms of conscience periodically overtook them, at least from the mid-sixteenth century onwards. The state discouraged excessive ostentation through its Magistrato alle Pompe and by sumptuary laws on the grounds that this soaked up the private fortunes on which the state must be able to draw for its own service. In the Scuole in particular, display was censured on the grounds that it discouraged all but rich spendthrifts from accepting office, and also that it distracted from almsgiving. In February 1543, the Council of Ten forbade banqueting in the Scuole, saying that

> The superfluous expenditure in the Scuole Grandi of this city on elaborate devices (*apparati*) and banquets has increased to such an extent that it has become an abomination, and if no provision is made against it much of the money of the Scuole which ought to go in alms to the poor will be consumed in abuses of this nature. As the Guardians and presidents of these Scuole spend extravagantly even of their own money, before long we shall find no men who want to enter there, because they cannot or do not want to compete with their predecessors in spending.[111]

The case against permitting such expenditure on the part of the officers, even if they were drawing on their own purses and not on the

---

[108] 'As Jesus Christ our Saviour to redeem the human race could not offer to the Eternal Father a more noble or gracious sacrifice upon the wood of the cross than himself, the Son of God, God and man, so is His Majesty pleased that we should sacrifice our hearts to him, as the noblest parts of our bodies, following the example of the fruits of the earth. Of the created things which we have to dispense in reverence to him we must choose the noblest and not the vilest, as it is written in the old law that the ancient priests used to do in the offerings they made to God in their sacrifices, and as Solomon did in building the temple which God had ordered his father David to build. . . . It is not because God delights in precious things but because it is our duty. The house which is to be the tabernacle of God should not resemble the dwelling place of men'—A.S.R., *Registro delle Terminazioni 4*, ff. 6v.–7.

[109] *Ibid.*, ff. 67v.–68.

[110] See below, p. 185.

[111] A.S.V., *Consiglio dei Dieci, Registro Comune 1542*, f. 107.

funds of the Scuole, was further stated by the Scuola di San Rocco in April 1553. It then proposed to appoint a commission of Reformatori to eliminate superfluous expenditure. At this time the numbers of the poor were said (as they often were) to be continuously growing, and to be imposing an increasingly heavy strain on the resources of the Scuola.

Again, men spend excessively out of their own pockets, which is an offence to the Majesty of God, and gives cause for criticism to those who see it, for they believe that these are the moneys of the Scuola which are being consumed in human luxuries when they ought to be dispensed to the poor—a thing which takes away devotion from the place, and causes prospective benefactors to change their minds (*cosa che leva la devotion al luoco, et a rimover li animi di quelli che forse hanno intention di lasiarli*). It would be better to moderate these abuses ourselves so as not to let this evil custom go any further—one day there will be nobody who wants to accept office, for not all men are of equal means and able to incur excessive expense, and these are also things which excite envy among the brothers, so that love is not preserved as it should be in fraternities.[112]

Although actual iconoclasm and neglect of the churches was unthinkable in Venice, the question of the rival claims of pomp and poor relief was at least raised there, both for religious and for social reasons. It was recognized that a building or a procession undertaken upon a religious pretext might in fact simply be a pretext for human display which was not to the glory of God. The Scuole provided the ideal mechanism for flaunting the magnificence of Venetian piety, and the Scuola di San Rocco in 1585 anticipated having to spend 300 ducats on a St Mark's day procession specially ordered by the Council of Ten.[113] The Scuole made charity seem splendid, but it was hard to find a satisfactory adjustment between the glory attached to office and its

---

[112] A.S.R., *Registro delle Terminazioni 2*, f. 134. For various examples of sumptuary legislation, A.S.V., *Scuola Grande di S. Rocco, seconda consegna*, vol. 46, f. 19, 87; A.S.R., *Registro delle Terminazioni 2*, ff. 270v.–271—this legislation is concerned with candles and palms used in processions; the tariff regulating the quantities of candle wax dispensed, of 15 May 1615, appears in A.S.R., *Registro delle Terminazioni 4*, ff. 224v.–225. A.S.V., *Consiglio dei Dieci, Registro Comune 1561*, ff. 48v.–49; *Consiglio dei Dieci, Registro Comune 1593*, ff. 115v.–116, 144: on the use of fragile but decorative stucco candlesticks for processions, instead of solid silver ones, deemed far cheaper in the end. A.S.V., *Inquisitori et Revisori sopra le Scuole Grandi, Capitolare I*, ff. 57v.–60 and *Consiglio dei Dieci, Registro Comune 1553*, f. 7, for a reverberating decree of the Carità against paying excessive salaries to musicians and its extension by the Ten to all the other Scuole. On this subject see Denis Arnold, 'Music at the Scuola di San Rocco', *Music and Letters*, vol. 40, no. 3 (July 1959); Denis Arnold, 'Music at a Venetian Confraternity in the Renaissance', *Acta Musicologica*, XXXVII.   [113] A.S.R., *Registro delle Terminazioni 3*, f. 99.

fundamentally sober purpose: the custody and administration of property left in trust for the poor of the Scuola. 'Do not your alms before men, to be seen by them' was a precept which commanded little respect from the officers of the Scuole Grandi, although Italian societies dedicated to the relief of *poveri vergognosi* often acted in such a spirit.[114] The expenditure of the Scuola di San Rocco on processions and state church-parades increased by about 160 per cent between the period 1551–70 and the period 1596–1615. Much of this apparent increase was certainly due to a fall in the purchasing power of the ducat, and no exact information about this is available. But it can usefully be compared with other increases taking place at the same time.

The figures in the accounts of the Scuola di San Rocco for the dispensation of alms, and for expenditure on candle-wax and other properties for use in processions, can be summarized as follows:

Period	Alms	Annual Average	Processions	Annual Average
		Measured throughout in ducats of account		
1551–1555	2,828	566	2,438	488
1556–1560	3,673	735	1,208*	403
1561–1565	3,326	665	2,212	442
1566–1570	3,337	667	2,531	506
1571–1575	3,697	739	3,835	767
1576–1580	4,152	830	3,722	744
1581–1585	4,226	845	3,426	685
1586–1590	4,738	948	3,439	688
1591–1595	4,809	962	4,923	985
1596–1600	6,022	1,204	6,027	1,205
1601–1605	5,840	1,168	6,295	1,259
1606–1610	5,773	1,155	6,072	1,214
1611–1615	6,005	1,201	3,362*	1,121

* The source gives figures for three of the five years only.[115]

Hence, if the sum spent on processions increased by 160 per cent, there was also an increase of about 100 per cent in the quantity of alms dispensed to the poor by the Scuola itself (as distinct from its trusts) between 1551–5 and the period 1596–1615. The Scuola by the early seventeenth century dispensed smaller quantities of alms to the poor than did its satellite trusts. The increase in ceremonial expenses was not wholly disproportionate to other increases taking place at the—

[114] See below, pp. 267–8, 373–4.
[115] A.S.V., *Scuola Grande di S. Rocco, seconda consegna*, vol. 387; an account book of the late seventeenth century compiled from the original books showing the expenditure of the Scuola itself and of its smaller trusts.

same time. The expenditure on materials used in processions tended to rise by sudden leaps, in the 1570's and in the 1590's. And if, at processions, much was spent on candle-wax and apparatus, much was also dispensed in alms and in paying men to do odd jobs.

Statements submitted by the Scuole di San Marco, the Misericordia and San Giovanni Evangelista, to the Senate and to the magistracy responsible for naval recruiting, at various dates between 1590 and 1627,[116] suggest that about half the net revenues of these Scuole were normally expended on poor relief. One-third to one-quarter was consumed in some form of display. In the poor Scuola di San Marco, the proportion of expenditure on display would naturally tend to be higher than in the rich San Rocco. Appearances among the intensely competitive Scuole had to be kept up to a certain minimum level, and none could spend much less than 600 ducats a year on public ceremonial. From the accompanying table, it appears that the situation changed radically in the Scuola della Misericordia between 1614 and 1627— between these dates, expenditure on charity proportionately increased. This resulted mainly from a lawsuit initiated by the Compagnia della Carità del Croceffisso, a society for the relief of prisoners founded in the 1590's.[117] The Ten ordained, in August 1615, that a much higher proportion of the revenues of a trust founded by Lorenzo di Tomasi in 1398 should be devoted to charitable uses, rather than to building. Expenditure on 'the decoration and building of the Scuola', from the Tomasi trust, had accounted for the large fraction of revenue (nearly 60 per cent) devoted by the Misericordia to display in 1614.[118]

The relationship of expenditure on charity and on 'display' to the total net revenues of the Scuole was as follows:[119]

| | | CHARITY | | DISPLAY | | |
	Date	(propor-tion) %	(amount) duc.	(propor-tion) %	(amount) duc.	Revenue duc.
San Marco	1590	54·51	1,239	34·45	783	2,273
	1611	51·39	1,060	28·61	590	2,063
San Giovanni						
Evangelista	1614	43·09	2,065	25·64	1,229	4,793
Misericordia	1614	27·01	1,043	58·17	2,247	3,863
	1627	48·25	1,897	22·61	889	3,932

[116] For a full analysis of these statements, see below, pp. 188–93.

[117] For the lawsuit, see A.S.V., *Consiglio dei Dieci, Parti Comuni, filza* 302, 17 August 1615. On the Compagnia della Carità del Croceffisso, see below, pp. 397–401.

[118] By 1627, 750 ducats was being dispensed in equal portions to prisoners, maidens and paupers, whilst 690 ducats was retained by the Scuola. (See the statement by the Scuola della Misericordia in A.S.V., *Milizia da Mar, fascicolo* 706.)

[119] See below, Appendix, pp. 188–93.

The Scuole had their critics, and they were obviously afraid of acquiring a reputation for spending money on things inessential to the care of the poor. In 1593 and in 1622, the state instructed its own Inquisitori and Revisori to inquire into superfluous expenditure and where possible to eliminate it.[120] But the Scuola di San Rocco at least had already appointed similar commissions, in 1553 and 1564, on the second occasion doing so for the express purpose of forestalling intervention by the Signoria.[121] In March 1587, the Council of Ten introduced a penalty involving a fine of up to 100 ducats, permanent disqualification for office and five years' continuous exclusion from the Chapter-General, for all who indulged in superfluous expenditure. Since 'most of the disorders arise in the time of the greatest devotion' the Guardians, Vicars and Guardians da Matin were to be summoned each year before the Heads of the Ten on the second day in Lent, and to swear that all regulations for controlling expenditure would be observed.[122]

Of the critics of the Scuole, few committed their thoughts to paper, and perhaps only Caravia has left a permanent record. The Scuola di San Rocco incurred his severest censures for its prodigal expenditure on building at the expense of the poor—especially as rival parties among the brothers repeatedly insisted on changes in the plan of the building. They were accused of spending 80,000 ducats on it when 6,000 would have sufficed.[123] This was an exaggeration for the sake of argument—but, according to a paper of uncertain origin in the Museo Correr,[124] between 1516 and 1564, when the erection of the great hall was in progress, the total expenditure incurred by the Scuola was just over 47,000 ducats for the building itself, and just under 2,500 for decorating the hall. These sums together were roughly equivalent to the total amount dispensed in all charitable uses by the Scuola and its satellite trusts between 1551 and 1572, including both years.[125] Subsequently, some further expenditure, which included gilding the ceiling of the upstairs room, laying the floor of the hall and paying for Tintoretto's paintings, amounted to about 5,500 ducats. Caravia suggested that such extravagance was destroying the confidence of testators who would otherwise have left their money to the Scuola—as the

---

[120] A.S.V., *Consiglio dei Dieci, Registro Comune 1593*, ff. 145v.–146; *Registro Comune 1622*, ff. 170v.–171v.

[121] A.S.R., *Registro delle Terminazioni 2*, f. 134r.–v.; *ibid.*, f. 265.

[122] A.S.V., *Consiglio dei Dieci, Registro Comune 1587*, f. 5r.–v.

[123] Caravia, *Il Sogno dil Caravia*, f. Dv.

[124] Biblioteca Correr, Venice, Gradenigo MSS. no. 194; Nicoletti, *Chiesa e Scuola di S. Rocco*, pp. 58–60.

[125] See below, p. 164.

officers of the Scuola uneasily anticipated in 1553 and 1564, when they established commissions to inquire into superfluous expenditure.

> There are many who abstain from making offerings because the poor are not benefited by them, and in Venice there are innumerable poor, hungry and barefoot and acquainted with hardship. Building cuts into the revenues of the poor, and it's not out of piety that they send their side-shows round the Piazza, with some new contraption every year, spending their money on crazy things. We should love Christ and for love of him use these ducats, which are now ill-spent, to clothe the naked and feed the hungry.[126]

Caravia was eccentric and obscure, scarcely a typical Catholic, though not necessarily heretical in his outlook. But in the mid-sixteenth century the officers of the Scuole themselves were obviously aware of some of the dangers he had pointed out. In Catholic Venice, fine building, ceremonial and pageantry were not proscribed either by the law of the state or by the doctrine and custom of the Church. But the Venetian government and Venetian religious institutions did not officially encourage rash and unlimited expenditure; they always sought to control it, and to forestall some of its dangerous consequences. They strove to protect the poor against the diversion of excessive quantities of revenue into ephemeral ostentation.

The Scuole Grandi existed to make Venetian religion and charity appear magnificent, to attract politically starved citizens into the service of Venice, to sublimate their energies—even, perhaps, to form another ruling oligarchy on a lower social level and with a more modest range. The citizens did not serve Venetian society as an independent middle class creating its own institutions, but as a lesser aristocracy cast in the image of the greater. Eventually, however, the taste for pomp turned sour, and the citizens began to shun the offices they had eagerly pursued in the days of Contarini and Caravia.

[126] Caravia, *Il Sogno dil Caravia*, f. Dv.

131

5

THE ACQUISITION OF PROPERTY AND
THE SERVICE OF THE STATE

The efficiency of charitable institutions during the sixteenth century depended, not only on the integrity of their officers, but also on their possessing reliable sources of income and enjoying opportunities to build up reserves. In an inflationary period like the second half of the sixteenth century, investment in land and real estate offered the best opportunities to religious and charitable corporations. They could scarcely risk their funds in commercial, industrial or financial speculation. Government bonds, though a respectable security, would tend to depreciate in real value with the rising cost of living, and in any case there was a risk that the principal consolidated loan funds might be liquidated. House property and land would, however, be likely to appreciate during periods of heavy population pressure, as in the second and third quarters of the sixteenth century. If population pressure augmented the numbers of the poor and forced up food prices, it might at the same time help to increase the incomes of corporations officially allowed to invest in houses and estates. Houses and shops in Venice itself, easily supervised and safe from the hazards of flooding which threatened certain mainland estates, constituted an especially desirable security.

However, there were good reasons why any sixteenth-century state should look askance at the acquisition of real property by the clergy and by religious corporations. This conflicted with the principle expressed in Bacon's famous aphorism, 'Money is like muck, not good except it be spread'. Money ought to be kept circulating through commerce, which benefited the community at large and swelled the prince's revenues, and excessive wealth ought not to be concentrated in the hands of any particular social order—especially of one whose members might own to loyalties outside the state. Bodin, indeed, boldly ascribed the religious revolutions of the sixteenth century to the unlimited acquisition of property by the clergy—property exempt from taxes and imposts, and never hazarded in the same way as the wealth of laymen.[1] During the sixteenth century, the Venetian government had some

[1] Jean Bodin, *Six books of the Commonwealth*, ed. M. J. Tooley (Oxford, 1955), Book V, ch. 2, pp. 160–1.

132

cause for concern. Admittedly, the famous thesis of Professor Carlo Cipolla maintains that in Northern Italy in the late Middle Ages the Church, for various economic and fiscal reasons, lost a substantial fraction of its patrimony. This may be true of the Duchy of Milan, of Cremona, Pavia, Lodi, Novara and Alessandria:[2] but whether it applies to the Veneto is much more dubious. During the fifteenth century, Benedictine abbeys like that of Santa Giustina in Padua had made very determined efforts to reconstitute their estates, and in the mid-sixteenth they participated in the general movement for the reclamation of land in the provinces nearest to Venice.[3] Towards the western border of the Venetian Republic, the province of Bergamo acquired the reputation of having fallen largely into the hands of the clergy and of religious corporations. Indeed, in 1605, the Capitano Bernardo Capello asserted that 'the property of the Church, of hospitals, and of other religious institutions' was constantly increasing in the Bergamasco through new purchases (made out of surplus revenue), through alms, and through pious bequests. Such institutions had already occupied two-thirds of the surface of the province, and there was a serious risk that without the intervention of the Venetian government all the land might pass to the Church.[4] Clerics and religious corporations did not have to make such progress to cause alarm in Venice—in the congested capital, space in which the laity could invest their wealth was always scarce and jealously guarded. In 1515, Gasparo Malipiero, Savio di Terra Ferma, complained that 'churches are erected in the centre of the city, like the Madonna dei Miracoli, Santa Maria della Fava, San Rocco and Santa Margarita, and other churches built in our own time, to the detriment of the Signory and of the city'.[5] Mortmain laws—restricting the bequeathal of real estate into the 'dead hand' of ecclesiastical institutions

---

[2] C. M. Cipolla, 'Une crise ignorée: comment s'est perdue la propriété ecclésiastique dans l'Italie du Nord entre le XIe et le XVIe siècle', *Annales: Économies, Sociétés, Civilisations*, II (1947).

[3] See Aldo Stella, 'La proprietà ecclesiastica nella Repubblica di Venezia dal secolo XV al XVII (lineamenti di una ricerca economico-politica)', *Nuova Rivista Storica*, XLII (1958), pp. 56–63, 67–8.

[4] A.S.V., *Collegio, Relazioni, busta* 35, report of Bernardo Capello, 2 April 1605. About 1608, the retiring Podestà Francesco Diedo explained that during the Interdict the Bergamasques had supported the Venetian Republic 'especially because it preserves property for laymen, this territory being owned for the most part by ecclesiastics'—*ibid.*, under date. Capello's remarks are repeated in the report of Benedetto Moro, Provveditore Generale in Terra Ferma, of 14 January 1607 Venetian style, at f. 6v.—*ibid., busta* 52.

[5] D.M.S., XIX col. 380, 16 January 1514 Venetian style; XX, col. 138, 23 April 1515. Malipiero was opposing a request made by the Scuola di San Rocco, which had purchased houses from the parish priest of San Pantalon, that the land on which these houses stood should be exempted from the lay impost or *decima* on real property.

—came much sooner to the city of Venice itself than to its subject regions.

Landed wealth bequeathed to the clergy or to religious corporations risked being withdrawn from state control and having its yield exported from the Venetian Republic. Capital might escape from the state through taxation imposed by the Holy See, through contributions sent by religious houses to the general treasurers of their congregations, or through the charges laid on Venetian ecclesiastical revenues for the support of foreign cardinals.[6] The question also arose of the state's right to tax ecclesiastical institutions. Very occasionally, the Venetian government was prepared to insist on this openly, as a vital matter of principle. In 1606, when the question was most expressly discussed, Sarpi argued that the Prince enjoyed rights over the property of all his subjects—rights superior to those of the private man who actually owned the property. The Prince had a right to dispose of the property of every private man 'as the need and profit of the common weal demands (si come ricerca la necessità ed utilità del ben publico)'—he exercised a maiestà or sopranità greater than the dominion of a private man.[7] In the words of the Senator Antonio Querini, also uttered during the Interdict, the Prince's rights were de jure divino and the subject's rights in his own property merely de jure humano.[8] When a man bequeathed property to the Church—so runs Sarpi's argument—he could transfer to it only his own inferior rights. He could not transfer the Prince's rights. The Prince therefore retained the same rights over ecclesiastical property as he had enjoyed when that property rested in the hands of laymen. Again, the Prince exercised a jus defensionis over all property, including ecclesiastical—'that is, a right to take useful measures to defend and maintain it, not at the expense of the defender, but (according to the laws of protection) at the expense of the thing defended'.

However, Sarpi's clear formulation of these views was a response to a crisis, when the party which favoured compromise had for once been defeated. The Venetians were not normally prepared to maintain that the clergy were as liable for taxation as the laity. The state levied a tax on real property held by clerics—the Decima al clero. But it was desirable to obtain the Pope's co-operation before trying to exact it.[9] Paul II,

---

[6] Cf. Stella, 'La proprietà ecclesiastica', pp. 52, 72.

[7] Paolo Sarpi, 'Consiglio in difesa di due ordinazioni della Serenissima Repubblica', in Istoria dell'Interdetto e altri scritti editi o inediti, II, ed. Giovanni Gambarin (Bari, 1940), pp. 12, 14.

[8] Cornet, Paolo V e la Repubblica Veneta, Appendice XI, pp. 290–1.

[9] F. Besta, Bilanci generali della Repubblica di Venezia, Introduzione, pp. CLIII–CLIV; docs. 154–6, pp. 203–7.

ENTRANCE TO BUILDINGS OF THE SCUOLA DELLA MISERICORDIA

Brothers of the Scuola, dressed as flagellants, can be seen sheltering under the robe of the Madonna della Misericordia.

facing p. 134

CORPUS CHRISTI PROCESSION

This drawing, published in the early seventeenth century, gives some idea of the probable scale and appearance of the grand ceremony of 1606 described above, pp. 59–60.

facing p. 135

Clement VII and Gregory XIII all, in their dealings with Venice, at one time or another, withheld their goodwill. In 1464 a Bull of Pius II asserted the principle that it would henceforth be necessary to ask the Pope's permission in order to levy this tax.[10] In 1510 Venice, faced with the League of Cambrai, bought off Pope Julius II partly by promising not to lay imposts on the clergy, or on ecclesiastical persons, monasteries, religious institutions or hospitals.[11] In 1574, the financier Giovanni Francesco Priuli, discussing the imposition of a general clerical tax, to be paid by monks (among others), assumed that a grant of clerical taxes from the Pope 'would stop everybody's mouth and make the matter go through absolutely peacefully'.[12] It was therefore advisable to take preventive measures, and to try to curb the acquisition of real property by the clergy, especially in the city of Venice itself: though it would scarcely have profited the state had it forbidden the clergy to invest in government loan funds. This possibility remained open to them until the early seventeenth century.

Lay corporations in Venice, even those associated with religious activities, received at the hands of the state treatment different from that accorded to hospitals and *luoghi pii* under clerical management. They were permitted to acquire real property in Venice itself (even after the mortmain law of 1536) on the understanding that they would contribute to the needs of the state in an emergency. This gave them, on the one hand, a better chance of acquiring a steady income, independent of voluntary contributions. On the other, the Scuole Grandi incurred very heavy fiscal obligations to the state, which, especially in the early seventeenth century, somewhat diverted them from their charitable activities. But—again in the early seventeenth century—the Scuole Grandi enjoyed considerable advantages over institutions under clerical management, when the principal government consolidated loan funds were liquidated, whilst at the same time opportunities for investing in real property were officially closed to the clergy.

During most of the period under review, the Scuole Grandi escaped the operation of the mortmain laws and acquired land and house property—their right to do so seems to have been called in question only occasionally. In 1472, 1536 and 1605, the Venetian Senate passed laws designed to limit the acquisition of real property by the clergy,

[10] Cecchetti, *La Repubblica di Venezia e la Corte di Roma*, I, pp. 153–5.

[11] The Council of Ten registered a secret protest against this agreement, declaring the conditions null and void, because they were exacted under duress—Romanin, *Storia di Venezia*, V, pp. 240–2.

[12] Daniele Beltrami, 'Un ricordo del Priuli intorno al problema dell'ammortamento dei depositi in Zecca del 1574', in *Studi in onore di Armando Sapori* (Milan, 1957), II, pp. 1081–7—at p. 1085.

135

K

and to restrict the bequeathal of such property either '*ad pias causas* (to religious uses)' or to institutions classifiable as *luoghi pii*. Hospitals were undoubtedly *luoghi pii*, religious institutions; it was doubtful whether the Scuole were so classifiable, though some of the uses to which they applied their money were undoubtedly *piae causae*. The law of 1472 was designed to correct the abuse whereby 'monasteries, churches, hospitals and priests' acquired the property of lay citizens by legacies or other means, and whereby this property became subject only to the two tithes imposed at intervals upon the clergy by the Venetian state with the Pope's consent—'things which act to the detriment of our dominion'. Henceforth all property so transferred must remain subject to lay taxation, as if no such transaction had ever taken place.[13] In 1536, the Senate forbade the bequeathal, or donation by living persons, of real property, '*ad pias causas*', to religious uses, for any period of more than two years.[14] This decree, however, applied only to the city of Venice itself, and left ecclesiastical or other concerns affected by it free to acquire property on the mainland. However, some sixteenth-century Venetians refused to regard such property as a safe investment comparable with houses or shops in the city itself, for large areas of the mainland near to Venice were liable to flooding.

No attempt was apparently made until 1592 to apply the law of 1536 to the Scuole Grandi: although in 1566 the Guardians explained to the Council of Ten that some revenues had been left to them to be dispensed '*ad pias causas*', and that they used them to pay for

[13] A.S.V., *Dieci Savii sopra le Decime in Rialto, Capitulare I*, ff. iiv.–iii.

[14] This was an extension of an earlier law which had fallen into desuetude—it forbade the bequeathal or donation of real property *ad pias causas* for a period of more than ten years. According to the decree of 1536, after a period of two years the property was to be sold at a public auction by the fiscal office of the Dieci Savii sopra le Decime and the proceeds handed over to the Procurators of St Mark's, after deducting a tax of 2 per cent which was then appropriated by the Dicci Savii. The Procurators and the trustees or executors of the will, if any, were then made responsible for distributing the proceeds as far as possible in accordance with the wishes of the testator (*ibid.*, ff. 43r.–v., and *Capitulare II*, f. LXVr.–v.; A.S.V., *Senato, Terra*, reg. 1536/1537, ff. 83v.–84). In 1582 the Dieci Savii determined that no respite beyond the two year period could be granted to any pious institutions or *luoghi pii* except by two-thirds of the votes of the Dieci Savii (*Capitulare II*, f. 149v.). In 1598 the Senate clarified the law of 1536 by announcing that all real property left to 'ecclesiastics and pious works before the year 1536' was to be allowed to remain in their hands (*ibid.*, f. 177r.–v.). There is no evidence easily available about the enforcement of the mortmain law of 1536, but various edicts of the Dieci Savii, issued in 1611, 1612, 1633 and 1642, reflect some difficulties in enforcing it occasioned by the disobedience of notaries —who were held responsible for informing the Dieci Savii of any bequests, gifts or other alienations of real property 'to religious institutions, ecclesiastical persons and religious uses (*a luochi pii, persone ecclesiastiche, et ad pias causas*)' (*ibid.*, ff. 185v., 189r.–v., 220, 237v.–238).

two doctors who are maintained by each Scuola to visit all their sick, to pay for all their medicines, and to assist them so that they do not die of want; for things for processions and for numberless salaried servants of the Scuole; and in alms dispensed on the first Sunday of every month to the brothers who accompany corpses to the grave.[15]

The principal activities of the Scuole could thus be described in Venetian officialese as *piae causae*. These ought not, theoretically, to be financed out of revenue from real property. In July 1592, the officials of the Dieci Savii sopra le Decime, chiefly responsible for the execution of the mortmain laws, attempted to check the further bequeathal of real property to the Scuole Grandi.[16] But the Guardians successfully appealed to the Heads of the Ten. They protested that the law of 1536 was obviously directed only against ecclesiastics—its preamble in fact declared that 'It is not to be permitted that all real property pass to ecclesiastics, by way of legacies or donations made to religious uses, as a large part of it already has'. The Guardians argued that the Scuole were not under ecclesiastical surveillance and that all questions concerning their administration were dealt with by the Council of Ten. They paid their taxes like laymen, and they provided or financed galley crews in preparation for national emergencies at the behest of the Ten. They pleaded that they did socially valuable work and that, together with the great textile guilds, the Arte della Lana and the Arte della Seta, they fed and maintained 'almost all the common people of this city'. If they were forced to sell their property in Venice itself, dubious acquisitions would have to be made on the mainland,

> where revenues are now dissipated by tempests,[17] by defaulting tenants, and by other things, contrary to the express orders of these acts, which, neither by the words which they contain, nor by the continuous interpretation of nearly seventy years (*sic*), nor by the decrees of this Council, can have any effect on the Scuole Grandi.

The Heads of the Ten were prepared to agree that these considerations

---

[15] A.S.V., *Inquisitori et Revisori sopra le Scuole Grandi, Capitolare I*, f. 80v.

[16] *Ibid.*, ff. 100–1.

[17] For examples of property owned by the Scuola di S. Rocco on the mainland being damaged by flooding, cf. A.S.R., *Registro delle Terminazioni 2*, ff. 347v.–348 (in May 1574: part of it, which occurred near Legnago, was the result of the Adige and Po breaking their banks): *Registro 3*, f. xxxix v. (in May 1579 at Cologna and Rovigo, where the most important possessions of the Donà, Moro and Zucca trusts were situated); *Registro 4*, f. 245r.–v., caused by the Adige in April 1617. In July 1617, Lodovico Ziletti, who rented from the Scuola estates in the Trevigiano at 366 ducats a year, spoke of 'the great losses he has suffered from tempests, from the death of vines the year of the great frost and from other mishaps, and none of it has ever been made good, and he says the slight value of the revenue at present causes him a heavy loss'—*ibid.*, f. 249.

should entitle them to undisturbed ownership of real property in a safe place, the city of Venice itself.

In the early seventeenth century new complications arose, which adversely affected the Scuole Grandi, but did not oppress them as severely as they did the clergy. Both the clergy and the Scuole had long been able to invest in government consolidated loan funds. The oldest fund was the Monte Vecchio, whose origins (though not the name) went back to 1262. A Monte Nuovo had been established in 1482, during the war of Ferrara, but was probably liquidated during the 1540's.[18] Further loan funds, the Monte Nuovissimo and Monte di Sussidio, arose during the Italian wars of the early sixteenth century, and were still in existence, with the Monte Vecchio, in the 1590's. All were forced loans to which Venetians had contributed in proportion to their wealth. They had received in exchange transferable securities whose existence was recorded on the books of the Camera degli Imprestiti, and on which the government paid interest at varying rates of 5 per cent or less.[19] In 1538, a new system of voluntary public loans came into operation, coexisting with the older funds. Deposits were made in the Mint, and remained in government hands for a limited period—unless the investor died meanwhile, in which case they passed permanently to the state, which recognized no obligation to his heirs.[20] The Scuola di San Rocco (which may have been reasonably typical of all the Scuole Grandi) placed capital on temporary loans to the Mint at interest rates which varied between 7 per cent and 3 per cent in the middle of the century.[21] Subsequently, the war of Cyprus created (by Venetian standards) so vast a debt, which so burdened the public

[18] On the origins of the Monte Nuovo, see Gino Luzzatto, *Storia economica di Venezia dall' XI al XVI secolo* (Venice, 1961), pp. 207–11. A Senatorial decree of 27 September 1541 alludes to 'the liquidation of the Monte Nuovo, of whose income of 130,000 ducats we shall be able to avail ourselves when it is freed', and takes steps to further the process—A.S.V., *Senato, Terra, registro* 1540/41, f. 149v. Cf. also the proposal of Antonio Grimani, Savio di Terra Ferma, for the liquidation of Monti— *ibid.*, f. 88, 22 January 1540 Venetian style.

[19] On the Monte Vecchio, see especially the summary of F. C. Lane, 'The funded debt of the Venetian Republic, 1262–1482', in *Venice and history: the collected papers of Frederic C. Lane* (Baltimore, 1966). On the origins of the Monte Nuovissimo, see F. Besta, *Bilanci generali della Repubblica di Venezia*, docs. 145 and 147, pp. 187–9, 191–2; on the Monte di Sussidio, *ibid.*, doc. 158, pp. 209–10.

[20] *Ibid.*, doc. 162, pp. 216–18.

[21] A.S.V., *Scuola Grande di S. Rocco, seconda consegna*, vol. 47, ff. 80, 120v. (January 1548, February 1552); A.S.R., *Registro delle Terminazioni 2*, ff. 152, 198 (August 1554, January 1559). The rate paid on some capital was 7 per cent in 1544, descending in stages to 4 per cent by the beginning of 1548. In 1554 interest of 4 per cent, paid on capital of 4,680 ducats belonging to the Donà trust, was reduced to 3 per cent. The Scuola at first resolved to leave the capital there for one year only, but in 1559 it was still in the Mint.

revenues, that responsible men were stimulated into trying to get rid of it. They did so on the grounds that vast quantities of public money were disappearing into the pockets of private individuals.[22] The debt then amounted to 5,714,439 ducats, and the interest paid on it yearly, at rates varying between $7\frac{1}{2}$ per cent and 14 per cent, to 514,993 ducats.[23] However, on an ingenious plan suggested by Giovanni Francesco Priuli, this debt was successfully liquidated: the process was completed in 1584.[24]

The success of the Venetian government in disposing of this latest instalment of debt inspired new efforts at the close of the century. An assault was then launched on the older loan funds, beginning, in 1596, with the Monte Nuovissimo. The Nuovissimo then amounted to 1,200,000 ducats.[25] The liquidation of the Monte Vecchio, which had amounted to 8,284,279 ducats in 1520 (the nearest date for which precise information is available),[26] began in 1599 and was not completed until about 1620.[27] The historian Nicolò Contarini mentioned the difficulties which resulted from capital in the Monti having 'passed with the progress of time from one heir to another, many conditions being imposed in order to fulfil the wishes of testators; the money had

[22] Beltrami, 'Un ricordo del Priuli', p. 1079; N. Contarini, *Historie Venetiane*, extracts in Cozzi, *Il Doge Nicolò Contarini*, p. 313.

[23] F. Besta, *Bilanci generali della Repubblica di Venezia*, doc. 183, p. 253.

[24] In 1574 a deposit had been formed out of the principal direct taxes, the *decima* and *tansa*, for the purpose of replenishing the depleted treasury, with a proviso that it was not to be touched unless war broke out. Priuli proposed to start a sinking fund by withdrawing from the deposit a sum of 120,000 ducats for every year it had existed and using this for the repayment of the capital. The money which would otherwise have been devoted to the payment of interest on the capital which had been liquidated was also to be used for the repayment of more capital. Thus the process gathered momentum. *Ibid.*, doc. 182, pp. 250–3 (the decree of the Council of Ten adopting and outlining Priuli's scheme); N. Contarini, *Historie Venetiane*, in Cozzi, *Il Doge Nicolò Contarini*, pp. 313–15; Ugo Corti, 'La francazione del debito pubblico della Repubblica di Venezia proposta da Gian Francesco Priuli', *Nuovo Archivio Veneto*, VII (1894), pp. 342–64—the most detailed account of the process of liquidation.

[25] The rate of interest payable on the Nuovissimo, formerly 5 per cent, had since been reduced to $4\frac{1}{2}$ per cent; many separate sources of revenue were pledged to paying it—N. Contarini, *Historie Venetiane*, in Cozzi, *Il Doge Nicolò Contarini*, pp. 316–17.

[26] F. Besta, *Bilanci generali della Repubblica di Venezia*, doc. 153, pp. 201–3. This consisted of 2,588,113 ducats at 4 per cent and 5,666,166 ducats at 2 per cent, including a few securities at 3 per cent: theoretically, the interest paid on this should have amounted to at least 217,000 ducats. In 1587 and 1594, the sum total of interest payable on the Sussidio, Nuovissimo and Monte Vecchio was about 225,000 ducats, falling to 197,501 in 1602, when the liquidation was sluggishly proceeding (*ibid.*, doc. 194, p. 369). In 1613 Giulio Ziliol, Cancelliere Inferiore and notary to the Camera d'Imprestidi, said that the Monte Nuovissimo and Sussidio had contained a million and a half, and the Monte Vecchio eight million, ducats in gold—A.S.V., *Consiglio dei Dieci, Parti Comuni, filza* 291, under date 26 March 1613.

[27] Corti, 'La francazione del debito pubblico', p. 338.

to be placed in other investments'.[28] Much of it (as will appear later) remained 'dead' in the Mint or in the hands of the Scuole Grandi for years afterwards, yielding no income. Investment in building was regarded by the Scuola di San Giovanni as a poor substitute for investment in Monti[29]—if government securities tended to deteriorate in real value during inflationary periods, at least they involved no overhead expenses. There were no stewards or rent-collectors to be paid, no repairs to be undertaken. But the Scuole were better placed than the clergy. Some concessions were made to the clergy,[30] but at the turn of the sixteenth century they found two highly-favoured forms of investment barred to them. In 1605, the mortmain law of 1536 was extended to the whole Venetian dominion.[31] The liquidation of the Monti was an event ignored by Sarpi in his account of the Interdict, but the chronicler Sivos described it as one of the most serious grievances of the clergy reported to the Pope by the nuncio Orazio Mattei. As part of the Interdict settlement, a special loan-fund of 600,000 ducats at 4 per cent had to be opened by the government in order to receive a small token proportion of the moneys released by the older Monti. Sivos welcomed this measure as highly beneficial to the Scuole Grandi and to the Procuracies of St Mark's, which, he said, had to leave capital to the value of 208,000 ducats lying idle in the Mint.[32] The Interdict was rooted partly in economic causes.

In 1636-7, the question of which corporations were subject to the restrictions imposed by the mortmain laws arose once more—this time in a case involving the guild of fruiterers, which was recorded as a precedent on the Capitulary of the Inquisitori et Revisori sopra le Scuole Grandi.[33] The fruiterers' guild obtained exemption from the

---

[28] N. Contarini, *Historie Venetiane*, in Cozzi, *Il Doge Nicolò Contarini*, p. 316.

[29] See below, p. 173.

[30] A senatorial decree of September 1600 permitted the clergy to lend money released from the Monti to laymen upon the security of real property, with a proviso that should this property actually be forfeited to the clergy it must be sold within two years in accordance with the provisions of the mortmain Act of 1536—Cecchetti, *La Repubblica di Venezia e la Corte di Roma*, II, p. 126.

[31] A.S.V., *Dieci Savii sopra le Decime in Rialto, Capitulare II*, f. 178v.; Romanin, *Storia di Venezia*, VII, pp. 20-1; Cornet, *Paolo V e la Republica Veneta*, Appendice I, p. 265. In May 1602 a case brought before the Senate by Doctor Francesco Zabarella and the commune of Padua on the one hand and the Benedictine monks of Praglia on the other had deprived the clergy of certain rights of pre-emption (*prelatione*) which had formerly been a valuable legal instrument for the acquisition of property. (*Ibid.*, Appendice IV, p. 269, and the article 'Prelazione' in Ferro, *Dizionario del diritto*, II, pp. 489-94).

[32] Biblioteca Marciana, Venice, MSS. Italiani, Classe VII, 1818 (9436), ff. 81v., 128v.-129. Cf. A.S.R., *Registro delle Terminazioni 4*, f. 139v.

[33] A.S.V., *Inquisitori et Revisori sopra le Scuole Grandi, Capitolare I*, ff. 153-4. The papers relating to this case are to be found in A.S.V., *Senato, Terra, filza* for

mortmain laws on the grounds that every guild was bound to furnish the reserve fleet with a certain number of galleots, and that the guilds were better equipped to raise loans for this purpose if they possessed real property to pledge as security. If prevented from investing their funds in sound securities, they might embezzle or otherwise waste them, and would be unable to build up reserves against a crisis. A second argument in favour of the fruiterers was that they formed a purely lay association, 'una Arte mera laica'. Not only were they laymen themselves, free of the jurisdiction of any ecclesiastical superior, but they had 'no religious duties or obligations, and no indulgences or anything similar, as have pious and religious institutions'. On this occasion, it was assumed that acquisitions of real property were prohibited by the Senate 'to monasteries, to religious persons, and to hospitals and Scuole of devotion, great and small'. Two of the Presidenti delli Dieci Savii, involved in the debate on the fruiterers' case, referred to a Senatorial decree of December 1596, in which the Scuole Grandi were classified as *luoghi pii*. The context is important. The decree was one regulating the liquidation of the Monte Nuovissimo and Sussidio, and it provided that the order in which creditors should be repaid must be determined by lottery. One clause declared that

> It is appropriate that this godly and Christian Republic should extend particular care and protection to religious institutions (*lochi pii*). There are many convents of nuns and of other religious persons who have capital in the Monti and interest due thereupon which is tied there for as long as these nuns shall live—as also have various other churches, chapters, hospitals, chantries (*mansonarie*), Procuracies, Scuole Grandi and small Scuole to a total of some 340,000 ducats. Be it therefore resolved that these *luoghi pii* shall not go into the lottery as yet, but shall continue for the time being to draw the interest on the capital that they now possess, just as they have done in the past; and they shall do so until all other holdings have been repaid. Meanwhile, this Council shall determine what is to be done with the aforesaid capital.[34]

For these purposes, the Scuole Grandi had certainly been lumped together with churches and monasteries under the heading of *luoghi pii*.

February 1636 Venetian style, under the date 13 February. They consist of (a) two petitions of the fruiterers' guild to the Serenissima Signoria, dated 7 July and 10 December 1636; (b) a report of two of the Presidenti dei Dieci Savii, Giovanni Andrea Pasqualigo and Pietro da Molin, dated 29 September 1636, with a dissentient report from the third, Giacomo Donà or Donado, dated 20 August 1636; (c) a report from the Presidenti alla Milizia da Mar, dated 14 November 1636; (d) a copy of a decision made by two of the Savii sopra le Vendite, a sub-department of the Dieci Savii sopra le Decime, on 27 May 1628, in favour of the fruiterers when the question of their right to acquire real property had first been raised.

[34] A.S.V., *Senato, Deliberazioni (Secreta), registro* 1596/1597, f. 81, 16 December 1596.

But this classification acted only in their favour, and not to their disadvantage. It did not in practice prevent them from acquiring house property and land in the first twenty years of the seventeenth century—whatever happened after that time. Like the corporation of fruiterers, they were not under clerical management or subject to ecclesiastical jurisdiction. Like the fruiterers, they supplied the navy with the funds to support galleots. They were prepared to tax moneys bequeathed to religious uses in order to raise funds to maintain crews, and were ready to use their charitable resources to offer to the poor inducements to serve the state in the galleys.

During the Interdict, Antonio Querini wrote a vigorous pamphlet in which he depicted the transfer of property to the clergy as a process which sapped the strength of the Prince, and impaired his ability to defend Christendom against the infidel.[35] Speaking in the Senate, he declared that 'giving to churches and to ecclesiastics is not the only form of piety—piety includes every other work of virtue and in the service of God, such as giving to one's country or preserving wealth for one's own children. . . .'[36] Indeed, the Scuole Grandi had, at least since the Turkish war of 1537–40,[37] been acquiescing in the theory that the Prince, in his holy duty of guiding Venice, the advance guard of Christendom against the Turk, was entitled to take a toll of revenues destined for religious purposes. In 1537 and 1539 the Scuole obtained permission to raid trust funds, although these were subject to conditions imposed by testators, in order to tide them over financial difficulties resulting from the state's demands.[38] The Ten might, as in 1547, issue a decree demanding the strict execution of the wishes of all testators who had founded charitable trusts.[39] But revenues bequeathed to the Scuole Grandi were not beyond the grasp of the state at a time

[35] Antonio Querini, *Relatio rationum Serenissimae Reipublicae Venetae, difficultatibus Pauli V Pontificis oppositarum,* in Melchior Goldast, *Monarchia Romani Imperii, sive de jurisdictione imperiali,* III (Frankfurt, 1668), pp. 312–25.

[36] Cornet, *Paolo V e la Repubblica Veneta,* Appendice XI, p. 291.

[37] In June 1537 the Carità responded eagerly to the call for galley crews with a declaration that 'We must with all vigilance and solicitude act as is appropriate to our good faith and as the observance of and zeal for the Christian religion and faith and the love of our country, of liberty and the common weal demand, particularly of every loyal subject of this most illustrious and Christian Dominion, shield and buckler of the most holy faith, and an example of justice and equity to all the world'. A.S.V., *Scuola Grande di S.ta Maria della Carità,* vol. 236, f. 51; cf. also A.S.V., *Scuola Grande di S. Giovanni Evangelista,* vol. 2, f. 81, and, for a later example, A.S.R., *Registro delle Terminazioni 2,* f. 345, 11 March 1574.

[38] A.S.V., *Scuola Grande di S. Giovanni Evangelista,* vol. 2, f. 82r.–v., 85r.–v.; *Scuola Grande di S. Marco,* vol. 18, f. 143v.; *Scuola Grande di S.ta Maria della Carità,* vol. 236, f. 54; *Scuola Grande di S. Rocco, seconda consegna,* vol. 46, ff. 68v.–69. *Consiglio dei Dieci, Registro Comune 1537,* ff. 39v.–43v., 44–45v.

[39] A.S.V., *Consiglio dei Dieci, Registro Comune 1547,* f. 7.

of urgent need. In 1566 the Guardians of the Scuole Grandi said, apparently without irony, to the Heads of the Ten that 'As it appears to your most illustrious lordships that sending men to the galleys on behalf of their Prince is a pious work (opera pia), all funds must contribute equally to this, the trusts as well as every other sort of moneys'.[40] In the first quarter of the seventeenth century, the trusts were taxed, even to the extent of 15 per cent, 25 per cent and possibly 30 per cent.[41] Dissentient voices were sometimes raised—in 1614, Bortolamio Cavazza, Guardian Grande of the Scuola della Misericordia, begged the Collegio alla Milizia da Mar, the office responsible for naval recruiting, to reduce the quota of galleots required of his Scuola. He implied that galleots ought not to be raised at the expense of schemes for the welfare of the poor, asserting fervently that

> if human efforts and human measures can resist the force of enemies, the humble and devout prayers of the poor we have assisted, of the orphan girls we have married, and of the wretched wards we have aided through the pious bequests of other men entrusted to the Scuole, have an equal or perhaps a greater power to stay the all-powerful hand of God from his just anger against us.[42]

But the magistrates persisted in believing that God was on the side of ← NLϲϹ the larger fleet.

During most of the sixteenth century (at least after 1530) the Venetian Republic was a mercantile state which desired peace but at intervals found war at sea thrust upon her. She was compelled to maintain the high level of naval preparedness demanded of a small state placed between two war-like empires—the Turkish and the Spanish. Venice later became a bar to communication between the eastern and western Habsburg empires and an impediment to the movement of

---

[40] A.S.V., Inquisitori et Revisori sopra le Scuole Grandi, Capitolare I, f. 81.

[41] In February 1609 the Scuola di S. Rocco imposed a 15 per cent tax on all trusts to help meet expenditure of 9,296 ducats incurred in the armament of 146 men in 1607 (A.S.R., Mariegola, f. 61). It imposed a tax of 25 per cent in September 1618 (A.S.R., Registro delle Terminazioni 4, f. 261), when, during the recent armament crisis, the Scuola had borrowed 12,118 ducats at 5 per cent interest. Angelo Zaguri, Guardian Grande of the Scuola di S. Giovanni Evangelista in 1614–15, attempted to raise a 15 per cent tax on the trusts in the Scuola. This was designed to pay off the 6,000 ducats due to be deposited by the Scuola in the Mint as a reserve fund against the next emergency in which galleots must be provided. It was also to be used to pay off capital of 3,000 ducats borrowed by the Scuola to raise galleots. A statement indicating the revenues of the Scuola and the uses to which they were tied (sent by the Scuola to the Collegio alla Milizia da Mar at the same time) shows that a 30 per cent tax on trusts was pending, if not actually imposed (A.S.V., Milizia da Mar, fascicolo 706).

[42] Ibid.; for the date of Cavazza's guardianship, M.C.V., Gradenigo MSS. no. 194—a list of Guardians of the Scuola della Misericordia.

Habsburg troops. Hence she faced the danger that she might, in Habsburg eyes, become a bottle-neck that could not be by-passed, but must be destroyed. Turkish expansion was a perpetual danger to Venice, who, especially in Crete and Cyprus, had great possessions in the east whose loss she feared. Moreover, in the Mediterranean there was no steady alignment of Christian powers against the infidel, and the Turk might easily be stung into action against the Venetians by Spanish *agents-provocateurs* operating at the Sublime Porte. Sometimes, as in the 1590's, the object of the intrigues was to force Venice into participating in a grand alliance of Catholic powers against the Sultan[43]— much against her will, for she was anxious to do nothing that might jeopardize the markets for her textiles in the Levant or prejudice the security of her outlying possessions. On other occasions, the Spanish purpose was, less subtly, to incite the Turks to damage Venice, and so make the task of the Habsburgs easier.[44] After the war of Cyprus and Lepanto in the early 1570's, Venice needed to protect her merchant shipping against the menace of piracy—against the Uskoks in the Adriatic, against the Knights of Malta, the Florentines and the Spaniards; and, finally, against the English and Dutch, who triumphed as merchants in the Mediterranean partly through the superior fighting quality of their ships and crews.[45] Through peace and prosperity, and perhaps through the development of the woollen industry in Venice itself, Venetian subjects had begun to lose their appetite for war and their love for the seaman's craft. Yet there was a chronic danger of serious emergencies in which many recruits would have to be drawn from the urban and land-bound population of the Venetian Republic.

Voluntary recruits had, by about 1540, become embarrassingly difficult to find. It was impossible to raise enough to equip even the regular fleet which carried out routine duties in peacetime, such as policing the Adriatic and protecting merchant vessels against pirates. In his treatise *Della milizia da mar*, probably written about 1553–4,[46] the naval commander Cristoforo Da Canal attributed the shortage

[43] C.S.P.V., IX, docs. 169, 264, 273, 315, 332, 335.

[44] For various examples, see N. Contarini, *Historie Venetiane*, in Cozzi, *Il Doge Nicolò Contarini*, p. 318; Sarpi, *Istoria dell'Interdetto*, I, pp. 99–102; Mario Nani Mocenigo, *Storia della marina veneziana da Lepanto alla caduta della Repubblica* (Rome, 1935), p. 94; C.S.P.V., XIV, doc. 828.

[45] Cf. the theme of Alberto Tenenti, *Piracy and the decline of Venice*, transl. Janet and Brian Pullan (London, 1967); also Ralph Davis, 'England and the Mediterranean, 1570–1670', in *Essays in the economic history of Tudor and Stuart England in honour of R. H. Tawney*, ed. F. J. Fisher (Cambridge, 1961), pp. 129–32.

[46] Cristoforo Canale, *Della milizia marittima libri quattro*, ed. Mario Nani Mocenigo (Venice, 1930). Nani Mocenigo dated this treatise in 1540, but Professor Alberto Tenenti argues that it was in fact written in 1553–4. Cf. Alberto Tenenti, *Cristoforo Da Canal: la marine venitienne avant Lepante* (Paris, 1962), pp. 17–19.

partly to the depopulation of the Greek and Slav colonies of the Republic which had once abundantly supplied galleots. These provinces had seen much emigration, caused by Turkish invasions and by a natural desire to move off to acquire wealth in richer places. The Venetians themselves could no longer supply galleots as they had done in the past, 'For at present prosperity is so great (è al presente talmente comodo dei beni della fortuna) that nothing but the most urgent necessity could ever induce them to enter the galleys voluntarily . . . the galleys that are being armed at present in this city are the worst of all—because only the beggars and down-and-outs who live among the people will go there, and good men shun them'.[47] In fact, beggars were not only serving voluntarily—at least from 1539 onwards, the Provveditori alla Sanità had been sentencing them to forced labour on the galleys. These magistrates had begun to enforce provisions in the poor law of 1529 which related to the employment of beggars and of vagabond children both in the Venetian navy and in the merchant marine.[48] In 1542, Cristoforo Da Canal (then still a mere sopracomito, or galley-captain) had suggested the introduction of a squadron based mainly on convict labour. The Senate eventually created such a unit in 1545, though this source of man-power scarcely proved as efficient as Canal had hoped.[49]

There remained, however, the major problem of the reserve fleet, which would have to be mobilized on the outbreak of war. For this the more respectable inhabitants of Venice and of its subject cities were held responsible—required to serve in person or to provide substitutes. Venice organized recruiting for the reserve fleet fairly systematically.

Up to the year 1545, the reserve fleet equipped by the Venetians consisted of fifty light and six great galleys. It was subsequently increased to a hundred light and twelve great galleys, with, from 1565, six galleasses, though this total was not always maintained.[50] Heavy conscription would be necessary to provide man-power, should such a fleet be called out for service. City corporations, whether professional and religious or purely religious, offered the state the best means of approaching the respectable workers of Venice. The corporations were the cell-structure of the greater organism of the state, responsible for

[47] Canale, Della milizia marittima, pp. 173–4; cf. Tenenti, Cristoforo Da Canal, pp. 69–72.

[48] See below, pp. 252, 297, 306–9.

[49] See Tenenti, Cristoforo Da Canal, pp. 9, 81–8; Nani Mocenigo, Storia della marina veneziana, pp. 5–6, 42–3; Alberto Tenenti, Naufrages, corsaires et assurances maritimes à Venise, 1592–1609 (Paris, 1959), pp. 53, 57.

[50] Ibid., p. 54; Romano, 'Economic aspects of the construction of warships', pp. 68 f.; A.S.V., Senato, Mar, registro 1545/46, f. 61, 62v.

transmitting its commands to the lower levels of society. A Scuola Grande, a guild formed out of a combination of a Scuola and an Arte or craft organization, or a union of boatmen (*traghetto*), possessed some disciplinary mechanism for persuading its members to obey the state. The Scuole Grandi disposed of privileges and material resources which could be offered as inducements to men to serve in the galleys, or be withheld from those who refused. They could provide insurance for the galleot and his family against the possibility of death or maiming. Each Scuola Grande had a dual personality—on the one hand as a religious fraternity existing to do everything that contributed to the salvation of the soul, and on the other as a subject corporation potentially useful to the Venetian state. Occasionally these two personalities came into conflict, when the fiscal obligations of the Scuole interfered with their obligations to the poor.

At intervals, the Venetian state called upon the Scuole Grandi to provide naval recruits at least from the time of the war of Ferrara—when, in 1482, they were ordered to find 100 men each to serve in the navy.[51] During the Italian wars of the first third of the sixteenth century, the state raised loans and taxes from the Scuole Grandi, and also instructed them on at least one occasion to use their resources to reward mariners who had served the state. It is not clear that all the moneys paid by the Scuole Grandi to the state were in fact used for the support of mariners. In October 1509, the Scuole Grandi and Scuole Piccole were included in a general levy. The Scuole Piccole paid sums varying between 1 and 25 ducats each, according to their resources. The four senior Scuole Grandi were each assessed at 200 ducats, and the relatively new Scuola di San Rocco at only 100 'because it is poor'.[52] It had had only thirty years to accumulate wealth.[53] Then, in January 1511, the four senior Scuole Grandi received orders to provide sums sufficient to equip ten small boats (*barche*) each, for service on the Po.[54] By 1514, there were signs of the system of rewarding ex-servicemen which became so highly developed later in the century. Already, in 1503, when the newly-founded Hospital at Sant' Antonio was dedicated to the support of aged ex-servicemen, the Senate had clearly recognized the need to provide this kind of security.[55] In 1514, the state required 'the greatest possible number of valiant and faithful mariners, who have been to sea, or citizens of this our city' to serve the Signoria for six months at Padua or Treviso. On their return, they were

[51] A.S.V., *Inquisitori et Revisori sopra le Scuole Grandi, Capitolare I*, f. 18r.–v.
[52] D.M.S., IX, coll. 245, 247, 11/12 October 1509.
[53] See below, pp. 157–8.
[54] D.M.S., XI, col. 732, 12 January 1510 Venetian style.
[55] See below, pp. 213–15.

to be rewarded with almshouses distributed by the Procurators of St Mark's, by the Scuole, by the hospitals, and by what were somewhat vaguely termed 'the trusts'. The order of priority was to be settled by lotteries. These veterans themselves would be entitled to enjoy the houses for life, whilst if they died on active service their families would be entitled to occupy them for a period of ten years[56] (time enough, perhaps, for young children to grow into adolescents and start earning).

By 1527, the method of taxation had temporarily changed, for the Senate was now levying forced loans on the Scuole Grandi and assigning them credits on the Monte di Sussidio. In August of that year, the Senate fixed their contribution at a total of 10,000 ducats, to be apportioned among them by the commission known as the Sette Savii sopra il Clero.[57] Three weeks later, these commissioners assessed the Scuole Grandi in the proportions:

Scuola della Misericordia	2,000
Santa Maria della Carità	1,200
San Giovanni Evangelista	1,000
San Marco	500
San Rocco	500
	5,200[58]

This presumably meant that the Misericordia would be bound to contribute just under 4,000 ducats to the levy of 10,000, the Carità just under 2,400, and so forth. In fact, they seem to have contributed only 7,000 out of this 10,000 ducats.[59] In 1529, a further forced loan of 8,000 ducats was levied.[60] But in addition to this, the government persuaded the officers of the Scuola della Misericordia to invest two large legacies they had recently received—the moneys of one Grifalconi, and those of the jeweller Bortolamio Gruato—in credits on the Monte di Sussidio. These last were voluntary, rather than forced loans.[61] How these moneys were used is not known—though, nearly ninety years later, officers of the Scuola della Misericordia informed the Council of Ten that 'from 1513 to 1530, in the wars introduced by Ludovico Sforza into Italy, the Scuola maintained at its own expense five armed ships upon the sea, and a good number of bowmen'.[62]

[56] A.S.V., *Inquisitori et Revisori sopra le Scuole Grandi, Capitolare I*, f. 24r.–v.
[57] D.M.S., XLV, col. 625, 17 August 1527.
[58] Note of the assessment made by these commissioners on 3 September 1527, D.M.S., LVI, col. 143, 10 April 1532.
[59] D.M.S., XLIX, col. 419, 3 February 1529.
[60] D.M.S., XLIX, col. 426, 6 February 1529.
[61] D.M.S., XLV, coll. 77–8, 11 May 1527; XLVIII, coll. 363–4, 11 August 1528.
[62] A.S.V., *Consiglio dei Dieci, Parti Comuni, filza* 302, 17 August 1615.

Perhaps this statement was based on authentic records, rather than merely on tradition.

Certainly from 1537 onwards the Scuole Grandi were regularly required to provide inducements to serve in the navy. In the summer of 1537, at the outset of the war with the Turk, the Scuole Grandi (doubtless on orders from above) presented for the approval of the Ten their schemes for raising quotas of 100 galleots each. Brothers who departed for the wars were to receive priority in all distributions by the Scuole Grandi of alms, of small monthly pensions, of almshouses, and of dowries for marriageable daughters. The normal rule, that nobody was eligible for the benefits of the Scuola unless he had been enrolled for five years, was suspended in favour of the galleots. Each Scuola was to disburse one ducat per month to support the family of every galleot during his absence on active service.[63]

On 15 June 1537, the Scuola di San Marco anticipated having to pay up to 4 ducats for each galleot under this system. But on 25 July, other methods of recruiting having failed, the governors of the Scuola decided almost unanimously that if necessary they would pay each galleot a lump sum of 8 ducats without admitting him to the benefits of the Scuola on special terms.[64] The Scuole Grandi did not—certainly at this stage, and probably at no time during the sixteenth century— assume the entire responsibility for paying the galleot. They merely offered incentives additional to those provided by the state and by its naval officers—which consisted both of basic pay, and of a bonus dispensed to the oarsmen by the galley-commander or *sopracomito* to enable them to equip themselves.[65] Basic pay disbursed by the state (some of it in the form of victuals) seems, according to Cristoforo Da Canal's calculations, to have amounted to 17–20 ducats a year some sixteen years later.[66] As yet, the Council of Ten were not prepared to approve any system whereby the brothers of the Scuole paid substitutes to serve in the galleys for them. One decree included a declaration 'that they cannot send anybody other than members of the Scuola di San Giovanni'—for the Ten were evidently prepared to trust only men reliable enough to be members of a Scuola Grande. Nor would they allow charitable benefits to be extended to the families of men who

[63] A.S.V., *Consiglio dei Dieci, Registro Comune 1537*, ff. 39v.–43v., 44–45v.

[64] A.S.V., *Scuola Grande di San Marco*, vol. 18, f. 143v., 144v.

[65] For this information, and for much valuable assistance with this chapter, I owe many thanks to Professor F. C. Lane.

[66] According to Canale, payments to the crew of each galley 'amount to 3066 ducats in the first year that the galleys are armed and 2616 in subsequent years'— there were 150 galleots to a crew. This sum evidently included a total of up to 1,320 ducats, which was spent each year on feeding the crews. Canale, *Della milizia marittima*, pp. 166–7.

had died on active service. In the summer of 1539 a second instalment of galleots was demanded of the Scuole, the Misericordia having to produce as many as 150.[67] On both occasions, 1537 and 1539, the Scuole were authorized to draw on trust funds in order to meet their obligations, and to repay the trusts later.

In July 1539, a Senatorial decree united the Scuole Grandi, the Procuracies of St Mark's, and all the professional corporations of the city in an elaborate scheme for rewarding volunteers. Veterans on their return were to be entitled to 'matriculate' in the guilds without paying the usual fee, though they were still obliged to carry out the usual tests to prove competence at their trades. Vacancies at the ferry stations or *traghetti* were to be filled only by boatmen who had served in the galleys. The Scuole Grandi and the Procuracies of St Mark's were obliged to reserve to the families of galleots engaged in active service one fifth of the alms they distributed every year, and one quarter of the dowries administered by the Procuracies was earmarked for the daughters of those who had served at sea. On this occasion the Senate specifically provided that the sons of men killed fighting the Turk should be eligible to occupy almshouses disposed of by the Scuole or Procuracies. If the dead had no male children, the houses should pass to their daughters for a period of ten years. The government itself reserved for the galleots certain fields of minor, menial but profitable office in government departments and customs houses.[68]

In 1545, when the reserve fleet was doubled, the obligations of the Scuole Grandi to equip a substantial portion of it were doubled also. Over 10,000 rowers—enough for fifty galleys—were to be provided by the city of Venice itself and by the Dogado, of whom 1,200 were to be the responsibility of the Scuole Grandi. The Scuola della Misericordia was bound to contribute 300 men, San Rocco (now among the richer Scuole) 260, the Carità 240, and the other two Scuole Grandi 200 men each.[69]

After the 1540's, the monetary payments made by the Scuole Grandi became increasingly heavy. The cost to them of retaining and later supporting a galleot rose substantially during and after the war of Cyprus. The scarcity of recruits, the high level of conscription, and some reluctance on the part of Venetians to serve at sea contributed to this increase, so that the element in the galleot's pay provided by the Scuole Grandi seems to have far outstripped the price rise. More of the

[67] A.S.V., *Consiglio dei Dieci, Registro Comune 1539*, f. 38.

[68] A.S.V., *Senato, Mar, Registro 1539*, ff. 46–8.

[69] The 'obligo vecchio'—see A.S.V., *Milizia da Mar, fascicolo* 707, and below, p. 153.

responsibility for maintaining these expensive galleots was shifted on to the Scuole Grandi, and that is the major fact that must be discussed here. The Scuole were ordered, both in 1562[70] and in 1594, to enforce conscription by expelling from their ranks any member who refused to serve in the navy. However, in November 1562, six months after the Council of Ten had issued orders to this effect, the soft-hearted officers of the Scuola di San Rocco surreptitiously readmitted all who had been expelled for refusing, as they pleaded, 'not because we did not wish to serve in the name of this blessed institution, but because there were various reasons why we could not—some for sickness, some because of the very great poverty of their families'.[71] In August 1594 the Scuole were instructed to organize a lottery for all their members between the ages of 18 and 40, and to expel all those who, having been chosen by lot, refused to do their duty.[72] A senatorial decree of the following month revealed that several of the Scuole and guilds had failed to fulfil their obligations; fortunately the emergency had passed. They were curtly ordered to repair the deficiencies within four months, so that men should be held in readiness.[73]

The chaos which accompanied this attempt to equip fifteen galleys in the summer of 1594 caused the Senate and the Collegio alla Milizia da Mar to compile systematically a register of reservists, the first since 1539, on which 23,000 names were placed. It was completed by the end of November 1595, when the Senate ordered 9,000 men to be selected from this mass, 8,000 of whom would be liable for immediate service in an emergency, whilst the other thousand were to be held back as a second line of reservists. If within a month the guilds or Scuole had not produced their quotas, the Presidenti alla Milizia da Mar were to organize a lottery within each of them for all men aged between 18 and 45.[74] At some succeeding date, between 1595 and 1639, the Scuole Grandi were exempted from the obligation to use the device of the lottery to force their members into the navy—certainly the brothers of San Rocco were in a position to refuse the exhortations of the Guardian Millan Millan in 1601.[75] The Scuole Grandi had long

[70] A.S.V., *Consiglio dei Dieci, Registro Comune 1562*, ff. 103v.–104.

[71] A.S.R., *Registro delle Terminazioni 2*, f. 256v.

[72] A.S.V., *Consiglio dei Dieci, Registro Comune 1594*, f. 65.

[73] A.S.V., *Senato, Mar, Registro 1594*, ff. 67v.–68v.

[74] *Ibid., Registro 1595*, ff. 200–3.

[75] At four o'clock in the afternoon of 23 September 1601 the brothers of the Scuola di S. Rocco were summoned *en masse* to the hall and exhorted by the Guardian Grande, offering them all the statutory benefits, to serve the state in the galleys. But 'without giving any reply, they took to shrugging their shoulders and one by one went out of the hall, and amongst this number there were only two who offered themselves'—one of the two was a weaver named Valentin, fifty years of age, anxious

abandoned any attempt to provide their quotas solely by drawing on their own members, although these were better people to deal with wherever possible, and less given to inexplicable disappearances.[76] In 1639 the Presidenti alla Milizia da Mar rejected proposals for compulsory service, and expressed their disapproval of any system of selecting galley crews by lot. This, they said, threatened to interfere with the trades of the city by depriving them of anything up to 10,000 good men, and, in their indignation at such treatment, Venetian artisans would be of scant use in the galleys and would only do their best to desert. As far as possible, Venetian reserve crews should be selected from foreigners, vagabonds and any guildsmen prepared to volunteer. The obligations of the Arti should be purely financial, and a gradual tax or *tansa insensibile* should be imposed to organize them into meeting them.[77] This was another confession that the Venetians had now become landbound and unwarlike.

In 1537 the Scuole Grandi had not anticipated having to pay more than four or five ducats for the support of each galleot and his dependants. In 1558 the situation was still much the same—the galleots were to have five ducats each for the voyage,[78] though the Scuola di San Marco then deemed it wise to raise 750 ducats for the support of 100 galleots.[79] In 1562 the Scuole were instructed by the Council of Ten not to pay any galleot more than ten ducats for a campaign,[80] and in March 1570 the Scuola di San Rocco proposed to pay for the support of its 130 men by raising a loan of 1,300 ducats.[81] But in July 1571 it was asked for another 50 galleots 'and there is no money in the Scuola to pay them at the rates which are now in force, because of the great shortage of men, who have been paid at excessive rates by banished men and others'.[82] The Signoria was then adopting the expedient of cancelling sentences of banishment on condition that the exiles provided a certain number of galleots.[83] The Scuola di San Rocco chose to raise funds by borrowing from its trusts, and later repaying them with 10 per cent

not to be deprived of the almshouse granted him, which he was illicitly subletting—A.S.V., *Scuola Grande di S. Rocco, seconda consegna*, vol. 48 (*Notatorio* 1596–1620), f. 7v.

[76] A.S.R., *Registro delle Terminazioni 2*, f. 296r.–v., 350: decrees of 15 June 1568 and 20 June 1574.

[77] F. Besta, *Bilanci Generali della Repubblica di Venezia*, doc. 232, p. 542.

[78] A.S.V., *Scuola Grande di S. Marco*, vol. 21, f. 151.

[79] *Ibid.*, f. 152v.

[80] A.S.V., *Consiglio dei Dieci, Registro Comune 1562*, ff. 103v.–104.

[81] A.S.R., *Registro delle Terminazioni 2*, f. 310.

[82] *Ibid.*, f. 328.

[83] *Cronaca Agustini over Savina*, in B.M.V., MSS. Italiani, Cl. VII, 134 (8035), f. 336.

L

THE ACQUISITION OF PROPERTY

interest.[84] Even so, there was a serious reduction in the charity dispensed by the Scuola, which fell from a total of 6,011 ducats in the two years 1569 and 1570 to one of 4,920 in the years 1571 and 1572, though the bottom of the trough came only in the mid-70's.[85] In 1574, the price of a galleot was obviously high—the war of Cyprus had probably made a substantial difference to it. A few stray papers in the archive of the Milizia da Mar show the guild of almondsellers (*mandoleri*) contracting with a silkworker from Bergamo to serve on their behalf when required at a fee of 38 ducats for the whole campaign—which he was to receive in addition to 'the pay of St Mark'. This was in March 1574; in April the almondsellers succeeded in contracting with another galleot for as little as 25 ducats.[86]

The guilds would not have to pay these sums to the galleots unless an emergency arose. However, from 1574 onwards they were legally obliged to set aside, in locked chests kept on their own premises, a deposit which would help to support their galleots.[87] In 1582, these measures having proved inadequate, all the guilds were ordered to make reserve deposits in the Mint.[88] An allowance of 25 ducats was to be made for each man: in the 1590's this represented about half the anticipated cost of supporting one galleot for one campaign.[89] For a time the Scuole Grandi escaped inclusion in the decree of 1581, on the somewhat inadequate grounds that one of them, the Scuola della Carità, had voluntarily opened a deposit of its own in 1558. In April 1586 this contained 960 ducats, which would hardly go very far towards the support of 240 galleots, the maximum number that might be required at its hands. It may have been intended to provide only retainer fees. In the summer of 1587, when the deposits made in the

[84] A.S.R., *Registro delle Terminazioni 2*, ff. 328v.–329.

[85] See below, p. 164.

[86] The terms of the contract specified that Zuanne di Zuan Piero was 'to go and serve our Serenissima Signoria as a galleot on behalf of the guild of almond sellers upon whichever galley the most worshipful Provveditori sopra l'Armar shall decide; and for the time he is on active service Missier Antonio di Zuane, almondseller, and his fellow assessors (*tansadori*) pledge themselves to give him a fee of 38 ducats at 6 *lire* 4 *soldi* the ducat, together with the ordinary pay of St Mark—here in my presence 5 ducats as a retainer (*per capara*), whilst they promise without fail to give him the remainder one half when he has taken the pay of St Mark and the other when he has completed his service on board the galley to which he is assigned'. (A.S.V., *Milizia da Mar*, fascicolo 755, under dates 22 March 1574 and 21 April 1574).

[87] F. Besta, *Bilanci Generali della Repubblica di Venezia*, doc. 181, pp. 249–50.

[88] *Ibid.*, doc. 188, pp. 280–1.

[89] According to a paper in M.C.V., MSS. P(rovenienze) D(iverse) c. 951, *fascicolo* 60, dated 26 June 1636, the deposit was designed to raise 225,000 ducats for the support of 9,000 galleots, and the sum actually deposited by the Scuole and other associations between 1582 and 1636 was 183,580 ducats.

Mint by the guilds had reached a total of 80,462 ducats, the Scuole Grandi were included in this new and provident system.[90] The rates at which they were to contribute were arbitrarily fixed by the Milizia da Mar on 4 August 1587, in a manner which soon drew agonized protest from the poorest of the older Scuole, the Scuola di San Marco. The Scuola di San Rocco was to contribute 6,500 ducats to the deposit at the rate of 70 ducats a month, the Carità 6,000 at 50 a month, the Misericordia 5,000 at 55 a month, San Marco 5,000 at 50 a month, and the Scuola di San Giovanni 5,000 at 30 a month. The governors of the Scuola di San Marco complained that this assessment was flagrantly unfair, since when it came to paying income taxes the Scuola di San Giovanni was rated at 362 ducats' *decima* and 120 ducats' *tansa*, the Scuola di San Marco at only 65 ducats' *decima* and 45 ducats' *tansa*. In October 1590 the rate at which the Scuola di San Marco was obliged to contribute was halved, and reduced to only 25 ducats a month: but not before its normal activities had been interrupted by the sequestration of revenues derived from the government Monti, in an effort to force it to pay.[91] The burden on most of the other Scuole was proportionately much lighter. There is certainly no sign of any reduction in the charity dispensed by the Scuola di San Rocco, which, both in its face value and in its probable real value, soared to unprecedented heights during the 1590's and attained its zenith in 1599–1600.[92]

In 1595 and 1603 the obligations of the Scuole Grandi were increased still further. Their responsibility for 12 per cent of the reserve fleet provided by Venice and the Dogado rose until they became answerable for 17–18 per cent. The quotas or *carattade* of the individual Scuole rose as follows:

	'Before 1595'	Assessment 1595	Assessment 1603	Assessment 1610
San Marco	200	250	313	313
Misericordia	300	400	500	500
San Rocco	260	350	438	438
Carità	240	250	313	313
San Giovanni	200	250	313	313
	1,200	1,500	1,877	1,877

[90] A.S.V., *Senato, Mar, filza* 96, under the date 19 June 1587. *Scuola Grande di S.ta Maria della Carità*, vol. 236, ff. 68v.–69.

[91] A.S.V., *Senato, Mar, filza* 109, under date 27 October 1590. A much clearer statement than any in the file of the relationship between the assessments for ordinary taxes and the assessments for galleots laid upon the Scuole is contained in Biblioteca Correr, Venice, MSS P(rovenienze D(iverse) c. 951 (Dandolo), *fascicolo* 45, marked 'Informatione per la supplica della Scola di S. Marco per diminuir l'imposizione per i Galeotti'.   [92] See below, p. 165.

The responsibility for this reserve force was divided between guilds, places subject to the Dogado, the Scuole Grandi and the ferry stations as follows:

	'Before 1595'	Assessment 1595	Assessment 1603	Assessment 1610
Guilds	5,548	4,947	5,224	5,971
Places subject to the Dogado	2,340	2,088	2,664	2,664
Scuole Grandi	1,200	1,500	1,877	1,877
Ferry stations	974	347	632	690
	10,062	8,882	10,397	11,202

By 1603 the Scuole della Misericordia and San Rocco had become the two Venetian corporations with the heaviest responsibilities—their nearest rivals were textile workers.[93]

No doubts are possible about the potential importance of the Scuole Grandi to the preparations anxiously made by the Venetian state against a possible outbreak of war. How much were they actually required to pay? There was an alarming increase, not only in the number of galleots chargeable to the Scuole, but also in the price of each man's service. During the Interdict in 1607 the Scuola di San Rocco was required to furnish 146 oarsmen at a cost of 8,994 ducats, contracting with them at an average rate of about 60 ducats each;[94] the Scuola di San Marco produced 104;[95] and in 1611 Francesco de Medici, formerly Guardian Grande of the Scuola della Misericordia, somewhat vaguely informed the Milizia da Mar that he remembered on this occasion having provided 170 or 180 galleots, contracting with them at rates which varied between 40 and 70 ducats each.[96] The Scuola di San Rocco had furnished some of the money by withdrawing 3,650 ducats from the deposit made in the Mint in the 1590's. This deposit did not, when it came to the point, cover more than a small fraction of the total sum paid to oarsmen by the Scuola. The rest was

[93] A.S.V., *Milizia da Mar, fascicolo* 707, marked 'Carattade diverse de Galeotti fatte in diversi tempi per l'armar delle cinquanta Galere. In essecution delle Deliberationi dell'Ecc. mo Senato *1595* et *1602*'. Wool combers and carders (*laneri*) were bound in 1603 to produce 375 galleots and in 1610 383. The obligation of the silk-weavers, fixed at 414 galleots in 1595, sank to only 250 at each of the subsequent assessments, and weavers of wool were assessed at 250 both in 1603 and in 1610.

[94] A.S.V., *Scuola Grande di S. Rocco, seconda consegna,* vol. 705, p. 7: entitled 'Compendio delle spese che furono fatte dalla Veneranda Scola di S.n Rocco per conto dell' impositione de galeotti dell'anno 1587 18 Ottobre', a late seventeenth- or eighteenth-century copy of earlier documents.

[95] A.S.V., *Milizia da Mar, fascicolo* 723, petition under date 1 March 1608.

[96] *Ibid.,* under date 19 February 1610 Venetian style.

raised by loans, and in 1609 a tax of 15 per cent was imposed on all the trusts for the purpose of repaying the capital and meeting the interest.[97]

Acute shortage of man-power forced the price of hiring the galleot to spectacular peaks in 1617–18. The extent to which this form of war taxation interfered with the normal charitable activity of the Scuola di San Rocco will be discussed in the next chapter. It is enough here to point out that in April 1617 the Scuola secured the services of eleven men at an average rate of just over 90 ducats each[98]—half as high again as in 1607. Each of the 122 men exacted from the Scuola in 1617 cost it 115 ducats, and the four greater Scuole laid out 50,485 ducats between them in providing 437 galleots at the same rate.[99] In March 1618 the Scuola di San Rocco bargained with a small group of 17 men at rates varying from 106 to 125 ducats.[100] In April 1618 the officers of the most heavily taxed of the Scuole Grandi, the Misericordia, announced that they had raised loans amounting to 16,850 ducats. They anticipated that their total expenditure on furnishing 182 galleots the previous summer would prove to have been about 22,000 ducats.[101] Between 1587 and the end of the year 1621 the Scuola di San Rocco spent a total of 44,095 ducats on the provision of galley crews[102]—in direct payments to the men themselves, contributions to the deposits in the Mint (which accounted eventually for only just over a fifth of the total), interest on capital borrowed to supply galleots, and various miscellaneous expenses. This sum was about equivalent to the entire sum dispensed by the Scuola in various forms of charity over a period of ten fairly prosperous years between those two dates.

Increasing war taxation did not, in the Scuola di San Rocco, usually reduce the quantity of charity actually dispensed by the Scuola, though it did prevent the sum total of the charity from increasing. The only

---

[97] A.S.R., *Mariegola*, f. 61r.–v.

[98] A.S.V., *Scuola Grande di S. Rocco, seconda consegna*, vol. 705, p. 11.

[99] *Ibid.*, p. 13: entry for 14 January 1617 Venetian style, probably for expenses incurred the previous summer.

[100] *Ibid.*

[101] A.S.V., *Consiglio dei Dieci, Parti Comuni*, filza 314, under date 9 April 1618.

[102] A.S.V., *Scuola Grande di S. Rocco, seconda consegna*, vol. 705, p. 17.

Money employed in providing galleots	duc. 31,089 gr. 8
The Office of the Mint on account of the deposit to pay galleots	9,473 gr. 9
Interest on capital borrowed by mortgage to provide galleots	2,631 gr. 17
Brokage and other expenses	720 gr. 23
The Office of the Presidenti of the Collegio alla Milizia da Mar	180 gr. –
	duc. 44,095 gr. 9

hiatus in its activities as a charitable institution occurred during the years 1616–18, with a partial recovery in 1619.[103] But for this heavy taxation, the 'charitable output' of the Scuola might have been greater by up to 30 per cent between the 1590's and 1620's. But the Scuole Grandi were both tolerated and encouraged by the Venetian government, and allowed to acquire real property as the foundation for a regular income, on condition that they should be exploitable. Some of their strength and much of their weakness lay in their being, not only a religious and charitable concern, but also a lay corporation whose administrative machinery could be adapted by the Council of Ten and the Senate to the purposes of the state. It could be used, where possible, to cajole a reluctant populace into doing the Prince's bidding. If they could not furnish men and money, they must at least furnish money. The bonds of the dead testator's wishes did not prevent the diversion to the galleot of moneys intended for men judged deserving by somewhat different criteria. The service of the Scuole Grandi to the Venetian state as a whole sometimes apparently conflicted with their service to individual Venetians. However, the galleots on whom they bestowed their charitable benefits were probably poor men, and there was an urgent need for some form of insurance against death or disablement on active service.

[103] See below, p. 166.

156

6

WEALTH AND ITS USES

In their initial stages the Scuole Grandi probably, like San Rocco in the early sixteenth century, depended for support mainly on the payment of subscriptions and on the generosity of their officers. Those fortunate enough, like the Scuola di San Rocco, to possess spectacular relics, could make a considerable income out of pilgrims and sightseers. Later, however, the Scuole Grandi derived most of their revenue from permanent endowments and were able to administer charity much more systematically. However, in the poorer Scuola of San Marco, collections were often taken among the officers at the annual distribution of dowries in order to supplement funds available from the revenues of trusts.[1] Pious promises, to be fulfilled in the lifetime of the person pledging himself, were made legally enforceable in the Scuola di San Rocco in 1574.[2] For a Scuola to maintain its reputation for external splendour, it clearly depended on the willingness of its officers to draw lavishly on their own purses. In 1581 Sansovino declared, in praise of the recently-promoted Scuola di San Teodoro, that, although it had as yet no source of regular income and 'was founded only upon the purses of the brothers', it was in no way inferior to the rest, either in display or in acts of charity.[3] Even in longer established Scuole the officers were required, not only to govern, but also to be generous to the corporation they administered.

The Scuola di San Rocco, which must be taken as the main example here, accumulated virtually all its wealth, from very insignificant beginnings, in the course of the sixteenth century. It started by relying heavily on the casual gifts of the faithful, especially on those of pilgrims

[1] In the Scuola di S. Marco, between 1550 and 1560, a total of 6,205 ducats was voted to 334 maidens out of the revenues of dowry trusts, and members of the Banca and Zonta voted out of their own pockets a further 1,721 ducats to 112 maidens who had been candidates for dowries but had drawn out of the lottery box the slip somewhat exasperatingly marked 'patientia' at the annual distribution—see below, Appendix.

[2] A.S.R., *Registro delle Terminazioni 2*, f. 342.

[3] Sansovino and Martinioni, *Venetia*, p. 289. This was not strictly true—at the time when Sansovino wrote, 1581, according to the tax returns, the Scuola di San Teodoro enjoyed an income of 199 ducats a year from real property (A.S.V., *Dieci Savii sopra le Decime in Rialto*, busta 158, fascicolo 1038). By 1620, a number of shops at San Salvador, under construction at the time of the fiscal survey of 1581, yielded an annual income of 293 ducats (A.S.V., *Consiglio dei Dieci, Registro Comune 1620*, f. 199v.).

who came to see the body of San Rocco displayed, and who contributed generously to building the Scuola's new and magnificent premises. The golden age of such munificence, often recalled with sincere or formal nostalgia by subsequent generations of officers, was the 1520's.[4] After 1551 the body of San Rocco was displayed four times a year,[5] but by 1590 devotion to his cult was cooling so fast that it proved necessary to reduce the number of annual displays to two.[6] Pilgrims, indulgences and offertory boxes no longer yielded a large income. At the end of the century entrance fees and annual subscriptions together did not account for more than 5 per cent at the most of the income of the Scuola itself[7]—and this calculation does not take account of the income of the great satellite trusts which had formed round it. Free gifts by living persons to the Scuola may have accounted for much of the sum it dispensed in alms on its own account, but investments and endowments furnished most of the income of the Scuola and the trusts together.

The Scuola had made its first investments in consolidated loan funds in 1498 to make certain of being able to pay its rent to its landlords, the Franciscans.[8] In 1527, however, it embarked on a more systematic policy of investing a certain proportion of the alms and other income which passed through its hands, saying that

> we should have provided ourselves with some income years ago and not have spent so much on building, but have set some aside so that now there would be a goodly sum coming in, for we ought to reflect that today our expenses are 700 ducats a year, and we have not a single ducat of regular income.

One-third of the annual income ought to be put in a special deposit and subsequently invested. After 1534 this practice died out, though it was still regarded as good in principle.[9] In 1528 the legacy of Maffeo

---

[4] In May 1527 the officers of the Scuola spoke with enthusiasm of 'so many benefits and alms which have been pouring in daily in the past seven years—it must be a heavenly miracle that there is such a concourse of people and so much devotion and we have such a reputation both in this illustrious city and in all Christendom. God in his mercy grant us grace to enjoy it for a long time'—A.S.V., *Scuola Grande di S. Rocco, seconda consegna*, vol. 45, ff. 53v.–54. Cf. also f. 6, for further references to pilgrims.

[5] A.S.V., *Scuola Grande di S. Rocco, seconda consegna*, vol. 47, ff. 109v.–110.

[6] A.S.R., *Registro delle Terminazioni 3*, f. 180r.–v.

[7] A.S.V., *Scuola Grande di S. Rocco, seconda consegna*, vol. 387.

[8] A.S.V., *Scuola Grande di S. Rocco, seconda consegna*, vol. 44, f. 45r.–v.

[9] A.S.V., *Scuola Grande di S. Rocco, seconda consegna*, vol. 45, ff. 53v.–54. The principle that these deposits ought to be made if possible was maintained at least until 1573 and sometimes even after that year: after 1534 the Guardians would usually give their reason for not making the deposit (cf. A.S.R., *Registro delle Terminazioni 2*, ff. 389v.–390; *Registro delle Terminazioni 3*, f. 10).

di Bernardo Donà, much disputed by his family, eventually passed to the Scuola and guaranteed it unconditionally two-thirds of the annual revenue from Donà's estate.[10]

Donà's was the first large endowment of many. Between 1509 and 1616, Venetian testators founded or provisionally founded 60 trusts, involving the Scuola di San Rocco either directly or indirectly.[11] A bequest might be made to the Scuola to be dispensed *ad pias causas* at the discretion of the Banca and Zonta, or it could be tied specifically to a particular charitable use. The officers of the Scuola might be asked to combine with trustees outside it and to dispense charity to their own members or to outsiders. In such cases, the trust, though closely associated with the Scuola, retained an existence separate from it, and is best described here as a satellite trust. Trusts committed to outside trustees could be administered in favour of the poor brothers of the Scuola. Bequests made to the Scuola di San Rocco can be classified as follows:

> *Indirect conditional legacies:* 23.
> *Mansonarie:* 9.
> *Mixed trusts:* 8.
> *Dowry trusts:* 17.
> *Other legacies:* 3.

The term 'indirect conditional legacy' is a fairly serviceable description of the common arrangement whereby estates were entailed on the relatives of the testator, and the Scuola was used merely as a longstop for the legacy lest the supply of heirs from within the family should fail. The Scuola might also be used to provide sanctions against misconduct on the part of the immediate heirs and beneficiaries. They would then be warned that the Scuola would inherit if they disregarded the wishes of the testator, or should they commit certain notorious malpractices, such as damaging timber or buildings on estates they were forbidden to sell outright by the terms of the entails.[12]

Such wills reflected a somewhat unequal struggle in the testator's mind between the claims of his own family—including those of nephews and nieces and their descendants—and those of humanity at large. It had been a principle of medieval charity that charity should

[10] A.S.V., *Scuola Grande di S. Rocco, Libro dei Testamenti,* in *prima consegna,* busta 438, ff. 19–33, 41; D.M.S., XLIV, col. 445; XLVI, coll. 401, 417.

[11] Official copies of wills benefiting the Scuola di S. Rocco are contained in the *Libro dei Testamenti,* A.S.V., *Scuola Grande di S. Rocco, prima consegna,* busta 438, and in the *Catastico dei Testamenti, prima consegna,* buste 64, 65, 66, 67.

[12] For examples see the *Libro dei Testamenti,* ff. 241, 322r.–v., 345; *prima consegna,* busta 66, *fascicolo* LIII.

begin at home, with one's own immediate family, and subsequently radiate outwards.[13] Testators were not usually content to ensure that their families were provided with the necessities of living, and then to leave the superfluities to poor persons outside the family. They were often anxious to leave the family a patrimony which would equip them to withstand any possible future disaster. The tendency of the family's claims to triumph outright over those of the poor was probably further enhanced when rich Venetians began to concentrate less on increasing their wealth through commerce and more on preserving it through landed investment. They were evidently doing this to some extent in the middle of the sixteenth century.[14]

Venetian testators were rarely explicit about their mental conflicts. Marco Zusberti, a self-made man disposing of his property in 1561, was unusually so by the standards of the time and place. He declared that

> God has given me this small property by means of my own labours, sweat and efforts, and I acknowledge it all from God because I received nothing from my father or mother. All the more sweat have I expended on the preservation of this little property, for so many years that this must be the last. Praise God: it is meet and right that what God has lent me should after a certain time return into his hands.

The property should be enjoyed for a hundred years by his son and nephew and their heirs, and when the century had passed a dowry trust should be founded and administered by the Scuola di San Teodoro. In 1567 Zusberti substituted the Scuola di San Rocco. Even then preference should be given to girls of his own kin, though, should there be more than one at any given time,

> I say that once one has been married or helped to enter a convent the other cannot be married until three years have passed, so that other poor girls can enjoy this benefit, because all men form one family and are all descended from Missier Adam.[15]

The Scuola was sometimes troubled by petitions from the relatives of testators who, in their anxiety to be generous to the Scuola, had failed to provide adequately for their own kin.[16] The officers of San Rocco were told by the children of Valentino di Capis in 1569 that

[13] Cf. Brian Tierney, *Medieval poor law: a sketch of canonical theory and its application in England* (Berkeley, Los Angeles, 1959), p. 57.

[14] For some examples, see Aldo Stella, 'La crisi economica veneziana della seconda metà del secolo XVI', *Archivio Veneto*, LVIII (1956), pp. 29, 33.

[15] A.S.V., *Scuola Grande di San Rocco, Libro dei Testamenti*, in *prima consegna*, busta 438, ff. 202v.–203v.

[16] E.g. the case of the Burato family, A.S.R., *Registro delle Terminazioni 2*, f. 173v., 214v.–215.

they will help the people of the world to make bequests to this blessed confraternity if they see that the descendants of benefactors are not left destitute.[17]

This was, indeed, a very necessary condition of any charitable bequest.

The labyrinthine will drawn up in 1604 by Giulio Fonte, in obedience to the wishes of Santo, his autocratic uncle, embodies the Venetian sense of the paramount claims of the family on the property of the man facing death. It also reflects the complementary anxiety, as the prospects of commercial success became more uncertain, to preserve the patrimony for the family at all costs. The preamble to the will appears to be more than a formula, and to reflect certain interesting assumptions of the man of property in Venice.

All men are born mortal, and, apart from the hope of enjoying eternal goods, human frailty receives no consolation in abandoning the spoils of this world other than a praiseworthy death and the sense of having disposed of the fruit of its honest labours, with some memory of itself, for the aid of its posterity, as both divine and human laws ordain. It is fitting that those whom God has favoured in the course of their life and permitted, running various risks and dangers, honourably to acquire property by their own industry, should at the end of their days have at least some certainty of being able to preserve it in their own families. To this end, many have tied their property by conditions, and instituted very strict entails (*fideicommissi*), with which they have greatly assisted their posterity, and many families have maintained themselves in some comfort when they might otherwise have sunk into poverty.

Santo Fonte had accumulated wealth to a total value of 150,000 ducats, invested partly in mortgages (*livelli*) and partly in business enterprises at the time when he finally considered disposing of it. He wanted it all solidly invested and tied by conditions, but his nephew Giulio was unwilling to do this immediately. He suggested that his own four sons, Giulio the younger, Santo, Fabio and Evangelista, who were engaged in traffic with the Indies, should for a time employ the capital in business so as to earn some money of their own. But he left strict instructions that the whole of the 150,000 ducats must be invested within the next twenty years in estates on the mainland, which were to be tied by strict entail. One-tenth of the annual revenue from land so acquired must be ploughed back each year into further acquisitions. The aid of the Scuola di San Rocco was invoked only for the purpose of enforcing obedience to the conditions of Giulio Fonte's will, and of inheriting

[17] *Ibid.*, ff. 304v.–305.

161

and putting the property to good use should the line of Fonte heirs die out.[18]

The selection of Venetian wills contained in the records of the Scuola di San Rocco is too small to be really indicative of the way in which Venetian testators in general were thinking. It shows—for what this evidence is worth—a marked increase in the proportion of indirect to direct legacies, becoming perceptible during the last quarter of the sixteenth century, as follows:

	Direct	Indirect
Before 1550	14	6
1550–1575	14	7
1575–1600	7	5
1600–1620	2	5

These figures probably reflect the process whereby the Scuola reached a saturation point, and testators decided that it was rich enough and did not require any further assistance. Yet it may be generally true that the increasing use of entails meant a reduction in the amount of liquid or easily disposable wealth left in the hands of the rich in Venice. It may have produced more complications about testamentary disposition, which could well increase the difficulty of transferring property to charities outside the family.[19] An estate entailed upon the testator's kin was not irrevocably lost to a Scuola. But the greater the lapse of time, the more difficult it became to keep track of all provisional legacies made to it.[20]

It is impossible, however, to regard this as evidence of flagging generosity among the Venetians. Wills can never tell the whole story about the charity of a particular age or people—however formidable the possibilities which Professor Jordan has demonstrated. It may be that some felt less entitled to dispose of goods outside the family at the moment when they faced death than at any earlier stage in their lifetime. To quote an admonition of Francis Bacon's: 'defer not charities till death, for certainly, if a man judge it rightly, he that doth so, is rather liberal of another man's than of his own'.[21]

Of the testators who made direct bequests to the Scuola, eight founded 'mixed' trusts, assigning their revenues in various proportions to several different charitable uses. The most popular of these were

[18] A.S.V., *Scuola Grande di S. Rocco, Libro dei Testamenti*, in *prima consegna*, *busta* 438, ff. 308–312v.

[19] Cf. G. R. Elton, Review in *The Historical Journal*, III (1960), p. 91.

[20] A.S.V., *Consiglio dei Dieci, Registro Comune 1576*, ff. 153v.–154: confirmation of a decree of the Scuola della Misericordia which appointed *conservatori et defensori* to undertake the specialized work of keeping track of wills which benefited the Scuola.

[21] Francis Bacon, Essay 'Of Riches'.

distributions of dowries and of alms. Hospitals and poor prisoners formed secondary objects of charity. Five of the mixed trusts were conspicuously larger than the others, each developing virtually into a charitable institution in its own right, and disposing of an income of anything from 500 to 3,000 ducats annually at the peak of its material prosperity.

Among the remaining testators, by far the most popular form of charity was the scheme for the marriage of poor maids. Such trusts arranged for the provision of dowries to young women chosen by the Banca and Zonta, usually by a mixture of chance and of careful selection. Seventeen testators making bequests to San Rocco pinned all their faith on this form of charity, which was also the one most favoured by testators who made indirect conditional bequests. The Scuola di San Giovanni laid even heavier emphasis on the dowry trust. It was famous for a large communal dowry fund known as the *sacho*, founded by permission of the Council of Ten in 1422 and then financed out of revenue from government bonds.[22] Dowries were less popular in the Misericordia, but, by 1627 at least, this Scuola was dispensing fairly large sums in another constructive form of charity, the relief of poor persons imprisoned for debt.[23] The benefactors of San Giovanni and the Misericordia showed a stronger tendency than those of San Rocco to leave money to be freely disposed of by the officers of the Scuola, without specifying how it was to be used.

Estimates showing what proportion of the wealth of the Scuole was dedicated to which charitable use naturally give heavy weight to the wishes of a few rich men. Most of the wealth of San Rocco came from only five major bequests. This consideration applies less to the Scuola di San Giovanni Evangelista, whose wealth was accumulated from over forty much smaller bequests. It is difficult to obtain information with reasonable rapidity, because of the absence of centralized sources from the copious papers of the Scuole themselves. In the Scuola di San Rocco, each of the major trusts had its own series of account books, kept separately from the accounts of the Scuola itself. To compile a year-by-year statement of the charitable activities of all the Scuole, and of the trusts in orbit round them, would be a disproportionately long task, even if the state of cataloguing in the Venetian archive

---

[22] A.S.V., *Scuola Grande di San Giovanni Evangelista*, vol. 8, ch. 63, ff. 28v.–29. In 1614 the *sacho's* funds were reinvested in house property and yielded 717 ducats a year, of which 465 came from sources not disclosed in the statement submitted by the Scuola to the Milizia da Mar. Apart from this anonymous fund, out of 48 testators listed on the statement 16 were anxious to establish dowry trusts or to contribute to the *sacho*. (A.S.V., *Milizia da Mar, fascicolo* 706, and Appendix, below.)

[23] *Ibid.*

163

THE CHARITY DISPENSED BY THE SCUOLA GRANDE DI SAN ROCCO
AND ITS SATELLITE TRUSTS
1551–1620

Measured in ducats of account

Date	Alms	Dowries	Hospitals	Prisoners	Medicines	Total	Average
1551	757	412	55	–	54	1,278 }	1,357
1552	768	237	368	–	63	1,436 }	
1553	786	362	416	–	56	1,620 }	1,724
1554	1,054	297	417	–	60	1,828 }	
1555	887	347	255	–	86	1,575 }	1,652
1556	1,054	288	307	–	80	1,729 }	
1557	996	273	245	–	105	1,619 }	1,634
1558	1,046	273	225	–	105	1,649 }	
1559	946	998	200	–	76	2,220 }	2,400
1560	1,837	518	190	–	35	2,580 }	
	10,131	4,005	2,678	–	720	17,534	
1561	2,102	726	105	–	128	3,061 }	2,492
1562	888	666	319	–	50	1,923 }	
1563	2,122	916	–	–	70	3,108 }	2,709
1564	1,033	1,086	141	–	50	2,310 }	
1565	2,267	1,036	44	–	31	3,378 }	2,626
1566	768	814	226	–	66	1,874 }	
1567	2,449	979	200	–	40	3,668 }	3,027
1568	1,142	899	233	–	112	2,386 }	
1569	2,593	1,189	96	–	–	3,878 }	3,006
1570	1,407	694	32	–	–	2,133 }	
	16,771	9,005	1,396	–	547	27,719	
1571	1,624	740	5	–	173	2,542 }	2,460
1572	1,139	740	292	–	207	2,378 }	
1573	2,105	620	205	–	163	3,093 }	2,580
1574	931	835	190	–	112	2,068 }	
1575	1,286	695	165	–	101	2,247 }	2,015
1576	935	605	163	–	80	1,783 }	
1577	1,658	745	239	–	61	2,703 }	2,548
1578	1,123	1,125	140	–	5	2,393 }	
1579	2,012	940	357	–	85	3,394 }	2,915
1580	1,239	680	300	–	216	2,435 }	
	14,052	7,725	2,056	–	1,203	25,036	

164

Date	Alms	Dowries	Hospitals	Prisoners	Medicines	Total	Average
1581	2,263	1,015	615	–	70	3,963⎱	3,259
1582	1,265	780	362	–	148	2,555⎰	
1583	2,364	1,260	481	–	112	4,217⎱	3,475
1584	1,396	905	241	–	190	2,732⎰	
1585	2,395	1,210	861	–	84	4,550⎱	4,180
1586	2,119	1,015	540	–	135	3,809⎰	
1587	2,516	1,535	385	–	49	4,485⎱	4,133
1588	2,165	1,065	470	–	80	3,780⎰	
1589	2,408	1,610	455	–	25	4,498⎱	3,840
1590	1,655	1,175	320	17	14	3,181⎰	
	20,546	11,570	4,730	17	907	37,770	
1591	2,587	1,475	680	31	–	4,773⎱	4,472
1592	2,393	1,550	210	18	–	4,171⎰	
1593	2,480	1,825	1,065	45	–	5,415⎱	4,617
1594	2,104	1,225	360	130	–	3,819⎰	
1595	2,544	1,950	665	80	–	5,239⎱	4,866
1596	2,399	1,600	460	34	–	4,493⎰	
1597	2,804	1,910	305	70	–	5,089⎱	4,858
1598	2,322	1,435	710	161	–	4,628⎰	
1599	2,901	2,420	455	26	–	5,802⎱	5,426
1600	2,460	1,815	640	135	–	5,050⎰	
	24,994	17,205	5,550	730	–	48,479	
1601	2,861	1,475	665	110	–	5,111⎱	4,735
1602	1,985	1,550	660	164	–	4,359⎰	
1603	2,590	1,825	455	35	–	4,905⎱	4,360
1604	2,212	1,225	310	67	–	3,814⎰	
1605	2,555	1,950	988	69	–	5,562⎱	5,078
1606	2,548	1,510	490	45	–	4,593⎰	
1607	2,815	1,890	439	75	–	5,219⎱	4,842
1608	2,436	1,435	560	34	–	4,465⎰	
1609	2,669	2,160	355	42	–	5,226⎱	4,955
1610	2,598	1,415	610	61	–	4,684⎰	
	25,269	16,435	5,532	702	–	47,938	

Date	Alms	Dowries	Hospitals	Prisoners	Medicines	Total	Average
1611	2,603	2,185	305	71	–	5,164 }	4,984
1612	2,724	1,580	393	106	–	4,803 }	
1613	2,736	2,370	455	91	–	5,652 }	4,994
1614	2,345	1,555	310	125	–	4,335 }	
1615	2,743	2,260	355	58	–	5,416 }	4,076
1616	294	1,555	855	33	–	2,737 }	
1617	282	2,030	365	22	–	2,699 }	2,450
1618	327	1,420	410	44	–	2,201 }	
1619	1,164	2,045	555	69	–	3,833 }	4,469
1620	2,577	1,870	560	98	–	5,105 }	
	17,795	18,870	4,563	717	–	41,945	

[24]

permitted it to be undertaken. Here it is possible to present only statements which describe the dispensation of charity by the Scuola di San Rocco and its satellite trusts in every year between 1551 and 1620.

The Scuole Grandi were, however, induced to draw up single comprehensive balance-sheets by the demands of the Collegio alla Milizia da Mar for galley crews—such demands sometimes caused the Guardians of the Scuole to present petitions complaining of the burdens flung upon their shoulders, together with balance-sheets showing how their revenues were already tied to this or that charitable use. The Scuola di San Marco presented one such statement to the Senate in 1589 or 1590. In 1611, 1614–15 and 1627 similar statements, framed in much the same spirit, were submitted to the Collegio alla

[24] The sources from which these figures are compiled are as follows:

For the Scuola itself and the minor trusts, mostly dowry trusts, administered by it:

A.S.V., *Scuola Grande di S. Rocco, seconda consegna*, vol. 387: a late seventeenth- or early eighteenth-century copy of the original accounts of the Scuola, which do not appear to survive.

For the Maffeo Donà trust, *ibid., prima consegna*, vols. 606, 607, 608, 609 (*Giornali della Commissaria Donà*); *prima consegna*, vol. 22, entitled 'Summario di tutte le dispositioni e spese fatte dalla Veneranda Scola di S. Rocco per conto della Commis.a del q.m. N. H. Maffio Donà fu de Bernardo (1527–1743)'.

For the Niccolò Moro trust, *ibid., prima consegna*, vols. 545, 546, 547; the balance-sheets of the trust, in *seconda consegna*, pacco X, *fascicolo* 650/III.

For the Zucca trust, *ibid., prima consegna*, vols. 586, 587, 588, 589, 590; *ibid.*, vol. 657, entitled 'Registro della Commissaria Zucca: Bilancio 1557–1742'.

For the Dalla Vecchia trust, *ibid., prima consegna*, vols. 570, 571, 572.

For the trust founded by Costantino di Teodoro Marcora, *ibid., seconda consegna, pacco 716*, two registers running from 1564–91 and 1591–1617.

For information about the sums dispensed to prisoners and in medicines, the two receipt books running from 1487–1564 and from 1564–1623, in *seconda consegna, busta* 423.

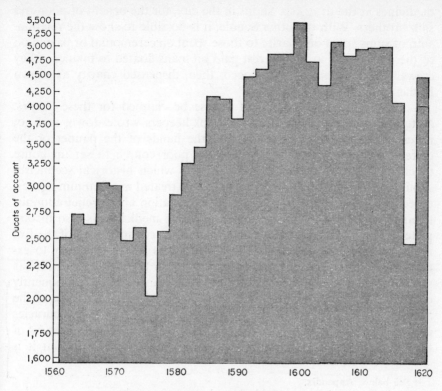

CHARITABLE OUTPUT OF THE SCUOLA GRANDE DI
SAN ROCCO 1561–1620
(*semi-logarithmic graph*)

Milizia da Mar by the Scuole di San Marco, San Giovanni Evangelista
and the Misericordia. Each of the balance-sheets theoretically described the financial arrangements in a typical year. Probably, like most
tax returns, they represented somewhat pessimistically the financial
circumstances of those who submitted them; though the returns could
doubtless have been verified by the accountants of the Milizia da
Mar.[25]

In dealing with the Scuola di San Rocco, I have attempted to show
only the sums spent on the various forms of charity, and the relationship of these to one another. They consisted of distributions of alms;
of schemes for the provision of dowries to poor maids; of payments
made under trust to hospitals; of sums dispensed for the relief of
prisoners (especially in the debtors' prisons); and of money used to buy

[25] See below, Appendix.

167

M

medicines at the druggists' shops in the city, for the benefit of poor and sick brothers. With the other Scuole, it is possible to show the relationship of sums spent on charity to those spent on ceremonial or passed on to the clergy, and to the interest paid on loans floated to finance galley crews.[26] The Scuola di San Rocco, then, dispensed charity as shown in the table on pp. 164–6.

Complete accuracy cannot of course be claimed for these figures. Naturally they represent what the book-keepers wrote down, and not necessarily what found its way into the hands of the pauper or the coffers of the hospital, or enabled the poor couple to set up house together. There is a limit to the extent to which historical scepticism should be stretched. All the figures must be treated as minimum figures, especially the estimate for dowries.[27] Information about relief administered to prisoners and about expenditure on medicines is also incomplete.[28] The bulk of the data comes from the account books of the five major trusts administered by the Scuola. It is reasonably easy to extract the relevant figures from them, though for the sake of speed it has sometimes been necessary to rely on the balance-sheets subsequently compiled, during an eighteenth-century inquiry into the finances of the Scuola, by expert accountants working on their books.[29] Inaccuracies are inevitable and small lacunae numerous, despite the copiousness of the trust records and the care with which they were kept. But it is

26 See below, Appendix.

27 A significant proportion of this figure is composed of the revenue from minor dowry trusts—an eighth or so in the 1560's, rising to a quarter in the '70's, but thereafter descending to about one-sixth only. These trusts are not commemorated by separate series of records. The accounts of some, but by no means all, were kept together with the accounts of the Scuola itself from the middle of the century until 1593. After 1593 pretty well all of them were placed on one reasonably comprehensive balance-sheet, which showed (a) how the Scuola dispensed the moneys which had been left to it to be administered at its own discretion, and (b) how it administered the minor trusts and the revenue derived from them which was tied to specific charitable uses. The accounts of the greater trusts were still kept separately. Before 1593 the information is especially incomplete: no payments are recorded on the book for some trusts for a period of several years after they are known to have come into operation.

28 This information is derived from a receipt book—not necessarily containing all the receipts issued for payments made for this purpose—which was used, until about 1590, to record payments to druggists for medicines, and after 1590 for payments made on behalf of prisoners to the gaolers of debtors' prisons. Receipts for medicines were taken elsewhere—where is not known.

29 The least comprehensible trust records are those which commemorate the charity founded by Constantino di Teodoro Marcora, which distributed alms and dowries in alternate years and made payments to convents. Here it has often been necessary to deduce the sums which were or ought to have been distributed for one particular charitable purpose from the amounts which—according to the entries on the books— actually were distributed to fulfil another.

unlikely that any inaccuracy would be gross enough to make a substantial difference to the general impression of the relationship of the various charities to one another, or of the fluctuations in the total quantity of charity dispensed by the Scuola.

The figures given under the heading of 'Dowries' are estimates of the total value (in ducats) of dowries actually collected by the girls to whom they were voted. Maffeo Donà, who set the pattern for the dowry trusts of the Scuola di San Rocco, stipulated that dowries provided out of the revenues from his bequest should be used as a lever to enable girls to obtain a husband. They should be voted to young women of deserving character who were neither married nor betrothed, and could only be collected when the wedding was a *fait accompli* and when the bride presented the trustees with a certificate to that effect from her parish priest.[30] In practice, to judge by the records of the Zucca and Dalla Vecchia trusts, about 80 per cent of the sum voted was in fact collected. It went, not only to maidens (*donzelle*) who had found husbands, but also to those who had determined to enter convents instead, or to become female Franciscans (*pizzochare*), with advancing years and growing disappointment.[31] In dealing with figures which seem to represent the sums voted by trustees rather than those claimed by beneficiaries, I have reduced by 20 per cent the figure which appears on the book.

In assessing the importance of the increase in the 'charitable output' of the Scuola, it is best to concentrate on increases which occurred after the year 1560. By 1560, the Scuola di San Rocco was certainly a well-established Scuola Grande. Comparatively small increases in the wealth of an established institution, if consistently maintained over a long period, are often far more significant than 500 per cent increases in the wealth of an institution in the preliminary stages of its development. The increase of 73 per cent in the charity of the Scuola between the decades 1561–70 and 1601–10 is more important than the increase of 175 per cent between 1551–60 and 1601–10. Taking the decade 1561–70 as the base, and ignoring temporarily—but only temporarily —the fact that a ducat in 1600 would buy far less than in 1550, the

[30] A.S.V., *Scuola Grande di S. Rocco, Libro dei Testamenti, in prima consegna, busta* 438, f. 28v.; A.S.R., *Registro delle Terminazioni* 2, f. 213.

[31] Between 1588 and 1621 the Zucca trustees voted a total of 25,275 ducats to 921 maidens (*donzelle*), of which they actually paid 19,825. In the first two decades of the new century, the Dalla Vecchia trustees voted 7,410 ducats and 6,190 were actually collected. What happened to the unclaimed dowries is not known—they may have been reinvested. The regularity of the sums which appear on the book of the Scuola di S. Rocco which records the operation of the minor dowry trusts suggests that they represent the sum voted rather than the sum collected in dowries—for the amounts collected would certainly have varied more between one year and another.

increase in the face value of the charity dispensed by the Scuola di San Rocco can be summarized as follows:

Period	Charity dispensed, in ducats		
1551–60	17,534	63·2	
1561–70	27,719	100·0	
1571–80	25,036	90·3	− 9·7
1581–90	37,770	136·2	+45·9
1591–1600	48,479	174·9	+38·7
1601–10	47,938	173·0	− 1·9
1611–20	41,945	151·3	−21·7

*want—> *
total'n

This table, and the graph on p. 167, show that the Scuola di San Rocco dispensed its largest sums in charity in the twenty years from 1591 to 1610, when its output was higher by 73–75 per cent than in the 1560's. The two slumps, in the 1570's and in the decade 1611–20, coincided with naval wars, and, on the second occasion at least, with heavy taxation. Hardly any alms were dispensed in 1616, 1617 or 1618, and by 1619 only a partial recovery had apparently taken place. War taxation affected the Scuola much more adversely than did the liquidation of the Monti.

The increase in the money revenue of the Scuola was due partly to new legacies accruing to it, and partly to an increase in the money rents paid by tenants of the Scuola in Venice or on the mainland. Rents were passably quick to take part in the price rise. Most of the investments made by the Scuole were in urban properties. On the mainland, they were careful to use short-term leases which did not bind them to accept exactly the same rent over a long period of years. In 1614–15 and in 1627, four-fifths of the gross revenue of the Scuola della Misericordia was derived from houses and shops in the city of Venice;[32] in 1614–15 the Scuola di San Giovanni received about two-thirds of its income from that source.[33] A petition of the Guardians of

[32] In 1614–15 the income of the Scuola della Misericordia from all sources was about 4,440 ducats, of which 3,550 came from houses, shops and real property in the city of Venice itself, 305 from houses and estates outside Venice, 435 from mortgages to private persons and 150 from *luminarie*, the annual tax payable by members of the Scuola. In 1627—the figures are computed on a different basis more suited to the way in which the balance-sheet was compiled, but the proportions are still comparable if not the total—the total income appears on the balance-sheet as duc. 5,070. Venetian properties yielded duc. 4,050 and outside investments in real estate duc. 480, mortgages duc. 390 and the *luminarie*, again, probably about 150. (A.S.V., *Milizia da Mar, fascicolo* 706.)

[33] In this year the income of the Scuola appears, from the statement of account submitted by Angelo Zaguri, the Guardian Grande, as duc. 6,535: from Venetian properties, duc. 4,386; houses and estates outside Venice, duc. 1,275; mortgages, duc. 582; uncertain sources, duc. 255; annual taxes and entrance fees, duc. 36. *Ibid.*

all the Scuole Grandi in 1592 testified to their lingering distrust of mainland investment, even at the close of the sixteenth century.[34]

In 1545 and 1550 the Scuole di San Rocco and San Marco made it compulsory to auction the tenancies of houses which were newly to let. The governors of San Marco stipulated that two separate auctions must be held, after which the house would finally be let to the bidder offering to pay the highest rent.[35] In 1553 the Scuola di San Rocco modified its policy so far as to allow the governors to let the houses by private treaty if they saw fit.[36] To judge by the records of the Donà trust, they were often passed to relatives of a deceased tenant.[37] In August 1559 the governors of San Marco determined that mainland properties should be auctioned afresh every five years.[38] The complaint of a certain 'poor Salvador', a tenant of the Scuola di San Marco in 1551, suggests that it was the tenant rather than the Scuola who suffered.[39]

The Scuola di San Rocco would occasionally let houses in the city for periods of not more than two years, but as a rule they changed hands only on the death of a tenant. Occasionally a long-lived occupant damaged the Scuola's finances. At his death, the rent of the house would rise abruptly. Once, in the space of only eight years, the rent of a dwelling-house at Santa Maria Zobenigo was raised from 115 ducats (in 1578) to 198 (in 1586).[40] Between 1581 and 1627, there were some impressive increases in the yield from house property owned by the Scuola della Misericordia. Houses and shops in the important commercial street of the Merceria, near the church of San Zulian, which had yielded 685 ducats before the deduction of tax in 1581, yielded 1,480 in 1614–15, an increase (in terms of money) of nearly 120 per

---

[34] See above, p. 137.

[35] A.S.V., *Scuola Grande di San Rocco, seconda consegna*, vol. 47, ff. 39v.–40; *Scuola Grande di San Marco*, vol. 20, ff. 114v.–115.

[36] A.S.R., *Registro delle Terminazioni 2*, ff. 134v.–135.

[37] Numerous examples of this occur in the records of the Donà trust: A.S.V., *Scuola Grande di San Rocco, seconda consegna*, vol. 21, *Quaderno Affittuali Commissaria Donà*, 1557–82; and the *Giornali* of the trust itself, *ibid.*, *prima consegna*, vols. 611, 612.

[38] A.S.V., *Scuola Grande di S. Marco*, vol. 21, f. 173v.

[39] *Ibid.*, vol. 20, f. 143. Salvador owned 46 *campi* at Botenigo. He said that for twenty years he had paid rent at the rate of 12 *grossi* or half a ducat per *campo* every year, before the property passed into the hands of the Scuola and for a short time afterwards. It was then put up for auction and Salvador, in order to retain it for another five years, was compelled to pay rent at 1 ducat 13 *grossi* per *campo*, three times the previous rate. His downfall was completed by flooding—his land remained under water for one month. For a similar example, which dates from February 1554, *ibid.*, vol. 21, f. 46.

[40] A.S.V., *Scuola Grande di S. Rocco, seconda consegna*, vol. 21, f. 169v.; A.S.R.. *Registro delle Terminazioni 3*, f. 143.

cent.[41] In these estimates it is impossible to take account of improvements in the property, involving considerable investment of capital, which may have been effected meanwhile. But it seems that real estate was a fairly rewarding investment, even if there was a rise in the cost of living and some danger arose from long tenancies. The Council of Ten, formulating the commission to the Inquisitori et Revisori sopra le Scuole Grandi in October 1622, admonished them that

> There are many people who for a long period of years continue under the terms of their original leases without making any alteration in the rent they pay, notwithstanding the great variation and increase in all prices. Hence the Scuole do not receive the profit which is due to them. Very old agreements of this nature must be reviewed.[42]

The Monti, of course, had great advantages—there were no administrative expenses, and no repairs to be undertaken. The Camera d'Imprestidi, unlike the private tenants of the Scuole, paid promptly except in wartime. But there was always the possibility that the Monti might be liquidated, and it was unwise to invest in them heavily to the exclusion of all else. The Scuola di San Marco was precariously situated—in 1590 nearly 70 per cent of its income came from the Monti.[43] In 1552 the governors had reflected that over 1,300 ducats of their annual revenue was derived from capital in the Monte Vecchio, and that should it be liquidated the Scuola would have to be closed. For there was not enough revenue from other sources even to meet everyday expenses and to finance processions. But their only remedy was to provide that the sum of 100 ducats a year should be transferred from the Monte Vecchio to the other loan funds: to the Monte Nuovissimo or Sussidio; 'or to some other good and sound investment'.[44] They did not envisage the possibility that all the Monti might be liquidated within a few years of one another. When this happened, the Scuola suffered heavily, but it was able to move its capital into land, and gradually to repair its fortunes, though only with the aid of a substantial new legacy. A minor revolution in investment is reflected in three statements submitted by the Scuola to the Senate and to the Milizia da Mar, in 1590, 1611 and 1614–15.[45]

[41] A.S.V., *Dieci Savii sopra le Decime in Rialto*, busta 164, fascicolo 1160; A.S.V., *Milizia da Mar, fascicolo* 706.

[42] A.S.V., *Consiglio dei Dieci, Registro Comune 1622*, ff. 170v.–171v.

[43] A.S.V., *Senato, Mar, filza* 109, under the date 27 October 1590.

[44] A.S.V., *Scuola Grande di S. Marco*, vol. 20, f. 175; *Consiglio dei Dieci, Registro Comune 1552*, ff. 148–9.

[45] A.S.V., *Senato, Mar, filza* 109, under date 27 October 1590; *Milizia da Mar, fascicolo* 723, under the date 22 February 1610 Venetian style, and *fascicolo* 706.

REVENUES OF THE SCUOLA DI SAN MARCO AND THEIR SOURCES

Measured in ducats of account

	1590	1611	1614–15
Loans and loan funds	1,855 (69·88%)	196 (10·80%)	328 (15·36%)
Real property in the city	481 (18·12%)	922 (50·79%)	1,118 (52·28%)
Estates and *daie* on the mainland	318 (12·00%)	698 (38·41%)	692 (32·36%)
	2,654 (100·00%)	1,816 (100·00%)	2,138 (100·00%)

In 1590 the source which provided the Scuola with two-thirds of its total gross income was the government Monti, whilst a thin trickle of revenue also derived from investment with the Procuracies of St Mark's. Only 30 per cent of the income of the Scuola was derived from investment in real property. Between 1590 and 1611, the total revenue of the Scuola fell by 31·58 per cent. Much of the capital formerly invested in the Monti was transferred to real estate, and some of it was used to buy the right to receive *daie*, taxes paid by the communes of mainland villages. Again, in 1611 only just over one-tenth of the total income of the Scuola was derived from loans to the government or to private individuals. Some of the money had entered the new 4 per cent loan fund opened for the benefit of the clergy and of religious institutions by order of the Senate in 1607. In the course of the next three or four years, the Scuola evidently continued to place its capital both here and in real property in the city. Its income rose by over one-sixth, though in 1614–15 it was still lower than in 1590 by nearly 20 per cent. San Marco's was an extreme case, but in 1614–15 Angelo Zaguri, Guardian Grande of the Scuola di San Giovanni Evangelista, claimed that the liquidation of the Monti had cost his Scuola revenue of 1,565 ducats a year, even 'having invested the capital taken from them in building, at a very remarkable disadvantage'. At this time the total gross income of the Scuola was in the region of 6,500 ducats.[46]

The Scuola di San Rocco, however, showed unusual skill in avoiding the ill-effects of the liquidation of the Monti. Between the peak years 1599–1600 and the years 1603–4 there was a decline of about 20 per cent in the charity dispensed by the Scuola, but between 1605–6 and 1613–14 it maintained its charity at the impressively high level of the mid-1590's. Admittedly, in June 1604

The capital belonging to our Scuola and trusts in the Monti has been removed from them and has remained dead for a long time since, to the

[46] A.S.V., *Milizia da Mar, fascicolo* 706.

173

great loss of the poor to whom the interest ought to come, whilst the souls of those who have made bequests suffer considerably.[47]

Committees were appointed with powers to act quickly and to snap up any promising bargain that presented itself—much property was auctioned by government offices which had confiscated it or foreclosed on persons in debt for the payment of taxes. Even so, in July 1610 a total sum of 19,006 ducats, capital belonging to minor trusts, was still uninvested, and the Scuola undertook to pay, itself, 3 per cent interest on this capital.[48]

The fact that the charity dispensed by the Scuola did not seriously diminish as a result of the liquidation of the Monti was related to the extent to which it had invested in real property. This, though more troublesome to maintain, was less at the mercy of the Venetian government than were the Monti. Even if the Venetian government kept, by sixteenth-century standards, good faith with its creditors, it could still cause great inconvenience when it chose to terminate its contract.

Nevertheless, the Scuola di San Rocco suffered financial stress in 1616–18, partly (if not wholly) as a result of war taxation. Between 1614 and 1621 the Scuola was compelled to disburse a total of 25,767 ducats to galleots, including over 15,000 in the financial year running from March 1617 to March 1618:[49] a massive sum to devote to a purpose unrelated to the original aims of the Scuola. The hiatus caused by war taxation in the normal charitable activities of the Scuola can be partly judged by the following table:

Date	Charity		Payments to galleots
1612	duc. 4,803		
1613		duc. 5,652	
1614	4,335		duc. 1,073
1615		5,416	1,082
1616	2,737		1,123
1617		2,699	15,239
1618	2,201		2,839
1619		3,833	109
1620	5,105		nil
1621			4,302

Between 1616 and 1618 the almsgiving charities appear to have been virtually extinguished. On 30 December 1616 the Scuola, casting desperately about for new sources of revenue, determined in future to

[47] A.S.R., *Registro delle Terminazioni 4*, f. 99.
[48] *Ibid.*, ff. 173v.–174v.
[49] A.S.V., *Scuola Grande di S. Rocco, seconda consegna*, vol. 705, pp. 9–17.

let all its almshouses, saying that they had originally been built by the Scuola out of its own moneys, 'and it is fitting that in time of need we should avail ourselves of what is our own'.[50] The conflict between the duty of the Scuola to the Venetian poor and its obligations to the state as a whole had never been more acute.

The other Scuole did not escape. In 1617–18 the four largest Scuole were required to contribute 50,485 ducats to the Venetian navy, apportioned as follows:

The Scuola della Misericordia for its part in the two great and light galleys most recently armed, 143 men at the rate of 115 ducats each.....duc. 16,448
The Scuola della Carità for a similar quota of 87 men at 115 ducats each
duc. 10,005
The Scuola di San Giovanni, for its part in these galleys, 87 men at 115 ducats .... duc. 10,005
The Scuola di San Rocco likewise 122 men at 115 ducats.........duc. 14,030[51]

It is therefore likely that there was a similar hiatus in the dispensation of charity by the other Scuole Grandi. All besieged the Council of Ten for permission to raise loans by pledging their own property or that of the trusts they administered. The Scuola di San Rocco borrowed 12,118 ducats at 5 per cent, and imposed a tax of 25 per cent on the net revenues of all its trusts to pay off the capital and meet the interest payments.[52] Between March 1617 and May 1621 the taxed and harassed Scuola della Misericordia obtained permission to raise at least 16,500 ducats by loan,[53] San Giovanni Evangelista 9,500,[54] the Carità 8,500[55] and the Scuola di San Marco 7,000.[56]

Should a charitable corporation be recognized by the Venetian state as useful to itself, the penalties were at intervals heavy. The Scuole found themselves sinking into financial difficulty, and gravely distracted from their purpose of assisting the poor. The Venetian government, instead of itself raising and paying interest on loans, proposed to

[50] A.S.R., *Registro delle Terminazioni 4*, f. 237r.–v.

[51] A.S.V., *Scuola Grande di S. Rocco, seconda consegna*, vol. 705, p. 12. Even this (see above, p. 155) does not represent the full extent of the contributions exacted from the Scuole.

[52] A.S.R., *Registro delle Terminazioni 4*, f. 261.

[53] A.S.V., *Consiglio dei Dieci, Registro Comune 1617*, f. 21, 48v., 59r.–v., 93v.–94, 142r.–v.; *Registro Comune 1618*, f. 13v.; *Parti Comuni, filza* 320, under date 15 July 1619; *Registro Comune 1621*, f. 56v.

[54] A.S.V., *Consiglio dei Dieci, Registro Comune 1617*, f. 64r.–v., 142r.–v.; *Parti Comuni, filza* 313, under date 9 January 1617 Venetian style; *filza* 315, under date 13 July 1618; *Registro Comune 1621*, f. 16v.

[55] A.S.V., *Consiglio dei Dieci, Registro Comune 1617*, f. 54r.–v., 142v.

[56] A.S.V., *Consiglio dei Dieci, Registro Comune 1617*, f. 29v., f. 53v.; *Registro Comune 1621*, f. 16v.

tap the reserves of wealth administered by the Scuole Grandi, and to make them, together with other lay corporations like the fruiterers' guild, partially responsible for borrowing on behalf of the state. But the corollary of this was that the Scuole Grandi were allowed to invest in real property, and they were therefore built upon a solid rock— more so, indeed, than those institutions which relied, for their upkeep, on voluntary offerings which were not invested but were dispensed immediately to their dependents. Rents did to some extent participate in the general upward movement of prices. The books of a San Rocco trust—that founded by Maffeo Donà—show how the revenues of one trust (based both on landed investment and on holdings in Monti) behaved during the period 1550–1620. The movement of this revenue is shown in the table below, and in the graph plotted from it.[57]

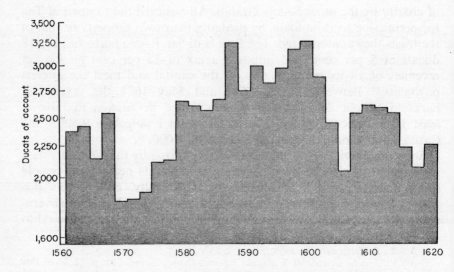

NET REVENUES OF THE DONÀ TRUST ADMINISTERED BY
THE SCUOLA GRANDE DI SAN ROCCO 1561–1620
(*semi-logarithmic graph*)

[57] The figures are extracted from A.S.V., *Scuola Grande di S. Rocco, prima consegna*, vols. 606, 607, 608, 609 (*Giornali della Commissaria Donà*): from the summaries of the net revenue, and of the way in which it was or ought to have been divided, which occur at fairly regular intervals throughout the Giornali.

NET REVENUES OF THE DONÀ TRUST ADMINISTERED BY THE
SCUOLA GRANDE DI SAN ROCCO, 1551–1620

Measured in ducats of account

1551	2,253	} 2,251	1561	2,364	} 2,357	1571	1,586	} 1,853
1552	2,248		1562	2,350		1572	2,120	
1553	2,150	} 2,330	1563	2,516	} 2,403	1573	1,525	} 1,902
1554	2,511		1564	2,289		1574	2,278	
1555	2,424	} 2,257	1565	2,308	} 2,144	1575	2,527	} 2,120
1556	2,090		1566	1,979		1576	1,713	
1557	2,589	} 2,534	1567	2,474	} 2,520	1577	2,020	} 2,139
1558	2,478		1568	2,565		1578	2,258	
1559	2,367	} 2,175	1569	2,490	} 1,840	1579	2,564	} 2,638
1560	1,982		1570	1,190		1580	2,712	
	23,092			22,525			21,303	
1581	2,640	} 2,596	1591	3,151	} 2,996	1601	3,244	} 2,883
1582	2,553		1592	2,841		1602	2,521	
1583	2,695	} 2,545	1593	2,887	} 2,816	1603	2,364	} 2,434
1584	2,395		1594	2,744		1604	2,503	
1585	2,532	} 2,645	1595	3,008	} 2,979	1605	1,846	} 2,048
1586	2,757		1596	2,950		1606	2,250	
1587	3,340	} 3,250	1597	3,220	} 3,185	1607	2,634	} 2,525
1588	3,160		1598	3,150		1608	2,416	
1589	2,734	} 2,748	1599	3,450	} 3,287	1609	2,743	} 2,598
1590	2,761		1600	3,124		1610	2,453	
	27,567			30,525			24,974	

1611	2,539	} 2,580
1612	2,620	
1613	2,591	} 2,526
1614	2,461	
1615	2,328	} 2,237
1616	2,145	
1617	2,400	} 2,076
1618	1,752	
1619	2,400	} 2,250
1620	2,100	
	23,336	

177

The following table compares the movement of the trust's net revenues with that of the total volume of charity dispensed by the Scuola and by its satellite trusts, using the decade 1561–70 as a basis for the comparison.

Period	Output of Scuola			Net revenue of trust		
1551–60	17,534	63·2		23,092	102·5	
1561–70	27,719	100·0		22,525	100·0	
1571–80	25,036	90·3	− 9·7	21,303	94·6	− 5·4
1581–90	37,770	136·2	+ 45·9	27,567	122·4	+ 27·8
1591–1600	48,479	174·9	+ 38·7	30,525	135·5	+ 13·1
1601–10	47,938	173·0	− 1·9	24,974	110·9	− 24·6
1611–20	41,945	151·3	− 21·7	23,336	103·6	− 7·3

It is therefore likely that the rise in the face value of the 'charitable output' of the Scuola over the last quarter of the sixteenth century was partly due to moderate increases in the yield of investments of the Scuola made before the price rise began. These investments could provide a moderately buoyant platform on which the superstructure of new legacies could be erected. The liquidation of the Monti was bad but not disastrous for the Donà trust, which must have suffered more heavily than most charities administered by the Scuola at this time. Even if the increases in trust revenue were not spectacular, the steadiness of this revenue was an important asset.

Hitherto, this discussion has dealt only with increases in the face value, and not with increases in the purchasing power, of the charity dispensed by the Scuola di San Rocco. Naturally, 500 ducats dispensed by the Scuola to its poor brothers in 1600 bought far less bread, wine, oil or firewood than 500 ducats in 1550. Unfortunately, no comprehensive cost-of-living index has yet been constructed for sixteenth-century Venice—though something is known about fluctuations in the price of the staple commodity, wheat, during the last quarter of the century. From valuable data recently published by M. Maurice Aymard, it appears that the average price of one *staio* or bushel of wheat in Venice was 12 lire 10 soldi (about 2 ducats of account) in 1567–76, rising to 23 lire 17 soldi (about 3·85 ducats of account) in 1589–98.[58] Over the period 1567–76, the Scuola di San Rocco dispensed 26,176 ducats in

---

[58] See Maurice Aymard, *Venise, Raguse et le commerce du blé pendant la seconde moitié du XVI siècle* (Paris, 1966), p. 109. According to M. Aymard's information, the optimum annual consumption of wheat per person was reckoned to be 4 *staia* in 1555, and the minimum necessary at 3 *staia* in 1586–94—*ibid.*, p. 17. Of course, in reality, much of the charity was actually dispensed in the form of marriage-portions, and was not intended for the purchase of bread or foodstuffs.

charity, the equivalent of just under 13,000 *staia* of wheat. Over the years 1589–98, the Scuola dispensed 45,306 ducats in various forms of charity, then equivalent to just under 11,800 *staia* of wheat. The loss in purchasing power in terms of wheat in the last third of the sixteenth century may therefore be reckoned at about 9·3 per cent. Similarly, in 1567–76, the revenues of the Donà trust (amounting to a total of 20,468 ducats) could have purchased over 9,900 *staia* of wheat. In 1589–98, they amounted to 29,446 ducats, equivalent to some 7,650 *staia* of wheat. Hence, these revenues lost about 22 per cent of their purchasing power in terms of wheat. This suggests that, owing to the accession of new legacies, the Scuola di San Rocco was able to continue dispensing charity whose real value did not fail very seriously to keep pace with rising food prices—even in a decade when these, owing to a general subsistence crisis affecting most of the Mediterranean, were extremely high.[59] It is quite possible that Venetian grain prices fell during the next two decades, as they did in Chioggia (to the south-west of Venice) and in Udine, to the north-east.[60] If this happened, it may be that between the early seventeenth century and 1615 the power of charity dispensed by the Scuola to purchase food was near to what it had been in 1567–76.

The movement of charity can also be related in some degree to the movement of wages over the period 1560–1620. Wage movements were affected by the price-rise and in their turn contributed to it. The information available concerns the money-wages of builders employed by the Scuola di San Rocco—both of master-builders (*mureri et marangoni*) and of journeymen (*lavoranti*).[61] These wage-figures can, of course, reflect only imperfectly the general state of the labour-market, but they are unlikely to be altogether misleading. It may be of some use to convert the charity dispensed by the Scuola di San Rocco in various years into its equivalent in builders' wages, to form some idea of what it meant to Venetian workmen. Master masons, but more especially journeymen (who earned only 60–70 per cent of a master's wage), belonged to economic groups which might from time to time need their earnings supplemented by charity—in years of famine, or at times when they personally suffered from old age, sickness or disablement.

[59] See below, pp. 355–60.

[60] Cf. Fernand Braudel, 'La vita economica di Venezia nel secolo XVI', in *La civiltà veneziana del Rinascimento* (Florence, 1958), p. 91; Fernand Braudel, Pierre Jeannin, Jean Meuvret and Ruggiero Romano, 'Le déclin de Venise au XVIIème siècle', in *Aspetti e cause della decadenza economica veneziana nel secolo XVII* (Venice–Rome, 1961), pp. 25 f.

[61] On this question, and for the statistics on which the following tables are based, see Brian Pullan, 'Wage-earners and the Venetian economy, 1550–1630', *The Economic History Review*, XVI (1964).

Date	Charity dispensed ducats	Average daily wage of		Equivalent of charity in days' wages of	
		Masters soldi	Lavoranti soldi	Masters	Lavoranti
1561–65	13,027	30·20	22·98	53,485	70,290
1566–70	10,692	32·04	19·82	41,376	66,887
1571–75	12,096	34·91	24·14[62]	43,220	63,048
		33·71	22.18		
1576–80	12,940	33·71	22·18[63]	43,413	70,818
		38·33	22·84		
1581–85	17,647	44·37	26·82	49,320	81,590
1586–90	20,124	42·47	27·08	58,755	92,146
1591–95	23,044	46·95	33·30	60,861	85,810
1596–1600	25,435	50·24	36·70	62,780	85,938
1601–05	23,267	52·64	38·06	54,810	75,805
1606–10	24,672	61·27	37·96	49,932	80,593
1611–15	24,028	61·76	41·63	48,241	71,568
1616–20	17,914	63·65	38·77	34,900	57,297

124 soldi = 1 ducat of account

The next table shows the proportional changes in the equivalent of the charity and its fluctuations from one five-year period to another. It uses the years 1561–5 as a base, with the index number 100.

	Equivalent of charity in days' wages of	
Date	Masters	Lavoranti
1561–65	100	100
1566–70	77·4 (– 22·6)	95·2 (– 4·8)
1571–75	80·8 (+ 3·4)	89·7 (– 5·5)
1576–80	81·2 (+ 0·4)	100·7 (+ 11·0)
1581–85	92·4 (+ 11·2)	116·1 (+ 15·4)
1586–90	109·9 (+ 17·5)	131·1 (+ 15·0)
1591–95	113·8 (+ 3·9)	122·1 (– 9·0)
1596–1600	117·4 (+ 3·8)	122·3 (+ 0·2)
1601–05	102·5 (– 14·9)	107·9 (– 14·4)
1606–10	93·4 (– 9·1)	114·7 (+ 6·8)
1611–15	90·2 (– 3·2)	101·8 (– 12·9)
1616–20	65·3 (– 24·9)	81·5 (– 20·3)

It therefore seems that in terms of the wages of journeymen builders (which are perhaps most indicative) the real value of the Scuola's charity fell between 1566 and 1575, but climbed to a significantly higher level during the 1580's, dropped somewhat during the 1590's,

[62] Here it is necessary to distinguish between wages paid in pre-plague years and wages paid during the plague year 1575. The first figure given, for masters and for *lavoranti*, shows the rates paid in 1571–4; the second, the rates paid in 1575.

[63] Here again, the first figure shows the rates paid in the plague period, in the year 1576 and the period up to July 1577. The second figure shows the rates paid between August 1577 and the end of 1580.

and showed a tendency to fall during the period 1601–15. The rise during the 1580's is partially a reflexion of the low level of journeymen's wages during that decade. The fall over the period 1601–15 reflects the fact that they had then become significantly higher than in the early 1590's: probably in real terms, as well as in terms of money. Where wages are high, the general need for charity may be less, and vice versa—so these figures may give a very rough indication of the usefulness of the Scuola's charity to working men. Masters' wages behaved somewhat differently from those of journeymen, rising much more rapidly in 1577–85 and after 1605. But here again it is possible to discern a depression in the real value of the Scuola's charity—measuring by this criterion—over the period 1566–85, followed by a modest improvement extending over the years 1586–1605, and thereafter by another depression. At least in 1577–85 and 1606–15, 'depressions' were caused by substantial increases in the money-wages of masters.

From these figures, one may tentatively conclude that the main achievement of the Scuola di San Rocco was to dispense charity which, between about 1580 and 1615, roughly maintained the same real value as in 1561–5. It seldom—to judge by any of the available criteria—rose above this level by more than some 20 per cent, or fell below it by more than 10 per cent. It needed new charitable bequests in order to achieve this. There were no spectacular increases in the volume of charity dispensed (in real terms)—but disastrous reductions were rare. The Scuola di San Rocco had to face many difficulties—the famines of the 1590's, the need to reinvest a proportion of its wealth, the demands of the state for galley crews. But its foundations were stable enough to support it throughout, and to equip it to render valuable service to the poor as well as to the state.

Finally, some comments should be made on the methods adopted by the Scuole Grandi in the dispensation of charity. The statistics for the Scuola di San Rocco, presented above, suggest that between 50 per cent and 60 per cent of the charity distributed by the Scuola was, during most of the period under review, disbursed in the form of alms. Almsgiving is sometimes represented as a fairly elementary and unsophisticated form of charity—a palliative measure, which does not cut at the roots of poverty and leaves the recipient in essentially the same condition as before. Alms, however, must often have served to tide families over temporary difficulties, when work was unavailable or when the wage-earner fell sick. A high proportion of the alms found its way to brothers of the Scuola, and therefore to persons whose needs the governors were in a position to know. But in the sixteenth century,

181

as the Scuola increased in wealth, the humbler 'brothers of the discipline' became automatically entitled to charitable benefits, and did not have to go to such lengths to prove their worthiness. The trustees of Maffeo Donà were not always wholly discriminating in the methods they employed. Their records, about the middle of the century, suggest that they distributed a certain proportion of their alms to persons whose names they carefully noted on their lists, but then tossed the rest to a large, anonymous crowd which had collected in or outside the headquarters of the Scuola. In the 1550's, the trustees ensured that the poor brothers of the Scuola were provided for—284 in 1550, 363 or more in 1552, and 406 in 1554.[64] But in 1566 obstreperous crowd behaviour prevented the distribution from being noted in any sort of detail[65]—under such conditions, discriminate almsgiving must have been virtually impossible. In 1563, the officers discussed the possibility of systematically distributing the income of the newly established Zucca trust, and of allotting a certain proportion to each sestiere 'because some have more poor than others'. But they rejected it.[66]

However, during the 1580's, the officers of the Scuola di San Rocco did begin to administer the new Dalla Vecchia trust on this principle—taking alms into the sestieri, rather than waiting for the candidates to appear at the Scuola.[67] The table on page 183 shows how these alms were distributed over the years 1586–1614.

This evidence tentatively suggests a reasonably intelligent distribution of charity. Apparently two of the sestieri on the Frari side of the Grand Canal, i.e. Dorsoduro and Santa Croce, were treated over-generously at the expense of the three sestieri on the opposite side—Cannaregio, Castello and San Marco.

However, Dorsoduro and Santa Croce were the areas in which the general level of rent for dwelling-places was lowest—according to the statistics compiled by Professor Beltrami from tax returns submitted in 1661. This is the nearest available figure, and it is unlikely that the situation greatly changed between the beginning and the middle of the seventeenth century. By the same criterion, San Marco was by far

[64] A.S.V., *Scuola Grande di San Rocco, prima consegna*, vol. 607, ff. 76–9, 102–8, 144–9. With time, the proportion of alms distributed to known recipients fell. More tended to disappear into the clutches of the unknown crowd. Between 1550 and 1558, the crowd seldom in any one year absorbed more than about half the sum distributed, and usually much less. But in 1560, 179 ducats went to the crowd and only about 36 to identifiable persons (104 in number)—*ibid.*, ff. 230v.–231v.

[65] *Ibid.*, vol. 608, f. 91v.

[66] A.S.R., *Registro delle Terminazioni 2*, f. 263.

[67] See below, p. 354, for the attempts made by Leonardo Donà during the 1590's to persuade the Procurators of St Mark's to distribute alms in the parishes, rather than over the counter in the Procuratie.

Sestiere	Alms distributed 1586–1614[68] duc.	Proportion % to the total sum distributed in all Venice	Proportion % of population of sestiere to total population of Venice 1581 and 1624[69]
Dorsoduro	2,448.20. –	26·91	21·22
Cannaregio	1,652. 3. –	18·16	22·84
Castello	1,628. 2.10	17·90	21·68
Santa Croce	1,622. 1.17	17·84	11·82
San Marco	917. –. –	10·12	15·04
San Polo	824.20.16	9.07	7·40
duc.	9,092.23.11	100·00	100·00[70]

the most prosperous sestiere.[71] Moreover, the Scuola itself stood in
Dorsoduro, and may have drawn most of its members from its
immediate neighbourhood in Dorsoduro and Santa Croce. The books
of the Dalla Vecchia trust do in fact suggest an advance towards more
systematic methods of almsgiving in the course of the sixteenth century, and balance the rather different impression left by the Donà
records.

Moreover, a high proportion of the Scuola's charity was devoted to
constructive uses—more than 10 per cent was usually distributed to
hospitals, and therefore devoted to indoor relief rather than casual
outdoor relief. Especially popular was the dowry trust, or scheme for
providing marriage portions to poor maids. Venetian charity in general
showed a marked preoccupation with the plight of young women—
they must be protected from the dangers and temptations of the world
by being provided with a husband, or being safely accommodated in a
nunnery.[72] Dowry trusts were designed to make marriage economically
possible for persons who could not otherwise have afforded to set up
house on their own, and they enabled women to do their proper job,

[68] Figures in this column are given in ducats, *grossi* and *piccoli*: there were 24
grossi to one ducat, and 32 *piccoli* to each *grosso*.

[69] Beltrami, *Storia della popolazione*, p. 61.

[70] *Giornali della Commissaria Dalla Vecchia*, A.S.V., *Scuola Grande di San Rocco*,
prima consegna, vols. 570, 571, 572.

[71] The average rent of dwelling-places in Dorsoduro in 1661 was 23 ducats—rents
were lower only in the island of Murano which, being then under the separate
government of a Venetian *podestà*, was not officially part of Venice. In Santa Croce
the average rent was 30 ducats, in Cannaregio 35, Castello 36, San Polo 38 and San
Marco 45: Beltrami, *Storia della popolazione*, Appendice, Tavola N.15.

[72] For the preoccupation of the new philanthropic movements of the sixteenth century with saving young women from disease and prostitution, see below, pp. 375–94.

N

entering into their preordained place in society. Capital was needed to provide dowries for daughters or orphaned nieces, and capital, for a poor man living at or near the poverty line, was hard to accumulate.

The records of the Scuola di San Rocco suggest that, throughout the period under review, 30–35 per cent of the charity dispensed by the Scuola went to provide dowries for poor maidens. In the course of about seventy years, there is no sign of a significant alteration in the relative popularity of the various kinds of charity favoured by the Scuola. More money was expended in alms than in marriage subsidies, but more testators favoured dowry trusts than favoured almsgiving. Dowry trusts, indeed, were almost the only form of charity in which the less rich testators reposed any faith.

FORMS OF CHARITY ADMINISTERED BY
THE SCUOLA GRANDE DI SAN ROCCO, 1551–1620; THEIR RELATIONSHIP
TO THE TOTAL SUM DISPENSED IN CHARITY

Period	Alms	Dowries	Hospitals	Prisoners	Medicines
1551–60	57·80%	22·82%	15·27%	—	4·11%
1561–70	60·50%	32·49%	5·04%	—	1·97%
1571–80	56·14%	30·85%	8·21%	—	4·80%
1581–90	54·45%	30·64%	12·45%	0·05%	2·41%
1591–1600	51·55%	35·49%	11·45%	1·51%	—
1601–10	52·70%	34·30%	11·54%	1·46%	—
1611–20	42·41%	45·00%	10·88%	1·71%	—

In the decade 1611–20, the proportional increase in dowries at the expense of alms was one of the effects of war taxation in 1616–18. This seems to have affected alms, but not, for some reason, dowries.

There is no continuous record of the activities of other Scuole Grandi. But their statements made to the Senate and to the Milizia da Mar in the late sixteenth and early seventeenth century are of some value. They make it possible to compose a general picture of their charitable activities at that time, as shown in the table on page 185.[73]

The methods adopted for the administration of dowry trusts—universally popular, as this table shows—give the impression of being fairly systematic. They were based on a combination of 'scrutiny' and lottery. In the Scuola di San Rocco, the first stage in the process of selection consisted of examining the qualifications of each candidate and especially of establishing whether she enjoyed a good reputation among her neighbours. Lotteries were used to make the final choice, once the board of governors had decided that all the candidates were deserving, and this may have had the effect of checking favouritism.

[73] For the S. Rocco figures, see the table above, pp. 164–6. For the others, see below, Appendix.

Scuola	Date	Alms	Hospitals	Dowries	Medicines	Prisoners
San Rocco (44 almshouses, 1581)[74]	1609–14 (average)	2,613 (52·48%)	405 (8·14%)	1,877 (37·70%)	—	83 (1·67%)
		TOTAL: duc. 4,978				
San Giovanni (76 almshouses, 1581)[75]	1614	181 (8·77%)	206 (9·98%)	1,560 (75·53%)	118 (5·72%)	—
		TOTAL: duc. 2,065				
Misericordia (60 almshouses, 1581)[76]	1614	247 (23·70%)	75 (7·20%)	355 (34·07%)	108 (10·36%)	257 (24·67%)
		TOTAL: duc. 1,042				
	1627	707 (37·29%)	—	488 (25·74%)	158 (8·33%)	543 (28·64%)
		TOTAL: duc. 1,896				
San Marco (26 almshouses, 1590)[77]	1590	610 (49·23%)	117 (9·44%)	412 (33·25%)	100 (8·07%)	—
		TOTAL: duc. 1,239				
	1611	376 (35·48%)	72 (6·79%)	540 (50·94%)	72 (6·79%)	—
		TOTAL: duc. 1,060				

Favouritism should theoretically have been discouraged by the size of the board responsible for administering the charity—which would doubtless make collusion difficult. For example, in February 1546, 214 *donzelle* competed for twenty dowries of fifteen ducats each, provided by the revenues of the Maffeo Donà trust. One ballot reduced their numbers to 94 and a second to 59—on each of these occasions every maiden who failed to obtain the unanimous approval of all the trustees was disqualified. In theory at least, there should have been 32 selectors on the board. Finally, 59 pellets were placed in an urn, twenty being golden and the remainder silver. Those who drew the golden pellets from the urn received the dowries.[78] However, when some of the greater trusts administered by the Scuola became embarrassingly popular, it became less practicable to exercise discrimination upon all the maidens who presented themselves. By November 1573 there were 2,000 candidates for the bounty of the Zucca trust. Voting on their qualifications consumed an excess of time for the 28 members of the Banca and Zonta, all of whom must in theory be present for the distribution to be valid. The lottery was now used in the first stage of the process of selection, for the purpose of reducing the number of candidates to reasonable proportions. Three-quarters of them were now

[74] A.S.V., *Dieci Savii sopra le Decime in Rialto*, busta 171, fascicolo 1185.
[75] *Ibid.*, busta 166, fascicolo 449. This figure does not include houses granted free of charge to chaplains of the Scuola and to *pizzochare* or female Franciscans.
[76] *Ibid.*, busta 164, fascicolo 1160.
[77] A.S.V., *Senato, Mar, filza* 109, under date 27 October 1590.
[78] A.S.V., *Scuola Grande di S. Rocco, seconda consegna*, vol. 47, f. 49.

eliminated by the lottery, without having their qualifications examined.[79] Similarly, in the regulations adopted for the Moro trust in 1578, it was provided that at least three hundred maidens (or one quarter of the total number presenting themselves at the first round) must have their qualifications examined:[80] it would not be enough to eliminate them by chance.

The history of the Scuole Grandi during the sixteenth and early seventeenth century testifies to the continued popularity and efficiency of a form of religious institution whose origins were rooted in the thirteenth and fourteenth centuries. The Scuola di San Rocco, founded in 1478, rapidly gained in wealth and status, until (by the early seventeenth century) it was probably the richest Scuola in Venice, and certainly the most generous to the poor. The character of the Scuole Grandi had undoubtedly changed over the centuries. They had lost their penitential character and had become increasingly worldly and ostentatious—expressing the magnificence and material splendour of Venetian piety, rather than any sense of human unworthiness or of the frailty of life on earth. From devotional societies they had developed into charitable institutions, channelling the gifts and bequests of the rich towards the poor. Fraternities of equals had divided into separate orders of rich and poor. The Scuole Grandi had been absorbed into the structure of the Venetian state, sometimes expressing its official propaganda, providing dignity, employment and honour to its estate of citizens. They were required to pass on the commands of the state to their lesser members, and to offer incentives to serve in the galleys of the Venetian navy—a duty which occasionally deflected them from their services to the poor. Nevertheless, the Scuole Grandi, for all these processes of adaptation, provided a link between the sixteenth century and its predecessors, an important inheritance from the past. The new forms of philanthropy introduced during the late fifteenth and the sixteenth century complemented these still-developing organizations of medieval origin—contrasting, but seldom conflicting, with them. The Scuole Grandi existed to serve the established, resident, respectable poor. They dealt with chronic poverty, of a kind endemic rather than epidemic in society. They did not cater primarily for vagrants or displaced persons, or cope with acute diseases requiring segregation and specialized care. They provided for the pious, respectable poor, not for criminals or prostitutes: their charity was geared to men punctilious

[79] A.S.R., *Registro delle Terminazioni 2*, ff. 337v.–338.
[80] *Ibid.*, *Registro delle Terminazioni 3*, f. 6.

in devotion, or young women of blameless reputation. They admitted many artisans, but did not plumb the lower depths of society. However, from the late fifteenth century onwards, and in the era of the Counter-Reformation, new religious movements collaborated with a state increasingly willing to extend its authority, and developed a programme of poor relief which extended and complemented the old machinery. With these new movements, the next part of this book will deal.

APPENDIX TO PART I

SUMS DISTRIBUTED BY THE SCUOLE GRANDI
IN CHARITY AND OTHER USES

A. *The Scuola di San Marco, 1550–60.*
(Compiled from entries on the Notatorii or minute books of the Scuola:
A.S.V., *Scuola Grande di S. Marco*, vols. 20 and 21, *Notatorii V* and *VI*).

(i) *Methods of dispensing charity*

TRUSTS: duc. 6,354, 500 *staia* (about 145 quarters) of flour, 250 *quarte* of wine, 16 cloaks.

Voted by members of the Banca and Zonta out of their own pockets to maidens who drew the slip marked 'Patientia' at the annual lottery in January: duc. 1,721.

Voted by the Banca and Zonta out of the funds at the disposal of the Scuola on receipt of a petition which had, from 24 August 1552 onwards, to be approved by two-thirds of them: duc. 485.

To the upkeep of the Hospital: approximately duc. 840.

To the surgeon: duc. 32.

To poor pensioners who received a regular monthly payment: duc. 500.

(ii) *Forms of charity*

Dowries		
By trust	duc. 6,205 to 334 *donzelle*	
By the Banca and Zonta	1,721 to 112 *donzelle*	
On petition	137 to 13 *donzelle*	
	duc. 8,063	

Outdoor relief

By trust	500 *staia* of flour
	250 *quarte* of wine
duc.	649 in cash
	16 cloaks

Relief of debtors
    duc. 213 on receipt of 35 petitions
Contribution to dowries for nuns—'per vestir per andar monacha'
    duc. 63 on receipt of 9 petitions
For relief of misery and sickness
    duc. 48 on receipt of 11 petitions
For the ransoming of slaves
    duc. 24 on receipt of 4 petitions

To the hospital
> duc. 840

To the surgeon
> duc. 32

130–40 marriageable girls regularly presented themselves at the annual balloting of *donzelle* for dowries every January. In each year ten would already have been disqualified as beneficiaries under the Tommaso Morosini trust. The Scuola di San Marco was thus meeting about one-third of the demand for dowries which was regularly put upon it. The average dowry which its resources enabled it to provide—excluding the special grants on petition—was about 18 ducats.

In the other tables in this Appendix I have accounted for the sums distributed by the Scuole after defraying the normal administrative expenses—salaries to the permanent staff, repairs to house property, ordinary taxation (*decime* and *tanse*, as distinct from war taxation to finance galley crews, etc.), and so on.

B. *The Scuola di San Marco, 1590, 1611 and 1614.*

CATEGORY A.

On the relief of the poor and sick		*1590*	*1611*	*1614*
Dowries to poor maidens	duc.	412	540	
Alms distributed at processions and charity burials, and to *faticanti*		470	372	332
To the paupers in hospital		117	72	
Salaries of doctors and medicines		100	72	86
Regular distributions of alms to the poor		90	4	24
Special grants to imprisoned debtors and others in distress		50		
	duc.	1,239	1,060	

CATEGORY B.

Ceremonial expenses				
Wax, *luminarie*, palms, etc.	duc.	603	500	600
Habits for brothers (*cape*)		60	60	
Musicians and singers		120	30	
		783	590	

CATEGORY C.

Payments to the clergy, churches, monasteries and religious congregations	*1590*	*1611*	*1614*
To chaplains and *mansonarii* appointed under trusts	179	163	
To churches, monasteries and congregations	40		
To the chaplain and acolyte of the Scuola itself	32		30
	251	163	

CATEGORY D.

Payments for the support of galley crews

Interest on a loan, probably made to help the Scuola
maintain its quota of galleots by a man named
Cubli, and the sum set aside annually to pay off
the loan   250

SUMMARY.	*1590*	*1611*
Category A	duc. 1,239 (54·51%)	duc. 1,060 (51·39%)
Category B	783 (34·45%)	590 (28·61%)
Category C	251 (11·04%)	163 (7·89%)
Category D	—	250 (12·11%)
	duc. 2,273 (100·00%)	2,063 (100·00%)

SOURCES: for 1590, A.S.V., *Senato, Mar, filza* 109, under date
27 October 1590.

for 1611, A.S.V., *Milizia da Mar, fascicolo* 723, under
date 22 February 1610 Venetian style.

for 1614, A.S.V., *Milizia da Mar, fascicolo* 706.

C. *The Scuola di San Giovanni Evangelista, 1614.*

CATEGORY A.

On the relief of the poor and sick

Dowries to poor maidens	duc. 1,560
Alms	
To the poor in the hospital of the Scuola and the neighbouring hospital of Ca' Badoer	206
To poor brothers of the Scuola (including an item entered as 'Despensa del Vedoa')	119
To poor men outside the Scuola, in Malamocco and possibly Castello	44
Odd jobs usually done by poor men	18
	387

Medical Attention

To doctors	(48)
To medicines	70
	118

Total expenditure in Category A: duc. 2,065.

190

CATEGORY B.
Ceremonial expenses
On properties for processions

Wax for processions and small church expenses	duc. 574
Processions and the festivals of St John and	
Holy Thursday	420
Palms and charity burials	60
Habits for brothers (*sachi e capi*)	60
	1,114
To musicians, organist and singers	(115)

Total expenditure in Category B: duc. 1,229.

CATEGORY C.
Payments to the clergy

To *mansonarii*	duc. 407
To chaplains and priests of the Scuola	260
To monasteries, parish churches and parish priests	42

Total expenditure in Category C: duc. 709.

CATEGORY D.
Payments for the support of galley crews

30 per cent tax on the trusts and the fund for the provision of dowries (*sacho*), to contribute to the sum exacted from the Scuola for the support of galley crews	duc. 640
Interest on loans made to the Scuola to enable it to provide galley crews	150
	790

SUMMARY.

Category A	duc. 2,065	43·09%
Category B	1,229	25·64%
Category C	709	14·79%
Category D	790	16.48%
	duc. 4,793	100·00%

SOURCE: A.S.V., *Milizia da Mar, fascicolo* 706.

D. *The Scuola della Misericordia in 1614 and 1627.*

CATEGORY A.

		1614	1627
On the relief of the poor and sick			
Alms			
To the poor in general, probably most of them brothers of the Scuola	duc.	168	591
To five poor in the Ospedaletto		75	
To six poor at *lire* 7 each per month			81
To two poor orphans in the parish of S. Marcilian		10	10
		253	682
To dowries for poor maidens		355	489
To the liberation of prisoners		258	543
Medical Attention			
To medicines	duc.	60	110
Salaries to two doctors		48	48
		108	158
Charity burials		50	
Repairs to almshouses		19	25
Total expenditure in Category A:	duc.	1,043	1,897

CATEGORY B.

Ceremonial expenses: building and processions

		1614	1627
For the building and adornment of the Scuola	duc.	1,174	
On properties for processions			
Wax for processions		865	620
Other expenditure on apparatus			160
Palms		65	50
Bread for *luminarie*		40	
Habits for brothers (*sachi*)		15	
		985	830

		1614	1627
To four musicians and singers	duc.	88	59 (includes payments to sextons also)
Total expenditure in Category B:	duc.	2,247	889

192

CATEGORY C.

*Payments made to chaplains and mansonarii, and to
churches, monasteries and religious congregations.*

To chaplains and *mansonarii* of the Scuola itself	duc.	190	152
To *mansonarii* appointed under trust		40	40
To monasteries and nunneries		43	84
		273	276
Total expenditure in Category C:	duc.	273	276

CATEGORY D.

Payments for the support of galley crews

Interest on capital borrowed to help furnish galley crews		300	870

SUMMARY.		*1614*		*1627*	
Category A	duc.	1,043	(27·01%)	1,897	(48·25%)
Category B		2,247	(58·17%)	889	(22.61%)
Category C		273	(7·06%)	276	(7·02%)
Category D		300	(7·76%)	870	(22·12%)
	duc.	3,863	(100·00%)	3,932	(100·00%)

SOURCE: A.S.V., *Milizia da Mar, fascicolo* 706.

PART II: THE NEW PHILANTHROPY

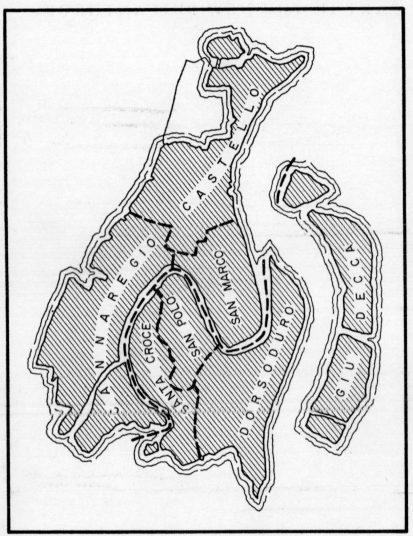

THE SIX SESTIERI OF VENICE AND THE GIUDECCA

1

HOSPITALS DURING THE FIFTEENTH CENTURY

Following leads given by German predecessors, English historians have often credited sixteenth-century Europeans with devising a new approach to philanthropy and poor relief. According to this thesis, the charity of private individuals and the social legislation of governments and town councils abruptly became more rational and systematic. There was, arguably, a significant move in this direction during the years which ran from 1520 to 1560, or over some fraction of that period. At this point, men began to concentrate, not on obtaining spiritual benefits for almsgivers, but on promoting the physical welfare of the recipients of charity and relief, and on furthering the interests of the society of which both giver and receiver formed part. Professor Jordan, in his studies of English philanthropy between 1480 and 1660, sets out to discuss 'the momentous shift from men's primarily religious preoccupations to the secular concerns that have moulded the thought and institutions of the past three centuries'.[1] Some sociologists and students of philanthropy, among them Professor Jordan, have connected this shift with the triumph of the Protestant Reformation and with the enforced reduction in opportunities for leaving money to religious uses.[2] Writers of an older generation, such as William Ashley and the Webbs, concentrating on public legislation rather than private initiative, reminded their readers that the introduction of rational, discriminating and occasionally brutal poor laws was not peculiar to Protestant countries in the sixteenth century. Many west European cities and states responded to a common economic challenge in a broadly similar way—the root explanation lay, if anything, in a general willingness on the part of local or greater governments to extend their competence and assume wider responsibilities, in the name of humanity, discipline and public order.[3] Some of these authors, nonetheless,

[1] W. K. Jordan, *Philanthropy in England, 1480–1660* (London, 1959), p. 16.

[2] For some interesting examples of this view, culled from recent historical writing, see Natalie Zemon Davis, 'Poor relief, humanism and heresy: the case of Lyon', *Studies in medieval and Renaissance history*, V (1968), pp. 218–20. Cf. also the remarks of R. H. Bremner, 'Modern attitudes towards charity and relief', *Comparative Studies in Society and History*, I (1958–9), p. 377; and above, Introduction, pp. 11–12.

[3] W. J. Ashley, *An introduction to English economic history and theory* (London,

pointed a dramatic contrast between the undiscriminating, haphazard and decentralized charity of the medieval Catholic Church, and the relatively well-conceived policies of sixteenth-century magistrates. Albert Emminghaus, a German student of social problems, advanced in its crudest form the doctrine that the aims of Church and State were fundamentally divergent—the one over-indulgent, the other harshly repressive;[4] the Webbs retained this view in a moderated form.[5]

These classic opinions are, however, open to serious objections. No sharp contrast can fairly be drawn between undiscriminating, Church-dominated, 'medieval' charity (using the term 'medieval' to mean 'before the sixteenth century') and discriminate, lay-controlled, 'early modern' social policies. Moreover, these chapters will set out to show that at least in the sixteenth-century Catholic state of Venice there was no obvious divergence of attitude to the problems of poverty between the Venetian government and the new religious Orders within the Catholic Church. It is impossible to demonstrate which inspired the other—one should, perhaps, abandon the notion that there was any such simple one-way relationship between the two, and merely stress that their aims were fundamentally similar. Certainly, the relief of the poor was not, in any simple sense, 'secularized'—save that members of the laity remained prominent in the administration of funds destined for the poor, and permanent lay magistracies acquired increased powers of supervision over charitable institutions. At least in theory, the professed aims of poor relief were spiritual as well as corporal, and they were closely connected with the determination of religious reformers to reclaim souls through the raising of moral standards and the assertion of the power of the sacraments.

In general, poor relief in western Europe in the fourteenth and fifteenth centuries fails in many respects to conform to the image created by later historians of the persuasion described above. Many changes once supposedly located in the sixteenth century were anticipated, at least in theory and in principle, by earlier generations. Very likely, some sixteenth-century changes in philanthropy and social legislation were changes in degree rather than in kind; quantitative changes, rather than changes in principle; changes stimulated by graver economic needs, rather than by radical alterations in intellectual attitudes. The new religious movements of the sixteenth-century Catholic Church

1893), Part II, ch. 5, pp. 305–76; F. R. Salter, *Some early tracts on poor relief* (London, 1926); Beatrice and Sidney Webb, *English poor law history*, Part I: *The old poor law* (new edition, with an introduction by W. A. Robson, London, 1963), pp. 30 f.

[4] Albert Emminghaus, Introduction to *Poor relief in different parts of Europe* (London, 1873), pp. 7–8.

[5] Webbs, *English poor law history*, Part I, pp. 23 f.

often embodied a conscious effort to return to pure originals, to ideals forgotten or corrupted by the passage of years, and Franciscan attitudes to the poor, formulated in the thirteenth century, flourished again in the sixteenth. To say this is not to belittle the achievements of sixteenth-century Europeans, for much significant historical change is quantitative rather than qualitative, and much revolution is accomplished by revival.

Possibly, in the sixteenth century, the scale of the problem of urban poverty changed still more than the principles on which it was solved. Certainly in some parts of Europe, including Brabant, there occurred a very marked increase in the proportion of poor persons in large and small towns, between the early fifteenth and the early sixteenth century, as a result of heavy immigration in search of work or relief from a countryside already beggared by agricultural depression over the years from about 1380 to 1450.[5a]

Medieval Catholicism has often been accused of encouraging haphazard and even actively pernicious charity by encouraging the giver to think only of the benefit to his own soul, and not of the effect of his alms on their recipient. Judging by later history, it is dangerous to assume that at any given time one can distinguish a single, unitary Catholic attitude to the problem of the poor—in the sixteenth century, the views of Mendicants in Flanders and Spain differed radically from those of Ignatius Loyola, of Italian Jesuits and of the Somaschian Order.[6] Then, at least, there was a wide spectrum of opinion among the Catholic clergy, with no clear consensus emerging. One can only seize on particular sectors of Catholic opinion. It is certain that twelfth-century canonists, expounding conflicting patristic texts in Gratian's collection, concluded that almsgivers were bound to exercise a certain discrimination, and to choose carefully on whom they bestowed their charity. Some merely argued that this choice should be exercised when funds were inadequate to supply all the poor who asked for assistance. Others held that there were undeserving paupers who, being idle or dishonest, would be corrupted by the receipt of charity, and ought to be denied it on principle.[7] Medieval Kings of France—Louis IX in the

---

[5a] Cf. Bronislaw Geremek, 'La popolazione marginale tra il Medioevo e l'èra moderna', *Studi Storici*, IX (1968).

[6] See below, pp. 281–6.

[7] Brian Tierney, 'The Decretists and the "deserving poor"', *Comparative Studies in Society and History*, I (1958–9); Brian Tierney, *Medieval poor law: a sketch of canonical theory and its application in England* (Berkeley–Los Angeles, 1959), pp. 47 f. On the other hand, R. F. Bennett, *The early Dominicans* (Cambridge, 1937), pp. 114–115, holds that, although the need to discriminate was certainly mentioned by some early Dominican preachers, it was not heavily stressed.

O

thirteenth century, John II in the fourteenth—attacked idle vagrants with legislation, and John II ordered the wardens and governors of French hospitals on no account to grant them shelter.[8] There is no reason to think this a policy promoted by a state in conflict with the Church, adopting a social attitude essentially different from the official ecclesiastical position. With good reason, in the early sixteenth century the city government of Ypres, a pioneer of poor relief, justified its schemes by saying that 'the canon laws do determine that alms should be given to feeble and weak persons, to such as are broken with sickness or forgone in years and to them that through impotency be not able to get their living: and seeing also that the same laws reckon those whole and strong persons that take alms as thieves and robbers'.[9] It found support in established ecclesiastical theory.

Legislation against vagrancy, and the open condemnation of idleness in poverty, were no new phenomena in the sixteenth century. The dislocation of the economy, and the drastic reduction of population in parts of Europe by the famines and epidemics of the fourteenth century, evoked many laws of this nature. Some, like the English Statute of Labourers of 1349, have been interpreted simply as the attempt of the rulers to 'freeze' the population—to deny economic improvement or geographical mobility to poor persons who had gained bargaining power by the shrinking of the labour force. Others, like the Statute of 1388, proved more constructive. They provided, not only for the suppression of vagrancy, but also for the relief of 'impotent' paupers genuinely unable to earn a living.[10] Again, in Spain, a law issued in 1387 at Bribiesca by John II, King of Castile, later provided the foundation for more constructive poor laws introduced into Castile after 1540.[11] Indeed, as the Belgian historian Bonenfant suggested, the readiness of so many sixteenth-century governments to introduce poor laws during and after the 1520's may partly be explained by the existence of many medieval precedents for them.[12] Certainly, in England in 1547, such theologically conservative bishops as Tunstal, Bonner,

---

[8] Jean Imbert, *Les hôpitaux en droit canonique (du décret de Gratien à la secularisation de l'administration de l'Hôtel-Dieu de Paris en 1505)* (Paris, 1947), pp. 118–19.

[9] Salter, *Tracts on poor relief*, pp. 50–1.

[10] Ashley, *English economic history*, pp. 336–7; E. M. Leonard, *The early history of English poor relief* (Cambridge, 1900), pp. 3 f.; Webbs, *English poor law*, I, pp. 24–6.

[11] Domiñgo Soto, *Deliberacion en la causa de los pobres* (Salamanca, 1545), ff. 3v.–4.

[12] Paul Bonenfant, 'Les origines et le caractère de la reforme de la bienfaisance publique aux Pays-Bas sous le règne de Charles-Quint', *Revue belge de philologie et d'histoire*, V–VI (1926–7).

Aldridge and Day were fully prepared to vote for the bill introducing the most savage of the vagrancy laws.[13]

In the domain of private charity, as distinct from public policy, recent inquiries into the habits of London testators in the fifteenth and early sixteenth century have suggested that many of the philanthropic principles of Tudor merchants were already present in the minds of their fifteenth-century predecessors. The real changes of principle occurred in the spheres of education and religion, rather than in that of poor relief—for Londoners of the post-Reformation years undoubtedly showed a greater concern with secondary, rather than with university, education, whilst 'changes in belief ended the endowment of chantries and other forms of prayers for the dead, and, incidentally, freed money for other charitable ends'. Otherwise, Londoners of the fifteenth and of the late sixteenth century willed their wealth to the seven bodily works of mercy in much the same way—the scale of the charity altered, rather than the principles behind it.[14]

Likewise, in some parts of Tuscany, testators and benefactors were already showing marked interest in the foundation and endowment of hospitals during the fourteenth and fifteenth centuries. Here, in the city and district of San Gimignano, generous legacies at or about the time of the Black Death began to increase the proportion of landed wealth held, not by private persons, but by ecclesiastical bodies, including hospitals. The share of ecclesiastical corporations in the taxable wealth of the region rose from 12 per cent in 1315 to 28·8 per cent in 1475. Within this general category, the landed property of hospitals expanded far more rapidly than that of any other religious corporations, and their economic gains outstripped those of monasteries and convents—which, however, recovered a very substantial lead by 1549 and had greatly increased it by 1674.[14a] Hence, in this area at least, testators showed a stronger preoccupation with social and charitable work in the fourteenth and fifteenth centuries than in the sixteenth and seventeenth—when the hospitals had apparently reached the limits of their expansion. Similarly, in Pistoia, urban hospitals were amassing wealth in the later Middle Ages. The Hospital of the Ceppo, founded about 1277, had by 1428 become the richest religious corporation in the town, and, over the same century and a half, the number of

[13] C. S. L. Davies, 'Slavery and Protector Somerset: the Vagrancy Act of 1547', *Economic History Review*, XIX (1966), p. 540.

[14] J. A. F. Thomson, 'Piety and charity in late medieval London', *Journal of Ecclesiastical History*, XVI (1965).

[14a] See Enrico Fiumi, *Storia economica e sociale di San Gimignano* (Florence, 1961), pp. 216–18, 220–3.

hospitals rose from four to eleven. Here were signs, as Pistoia's latest historian holds, of 'a new, charitable and social emphasis in religious practice'.[14b]

In Italy, too, a new movement towards the reorganization of poor relief was unmistakably gaining impetus by the middle of the fifteenth century. This was closely linked with the activities of Observant Franciscan preachers, who helped to publicize and disseminate certain new forms of charitable organization. Identifying themselves with the poor, they strove to promote their interests, to defend them both against exploitation by usurers and against theft of their rightful property by maladministered charities. The Observance attempted to return to the strict, literal interpretation of the Rule and ideals of Francis of Assisi. Its status had risen substantially in the fifteenth century through the personal prestige and influence of some of its leaders, such as the Vicars-General Bernardino of Siena and Giovanni of Capistrano, who stood high in papal favour. The most famous and permanent memorials to the Franciscans were the Monti di Pietà, low-interest Christian loan banks originally designed to relieve the poor of dependence on Jewish and Christian moneylenders, and inspired by a mixture of religious and economic motives. The question of moneylending is complex enough to demand treatment in a section of its own, and so its discussion must be deferred.[15] But some Franciscan preachers concerned themselves with other forms of institution, less essentially connected with their Order. In the western, Lombard provinces of the Venetian Republic and in the Duchy of Milan they helped, about 1450, to found large, centralized general hospitals in the interests of greater administrative efficiency.

Before the close of the fourteenth century, Gian Galeazzo Visconti, first Duke of Milan, had taken steps to increase his authority over charitable institutions, and to provide more efficient means for the care of the sick and begging poor in his capital. In 1396, in Milan itself, he appointed a commission to patrol the city in search of sick paupers and beggars requiring accommodation in hospital. The *Officium Pietatis Pauperum*, established in 1405, after his death, consisted of a mixed board of ecclesiastics and laymen, subject to the Vicar-General of the diocese, and charged with sheltering the poor who wandered through Milan. From 1401, a lay nobleman acted as

---

[14b] Cf. David Herlihy, *Medieval and Renaissance Pistoia: the social history of an Italian town, 1200–1430* (New Haven–London, 1967), pp. 245–9.

[15] See below, Part III. For a recent account of the origins of the Observance, see John Moorman, *A history of the Franciscan Order from its origins to the year 1517* (Oxford, 1968), pp. 369–77, 441–56.

'governor and rector' of all hospitals in the Duchy.[16] Clerical and lay authorities were both contributing to a more systematic and less casual policy. In Milan and in Venetian Lombardy, the bishops began to take the lead in the middle of the century. The citizen council of Brescia put forward, in 1427, a project to establish a centralized 'great hospital'. But the outbreak of war between the Venetian Republic and the Duchy of Milan temporarily smothered the plans. The restoration of peace fourteen years later did, however, bring their revival. At this point, Alberto of Sarteano, a prominent Observant preacher, encouraged the citizens. In April 1442, Pope Eugenius IV wrote to the Brescians expressing his approval of their proposals, and announcing his intention of sending his own favourite, Pietro del Monte, as Bishop of Brescia. Del Monte would carry the plans through: if the Brescians wanted their hospital, they must accept the Bishop nominated by the Pope. In collaboration with Alberto of Sarteano, Pietro del Monte smoothed the way to the official foundation of the new general hospital in May 1447.[17]

This Brescian foundation formed part of a wider movement in Lombardy in the late 1440's. The general hospital of Milan, where Visconti rule had favoured centralization, was founded in the spring of 1448.[18] Again, on 8 April 1449, the Venetian governors of Bergamo and its leading native magistrates, the Anziani, determined to unite the small hospitals of the city into a single comprehensive one.[19] At least in Milan, the pattern of events resembled that of Brescia. Enrico Rampini, the Cardinal Archbishop, was the public dignitary most obviously responsible for the new foundation; an Observant Franciscan, Michele Carcano of Milan, may have helped to rouse enthusiasm for it; papal confirmation followed. The history of the general hospitals of Milan and the Venetian Republic does not support the view that the Catholic Church as a whole was fundamentally inefficient or corrupt in its administration of charity at the close of the Middle Ages. Co-operation between ecclesiastical and lay authorities produced these hospitals: it found symbolic expression in the opening ceremonies held at Brescia in April 1447. The Bishop himself laid the first foundation stone, and was followed by the two Venetian governors of the city.

[16] G. C. Bascapè, 'L'assistenza e la beneficenza a Milano dall'alto medioevo alla fine della dinastia sforzesca', Fondazione G. Treccani degli Alfieri, Storia di Milano, VIII (Milan, 1957), pp. 394–6, 400–1.

[17] Agostino Zanelli, 'Pietro del Monte', Archivio Storico Lombardo, anno 34 (1907), vol. VIII, pp. 57–9.

[18] Bascapè, 'L'assistenza a Milano', pp. 402 f.

[19] Bortolo Belotti, Storia di Bergamo e dei Bergamaschi (3 vols., Milan, 1940), II, pp. 83–4.

Then came the Abbot of San Faustino Maggiore, of the Venetian family of Marcello. The fifth and sixth stones were laid by Brescian citizens, one of them the chronicler Cristoforo Da Soldo, who duly recorded the event.[20]

Behind the new foundations lay dissatisfaction with the inefficiency and corruption of the small, separate hospitals, unco-ordinated and unsupervised by any effective central organization. This dissatisfaction had parallels elsewhere in Europe: it was mirrored, for example, in the preamble to the English Statute for the reformation of hospitals, in 1414, and in the complaints of the Commons under Henry IV and Henry V.[21] The foundation decree of the Great Hospital of San Marco in Bergamo, officially enacted on 5 November 1457, clearly stated the motives which lay behind its establishment. There was, as yet, no 'worthy and well-founded' hospital in Bergamo,

> though both in the city and in its suburbs there are many hospitals and religious institutions in which divine worship, the fabric, and the relief of the poor are neglected, and where the revenues are consumed in uses to which they have not been assigned. This arises because of negligence on the part of their staff, because of their lack of funds, and because of the misgovernment of the many men who are necessary to run them. We have therefore decreed that in this great city, which has offered to carry out this holy, pious and praiseworthy work, one single great general hospital with a chapel ... should be constructed.

This hospital should be formed by the fusion of eleven small hospitals, some of which were ancient foundations, of the eleventh and twelfth centuries. The statute declared that the union had been effected by Giovanni Barozzi, Bishop of Bergamo, and by the Vicepodestà and Capitano, in collaboration with the prelates of the cathedral and the cathedral chapter, and with the Anziani and the whole citizen council. The Bishop and clergy enjoyed the power to influence and sometimes actually control the appointment of the hospital's leading officials, especially of the Patrone, responsible for defending the civil and property rights of the hospital. The governors of the city and the native Bergamese Anziani collaborated with the Bishop in the election of a board of hospital governors, to hold office for one year, with the possibility of confirmation for a second. Like most of the greater medieval hospitals, this institution assumed responsibility for the souls

[20] Cristoforo Da Soldo, *Memorie delle guerre contra la Signoria di Venezia dall'anno 1437 fino al 1468*, in L. A. Muratori, *Rerum Italicarum Scriptores*, XXI (Milan, 1732), coll. 839–40.

[21] R. M. Clay, *The hospitals of mediaeval England* (London, 1909), pp. 212, 222, 228–9.

of its inmates, as well as for their bodies: as a 'cure of souls', it was subject at least in certain respects to episcopal jurisdiction. The Patrone, and the governing board of 'ministers' and counsellors, elected a chaplain to care for the souls of the poor and to celebrate Mass daily in the chapel. The appointment must be confirmed within eight days by the cathedral chapter, and the candidate must finally appear before the Bishop, 'from whom he shall receive his licence to exercise this cure of souls and to do the other things which pertain to his office'.[22] In view of the essentially religious character of most major hospitals, some episcopal intervention was almost inevitable in their establishment and subsequent administration.[23] This was so at least in the recently absorbed Lombard provinces of the Venetian Republic, which did not share Venetian distrust of the clergy as administrators.

In the Lombard cities, the centralization of hospitals was not all-embracing. Some institutions retained a separate existence—certainly in Milan and Bergamo. The Hospital of San Marco in Bergamo did not absorb the hospital of the Maddalena, a relatively large institution governed by the local fraternities of the Disciplinati. This was originally a general hospital, lodging beggars, pilgrims and other paupers; but at some stage in its career, before the last quarter of the sixteenth century, it acquired an unusually specialized function—the care of the insane, the senile and the mentally defective.[24] Nevertheless, the mid-fifteenth century saw a significant tendency towards greater concentration in the interests of greater efficiency. To judge by later evidence, the general hospitals probably assumed the double function of caring for the sick and aged, and of caring for foundlings and orphans—often through an elaborate system of farming them out to wetnurses and foster-mothers. Such, at least, were their duties by the end of the sixteenth century.[25] It may be that the ultimate source of these new foundations lay in Tuscany and Siena. Alberto of Sarteano, himself from the region of Siena, had encouraged the Brescians to copy the hospitals of Florence and Siena. Even before this, in 1401, Gian

[22] Foundation charter of the Bergamese hospital, printed in A. G. Roncalli and Pietro Forno, *Gli atti della visita apostolica di San Carlo Borromeo a Bergamo, 1575* (2 vols. in 5, Florence, 1936–57), I/ii, pp. 218 f.

[23] On this question in general, cf. Imbert, *Les hôpitaux*, pp. 67 f. Cf. also Clay, *Mediaeval hospitals*, pp. xvii–xviii: a hospital 'was an ecclesiastical, not a medical, institution. It was for care rather than cure: for the relief of the body, when possible, but pre-eminently for the refreshment of the soul. By manifold religious observances, the staff sought to elevate and discipline character. They endeavoured, as the body decayed, to strengthen the soul and prepare it for the future life.'

[24] Roncalli and Forno, *Atti di Borromeo*, I/ii, pp. 133–5, 216–17; A.S.V., *Sindici Inquisitori in Terra Ferma*, busta 63, ff. 70, 111.

[25] Roncalli and Forno, *Atti di Borromeo*, I/ii, pp. 246 f.; A.S.V., *Sindici Inquisitori in Terra Ferma*, busta 63, ff. 70, 110r.–v.; *ibid.*, busta 64, ff. 57–8.

Galeazzo Visconti had declared that the hospitals of his capital and Duchy 'shall be governed and regulated in the same way as the hospital of the city of Siena'.[26]

The movement continued in Lombardy in the second half of the fifteenth century, though how far it affected the Veneto as a whole remains uncertain. The Observant Michele Carcano publicized the new system by earnestly 'recommending' it to the authorities of Como, of Piacenza (in 1471), and (in 1479) of the Venetian subject town of Crema.[27] The institution he inspired there may have been the large foundling hospital described long afterwards in the reports of Venetian governors.[28] Further east, the cities of Verona, Vicenza and Padua were less obviously affected by these recommendations, though they all acquired Monti di Pietà. In the sixteenth century, they apparently maintained no outstandingly large general hospitals as centres for the indoor relief of the poor. To the north-east of Venice itself, there seemed—again on the evidence of later governors' reports—to be more tendency to concentrate on one large, heavily endowed central institution, rather than on a variety of small ones. Udine possessed a single large hospital, that of the Misericordia, in the middle and late sixteenth century.[29] Still more conspicuous for wealth was the Hospital of Santa Maria dei Battuti in Treviso:[30] evidently founded or administered by fraternities corresponding to the Venetian Scuole Grandi. But how these concentrations arose, and on whose initiative, is not known.

The methods of the Venetians themselves diverged from those of their subject cities. They did not establish a general hospital or introduce a Monte di Pietà. The Venetian government viewed with qualified enthusiasm the campaigns of the Observant Bernardino Tomitano of Feltre, whose preaching they more than once restrained on account of its rabble-rousing powers[31]—although for a time Venice harboured Michele Carcano. Ecclesiastical authorities showed less tendency to take independent action in Venice itself. A great number of small

[26] Zanelli, 'Pietro del Monte', pp. 57–9; Bascapè, 'L'assistenza a Milano', p. 396.

[27] Paolo Sevesi, 'Il Beato Michele Carcano di Milano, O.F.M.', *Archivum Franciscanum Historicum*, III–IV (1910–11), III, pp. 658–60; IV, pp. 29, 32, 45.

[28] Cf. especially A.S.V., *Collegio, Relazioni, busta* 40, report of Zaccaria Balbi, 24 April 1633.

[29] A.S.V., *Collegio, Relazioni, busta* 49, reports of Girolamo Mocenigo, 27 August 1574; Stefano Viaro, 4 November 1599; Vincenzo Capello, 12 June 1615; Alvise Mocenigo, 3 August 1622; Federico Sanuto, 15 March 1635.

[30] A.S.V., *Collegio, Relazioni, busta* 48, reports of Pietro Pizzamano, 6 June 1564; Giovanni Michiel, 18 June 1578; Stefano Viaro, 6 December 1595; Antonio Mocenigo, 9 February 1605 Venetian style; Francesco Tiepolo, 4 September 1607; Alvise Moro, 17 March 1609; Vincenzo Pisani, 10 May 1612; Almorò Dolfin, 3 June 1625; Antonio Zeno, 4 April 1628; Paolo Querini, 1 July 1639.

[31] See below, pp. 463–4.

hospitals consequently retained their separate identities in Venice. There are no available estimates of their numbers from the late fifteenth century: but a survey compiled in the second half of the sixteenth century, certainly between 1561 and about 1600, lists over forty hospitals which were, almost certainly, of medieval origin.[32] Only one large hospital served the needs of the city as a whole: the foundling institute of the Pietà, with headquarters in the parish of San Giovanni in Bragora, near San Marco. The history of the Pietà remains all too obscure—but it had, apparently, been founded about 1346 by a Franciscan, Friar Pietro of Assisi. From his practice of wandering the streets, crying with a loud and tearful voice, 'Pietà, pietà!' he acquired the name of 'Friar Pieruzzo della Pietà'. The hospital was administered by two confraternities, one of men and the other of matrons, which probably bore a superficial resemblance to the other Scuole in their constitutional structure, and which devoted themselves to the specific work of supervising the relief of orphans.[33] The Pietà was partly an organization for farming out foundlings to wetnurses; in the mid-sixteenth century, the numbers ran to several hundreds—to 800 charges in 1551, and 1,200 in 1559.[34]

Apart from the Pietà, which specialized in this function, there is no evidence that Venetian hospitals were conceived on the grand scale before the early sixteenth century. Surviving information about the number of inmates of the older hospitals after 1560 suggests that the average size of a Venetian hospital enabled it to admit about ten people, often widows or old men. Seven women's hospitals—those of Ca Badoer, San Boldo, San Leonardo, the Crosecchieri, the Maddalena, Ca Bandi and Bernardo Pusco—contained about 70 inmates between them. The greater part of the forty-odd hospitals of Venice probably conformed to this pattern, with one or two larger institutions for between twenty and fifty poor or 'wretched' persons emerging from the broader mass. One fourteenth-century foundation, the hospital of San Giobbe, had as many as 120 almshouses in 1574.

There were two hospitals of a distinctively medieval character—a pilgrim hospital, and a leprosary dedicated to San Lazzaro and suitably isolated on a lagoon island. Another hospice for pilgrims had, in the fourteenth century, undergone conversion, and, by order of the Great Council, been turned into the Casa di Dio for some fifty respectable

---

[32] See below, Appendix, pp. 423–8.

[33] Pierluigi Bembo, *Delle istituzioni di beneficenza nella città e provincia di Venezia* (Venice, 1859), pp. 3–4; Giuseppe Tassini, *Curiosità veneziane, ovvero Origini delle denominazioni stradali*, ed. Lino Moretti (Venice, no date), p. 516.

[34] A.S.V., *Senato, Terra*, reg. 1550–1, f. 89v., 31 January 1550 Venetian style; reg. 1557–8, ff. 169v.–170, 18 February 1558 Venetian style.

widows.[35] Elsewhere in Europe, there were parallel signs of decreasing sympathy with the needs of pilgrims.[36] Leprosy was dying out, and the hospital for lepers held only five persons in 1528.[37] But another island haven, the Lazzaretto, existed to deal with the undiminished menace of bubonic plague.

Of the remaining institutions, twenty-four seem to have been designed for the reception of women. Nine of these hospices sheltered female Tertiaries or *pizzocare*, members of the Third Orders founded in the thirteenth century by St Francis and St Dominic to receive men and women whose married status or other circumstances precluded them from joining the first two Orders. Tertiaries promised to lead an austere life and to devote themselves to good works, which included almsgiving.[38] But the Third Orders performed another important social function, in providing a recognized status for those who joined them. They received women who did not choose or could not afford to marry or enter a cloister: who found difficulty in solving the economic problem of the dowry. Some of the institutions for Tertiaries were specifically described as hospitals: those of Santa Giustina in Castello, of San Canciano in Cannaregio, and of Santa Maria dei Carmeni in the parish of San Barnabà in Dorsoduro. Six others were listed as charitable institutions in the late sixteenth century.

Three professional associations—the guilds or crafts of bakers, tailors and silkspinners—possessed their own hospitals, which they probably reserved either to their own members or to their relatives and relicts. Among religious fraternities, the Scuole Grandi maintained five small hospitals between them, as well as the hospital for Tertiaries in San Canciano governed by the Scuola di San Giovanni Evangelista. Other hospitals of the 'closed' type, restricted to members of a narrow fraternity or social group, were the institutions serving the foreign communities of the city—especially the privileged group of German merchants or artisans whose headquarters, the Fondaco dei Tedeschi, lay at Rialto. Three hospitals served German residents or Germans passing through Venice, whilst an Armenian hospital stood at San Giuliano, off the Merceria. Finally, there were ten other hospitals, whose uses must remain uncertain, but which probably accepted aged paupers. The last major foundation of the fifteenth century, the Hospital of Gesù Cristo di Sant'Antonio, was eventually restricted to ancient

---

[35] Bembo, *Istituzioni di beneficenza*, p. 273.
[36] Cf. Clay, *Mediaeval hospitals*, pp. 6 f.
[37] D.M.S., XLIX, coll. 110, 115, 29, 31 October 1528.
[38] Cf. Bede Jarrett, art. 'Third Orders', *Catholic Encyclopedia*, XIV (New York, 1912), p. 637.

mariners and ex-servicemen, or to others who had deserved well of the state.

The small independent hospitals—especially those designed for widows or destitute women, a section of society with slight earning-power—remained typical of Venetian organization. There was little to draw them together. Admittedly, a few charities were placed under a single board of administrators—the Procurators of St Mark's. All monasteries, convents, churches and hospitals possessed Procurators or advocates to defend their temporal interests: but the Procurators of St Mark's had gained a unique prestige. This had inspired many testators to use them as trustees or executors for the administration of pious and charitable bequests—in much the same way as they employed the Guardians and governing bodies of the Scuole Grandi. The Procurators were magistrates of unblemished integrity, who had completed long careers of public service. They held office for life, and enjoyed precedence over all other magistrates; Doges were almost invariably recruited from their ranks. Their position conferred a perpetual place in the Senate, and, until the constitutional crisis of 1582–3, entry to the Council of Ten also. These privileges apart, the Procurators were charged with the specific duty of acting as guardians to Venetian orphans. As Gasparo Contarini explained in the 1520's:

> 'Their office is to take upon them the defence and tutorshippe of Orphelins, who being under age, and their fathers deade without making any will, have not any tutor or overseer appointed them.'[39]

Sixteenth-century writers, describing the history of the office, usually concluded that until the end of the twelfth century, there had been only one Procurator, who guarded the fabric of the church. But Sebastiano Ziani, Doge from 1173 to 1178, had left an extensive and complicated bequest which required the attention of a second Procurator to administer it. The Doge's example inspired many others. Contarini described how

> In times passed this office was of passing great and honourable estimation, not onely within *Venice*, but also in forrayne regions, in so much that not onely the subiectes and neere borderers, but also forreners and strangers, made them by testament their executors, and put wholly into their handes the administration of their goodes, during the minority of their children. Likewise great summes of money are committed to them,

---

[39] Gasparo Contarini, *De magistratibus et Republica venetorum* (Basel, 1547), pp. 116, 169–73—as translated by Lewes Lewkenor, *The Commonwealth and Government of Venice* (London, 1599), pp. 81, 122–5. Cf. also Gaetano Cozzi, 'Federico Contarini: un antiquario veneziano tra Rinascimento e Controriforma', *Bollettino dell'Istituto di Storia della Società e dello Stato veneziano*, III (1961), pp. 190 f.

to bee by their discretion dispensed and bestowed among the poore, so that in these times of ours great and mighty summes of money are committed to their fidelity, as well to the use of Orphelins, and the poore, as otherwise. This office was at the first instituted, to the ende that the heritages and substances of those citizens that should eyther die in service of their countrey, or in traficke of marchandise among forraine nations, shoulde not bee by fraude misemployed or diverted from their heires. . . .

By the time of Francesco Foscari, elected Doge in 1423, there was an establishment of nine Procurators, of whom three were simply concerned with supervising 'the royal, sumptuous and magnificent Temple of Saint *Marke*'. The remaining six carried out duties of wardship and acted as public trustees. They divided their responsibilities geographically, and three Procurators presided over the area to the right of the Grand Canal, three over the other side of the city. This division into the Procuratia de Ultra and the Procuratia de Citra dated from the reign of Doge Renier Zeno, about 1270. In the course of the sixteenth century, the honour attached to the title of Procurator—no matter how acquired—inspired the creation and sale of supernumerary Procuratorships to raise money in such grave crises as the wars of the League of Cambrai and of Lepanto.[40]

The Procurators had thus acquired their influence over Venetian charities by the spontaneous desire of testators, not by the determination of the government to exercise surveillance over charities. In the mid-sixteenth century, the Procurators administered eight hospitals. These included the pilgrims' hospital in Castello; the Hospital for Poor Armenians, reputedly part of Doge Ziani's ancient legacy; three hospitals for women; a block of tiny houses for Tertiaries, known as the Corte delle Pizzocare, at San Moisè; and two other hospitals, the Trinità in Castello and the Veriseli at the Santi Apostoli.[41] In addition, they disposed of substantial numbers of almshouses, which probably differed technically from hospitals in that they provided only shelter, and not spiritual services. The situation was probably essentially similar at the close of the fifteenth century. Thus, only about one-sixth of the hospitals in Venice were united even by subjection to the same board of governors—let alone by concentration under one roof. The Scuole Grandi were subject only to the general surveillance of the Council of Ten, and the professional hospitals to that of the Giustizia Vecchia. Neither of these magistracies was specifically concerned with

---

[40] Summary of the history of the institution, compiled from the study of various writers on Venice, in Lewes Lewkenor, *Divers observations upon the Venetian Commonwealth*, appended to his translation of Contarini, at pp. 160–2. Cf. also Girolamo Bardi, *Delle cose notabili della città di Venetia* (Venice, 1606), pp. 22–3.

[41] See below, Appendix, pp. 423–8.

charity. There was nobody to check on the Procurators: despite their vaunted integrity, their methods were (on investigation in the late sixteenth century) found wanting.[42]

The Venetians, however, were not completely insensitive to the unsatisfactory state of their largely unsupervised charities. In 1489, they set up an *ad hoc* commission to examine hospitals in Venice, and proclaimed, in words which recalled the English statute of 1414 or the Bergamese of 1457, that

> Our pious ancestors have built and bequeathed hospitals in substantial numbers in this our city, which, as is well known, are constituted in various different ways and excellently endowed. But the greater part of them are in a poor condition and even decayed, which is an offence to God and to the honour of our State, on account of the complaints of the poor who are not receiving their dues as they ought, or in accordance with the bequests and instructions of testators. God does not ignore these laments, for it is written: '*Non sum oblitus clamore pauperum*'.

The Venetians did not intend to ignore them either. The fault lay both with the governors of the hospitals, and with the priors or prioresses who dealt with their domestic administration; many were simply neglecting their duties and appropriating the revenues themselves. The Senate therefore created a commission empowered first to examine all testaments establishing hospitals, and then to inspect the living quarters both of the unfortunate inmates and of their priors and prioresses, to discover whether the founders' wishes were being respected. But whatever action this commission took, it effected nothing so drastic as the concentrations of hospitals in Lombardy and the Milanese. Another *ad hoc* commission, modelled on that of 1489, was to appear in 1526;[43] but there was no permanent magistracy to perform these tasks in Venice until 1561.[44]

In 1497, Battista Sfondrato, the Milanese Ambassador to the Venetian Republic, was asked by his master, Ludovico Sforza, to describe the religious and charitable institutions of Venice. He replied, with satisfaction, that 'in this city there is no famous hospital which in any way resembles that of Milan'. Patriotism, perhaps, prompted him to add that there was one hospital whose construction was now in progress, which owed its foundation to the Milanese Observant Franciscan Michele Carcano.[45] The early history of this institution, almost certainly the Hospital of Gesù Cristo di Sant'Antonio, illustrates the

[42] See below, pp. 351–5.
[43] D.M.S., XLII, coll. 257 f., 28 July 1526: copy of the decree of 29 June 1489, renewed on 28 July 1526.
[44] See below, pp. 344–5.   [45] Sevesi, 'Michele Carcano', IV, p. 461.

nature and limitations of the Venetian concept of poor relief at the close of the fifteenth century. It also suggests that for a time the Venetians considered following the same course as the Milanese.

During the 1470's, when the Venetian government was facing the advancing Ottoman Turks, the problem of beggars, paupers and refugees forced itself upon the city's attention. The need to earn divine favour, which might bring success in this holy war, inspired the city to good works: a state, like an individual person, could collectively acquire merit in the sight of God, whilst moral corruption or un-Christian conduct invited divine punishment. After Christmas 1471, the Senate recognized the number of paupers dying of cold and hunger in the porticoes of St Mark's itself and round the adjacent Ducal Palace, and decreed that a temporary shelter be erected for them on Campo Sant'Antonio, a square in the region of the cathedral of San Pietro di Castello. The Ufficio del Sale, which financed public works out of the proceeds of the government salt monopoly, must provide funds for this operation. This temporary accommodation was not used merely during the winter: it was still occupied the following August. The inmates were evidently expected to support themselves by personally begging throughout the city, but the Senate now recognized that some were too aged and incapable to do this, whilst those who did beg often gathered insufficient to support life. 'Since our Lord God must be induced to favour us by means of alms and every other device', the corn commissioners or Provveditori alle Biave were ordered to send sacks of bread to the shelter at the rate of two *staia* a week. As the Turks pressed westwards towards Dalmatia, refugees flooded into Venice, and aggravated the government's problems. For the relief of Albanian refugees in August 1474, the Senate ordered further systematic measures. Apparently there was already an organization or fraternity of women in Venice who collected alms on behalf of poor prisoners—perhaps both criminals and debtors—who had no other means of support. The Senate now ordered them to distribute to the displaced Albanians bread made out of the official stocks of flour, and soup bought at the government's expense.

Light showed in the prevailing darkness abroad. The Venetian outpost of Scutari escaped Turkish occupation. By way of thanksgiving, in September 1474, the Senate determined to establish

> an institute of charity and a shelter for the poor and sick which shall be extensive and fitting, and shall bear the name of Missier Jesus Christ, out of the body of this city in whatever place this Council shall decide; and when this war ends it shall be expanded by our Signory as this Council shall determine.

212

They were aware of the Milanese model, and were anxious to study other such institutions abroad, elsewhere in Italy. To finance the project, they proposed to ask the Pope for a plenary indulgence, 'as the Duke of Milan has,' in favour of all who would give alms to the new hospitals. The commission in charge of the embryo hospital was to 'take information about similar worthy hospitals elsewhere in Italy'. As a further means of fund-raising, the Senate resorted to a device already used to assist the pesthouse or Lazzaretto in the lagoon. All notaries drawing up wills were henceforth obliged, in the face of drastic penalties, to remind testators of the existence of the hospital. Caught in this psychological moment, men contemplating death and the hereafter might not like to refuse, and the resources of the hospital might be augmented by numerous more or less voluntary contributions, exacted by moral pressure.[46] It may have been no coincidence that in 1476 the Council of Ten relaxed some of its former provisions forbidding the Scuole Grandi to bestow alms on any but their own members, and permitted them to give charity to institutions—hospitals, monasteries, convents and prisons. The foundation stone of the Hospital of Gesù Cristo di Sant'Antonio was laid on 7 April 1476,[47] and this fact lends plausibility to Sfondrato's claim that its inspirer was the Milanese Carcano. He was in Venice during a part of the years 1476 and 1477,[48] and, though there is no evidence that he conceived the original project, he had unrivalled experience, and was an obvious person to consult about its execution. The direct, not to say crude, eloquence of the Observants often proved highly successful in floating or reviving charitable projects. Certainly in the early sixteenth century they loudly maintained that there was a strong link between moral reform and success in war: the kind of assumption reflected in the Senate's decrees.[49]

In the 1470's, the Venetians may have conceived their policy on a much wider scale than usual, and—though they showed no determination to unite existing hospitals—have planned a hospital which would confront the urgent problem of poverty in the city as a whole, instead of merely nibbling at it with another small foundation. But the project lost some of its urgency, and was not completed until 1503. It then emerged as a much more conventional institution, which supplemented

[46] See the official copies of the Senate's legislation of 28 December 1471, 3 August 1472, 10 August 1474, and 7 September 1474, in A.S.V., *Compilazione delle Leggi*, *busta* 309, ff. 471–7v.
[47] Marino Sanuto, *Vita de' Duchi di Venezia*, in Muratori, R.I.S., XXII (Milan, 1733), col. 1205.
[48] Sevesi, 'Michele Carcano', IV, pp. 36 f.
[49] See below, pp. 484–5.

Like a
VA

the existing organizations for the security of ex-servicemen and Arsenal workers. The Great Council, decreeing financial support for the hospital, formulated its preliminary declaration of principle along familiar lines:

> The chief and most salutary means of obtaining divine favour for a state and republic, just as for private persons, is the maintenance of the poor, in whom the person of Our Lord Jesus Christ is represented; and hence the chief ornament of every most noble city is, and always has been, some excellent hospital for feeding the poor. Proceeding on these lines, our good and pious ancestors gave a notable beginning to the hospital at Sant'Antonio, which has now been completed, and where many paupers could be lodged if the means for their support were forthcoming.

It transpired, however, that the number of paupers to be accommodated at the beginning was only twenty-five or thirty;[50] and to judge by later evidence, from 1563, the hospital did not subsequently expand much beyond this level.[51] The Procurators of St Mark's were to take charge of this new institution, and the Great Council now adopted their recommendation that the hospital be confined to 'poor Venetians and mariners and others who have deserved well of our state'.

The Venetian government thus maintained a nice balance between conventional godliness and a shrewd determination to use charitable resources to encourage those pursuits most beneficial to the state and its economy. Mariners, ex-servicemen and Arsenal workers already enjoyed numerous special benefits. In particular, there was the group of pensioners known as the Poveri al Pevere. As Gasparo Contarini explained, in a brief account of the connexion between charity and state service,

> by an ancient statute it is ordained, that in all matters of buying and selling of rich marchandize, the one and the other, that is both the buyer and the seller, do pay according to the quantitie of the summe, a certain price which is devided among poore mariners, that having spent their time in that exercise, are through olde age unable anie longer to continue therein.[52]

The 'ancient statute' to which he referred was almost certainly the decree passed by the Great Council on 22 November 1362. By this act the Council had determined that the proceeds of the brokage tax on pepper (*officium missetarie piperis*) should be conferred on 'Venetian mariners and other men of respectable status who have spent their

---

[50] D.M.S., IV, coll. 810–12, 12 March 1503.
[51] A.S.V., *Provveditori sopra gli Ospedali e Luoghi Pii*, busta 17/21, *Atti e Terminazioni 1561–1575*, f. 7, 3 February 1562 Venetian style.
[52] Contarini, *De Republica*, Latin version, pp. 194–5; English translation, pp. 140–1.

youth, and indeed their whole lives, in our service and honour, rather than on outsiders who have not deserved so well of us'. The money should go to native Venetian seamen aged sixty or more, who were indigent on account of old age or incapacity. By 1403, the number had increased from about 30 pensioners (before 1386) to a total of 82—at which it still remained in 1651. The Poveri al Pevere owed their name to the tax on the exchange of pepper, but by 1403 they were receiving support from an increasingly complicated tariff of payments levied on such commodities as wool, cloth, tin, wax, spices, sugar and soap.[53] The state, moreover, encouraged trades vital to its existence as a naval and maritime power by providing special conditions of employment at the Arsenal, and special guarantees for the employment of 'veteran' craftsmen over the age of fifty-five.[54] Earlier chapters of this book have already discussed how the Venetian state used the pensions and almshouses controlled by the Scuole Grandi and by the Procurators in order to increase the incentives to serve the Venetian state in the galleys.[55]

By establishing the Hospital of Gesù Cristo di Sant'Antonio, the Venetian government was retreating on to an older, already established policy, embodied in the institution of the Poveri al Pevere. It was not establishing a general hospital capable of confronting the problem of poverty and begging in Venice as a whole; it focused attention, instead, on a particular sector of the poor. On the other hand, it is clear that, in the name of Christianity, the Venetian state was in fact exercising a highly discriminating policy, one designed to encourage some of the 'deserving' poor, of a kind who stood very high on the government's list of priorities. From the 1470's onwards, the state was unmistakably venturing further into the realms of social responsibility. Venice, however, proved more conservative than her subject cities, and no radically new principles were actually put into execution until the 1520's. Venice was not exposed to such forthright clerical influences—Franciscan and episcopal—as her own Lombard provinces. Clerical initiative weighed very heavily in the improved organization of poor relief in the mid-fifteenth century. Moreover, the centralization of charitable institutions in a town of over 100,000 inhabitants would have been a far more complex undertaking than in one of about 20,000 or 30,000, like Brescia or Bergamo.

[53] Official copies of legislation of 22 November 1362, 23 May 1368, 29 July 1386, 3 May 1395, 10 August 1403, 27/28 October 1416, 1/17 March 1490, in A.S.V., *Compilazione delle Leggi, busta* 309, ff. 386–425.
[54] F. C. Lane, *Venetian ships and shipbuilders of the Renaissance* (Baltimore, 1934), chapter on 'The craft guilds'.
[55] See above, pp. 146–9.

P

2

NEW INSPIRATIONS AND INCENTIVES

About 1500, a combination of economic, non-economic and intellectual forces heightened the existing awareness of the problem of poverty. Governments and private associations for the care of the poor showed an increased readiness to assume responsibility. Their concern extended, not merely to the respectable, resident, native poor for whom the Scuole had long catered: but also to the outcasts of society. It began to embrace men and women outside the framework of the brotherhoods, deprived of the security afforded by families and native towns or villages, beyond the pale of respectability and conventional morality. In the era of the Reformation and of Catholic reform, clergy, laity, governments and city magistrates displayed a new sensitivity to the spiritual and material needs of beggars, orphans and prostitutes. The new religious societies and religious Orders discharged a militant, evangelical function, directed ultimately at the salvation of souls imperilled by the ignorance and temptation which poverty brought in its train. It was impossible to launch a wholly successful physical attack on the corporal problem of poverty: but some of its evil consequences for the soul of the pauper could be eliminated.

In general surveys of Europe, increased population pressure is often invoked as the most satisfactory explanation for the increase of poverty and poor laws in the early sixteenth century. Sometimes, indeed, vagrancy laws are adduced as circumstantial evidence of the existence of this pressure—of the growth of a floating lumpenproletariat which the crowded land could not support. Vagrancy laws, however, had certainly been issued in the second half of the fourteenth century, in regions which suffered loss of population.[1] Labour shortages, and a consequent desire to employ all hands, were just as likely to produce laws against idle wandering as was the appearance of surplus labour and of resulting unemployment. It may be that, in Europe generally, the gaps blown in the population by the famines and epidemics of the fourteenth century were at last being filled by the beginning of the sixteenth. But one cannot be sure that in Venice and its subject pro-

[1] Cf. K. F. Helleiner, 'The population of Europe from the Black Death to the eve of the vital revolution', *The Cambridge Economic History of Europe*, IV: *The economy of expanding Europe in the sixteenth and seventeenth centuries*, ed. E. E. Rich and C. H. Wilson (Cambridge, 1967), pp. 29–30.

vinces population stagnated or seriously declined throughout the fifteenth century—still less that it substantially grew during the first third of the sixteenth, when some of the most important innovations were made in charity and poor relief. Over this significant period, such non-economic forces as war, and disease spread by war, were more obvious stimuli to the social conscience than was population pressure. Relief was designed to deal with forces that restrained the increase of the people. It is quite probable that in the Venetian Republic population may have gently increased in the middle and late fifteenth century, though the constant recurrence of epidemics of pestilence kept it under control. Some mountainous areas in Italy—including the Bergamese Alps—suffered from over-population in the course of the fifteenth century.[2] At least in some parts of the Republic, such as Verona and Brescia, war and disease cut back the population in the early sixteenth century; and there is no countervailing evidence of growth elsewhere. Convincing evidence of population pressure, provoking economic action, generally appears only in the second and third quarters of the sixteenth century,[3] when it brought about the renewal and re-application of many of the principles devised earlier in the century.

The evidence of censuses compiled for the city of Verona suggests that its population followed this course, and that it may have suffered very substantial losses in the early years of the century, for which it was barely compensating in the 1550's. Even if one mildly distrusts the totals given by the censuses and eliminates the high figure for 1501, there is certainly no evidence of demographic increase at the beginning of the century: at best, population tended to stagnate.

The movement of population in Brescia may have been broadly similar. Surviving information for the fifteenth and early sixteenth century is of two kinds: it includes estimates for the number of citizen heads of households liable to contribute to taxation, and estimates of the total number of inhabitants of the city. The number of contributing citizens decreased between 1388 and 1416, but later rose from 1,607 in 1434 to 5,721 in 1459: an increase too great to be accounted for merely by improved administration and heavier fiscal pressure, and almost

---

[2] Cf. P. J. Jones, 'Medieval agrarian society in its prime: Italy', *The Cambridge Economic History of Europe*, II: *The agrarian life of the Middle Ages*, second edition, ed. M. M. Postan (Cambridge, 1966), pp. 361–2. Léopold Génicot, 'Crisis: from the Middle Ages to modern times', *ibid.*, pp. 664–6, also thinks it doubtful that the countryside of northern and central Italy was seriously depleted in the fifteenth century.

[3] Cf. Brian Pullan, 'The famine in Venice and the new poor law, 1527–9', *Bollettino dell'Istituto di Storia della Società e dello Stato veneziano*, V–VI (1963–4), pp. 181–3; Helleiner, 'The population of Europe', pp. 33 f.

The population of the city of Verona in the sixteenth and early seventeenth century

1472	29,541	1555	48,828	1614	52,988
1491	38,322	1557	49,280	1616	50,032
1501	50,084	1558	52,262	1625	53,052
1514	31,184	1572	52,120	1627	52,933
1518	29,014	1577	51,265	1630	53,036
1529	30,072	1583	46,992	1631	20,987
1541	35,574	1593	56,179	1633	26,670
1545	41,667	1603	54,709	1652	26,636

[4]

certainly reflecting a rise of population. Censuses of 1493 and 1505 estimated the total population of Brescia at 56,060 and 65,000 respectively, and these estimates were substantially higher than the figures of 40,000–50,000 found in the reports of provincial governors and other sources over the years 1546–57. There is a certain ambiguity in the figures, since some may include the area known as the Chiusure on the borders of the city, and others not. But it seems as though the growth in Brescian population was almost certainly halted by the events of 1512–16. After three years of French occupation from 1509–12, the Venetians temporarily recovered control of Brescia: but the city was viciously sacked by French troops under Gaston de Foix, and for the next four years became the object of dispute between the forces of the Venetian Republic and those of the Spanish–Austrian League which had defeated the French. Death and emigration probably took a heavy toll of the people, though the number of heads of households contributing to the fisc slowly rose, from 3,643 in 1517 to 4,195 in 1534. Here again, one cannot speak with confidence of increasing population pressure over the first quarter of the sixteenth century.[5]

For Venice itself, and for the regions adjacent to Venice, there is again no evidence of increasing pressure before about 1540, though refugees certainly fled into Venice itself during and after 1509 and during the 1520's, thereby overcrowding the city and adding to its burdens. Jewish refugees formed a conspicuous group among them, and famine as well as military invasion drove the people to the capital.[6]

[4] See Pietro Donazzolo and Mario Saibante, 'Lo sviluppo demografico di Verona e della sua provincia dalla fine del secolo XV ai giorni nostri', *Metron*, VI, nos. 3–4 (1926), p. 71; also Daniele Beltrami, *La penetrazione economica dei veneziani in Terraferma: forze di lavoro e proprietà fondiaria nelle campagne venete dei secoli XVII e XVIII* (Venice–Rome, 1961), Appendice al Capitolo I.

[5] Carlo Pasero, 'Dati statistici e notizie intorno al movimento della popolazione bresciana durante il dominio veneto (1426–1797)', *Archivio Storico Lombardo*, series 9, vols. I–II, *anno* 88 (1963).

[6] See below, pp. 243 f., 478, and Pullan, 'The famine in Venice'.

Here, the displacement of the people was more obviously responsible for Venice's difficulties than was any increase in their numbers. Famine, disease and war all threatened to check such increase.

Venice itself and some of its subjects had long been suffering from recurrent outbreaks of pestilence. Only in the second quarter of the sixteenth century did these become relatively infrequent. Pestilence—which was probably bubonic plague—invaded Venice in 1361, 1381–2, 1391, 1397, 1403, 1411, 1438, 1447, 1456, 1464, 1468, 1478, 1485, 1490, 1498, 1502, 1507, 1510, 1511, 1513, 1523 and 1528.[7] Alvise Cornaro, a pioneer of land-reclamation in the provinces adjacent to Venice, later suggested that these epidemics had sometimes carried off as much as one-fifth of the total population of the city, and attributed the growth of population after 1528 partly to the removal of these checks on its expansion. He may have exaggerated the extent of the damage: but he was probably right to draw a contrast between a period of relative stagnation before 1528 and one of rapid growth thereafter.[8] Likewise, Verona suffered from plague in the years 1399–1400, 1424, 1437–8, 1451, 1474, 1478, 1490, 1500, 1510, 1511, 1512, and 1527.[9] Admittedly, plague may have been largely a scourge of cities, and may not have inflicted comparable losses on the countryside.

In Venice, the threat of plague eventually brought the establishment of permanent machinery for dealing with the problem of vagrancy—from the point of view of a state determined to protect itself and its reserves of manpower against disease. From 1486 onwards, Venice possessed a permanent magistracy in charge of public health—the Provveditori alla Sanità. The Venetians had appointed temporary commissions for this purpose—as in 1459[10]—but probably established no enduring organ of government before the late fifteenth century. Plague raged in the summer of 1485. The Senate, in the following winter, chose to appoint a commission of 'three dignified and honourable noblemen' to take prophylactic measures against the return of plague, and to eliminate 'the materials on which it might feed (*li nutrimenti per li qualli quela se potesse conservar*)'. This was a matter involving 'the safety of all the people (*la comune et universal salute*)'. These commissioners were to be chosen every year, and were empowered to

---

[7] Ernst Rodenwaldt, *Pest in Venedig 1575–1577. Ein Beitrag zur Frage der Infektkette bei den Pestepidemien West-Europas, Sitzungsberichte der Heidelberger Akademie der Wissenschaften*, Mathematisch-naturwissenschaftliche Klasse, Heidelberg, 1953, p. 66, n. 1.

[8] Quoted at length in Daniele Beltrami, *Saggio di storia dell'agricoltura nella Repubblica di Venezia durante l'età moderna* (Venice–Rome, 1955), pp. 32–3.

[9] Donazzolo and Saibante, 'Sviluppo di Verona', p. 63.

[10] Malipiero, *Annali veneti*, p. 653.

funding provided

use funds derived from the government salt monopoly to take all steps necessary for the preservation of public health.[11] In this era, sanitary authorities believed that plague was a contagious disease communicated between man and man, and one also conveyed by various forms of merchandise, such as textiles. Centuries had still to pass before investigations of the great pandemics in the late nineteenth century suggested that plague was a disease of rats, conveyed to human beings by the bite of a flea attacking the rat, and migrating to man when its former host had died of plague.[12] However, diseases can change their characteristics over a long period of time, and there is a certain possibility that the human flea was more important as a plague-carrier in the sixteenth century than it subsequently became.[13] In any case, the belief that there was a strong link between the movement of men and the spread of plague drew the attention of the authorities to the question of vagrancy; and they were concerned with other contagious or supposedly contagious diseases. At first they made no attempt to stamp out begging altogether. They simply tried to regulate it, to control immigration in the interests of public health, and to prevent fraudulent begging.

In 1495, for example, the Provveditori alla Sanità insisted that all lepers who kept houses in the city in which they lodged fellow-sufferers should immediately repair to the island of San Lazzaro, the established leper colony. They could still beg in the city, but must confine themselves to squares and wide open spaces, and not infest narrow alleys where they might brush against passers-by.[14] The Provveditori alla Sanità also attempted to control the lodging-houses in the town which habitually accommodated rogues, vagabonds, casual labourers and other people of uncertain provenance, who might import disease into Venice. In 1495, they tried to limit the number of persons who could be lodged in any one establishment to a maximum of four. In the plague year 1498, the new magistracy decreed that all lodging-house keepers must obtain licences—a measure justified in the interests of public health, for the purpose of preventing overcrowding and unrestricted immigration.[15] Later, in the early 1520's, the Provveditori alla Sanità seemed to be expecting large seasonal migrations of beggars, in late August or early September:

[11] A.S.V., *Provveditori alla Sanità, Notatorio I*, vol. 725.
[12] Cf. L. F. Hirst, *The conquest of plague: a study of the evolution of epidemiology* (Oxford, 1953), pp. 152 f.
[13] Rodenwaldt, *Pest in Venedig*, pp. 218 f.: Helleiner, 'Population of Europe', p. 7, n. 1.
[14] A.S.V., *Provveditori alla Sanità, Capitolare I*, f. 30.
[15] *Ibid.*, ff. 30, 40.

The time is now approaching when the rogues, beggars and vagabonds (*burbanti, furfanti et mendicanti*) from various regions repair to this city, who, both because of their condition, since they are persons who go begging, and because they might be coming from unknown places infected with disease, could easily infect our own city with the pestilence.

Hence the magistrates forbade ferrymen to bring in beggars from Padua, Marghera and elsewhere.[16]

The fear of disease and the desire to take systematic measures against it heightened awareness of the problem of vagrancy. Public health, as well as public order, demanded its control. Early in 1506, the Provveditori alla Sanità attempted to introduce some mechanism to enable the general public to discriminate between fraudulent beggars and those genuinely suffering hardship. They complained that

there are many rogues and persons of low and wretched condition, both male and female, who go seeking alms throughout the city, the women covering their faces with cloaks and the men with sacks so that they shall not be known. They pretend to be good citizens and to come of excellent families reduced to poverty; nor does anyone know whether they are Venetians or foreigners, or where they come from, and they might easily come from an infected region, and cause a great epidemic of plague to break out. Moreover, by this means they extort money from many people, and they are the reason why many needy persons who are in fact reduced to great poverty come to suffer as a result of their deception.

The Provveditori alla Sanità then ordered that no-one should in future beg with his or her face covered unless he had, with the support of his parish priest, obtained a licence to do so from their offices. Any decayed gentlefolk who chose to follow this procedure would have their identity kept strictly secret. Imprisonment and flogging from San Marco to Rialto now awaited anyone who presumed to beg incognito without a licence.[17] This decree of the Provveditori evidently assumed that anyone could distinguish between a sturdy rogue and a genuine pauper if the face were uncovered. Further than this, it did not go. But it maintained the principle that almsgivers must be encouraged to discriminate; and it showed an interesting concern for the category of poor later described as the *poveri vergognosi*, who stood high among the priorities of sixteenth-century religious reformers.[18] The establishment of a per-

---

[16] A.S.V., *Provveditori alla Sanità, Notatorio II*, vol. 726, f. 45, 25 August 1522; *ibid.*, f. 99v., for a similar decree of 12 October 1525.

[17] A.S.V., *Provveditori alla Sanità, Capitolare I*, f. 30r.–v., 23 January 1506; also printed in P. G. Molmenti, *La storia di Venezia nella vita privata dalle origini alla caduta della Repubblica*, II (Bergamo, 1925), p. 477.

[18] See below, pp. 229–31, 267–8, 373–4.

manent magistracy for the protection of public health was contributing to a more coherent policy, though as yet there were few facilities—other than the licence to beg—for the relief of deserving cases of poverty.

Disease could turn the pauper at once into an object of pity and into one of fear and disgust. Contagious diseases—such as leprosy—had in the past stimulated municipal action. In the early sixteenth century, leprosy found a successor, in the form of syphilis, which was now spread abroad in a virulent, epidemic form. Syphilitic patients became the new lepers of the sixteenth century. In the high Middle Ages, lepers were at once the repulsive, disfigured outcasts of human society, and, in a peculiar sense, the 'poor of Christ', dead to the world, their only hope lying in patience and spiritual consolation. They acquired special sanctity from the confusion between Lazarus, the beggar covered with sores in the parable of Dives and Lazarus, and Lazarus of Bethany—the Lazarus raised by Christ from the dead—although there was no biblical evidence to connect him with leprosy. St Lazarus, therefore, was their patron saint.[19] The care of lepers was at once a form of self-mortification and self-humiliation, and a means of meeting a genuine social need. Francis of Assisi had called upon his followers to identify themselves with the outcasts, to become as the poor themselves were. In the words of the *Mirror of Perfection*,

> at the commencement of the Order, he wished the friars to live in leper-houses to serve them, and by so doing to establish themselves in holy humility. For whenever anyone, whether noble or commoner, entered the Order, among the other instructions given him, he was told that he must humbly serve the lepers and live with them in their houses.

Or, as the First Rule prescribed,

> Let them (the friars) be happy to associate with humble and insignificant people, the poor and the weak, the sick, the lepers, and the beggars on the roads. . . .[20]

[19] See Charles Creighton, *A history of epidemics in Britain*, new edition, with additional material by D. E. C. Eversley, E. Ashworth Underhill and Lynda Ovenall (2 vols., London, 1965), I, pp. 79 f.; Clay, *Mediaeval hospitals*, pp. 35 f., 50 f., 251–252; Imbert, *Les hôpitaux*, pp. 149 f. In the Veneto there were several places named after San Lazzaro and situated just outside the walls of towns—circumstantial evidence of the existence of leprosaries—at Udine, Cividale, Portogruaro, Verona and Treviso, whilst Venice itself had its leprosary on the island of San Lazzaro in the lagoon—see Emilio Nasalli-Rocca, 'Gli ospedali italiani di San Lazzaro o dei lebbrosi', *Zeitschrift der Savigny-Stiftung für Rechtsgeschichte, kanonische Abteilung*, 27 (1938), pp. 266–7.

[20] As translated in L. D. Sherley-Price, *St. Francis of Assisi: his life and writings as recorded by his contemporaries* (London, 1959), pp. 57, 212.

However, it is possible that the term 'leprosy' was used very loosely to describe many varieties of skin disease, including venereal diseases —hence the belief found at least in the fourteenth century that leprosy was conveyed through sexual acts, as well as through the polluted breath of the sufferer.[21] There were, therefore, many precedents for the special concern with syphilitic patients shown by charitable people in the sixteenth century.

In the late fifteenth century, syphilis probably existed in the South of France, and in such ports of Spain as Barcelona and Valencia, from which it was imported to Italy as a result of Charles VIII's invasion in 1494. Contemporary and sixteenth-century writers traced it to the siege of Naples in 1495, and to the subsequent dispersal of the French King's international armies. Hence its description—in Aberdeen in 1507—as the 'seiknes of Nappillis'; and the observation, by John Jones, in his *Dyall of Agues* of 1563, that 'the Neapolitans, or rather the besiegers of Naples, with the pockes, spread hence so far abroad through all the parts of Europe, no kingdom that I have been in free— the more pity'. Soon after the siege of Naples, syphilis was known to Venetians. Marcellus Cumanus, an army surgeon, described the advent of the disease among Venetian and Milanese troops banded against the French invader at the siege of Novara in 1495.[22] Again, on 8 July 1496, the Venetian diarist and chronicler Marino Sanuto commented on the disease. It had appeared in Italy with the French invasions, and hence was known to Italians as the French disease and to Frenchmen as the Italian disease—though it was also prevalent in Spain and Greece, and, indeed, throughout the whole world. Manifested in the form of pustules and ulcers all over the body, it brought such agony that the victims cried out for death, though few in fact died of it. Sanuto recognized that it was contagious in the sexual act, but not by other means.[23]

In the early sixteenth century, Italian societies were thus facing the challenge of widespread warfare, on a scale unknown during the relative equilibrium of the years 1454–94, and that of the disease which war brought in its train. These supplemented the forces of the old enemy, bubonic plague. Intellectual change shaped the response to the challenge of circumstances. The philosophy of humanism bred impatience and scepticism towards the pursuit of salvation through the mere performance of a series of finite, mechanical good works. Before

---

[21] Creighton, *History of epidemics*, I, pp. 72 f.

[22] *Ibid.*, I, pp. 417 f. See also J. Johnston Abraham, 'The early history of syphilis', *The British Journal of Surgery*, XXXII (1944–5).

[23] D.M.S., I, coll. 233–4. Also quoted in *Leggi e memorie venete sulla prostituzione* (Venice. For Lord Orford. 1870–2), p. 253.

and after the Reformation, Christian humanism may have been a potent force contributing to a new attitude to the poor, both in Protestant and in Catholic societies.[24] It stressed the importance of consistent and righteous conduct, rather than the mystical or magical facets of religion.[25] Charity must be charity in the Pauline sense of the term: a way of life demanding continual self-sacrifice, and devotion to the good of one's neighbour, including the most needy. There was no point in haphazard, indiscriminate almsgiving, done without love, or for purely material and superstitious ends. Erasmus wrote with contempt of those who 'assign and name certain portion of their winning to poor men, lest their merchandise should perish by shipwreck'.[26]

Erasmus's *Enchiridion militis christiani*, composed at Saint-Omer in 1501, appeared at Antwerp in 1504; it was reissued in 1518, as the manifesto of Erasmianism in the early debates of the Reformation. The extent of Erasmus's influence on thinking-men in Venice is hard to gauge; but it is certain that he came to Venice late in the year 1507, attracted by the high reputation of Venice as a centre of Greek scholarship, and ready to feed into the press the new edition of his *Adagiorum Chiliades*. He remained there till the autumn of 1508, when he departed to tutor a royal pupil at Padua, and thence, faced with the growing threat of war, made for Ferrara. He undoubtedly retained admirers and supporters at Venice and Padua.[27] Two other eminent sympathisers—both concerned in the late 1520's with the promotion of organized charity in the diocese of Verona—were Gian Matteo Giberti, Bishop of Verona, and Count Ludovico di Canossa, formerly Bishop of Bayeux.[28] How far their Erasmianism influenced their ideas of charity it is impossible to say: one can only draw attention to the possibility of a link. At least by the late 1520's, Erasmus commanded a following in Brescia, where the chancellor, Emilio de' Migli, was a passionate admirer, who in 1529 completed an Italian translation of the *Enchiridion*.[29] In general, Erasmus's books were

[24] For this argument, focused especially on Lyons, cf. the article of N. Z. Davis, 'Humanism, heresy and poor relief', cited above.

[25] For the general theme, see H. A. Enno van Gelder, *The two Reformations in the sixteenth century: a study of the religious aspects and consequences of Renaissance and humanism* (The Hague, 1964).

[26] Erasmus, *Enchiridion militis christiani* (London, 1905), pp. 134–6. Cf. Armando Sapori, 'La beneficenza delle compagnie mercantili del Trecento', in his *Studi di storia economica medievale* (2nd edition, Florence, 1946).

[27] See Auguste Renaudet, *Érasme en Italie* (Geneva, 1954), pp. 37, 75–87, 130, 219–220. For the example of Erasmus's correspondent, the Cavalier Sebastiano Giustinian, see below, p. 237.

[28] See below, pp. 270–3.

[29] Renaudet, *Érasme en Italie*, pp. 222–3; Erasmus, *Opus Epistolarum*, ed. P. S. and H. M. Allen (12 vols., Oxford, 1906–58), VIII, pp. 143–4, 175–7.

among the most widely read by the intelligentsia of Europe in the early sixteenth century, and there is no reason to think that Venice was insulated from their message.

The *Enchiridion* inveighed against all distractions, in the form of rites, ceremonies and legalism, from the true 'philosophy of Christ', and from true piety. This true piety lay in righteous conduct, in the love of God and one's neighbour, and in the sense of being part of the body of Christ: of possessing nothing for oneself alone. Righteous conduct towards one's neighbour in general naturally included the defence and aid of the poor.

> Paul everywhere (as I have said) commendeth charity, but specially writing unto the Corynthes he preferreth charity both before miracles and prophecies, and also before the tongues of angels. And say not thou by and by that charity is, to be oft at the church, to crouch down before the images of saints, to light tapers or wax candles, to say many lady psalters or Saint Kathryne's knots. God hath no need of these things. Paul calleth charity to edify thy neighbour, to count that we all be members of one body, to think that we all are but one in Christ, to rejoice in God of thy neighbour's wealth even as thou doest of thine own, to remedy his incommodities or losses as thine own. If any brother err or go out of the right way, to warn him, to admonish him, to tell him his fault meekly, soberly and courteously: to teach the ignorant: to lift up him that is fallen: to comfort and courage him that is in heaviness: to help him that laboureth: to succour the needy. In conclusion to refer all riches and substance, all thy study, all thy cares to this point, that thou in Christ shouldest help as much as thy power extendeth to. That as he neither was born for himself, nor lived to his own pleasure, neither died for himself but dedicate himself wholly to our profits: even so should we apply ourselves, and await upon the commodities of our brethren, and not our own....[30]

Erasmus, moreover, attacked not only pedantic ritualism as a distraction from true charity, but also the mistaken belief that one had an absolute right in one's own property, and was entitled to live luxuriously and enjoy a superfluity of goods. All men were the body of Christ:

> in another place he biddeth every man to bear one another's burden, because we be members one of another. Look then whether they pertain unto this body whom thou hearest speaking everywhere after this manner, it is my good, it came to me by inheritance, I possess it by right and not by fraud, why shall not I use it and abuse it after mine own mind, why

[30] Erasmus, *Enchiridion*, pp. 171–2. N. Z. Davis, 'Humanism, heresy and poor relief', also draws attention to this passage.

should I give them of it any deal at all to whom I owe nothing? I spill, I waste, I destroy, that which perisheth is mine own, it maketh no matter to other men. Thy member complaineth and grinneth for hunger and thou spuest up partridges. Thy naked brother shiverest for cold, and with thee so great plenty of raiment is corrupt with moths and long lying. One night's dicing hath lost thee a thousand pieces of gold, while in the mean season some wretched wench (need compelling her) hath set forth her chastity to sell, and is become a common harlot, and thus perisheth the soul for whom Christ hath bestowed his life.[31]

The Observant Bernardino of Siena had already expressed such sentiments in the first half of the fifteenth century.[32] In the years to come, other reformers were to return to this doctrine, latent in patristic writings, that all goods were ultimately common in the sense that they must be shared in time of necessity, and that no-one was entitled to heap up a surplus of property when others were in need.[33] The return to the original sources of Christian knowledge, in the Bible and the Fathers, re-emphasized such theoretical justifications for charitable giving, which were appreciated by Catholics and Protestants alike. Erasmus also argued explicitly that voluntary poverty was not merely enjoined upon monks or friars.[34] Every Christian was bound to practise such poverty—to cultivate readiness to give away goods which he possessed by earthly law, but could not own absolutely in the sight of God.

Sentiments akin to those of Erasmus appeared in a treatise written in 1516 by the Venetian patrician Gasparo Contarini. Contarini, the future Cardinal Bishop of Belluno, was a prominent advocate of Catholic reform. In the fifteenth and early sixteenth century, spontaneous attempts at reform by individual religious houses, branches of religious orders, individual bishops and groups of clergy and laity long preceded any general programme of ecclesiastical reform promoted by Popes or General Councils of the Church. They also preceded the challenge of the Lutheran Reformation. Contarini belonged to a small group of devout young men living communally in Venice on the island of Murano. Two members of this group, Tommaso Giustinian and Vincenzo Querini, entered the Order of Camaldoli, whilst Contarini himself and Nicolò Tiepolo remained in the world. Later, after his

---

[31] Erasmus, *Enchiridion*, pp. 211–12.

[32] Cf. Iris Origo, *The world of San Bernardino* (London, 1964), p. 106.

[33] For this doctrine, as interpreted by medieval canonists, see Tierney, *Medieval poor law*, pp. 29 f. Cf. P. J. Klassen, *The economics of Anabaptism, 1525–1560* (The Hague, 1964), pp. 29 f.; André Biéler, *La pensée économique et sociale de Calvin* (Geneva, 1959), pp. 245, 338 f.

[34] Erasmus, *Enchiridion*, pp. 216, 265.

promotion to the College of Cardinals by Pope Paul III in 1536, Contarini had the chance to repeat, in the famous *Consilium de emendanda ecclesia*, many of the proposals already advanced by Giustinian and Querini in a memorandum addressed to Leo X.[35] The treatise of 1516 also anticipated one of the most prominent features of later Catholic reform, in its determination to instil into the bishop a proper sense of his own obligations. Contarini's *De officio episcopi* was addressed to his friend Pietro Lippomano, recently appointed Bishop of Bergamo; the immediate practical inspiration probably derived from the pastoral work of Pietro Barozzi, Bishop of Padua in the late fifteenth century;[36] the ultimate theoretical inspiration may have lain in patristic writings—Gregory's *Regula pastoralis*, the *De officiis* of Ambrose, and so forth.[37]

In Erasmian fashion, Contarini emphasized the paramount importance of the spirit of charity in guiding all the actions of the bishop, who ought not to think merely in terms of his legal obligations, when he made the decision as to how to apportion his revenues. As he wrote,

> the theologians list three virtues, of which the first, which is faith, pertains to the intellect, whilst the two others, hope and charity, belong to the will. The first of these is faith, but the most indispensable is charity, without which none of the other virtues have any power at all. . . . The soul of man rises so high through this virtue that it begins to live, not in itself, but in God. . . .[38]

Beyond this, Contarini made a number of specific, practical recommendations on the subject of poor relief—on its position among the duties of the bishop, and on the order of priorities to be observed in the dispensation of funds to the poor of the diocese. He reminded the bishop of his duty to administer faithfully the goods entrusted to him by testators for the purpose of promoting divine worship and meeting

[35] See Hubert Jedin, *A history of the Council of Trent*, trans. Ernest Graf, I (Edinburgh, 1957), pp. 128–30, 139–48.

[36] See Franz Dittrich, *Gasparo Contarini, 1483–1542* (Braunsberg, 1885), p. 284; O. M. T. Logan, *Studies in the religious life of Venice in the sixteenth and early seventeenth centuries: the Venetian clergy and religious Orders, 1520–1630* (Ph.D. thesis, University of Cambridge, 1967), pp. 114 f. I am indebted to Dr Logan for drawing my attention to the importance of Contarini's treatise. Barozzi occupied the see of Belluno from 1471 to 1487, and that of Padua from 1487 to 1507—see *Hierarchia Catholica*, II, pp. 103, 210; III, p. 284. See below, pp. 460–1, for Barozzi's collaboration with Bernardino of Feltre to found a Monte di Pietà in Padua. Pietro Lippomano held the see of Bergamo from 1516 until his appointment as successor to Giberti in Verona in 1544—*Hierarchia Catholica*, III, pp. 147, 351.

[37] Jedin, *History of the Council of Trent*, I, p. 163.

[38] Gasparo Contarini, *De officio episcopi*, in his *Opera* (Paris, 1571), pp. 410–11, 428.

the needs of the poor. If laymen were bound by the Scriptures and the Fathers to devote a certain proportion of the goods earned by their own labour to the support of the poor, then how much more were bishops obliged to give their revenues to the poor. Luxurious or ostentatious living was inappropriate to a bishop,

> but I think it appropriate to the style of a bishop that, first of all, he should be most generous towards the poor and should construct large hospitals in which food and medical care may be provided for the poor, especially when they fall sick; and, secondly, that he should have fine and richly decorated churches, vessels, vestments and other things pertaining to divine worship, in so far as it is possible to do so without neglecting his duty towards the poor.[39]

The duty to provide for the worship of God, as Contarini later stated, took precedence over duty to the poor: but it was chiefly important to secure certain standards of decency, rather than provide for the beauty of holiness.

> Let the bishop first assign the necessary portion to the worship of God, and then distribute the rest to the poor. But should the need of the poor be so great that it became necessary, in order to save their lives, to reduce the normal expenditure on divine services, then I think that the bishop would be acting very much in accordance with his Christian duty if he worshipped God with less splendour in temples of stone in order to repair and enrich those temples of God which are not of unfeeling marble, but possess life and intelligence. 'For you are the temples of God', he says. But if there is no such necessity, let the bishop conduct divine service with as much splendour as accords with custom and with the dignity of the city. Let him distribute the remainder to the poor, and regard himself as the advocate and guardian of the poor, rather than as their lord. If there is anything left over, then let him apply it all to the adornment of the church.

Not only was the state moving towards a greater sense of responsibility towards the poor: the higher ecclesiastical authorities were also being reminded of their essential duty to support and guard them. Contarini then proceeded to suggest an order of priorities, to decide whom to prefer in dispensations of charity. Many of his recommendations at least coincided with the principles adopted by municipal or state governments formulating poor laws a few years later, and with the preoccupations of such charitable societies as the Oratories of Divine Love. On the example of Pietro Barozzi, who had chosen to prefer inhabitants of his diocese of Padua to his fellow Venetians,

[39] *Ibid.*, pp. 407, 428.

228

Contarini advised the bishop to take care first of his own local poor. Within this framework, he must dispense charity on moralistic principles, preferring good men and women of good reputation to criminals and rogues. 'For they are nearer both to Christ and to ourselves than are dishonest and wicked persons.' The bishop, however, must not neglect criminals in extreme want—'Let him imitate God, who, as Holy Scripture tells us, causes his sun to rise upon the just and the unjust alike'. Contarini then declared that, once these conditions had been fulfilled, charity should first be bestowed on persons of high social rank who had been plunged into poverty. He justified this preference expressly on the grounds that poverty, because it was not their natural condition and because of the disgrace it carried, caused such people additional suffering. Their upbringing did not equip them to earn wages—in Venice and its subject cities engaging in manual or retail trades disqualified or 'derogated' from noble rank, as it did in most other parts of western Europe. They must not be expected to go out and beg for themselves: rather, alms must be brought to them, and if possible handed over without their knowledge.[40] Behind this tenderness for the 'shamefaced poor', or *poveri vergognosi*, there probably lay certain reasons of government: a general desire to control begging by undermining it, and by anticipating the needs of the very poor; a specific determination to prevent the gently-born poor from bringing the ruling classes into disrepute by going on the streets and publicly begging. The purpose of sixteenth-century poor relief was always to preserve the existing social order, and not to modify or improve it through the redistribution of income or property on a large scale.

As a Venetian, Gasparo Contarini had every reason to be acquainted with the problem of noble poverty. Theoretically, Venetian patricians did not lack opportunities for employment: there was the possibility of service at sea, the opportunities for small-scale investment in the cargoes of galleys and roundships, above all the noble monopoly of magisterial offices, some of which carried modest salaries. Overseas trade, however, though not permanently crippled by the geographical discoveries of the early sixteenth century, was suffering disruptions and setbacks.[41] In 1509, the pessimistic diarist Priuli was writing his jaundiced account of the ignominious flight to the land by Venetian investors—a process likely to damage the prospects of the small investor.[42]

[40] *Ibid.*, p. 429.

[41] Cf. F. C. Lane, 'Venetian shipping during the commercial revolution', *American Historical Review*, XXXVIII (1933), p. 229.

[42] Girolamo Priuli, *I Diarii*, IV, ed. Roberto Cessi (Bologna, 1938), pp. 50 f., 6 June 1509. Cf. also J. C. Davis, *The decline of the Venetian nobility as a ruling class* (Baltimore, 1962), pp. 35 f.

Moreover, in the early sixteenth century, the number of noblemen qualified by birth and age to hold magisterial office was over 2,500,[43] whilst by the mid-sixteenth century the number of available offices was in the region of 600–700 only, and by no means all of these conferred either salaries or outstanding chances of illicit profit. Offices were rotated, and few lasted more than one or two years: there was no security of tenure. This system was designed to satisfy the maximum number of people, but in practice it allowed the formation of those groups of permanent Outs which it tried to eliminate.[44] In 1499, one Andrea Contarini had appeared before the Signoria, and said that he had an income of only 16 ducats a year, with nine dependent children. He had held no office for sixteen years, and had recently been forced to sell his house to pay off his debts to the treasury.[45] Demagogic leaders periodically arose to exploit the grievances of the poorer nobility, seen as a springboard for the politically ambitious. In 1492, for example, the Council of Ten had banished Gabriele di Felice Bon and Francesco di Piero Falier for their refusal, after official warnings, to abandon their proposal to dispense some 70,000 ducats a year to poor noblemen who held no office. They suggested that men over sixty should receive 100 ducats a year, and men aged twenty-five to sixty 50 ducats a year. The money should be raised by deductions from the salaries of Venetian governors. Learnedly recalling the Roman agrarian law, the Collegio had taken alarm at the plan, reflecting that

> it was not to be permitted that anyone should attempt to increase his standing through the expenditure of public money; and that by this means a faction might be created in the city; and that eight hundred noblemen would be attracted here from Crete; and that the city would be prevented from availing itself of money in time of need. . . .[46]

The existence of numerous poor nobles, known as the Swiss on account of their corruptibility and mercenary habits, provided in the early sixteenth century numerous opportunities for the *broglio* or intrigue so strongly condemned in theory by Venetian laws. No matter how ignobly poor, a nobleman over twenty-five enjoyed a vote in the Great

---

[43] *Ibid.*, p. 58.

[44] For this, and for the general question of poverty among Venetian noblemen, cf. Brian Pullan, 'Poverty, charity and the reason of state: some Venetian examples', *Bollettino dell'Istituto di Storia della Società e dello Stato veneziano*, II (1960); Brian Pullan, 'Service to the Venetian state: aspects of myth and reality in the early seventeenth century', *Studi Secenteschi*, V (1964).

[45] D.M.S., II, col. 502.

[46] Malipiero, *Annali veneti*, pp. 691–2; see also Pietro Bembo, *Historiae venetae*, in *Istorici delle cose veneziane*, II (Venice, 1718), pp. 30–2.

Council which elected to the highest magisterial offices; and, as Sanuto wrote censoriously in 1519,

> if anyone wants honour, he now has to give money to certain poor noblemen, known as the Swiss.[47]

Considerations of this kind may well explain the high priority which Contarini accorded to the poor of noble origin, or *poveri vergognosi*. This concern, as will appear later, was by no means original or peculiar to Contarini. He may have reflected current opinion as much as he shaped it. He went on to prescribe that, in the care of other paupers,

> care must be taken lest, as frequently happens, certain lazy creatures be led astray by such liberality into giving themselves to idleness and leading a slothful and wicked life.

The condemnation of idleness was certainly not peculiar to secular legislators or to Protestant clerics; idleness among the poor threatened to disrupt any social order. Finally, Contarini reminded the bishop of his duty to exercise surveillance over '*Nosodochia*, or, to use the new word, hospitals'; and to restrain public officials in towns and villages from oppressing the poor and misappropriating funds designed for their relief. He concluded that the bishop should carry out his good works in public, not out of personal ambition, but to inspire others with his own example.[48]

Later in the century, the ideals formulated by Contarini would certainly be translated into action—by Giberti of Verona, and later, in the same diocese, by Agostino Valier; by Pietro Lippomano himself, who as Bishop of Bergamo became the patron of Girolamo Miani and of his movement for the foundation of orphanages and training-schools for the employment of beggar-children; by Carlo Borromeo, as Archbishop of Milan and in his visitations of the Venetian regions of his metropolitan diocese. Contarini himself made substantial legacies to the poor of his own diocese of Belluno.[49]

Magistrates and bishops both proved prepared to act on behalf of the poor with renewed intensity, faced with the special challenges of the early sixteenth century. The Societies of Divine Love, or Compagnie del Divino Amore, formed another mainspring of action. They were mixed societies of priests and laymen which, in their origins, owed much to the medieval Scuole, and out of which new congregations of regular clerks, devoted to charity and evangelism, were later

---

[47] D.M.S., XXVIII, col. 65, 11 November 1519.
[48] Contarini, *De officio episcopi*, pp. 429–30.
[49] See below, pp. 270–3, 278–9, 336–9, 362–3.

Q

to develop. Their foremost preoccupations, in the realm of philanthropy, were the care of syphilitic patients and the care of the 'shamefaced poor'. For some of their activities, there were medieval precedents
—especially in the fraternity of the twelve Buonomini di San Martino,
founded in 1442 by Sant' Antonino, Archbishop of Florence. The tire-
less Observant, Bernardino of Feltre, had also established two fraternities in Vicenza in 1492–3, for the care of poor persons of noble stock
who were ashamed to beg. The original Compagnia del Divino Amore
was founded by Ettore Vernazza in Genoa in 1497.[50] Superficially, its
constitutions somewhat resembled those of the Venetian Scuole. The
society was to consist, at the most, of 36 laymen and four priests. Its
devotional activities at first included the use of the discipline—in
private[51]—though this was no longer prescribed in the statutes of the
fraternity later established in Rome.[52] Like the Scuole dei Battuti, the
society was spiritually linked to the Mendicant Orders.[53] The statutes
of the Genoese society proscribed usurers, blasphemers and evil-livers,
and strictly forbade its members to indulge in any form of gambling.
On familiar lines, they laid down procedures for the administration of
spiritual and corporal charity, and especially for the visitation of sick
members. The society seemed dedicated chiefly to mutual aid; alms
given by its members were reserved chiefly to members of the Compagnia. However, instead of remaining merely another self-centred
organization, the Compagnia del Divino Amore developed into a body
devoted to the care of outcasts and outsiders, and to the systematic
maintenance of hospitals for the chronically sick. From the first, members proposed to perform their good works under conditions of secrecy,
and not with the ostentation of some of the rich medieval fraternities.
Moreover, they helped to create the bond between the practice of
charity and the frequent use of the repeatable sacraments of the Church
which later became characteristic of many Catholic movements of the
sixteenth century. By later standards, their original insistence on
monthly confession and on communion being taken four times a year
was not impressively rigorous. But it went much farther than the
minimum—annual communion and confession—laid down in 1215 by

[50] See especially Pio Paschini, 'Le Compagnie del Divino Amore e la beneficenza
pubblica nei primi decenni del Cinquecento', in his *Tre ricerche sulla storia della
Chiesa nel Cinquecento* (Rome, 1945); also Pastor, *History of the Popes*, X, pp. 388 f.;
Pietro Tacchi Venturi, *Storia della Compagnia di Gesù in Italia* (2 vols. in 4, Rome,
1950–1), I/i, pp. 401–2.

[51] For the statutes of the Genoese society, see Tacchi Venturi, *ibid.*, I/ii, pp. 25–38.

[52] For the statutes of the Roman society, see Antonio Cistellini, *Figure della riforma
pretridentina* (Brescia, 1948), pp. 273–7.

[53] Paschini, 'Le Compagnie del Divino Amore', p. 20.

Innocent III's Lateran Council.[54] Members of these societies experienced the love of Christ through the Eucharist, the bloodless re-enactment on the altar of the Redeemer's sacrifice for mankind. They expressed the love of Christ through the service of the poor—'In so far as you have done this to one of the least of these my brothers, you have done it to me'.[55]

Syphilitic patients were among the first objects of the charity of these societies, and came to occupy in their sight something of the same position as the lepers of the thirteenth century in the spiritual experiences of Francis of Assisi. Care for the incurably sick was a form of asceticism more socially valuable than mere personal austerity or self-torture; it was a means, not only to self-sanctification, but of equipping oneself for tough and demanding evangelical work. Although syphilis appeared to be the successor of leprosy, and although leprosy had largely disappeared by the early sixteenth century, the Compagnie did not merely take over the existing lazar-houses. Instead, they began to establish specialized hospitals of a standardized type, known as hospitals for Incurabili, which refused to admit either lepers or victims of plague. The Compagnia began to put out branches; by the second decade of the sixteenth century, it was established in Rome, where it administered the hospital for Incurabili at Santa Dorotea in Trastevere, whose foundation Leo X authorized in 1515.[56] The Roman society and hospital were excellently placed to become the seedplot for others. Two citizens of Venetian towns, Gaetano Thiene of Vicenza and Bartolomeo Stella of Brescia, priests in early middle age attracted to Rome, helped to import these institutions to Venetian territory. Among the first was the Hospital of the Misericordia in Verona. According to a local historian writing at the close of the sixteenth century, the city council authorized the establishment of the hospital on 11 April 1515, on the instigation of a certain Alessandro Sellaro. He, together with a group of friends and relatives, had decided to found a hospital 'where, by their own poor efforts and out of their own slender property, they might direct and maintain those wretched persons who, being sick, especially of incurable diseases, had no means of support and no medical care'.[57] On this later evidence, it is difficult to be certain that the hospital did in fact admit incurables from the moment of its inception. Thiene was certainly connected with charitable work in Verona

[54] IV Lateran c. 20: Mansi, *Concilia*, XXII, coll. 1007–10.

[55] Matthew xxv, 35–40.

[56] Paschini, 'Le Compagnie del Divino Amore', pp. 34 f.

[57] Girolamo Dalla Corte, *Istorie della città di Verona* (3 vols., Venice, 1744), III, pp. 220–1.

at a slightly later date—in 1517, he obtained a papal brief in favour of a local society, the Confraternità Segreta del Santissimo Corpo di Cristo. Early in 1519, in his native town of Vicenza, Thiene helped to revive the Compagnia Segreta di San Girolamo, originally founded by Bernardino of Feltre, and (in 1521) to re-establish a local hospital—that of Santa Maria della Misericordia in Borgo Pusterla—as an institution catering specifically for syphilitic patients.[58]

Bartolomeo Stella was one of at least five Brescian members of the Compagnia del Divino Amore in Rome, and became one of the officials of its hospital in 1519. The following year he carried both institutions to his native city, where the foundation stone of the Incurabili was laid in 1521.[59] Both in Brescia and in Venice itself, these new hospitals became centres for evangelical work, pivots round which the activities of several devout societies revolved.[60] Those interested in a revival of devotional activity seemed naturally attracted to the Incurabili. Associated with the origins of the Brescian hospital were Gerolamo Patengola and Agostino Gallo, citizens of Brescia and admirers of Angela Merici, the evangelist and Tertiary from Desenzano who later became the foundress of the Ursulines.[61] In the early 1520's, Bartolomeo Stella drafted statutes for a Compagnia, now styled Amicizia or Society of Friends. Many phrases recalled the Genoese and Roman models; the purpose of the association was 'to sow and plant charity in our hearts, exhorting all the Friends to true humility, from which all good conduct proceeds'. However, these statutes clearly bound the brothers, not merely to mutual aid, but to assist outsiders beyond the pale of their fraternity. They were bound to follow a life devoted both to prayer and to works of mercy.

> The Friends shall contrive to meet and converse with one another frequently (things which give pleasure to God), and to employ themselves as much as they can in works of mercy, and to set a good example to their neighbours in all their actions, especially in the support of the sick poor in the Hospital of the Incurabili, whom they must visit and assist to the best of their ability; and they must do likewise to prisoners, and carry out other activities that may arise from day to day, as shall be decided in the congregation by the Head of the Society and his Counsellors.[62]

[58] Paschini, 'Le Compagnie del Divino Amore', pp. 47–8, 61–4; also Pastor, *History of the Popes*, X, pp. 396–7; René de Maulde la Clavière, *Saint Cajetan*, trans. G. H. Ely (London, 1902), pp. 47–8; Giovanni Mantese, *Memorie storiche della Chiesa Vicentina*, III/2 (Vicenza, 1964), pp. 683–8.

[59] Cistellini, *Figure della riforma*, pp. 69–83; Paschini, 'Le Compagnie del Divino Amore', p. 57.

[60] Cf. Cistellini, *Figure della riforma*, p. 93.

[61] *Ibid.*, p. 21.

[62] Draft statutes of the Brescian Amicizia, in Cistellini, *ibid.*, pp. 277–82.

Other foundations at Venice itself and Padua roughly coincided with those of Stella and his Brescian associates. By the summer of 1522, in a letter dilating on the boundless love of Christ and his powers as healer and worker of miracles, Paolo Zabarella, Vicar-General to Marco Cornaro, Bishop of Padua, had approved the foundation of a Compagnia del Divino Amore in his diocese.[63] Four years later, the Pope was granting indulgences in favour of 'the Hospital of San Francesco at Padua for the incurable sickness'.[64] At some stage in the sixteenth century, both Crema and Bergamo acquired such hospitals: Bergamo by 1572, Crema before 1584.[65]

The dispersal of members of the Compagnia del Divino Amore from their nucleus in Rome spread these new institutions. The Vicentine Gaetano Thiene brought them to Venice, at some time before 1522. He joined forces with two women of noble birth, Maria Malipiera Malipiero and Marina Grimani, to take into the shelter of a house at the Spirito Santo three poor women suffering from syphilis whom they had found near the Scuola di San Rocco.[66] The project rapidly attracted support, both from individual noblemen and women, and from the state itself. This was not a state foundation in the same sense as the hospital for ex-servicemen at Sant'Antonio, but the new establishment was soon approved by the Provveditori alla Sanità, acting in the interests of public health. On 22 February 1522, they issued a proclamation ordering all beggars afflicted with syphilis or other offensive evils to enter the hospital forthwith. Private charity, inspired by religious motives, was fully in harmony with the aims of public authority. In the words of the proclamation,

The Most Reverend Monsignor Patriarch has made it known' that many of our gentlemen, gentlewomen and others have been moved with pity for many persons sick and afflicted with the French pox and other ills, some of whom in their impotence loiter on the streets and in the passageways of churches and public buildings both at Rialto and at San Marco to beg for their living; and some of whom, being accustomed to such squalor

[63] Text of the letter, *ibid.*, pp. 291–5. A letter of Hieronimo de la Lama, of 1 October 1524, suggests the existence of Compagnie del Divino Amore in Venice, Padua and Brescia—D.M.S., XXXVII, coll. 35–7.

[64] D.M.S., XLI, coll. 70, 82, 12, 16 March 1526; Paschini, 'Le Compagnie del Divino Amore', p. 71.

[65] Roncalli and Forno, *Atti di Borromeo*, I/ii, p. 250—new regulations for the General Hospital of San Marco (dated 6 September 1572) mention the comparatively recent addition of an infirmary for incurables; A.S.V., *Collegio, Relazioni, busta* 40, report of Pietro Zane, 28 May 1584.

[66] D.M.S., XXXVI, coll. 102–3, 23 March 1524. Entries in the Diaries of Sanuto relating to the Hospital of the Incurabili are collected in E. A. Cicogna, *Inscrizioni veneziane* (6 vols., Venice, 1824–53), V, pp. 305–9.

(*gogioffaria*), do not want to take steps to be cured and recover their health, but stay in those places emitting a great stench and infecting their neighbours. Hence it is a very serious cause for complaint, not only to our people but to all who visit this our city, that there is no provision made for such misery, as there is in every other place in Italy, on our own territory and elsewhere: especially as we are informed that, as a result of this great foetor, contagion and disease might ensue, to the universal detriment and ruin of this our city.[67]

It was popularly believed, of syphilis as of leprosy, that the disease could be transmitted, not only through sexual or other contact, but also through the polluted breath of the sufferer.[68] Afflicted beggars were offered the choice either of entering the new hospital or of being expelled from the state at the expense of the Provveditori alla Sanità. The provision, by private enterprise, of better hospital accommodation enabled the state to attack at least one sector of the problem of begging more systematically.

The number of inmates, as well as the number of supporters, grew rapidly. Within two or three years, the Incurabili had become substantially larger than the average medieval hospital. In 1524, according to the diarist Sanuto, it contained 80 patients, male and female, maintained at a daily cost of about ten ducats overall. By April 1525, the number had reached 150.[69] These early years saw the formation of a governing body of men who expressed an earnest interest in new charitable methods and new forms of devotion. They assumed the name of 'Procurators', or advocates, bound to defend the temporal interests of the new hospital. Acting as a body, they attempted unsuccessfully in 1523–4 to procure the foundation of a Monte di Pietà in Venice, which had so far resisted these Franciscan creations.[70] Among them, Vincenzo, son of the late Doge Antonio Grimani, was a man of piety, the patron of a working woman named Chiara,

a most devout creature, who often goes publicly into ecstasy in the churches of the Carità and San Vio and elsewhere, and has now taken communion and heard Mass every day for fifty days at the Carità; for fifty days she has eaten and drunk nothing, and lives only off the communion.[71]

[67] A.S.V., *Provveditori alla Sanità, Capitolare I*, ff. 31r.–v., 22 February 1522; also printed in Orford, *Leggi sulla prostituzione*, p. 97.

[68] Cf. Creighton, *History of epidemics*, I, pp. 72–3, 422.

[69] D.M.S., XXXVI, coll. 102–3, 23 March 1524; XXXVIII, coll. 140–1, 1 April 1525.

[70] See below, pp. 499–504.

[71] D.M.S., XXXIII, col. 562, 1 January 1523.

This accorded well with the ideals of the Compagnia del Divino Amore, and perhaps compensated a little for the agonized cry of the evangelist Gaetano Thiene:

> I care nothing for outward works or almsgiving if they are not salted with the blood which was shed for us with such burning love. As for this splendid city, *heu, heu, flendum est super illam*. Certainly there is no-one who seeks Christ crucified. It is terrible that, perhaps on account of my sins, I have not found a single noble in such a city who is willing to spurn his honour for the love of Christ. Alas, alas! not one! Christ waits, and no one moves. I do not say there is nobody who means well, *sed omnes stant propter metum Iudaeorum*,[72] and are ashamed to be seen at confession or communion. Father, I shall never be content until I see Christians going to the priest like famished men to eat with pride and not with shame.[73]

Years afterwards, Vincenzo Grimani contemplated entering the newly-established Order of the Theatines, which had grown out of the Compagnia del Divino Amore in Rome.[74] At least two of the other Procurators, Sebastiano Giustinian and Pietro di Zaccaria Contarini, were, or later became, acquainted with leading figures in the pioneering movements for Catholic reform. Sebastiano Giustinian, formerly Venetian Ambassador to England, had met Gian Pietro Caraffa, Bishop of Chieti, later to become co-founder with Thiene of the congregation of Theatines, Cardinal and Pope Paul IV. He had written of Caraffa eulogistically to Erasmus.[75] Pietro Contarini later befriended Ignatius Loyola, and drew him and his band of companions to the hospital of the Incurabili.[76]

In Venice, as in Brescia, the hospital served as a centre and a springboard for a wide variety of evangelical activities among the poor. As its very name suggests, there was little to be done to cure the physical sickness of the sufferers: they could be cleaned and fed and sheltered; but otherwise the main business of the hospital was to provide spiritual consolation. It presented its servants and governors with the opportunity to undertake calculatedly unworldly actions, like the ceremony of washing the feet of poor inmates performed on 24 March 1524— 'There were plenty of people to see it, and many were moved to devotion when they saw these men and women, among the first in the state,

---

[72] Cf. John vii, 13; xix, 38; xx, 19.

[73] Letter of Gaetano Thiene to Paolo Giustinian, a hermit of Camaldoli, 1 January 1523: full text in *Le lettere di San Gaetano da Thiene*, ed. Francesco Andreu (Vatican City, 1954), pp. 52–7. Also quoted in Pio Paschini, *San Gaetano Thiene, Gian Pietro Carafa e le origini dei Chierici Regolari Teatini* (Rome, 1926), p. 24.

[74] D.M.S., XLIX, coll. 367–8, 18 January 1529.

[75] Paschini, *San Gaetano Thiene*, pp. 32–3; Erasmus, *Opus Epistolarum*, ed. Allen, II, pp. 594–7.   [76] See below, p. 264.

carrying out such a pious work'. Sanuto's claim that 'the first in the state' were involved was perfectly just.[77] Some of the Procurators were of sufficient rank and wealth to hold important governorships on the mainland of Italy, and one of them—Agostino Da Mula—served on more than one occasion as a fleet commander or Provveditore in Armata.[78]

By the middle 1520's, some of the machinery later to be used for the care and discipline of the Venetian poor already existed in embryo form, and many of the principles afterwards applied had already been formulated. In the permanent Magistrato alla Sanità, Venice had machinery which could implement state policy towards vagrants. The duty to preserve public health stimulated state intervention in the question of poor relief. Venetian opinion condemned fraudulent begging, and upheld the principle that almsgivers ought to discriminate between the worthy and the unworthy. No attempt to stamp out begging could ever succeed unless its roots were pulled up—unless hospital accommodation was provided, and unless the needs of the poor were anticipated through systematic inquiries into their circumstances and through the distribution of alms to them in their homes. The Venetian authorities had not eliminated all begging, but tried to control it both through the issue of licences to the deserving local poor and through compelling those afflicted with infectious diseases to take advantage of the hospital provided. Sixteenth-century legislators have often been accused of making only the crude distinction between the 'able-bodied' poor, who did not deserve relief, and the disabled, or 'impotent', who did. In fact the Venetians, from an early date, recognized the existence of at least one intermediate category—that of the *poveri vergognosi*, who, though physically whole, could not be expected to work on account of their upbringing. In this, the Venetians were not alone. The extraordinary circumstances of the late 1520's were soon to intensify the demand for organized relief, when famine, disease and the indirect impact of war disrupted many established social securities.

[77] D.M.S., XXXVI, coll. 102–3, 24 March 1524.
[78] D.M.S., XXXV, coll. 184–5; XXXVIII, coll. 140–1.

3

POOR LAWS AND PRIVATE SOCIETIES, 1528–1540

In western Europe, during the decade 1520–30 and the years which followed, the volume of systematic social legislation issued by city authorities markedly grew. At least in Italy, these years witnessed a comparable increase in the number of lay and clerical societies which combined evangelism with poor relief, and which shared both the preoccupations and the attitudes of public legislators. In March 1528 and April 1529, the Venetian Senate made two ambitious attempts to coordinate the organization of poor relief and the dispensation of charity.[1] Many other cities had reacted, or later came to react, to the problem of poverty in an essentially similar way—in Germany in the early 1520's, in the Southern Netherlands from 1524–5, in France by the 1530's, in Spain after 1540.[2] They offered a number of solutions to the problem of poverty which, taken individually, were not completely original—though in the combination, and in the widespread movement towards organized public poor relief, there was surely something new. These schemes for the relief of the poor sought to introduce more efficient machinery for discriminating between the worthy and the unworthy poor, and to establish an official order of priorities in the bestowal of relief. Not only should the available funds be increased, but they should be dispensed in the most effective manner possible, and social parasites be eliminated. The schemes made a broad distinction between paupers who were physically handicapped, and paupers who were able-bodied but not employed; often they recognized a third category, of persons who were physically whole but were ill-equipped

---

[1] For the decree of March 1528, see D.M.S., XLVII, coll. 81–4, and Molmenti, *Storia di Venezia*, II, pp. 477–8. For that of April 1529, A.S.V., *Senato, Terra, reg. 1529*, ff. 125v.–127, and *Documenti per la storia della beneficenza in Venezia* (Venice, 1879), p. CCCXIII. For the history of these laws, see also Pullan, 'The famine in Venice', cited above.

[2] See Ashley, *English economic history*, pp. 340 f.; Salter, *Early tracts on poor relief*; Webbs, *English poor law history*, Part I, pp. 30 f., with many references; Bonenfant, 'Bienfaisance aux Pays-Bas'; Marcel Fosseyeux, 'La taxe des pauvres au XVIe siècle', *Revue d'histoire de l'Église de France*, XX (1934); Ernest Coyecque, 'L'assistance publique à Paris au milieu du XVIe siècle', *Bulletin de la Société de l'Histoire de Paris et de l'Île de France*, XV (1888); N. Z. Davis, 'Humanism, heresy and poor relief'; María Jiménez Salas, *Historia de la asistencia social en España en la Edad Moderna* (Madrid, 1958).

by their upbringing to do manual labour. The largest possible fraction of the community must become self-supporting, independent of relief. The able-bodied should be furnished with opportunities to work, and if necessary be forced to take advantage of these, on pain of expulsion or corporal punishment. Beggar-children must be educated to working, and, where possible, be absorbed into the economic system. The 'impotent' or 'shame-faced' poor, the aged, the crippled and the genteel, must be helped through accommodation in hospitals, through the automatic and regular distribution of alms to their houses, or, in the last resort, through licences to beg designed to establish their worthiness in the sight of the discriminating public. Voluntary aids or compulsory poor-rates must supplement the available funds. Paupers must be the responsibility of their own native places, and native paupers should therefore enjoy priority over outsiders. To make this possible, the laws provided for some centralization in the administration of poor relief funds, designed to procure greater efficiency, to promote a common policy, and to suppress the professional beggar class. There must be some municipal organ to supervise the administration of relief, even if not all institutions were required to deposit their moneys in some Common Chest. The city must appoint experts, municipal deputies who would specialize in knowing all the poor and their circumstances, and in assigning them appropriate quantities of money, victuals or clothing.

During the past forty years, Venice had taken tentative steps in this direction, both on public and on private initiative. But the events of the late 1520's were needed to force the city to formulate a really comprehensive policy, in the face of extraordinary but not unprecedented challenges from famine, disease and the indirect impact of war. Venice did not suffer as tragically or as grievously as Rome or Florence in the late 1520's; no siege was laid to her; there was no threat to overturn the fabric of the state. Nevertheless, a combination of natural disasters with heightened religious ardour produced a new solution to the increasingly acute problem of poverty, on which, in these years, many religious reformers and many responsible magistrates were forced to pronounce.

Thanks to Sanuto's voluminous Diaries, much can be known about the circumstances which attended the issue of the Venetian poor law. During the critical years, 1527-9, much of northern and central Italy lay in the grip of famines and epidemics, heightened by siege warfare and by the invasions of marauding armies which requisitioned and destroyed crops. Regions such as the Veneto, no theatres of war, suffered from drought and flooding against which their agriculture possessed no defence. During this time, Venice was heavily involved in the last attempt, before the signing of the Peace of Bologna, at delivering Italy from Habsburg predominance. Therefore, central European regions, especially Austria and Hungary with their abundant supplies of grain and meat, were inaccessible to Venetian buyers.[3] In the summer of 1527, cloudbursts, remorseless rain and flooding from the Po, the Adige, the Brenta and the Piave partially or completely destroyed the harvests on which Venice depended, and created serious transport difficulties.[4] Much of the seed-corn for the following harvest may have been destroyed or consumed as a result of the shortages of 1527–8, and this may explain a further very poor harvest in 1528. There was, moreover, a serious shortage of labour to gather the harvest in, for famine and plague had depleted the countryside, and the famines had prompted emigration from the villages.[5] Only the abundant harvests whose safety was assured by 19 June 1529 brought relief from the scourge of famine.[6] Between the beginning of 1527 and the spring of 1530, the minimum price of a Venetian bushel or *staio* of good Paduan wheat recorded by Sanuto was 4 lire. The maximum official controlled price—let alone the black-market price—of this quantity of grain was 15½ lire: nearly four times as great. Official prices at the public granaries of San Marco and Rialto actually stood at or near this high level for months at a time. The longest stretch of acute famine ran from the autumn of 1528 to the summer of the following year, when prices fell into the region of only 6–8 lire.[7] In mid-July 1527, a speaker in the Senate remarked that the price of flour had touched some 15 lire the *staio*, 'a thing he had never seen before in all his fifty-one years'.[8]

In severe dearths, the towns attempted to suck the surrounding countryside dry of the victuals it produced. Many citizens were landowners; the patriciates of many medieval Italian cities had been landowning associations.[9] At least since 1455, laws had existed to provide that Venetians must transport to Venice all corn yielded them by their estates, leaving behind only enough to sow the next crop.[10] By 1520, perhaps one-sixth of the cultivated area of the Padovano had passed

---

[3] D.M.S., XLVI, coll. 354, 457; XLVIII, col. 209; LII, col. 296.
[4] D.M.S., XLV, coll. 177, 225, 244, 283, 305; XLVI, col. 106.
[5] D.M.S., XLVIII, col. 87.
[6] D.M.S., L, coll. 500, 507.
[7] Pierre Sardella, *Nouvelles et speculations à Venise au début du XVIe siècle* (Paris, 1948), pp. 25–9; Pullan, 'The famine in Venice', pp. 146–7, and Appendix I, pp. 195–9.
[8] D.M.S., XLV, col. 491.
[9] Cf. P. J. Jones, 'Italy', pp. 348 f.
[10] See Luigi Dal Pane, 'La politica annonaria di Venezia', *Giornale degli economisti e annali di economia, nuova serie*, V (1946), p. 345.

into Venetian hands—after the conquest of Padua in the early fifteenth century, the confiscation of the estates of the ruling family of Carrara had provided excellent opportunities of acquiring further property on the mainland, with the approval and financial encouragement of the Senate.[11] Poorer regions like the Veronese, however, were less penetrated by Venetian capital.[12] Decrees issued in 1527 and 1528 applied to the nearer provinces of the Polesine, Padua, Vicenza, Verona, Treviso and Friuli. They ordered all residents of Venice, all prelates, priests and friars, all monasteries, convents, hospitals and religious corporations of Venice to bring to the city any corn they possessed in those provinces, leaving only seed behind.[13] Roving commissioners were sent out to supervise the process. The interests of peasants in the countryside were less effectively safeguarded than were those of towns, with their stocks of grain, price-controls and landowning citizenry. Moreover, Venice was a grain port: the orifice through which foodstuffs, imported especially from the eastern Mediterranean, could enter and relieve the distress of northern Italy. Venice drew grain from its colony of Cyprus, in the second half of 1527, before Cyprus too sank into distress.[14] Supplies from the Ottoman Empire bulked large, and Venetian ships laded first corn and then huge consignments of beans (an invaluable substitute) in Alexandria.[15] At longer intervals, they took on substantial cargoes in Salonica.[16] Occasionally, on the other hand, merchants managed to transport supplies from Sicily also.[17]

Straddling the grain-route, the Venetians secured their own interests first. Professing a paternal solicitude for their dominions on the mainland, they failed to include them in the same category as themselves. Their needs were urgent and visible; those of their subjects remote if greater. Venetian policy restricted large-scale re-export to the mainland, and the government frequently offered higher bounties to merchants on condition they did not re-export.[18] Occasionally, however, the

[11] Antonio Pino-Branca, 'Il comune di Padova sotto la Dominante nel secolo XV (rapporti amministrativi e finanziari)', *Atti del Reale Istituto Veneto di Scienze, Lettere ed Arti*, XCIII (1933–4), pp. 354–5; Vittorio Lazzarini, 'Beni carraresi e proprietari veneziani', *Studi in onore di Gino Luzzatto*, I (Milan, 1949).

[12] Michele Lecce, 'Le condizioni zootecnico-agricole del territorio veronese nella prima metà del '500', *Economia e Storia*, V (1958), p. 50.

[13] D.M.S., XLVI, coll. 72–3, 184; XLVIII, coll. 24, 59, 152–3.

[14] D.M.S., XLV, coll. 34, 141, 226; XLVI, coll. 380, 479; XLVII, col. 523; XLVIII, col. 296.

[15] D.M.S., XLVI, col. 383; XLVIII, coll. 231, 268; XLIX, coll. 184, 303; L, coll. 11, 71, 373, 385, 425, 474.

[16] D.M.S., XLVI, col. 291; XLVIII, col. 375; XLIX, coll. 422–3.

[17] D.M.S., XLVI, col. 568; XLVII, col. 237.

[18] D.M.S., XLV, coll. 340–1; XLVI, coll. 71–2, 192, 511; XLVIII, coll. 172–3, 214–215, 252–3.

Venetians approved official consignments of grain to distressed provincial cities, such as Verona and Vicenza.[19] Doubtless some grain percolated illicitly through from Venice to the mainland, but it was conveyed by speculators whose motives were scarcely philanthropic, and who were unlikely to observe the price controls theoretically extended by the government from Venice to Padua, Treviso, Vicenza and Cologna early in 1528.[20]

Famines displaced the people of the countryside, breaking up families and destroying the normal securities of village life. Migrations occurred partly, no doubt, because of a blind and helpless instinct to wander in search of food, in the certainty that things could not possibly be worse elsewhere. Perhaps, also, there was genuine knowledge that there were better opportunities for finding food in the towns, and a compelling desire to follow the loads of grain carried off there. Certainly, in years of famine, floods of migrant peasants inundated the towns, swelling and perhaps dwarfing the numbers of the regular professional beggars. In late March 1528, Luigi Da Porto, a noble of Vicenza, wrote that the poor were relentlessly invading the streets, courtyards and even the private dwellings of his native city:

> Give alms to two hundred people, and as many again will appear; you cannot walk down the street or stop in a square or church without multitudes surrounding you to beg for charity: you see hunger written on their faces, their eyes like gemless rings, the wretchedness of their bodies with the skins shaped only by bones.

Everywhere they died; the air rang with their cries, the town stank with their odour.

> Certainly all the citizens are doing their duty with charity—but it cannot suffice, for a great part of the country has come hither, so that, with death and the departure of the people, many villages which lie in the direction of the Alps have become completely uninhabited.[21]

In the greater city of Venice, the problem was at least as acute. Even before the development of famine, Venice and its neighbour Chioggia, secure against invasion, had become heavily burdened with foreign refugees. On 30 April 1527, Sanuto had written: 'There are many foreigners in this city, some fled hither, some come to live; and many from the Romagna have come to Chioggia, though, since the battle-

[19] D.M.S., XLVII, col. 325.
[20] D.M.S., XLVI, coll. 413, 417, 423; XLVII, col. 85.
[21] D.M.S., XLVII, coll. 148–9; also in Luigi Da Porto, *Lettere storiche dall'anno 1509 al 1528*, ed. Bartolomeo Bressan (Florence, 1857), pp. 327–8.

fields have shifted to Tuscany, they are now returning home.'[22] A few weeks later, reciting the famine prices, he observed sourly: 'The trades at a standstill because of the wars, plenty of wine and idleness but all the rest dear, poultry and fish costly because of the great multitude of foreigners in this city.'[23] Apart from the effects of war, high food prices would tend to paralyse trade and industry, since bread would absorb most of the money of humbler people and thus destroy the demand for other products. Artisans and labourers were liable to suffer both from high prices and from unemployment.

Sanuto tersely described the Venetian scene in the winter of 1527–8:

16 December 1527. 'Everything is dear, and every evening, on the Piazza San Marco, in the streets and at Rialto stand children crying "Bread, bread! I am dying of hunger and cold!", which is a tragedy. In the morning, dead have been found under the portals of the palace. Yet no measures are taken.'[24]

2 February 1528. 'After dinner a Cabinet meeting was held, the city full of feasting and many masquerades; and, by contrast, a great horde of poor by day and by night; and many peasants are beginning to come here with their children, looking for food, because of the great famine outside. Yet this morning we heard that some ships were arrived with corn. . . .'[25]

20 February 1528. 'I must record a notable thing, which I want to be a perpetual memorial of the great famine in this city. Apart from the poor who belong to Venice and are crying in the streets, they have come from the island of Burano, mostly with their clothes upon their heads and children in their arms, asking for charity. And many have come from the provinces of Vicenza and Brescia—a shocking thing. You cannot hear Mass without ten paupers coming to beg for alms, or open your purse to buy something without the poor asking for a farthing. Late in the evening they go knocking at the doors, and crying through the streets "I am dying of hunger!" Yet no public measures are taken against this.'[26]

Sanuto's comments seem to betray a sense that this famine was somehow uniquely terrible. His reproachful refrain, 'Yet no public measures are taken', recognized implicitly that the situation was beyond the grasp of private philanthropists and almsgivers. The Vicentine Da Porto had also told how private charity could not suffice. In fact, the government had, in December 1527, organized distributions of rye bread to the poor in the parishes every week.[27] But this did not solve the problem of displaced persons and homeless beggars. The only remedy lay in steps towards formulating a poor law of the type already

22 D.M.S., XLIV, col. 599.   23 D.M.S., XLV, col. 356.
24 D.M.S., XLVI, col. 380.   25 D.M.S., XLVI, col. 550.
26 D.M.S., XLVI, col. 612.   27 D.M.S., XLVI, col. 413,

enforced in Germany and the Southern Netherlands: in drastic measures to clear the streets, yet at the same time provide humanely for the starving; to spread responsibility for the poor over the entire community; to assess the relative claims on charity of Venetians and of immigrants from outside Venice. This action followed when the problem unmistakably presented itself in the form of a threat to public health, with which the Provveditori alla Sanità were charged to deal. The fear of disease underlined the need to control immigration, and to segregate the poor from the healthier members of society. The Senate's decree of March 1528 declared that

> Failure to provide for the multitude of poor at present in the city and increasing day by day would not only cause much greater famine than there is now, but would also (and this is even worse) import disease of the kind which has been seen in many cities of Italy, and which no human remedy has been able to extinguish.[28]

In all probability, the disease which immediately threatened the Venetians was typhus, the *mal di petecchie* or 'spotted sickness'. Epidemics of typhus and of bubonic plague tended to run concurrently, with typhus reaching its peak in the colder months of the year: it was a disease conveyed by body lice (though this fact was unknown to contemporaries), and therefore flourished in seasons when people wore the maximum quantity of infested clothing and personal hygiene was at its lowest level. Conditions of famine, homeless wandering, abject poverty and constant warfare were ideal for the spread of typhus.[29] Some form of pestilence was an expected consequence of famine. The previous April, Giovanni Contarini, Governor of Vicenza, had announced in a proclamation that the poor peasants 'and all their families were living like animals, for the most part off grass and water . . . with manifest peril of introducing an uncommon pestilence into the country' —though he may have been referring to some form of food poisoning as well as to the threat of typhus fever.[30] There were few or no precise clinical descriptions of typhus before the first half of the sixteenth century, when the fever was described by Girolamo Cardano in 1525 and by the Veronese physician Girolamo Fracastoro in 1546.[31]

---

[28] D.M.S., XLVII, coll. 81–4.

[29] Cf. Raymond Crawfurd, 'Contributions from the history of medicine to the problem of the transmission of typhus', *Proceedings of the Royal Society of Medicine*, VI: *Section of the History of Medicine* (1913); Hans Zinsser, *Rats, lice and history* (London, 1935), pp. 236 f.; W. P. MacArthur, 'Old-time typhus in Britain', *Transactions of the Royal Society of Tropical Medicine and Hygiene*, XX (1926–7).

[30] D.M.S., XLV, col. 20.

[31] See Girolamo Cardano, *De methodo medendi*, ch. xxxvi, revised edition in his *Opera omnia*, VII (Lyons, 1663), p. 216; Girolamo Fracastoro, *De contagione et*

Cardano, a native of Pavia, had lived in Saccolongo, near Padua, from 1526 to 1529, whilst his own country was 'being devastated by all manner of evils':[32] he had opportunities of seeing the spotted fever at large in the Veneto. Although severe 'famine fevers' had broken out in medieval Europe,[33] sixteenth-century physicians evidently believed that the disease was comparatively new, at least to western Europe. According to Fracastoro, 'the fever which they call lenticular or punctate or petechial' had first appeared in Italy in 1505 (another famine year) and again in 1528, 'although in certain nearby regions, in Cyprus, and in neighbouring islands, it was known to our ancestors'.

In March 1528, Luigi Da Porto wrote an account of the mysterious disease afflicting the city of Vicenza, which was teeming with beggars who had invaded it from the countryside.[34] This coincides in important details with the descriptions by Cardano and Fracastoro.

> Some days, the clergy of the city cannot suffice to bury even the noblemen who are dying, oppressed by a certain malignity of humours which are hidden, and all but unknown to physicians, so that many have died whilst still saying they did not feel ill at all, and others at the first onset made their bodies completely still, suffering from a very severe headache. None had very obvious fever in the outward parts of the body, but there was a certain malignancy which went to their hearts and at once vanquished the soul and the spirit of life at a single blow, so that little could be done for many of them, because they were not strong enough to respond to treatment. Spots (*petecchie*) have been discovered on some, but not on others, on some livid and as wide as small coins, on others tiny as chickpeas, red, raised up and pointed, very similar to the measles which appear on children.[35] Some of both sorts have recovered. . . .

The disease could well have been spread by overcrowding in the cities resulting from the mass movements of population in the Veneto. Da Porto offered a very different explanation—

> I think not that there is any contagion in the air, but only a sickness in the souls of men, caused by pity for these things (i.e. the sufferings of the poor), which breeds poisonous humours in the body.

contagiosis morbis et eorum curatione (Lyons, 1550), pp. 321 f., 459 f. Both these clinical descriptions are translated in R. H. Major, *Classic descriptions of disease with biographical sketches of their authors* (London, 1945), pp. 163–5.

[32] Girolamo Cardano, *The book of my life (De vita propria liber)*, trans. J. Stoner (London, 1931), pp. 13–14.

[33] MacArthur, 'Old-time typhus', p. 490.

[34] D.M.S., XLVII, coll. 147–8; Da Porto, *Lettere storiche*, pp. 326–7. For diagnosis of the disease, and for much valuable help, I am indebted to Dr D. B. Cater, Dr Arthur Rook and Dr W. A. H. Rushton.

[35] Cf., the fact that Cardano took pains to distinguish typhus from measles.

246

DIVES AND LAZARUS (IL RICCO EPULONE)

Here Bonifacio de' Pitati (c. 1487–1553), a Veronese artist working in Venice, depicts the extremes of irresponsible wealth and abject poverty. For the significance of Lazarus, see above, p. 222.

facing p. 246

St Omobono giving alms to a beggar

St Omobono (or Homo-bonus) was a twelfth-century merchant of Cremona, renowned for his charity, and became the patron saint of tailors and cloth-makers—hence the scissors. This painting, dated 9 November 1533, was executed for the Guild of Tailors in Venice.

facing p. 247

Fracastoro was later to classify the disease as 'malignant' rather than 'pestilential', because its mortality rate was lower than that of plague. But its effects in Venice were devastating, when combined with those of starvation and unemployment. It greatly sharpened the demand for state action to direct and supplement private philanthropy.

On 13 March 1528, the Ducal Counsellor Alvise Mocenigo, and Giovanni Francesco Emiliani, one of the Heads of the Quarantia, joined with the Provveditori alla Sanità in introducing proposals in the Senate. They suggested erecting 'two, three or more' large temporary refuges, shelters constructed out of boards and supplied with straw to sleep on, and lodging the poor therein. All paupers must enter these hospitals: begging was strictly forbidden, on pain of arrest, corporal punishment and subsequent expulsion from the city. Boatmen must inform all persons ferried to the city of the penalties for begging. No paupers from outside Venice were in future to be admitted to the rudimentary hospitals. These hospitals now became the responsibility of the whole community, and taxation was to be systematically levied for their maintenance. This poor-rate would be assessed according to the rent paid by each inhabitant of the city, and it amounted to a tax of about $2\frac{1}{2}$ per cent, or 3 soldi per ducat of rent. Persons who owned their houses would probably be assessed according to the rateable value attributed to them at the last fiscal survey of real property, on which the apportionment of the secular, state-imposed tithe or Decima was based. The collection of the tax should be conducted through the parish, by means of the parish priest and two lay deputies appointed in each parish. The Provveditori alla Sanità must receive the moneys collected through parochial machinery, and dispense them in the interests of the poor. Lists of those who refused or failed to pay the tax would be entered on the books of the Provveditori alla Sanità, and the roll of their names would then be read from the parish pulpits at High Mass on festival days: a species of formal disgrace which few would care to face with equanimity. Finally, the legislators appended a clause to the effect that the new system should not interfere with the existing machinery for the distribution of alms to the house-poor or *poveri vergognosi* of each parish. The Senate proposed to accept responsibility for the poor until the following June, when the harvest could be expected to relieve the famine. The poor from the hospitals were then to be transported to the mainland, and dismissed with a solemn threat of being flogged from San Marco to Rialto should they return to beg.[36]

Enforcement of the decree then proceeded. By the beginning of April, the Venetians had run up four hospitals—three situated in the

[36] D.M.S., XLVII, coll. 81–4.

R

sestiere of Castello at SS. Giovanni e Paolo, San Giovanni in Bragora and Sant'Antonio, the fourth at Ca' Donà on the Giudecca.[37] San Giovanni in Bragora already contained the headquarters of the foundling hospital of the Pietà, Sant'Antonio the hospital of Gesù Cristo. Many immigrant peasants had no wish to be immured there, and continued to beg in spite of all the prohibitions. The hospitals did not present themselves as attractive, humanitarian institutions, and the Provveditori alla Sanità had to protect the servants of SS. Giovanni e Paolo from insults and violence.[38] By the middle of the month, about a thousand immigrants had been lodged in the hospitals, where they received bread, wine and soup, but many deaths were occurring there, and begging persisted. Attempts to prevent further immigration and to round up the poor continued. By 18 April 1528, the Provveditori alla Sanità had undoubtedly adopted the proposal—advanced during the debate in March—that healthy immigrants should be expelled, and only the sick be lodged in the hospitals.[39]

The law of 13 March 1528 embodied the first attempt made by the Venetian government at the total elimination of begging. It was a measure designed to meet a severe temporary crisis, in which mere private almsgiving, and even organized distributions of bread through the parishes, proved inadequate to meet the needs of the poor. It did, however, assert the principle that in such a crisis the state could levy taxation in the combined interests of humanity and public health for the support of the poor. It carried into execution the already formulated principle that where the need was acute poor relief should be dispensed in a highly discriminating manner, and in accordance with an order of priorities that placed the sick above the healthy and the native above the foreigner. It did not lack all precedent: the processes which led to the foundation of the hospitals of Gesù Cristo di Sant'Antonio and of the Incurabili were moves in the same direction, but not convincing attempts to prevent begging entirely. In part, this poor law was the defensive measure of a city menaced by famine and disease, its streets overrun by poor immigrants from as far afield as the province of Brescia, about 120 miles to the west. Its own policies had done much to provoke this immigration. But the Venetians did not take the least responsible way: they may have enforced prohibitions on migration to Venice both by beggars and by casual labourers pretty consistently from March 1528 onwards,[40] but they at least did some-

[37] D.M.S., XLVII, col. 178.

[38] A.S.V., *Provveditori alla Sanità, Notatorio II*, vol. 726, f. 132v.

[39] D.M.S., XLVII, col. 252.

[40] A.S.V., *Provveditori alla Sanità, Notatorio II*, vol. 726, ff. 130v.–131, 141v., 142v., 167, 173.

thing to help those who had already arrived before the issue of the poor law. Nevertheless, their policy was in fact likely to promote the disease rather than to quell it, since typhus throve on overcrowding, and so, in later centuries, acquired the name of ship-, camp-, gaol- or hospital-fever. To herd the poor together was to imperil their lives. During the months March, April and May 1528, the death toll from all causes in the city of Venice was formidably high—666 reported dead in March, 1,041 in April, and 1,439 in May. Over this period, 293 deaths occurred in the hospital of SS. Giovanni e Paolo alone.[41] Probably a high proportion of these deaths—which increased as the last grain supplies shrank in the months before the new harvest— resulted from starvation. Sanuto's first mention of the spotted fever was made on 6 May 1528,[42] but it may well have invaded the city at an earlier date. The meaning of these mortality figures is hard to assess: but one can grasp something of it by a comparison with the statistics for the following year. In the months of April and May 1529, the number of deaths recorded was between 900 and 950, as compared with nearly 2,500 in April and May 1528. Even in 1529, food prices were high, and Venice was suffering from a relatively controlled out- break of pestilence, of which there were over 100 cases in those two months. This was not likely to have been an exceptionally good year.[43]

Official precautions against disease were inadequate to prevent the spotted fever from being succeeded by the pestilence. A disease des- cribed as *peste* on the bills of mortality began to attack Venice in the summer of 1528. To judge by its seasonal incidence, it was probably bubonic plague: it resembled the great seventeenth-century epidemics of London and Leyden, and the Marseilles outbreak of 1720, in mounting to a climax in late summer and early autumn.[44] It claimed most victims in September and October, and thereafter declined abruptly with the onset of winter, the season least favourable to the breeding of fleas. *Peste* had room to itself on the bills of mortality. From those summarized by Sanuto, it can be calculated that between mid-July and mid-August there were probably at least 225 deaths from bubonic plague and 850 from other causes; in the next month 200 or more deaths from plague and 550 from other causes; then 285 or more deaths from plague and 410 from other causes. The pattern continued:

[41] This summary, probably drawn up by the Provveditori alla Sanità, was repro- duced by Sanuto in his entry for 31 May 1528 under the heading *Copia tratta de li morti moreno per la terra*—D.M.S., XLVII, col. 550.

[42] D.M.S., XLVII, col. 370.

[43] See Pullan, 'Famine in Venice', Appendix II, pp. 199–202.

[44] Hirst, *Conquest of plague*, pp. 260–1; cf. also the figures showing the seasonal incidence of plague in Vicenza in 1577, in Rodenwaldt, *Pest in Venedig*, p. 110.

the number of deaths from plague increased, whilst the toll from other causes proportionately diminished.[45] Sanuto believed that typhus had departed by the end of August, only to reappear in February and March 1529, though it did not attack the population as viciously as before, and on 18 June 1529 he felt able to say that it had disappeared.[46] Between April 1528 and November 1529, the number of plague cases noted by the Provveditori alla Sanità was probably in the region of 1,850, though not all of these were necessarily fatal.

Again, to assess the meaning of these figures in terms of a proportional reduction in the population of Venice is nearly impossible. There is no accurate estimate of the total population of the city for any year near to 1527–9, and in any case the population must have fluctuated unusually rapidly during this period: the city was swarming with temporary migrants in constant movement—into Venice, impelled by hunger, and out of it again, expelled by agents of the Provveditori alla Sanità. Many of the deaths occurred among this unsettled, floating population. But according to the figures for the population of Venice accepted by Professor Beltrami, the city had about 115,000 inhabitants in 1509, rising to some 130,000 by 1540.[47] It is doubtful whether the extraordinary mortality from hunger and disease occurring in Venice in 1528 was equivalent to more than about 4 per cent of the more settled population. This, compared with the great plagues of 1575–7 and 1630–1, was destruction on a relatively small scale: but the Venetians were accustomed to a different incidence of epidemic disease in the late fifteenth and early sixteenth century—of smaller but much more frequent outbreaks. With this their social legislation was designed to deal, and it was to survive into a period in which the demographic pattern changed. A preamble of October 1528 implied that the current epidemic was believed to be the severest for the past fifty years. Some sort of contagion had invaded the city every seven or eight years since the great plague of 1478, but had proved relatively easy to scotch 'since the cities of Italy, especially those which belong to our own state, and also neighbouring cities in foreign states, were free of the pestilence'. The situation was now much more ominous, 'since the whole of Italy, and especially the coastal cities, are oppressed by this disaster'. To control the epidemic would therefore be far more difficult.[48] Here, again, there was a certain belief in the peculiar severity of the current situation, a sense that it demanded peculiar measures.

[45] Pullan, 'Famine in Venice', Appendix II, pp. 199–202.

[46] D.M.S., XLVIII, col. 423; XLIX, col. 483; L, col. 11, 132, 507.

[47] Daniele Beltrami, *Storia della popolazione di Venezia dalla fine del secolo XVI alla caduta della Repubblica* (Padua, 1954), pp. 57–8.

[48] D.M.S., XLIX, col. 43.

Plague aggravated the problem of poverty, because the quarantine regulations it demanded threatened to paralyse the economy. The belief that plague, even in its bubonic form, was an ordinary infectious disease communicated directly between man and man, caused the sanitary authorities to concentrate on limiting the movements of human beings, and on fumigating or destroying goods which had been in immediate contact with victims. The emphasis on the restriction of human movement caused the Venetian authorities to pursue what a modern writer has called the 'tragically mistaken' policy of locking up members of a household in which a death from plague had occurred in the stricken house itself, to prevent them from spreading infection.[49] Should people be isolated in their own boarded-up homes, or transferred to the dreaded pesthouse, the Lazaretto Nuovo, they were usually prevented from earning their living in the normal way. Poor families with no reserves of cash or realizable assets to fall back on urgently needed support from charity or from public funds. Therefore, on 21 August 1528, the Senate again announced a levy on the propertied members of the community. The tax was raised on exactly the same principles as before, but at the rate of 1 soldo per ducat or about 0·8 per cent only. Any sums remaining from the previous poor-rate must be devoted to the same end: the support of the *serrati*, of persons confined in their homes as a quarantine measure.[50] Further difficulties, and a further need for subsidies, arose from the determination to destroy clothing and bedding once in contact with the disease. At first, the magistrates formed huge dumps at the pesthouses in the lagoon, but they judged a period of forty days necessary before the goods would be free of infection. Not surprisingly, by December 1528, the dumps were overflowing, and it seemed impossible to fumigate the bedding adequately and still preserve it. The Signory therefore gave orders to burn all bedding, pillows, eiderdowns, quilts and similar objects in the pesthouses—but at the same time instructed the Provveditori alla Sanità to have the goods valued first and to pay compensation to the owners.[51]

Disease, therefore, called upon the state to assume extensive responsibility for the poor, whose livelihood and property had suffered, not only from the disease itself, but also from the regulations necessary to bring it under control. The first poor law had been put into operation as an emergency measure in the face of immediate and formidable danger. There is no record in Sanuto's journals of further mass immigration to Venice. Perhaps the stringent quarantine regulations

[49] Cf. Hirst, *Conquest of plague*, pp. 406 f.
[50] D.M.S., XLVIII, col. 394.   [51] D.M.S., XLIX, col. 241; cf. also col. 371.

designed to control the plague had frustrated it, though plague itself could only worsen the circumstances of the poor. But the Senate proceeded to pass a still more elaborate statute on 3 April 1529,[52] evidently formulated at greater leisure. The principles were those familiar to many other municipal authorities in Europe at this time and in the decades which followed. According to the preamble, the decree was formulated both in a spirit of charity and in a desire to preserve order and discipline. It set out

> to watch over the welfare of the poor and the health of the sick, to give bread to the hungry, and not to fail to aid and favour those who are capable of earning their own living in the sweat of their brow.

Its sterner purpose was to rid the city of the 'knavery and mendicity' which was plaguing it. Accordingly, all 'foreign' (i.e., non-Venetian) beggars who entered the city must be sent away with letters of commendation to the governors of the places from whence they came. These governors were instructed to take care of them and not allow them to return. Everyone was the responsibility of his native place or *patria*.

Once this preliminary distinction had been made, natives or inhabitants of Venice (*terrieri*) should be classified either as impotent or as able-bodied. 'Impotent' poor who possessed their own houses should retire to them and put themselves in the hands of their parish priests: on no account should they go forth and beg on their own initiative. The homeless 'impotent' poor should be drafted into hospitals or other suitable places of refuge. As for the able-bodied, the real sturdy and obstreperous beggars should be embarked on ships. Masters of merchant vessels would be asked to take as many poor as possible; they must pay their expenses as they did for other sailors, but were entitled to offer them only half the usual pay. Perhaps without this inducement it would scarcely have been possible to persuade captains to accept so dubious and inexperienced a crew. Likewise, the magistrates in charge of naval recruiting received orders to load light galleys and *fuste* with appropriate consignments of poor recruits. Venetian galleys, propelled by oars as well as sails, were prodigal of manpower, and the Venetian government could neglect no opportunities of raising supplies. In 1545, at the instigation of Cristoforo Da Canal, the Senate was to resort to convict labour.[53] Some years earlier, it had appreciated the possibilities of vagabond labour as well. Service at sea promised at once to benefit the state and the economy, and to discipline and deter the poor. The Senate then proceeded to call upon the officers of the

---

[52] A.S.V., *Senato, Terra, reg. 1529*, ff. 125v.–127.   [53] See above, pp.144–5.

guilds, hinting that each guild ought to accept three or four poor apprentices and teach them its craft, whilst providing them with food and wages as seemed necessary. There remained, however, the serious problem of widows and other women with young dependent children, who had acquired no skills and could not ply any of the trades. Somewhat vaguely, the Senate instructed parish priests and deputies to put them in the way of any work they could do—perhaps odd jobs or domestic service—and to supplement their income out of charitable funds if they proved unable to support themselves.

The decree made no attempt to establish a single central bureau, a General Almonry or Common Chest, to control all funds destined for the poor. It allowed monasteries, hospitals and Scuole to distribute charity independently, under the usual distant supervision of their magistracies, and merely reminded them (together with prelates, churchwardens and 'others who enjoy abundant property') of their general duty to the poor. The Senate's decree called on the superiors of nunneries to consider, and where possible to admit to their convents, poor girls of good morals recommended to them by parish deputies. It also imposed responsibility for exhorting the people to charity upon the so-called Scuole del Corpus Domini. These fraternities probably owed their existence to a comparatively recent movement in Italy to guarantee due reverence for the sacrament and to save it from desecration: a movement with which certain Friars, such as Bernardino of Feltre, had been associated.[54] Their accounts and those of other small Scuole were to be reviewed by the parish deputies.

The poor law of April 1529 was ultimately designed to ensure that the work of these established organizations should be supplemented by the parishes. The Senate stipulated that the parish priests should summon their parishioners once a year to elect by ballot a committee of two nobles, one citizen and one 'artisan' or guildsman to look after the welfare of the parish poor 'and not allow the Majesty of God to be offended in their parishes, as far as that is possible'. They then appealed to the assembly to vote an aid or 'voluntaria taxa' to be dispensed to the poor. Parish priests were to be ordered, both by the Patriarch and by the Provveditori alla Sanità, to appeal to the rich inhabitants of every parish for charity. On penalty of a fine of ten ducats, priests must draw their parishioners' attention to the new law at High Mass every high festival. Preachers must preach charity sermons, and a poor-box be placed in every parish church, with the priests and deputies holding

[54] Cf. Tacchi Venturi, *Storia della Compagnia di Gesù*, I/i, pp. 219 f. Cf. the references to Scuole del Corpo di Cristo in D.M.S., XIX, col. 462, 28 February 1515, and XX, col. 98, 6 April 1515; see also above, p. 121.

its keys and keeping accounts of how the contents were dispensed. These accounts were to be audited annually by the judges of the palace courts. The Senate evidently preferred to keep poor relief on a voluntary basis, using only moral pressures to prick the conscience of donors; and to impose compulsory taxation by Senatorial decree (as in March 1528) only in grave emergencies.

This more elaborate law was thus placed on the statute-book in the spring of 1529—but it was probably not fully enforced in Venice itself until 1545 and afterwards.[55] The immediate incentives for the enforcement of the law abruptly diminished in the summer of 1529, with the abundant harvest and the fall in grain prices about 20 June. Not more than forty or fifty cases of plague were recorded in any one summer month.[56] In the years to come, population pressure, rather than the diseases which cut population back, created the demand for the enforcement of the law.

The explanation for the form of this poor law cannot lie merely in economic expediency. Although the Venetians believed that the crisis was peculiarly severe in 1528, similar situations must have arisen in earlier years (as in 1505)[57] without being met by comparable legislation. Changes of attitude as well as changes of circumstance were required in order to produce this result. One possible explanation lies in external influences—in the example of other cities abroad. A plausible thesis, advanced by the Belgian historian Paul Bonenfant, traced the poor law schemes to the influence of Lutheranism, and suggested that they began to spread from Saxony in 1522–3 to Nuremberg and Strassburg. These acted as foci for the dissemination of the poor laws, first across the Flemish and later across the French frontier. In such cities, some of Luther's principles were blended with older laws on poverty, charity and vagrancy which were familiar and not repugnant to orthodox Catholics. Nevertheless, the reform of poor relief resulted from 'a curious and doubtless generally unconscious introduction of Lutheran principles into the legislation of Catholic towns and countries'.[58] One cannot rule out the possibility that German influence contributed to the Venetian poor law, though there is no direct and concrete evidence to support such an argument. The Venetians could easily have heard what was happening in Nuremberg. This was one of the most internationally active of German commercial cities, and about 1500 there were 232 Nuremberg merchants in Venice, as

[55] See below, pp. 297 f.

[56] Pullan, 'Famine in Venice', Appendix II, pp. 199–202.

[57] Priuli, *Diarii*, II, pp. 348 f., especially the entry for 15 February 1505 at pp. 368–9.

[58] Bonenfant, 'Bienfaisance aux Pays-Bas', VI, pp. 221 f.

compared with not more than five from Strassburg and 62 from Augsburg.[59] The presence of so large a body of Nurembergers on Venetian territory gave rise to much correspondence between the two city governments.[60] Nuremberg had been sensitive to the influence of the Wittenberger reformers since 1517, had failed to enforce the Edict of Worms against Luther, and had by 1522 appointed a Wittenberg student and graduate to the parish churches—though it did not officially turn Lutheran until 1525.[61] In 1522 it had introduced a scheme for the systematic administration of poor relief and control of begging.[62] It is, however, doubtful how far such schemes ought to be identified with 'Lutheranism'. Some of what Luther said and wrote bore his own peculiar stamp; many of the opinions he voiced on social questions did not, and were perfectly acceptable to persons who did not opt for the Reformation. Certainly, attempts were sometimes made to discredit the new poor laws in Catholic towns on the score that they were defiled by the Lutheran heresy, or might lead to the spoliation of ecclesiastical property.[63] But, in the words of a Catholic priest in Ypres, writing in August 1531,

> It is no good confronting us with the Germans. Where, I ask you, did you ever read that among their condemned doctrines is the opinion that they ought to maintain their poor out of a Common Chest, and prohibit vagrancy and idle begging? Nowhere: and this supports our case, for otherwise the censors of doctrine would never have passed it. Because they saw it was a useful Christian measure, they allowed it to stand.[64]

Certainly, Luther argued in general that the sovereign remedy for social evils was the elimination of the parasitic classes in society— including beggars—and the abandonment of socially useless or pernicious piety.[65] But his was only one of several impulses in this

[59] Cf. Hans Baron, 'Religion and politics in the German imperial cities during the Reformation', *English Historical Review*, LII (1937), p. 616.

[60] See documents in Henry Simonsfeld, *Der Fondaco dei Tedeschi in Venedig und die deutsch-venetianischen Handelsbeziehungen* (2 vols., Stuttgart, 1887), vol. I.

[61] See, for example, Gerald Strauss, *Nuremberg in the sixteenth century* (New York, 1966), pp. 160 f.; Gerald Strauss, 'Protestant dogma and city government: the case of Nuremberg', *Past and Present*, no. 36, April 1967.

[62] For the text of this scheme, see Otto Winckelmann, 'Die Armenordnungen von Nurnberg (1522), Kitzingen (1523), Regensburg (1523) und Ypern (1525)', *Archiv für Reformationsgeschichte*, X (1912–13), pp. 258 f. The broad similarity between the laws of Nuremberg and those of Venice is already noticed by Tacchi-Venturi, *Storia della Compagnia di Gesù*, I/i, pp. 419–20.

[63] For examples, cf. N. Z. Davis, 'Humanism, heresy and poor relief'.

[64] Letter of Joos de Wulf, printed as doc. 21 in J. Nolf, *La réforme de la bienfaisance à Ypres au XVIe siècle* (Ghent, 1915), p. 143.

[65] For his views specifically on the question of begging, see the 'Address to the Christian nobility of the German nation', trans. in B. L. Woolf, *Reformation writings*

direction, and his impatience with those superstitious 'good works' that distracted from true charity was certainly shared by humanists whose position ultimately differed sharply from the Lutheran.

With these qualifications, one can accept the possibility that German influences contributed to the poor law of 1529—though not the belief that this marked an infiltration of heresy into Venice. There were many instances, in the sixteenth century, of city authorities studying one another's laws with a view to learning from them. Somewhat later in the century, the poor laws of Ypres, Paris and Lyons became important models for others.[66] As it happened, the Nurembergers in 1505 had asked for copies of Venetian laws on wardship,[67] and it is quite plausible that in the late 1520's the reverse process could have occurred, and laws of German origin been promulgated in Venice. Again, the Senate was in a position to know of the action taken by the Florentines: the Venetian Antonio Surian, who served as Ambassador to the last Florentine Republic under siege conditions from January 1528 to April 1529, told on his return of

the kindness of the city, for in such a famine not one pauper was turned away, but all were fed, though an enormous number assembled here. Apart from public assistance, they made a provision that ecclesiastical benefices should pay the poor a certain portion, as the sacred canons ordain that a part of the revenue be converted to the use of the poor; and again, that when such benefices fall vacant, all the revenue should devolve upon the poor. They have deputed four citizens to see that this is done.[68]

Moreover, as a possible remedy against the spread of plague, the Florentines found shelter for roaming beggar children who had formerly spent the night slumbering in heaps under the cover afforded them by the Mercato Vecchio.[69]

Finally, to conclude this speculation about possible external influences on the Venetian scheme for poor relief, it is worth mentioning

of Martin Luther (2 vols., London, 1952–6), pp. 172–4; his Leisnig ordinance, trans. in part in Salter, *Tracts on poor relief,* pp. 84–96.

[66] Salter, *Tracts on poor relief,* pp. 33–76, prints the English translation of the Ypres scheme of poor relief by William Marshall. See G. R. Elton, 'An early Tudor poor law', *Economic History Review,* second series, VI (1953–4), for the probable activities of Marshall as a poor-law reformer. For French examples of the exchange of statutes on poor relief between cities, see Fosseyeux, 'La taxe des pauvres', pp. 417, 418, 427, 414.

[67] Samuele Romanin, *Storia documentata di Venezia* (10 vols., Venice, 1912–21), VI, pp. 451–2.

[68] 'Relazione di Antonio Suriano', in Eugenio Alberi, *Relazioni degli ambasciatori veneti al Senato,* II/v (Florence, 1858), p. 428.

[69] Benedetto Varchi, *Storia fiorentina: nella quale principalmente si contengono l'ultime revoluzioni della Repubblica fiorentina e lo stabilimento del principato nella Casa de' Medici* (Cologne, 1721), p. 186.

that in the middle 1520's Venice sheltered Michael Geismayr, formerly confidential secretary and tax-collector to the Bishop of Brixen. He, in 1525, had led the Tyrolese peasants' revolt; he was assassinated in 1528.[70] The Venetians would scarcely have approved some of the proposals in his imaginary constitution—for the abolition of cities, the public ownership of mines, the centralization of business enterprises and marketing. But they could well have appreciated the suggestion that, even while the poor were supported from the proceeds of the tithe, 'such regulations shall be made as will do away with house-to-house begging, so that idle loafers may no longer be permitted to collect charity'; that officials should be specially deputed to looking after asylums and paupers; and that in the last resort private charity should be supplemented out of public funds, if it proved inadequate. Geismayr's proposals for converting the monasteries and houses of the Teutonic Knights into asylums for the sick, for the aged and for 'poor, uneducated children' were also too radical for the Venetians—though a few years later, Andrea Lippomano, Prior of Holy Trinity and holder of two substantial commendams, did feel a compelling urge to convert his revenues to charitable uses.[71]

In any case, the home demand for ampler and more intelligent philanthropy was very strong. The complex of charitable activities revolving round the Incurabili and its governing congregation began to expand. Already, in 1523–4, the governors had made an abortive attempt to erect a Monte di Pietà.[72] On 16 June 1525, a patent issued by the Patriarch Girolamo Querini, entitling the hospital to seek alms in his diocese, referred to it as the house 'in which the sick, male and female children, orphans and sinful women converted to God' were lodged and maintained.[73] In Brescia and Bergamo, the hospitals for Incurabili were absorbed into the existing general hospitals. But in Venice, the Incurabili itself emerged as the first general hospital. Naturally enough, concern with venereal disease hinged over into an anxiety to prevent and control prostitution—both as a prophylactic measure in the interests of public health, and as a move in the campaign for the salvation of souls. By following the sublime example of Mary Magdalen, the harlot could, by deliberately forsaking her former way of life and vowing herself to austerity and repentance, expunge her sins and attain salvation. The Compagnie del Divino Amore and their associates had begun to revive a form of institution, the house for

[70] See J. S. Schapiro, *Social reform and the Reformation* (New York, 1909), pp. 145 f., with the text of Geismayr's project: 'This is Geismayr's constitution when he dreams in his chimney corner and imagines himself a prince'.
[71] See below, pp. 263–4, 384.   [72] See below, pp. 499–504.
[73] Cicogna, *Inscrizioni veneziane*, V, p. 310.

repentant prostitutes, already found in Florence, Siena and Bologna in the fourteenth century, and recently revived in Paris also by the Franciscan Jean Tisserant in 1496.[74] One such institution was already flourishing in Rome by 1524, and in Brescia Bartolomeo Stella, founder of the local Incurabili, contemplated the establishment of another in the mid-1520's.[75] Evidently, the repentant sinners of Venice occupied a wing of the general hospital of the Incurabili, until in the early 1540's they moved to their own premises, the nunnery of the Convertite on the Giudecca.[76]

The sack of Rome by imperial troops in 1527 made Venice, for a few years, the headquarters of the religious and charitable movements branching out from the Compagnie del Divino Amore. Gaetano Thiene himself had left Venice for Rome in 1524. There he had joined with Gian Pietro Carafa, Bishop of Chieti and holder of the Archbishopric of Brindisi in commendam, formerly (like Thiene himself) a career priest, to found a new Order of Regular Clerks. This proposed Order was to devote itself to evangelical work—it must not be involved in the need to administer temporal estates; must not be committed to parochial duties or to the recitation of an elaborate liturgy; nor, like the Mendicant Orders, should it beg for support. Its members were to renounce any benefices they might hold, and the society should depend entirely on voluntary contributions. The four original members of the new Order, Thiene, Carafa, Bonifacio de' Colli and Gislerio Consiglieri, were all members of the Compagnia del Divino Amore. Both the foundation of the Order, and its charitable activities in the anarchy which accompanied the sack of Rome, were described to members of the Compagnie in cities abroad by enthusiastic correspondents. Early in 1527, the governing congregation of the Incurabili appointed Carafa and Thiene to represent their interests at the Roman Curia. Soon, they had occasion to offer them hospitality as refugees. The congregation escaped from Rome, taken off at Civitavecchia by a part of the Venetian fleet, and on 17 June 1527, at the beginning of the dark years of famine and sickness, they were welcomed to Venice by the Procurators of the Incurabili. After occupying two temporary homes, the small community accepted the offer of the pious fraternity of San Nicolò da Tolentino to consign them both an oratory and living quarters on their own premises near the Chiovere, in the sestiere of Santa Croce. Carafa, the most forceful figure in the company, remained in Venice until his

[74] Tacchi-Venturi, *Storia della Compagnia di Gesù*, I/i, p. 383 n. 1.

[75] Paschini, 'Le Compagnie del Divino Amore', pp. 50–2, 57; Cistellini, *Figure della riforma*, pp. 91, 237–8.

[76] See below, p. 377.

summons to Rome to be raised to the purple by Paul III in 1536. The name Theatines, applied to the new congregation, derived from the Latin name of Carafa's bishopric of Chieti, of which he retained the title but not the revenues. This group of spiritual directors at San Nicolò da Tolentino formed a nucleus for ardent philanthropists, and for devout men and women strongly interested in the Catholic revival.[77]

Beside the formidable Carafa, there arose the milder figure of Girolamo Miani. Born in 1481 of a minor Venetian patrician family, he came of the same generation as Thiene and Carafa; he had seen much active service as a soldier, but during his military career had been converted to the notion of a Christian life. His preoccupations closely resembled those of the governors of the Incurabili, and he later became associated with them. According to his seventeenth-century biographer, Agostino Tortora, he at first showed an especial concern for virgins whom destitution might drive to prostituting their bodies; and did his best to support *poveri vergognosi* whom modesty restrained from venturing out to beg.[78] Later, however, under the stimulus of the famine of 1527–9, he began to specialize in the problem of educating orphaned child beggars, both in the Christian life and in some trade which would enable them to become self-supporting. Orphans and foundlings had presented a recognized challenge in earlier centuries, and the Pietà existed to take care of foundlings. But in the 1520's, given the epidemics and mass-migrations, many orphans appeared who were not foundlings, and the resources of the Pietà could scarcely be stretched any further to cope with them. In August 1525, the Senate heard that the Pietà was gravely embarrassed for lack of funds. The number of children had grown so that some of the wetnurses had to feed as many as four babies, and the hospital was in debt to these foster-mothers to the tune of 3,000 ducats, for arrears of wages. The Senate agreed to bolster up the Pietà by assigning it the right to sell or hire out one of the boats in each of the ferry-stations in Venice; by authorizing it to send out a band of musicians, with a standard or *penello*, to collect alms throughout the city; by resolving to obtain from Clement VII an indulgence in favour of all who gave alms to the hospital; and, finally, by earmarking to the Pietà a certain proportion of the revenue from judicial fines imposed by Venetian magistracies.[79] Later, in 1526, the Senate resolved to renew demands originally made in 1489—when the Venetians had tried to secure some regular income

[77] For this, see Paschini, *San Gaetano Thiene*, pp. 41 f.

[78] Agostino Tortora, *Vita Hieronymi Aemiliani*, in *Acta Sanctorum*, February, II (Antwerp, 1658), p. 230.

[79] D.M.S., XXXIX, col. 300, 11 August 1525.

for the Pietà by asking the Pope to attach to it ecclesiastical benefices yielding an annual income of 1,000 ducats.[80] But even with these measures to back it, the finances of the Pietà were scarcely robust, and this was hardly the time to accept the added burden of orphans of more advanced age. Apart from the Pietà, there remained only one long-established orphanage—that of the Scuola di Sant'Agnese, in the parish of San Barnabà. This shared some of the aims connected with the avant-garde philanthropy, but catered only for very small numbers, and only for the children of members of the Scuola: it had recently, in 1525, been returned by senatorial decree to the Scuola's control, after some years under the Procurators of San Marco.[81] Sanuto described how, on the festival of St Agnes, 21 January 1526,

> I went to her church to see a novelty, i.e. the six children of eight or nine years who are daughters of members of the Scuola. They were placed on a platform, dressed half in white and half in red, with hair falling down to their shoulders and garlands of flowers on their heads. They live in a house at San Barnabà which is devoted to this purpose, with a governess who is paid 40 ducats a year; and their expenses are met, and they are taught to read and work until they reach the right age for marriage or some other destiny; and they receive marriage portions out of the moneys of the Scuola: all this from the proceeds of a certain legacy collected in the past by the Procurators of San Marco—but, by a decree passed this year in the Senate, the government has been transferred to members of the Scuola. . . . They are obliged to support twelve girls, but for the time being they have only six, who are chosen by members of the Scuola according to a very sensible procedure.[82]

During the 1520's, both Miani himself and the governors of the Incurabili increased the resources available for caring for orphans. Spurred on by the famine, he took a house near the church of San Rocco, and sheltered in it the orphans he collected from the streets and squares of the city. According to the later traditions of the Somaschians, members of the Order which traced its origin to Miani's activities, he offered wages to artisans to instruct them in sedentary trades which would help them to overcome their present poverty, to become self-supporting, and if necessary to maintain families when they grew up.[83] None should go begging, for Miani thought it disgraceful that healthy and robust persons should get their food by this means—unless they did so as a means of practising Christian humility, in obedience to a

[80] D.M.S., XLI, col. 160, 9 April 1526; Malipiero, *Annali veneti*, p. 685, 6 July 1489.
[81] D.M.S., XXXVII, coll. 670–1, 27 February 1525.
[82] D.M.S., XL, coll. 696–7, 21 January 1526.
[83] Tortora, *Vita Hieronymi Aemiliani*, pp. 237 f.

religious Rule, or in response to 'imperious necessity'. Idleness must be condemned, and 'tender age' must never be corrupted by 'inert and slothful mendicity'. St Paul's precept 'If a man does not work, then neither shall he eat' (a favourite text for poor law reformers) deserved to be obeyed.[84] The orphans were taught to pray, to recite their devotions, to invoke the saints and to sing hymns and psalms in the intervals of work. Whilst actually engaged in work, they must hold their tongues and listen to sacred readings or improving discourses. Every day, there were two sessions of instruction in Christian doctrine and in the articles of the Catholic faith, accompanied by practical instruction in reading, writing and arithmetic. On feast-days, the orphans marched out in procession to the public squares, carrying the Cross, chanting, and invoking the saints—an excellent advertisement which attracted many curious visitors to the house itself.

It is, of course, possible that Miani's biographer projected back into the 1520's too many of the established practices of a later era. He prefaced his account with the remark that 'although he [Miani] had not yet drawn up specific regulations on this matter, nevertheless the discipline of the orphans was not neglected'.[85] However, there is a little contemporary evidence to show that Miani did indeed begin in this way. In May 1531, the Senate was asked to grant a twenty-year patent to one Arcangelo Romitano, a native of Vicenza, described as 'instructor to the orphan children (*mestro di puti derelicti*)'. He had made the application on the instigation of Girolamo Miani, 'who has erected a workshop for making paper and other trades under his control, for the support of these poor orphan children'. Romitano had invented a water-driven fulling-mill, and any profits realized by this device were to be shared between him and the orphans he taught.[86] A few years later, in a letter addressed to a Bergamese correspondent, Ludovico Scaino, Miani described how he had introduced other similar trades to the orphanages he founded in Lombardy and the Veneto.[87] Moreover, Miani's views on the subject of begging and idleness were perfectly consonant with those generally accepted in Venice in 1528, and translated into official government policy. There is every reason to think that private initiative on the part of religious reformers was pressing

[84] II Thessalonians, iii, 10. Cf. Ludovico Vives, *Il modo del sovvenire a poveri* (Venice, 1545), f. 53; Juan Medina, *De la orden que en algunos pueblos de España se ha puesto en la limosna: para remedio de los verdaderos pobres* (Salamanca, 1545), ff. A 6v., C 5v., C 7; Soto, *Deliberacion en la causa de los pobres*, f. 6.

[85] Cf. also Marco Tentorio, 'I Somaschi', in Mario Escobar, *Ordini e congregazioni religiosi* (2 vols., Turin, 1951–2), I, p. 615.

[86] D.M.S., LIV, col. 419; Cicogna, *Inscrizioni veneziane*, V, p. 368.

[87] *Ibid.*, V, p. 376.

forward in the same direction as state legislation. It is impossible to know whether Miani was simply repeating accepted notions and drawing inspiration from government policy; or whether, on the other hand, pressure from admirers of Miani or from the influential Procurators of the Incurabili helped to frame the legislation.

As well as starting his own private orphanage, Miani found himself attracted to one of the temporary hospitals erected in Venice early in 1528 on the orders of the Senate and Provveditori alla Sanità. This was the shelter for the poor at SS. Giovanni e Paolo, the only one of the four to develop into a permanent establishment. This refuge stood on a stretch of waste ground used both as a rubbish dump and as a firing-range for the training of gunners. Arsenal workers ran up temporary wooden sheds to meet the increasing demand on the part of poor immigrants for accommodation. Eventually, stone buildings replaced these wooden structures, and the hospital at SS. Giovanni e Paolo became the second large general hospital in Venice, discharging functions as varied as those of the Incurabili. It took the name of 'Hospital for the Destitute', or Derelitti. Its governors in 1542 described how the state had used the hospital

to meet all the needs of its poor, both outsiders (i.e., galley-crews, soldiers, mariners and sick persons) and other paupers from within the city: sick persons, wards, orphan girls, widows and destitute creatures of every social rank and of either sex. These have been benevolently received and assisted by this institution.[88]

There was obviously much sympathy between the Procurators of the Incurabili and those of SS. Giovanni e Paolo, whose primitive rule showed the same concern with the sacraments, and enjoined the governing congregation to take communion six times a year.[89] According to his letter to Scaino, Miani worked for about three years among the Derelitti in Venice: his interest may have contributed to the survival of the temporary asylum, and his own orphanage have merged with the general hospital at SS. Giovanni e Paolo. In April 1531, the governors of the Incurabili invited him and his orphans to come and live on their premises, taking charge of their own orphans and patients.[90] He did so for a short time, but soon afterwards left to continue his work on the mainland of Italy.

If the poor law itself remained unenforced in the improved condi-

[88] *Ibid.*, V, pp. 368–9.
[89] See *Capitoli et ordini per il buon governo del Pio Hospitale de Poveri Derelitti appresso SS. Giovanni e Paulo* (Venice, 1704), p. 2, which gives a brief extract from the original constitutions.
[90] Cicogna, *Inscrizioni veneziane*, V, p. 370.

PORTRAIT OF A VENETIAN PROCURATOR

For the duties, status and misconduct of the Procurators of St Mark's, see above, pp. 209–11, and below, pp. 351–5.

facing p. 262

PORTRAIT OF A VENETIAN SENATOR

facing p. 263

tions of the early 1530's, the hospitals of the Incurabili and Derelitti continued to flourish. In the summer of 1533, the Senate resolved to experiment with one of the proposals outlined in the statute of 1529, by drafting a number of orphans from both hospitals on to warships to be trained as seamen.[91] This might suitably extend the policy of Girolamo Miani, and at the same time benefit the state. Later, the Provveditori alla Sanità were to regard the sea as the panacea for all mendicity, and as the sovereign form of character-training for beggar-children; conveniently, it helped to meet the state's demand for mariners.

Carafa and the Regular Clerks at San Nicolò da Tolentino became confessors to a select group of devout and high-born persons who showed a strong interest in organized philanthropy, in the Pietà as well as in the two new general hospitals. In 1534, Carafa informed the absent Thiene that the circle round their congregation in Venice included Elisabetta Capello, Prioress of the Pietà, Pietro di Zaccaria Contarini, and Andrea Lippomano.[92] Contarini and Lippomano were to provide the link between the Regular Clerks, the Venetian hospitals, and the embryo Society of Jesus. Andrea Lippomano came of an ecclesiastical family which owed its advancement, not to political or financial leverage, but rather to its tradition of loyal service to the Papacy. He was the brother of Pietro Lippomano, the new Bishop of Bergamo to whom Contarini had dedicated his improving treatise in 1516.[93] His personal income derived from two priories of the Teutonic Order held in commendam, those of the Santissima Trinità in Venice itself and of Santa Maria Maddalena (otherwise the Precettoria dei Lambertani) in Padua. Sharing or actually inspired by the Theatine ideal of poverty, he lived in the severest personal austerity, and gave away all but a small remnant of the income to the poor. Evidently, he followed Venetian convention by providing dowries to young women, either for marriage or for the cloister.[94] With Carafa's aid, he made more than one unsuccessful attempt at legally renouncing the priories: on the second occasion, in 1533, his object was to help the Pietà to extricate itself from its chronic financial embarrassment and to provide it at last with some regular income. The new hospitals may have exercised, for voluntary contributors, a more fashionable attraction than the old, and have thereby increased the Pietà's difficulties. Antonio Venier and Bartolomeo Zane, Procurators of the Incurabili, were privy

---

[91] D.M.S., LVIII, col. 374, 26 June 1533.

[92] Paschini, *San Gaetano Thiene*, pp. 90–1, 193–4.

[93] Logan, *Studies in the religious life of Venice*, pp. 247–8, 256.

[94] See the 'Profilo' of Andrea Lippomano, written in the late sixteenth century by a Jesuit who knew him well during his lifetime (he died in 1574)—reproduced in Tacchi Venturi, *Storia della Compagnia di Gesù*, II/2, pp. 680–4.

S

to this plan; but it did not succeed. As it happened, Lippomano's revenues were eventually reserved for the support of the first Jesuits established in Venice and Padua.[95]

In all probability, it was Lippomano who offered hospitality to Ignatius Loyola when he first arrived in Venice in 1536. One of Lippomano's habitual acts of charity was to shelter pilgrims bound for the Holy Land, for which Venice remained an important transit-station.[96] Venice was the meeting-point for Loyola and the group of companions he had assembled in Paris, for they were contemplating a voyage to the Holy Land and hoping to obtain papal approval for it. The service of the poor was uppermost in their minds at this time. As Diego Laynez wrote in 1547,

> whilst we were in Paris, our intention was not to establish a congregation, but only to live as a community in perpetual poverty, and serve the Lord our God through the service of the poor in hospitals, and likewise to minister to the salvation of our neighbours. . . .[97]

Loyola had returned to his native town of Azpeitia in the Basque province to wind up his affairs and expunge the memory of his erratic youth, and had introduced there a comprehensive scheme for the relief of the poor and the elimination of begging.[98] Not surprisingly, when Loyola's companions joined him in Venice, they chose to devote their time to service in the fashionable hospitals of the Incurabili and SS. Giovanni e Paolo. Pietro Contarini, a governor of the Incurabili, offered them access to his hospital.[99] The polyglot company from Paris consisted of the Spaniards Francesco Xavier, Diego Laynez, Alfonso Salmeron and Nicolo Bobadilla; of two Frenchmen, Paschase Broët and Jean Codur; of the Savoyards Pierre Favre and Claude Le Jay; and of a Portuguese, Simon Rodriguez. Another Spanish recruit, Diego Hozes, had joined Ignatius in Venice. Whilst awaiting papal permission to depart on their pilgrimage, they spent the spring and summer of 1537 in the hospitals; in summer, their departure was frustrated by the outbreak of war between Venice and the Turks, and the company split up again and left for the Venetian mainland. Loyola and Hozes heard confessions; the rest went half to the Incurabili and half to SS. Gio-

[95] Paschini, *San Gaetano Thiene*, p. 96; Tacchi Venturi, *Storia della Compagnia di Gesù*, II/2, pp. 305 f.

[96] See Angelo Martini, 'Di chi fu ospite S. Ignazio a Venezia?', *Archivum Historicum Societatis Iesu*, XVIII (1949).

[97] From a letter of Diego Laynez to the chronicler Juan Alonso Polanco about the origins of the Society of Jesus, from Bologna, 16 June 1547, in M.H.S.J., *Fontes narrativi*, I, pp. 108–11.

[98] See below, p. 286.

[99] See Tacchi Venturi, *Storia della Compagnia di Gesù*, II/1, p. 82 n. 1.

vanni e Paolo. They underwent a rigorous ascetic experience which contributed much to Jesuit tradition and probably helped to establish service in hospitals as part of the Jesuit novitiate. Of the group, the Portuguese Rodriguez furnished, in his old age forty years later, the most elaborate account of their experiences in Venice.

They went to the hospitals to serve the beggars, to make the beds, to sweep the rooms, to clean out everything dirty, to wash the vessels used by the sick poor, to carry the bodies of the dead to decent burial and cover them reverently with earth, and to be at everyone's service by day and night with such diligence, fervour, pleasure and joy that all the inmates of the hospitals marvelled at it. When the word got about in the city, the nobles and most prominent members of the community talked about this, and visited the hospitals to see these men, forming a very high opinion of their learning and holiness.

I should also say that the fathers not only abandoned their higher studies to apply themselves to this menial work, but also with great care and diligence talked to the beggars about the word of God, and were accustomed to concern themselves deeply, in accordance with the need, with their spiritual welfare.

Whilst the fathers so employed themselves, they made a courageous attempt to overcome the physical repugnance induced by the filth and reek of the place and by their own horror at wounds and ulcers. A great deal could be said about this, but for the sake of brevity I will content myself with one or two examples. In the hospital of the Incurabili, a leper, or one suffering from a form of skin disease, covered all over by a kind of pestilential mange, called one of the fathers and asked him to scratch his back. The father diligently performed this service, but whilst he was doing so he was suddenly struck with horror and nausea, and with the terror of contracting the contagious disease. But since he wanted to master himself and to suppress his own rebellious spirit rather than take thought for the future, he put into his mouth a finger covered with pus and sucked it. Another day, he told one of his companions about it, and said with a smile: 'I dreamt last night that the sick man's disease had stuck to my throat, and that I tried to expel it by coughing and spitting it up, but in vain'. But for this father, who had done this act in good faith and fervour in order to conquer himself, the words of our Lord Jesus Christ were fulfilled: 'And if they drink anything deadly, it shall not harm them'.

Rodriguez added the story of one of the fathers serving at SS. Giovanni e Paolo, who had shared his bed with a beggar and had actually caught his disease, but had been miraculously cured.[100]

[100] Simon Rodriguez, *De origine et progressu Societatis Iesu*, Lisbon, 25 July 1577, in M.H.S.J., *Epistolae patrum Paschasii Broeti, Claudii Jaii, Joannis Codurii et Simonis Rodericii* (Madrid, 1903), at pp. 474–6; letter of Ignatius Loyola to Juan de Verdolay, Venice, 24 July 1537, in M.H.S.J., *Monumenta Ignatiana*, I, p. 119;

The story told by Rodriguez illustrated several of the ideals of charity associated with Catholic reform. Service in the hospitals was a form of asceticism, a means of winning victories over the rebellious flesh and spirit, a means, ultimately, of equipping oneself to do tough and demanding evangelical work. At the same time, the concept of charity was not merely confined to the fulfilment of bodily needs: hospitals also existed for the spiritual education and consolation of those near to death, or of those to whom the physical world extended no further hope, whose only corporal future lay in suffering. The revival or continuation of primitive Franciscan ideals was clear enough; Rodriguez referred to venereal and other skin diseases as 'leprosy'.[101] The Jesuits were also following the track laid down, more recently, by the Compagnia del Divino Amore and its Theatine offshoots. Carafa's congregation of Regular Clerks in Venice had occasionally used the period of service in a hospital as part of their novitiate—they had done so in 1534, in order to test a Bergamasque postulant, Simone Barrili.[102] However, it remained to the Jesuits to make this form of service a regular constituent of the novitiate.[103] Rules drawn up in 1541, after the official foundation of the Society of Jesus, established a preliminary term of three months' probation—thirty days of engaging in spiritual exercises, thirty days of serving the poor in hospital, and thirty days on pilgrimage, begging for support.

> For the space of one further month, he must serve the poor in hospital in whatever humble duties they may enjoin upon him, so that by becoming humble and overcoming worldly shame he may set himself apart and lose himself.[104]

Venetian experiences of serving the outcasts of the world and of identi-

Memoriale of Pierre Favre, in M.H.S.J., Fontes narrativi, I, p. 40; letter of Laynez to Polanco, cited above, ibid., pp. 108–11; M.H.S.J., Polanco, Historia, I, pp. 56–60. Laynez, followed by Polanco, says that it was Francesco Xavier who mastered himself by sucking the venereal ulcers.

101 Cf. the Testament of Francis of Assisi: 'The Lord granted me, Brother Francis, grace to begin to do penance, for while I was living in sin, it seemed a very bitter thing to look at lepers; but the Lord Himself led me among them, and I had compassion on them. And when I left them, the thing that had seemed so horrible to me was transformed into happiness of body and soul for me'—see Sherley-Price, S. Francis of Assisi, p. 200. Cf. also Tacchi Venturi, Storia della Compagnia di Gesù, II/2, pp. 29–30.

102 Letter of Carafa to Gaetano Thiene, 18 January 1534, in Paschini, San Gaetano Thiene, pp. 72, 192–3.

103 On this question in general, see Pietro Tacchi Venturi, 'La prova dell'indifferenza e del servizio negli ospedali nel tirocinio ignaziano', Archivum Historicum Societatis Iesu, I (1932); Tacchi Venturi, Storia della Compagnia di Gesù, II/2, pp. 30 f.

104 See the document 'Fundación de Collegio', of 1541, in M.H.S.J., Monumenta Ignatiana, III/1, Constitutiones Societatis Iesu, p. 54.

fying with their squalor and suffering almost certainly helped to inspire this constitution.

Again in the late 1530's, the small group of avant-garde charities and religious movements was augmented by the addition of a new lay fraternity specializing in the care of the 'shamefaced poor', and also by the arrival of the first Venetian Capuchins. The first poor law of March 1528 had assumed that some work was already being done to relieve in their houses those who were ashamed to beg.[105] But a voluntary society dedicated to this activity received official approval only in 1537. Members of the Compagnie del Divino Amore had originally shown interest in the *vergognosi*, as well as in the syphilitic; sometimes separate organizations, like the Archconfraternity of the Carità in Rome in 1519, had developed beside them, and devoted themselves to the *vergognosi*. Naturally, one of the most effective methods of undermining begging was to make it unnecessary by organizing house-to-house distributions of alms to the genuinely deserving poor. Only if machinery existed for doing this could the state justifiably forbid begging and flog, enslave or otherwise punish the recalcitrant. The aims of the new fraternity accorded well with those of the poor laws and with those of the Compagnia del Divino Amore and its offshoots; facilities for outdoor relief could now be increased, as well as the amount of hospital accommodation. The founding members applied in February 1537 for the Patriarch's approval, and in the course of the same year obtained that of the Heads of the Ten and of the Provveditori alla Sanità, now recognized as the magistracy responsible for poor-relief. The Provveditori described how

A number of faithful Christians, both noblemen and others, had been moved to pity by the great multitude of shamefaced poor and other sick and afflicted persons of various social ranks, some concealed and others revealed, noblemen and others, dispersed throughout this city.

The new organization evidently provoked the furious resentment of the professional beggars capable of earning a living, whose trade it undermined and to whom it refused alms. The Provveditori alla Sanità solemnly granted the fraternity protection against all who tried to molest its agents in the execution of their duty.[106] They then took the further step of recommending that similar fraternities be established in all the principal subject cities on the mainland. The initiative should

---

[105] See above, p. 247.
[106] A.S.V., *Provveditori alla Sanità, Notatorio III*, vol. 727, ff. 337–8, 1 June 1537; cf. also A. S. De Kiriaki, *La beneficenza elemosiniera a Venezia nel passato e nei nostri tempi* (Venice, 1897), pp. 13–16.

come from the lay governors of each territory, who must recommend to the bishop or to his vicar the establishment of such a fraternity, which would cater both for the spiritual and for the physical needs of the poor. Monasteries, convents, executors of pious legacies and all other dispensers of alms must be reminded of the existence of the deserving poor. The governors were expected

to make some provision that the healthy and prosperous who have been in the habit of getting a living by dishonest means may hitherto be able to live by their own honest efforts, as we have begun to do in this city of Venice.

The Provveditori alla Sanità recognized these fraternities as a force for 'the reformation of Christian life'[107]—perhaps because they proposed to dispense charity on strictly moral principles, denying alms to the wicked, and because they brought the sacraments to the poor. In Venice itself, they evidently raised funds by the systematic collection of alms: in or before August 1537, a certain Madonna Theodosia Scripiani presented a house on the Giudecca, free of charge, to eight collectors or *cerchanti* employed by the fraternity.[108] In 1541, the fraternity officially acquired the status of a *luoco pio*, one of the religious institutions which notaries were required to recommend in general terms to testators drawing up their wills.[109] Three years later, notaries were obliged to recommend the *poveri vergognosi* specifically to all testators.[110] At some stage, this new society adopted, as its patron saint, Antonino Pierozzi, the fifteenth-century Dominican reformer and Archbishop of Florence, canonized in 1523. Pierozzi had in 1442 founded what was probably the archetypal Italian society for *vergognosi*, that of the Buonomini di San Martino.[111] The dedication of the Venetian society recognized his contribution to philanthropy.

At some stage also, the society for the care of the *vergognosi* formed bonds with the Capuchins. The foundation of the Capuchins marked the second major and vital reform of the Order of St Francis, a renewed attempt to live according to the founder's primitive Rule. Clement VII had recognized this as a canonical reform of the Rule in 1528, and in the next eight years the total number of Capuchins had increased to about 500, many of whom were friars disillusioned with the corruption

[107] A.S.V., *Provveditori alla Sanità, Notatorio III*, vol. 727, ff. 338v.–339.
[108] *Ibid.*, f. 344v., 21 August 1537.
[109] A.S.V., *Provveditori alla Sanità, Notatorio IV*, vol. 728, f. 69, 6 July 1541.
[110] A.S.V., *Maggior Consiglio, Deliberazioni, Liber Novus*, f. 96.
[111] Paschini, 'Le Compagnie del Divino Amore', pp. 3–5; Tacchi Venturi, *Storia della Compagnia di Gesù*, I/i, pp. 401–2.

stealing into the Observance.[112] The new Order probably appeared in the Veronese between 1533 and 1535, and a Venetian province was created at the Chapter-General held in Rome in 1535.[113] Giovanni Pili of Fano became the first provincial, and, like Ignatius Loyola, stayed at the house of Andrea Lippomano on early visits to Venice to discuss the foundation of a Capuchin house there.[114] The Capuchins eventually entered Venice in 1539, on the wave of popularity created by the successful sermons of their General, Bernardino Ochino, who preached that year from the fashionable pulpit of the Santi Apostoli.[115] The Capuchins were not as obviously concerned with poor relief as some of their contemporaries, though they had done relief work during the plague at Camerino in 1527, and though Giovanni da Fano, following Miani's path, showed an obvious concern for orphans during his Lenten course of sermons in Brescia in 1536.[116] But there was some link with the Venetian fraternity for the *poveri vergognosi*: to them, the Venetian Capuchins turned in their troubles in 1542–3. The spectacular apostasy of Ochino, who had preached again in Venice in 1542, threatened to discredit the whole Order. It roused suspicion in Father Bonaventura, an Observant hermit originally from the friary of San Francesco della Vigna, who had invited the Capuchins to share the hermitage built for him on the Giudecca by his admirers. After the breach with Bonaventura, the Capuchin warden Michelangelo of Florence turned for support to the fraternity, whose members included an eminent Senator from the house of Barbarigo, and a Bergamese merchant or banker, Bartolomeo Stravazzeno. Stravazzeno was among the contributors who purchased a new site for the Capuchins elsewhere on the Giudecca.[117] The connexion between the new Orders and the new philanthropic organizations was clearly a strong one, though the precise nature of the link is often hard to illustrate.

During the 1530's, voluntary organizations, private initiative and ecclesiastical authorities pushed the frontier forward with state approval and co-operation. They, too, were largely responsible for the extension of the new machinery to the provinces of the mainland. The Venetian government made only sketchy attempts at legislation on a national rather than a merely municipal scale: in 1529 it vaguely commended 'foreign' beggars expelled from Venice to the governors of

[112] Davide M . . . da Portogruaro, *Storia dei Cappuccini veneti* (2 vols., Venice–Mestre, 1941–57), I, pp. 71–3, 92.
[113] *Ibid.*, I, pp. 97 f.　　[114] *Ibid.*, I, pp. 166–7.　　[115] *Ibid.*, I, pp. 173 f.
[116] *Ibid.*, I, pp. 70–1; Cistellini, *Figure della riforma pretridentina*, p. 19.
[117] Davide da Portogruaro, *Storia dei Cappuccini*, I, pp. 238 f., 280–1, 304–6. Stravazzeno was one of the subscribers who raised money in 1552 to enable the Capuchins of Roncone, near Padua, to move to a new site in Padua itself.

their native cities, but did not specify what these authorities were supposed to do about them.[118] Again, in 1537, it recommended the establishment of fraternities for the care of *vergognosi* in all subject cities, but again left the actual mechanics to local action.[119] Much research would be needed to give a proper impression of how widely these recommendations were adopted on the mainland. However, there is no doubt that the cities of Verona and Brescia did adopt important measures for the organization of systematic relief in this decade, whilst Girolamo Miani carried his concern for orphans across from Venice to the mainland.

Episcopal initiative weighed heavily in Verona. Matteo Giberti came near to translating into reality the ideal of a Christian bishop sketched in theory by Gasparo Contarini. Born in 1495, the bastard son of a Genoese admiral, Giberti had risen high as a curialist, through the favour of Cardinal Giulio de' Medici, later Pope Clement VII. During his patron's pontificate, when Giberti was serving in Rome as Datario, he received the diocese of Verona. With Clement's somewhat reluctant approval, he determined to carry forward the reform of the clergy and the revival of Christian belief and morality by the restoration of effective episcopal authority. In 1528, he came to reside in the diocese. A Venetian observer, Santo Querini, vividly described Giberti's immediate impact on the clergy—his rigorous examination of priests to test their efficiency, followed if necessary by suspensions or deprivations of benefices; the prisons filled with those who had lived in concubinage; the austerity of his household; his generosity in almsgiving; his ruthless pursuit of the superstitious, the sacrilegious, the usurer and the evil-liver.[120] Over the next fourteen years, Giberti systematically drew up a series of constitutions based partly on patristic writings and canon law, and partly on his own day-to-day experience of governing the see. These constitutions, first published in 1542, earned a reputation that extended far beyond Verona. Reprinted in Venice in 1563 at the instigation of an ardent admirer, Pietro Francesco Zini, the statutes received serious attention during the last sessions of the Council of Trent.[121]

As a philanthropist, Giberti shared the concerns of the Compagnia del Divino Amore and of its related associations in Rome, Venice and elsewhere. In 1530, he and the civilian governor, Alvise Contarini, prepared to put into execution a scheme very similar to that of the

---

[118] See above, p. 252.   [119] See above, pp. 267–8.
[120] D.M.S., XLIX, col. 161, letter dated 17 November 1528.
[121] See the Preface to Gian Matteo Giberti, *Opera* (Ostiglia, 1740), by Pietro Ballerini of Verona; Tacchi Venturi, *Storia della Compagnia di Gesù*, I/1, p. 374.

Venetian poor law. They proposed to assemble all beggars at one central depôt, and to expel from the city any who refused to go there. Those who could work, should be sent to the hospitals and provided with employment. Any who could not work, should be licensed to beg, whilst those too aged or crippled to beg should be maintained by alms collected for them by special collectors. However, it is probable that no action was ever taken on this comprehensive scheme:[122] during the early 1530's, economic pressure was perhaps not severe enough to force the authorities either in Verona or Venice to take such ruthless measures. Nevertheless, Giberti was able to extend the premises of the relatively new hospital of the Misericordia, founded in 1515 and perhaps already associated with the care of incurables. Like the Incurabili in Venice, the hospital now acquired an orphanage, run on the lines made familiar by Girolamo Miani in Venice, and perhaps actually with his assistance or that of his followers.[123] In these enterprises, Giberti enjoyed the support of a local aristocrat, Count Ludovico di Canossa. Canossa had, like Giberti himself, Thiene and Carafa, been a curialist, with ample opportunities for knowing of the latest developments in Rome. He was also a successful diplomat, who as nuncio to Leo X had rendered exceptional services to Louis XII of France, for which he was eventually rewarded with the lucrative Bishopric of Bayeux. In 1527, Francis I had employed him as French Ambassador to the Venetian Republic,[124] where he had given money for the support of the Theatine exiles from the sack of Rome, and had joined with the Procurators of the Incurabili in concern for their welfare.[125] Now, in 1531, having resigned his bishopric on account of ill-health, Canossa returned to his native Verona to die. Like Giberti, he admired and corresponded with Erasmus: he had met him in London in 1514, an occasion which Erasmus recalled affectionately at about the time of Canossa's death; and in 1516 had offered Erasmus a pension, which Erasmus, however, refused.[126] On his death on 30 January 1532, Canossa bequeathed 400 golden crowns to the orphans of Verona, to

---

[122] Dalla Corte, *Istorie di Verona*, III, p. 282; Ballerini, *Vita Giberti*, in his *Opera*, at p. xxxiv.

[123] P. F. Zini, *Boni pastoris exemplum*, in Giberti, *Opera*, p. 282; Ballerini, *Vita Giberti*, *ibid.*, p. xxi. According to Ballerini, this account of Giberti by Zini was originally composed during Giberti's own lifetime and was sent in 1555 to one Giovanni Francesco Stella, who was about to set out for England with Cardinal Reginald Pole; it was first printed at Venice in 1573.

[124] Dalla Corte, *Istorie di Verona*, III, pp. 215–17.

[125] D.M.S., XLV, col. 343, 17 June 1527; Paschini, *San Gaetano Thiene*, p. 65.

[126] Erasmus, *Opus Epistolarum*, ed. Allen, I, p. 562; II, pp. 382–3, 483; IX, pp. 105–6, 417–19; Renaudet, *Érasme en Italie*, p. 219. For Giberti's connexions with Erasmus, see *Opus Epistolarum*, VI, pp. 129, 348–50; VIII, p. 470; IX, pp. 30–1, 328–9; X, p. 21; Renaudet, *Érasme en Italie*, pp. 165, 238–9.

be spent on extending the buildings of the Misericordia to receive them. He left a further 2,000 golden crowns in trust, for the support of orphans, stipulating that it could be used to provide marriage portions of 10 ducats each to any of the girls who had reached marriageable age. Sanuto also reported that 'he has left to the poor all the moneys remaining to him from the bishopric which he held in France'.[127]

Under Giberti's patronage and with Canossa's financial support, the hospital of the Misericordia addressed itself to the beggar orphans who were straying about the city 'with great danger to body and soul'. They were brought up in the fear of God, and educated to a sense of Christian duty. The hospital staff taught them to read and write, and they graduated to higher studies if they showed exceptional talent.[128] Giberti, moreover, soon reformulated his plans for a comprehensive attack on poverty, to some extent drawing, again, on Roman models. His former patron, Cardinal Giulio de' Medici, had founded in Rome in 1519 a society specially devoted to three forms of charity. First, he 'Piously considered that paupers who are ashamed to beg suffer much greater need than those who do beg'; secondly, he was deeply concerned at the number of prisoners with no friends or advocates to take their part who languished forgotten in the gaols of Rome; and, finally, he was horrified at the number of poor corpses left by the roadside without decent Christian burial. The Cardinal had summoned a number of curial officials prepared to interest themselves in the solution of these problems, and had himself given some 2,000 gold ducats to the enterprise. By the following year, the society comprised about eighty members, and by virtue of a brief issued by Leo X early in 1520 this Confraternità della Carità became an Archconfraternity, to which all future fraternities aspiring to the same title were to become affiliated.[129] A few months later, the brethren of this society acquired a further commitment by becoming procurators, defenders of the temporal interests, of the recently-founded nunnery for repentant prostitutes in Rome. In this capacity, they were also responsible for vetting all prospective entrants.[130]

Giberti's solution to the problem of poverty in Verona and in the rest of his diocese lay in the introduction of a voluntary organization of this type which would enjoy the approval and support of the civil government. Tied by so close a personal bond to Giulio de' Medici, he

[127] D.M.S., LV, coll. 441–2, 5 February 1532.
[128] Zini, Boni pastoris exemplum, p. 282.
[129] Leo X, 'Illius, qui caritas', 28 January 1520, in M.B.R., V, pp. 739–42; Paschini, 'Le Compagnie del Divino Amore', pp. 50–2; Tacchi Venturi, Storia della Compagnia di Gesù, I/1, p. 402.
[130] Leo X, 'Salvator noster', 19 May 1520, M.B.R., V, pp. 742–8.

272

was almost certainly aware of the operations of the Carità and of the Compagnie del Divino Amore. In 1532, meeting Clement VII at Bologna, Giberti ensured that his proposed Compagnia della Carità should be admitted to the same spiritual benefits and privileges as the Archconfraternity in Rome.[131] During the 1530's, he did in fact assemble a small community of about thirty women, formerly of disreputable life, who were inspired by his words to repentance, and establish them in a nunnery where they were acquainted with the rigours of Christian asceticism.[132] But the actual erection of the multipurpose Compagnia della Carità waited till 1539, when its foundation was probably connected with the recurrence of famine. By April 1539, in the last months before the harvest, wheat prices were tripling after heavy rains. The city government raised funds for the purchase of foodstuffs partly by loans from private individuals, but partly also by drawing on the resources of the hospitals. The isolation hospital of San Giacomo and San Lazzaro contributed 5,000 ducats, the others 3,000. Since San Giacomo and San Lazzaro was used only during epidemics of plague, in the intervals between these outbreaks it accumulated a surplus of revenue which could be transferred to other, more immediate needs. From these sources, and from the gates of monasteries and nunneries, the government organized distributions of flour or bread to the poor.[133]

In such circumstances, Giberti and a group of commissioners drew up proposals for the foundation of a central board of guardians of the poor, to organize all relief work in the city, and to bear the title of Società or Compagnia della Carità. These proposals were presented to the city council by Pietro Dante Aligeri, 'Provveditore nel Consiglio', to be confirmed on 11 May 1539.[134] Within a year or two, legislation both of the Bishop himself and of the civil governors set out to extend this form of organization to all parishes in the countryside.[135] It also penetrated into at least one other town, that of Salò on the shores of Lake Garda, where there was an ardent group of pious men and women. These circles of devout Catholics had formerly gathered round the figures of Angela Merici, the foundress of the Ursulines, and of Laura Mignani, an Augustinian nun in the convent of Santa Croce at Brescia. Laura Mignani had probably put them in touch with Gaetano

---

[131] See Antonio Cistellini, 'La "Confraternità della Carità" di Salò (1542)', *Rivista di Storia della Chiesa in Italia*, I (1947), p. 394.

[132] Zini, *Boni pastoris exemplum*, pp. 284–6; Dalla Corte, *Istorie di Verona*, III, pp. 292, 321–2.

[133] Dalla Corte, *Istorie di Verona*, III, pp. 304–5.

[134] Giberti, *Opera*, pp. 228–9.

[135] *Ibid.*, pp. 229–31, and Giberti's *Constitutiones*, titulus v, ch. 8, *ibid.*, pp. 71–2.

Thiene, and he in turn had introduced them to Giberti's circle. Through his household, they also made contact with Girolamo Miani, and three of their number, Stefano Bertazzoli and the brothers Scaini, invited him to stay at Salò in 1535. In 1542, the Salodians founded both a Compagnia del Divino Amore and a Compagnia della Carità. The statutes of the Salodian organization have survived intact, whilst those of the Veronese are known only in a truncated form. There is good reason, however, to think that the Salodian statutes were originally copied from a Veronese model, and that they can be used as a guide to the original constitutions of these societies.[136]

The statutes of Verona itself and of Salò opened with the declaration that

> Since outward works of charity are of little or no value unless we have the true inner charity in our hearts, each of us shall be entreated to pray to our Lord God, the giver of every good thing, to light fires in icy souls with the rays of his grace, and to increase with his grace the godly ardour in souls already aflame.[137]

The allusion to the Pauline doctrine of charity was obvious—to a spirit of love giving an inner consistency and harmony to all physical acts of mercy which it inspired. The Salodian constitutions appeared to visualize a voluntary mixed society of priests and laymen under the protection of the higher civilian officials of the district. In Verona and Salò, the civil governors and the superiors of all religious houses were invited to attend monthly meetings at which the society reported on all its activities. At Salò, the town was divided into four quarters, for each of which two elected officials known as Presidenti were ultimately responsible. They were assisted by one priestly and three lay visitors chosen every four months to investigate the state of the poor in each quarter. These visitors were instructed to inform themselves

> how many poor there are, how great their needs are, and what their conduct and morals are like, so that alms may be dispensed judiciously and discreetly; and also how many sick persons there are, who they are, what their rank and what their needs. They must visit and comfort them, and in these duties avail themselves of the aid and assistance afforded by the parish priest or his deputy.

Moreover, these visitors were to try to co-ordinate the work of the existing charitable societies in Salò.

[136] Cistellini, 'La "Confraternità della Carità"'; Cistellini, *Figure della riforma pretridentina*, pp. 104 f.

[137] For what follows, see the sources cited above, notes 134–6, and the account of the weekly meetings of the Compagnia della Carità in Verona, in Zini, *Boni pastoris exemplum*, p. 295.

Because in this city there are by the grace of God many other persons who dispense much alms, and also the governors of hospitals and the stewards of the Scuole or confraternities of the Most Holy Body of Christ, of the Blessed Virgin, of St Joseph and others, it will be necessary to ensure that persons who are assisted by these other means do not get double rations, thereby taking shares that could be given to others. This is said because there will never be such plenty that everyone can be supplied. . . .

Like the proposed system of parish relief in Venice, the Salodian society set out to complement existing organizations, and to supply all deficiencies which they had left.[138] Likewise, the decree issued by the governors of Verona in January 1541, extending the organization of the Compagnia della Carità to all villages in the territory, provided for a commission of public officials, communal deputies, councillors of the voluntary society and the parish priest

diligently to seek out the poor of their villages, who have no means of meeting their expenses, and also those who have nothing to sell or pledge, and those who cannot work or help themselves in any way (for if we wished to make lists of all who appear to be poor, the numbers would be infinite)

The societies were thus ready to embark on a policy of highly discriminating charity, which they justified on the grounds that resources would never suffice for everybody, and that they must be applied in the most effective way—working according to economic and moral criteria similar to those outlined in theory twenty years before by Gasparo Contarini.[139]

In Salò, the Visitors and Presidenti were to seek lodgings for the night for persons who found themselves homeless,

taking care to perform this office only for persons whom they know to be in genuine need, and not making a living out of it.

The professional vagabond lurked in the consciousness of most philanthropists of the sixteenth century.

Again, in Salò, the visitation of the sick was a procedure combining physical and spiritual charity, and the statutes plainly declared that the spiritual charity which ministered to the soul was the higher form of this activity. The visitors must do their utmost

to make the sick confess, and this must be their first concern, since the infirmities of the soul are of greater consequence than those of the body.

[138] See above, pp. 252–4.   [139] See above, pp. 226–31.

They must enlist the aid, not only of relatives, but also of physicians attending the sick. This preoccupation with the salvation of the soul through the use of the sacraments, officially deemed the supreme form of charity, was becoming very characteristic of Catholic reforming movements. The ultimate inspiration for these clauses lay in a thirteenth-century decretal, 'Cum infirmitas', of Innocent III—which both Giberti and the Loyola group were seeking to revive. This law, promulgated at the Lateran Council of 1215, recalled the words of Jesus to the cripple healed at the pool of Bethesda: 'Go and sin no more, lest a worse thing befall you'. The Pope had construed the text as implying that physical sickness could be traced to spiritual roots, and had on the strength of this provided that a spiritual healer should always minister to the sick before an ordinary physician did so.[140] Giberti, in his constitutions, threatened with severe penalties all physicians who persisted in attending patients who failed or positively refused to confess. They would be allowed to visit them only twice. Every kind of pressure must be applied to the recalcitrant in the interests of the soul.[141] Loyola and his companions had begun to agitate for such measures in Rome itself about 1538, and by 1543 or 1544 had actually got them enforced, in spite of opposition from a medical profession understandably indignant at this curtailment of its freedom.[142]

The ultimate aim of the Compagnie della Carità was to promote the Catholic faith, to increase the use of the sacraments, to keep a watch on morality and to promote peace and harmony. They must seek out and protect all young women whose virtue was imperilled through poverty. They must try to eliminate all common prostitutes and whores, all public blasphemers, 'and especially all who in word or in deed show themselves to be departing from the Catholic faith'. Philanthropy and moral and religious censorship were thus fused together. The Visitors and Presidenti must try to settle all legal disputes in which the parties could be persuaded to compromise. A few advocates and notaries were expected to volunteer to provide free legal aid to the poor, and the society would direct to them paupers found entangled in litigation. In all these activities, they could call for assistance from the governors of the town. In spite of its semi-public character, the society remained largely if not exclusively dependent on voluntary contributions, raised in Salò by means of poor boxes and of collections taken at an annual procession for the benefit of the society. In Verona, the

[140] IV Lateran, c. 22, in Mansi, *Concilia*, XXII, coll. 1010–11; John, v, 14.
[141] Giberti, *Constitutiones, titulus* iv, c. 11, in his *Opera*, pp. 58–9.
[142] Tacchi Venturi, *Storia della Compagnia di Gesù*, II/2, pp. 190 f.

society had its own specially deputed collectors of funds. The dispensation of alms was always, in Salò, to be the occasion for moral admonitions—the poor were invariably to be warned to look to their own salvation, especially by frequent confession.

These Compagnie, therefore, were organizations which used physical and spiritual charity for the purpose of heightening the religious life, of establishing a severer and more moral atmosphere, and of leading the maximum number of souls to salvation. Censuses of the poor would enable members of the upper groups in local society to establish a tighter grip on the conduct of the poor through a more detailed knowledge of their way of life. Investigations of this nature might well lead to the discovery of heresy, as well as of ignorance and loose morality. The principle of indiscriminate charity was condemned: resources were too limited to cope with the pressing problem of poverty in years of bad harvests, and in any case the positive advantages of discriminating between the moral and the immoral candidate for alms were clearly very great. Giberti himself disapproved of the more haphazard forms of almsgiving sufficiently to suspend the traditional distributions of loaves from the gates of his episcopal palace. He obtained Pope Paul III's approval for this measure in 1542, on the grounds that such dispensations did not benefit the true poor. They merely led to cursing, blasphemy, violence, quarrelling and even sexual promiscuity on the part of the jostling and ungrateful crowd struggling to get a share. Giberti proceeded to transfer the revenues which had supported these distributions of food to his own creation, the nunnery of the Convertite, and to other inhabitants of the convent of the Santissima Trinità, where the Convertite were then lodged.[143]

Famine conditions in 1539 had stimulated the actual foundation of the Compagnie della Carità in Verona and its diocese; the shortage of resources in these years provided the official justification for more 'judicious and discriminating' charity. These circumstances forced the citizens of Brescia also to devise a more comprehensive policy to deal with the problem of the poor. In October 1539, commissioners appointed for the purpose reported that the town was, in consequence of grain shortages, inundated with about 4,000 poor who had entered from outside. The city council then declared that it

had not forgotten the commandments of God, by which we are clearly reminded to redeem our sins with alms, and that alms extinguish sin as water puts out fire,

[143] See the brief of Paul III, 3 February 1542, reproduced in Ferdinando Ughelli, *Italia sacra* (5 vols., Venice, 1717–22), V, coll. 979–81; Ballerini, *Vita Giberti*, in *Opera*, p. xxii.

and that it must not forget the words of the Saviour

that what is done to one of the least of these poor creatures is done to him.

The council evidently considered that only well directed almsgiving would produce these spiritual results, and promptly forbade all begging whatsoever, with a stipulation that all foreign vagrants should be expelled within a day on pain of a flogging. The genuinely poor of the city were to receive bread tickets entitling them to 8-ounce wheaten loaves and 10-ounce millet loaves. Evidently the alms which cancelled out sin did not have to be voluntary alms: all the citizens, for every 'trei danari d'estimo' (i.e. for every 3 deniers at which they were rated for the purposes of taxation), were bound to give at least one loaf to the poor before the next harvest. Since the Brescians already possessed a centralized General or 'Great' Hospital, founded in the fifteenth century, they did not need to devise such elaborate measures for the co-ordination of relief. The Great Hospital was deemed capable of providing bread for 1,700 poor. As in Venice, the Scuole and fraternities received a general admonition to carry out their obligations faithfully, and thereby to relieve the poor. The Brescian legislation used phrases strongly redolent of Gasparo Contarini's admonitions to the bishop: 'If laymen are forced to give away the goods they have acquired by their own labours, then how much more must such institutions be compelled to give the poor a part in the goods left specifically to the poor!'[144]

During the 1530's, also, Girolamo Miani continued his work on the mainland of Italy in several dioceses of Lombardy and the Veneto. He pursued the same group of aims as the Compagnie del Divino Amore, the Procurators of the Incurabili and the diocesan reformer Giberti. He maintained a close relationship with the Theatines, with whom his followers—known as the Somaschians, after the hamlet in the Bergamasco where the congregation was originally formed—were temporarily merged from 1546 to 1555.[145] A decree of Pietro Lippomano, Bishop of Bergamo, issued in 1538, described the principal duty of the Somaschian congregation as being to

take care of wandering boys and girls, of orphans and destitute persons, of sinners and of women converted to God, either in hospitals, especially those of Christ's Incurables, or in other places.

---

[144] Cistellini, 'La "Compagnia di Carità"', pp. 394–5; Cistellini, *Figure della riforma pretridentina*, pp. 127 f. Cf. Contarini, *De officio episcopi*, in his *Opera*, p. 428.
[145] Tentorio, 'Somaschi', pp. 612–14.

This closely recalled the activities of the Incurabili of Venice, as described by the Patriarch in 1525. The members of the society to whom the decree was addressed were mostly of Lombard origin—from Bergamo itself, Brescia, Milan, Pavia, Como, and (by way of exception) Genoa. They had resolved to withdraw from the world and to live as a community on the alms of the faithful,

> without adopting the habit of any approved religious Order, but each remaining within the calling wherein he was called.[146]

Visiting Brescia in 1532, Miani had lived in the hospital of the Incurabili, in the humblest possible conditions, and there founded an orphanage which was subsequently strengthened by a legacy of a Brescian citizen, Zaccaria Pezzano, who charged the Great Hospital to supply medicines and drugs to sick orphans, to furnish their church or chapel with suitable equipment, and to build them ampler premises.[147] Again, in Bergamo, Miani seems to have founded orphanages for both males and females. Through the personal initiative of a travelling evangelist, still a layman, identifying himself with the interests of the poor and especially of the young, the development of charity in some of the mainland cities proceeded on the same path as in Venice itself. Miani also inspired the foundation of a nunnery for repentant prostitutes in Bergamo.[148]

The first forty years of the sixteenth century constituted the formative period in which the principles of Catholic philanthropy were worked out, often with reference to ancient models and long-established precepts which now acquired a new relevance and a fresh urgency. After 1540, these principles continued to be applied and modified, seldom radically changed. The history of the Venetian Republic (not a great innovator, but very receptive to the new movements of the Catholic revival) tentatively suggests a number of conclusions which may be of wider significance for the history of Catholic societies. During these years, the most valuable initiatives did not come from organs or bodies that can be identified in any simple sense with either Church or State. They stemmed from the voluntary mixed society of clerks and laymen, which, once established in some cosmopolitan centre like Rome, proved highly exportable to other parts of Italy. Italian society could draw on several hundred years of experience in

---

[146] Decree reproduced in Ughelli, *Italia sacra*, IV, coll. 487–9.

[147] Tortora, *Vita Hieronymi Aemiliani*, pp. 240–1; Cistellini, *Figure della riforma pretridentina*, pp. 20–1, 93.

[148] Tortora, *Vita Hieronymi Aemiliani*, p. 242; Roncalli and Forno, *Atti di Borromeo*, I/2, p. 143; Belotti, *Storia di Bergamo*, II, p. 205.

T

formulating clearcut, precise and unambiguous constitutions which made these processes of export and dissemination both easy and possible. The new societies owed something to the medieval Scuole, but differed from them in showing a tendency to focus their activities essentially outwards, in order to benefit primarily persons not members of their own brotherhoods. Although the *vergognosi* formed one of the main objects of their charity, they did not concentrate only on the respectable, resident poor. To some extent, they dealt with outcasts and sinners; if they rejected the professional, fraudulent adult beggar, they showed an anxious concern with the education and welfare of beggar children.

Such societies rapidly gained support both from ecclesiastical authorities and from lay magistrates. This happened naturally enough in city-states like Venice, where a high-ranking patrician, his own attention attracted through good evangelical strategy, could quickly win the approval of government organs for a new and useful foundation. There was usually an essential coincidence of aim between the state and these societies, and state action may have influenced the programme of some of the private organizations: there is no ground for assuming that the process was entirely one-way. Clearly, the state could do some things that private societies could not, like expelling, flogging or otherwise suppressing beggars; private organizations, however, joined in and showed their approval of the principle by refusing alms to the sturdy rogue. The state, like the private organizations, held to the principle that almsgiving should be kept voluntary wherever possible—though under extreme stress governments were willing to levy a compulsory rate, evoked by famine and epidemic disease in Venice, and by similar conditions in Brescia some years later.

The purpose of poor relief, at least in the hands of these societies, was never formally 'secular': their work was never officially designed to procure the good of human society as an end in itself. Their highest professed aim was spiritual, and the relief of the poor was both a form of asceticism and an expression of the love of God through the service of the least of his children. They were partially concerned with self-sanctification, but also with the souls of others. They were never so self-regarding that they could not look at the needs of society. They were not distracted from their duty to deal with such physical evils and social problems as disease and prostitution, though they treated prostitution as an offence against divine law to be expiated by repentance, rather than as a social phenomenon. Spiritual aims and moral judgments governed all charitable acts, and even obtruded into the relationship between doctor and patient.

Both in theory and in practice, the relief of the poor by Catholics was governed by discrimination on economic and on moral grounds: to each according to his need, to each according to his conduct. Accentuation of the problem of poverty, for whatever reason, forced most western European societies to consider the best means of disposing of their resources, which would not suffice for all who claimed to be poor. Between 1520 and 1560, economic expediency spurred many West European societies into reorganizing their methods of poor relief. The redistribution of population and dislocation of the normal securities by war, weather, famine and disease; the weight of population pressure, reflected in the subdivision of land and in the shrinking of real wages; the greater opportunities and security enjoyed by townsmen, which stimulated panic migrations from the countryside in the desperate anxiety to share them; the need to secure labour for vital industries: all these economic incentives, universally occurring in some degree, helped to evoke poor laws and generally stimulate philanthropy. These problems transcended all religious or political barriers. However, one cannot find the root explanation merely in economic expediency. The motive surely lay partly in the common inheritance of both the Catholic and the Protestant churches. It lay in the Pauline doctrine of charity, in the canon law, in a general uneasiness and dissatisfaction with the immorality and ignorance of European society; it lay also in the widespread determination, common to humanists, Protestants and their conscious or unconscious imitators and followers, to resurrect first principles obscured by time and by irrelevant superstition.

It would, indeed, be fallacious to imply that in the European Catholic Church as a whole during this period there was any single, consistent view on the subject of charity and poor relief. There arose, in fact, an extensive theoretical debate in Flanders and Spain on the subject of the new schemes for the organization of poor relief and for the suppression of begging. The schemes received theoretical justification in the 1520's in the treatise of Juan Luis Vives, the Valencian humanist resident in Bruges, and in the 1540's from Juan Robles or Juan Medina, Benedictine Abbot of San Vicente in Salamanca, who had prepared his work after consultation with the Cardinal-Archbishop of Toledo in November 1544. Vives gave support to the schemes already introduced at Mons and Ypres, whilst Medina justified the methods employed by several towns of Old Castile and Leon—those of Zamora, Salamanca and Valladolid—in the early 1540's.[149] Most of the coherent and rational opposition to these schemes from within the body of the

[149] Vives, *Il modo del sovvenire a poveri*, cit.; Medina, *Remedio de los verdaderos pobres*, cit., ff. A2, A3v.

Catholic clergy was identified with the Mendicant Orders, who found the poor laws objectionable on theological and on practical grounds. In 1530-1, the Friars of Ypres challenged their validity and submitted them to the Sorbonne for adjudication, the Sorbonne passing the Ypres scheme on condition that nobody should be forbidden to give alms on his own initiative, that the poor laws should not be made a pretext for the secularization of church property, and that the Mendicants themselves should not suffer from the general condemnation of begging.[150] Again, in 1545, Domiñgo Soto, the Dominican theologian of Salamanca, debated the question exhaustively with the Benedictine Medina.[151] In 1564, the Augustinian Lorenzo de Villavicencio renewed the attack two years after Giles Wyts, Pensionary of Bruges, had tried to introduce into his city a scheme for poor relief on the familiar lines.[152]

Since the Friars have provided much ammunition for the argument that the Catholic Church favoured indiscriminate poor relief, it is worth briefly examining their contentions here, and relating them to the attitudes prevalent in Venice. The Friars represented begging as a fundamental human liberty of which no-one could rightfully be deprived unless he had committed a serious crime: whereas the magistrates and their supporters held it to be a disagreeable necessity of which it was a kindness to relieve the poor.[153] The Friars stood for individual action on the part of both pauper and benefactor, in the interests of the spiritual and physical welfare of every individual person; Vives, Medina and the magistrates for action by the civil authority to further the common weal, and thus indirectly to promote the good of each member of the community. The Friars advocated personal, amateur, irregular charity; their opponents a more impersonal, semi-professional charity, in the belief that regular assistance degraded the pauper less than alms for which he had to beg.[154] The Friars appealed to the divine law as the ultimate standard of conduct. Villavicencio at any rate proclaimed the absolute right of the clergy, men specially qualified to know and interpret the divine law, to intervene and even

---

[150] The complaints of the Friars and the replies of the magistrates of Ypres are printed as doc. 8 in Nolf, *Bienfaisance à Ypres*, pp. 40–76, in a French translation; for Latin versions of the Sorbonne judgment, *ibid.*, docs. 16–17, pp. 119–23, and for an English translation, from which I quote, Salter, *Early tracts on poor relief*, pp. 76–77.

[151] Soto, *Deliberacion en la causa de los pobres*, cit.

[152] Lorenzo de Villavicencio, *De oeconomia sacra circa pauperum curam* (Antwerp, 1564).

[153] Nolf, *Bienfaisance à Ypres*, pp. 56–7, 60; Soto, *Deliberacion*, ff. 9v.–10; Medina, *Remedio*, f. B v.

[154] For the last point, see Nolf, *Bienfaisance*, p. 45.

take the lead in every sphere of human activity—especially that of poor relief.[155] Vives, on the other hand, affirmed the omnicompetence of the magistrate acting for the common good within his commonwealth, and asserted his right to legislate on questions of poor relief as matters supremely relevant to its welfare and stability.[156] There was no disagreement in theory that idle and fraudulent beggars ought to be discouraged, but the Friars then unhelpfully questioned the right of the magistrate either to restrain the genuinely poor from seeking relief on their own account, or to inquire closely into anyone's claim to relief.[157]

The theoretical debate pivoted on the nature of mercy or *misericordia*, and on its relationship to justice. Mercy was held by Soto (and many of his opponents would surely have agreed) to possess a peculiar power to blot out the sins of its practitioner, or to maintain the righteous in a state of grace. Justice ranked lower in the scale of life-giving virtues, because it merely consisted of rendering each man his due. Soto chose to interpret mercy as being an act of pure grace done, in imitation of Christ himself, to somebody who did not deserve it. In man, mercy and justice were distinct and separate virtues: they coincided only in God.

> The subject of corporal mercy is solely the misery and need of the pauper . . . brotherly correction is quite another matter. And the punishment of evil-doers . . . pertains to the ministers of justice. It is one thing to be the judge of evil, and another to give alms to the poor.[158]

Hence the Friars rejected all attempts to discriminate between the deserving and the undeserving poor, and all attempts to use charity for the purposes of discipline and moral improvement.

Soto thus complained of the poor laws because they devalued acts of mercy by reducing them to the status of acts of justice. It was essential to all good Christians to enjoy opportunities of being merciful. When the authorities deprived a person of his right to beg for subsistence, they then incurred an actual obligation to provide him with support, and their doing so became an act of mere justice.[159] Anyway, on what grounds could the magistrate undertake to furnish the poor with subsistence? He had no right to force the rich to give, since relieving the poor could be conceived only as a voluntary act of mercy. It was true that the canon laws had always maintained that one must give alms to save a fellow-creature from dying of want, and that a rich

[155] Villavicencio, *De oeconomia sacra*, pp. 162, 230, 235–6, 280–1, 289–90, 208 f.

[156] Vives, *Il modo del sovvenire a poveri*, ff. 47v. f., 51v. f.

[157] Soto, *Deliberacion*, ff. 6–8v., 22v.–23, 45v.; Villavicencio, *De oeconomia sacra*, pp. 186–7, 240–3.

[158] Soto, *Deliberacion*, ff. 21v., 26–7.   [159] *Ibid.*, f. 34v.

man who out of his superfluous property relieved a pauper in extreme need was merely doing an act of justice.[160] The magistrate had no authority to go further than this, and could not force anyone to maintain the same pauper systematically over a substantial period save in extreme necessity.[161] The Friars further objected to measures which threatened to weaken the personal relationship between the pauper and his benefactor. Hence their disapproval of projects for removing the poor from streets and churches, and for confining them to their homes or accommodating them in hospital. They did not sympathize with the ideal cherished by the Benedictine Medina that it might be possible in hospital to cure the pauper of his ills and hence of his poverty. They argued that if the poor were not on public view the public would forget them, and give little or nothing to the municipal almonry or Common Chest on their behalf.[162] To Soto, mercy must include compassion, an inward emotional stirring which acquired merit even if he who felt it could not follow it up with an external act of mercy more tangibly affecting the pauper. No-one could be expected to feel this compassion unless he was directly confronted with the poor.[163] No-one could delegate charity to a board of officials—even were it possible to find anyone reliable enough to be entrusted with the funds.[164]

The Mendicant Friars certainly stated these positions. But they cannot be taken as representative of Catholic opinion in general. Medina directly answered them, often by resorting to the argument of expediency rather than of logic. Justice and mercy could not be separated: to believe that mercy should not be related to the merits of the recipient would perniciously cause the wicked to prosper at the expense of the good.[165] In mercy, there were two elements: compassion for suffering, certainly, but also the remedy for it; and the greater of these was remedy.

> No man of sense should doubt that it is better to cure the afflicted man than to give him every day a *blanca*, and better to maintain the pauper than to give him every day a *maravedi*.[166]

He pointed out that Christ himself had set the example of remedial charity, for

---

[160] Cf. Tierney, *Medieval poor law*, pp. 29 f.
[161] Soto, *Deliberacion*, ff. 9v.–10.
[162] Nolf, *Bienfaisance*, pp. 54–5; Soto, *Deliberacion*, f. 39r.–v.; Villavicencio, *De oeconomia sacra*, pp. 189, 264.
[163] Soto, *Deliberacion*, f. 39r.–v.; Villavicencio, *De oeconomia sacra*, p. 189.
[164] Cf. Nolf, *Bienfaisance*, p. 59.
[165] Medina, *Remedio*, ff. C2v.–C3v.   [166] *Ibid.*, ff. B4v.–B5.

we do not read that the Son of God extended to beggars any charity other than to take away from them the occasion to beg—giving them health, so that they could earn without the toil and shame of begging.[167]

Nobody, or so Medina most trenchantly argued, had any right to withhold remedies from the poor in order to benefit himself by manufacturing chances to be merciful.

> If a man is capable of relieving his brother of pain and misery and yet refrains from doing so, who doubts that he does evil? To do such evil in order to obtain the benefit of mercy for ourselves is certainly evil according to the doctrine of St Paul.... Although many occasions for acquiring merit are removed if there are hospitals endowed with revenues, nevertheless the man who builds these institutions and thereby meets the needs of the living poor is still doing the greatest good, even if they do relieve many sick and afflicted persons of the need to venture out in public.[168]

How did the new religious movements passing through the city and Republic of Venice react to the questions raised by the Friars? These movements collaborated with, and perhaps even inspired, state policy. The state tried to eliminate begging for the sake of public order and public health, and also on religious and humane grounds. It did not seek to eliminate voluntary effort, but to co-ordinate, supplement and use it. It levied compulsory rates only in exceptional circumstances, perhaps on the good canonical grounds that compulsion was justified in order to save humans from dying of want. There is no doubt that the new movements differed from the Friars in that they wished to eliminate begging—not by penal methods, but by making it unnecessary. Their object was, tactfully, to anticipate the needs of those who are still ashamed to beg, so that it would be unnecessary for them to venture on the streets, and to train beggar children to become self-supporting. Only such voluntary action could make it feasible or just for the state to suppress begging. The new movements did not wish to ignore the existence of the sinner: but they offered him charity on a moralistic basis, with a view to spiritual reclamation. They were not prepared, like the Friars, to exclude moral judgments altogether from the act of charity. Nor did they fear the results of increasing hospital accommodation, or of encouraging the largest number of people to take advantage of it. At the same time, they placed a high value on personal contact with the poor. These remarks apply in some degree to most of those who sympathized with the Compagnie del Divino Amore, the Compagnie della Carità, and the Fraternities for the care of the Poveri Vergognosi.

[167] *Ibid.*, ff. Ev.–E2. [168] *Ibid.*, ff. E8v.–F.

It may also be significant that when, in the spring of 1535, Ignatius Loyola returned to the Basque country, he persuaded the mayor and notables of his native town of Azpeitia to put into operation a scheme for the elimination of begging. This could have been the fruit of his own personal experiences over the past seven years, either in Paris or in Flanders. Poor relief in the village ought to be entrusted to two officials known as *mayordomos*, whose duty it would be to inquire into the affairs of the poor, and to deny alms to healthy inhabitants of the place who were capable of working for a living.[169] The founder of the Jesuits approved of the poor laws enough to import them to Spain. In the late 1530's, the future Jesuits in Rome tried to concentrate beggars in rough shelters or hospitals, and to teach them Christian doctrine as well as supplying their physical wants;[170] Loyola exhorted Pierre Favre to do the same in Parma in 1540.[171]

There is no record of any serious clerical protest against the Venetian poor laws, and their aims seem to have received episcopal endorsement, since they were clearly shared by Giberti. The legislators clearly assumed that they would enjoy the support of parish priests. There is an obvious need, not to talk in terms of a single 'Catholic standpoint' or social attitude, but to distinguish between differing sectors of Catholic opinion. One might, on the slenderest evidence, argue that, since the poor laws were a product of a time of flux and uncertainty, when Catholic and Protestant orthodoxies were not sharply defined, the new methods could have been inspired by Protestant influences acting on men who did not know what they ought to believe. However, it is certain that the methods evolved in the first half of the century were endorsed and employed in the post-Tridentine era, with the continued support of eminent churchmen. The next chapters will deal with the subsequent application of these principles.

[169] For the text of the ordinance, see M.H.S.J., *Monumenta Ignatiana*, IV/1, *Scripta de Sancto Ignatio de Loyola* (Madrid, 1904), pp. 539–43; also the letter of Ignatius Loyola to the citizens of Azpeitia, in M.H.S.J., *Monumenta Ignatiana*, I/1, pp. 161–5, August–September 1540. Cf. also Tacchi Venturi, *Storia della Compagnia di Gesù*, II/1, pp. 71–4; Heinrich Boehmer, *Ignatius von Loyola*, ed. Hans Leube (Stuttgart, 1941), pp. 128–30, 313–15.

[170] Rodriguez, *De origine et progressu Societatis Jesu*, in M.H.S.J., *Epistolae Broeti*, p. 500; M.H.S.J., Polanco, *Historia*, I, pp. 65–6; Tacchi Venturi, *Storia della Compagnia di Gesù*, cit., II/1, pp. 161–9.

[171] Letter of Pierre Favre to Pietro Codacio and Francesco Xavier, Parma, 25 March 1540, M.H.S.J., *Fabri Monumenta*, pp. 21–4; Tacchi Venturi, *Storia della Compagnia di Gesù*, II/1, pp. 239–41.

4

THE ENFORCEMENT OF THE POOR LAWS: TOWARDS A SOCIAL POLICY, 1540–1577

About 1540, the food situation in Venice itself and in the provinces which helped to supply it became alarmingly unstable. The incidence of epidemic disease decreased, but famine recurred more frequently and with no less menace. With the temporary removal of some of the checks on its growth, the pressure of population began to combine with the effects of storm and flood, to throw an expanding burden on supplies of food which might at any time suddenly contract. The systematic enforcement of the Venetian poor law formed part of a wider programme of social and economic action launched against this challenge: a programme which included the reclamation of land and the establishment of grain stocks as prophylactics against recurrent famine. This new phase in the internal economic history of the Venetian Republic extended into the early and middle 1570's, when epidemic disease reappeared on a scale unknown since the fourteenth century, and plague cut population back.

Famines, often causing peasant migrations like those of 1527–8, afflicted the Venetian Republic at ten-year, sometimes at five-year intervals. In the summer and autumn of 1539, famine stimulated action by civic and episcopal authority in Verona, Brescia and Bergamo.[1] The following summer, the Venetian Senate described itself as

> having in this present year seen by manifest experience how this city has been imperilled by extreme shortages of grain, so that one may truthfully say that only the Majesty of God, who extends his protection to our state, has by his special grace preserved this most numerous people from dying of hunger.[2]

In April 1540, the civil governors of Padua declared that with two months still to elapse before the harvest they had food in their granaries sufficient for only two days.[3] A few weeks later, the Senate found it necessary to extend to the Padovano a moratorium on all debts owed by the peasants of the region, in view of 'the dearths and disasters of

---

[1] See above, pp. 273, 277–8, and below, pp. 295–6.

[2] A.S.V., *Senato, Terra*, reg. 1540/41, f. 30v., 16 June 1540.

[3] See Angelo Ventura, *Nobiltà e popolo nella società veneta del '400 e '500* (Bari, 1964), p. 384.

287

these present times'. The exaction of these debts would be deferred till the next harvest.[4] The peasant's capacity for meeting his obligations either to private creditors or to the fisc depended closely on the excellence or otherwise of the harvest. Mass migrations of peasants and other beggars troubled the Venetians in 1544–5, the years when the systematic re-enforcement of the poor law of 1529 began.[5] In the small town of Bassano, the only region in the Venetian Republic for which a reasonably complete series of wholesale grain prices is available for this period, prices shot up to a high peak in 1545, two-and-a-half to three times as high as in 1541–3 or in 1546.[6] In Venice, a sixteenth-century chronicle described great dearths in 1549, which again caused peasant migrations to Venice; and bad harvests followed in 1550 and 1551. In April 1551, the Senate noted that many communes on the mainland were slumping into debt, failing to pay the direct tax or Sussidio on account of 'the grave dearths and famine of the present year'.[7]

Other, widespread disasters occurred in 1559, immediately caused by cloudbursts and heavy rains in May, when several rivers broke their banks; and these produced acute shortages spanning several months, from November 1559 to July and August 1560. Rain and flooding was severe enough to destroy some of the seed corn for the following year. The Senate adopted its usual measures—by granting the mainland extra time to pay the Sussidio, by issuing a moratorium on the payment of debts, and by suspending the *mostra generale*—the muster parades at which the mainland areas furnished their quotas of recruits to the Venetian armed forces.[8] Finally, the last really severe famine in this phase of expanding population arose in the autumn and winter of 1569. In the words of a contemporary, Francesco Da Molin,

> since there was no flour in the public warehouses, people crazy with hunger wandered through the city looking for baker's shops as if they were going to churches to obtain pardons and indulgences. Fortunate indeed were they who could get any bread. Matters reached such a pass that ship's biscuit had to be distributed and strictly rationed in order to feed the people. One *staio* of grain was valued at 7–10 golden crowns. For

[4] A.S.V., *Senato, Terra*, reg. 1540/41, f. 24, 24 May 1540.

[5] See below, pp. 297 f.

[6] See Gabriele Lombardini, *Pane e denaro a Bassano: prezzi del grano e politica dell'approvigionamento dei cereali tra il 1501 e il 1799* (Venice, 1963), Tabella II, pp. 58–60.

[7] M.C.V., Cicogna MSS. 2853, *Cronaca Agostini*, f. 88v.; A.S.V., *Senato, Terra*, reg. 1550/51, f. 116, 171, 17 April, 29 August 1551.

[8] M.C.V., Cicogna MSS. 2853, f. 110v., 124r.–v.; A.S.V., *Senato, Terra*, *filza* 29, 14 July, 16 August, 19 August 1559; *filza* 30, 7 September, 16 September 1559; *filza* 31, 11 March 1560. The area affected included the Padovano, Vicentino, Veronese, Bresciano, Udine, Legnago and Porto, Belluno and Crema.

the most part, the peasants of the Padovano, Trevigiano and Friuli ate roots and cooked herbs. . . .[9]

In 1572, Venice suffered from severe shortages, especially of flour, round Easter time—but these lasted for only fifteen days, as compared with several months in 1569–70.[10] In that year, famine had begun on 4 October, and prices were still exceptionally high by the end of the following June, when all controls had been removed in a desperate attempt to attract more grain to the city.

The most convincing explanation for this instability is that the expansion of population in Venice itself and in some of its subject regions was reducing the normal safety-margin which separated plenty from starvation, so that the people lay at the mercy of the weather. Censuses supply direct evidence of this increase, which is supported both by the general belief among responsible contemporaries that population was expanding, and by the circumstantial evidence of certain forms of economic activity, including projects for the reclamation of land and the fuller use of the soil. Censuses, taken by themselves, are not wholly reliable—but, as Professor Helleiner remarks,

> Man's capacity to appraise quantities in terms of 'more' or 'less', 'large' or 'small', 'growing' or 'declining'—as distinguished from his ability to guess at absolute numbers or rates of change—was probably not much less developed in the sixteenth and seventeenth centuries than it is now.[11]

Again, land reclamation might have been designed in part to repair the ravages of flood damage or compensate for exhausted soils, rather than to accommodate an expanding population. But it did occur in conjunction with other phenomena which seem to indicate that population was growing: the combination of all these phenomena points to population increase.

Venetian censuses returned the population of the capital city at about 130,000 in 1540, rising to nearly 160,000 in 1552 and 1555, and nearly 170,000 in 1563—an increase far too large to be explained away merely by variations in procedure or changes in the degree of administrative efficiency.[12] General consciousness of the problem of population

---

[9] B.M.V., MSS. Italiani, Classe VII, DLIII (8812), *Compendio di me Francesco Da Molino de Missier Marco delle cose, che reputerò degne di venerne particolar memoria*, p. 13.

[10] B.M.V., MSS. Italiani, Classe VII, CXXXIV (8035), *Cronaca Savina*, ff. 344v.–345.

[11] Helleiner, 'Population of Europe', pp. 2–3.

[12] The actual figures in the censuses are more exact, but it is best to treat them as approximations. There are often doubts as to whether they include foreigners, inmates of hospitals, etc. For extensive discussions of the sources, see Aldo Contento, 'Il

and victuals probably inspired the only surviving general census of the mainland cities, which was conducted in 1548, and which returned the total population of the Venetian mainland as 1,590,040.[13] In the next fifteen or twenty years, information supplied by the Venetian governors suggested substantial increases in the population of four provinces. The Padovano (including Padua itself) rose from 152,163 in 1548 to 180,000 in 1571; the Trevigiano (including Treviso) from 158,084 in 1548 to 181,268 in 1563; the Vicentino (including Vicenza) from 155,708 in 1548 to 170,470 in 1570; and the Bergamasco (including Bergamo) from 122,511 in 1548 to 165,106 in 1564 and 160,000 in 1572.[14] According to these official Venetian sources, the population of other regions remained more or less constant: but, on the other hand, the figures discovered locally by Donazzolo and Saibante in their investigations of the Veronese suggest that the population of that province grew from 145,298 in 1538 to 177,946 in 1577—an increase of about 25 per cent.[15]

Alvise Cornaro, a Venetian patrician and a pioneer of land reclamation, attributed this increase to the suspension of the series of plague epidemics 'which used, every eight or ten years, to carry off one-fifth of the people'. He also referred to a 'new way of making war' which eliminated far fewer people than the old.[16] Judging by the plagues of 1528–9, Cornaro was exaggerating the extent of the damage: but there was some truth in his assertion that disease was striking lighter blows. Admittedly, in the spring of 1535, one mysterious disease, which might have been pneumonia or influenza, gave the Provveditori alla Sanità enough concern to inspire them to order public post-mortem examinations in which over seventy physicians took part.[17] In 1555 and 1556, there were serious outbreaks of plague in several Venetian parishes, and a parallel epidemic in Padua, where the disease began at the end of April or beginning of May 1555.[18] Likewise, in the spring of 1570, an outbreak of typhus accompanied the prolonged famine in Venice, whilst in Friuli similar epidemics of typhus helped to reduce the population of the province from 165,941 in 1569 to 140,304 in 1572. In this, it combined with recruitment to the galleys of Venice during the war of

censimento della popolazione sotto la Repubblica Veneta', *Nuovo Archivio Veneto*, XIX–XX (1900); Julius Beloch, 'La popolazione di Venezia nei secoli XVI e XVII', *ibid.*, nuova serie, III (1902). See also Beltrami, *Storia della popolazione*, p. 59.

[13] Beltrami, *Veneziani in Terraferma*, Appendice al Capitolo I.
[14] *Ibid.*
[15] Donazzolo and Saibante, 'Sviluppo di Verona', pp. 108, 124.
[16] Beltrami, *Storia dell'agricoltura*, pp. 32–3; see also above, p. 219.
[17] A.S.V., *Provveditori alla Sanità, Notatorio III*, vol. 727, ff. 293–306.
[18] *Ibid.*, *Notatorio VI*, vol. 730, f. 24, 42v.–43, 257v.–262; A.S.V., *Senato, Terra*, reg. 1555/56, ff. 41v.–42, 148v.–149.

Lepanto and Cyprus, together with much emigration to avoid naval service.[19] However, these were mortality peaks rising out of a plain, and were not regular occurrences like the plagues of the half-century from 1478 to 1528. A more positive reason for the expansion of Venice doubtless lay in the existence of economic opportunities, which were growing more or less in step with the advance in the city's population. Over the decade 1530–9, the average annual production of broadcloth in Venice was about 5,200 cloths; in 1560–9, it had risen to 18,000 cloths.[20] Likewise, the great industrial complex of the Arsenal was expanding in proportion to the overall population increase: it employed 1,138 ship's carpenters, caulkers and oarmakers in 1536, 1,381 in 1538 and 2,346 in 1560. According to Professor Romano's calculations, the Arsenal employed about 2 per cent of the total population of Venice in the late 1530's, and perhaps $2\frac{1}{2}$ per cent in 1560.[21]

The growth of Venice almost certainly depended on a steady supply of immigrants from adjacent provinces, and only population pressure could guarantee a steady flow of such immigration. Padua, the rich agricultural region nearest to Venice, suffered acutely from Venice's determination to transfer its own shortages to its subject mainland areas. Venetian capital had penetrated deeply into the Padovano. A certain Podestà of Padua reported in 1558 that

> the lands of the Paduans have for the most part passed into the hands of gentlemen and citizens of Venice. The lands which remain to the Paduans and to all the clergy, even taking into account the revenues of the bishopric, are not sufficient to feed the city of Padua and supply it with bread, especially as many citizens and clergy of Padua convey their revenues to Venice, and hence the city of Padua loses many of its crops. For these reasons, and because of the proximity of Venice, grain is always more costly in Padua than in any of your other mainland cities.[22]

Again, in 1559, the governors of the city told the Venetian Senate that

> the needs of this town threaten to increase every year for two reasons. One is that, by the grace of God, the population hourly grows, since everybody wants to live under the peaceful protection of Your Serenity;

[19] Report of the governor Daniele Priuli, 16 March 1573, in A.S.V., *Collegio, Relazioni, busta* 49; Beltrami, *Veneziani in Terraferma*, p. 4, n. 1; M.C.V., Cicogna MSS. 2853, f. 187v.

[20] See Pierre Sardella, 'L'épanouissement industriel de Venise au XVI siècle', *Annales: Économies, Sociétés, Civilisations*, II (1947); Domenico Sella, 'The rise and fall of the Venetian woollen industry', revised English version in *Crisis and change in the Venetian economy*, ed. Brian Pullan (London, 1968), p. 109.

[21] See Ruggiero Romano, 'Economic aspects of the construction of warships in Venice', *ibid.*, pp. 75–6.

[22] A.S.V., *Collegio, Relazioni, busta* 32, *Miste*, vol. II, f. 94.

the other, that every year more of this city's landed estates pass into Venetian hands, so that their revenues are pledged to Venice and therefore have to be carried off there.[23]

Severe shortages in the region of the Padovano could well have swelled the numbers both of short-term and of long-term immigrants to Venice, thereby stressing the need for an effective poor law.

There is, unluckily, no evidence about the behaviour of Venetian prices before the last quarter of the sixteenth century; though it is known that in the second half of the century grain prices in Udine, to the north of Venice, and in Chioggia (to the south of the lagoon) began to move upwards.[24] The more or less continuous series of grain prices available for the town of Bassano indicates a continuous tendency to rise between about 1541 and 1593, passing through an especially acute phase in the '40's and '50's.[25] Unfortunately, there is no evidence about the movement of industrial prices in this area, to indicate how far prices were 'scissoring', and how far those of basic foodstuffs were outstripping others (as might be expected in a period of rising population). Rising prices were not confined to Bassano. Early in 1551, the citizen Council of One Hundred in Vicenza had occasion to declare that

Since, by the grace of God, the population of this city and its territory have so increased, wheat which formerly cost only 1 lira now costs 3 lire and sometimes more, and wine which used to cost 2 ducats now fetches 5 or 6 and sometimes more, so that the ancient custom of commuting rents paid in wheat into cash at the rate of 4 ducats per *staio* and wine at the rate of 40 ducats per *carro* has now ceased to be appropriate, on account of the excessively high prices.[26]

Concern at this situation produced public and private social and economic action. Schemes to reclaim and irrigate flourished, and were most ambitiously formulated by Alvise Cornaro, who proposed the systematic reclamation of the marshy tracts in the Basso Padovano and Basso Polesine. The Venetian families of Badoer, Bernardo, Bon, Contarini, Diedo, Dolfin, Foscarini, Priuli, Rinaldi, Sagredo and Sanuto all participated in these enterprises, though the work was often delayed by quarrels between the companies of contractors that sprang up everywhere.[27] In 1542, the government made an abortive proposal

[23] A.S.V., *Senato, Terra, filza* 29, 14 July 1559.

[24] Fernand Braudel, 'La vita economica di Venezia nel secolo XVI', *La civiltà veneziana del Rinascimento* (Florence, 1958), p. 91.

[25] Lombardini, *Pane e denaro a Bassano*, pp. 56, 58–60.

[26] A.S.V., *Senato, Terra,* reg. 1550/51, ff. 134v.–135, 3 January 1551 Venetian style.

[27] See Aldo Stella, 'La crisi economica veneziana della seconda metà del secolo XVI', *Archivio Veneto*, LVIII (1956), pp. 21 f.

to sell off a fraction of the untilled common lands (*beni comunali*) in Friuli and the Trevigiano to the north of Venice, and to reduce part of the residue to cultivation. The project was stopped, however, by protests to the effect that this would destroy the necessary reserves of pasture-ground.[28] In the autumn of 1543, a senatorial committee was considering the recovery of lands in the Valley of Santa Giustina in the Polesine, and declaring that 'Because of the increase of population, we must not fail to carry out this most fruitful work'. It would increase the national wealth and the revenue of the state, extend meadowland and pasturage, and improve the air (thus presumably reducing the risk of malaria).[29] Meadowland was vital: the spread of arable land in response to population pressure was probably cutting into the area available for pasture. Cattle were needed both to provide manure for the fertilization of land and to remedy the meat shortages of which the Venetians were conscious during the 1540's.[30]

In 1545, the Senate proceeded to appoint a new commission of three magistrates to inquire into the nature and extent of the uncultivated land subject to Venice. They hoped, thereby, to keep both the capital and the mainland abundantly supplied with grain, and to ward off the evil results of severe famines. Optimistically, they also hoped to reduce the flow of precious metals out of the country for the purchase of foreign grains.[31] A second commission, this time a permanent one, was finally established in the autumn of 1556. The Senate announced that

> In our lands of Padua, Vicenza and Verona, in the district of Asolo, in the Polesine di Rovigo and in Istria there are many untilled areas which could be brought under cultivation if they were watered, drained or irrigated; and a great quantity of grain could then be drawn from them.

It empowered its commissioners to examine all projects and recommendations put forward for this purpose by engineers, if necessary

[28] See Giannino Ferrari, 'La legislazione veneziana sui beni comunali', *Nuovo Archivio Veneto, nuova serie,* XXXVI (1918), pp. 15–16.

[29] A.S.V., *Senato, Terra,* reg. 1543/44, f. 31v. f., 11 September, 8 November 1543. On this occasion, the decree was not passed, perhaps because of objections to the methods recommended.

[30] A.S.V., *Senato, Terra,* reg. 1545/46, f. 75, 19 September 1545, refers to meat shortages caused by increases in the export taxes imposed by Ferdinand, King of the Romans; *ibid.,* reg. 1550/51, f. 98v., 21 February 1550 Venetian style, by which two Provveditori sopra le Beccarie were sent to the mainland to reduce the high price of meat to its former level; reg. 1551/52, f. 188v., 15 February 1552 Venetian style, which reflects the still greater need to encourage meat and cattle farming in Venetian territory, in view of the destruction of cattle in Hungary, Germany, Lombardy, Piedmont and elsewhere as a result of war. See also Lecce. 'Condizioni del territorio veronese'.

[31] A.S.V., *Senato, Terra,* reg. 1545–6, f. 74v., 19 September 1545.

going to the spot in order to inform themselves of what the plans would entail.[32] In 1560, the Senate recruited another commission specially devoted to the province of the Trevigiano, which had been omitted from the original instructions.[33] In practice, these Provveditori sopra i Beni Inculti seem to have confined themselves to approving the projects of the various private companies, and occasionally (where schemes seemed especially worthy and public-spirited) exempting contractors from the obligation to pay taxes for a period of ten years.[34]

A less laborious method of restraining famine lay in extending the machinery for the accumulation of grain stocks. This was designed mainly to frustrate the manoeuvres of speculators—the municipality would purchase grains in bulk in the month or two after the harvest, when the seasonal cycle of prices was usually at its lowest point, and then release them on to the market later in the harvest-year, at modest prices sufficient only to cover its own costs and administrative expenses. Bassano, for example, possessed an institution which had been engaging in this form of activity at least since 1485.[35] Other cities took steps to provide themselves with such machinery in the years 1540–60.

Importers of grain to Venice were officially allowed to keep only as much as was necessary for their own and their family's consumption; later in the century, about one-third of the grain consumed in Venice was eaten by the households of persons who had themselves imported it to the capital. Two-thirds of all the wheat brought to Venice was deposited in the two warehouses or Fondachi of Rialto and San Marco. Their officials dispensed it in the form of flour to persons baking their own bread, who accounted for 22·2 per cent of all consumption, and to the bakers of the Arte dei Pistori, who supplied, about 1600, 44 per cent of all civilian consumption. The government directed that the price of bread should be kept constant in famine years, but that the loaf should be proportionately lightened.[36] These Fondachi, which dealt mainly in wheaten flour, were already active by the close of the

[32] *Ibid.*, reg. 1555/56, f. 136r.–v., 10 October 1556. Reg. 1557/58, f. 40, 6 August 1557 provides for a survey ('sia fatto il ritratto') on valleys from Battaglia to Este bordering on 'the river or canal of Moncelese and the mountains around the valleys of Garzignan, Val Sanzibio, Arqua and Baon', with a further reference (ff. 94v.–95, 2 May 1558) to 'digging the Moncelesana canal'. *Ibid.*, f. 75, 29 January 1557 Venetian style, shows that the process was extended to 'valleys and other areas in our lands of Cologna, Montagnana, Este and Castelbaldo, and the areas of Vighizzuol, Val Grande, Val Urbana, Villa di Carmignan, Vescovana, Salesmi and Anguillara'.

[33] A.S.V., *Senato, Terra*, reg. 1560/61, ff. 14v.–15, 12 October 1560.

[34] Stella, 'La crisi economica', pp. 24–5.

[35] Lombardini, *Pane e denaro a Bassano*, pp. 29 f.

[36] See Maurice Aymard, *Venise, Raguse et le commerce du blé pendant la seconde moitié du XVIème siècle* (Paris, 1966), pp. 74–6.

1520's.[37] The Venetian government, however, decided in 1540 to provide against famine by the effective establishment of deposits of millet,
a much cheaper and humbler crop, in a warehouse at San Stai. The
magistracy in charge of grain policy, the Collegio alle Biave, had
apparently issued instructions for the creation of such a deposit in 1531
—but their orders had never been executed. The Senate now proposed
to finance the new deposit with the aid of 20,000 ducats subtracted
from the latest levy of the Sussidio on the Venetian mainland—a tax
expected to yield some 200,000 ducats overall.[38] They further supplemented the reserves by adding, in 1551, a deposit of *gran grosso*: a form
of grain which was cheaper and coarser than the finest Paduan wheat,
and which had served the Venetians extensively during the famines of
1527–9. This reserve deposit originally consisted of some 50,000 *staia*,
and had expanded to 80,000 by 1593, when a second such deposit (this
time of 60,000 *staia*) was added.[39] During famines, the government did
in fact retreat upon its reserves of millet and *gran grosso*, though such
measures proved violently unpopular. The Venetians, on all social
levels, were too deeply accustomed to wheaten bread, and in 1569–70,
Doge Pietro Loredan, the formal scapegoat for the supposed short-
comings of the government's victualling policy, earned the disgusted
epithet of 'the millet Doge (*il Dose dal meiotto*)'. Mobs shouted this at
his corpse when he died on 3 May 1570. The Venetians themselves
chose to purchase a very white and fine type of bread known as 'bread
of Lonigo', after 'a fortress in the Vicentino which enjoys the reputation of making the finest bread in Italy', though much of it had in
reality never been near the place.[40] In fact, on M. Maurice Aymard's
showing, over the rather later period 1566–91, Venice imported about
11·8 million *staia* of wheat, both from within Venetian territory and
from abroad, but only 3·1 million *staia* of vegetables and of the so-
called *biave menute*—the humbler and cheaper crops which included
millet, rye, barley and sorghum.[41]

Other major cities took the same action as Venice itself. In Bergamo
and Treviso, episcopal action joined with civic. In 1539, Bishop Pietro
Lippomano invited to the city a successful Dominican preacher,
Orsetti de' Gherardi, who had already been responsible for the estab-

---

[37] See Pullan, 'The famine in Venice'.

[38] A.S.V., *Senato, Terra*, reg. 1540/41, ff. 30v., 57v.–58, 16 June, 12 October 1540;
reg. 1542/43, f. 34, 2 June 1542.

[39] Aymard, *Venise, Raguse et le commerce du blé*, pp. 76–7; A.S.V., *Senato, Terra*,
reg. 1593, f. 56v., 17 July 1593.

[40] M.C.V., Cicogna MSS. 2853, ff. 164–8, 183, 187v.–188; Francesco Da Molin,
Compendio, B.M.V., MSS. Italiani, Cl. VII, DLIII (8812), p. 13.

[41] Aymard, *Venise, Raguse et le commerce du blé*, pp. 112–13.

lishment of grain deposits in other towns, and was now on his way to Como for the same purpose. In August 1539 he began preaching in Santa Maria Maggiore, and ten days later the grain deposit was started, bearing the title of Monte dell'Abbondanza. The citizens gave 'considering the hard times, generous alms amounting to 200 crowns', and the Bishop also contributed.[42] By 1553, the Monte dell'Abbondanza disposed of cash reserves amounting to 1,500 ducats, increasing by 1555 to some 2,500.[43] In Treviso, proposals for the establishment of a grain deposit were maturing in November 1548. According to a much later source, Cardinal Francesco Pisani, the rich, absentee, pluralistic Bishop of Treviso, contributed generously to the new institution.[44] By the end of 1550, the citizens of Verona were ready to bring into existence a Monte di Farine,[45] whilst in 1559 the governors of Padua proposed to remedy the unenviable conditions in their area by the establishment of a Monte di Carità to deal in grain and thereby complement the existing Monte di Pietà (which supplied small money loans to the poor).[46]

The enforcement of the poor law formed part of this programme for controlling the unstable situation which resulted from population pressure. One of the purposes of the poor law was to regulate immigration in the public interest, so as to preserve the city of Venice from the assaults of disease. During the 1530's the law had not been systematically executed, though the Fraternity of Sant'Antonino for the Poveri Vergognosi had by private initiative fulfilled some of its purposes. The Provveditori alla Sanità had at intervals—as in 1537[47] and 1539—carried out expulsions of beggars from the city. Indeed, in September 1539, the Council of Ten and Zonta congratulated the Provveditori alla Sanità on their success in repelling from the city a multitude of paupers and vagrants suspected of plague, discharged over the border by the states of Milan and Piedmont. They had also managed to dispose of 'four or five thousand persons, beggars and others, who had recently come to abide in this city'—by prohibiting begging without

[42] Roncalli and Forno, *Atti di Borromeo*, I/i, pp. 324–5, 381–5.

[43] A.S.V., *Collegio, Relazioni, busta* 32, *Miste*, vol. II, f. 32, report of Costantino di Priuli, 8 November 1553; *ibid., busta* 35, report of Pietro Antonio Barbarigo, 10 May 1555.

[44] A.S.V., *Senato, Terra*, reg. 1548/49, ff. 29v.–30, 16 November 1548; *Collegio, Relazioni, busta* 48, report of Paolo Querini, 1 July 1639.

[45] A.S.V., *Senato, Terra*, reg. 1550/51, f. 84v., 18 December 1550.

[46] *Ibid., filza* 29, 14 July 1559, and see below, p. 606.

[47] A.S.V., *Provveditori alla Sanità, Notatorio III*, vol. 727, f. 331, 5 April 1537.

licence, by sending many of the poor to serve on the galleys (for Venice was at war with the Ottoman Turks), and by accommodating young children in the hospitals.[48] A list of beggars sentenced to galley service in August 1539 revealed the extent of Venice's attraction for vagrants from all over Italy: it included the names of Gianetto of Riva di Trento, Angeletto of Friuli, Giovanni Battista Cerazzo (a Piedmontese), Martino of Friuli, Sebastiano from the Padovano, Leone of Arezzo, Battista of Milan, Giovanni Antonio of Sicily, Gianetto of Brescia, Bernardo the Frenchman, Piero the Brescian, Salvatore of Pisa, Giovanni Pietro of Milan and Giovanni, a stevedore from Venice itself.[49] The Provveditori continued to enforce the penal and repressive side of the law. At intervals they forbade boatmen to bring beggars to Venice (especially Piedmontese, who seemed peculiarly iniquitous or undesirable, at least in October 1542); they imposed severe prohibitions on the lodging of beggars and rogues (*furfanti et persone che vano mendichando*); and, in 1543, they renewed the legislation of 1506 against begging with faces covered for the purpose of deceiving potential almsgivers.[50] In 1542, they complained that they were obstructed in their labours to eliminate begging in Venice by the activities of the so-called Scuola dei Zotti. This was a devotional society of cripples, or at least of lame men, founded in the fourteenth century. By the mid-sixteenth, it owned a number of almshouses in the parish of San Samuele, and its members may have automatically enjoyed licences to beg. The magistrates remarked that every time they tried to get rid of some newly arrived beggar, he promptly went to seek admission to the Scuola dei Zotti, whose officials then came to defend him against the inhuman threats of the Provveditori alla Sanità. In order to eliminate this particular pretext, the magistrates forbade the Scuola dei Zotti to accept any new recruits without an official mandate signed by two of the Provveditori.[51]

However, it was only in February 1545 that the Venetian government made a comprehensive attempt to use the methods recommended in April 1529 for whipping up the spirit of charity and increasing the funds for the support of the resident, deserving Venetian poor. Parish priests and preachers must do everything in their power to encourage almsgiving. The Provveditori alla Sanità proposed to send them a set of printed instructions on how to do this every year on Carnival

---

[48] Orford, *Leggi e memorie sulla prostituzione*, doc. 98, p. 100.

[49] A.S.V., *Provveditori alla Sanità, Notatorio IV*, vol. 728, f. 8v., 25 August 1539.

[50] *Ibid., Notatorio V*, vol. 729, ff. 13v., 19v., 24v., 11 October 1542, 15 November 1542, 31 March 1543.

[51] *Ibid.*, f. 15v., 14 October 1542; M.C.V., Cicogna MSS., *busta* 2987/2988, *fascicolo* 19, ff. 10–11.

Sunday, immediately before the opening of Lent. Six deputies must be elected to assist the priest in every parish—two recruited from each of the three respectable 'estates' or conditions of men represented therein: two nobles, two citizens, two 'artisans' or guildsmen. As previously recommended in 1529, a poor box should be placed in every church—the magistrates, paying close attention to detail, now stipulated that it must bear the words 'For the Poor of the Parish' in big letters, and that these must be repainted every year. The box should have three keys, one for the priest, one to be kept by a noble deputy, the other by a citizen (the artisans were evidently not trusted enough to have one). The parish priest should then choose one of the paupers themselves, or 'some other respectable man', to collect for the poor every day in the parish, with a sack for gifts of food and a box for money offerings, likewise equipped with three keys. Furthermore, the parish priest, or his deputy the 'first priest', was bound to pay a personal visit to every house in the parish,

> earnestly recommending the poor of the parish, and making the house-holders understand that they will not be able to remain alive without their alms.

The parish deputies were then made responsible, with the priest, for distributing alms to beggars, *vergognosi* and sick persons. The Provveditori did not now envisage the possibility of eliminating begging altogether—perhaps the available accommodation in the hospitals was inadequate. But they did propose to restrict it to those who had, as especially deserving cases, been awarded licences by the Provveditori alla Sanità: thus harking back to the procedure of 1506. Apart from them, only friars and nuns might beg. The magistrates added stern warnings to the effect that nobody might, without their express permission, let houses either to beggars or to foreign immigrants—a measure which they justified on the grounds of preserving public health. Since even beggars had to shelter somewhere, this—together with their control over boatmen working on the ferries plying between Venice and the mainland—formed the magistrates' most effective means of limiting begging and immigration. All cases of disease among beggars, whether curable or incurable, must be reported on the day of discovery to the Provveditori alla Sanità.

These clauses incorporated modifications to and refinements of the law of 1529. The remaining clauses simply repeated the exhortations of 1529 to the parish deputies to find work for everyone who could possibly do it, including cripples: again,

Poor men and women beggars who are at present wasting their time must be informed that they shall not have alms, but must do some work, and the Reverend Parish Priest and the Deputies must give them every kind of assistance so that they can find it.

Beggar children must be lodged somewhere; the girls could if necessary be placed with convents, the boys put to some trade or sent to sea (the inevitable remedy).[52]

The purpose of this renewed legislation was, in effect, to project on to a much wider canvas the work already done by the Fraternity of the Poveri Vergognosi, and to use the official mechanism of parish deputies to ensure that it was systematically carried out. The principle that almsgiving was voluntary must be preserved, but every available kind of moral pressure should be applied to instil charitable sentiments into Venetian parishioners. The Provveditori also issued detailed instructions for the preaching of charity sermons on every Sunday, Wednesday and Friday during Lent and on every other festival, which should inform congregations of the work in progress, and stress that this depended on 'generous alms from your charitable hearts (*le large elemosine delle caritade vostre*)'. The magistrates also instructed confessors to recommend the poor to those who came to them.[53] Soon afterwards, the government, through the Great Council, resorted to a well-tried device. It instructed notaries drawing up wills to recommend to testators, not only the *poveri vergognosi* (as in 1544), but also the poor beggars approved by the Provveditori alla Sanità. The notary must then inform the Provveditori of the bequest.[54] The Provveditori followed up this measure by stipulating, in the summer of 1545, that the parish deputies should carefully review all the records of legacies to the poor to be administered by the parish priest or chapter, and ensure that they were properly executed.[55] Finally, by way of ensuring that existing resources were properly used and not misappropriated by fraudulent trustees, the Provveditori alla Sanità proposed to compile a comprehensive register of all legacies destined for religious uses (*ad pias causas*) and intended to support the poor of any kind. All bodies administering such legacies, including hospitals, monasteries and convents, must supply the necessary information in the course of one month.[56]

This all-embracing scheme demanded a high degree of support and

[52] A.S.V., *Provveditori alla Sanità, Capitolare I*, ff. 49v.–51v., 1 February 1544 Venetian style.
[53] *Ibid.*, ff. 51v.–52.
[54] A.S.V., *Maggior Consiglio, Deliberazioni, Liber Novus*, f. 108, 12 March 1545.
[55] A.S.V., *Provveditori alla Sanità, Capitolare I*, f. 55, 15 July 1545.
[56] *Ibid.*, ff. 57v.–58.

co-operation from the parish clergy and ecclesiastical authorities. There was little sign that they objected to the aims of the poor law, or to the state's assuming the right to treat parish priests as minor civil servants and to dictate to the pulpit and confessional. The parish clergy were locally elected[57] and long domesticated, so it was hardly surprising that they should collaborate. The scheme evidently enjoyed the support of at least one man connected with the avant-garde movements— of the Prior of the Trinità, Andrea Lippomano, pupil of the Theatines and patron of the Jesuits. At the end of March 1545, the Provveditori alla Sanità elected a standing commission to advise on all measures to be taken for the relief of the poor, and to guard all moneys left to them: probably all those bequeathed to the *poveri mendicanti e vergognosi* without further stipulation, and not entrusted to any particular parish authorities, fraternities or hospitals. The commission consisted of Andrea Lippomano, who was to keep the cashbox; of two other clergymen, Giovanni Trevisan, Abbot of San Cipriano di Murano, and Garzone di Garzoni; and of three lay patricians as 'coadjutors and co-operators', Andrea di Bernardino Falier, Alvise di Andrea Da Mula, and Pietro Maria di Zaccaria Gradenigo. They were empowered to co-opt other helpers, and to carry on their work under the protection of the Provveditori alla Sanità.[58] Unfortunately, nothing is known about the work of this standing committee—though Andrea Lippomano maintained some connexion with the Fraternity of the Poveri Vergognosi, and in 1551 took pains to introduce his Jesuit protégés to it.[59] Moreover, in the years to come, at least one eminent Jesuit is known to have given unequivocal support to the enforcement of the poor law during the severe famines of 1559–60. In September 1560, Cesare Helmi, one of the Jesuit fathers in Venice, wrote to the General Laynez describing the activities of the Provincial of Lombardy, Benedetto Palmio. He claimed that on Palmio's inspiration the government had taken measures to ensure that each of the 72 parishes in Venice raised the sum of 100 ducats every month for the support of the poor.[60] Helmi's description may even imply that in these exacting circumstances compulsory poor rates were levied, though neither the Senate records nor those of the Provveditori alla Sanità give any hint of so radical a measure being adopted.

[57] See Bartolomeo Cecchetti, *La Repubblica di Venezia e la Corte di Roma nei rapporti della religione* (Venice, 1874), I, pp. 443–4. For an example of a parish priest's election, relating to the parish of Santa Fosca, see A.S.V., *Senato, Terra*, reg. 1534/35, f. 122v., 9 April 1535.

[58] A.S.V., *Provveditori alla Sanità, Capitolare I*, ff. 53v.–54.

[59] M.H.S.J., Polanco, *Historia*, II, p. 210.

[60] M.H.S.J., *Litterae Quadrimestres*, VI, pp. 888–9.

The records of the Provveditori alla Sanità over the years from 1545 to 1560 do provide a reasonable indication of the way in which certain aspects of this programme were realized: though it is possible to know much more about the repressive side of the law than about its humane and constructive facets. During this period, the magistrates kept an informative, though not necessarily a complete, record of their judicial activity—from which it is possible to discover what kind of begging was actually suppressed, and what happened to the beggars. Occasionally, there are hints about the administration of parish funds, over which the Provveditori alla Sanità exercised general surveillance. They fined the parish priest of Santa Maria Formosa 8 ducats in eight weekly instalments in 1550 for misappropriating funds destined for the poor of the parish.[61] In 1556, they approved the parish deputies elected in San Cassiano, more or less according to the rules: the parish priest himself, two noblemen (Bernardo Venier and Luca Gritti), two citizens (Marco Zusberti, and 'Missier Marco, druggist at the Sign of the Hat'), and one artisan ('Missier Stefano, barrelmaker, at present Gastaldo of the Scuola del Sacramento').[62] But such occurrences were seldom recorded.

The policy of eliminating unlicensed begging was, at least in its early stages, successful. At the end of March 1545, the Provveditori alla Sanità received official congratulations from the Senate on reducing the total numbers of beggars in the city from over 6,000 to as little as 1,400, by the use of the methods prescribed in the legislation. Some of the 6,000 were outsiders, who had now returned to their native places. The Provveditori had introduced the system of parish deputies to the three sestieri which lay on the Frari-Santa Margarita side of the Grand Canal. It only remained to establish the same order in the three sestieri on the San Marco side, and to clear the streets and bridges as fully as possible of the remaining beggars. The Sanità, however, disposed only of a tiny force of four officers or beadles, known as Fanti. The Senate now gave them added power by authorizing them to make use of the services of all the police forces controlled by the magistracies of Venice, except that of the Council of Ten, over which the Senate claimed no jurisdiction.[63] The Provveditori undoubtedly used these forces, and dealt with them in a censorious and critical spirit. The officers of the watch in the sestiere of San Polo were drastically fined twelve ducats each for failing to suppress begging in the parish of Sant'Agostino, where their neighbours, the officers of Santa Croce, had found a beggar lurking in the church. A week later, however, they redeemed them-

---

[61] A.S.V., *Provveditori alla Sanità, Notatorio V*, vol. 729, f. 199v., 27 June 1550.
[62] *Ibid., Notatorio VI*, vol. 730, f. 42v., 15 January 1555 Venetian style.
[63] A.S.V., *Senato, Terra*, reg. 1545/46, ff. 11v.–12, 26 March 1545,

selves by catching Blind Francesco, a notoriously persistent beggar who had been banished with a price of 25 lire on his head. On the strength of this coup, they obtained a remission of their fine.[64] Likewise, the Provveditori, later in the year 1545, censured the officials of Rialto for their failure, in spite of repeated warnings, to suppress begging efficiently in their area.[65] This provides evidence both of the difficulty of suppressing begging, and of the determination of the Provveditori to see that their orders were carried out.

In the next few years, beggars, landlords guilty of lodging them and boatmen guilty of conveying them to Venice joined the shabby queues of bawds, prostitutes and insanitary householders waiting to be judged by the Provveditori alla Sanità. The magistrates dealt with flagrant cases of fraudulent begging, and, more subtly, with occasional cases of genuine cripples found to have secreted enough savings to enable them to live without soliciting alms. Early in 1545, they investigated the affairs of 'Antonio of Verona, called Vettore, a blind man', who was found to have savings to the tune of 325 ducats. These he had invested in the new 14 per cent loan funds in the Mint in January 1540, taking care to do so in the name of a man of straw, Antonio, a soapmaker at the German Exchange. Since the Mint yielded him an income of 45 ducats a year, the Provveditori understandably decided he had no need to beg, and forbade him to do so on pain of a fine of 25 ducats. When they later discovered, on 3 March 1545, that Antonio had accepted alms in the Piazza San Marco, they actually fined him 5 ducats.[66] Again, there was Blind Francesco, the son of a carpenter, who lived in the parish of San Samuele—possibly in one of the almshouses owned by the Scuola degli Orbi, another fourteenth-century association for the disabled. He received 24 ducats a year for attending to an alms-box in the church or Scuola della Carità, but chose to augment his income by going from house to house and offering prayers in return for alms. The Provveditori issued several warnings, but eventually lost patience and 'delivered him to the law'.[67] Some years later, in 1559, their agents arrested one Lame Tommaso, who normally wore clothes of excellent quality, but kept a collection of 'sorry garments' for the express purpose of going out begging. They tried mere expulsion from Venice first, but later were forced to send him to the galleys.[68]

The records afford brief glimpses into the Venetian underworld of

[64] A.S.V., *Provveditori alla Sanità. Notatorio V*, vol. 729, f. 80, 23, 31 July 1545.
[65] *Ibid.*, f. 85v., 22 October 1545.
[66] *Ibid.*, ff. 65v.–66, 71v., 9 January 1544 Venetian style, 3 March 1545.
[67] *Ibid.*, f. 74r.–v., 1 June 1545.
[68] A.S.V., *Provveditori alla Sanità, Notatorio VI*, vol. 730, f. 245v., 281, 5 October 1559, 3 July 1560.

professional beggars. On 16 December 1547, Giovanni Battista, from Friuli, was sentenced to appear in the punitive cage or *berlina* at Rialto, with a placard declaring that he had 'made himself yellow in order to go begging'.[69] Giacomo Antonio, of Vicenza, was banished for three years for 'pretending to have the shakes, with a bloodstained cap on his head, and yet he is robust and healthy'.[70] Giovanni Francesco, a native of Venice, had patrolled the city and its churches, begging, with a shrivelled arm round his neck, which he claimed had been severed from his own body—'although he was perfectly fit, and was defrauding good Christians to the detriment of the truly needy'.[71] The Provveditori always seemed to work on the official assumption that there was a limited fund of alms available, and that every penny given to a fraudulent beggar was in effect taken away from some deserving case. In 1555, Giovanni of Parma incurred heavy penalties for begging 'naked under a cloak';[72] and in 1559 Francesco, a Brescian, was found in the church of Santa Cattarina dressed as a woman and pretending to be lame, although he was in fact a perfectly healthy young man.[73] A certain Pietro Carota used a slightly different gambit in 1551, when he posed in the churches as an official collector for Venetian hospitals and converted the money to his own uses.[74] Finally, about 1559, the magistrates prosecuted a number of Fagins who trained children as beggars and rogues, like the Giuseppe Rossini and the 'Antonio, alias Quinto' whom they sent to the galleys in March of that year.[75]

The instructions sent to parish priests from 1545 onwards apparently respected the right of religious orders to beg. In practice, the magistrates did not recognize this without reservation, though the people whom they prosecuted or admonished were all non-Venetians, probably of dubious credentials, such as friars not attached to any religious house. On 5 March 1551, they sentenced one Friar Giovanni of Vicenza to three months' imprisonment or a fine of 20 lire, 'for going begging and committing knaveries'.[76] Friar Francesco of Vicenza suffered four years' banishment from Venice and environs in the summer of 1551.[77] Later, in 1557, Father Giraldo of Florence and a French priest whose name, in Venetian, became 'Piero di Sbansis', received a summary

---

[69] *Ibid.*, *Notatorio V*, vol. 729, ff. 136v.–137.
[70] *Ibid.*, f. 154v., 10 April 1548.
[71] *Ibid.*, f. 212, 14 March 1551.
[72] *Ibid.*, *Notatorio VI*, vol. 730, f. 3v., 12 January 1554 Venetian style.
[73] *Ibid.*, f. 250v., 29 November 1559.
[74] *Ibid.*, *Notatorio V*, vol. 729, ff. 214v.–215, 16 April 1551.
[75] *Ibid.*, *Notatorio VI*, vol. 730, f. 230, 230v., 237v.–238, 247v.–248, 17–18 March, 13 May, 31 October 1559.
[76] A.S.V., *Provveditori alla Sanità, Notatorio V*, vol. 729. f. 211v.
[77] *Ibid.*, f. 219, 1 June 1551.

admonition not to beg in Venice save in the course of celebrating Mass. They were curtly threatened with the galleys if they ignored the warning.[78] Again, in September 1559, the Provveditori dealt unceremoniously with two other undesirable friars, Friar Lorenzo and Friar Francesco, who lived in Venetian convents but were not in holy orders. They had gone 'soliciting alms in violation of all the rules, and quarrelled many times between them'. Since they were both foreigners, they were ordered to leave Venice within three days on pain of having their noses cut off.[79] Elsewhere in Europe, representatives of the Mendicant Orders had shown a certain apprehension lest the laws against begging reflect discredit on them, and lest they suffer the rigours of the law. The Sorbonne judgment on the Ypres case had demanded guarantees to protect the interests of the Mendicants.[80] Venetian experience suggests that their misgivings were not quite without substance, though there is no reason to think that the magistrates interfered except where shady clerks were committing obvious abuses. They were not prepared to concede absolute immunity to the friars or to any other clergy.

Very occasionally, the magistrates investigated cases of genuine hardship and tried to get provision made for them by their own families. In the early days, in February 1545, they attempted to resolve a dispute in the family of Stefano di Bartolomeo Sartorello, from the Bergamasco. He had begged because he had no trade: he had sold his smallholding in the Bergamasco to his brother Bartolomeo and another relative, who both lived in Venice, for the sum of 40 ducats, as appeared in a notarial document dated 28 March 1539. Of this, he had received only 28 ducats, and now wanted the whole arrangement cancelled. The magistrates summoned the parties before them, and eventually approved an arrangement whereby Stefano should return to the plot and should enjoy the proceeds or usufruct until his death, though his relatives would not be bound to pay him anything more—apart from one modest ducat, to cover his fares and expenses on the journey from Venice to Bergamo.[81] The magistrates acted in a similar spirit in May 1546, when a Dominican Tertiary named Donna Giovanna was found begging, and the trustees of her deceased daughter Orsetta were ordered to provide her with satisfactory accommodation and a tiny pension of 10 lire a month.[82] Such elaborate solicitude was rare, but in general the magistrates seem to have enforced the law with moderate humanity

see p 282

---

[78] *Ibid., Notatorio VI*, vol. 730, f. 128v., 8 March 1557.

[79] *Ibid.*, f. 245v., 28 September 1559.

[80] See above, p. 282.

[81] A.S.V., *Provveditori alla Sanità, Notatorio V*, vol. 729, ff. 69v.–70, 18 February 1544 Venetian style.

[82] *Ibid.*, f. 97, 18 May 1546.

and without excessive rigour. They frequently issued warnings before resorting to punishment.

Lodging beggars and ferrying them to Venice also constituted offences. At first these were met with light fines and orders to pay the costs of the prosecution or the cost of transporting the beggar back to the mainland, but later they earned public floggings, sentences of banishment and spells of exposure in the notorious *berlina* at San Marco or Rialto. One beggars' roost, repeatedly raided but never apparently destroyed, was Corte Contarina in the parish of San Moisè near San Marco, described in a somewhat later survey as a block of nine almshouses.[83] Giovanni, a capper, was expelled from the place in December 1547 for lodging a beggar;[84] Giacomo, a sievemaker, paid a fine of half a ducat for accommodating the dubious Friar Giovanni of Vicenza in Corte Contarina; and it appeared in June 1551 that Friar Francesco of Vicenza had found shelter in the same court.[85] Later, Giovanni of Verona and Marco Morfone were sentenced to be whipped from San Marco to Rialto for lodging beggars in Corte Contarina, and were ordered to leave the almshouses within three days. Morfone moved to San Samuele, where the law again trapped him eighteen months later.[86] Donna Lucia of Verona paid two *mocenighi* for a similar offence on 21 August 1554, and another inmate suffered five years' banishment for the combined offence of lodging beggars and failing to answer the summons.[87] Bortolo Scaleta, a neighbour from Calle delle Piere in the same parish, was sentenced to be whipped round Corte Contarina for lodging beggars on 28 April 1557.[88] This disreputable court incurred added notoriety during the pestilence of 1555-6, when the Provveditori alla Sanità identified it as a focus of infection.[89]

There remained, of course, the problem of what to do with the beggars before or after sentence: how to find them employment, whether merely to flog them and send them away to be a public menace somewhere else, or to shift the responsibility back on to their local authorities. Attempts on the part of some artisans to obey the law by accepting pauper apprentices roused indignation in their guild. In June 1546, the Provveditori heard the protests of the Gastaldo of

[83] M.C.V., Cicogna MSS., *busta* 2987/2988, *fascicolo* 19, f. 11v.

[84] A.S.V., *Provveditori alla Sanità, Notatorio V*, vol. 729, f. 137.

[85] *Ibid.*, f. 211v., 219, 5 March, 1 June 1551.

[86] *Ibid.*, f. 237, 276, 22 October 1552, 31 March 1554.

[87] *Ibid.*, f. 283v., 21 August 1554; *Notatorio VI*, vol. 730, f. 3, 12 January 1554 Venetian style.

[88] *Ibid.*, ff. 139v.-140.

[89] *Ibid.*, f. 260—mentioned in a resumé of measures taken against plague in 1555-6, drawn up in December 1559.

the coopers' guild, the Arte dei Barileri, against two of its members, Alessandro and Francesco, who had taken such apprentices. The magistrates duly defended the coopers against the charge of violating the constitutions of their guilds, and proclaimed that

> the said apprentices have been well and lawfully accepted, and that in future any member of the coopers' guild may take as apprentice any vagabond child, especially from among those who go about begging and who are deprived of assistance from their own families, so that by this means some provision may be made for their wretched condition.[90]

Nia

How far other guilds showed themselves willing to accept such apprentices is not known.

The Provveditori alla Sanità, however, undoubtedly did enforce the provisions in the poor law which related to the employment of beggars and vagabond children both in the Venetian navy and in the merchant marine. They had used this method to some extent in 1539 and 1545, as the congratulatory preambles of the Council of Ten and Senate bear witness.[91] In 1550, another famine year, they returned to the same clauses in the original act of April 1529, now specifying that all ships with a capacity of more than 100 butts would be actually obliged to take at least one pauper on board.[92] Hitherto, merchant captains and shipowners had merely been exhorted to take on their ships as many poor as they chose; only the navy had been forced to employ beggar seamen. The navy, at this time, was desperately short of galley crews, and the unsuccessful war of 1537–40 with the Ottoman Turks had served to underline its deficiencies. The loss of colonies in the eastern Mediterranean enhanced the problem. Galleys, propelled both by sail and by oar, were prodigal of manpower. The Spanish Ambassador, Diego Hurtado de Mendoza, told his master in 1546 that although the Venetians could produce if necessary a total of about 180 galleys in a wartime emergency, nevertheless they could not actually man more than about sixty of these without resorting to the highly unsatisfactory crews supplied by the mainland regions. In 1545, however, through the influence of a junior naval officer, Cristoforo Da Canal, the Senate agreed to draw on convict labour to supplement the deficiencies of the free labour force. The chief criminal courts of Venice, the Quarantie, had in practice begun to sentence criminals to service in the galleys at a rather earlier date, and from 1542 the governors of the mainland cities followed suit. By 1549, the Venetians had put into operation a squad-

[90] A.S.V., *Provveditori alla Sanità, Notatorio V*, vol. 729, f. 100r.–v., 28 June 1546.
[91] See above, pp. 296–7.
[92] A.S.V., *Provveditori alla Sanità, Notatorio V*, vol. 729, ff. 191v.–192, 22 March 1550.

ron of half a dozen galleys manned by convicts, whose normal zone of operations extended from Corfu to Crete.[93] It was understandable, therefore, that the Provveditori alla Sanità should join in the patriotic enterprise of providing unfree labour for the galleys. In April 1551, they passed an exemplary sentence of one year's service in the galleys on half pay on nine able-bodied men caught begging in spite of the prohibitions.[94] Previously, even during the Turco-Venetian war, they had hesitated to pass long sentences to such forced labour—in August 1539, they had sentenced fourteen beggars to four months at the oar and only one to as much as six months.[95] By 1557, they were increasing the usual sentence to eighteen months.[96]

By the middle 1550's, they were also dealing with beggar children by apprenticing them to the seaman's craft and sending them on board ship as cabin-boys, using, for this purpose, the services of an energetic beadle named Giovanni Giacomo di Giovanni. Commending his courage in dealing with sturdy beggars and breaking up rogues' kitchens where children were trained to be fraudulent beggars, the Provveditori alla Sanità charged him to go down to all ships leaving the port, and to compile a careful record of the number of pauper children they were taking with them. The captains were expected, at the end of the voyage, to bring the children back to the offices of the Provveditori, 'so that we may know the good effects produced by this good work', or at least to give some account of what had become of their charges.[97] Again, in 1559, the Provveditori professed concern at

the enormous increase in the number of child rogues and beggars, who wander round the squares of San Marco and Rialto, and sleep at night in the doorways, and do not exercise any trade, but become increasingly vicious, so that in the end they develop into thieves.

They were anxious to 'recall them from this evil way of life to good conduct, so that they can live by their own efforts, and not be vagabonds'. The sea was the simple, all-embracing solution. Smaller vessels, *marani* and *marciliane*, must take one pauper cabin-boy each; roundships of up to 500 butts, two cabin-boys; and any vessel of more than 500 butts, three cabin-boys. The captains must be compelled to report after the voyage, to prevent them from leaving the children to become infidels in Turkish lands; and if they had died or escaped on the voyage

[93] See Alberto Tenenti, *Cristoforo Da Canal: la marine vénitienne avant Lepante* (Paris, 1962), pp. 63 f.; also above, p. 145.

[94] A.S.V., *Provveditori alla Sanità, Notatorio V*, vol. 729, f. 213r.–v., 4 April 1551.

[95] *Ibid., Notatorio IV*, f. 8v., 25 August 1539.

[96] *Ibid., Notatorio VI*, f. 163v., 166, 169v., 18, 30 July, 11 August 1557.

[97] *Ibid.*, f. 4v., 29 January 1554 Venetian style.

the captains must come and explain the circumstances, producing witnesses to the official, Giovanni Giacomo.[98]

The Provveditori alla Sanità shared the consciousness—widespread in this age—that some form of education, however rough, was the best solution to the problem of poverty, and the best antidote to the criminal degradation into which vagabond children were so liable to sink. The solution was, admittedly, chosen because it was convenient to the state and the economy rather than because it suited the particular aptitudes of the children themselves. The sea was, it seemed, an excellent source of discipline and character-training, and Venice could never have too many mariners. Idleness was the worst sin, against the divine law and the social order: let the merchant marine purge it away. In their concern for the children forcibly articled to the sea, the Provveditori showed some flickers of humanity, and did not abdicate from responsibility. They did not, however, succeed in removing entirely (even if they wanted to) the penal aspect of the transaction. Beggar children waiting to be embarked were confined in prison; a decree of November 1562 sought only to guarantee them a supply of two loaves of bread a day each, like the other prisoners.[99]

After 1562, the records kept by the Provveditori alla Sanità unfortunately become far less informative; most entries merely relate to the intricate details of administration, to the salaries of minor officials, beadles and watchmen. However, entries at intervals do convey the information that the same policy for dealing with vagabonds and beggar children was still being applied in later years—in 1566–7[100] and in 1572–4. The process never proceeded absolutely smoothly, and many masters of ships and smaller craft tried to escape without accepting the prescribed quotas of cabin-boys for maritime training—unschooled children on board, for whom they were forced to accept some kind of paternal responsibility, often seemed a grave liability or at least a minor irritation. In 1573, however, the Provveditori declared optimistically that

the number of apprentice-seamen (*mozzi*) increases every year, and we are obtaining good results, as has manifestly appeared in the past, when navigation has benefited on account of these apprentices, and many excellent seamen have emerged, and this city is not as full as it was of little vagabond rogues.[101]

The following year, the magistrates relented far enough to permit the Chioggians, represented by the officers of the Scuola di San Nicolò at

98 *Ibid.*, f. 229, 4 March 1559.   99 *Ibid.*, f. 329v., 4 November 1562.
100 *Ibid.*, *Notatorio VII*, vol. 731, f. 21v., 40, 23 July 1566, 1 July 1567.
101 *Ibid.*, f. 184r,–v., 5 December 1573.

Chioggia, to place on their vessels their own children or nephews ('for they say they have many who are going to the bad') in preference to the beggar children huddled in Venetian prisons.[102] Incentives to the enforcement of the law were certainly not lacking, since after the outbreak of the War of Cyprus the city became crammed with an influx of Dalmatian and Slavonian refugees from the anticipated Turkish advance. These included a high proportion of small children, some of whom were lodged with private families and some introduced to the hospitals, though the hospitals were so heavily burdened with sick paupers and wounded soldiers that they could not accommodate all the children.[103]

Virtually no statistical information is available to indicate how far the application of the Venetian poor law succeeded in diminishing the number of beggars; there are only the rough estimates comprised in preambles like those of 1539 and 1545, indicating a sharp reduction, in 1545, from over 6,000 to about 1,400.[104] In 1563, which was not a famine year, census-takers counted a total of 539 beggars in a population of 168,627: it is possible that these were the legitimate, licensed beggars registered at the offices of the Provveditori alla Sanità, and that the figure did not include the elusive tramps who slept under archways or those who made a habit of begging occasionally to supplement meagre resources in hard times. In 1586, there was little change, with 447 beggars recorded in a total population of 148,637.[105]

As yet, little can be known about the schemes for the control of poverty and begging then being applied on the mainland possessions of the Venetian Republic. One can only say that in some places the mechanism existed, in the big centralized hospitals of the Lombard cities to the far west, and in Giberti's Compagnie della Carità in the important diocese of Verona in the heart of the Republic. Certainly, in this phase of expanding population, the need was urgent and obvious. During and after the 1560's, the westerly regions of the Bresciano and Bergamasco, which formed part of the province of Milan, were exposed to the influence of its formidable Cardinal-Archbishop, Carlo Borromeo, who set out to establish a tight control over the province. The records of his provincial synods of 1565, 1569 and 1573 leave little doubt that he strongly endorsed the principles implied in the poor laws, and exhorted both clergy and lay authorities to apply them: to deny alms to unworthy, idle and fraudulent beggars, and to compel

[102] *Ibid., Notatorio VIII*, vol. 732, f. 16, 2 September 1574.
[103] A.S.V., *Provveditori alla Sanità, Capitolare I*, ff. 158v.–160, 19 November 1571, 12 February 1571 Venetian style.
[104] See above, pp. 296–7, 301.
[105] See Beloch, 'La popolazione di Venezia', p. 27.

them to work, whilst at the same time assembling the genuinely sick in some centralized hospital. Priests in the province received instructions to concern themselves with the provenance of the beggars, with the state of their morals, with their knowledge or ignorance of the Christian faith, and with their use of the sacraments of the Church.[106] An admirer of Giberti, Borromeo likewise proposed to introduce the Compagnia della Carità as a standardized institution in all parishes of the province, to care for their poor.[107] How far Borromeo's aspirations were actually translated into reality is uncertain. But it is clear that at least one of the Veneto–Lombard cities, that of Bergamo, pursued a highly sophisticated policy in the administration of poor relief. Information submitted to Borromeo during the visitations he conducted in 1575 undoubtedly established this: though it is impossible to say here at what point in time the citizens of Bergamo had begun to execute the scheme.

According to the reports submitted by Pietro Sanuto, governor of the Bergamasco, in 1549, this was a region poor in natural resources but heavily populated. Its inhabitants found the solution to their problems partly in emigration, either seasonal or permanent, partly through the existence of numerous charitable institutions, both in town and countryside, which were known as Misericordie. In 1548, the total population of the city and province was over 124,600, plus another contingent of 4,000 made up of religious and of inmates of hospitals.[108] In 1564 and 1572, the population of the province was returned as being in the region of 160,000, whilst that of the city remained about 18,000–20,000 in the third quarter of the sixteenth century.[109] In the whole province, according again to Pietro Sanuto, the leisured class of those 'who do not live by industry' amounted only to some 2,000. The mountainous countryside produced only enough cereals for three months of the year, and the Bergamasques depended heavily on chestnuts and other fruits to eke out their victuals. They also imported grain heavily from elsewhere. Pietro Sanuto wrote at a time of serious economic depression, which may have been only a temporary slump; cloth production in the zone had fallen to barely 1,500 cloths a year where once it had been 14,000. The few iron-merchants and clothiers who remained operated a tommy-shop system, and gave victuals and clothing to their workmen

at prices so exorbitant that they have not enough to live on, and they are so heavily indebted as to become like slaves.

106 *Acta Ecclesiae Mediolanensis* (Milan, 1583), f. 21v., 29v., 87v.–88.
107 *Ibid.*, ff. 335v.–336.
108 A.S.V., *Collegio, Relazioni, busta* 35, report of Pietro Sanuto, 23 May 1549.
109 Beltrami, *Veneziani in Terra Ferma*, Appendice al Capitolo I.

In such an economy, the Misericordie were vitally important. The Misericordia in Bergamo itself formed an archetype or model, of which the numerous country institutions were smaller replicas. These institutions superficially resembled the Scuole Grandi of Venice, in that they devoted a proportion of their revenue to financing religious observances and the celebration of Masses, and used the remainder for the relief of the poor. The Misericordie were not, however, like the Scuole or Fraternities of the Disciplinati, inward-looking brotherhoods existing primarily to benefit their own poorer members. In Bergamo itself, the Misericordia consisted of a public board of trustees, guardians of the poor administering a species of general almonry, which, in size and scope, overshadowed all the other charities of the town—though there was no attempt at absorbing all charitable funds into a single Common Chest. Probably the funds of the Misericordia came largely from pious legacies voluntarily left in trust, and it owned extensive landed estates which furnished a regular income. More needs to be known about its history; the bare facts are that it owed its original foundation in 1265 to a Dominican Friar, Pinamonte Brembato, and that in 1449 it was entrusted with the care and administration of the large twelfth-century church of Santa Maria Maggiore. In 1575, its governing body consisted of a 'patron' or 'protector', a 'minister', twelve 'presidents' and a treasurer. In the Lombard areas, the principle that clerics must not intervene in the management of lay charities was not as strictly enforced as in Venice itself, and the 'patron' was always chosen from among the 'prelates or canons of the cathedral church of Bergamo'. The 'minister' came from among the leading citizens, and the 'presidents' always included two or three learned in the law.[110] In 1555 a Venetian governor assessed the revenues of the Misericordia at approximately 10,000 ducats a year; in 1596, 1617 and 1626 his successors put them at over 20,000 crowns.[111] The possession of so much land may well have enabled its revenues to rise with the inflationary curve. Some estates were directly controlled by the Misericordia itself through stewards or *massari*, whilst others were leased to tenants.[112] The governor writing in 1555 testified that in emergencies, as in the severe dearths of 1527-8, the Misericordia was prepared to employ, not only

---

[110] Roncalli and Forno, *Atti di Borromeo*, I/i, pp. 321-2, 356-65; Belotti, *Storia di Bergamo*, II, p. 83.

[111] A.S.V., *Collegio, Relazioni, busta* 35, reports of Pietro Antonio Barbarigo, 10 May 1555, and Bernardo Valier, 31 October 1617; *busta* 36, report of Francesco Zeno, 12 June 1626; A.S.V., *Sindici Inquisitori in Terra Ferma, busta* 63, ff. 109-11v.

[112] In 1575, 'The estates of Fara, Spirano, Spiranella Nova, Comun Nuovo, Grumello, Campagnola, Presezzo and Bonato di Sopra are placed under *massari*; and all the others are leased'—Roncalli and Forno, *Atti di Borromeo*, I/i, p. 357.

X

its revenues, but also the proceeds of the sale of capital goods for the purpose of relieving the poor. Generous donations in the meantime had fully compensated for this sacrifice.

In 1575, the Misericordia devoted some of its revenue to the celebration, in Santa Maria Maggiore, of over thirty Masses a day and of 'all canonical hours' 'as if it were a collegiate church'. Seventy-five clergy were needed to serve the needs of this church, including 25 maintained in a seminary designed

> to educate priests who will be Godfearing, learned and decorous, and who will be able to fulfil the obligations they incur, in view of the shortage of priests.[113]

In 1555, the governor Pietro Antonio Barbarigo supposed that only 10 per cent of the total revenue went to the support of these clerical enterprises; more plausibly, in 1626, Francesco Zeno stated that the organization spent some 25 per cent of its income on 'buildings, music and Masses', dispensing the remainder to the poor.[114]

Detailed descriptions of the technique adopted by this general almonry appear in the information submitted to Borromeo in 1575, and in the survey of Bergamo and the Bergamasco conducted in 1596 by the Capitano Giovanni Da Lezze.[115] Methods were based on a systematic census of the poor compiled every two years: in 1575 this revealed the existence of over 7,000 poor, 'registering only the aged, the sick, and children aged fifteen or less', and not the able-bodied; in 1596 about 5,000 poor were registered. Bergamo's population was 18–20,000 in the 1570's, and about 24,000 in 1596. Hence, 20–35 per cent of the inhabitants were apparently counted as poor, by these criteria, which in 1575 took account of all those who were not at the peak of their economic capacity or earning power as a result of youth, age or illness. The survey of 1596 clearly stated that the majority of these would receive alms on three to five occasions during the year, which almost certainly included Christmas, Easter and harvest-tide— 'and this is done without any confusion, because everyone goes to collect his portion at the allotted time'. Haphazard and indiscriminate distributions of alms aroused much disapproval in Bergamo, and at the time of Borromeo's visitation much excitement had arisen over the distributions of loaves to the poor made by the monks of Santa Maria Vallombrosa of the abbey of San Sepolcro at Astino. The objections were similar to those raised in Verona over the distributions of alms

---

[113] *Ibid.*, pp. 318, 357 f.
[114] Reports in A.S.V., *Collegio, Relazioni*, busta 35.
[115] A.S.V., *Sindici Inquisitori in Terra Ferma*, busta 63, ff. 109–111v.

from Giberti's episcopal palace: they caused violence, unseemliness and rioting, and attracted 8–10,000 persons or more, many of them up to no good. As in Verona, a scheme was devised for applying the funds to some more systematic form of charity: in Bergamo, to the ward for incurables in the general hospital.[116]

Within the main body of paupers, a smaller group of about a thousand persons was reckoned to be completely impotent and helpless, and received alms at much shorter intervals. The 1575 report referred to weekly distributions, that of 1596 only to monthly distributions of bread. Alms were dispensed in the form of food and not of money—perhaps to ensure that they were not dissipated in drink or gambling. The distribution was carried out by visitors known as *canevari*, who were members of the higher guilds, druggists, mercers, or men of comparable rank. The *cancelliere*, secretary to the governors, assigned bread-tickets to the *canevari* bearing the name of the pauper and the quantity of bread he was assigned. Equipped with this, the pauper went to the headquarters of the Misericordia to collect his bread. Each *canevaro* visited all the poor of his district every two or three days, and if he found any member of the family sick he was entitled to take action to get them placed on the rolls. In addition to the impotent poor, the Misericordia recognized the familiar category of *poveri vergognosi*, who received alms

> according to their needs and their status in the city (*civiltà*), and sometimes according to the merits of their ancestors who have left goods to this Christian institution, and according to their sickness and the size of their families.

Every year, the Misericordia appointed a special committee of deputies to inquire into any change in the circumstances of these *poveri vergognosi*.

This was the central operation carried out by the Misericordia: but it also discharged a variety of other functions. It subsidized orphanages, including those founded by Girolamo Miani, and, perhaps as an extension of this activity,

> If anyone wants to learn a trade, but has not the means to do so, the Misericordia will assign to their masters one or two *some* of grain a year, so that the man can learn a trade.

The governors were also prepared to subsidize poor students at a University. Members of religious orders were likewise included among the poor, and funds were assigned to Observantine and other nuns, as

[116] Roncalli and Forno, *Atti di Borromeo*, I/ii, pp. 11–12, 25, 40–9; for the Veronese case, see above, p. 277.

well as to Capuchins and *convertite*. Bergamese testators shared the usual predilection for assigning marriage portions to deserving young women, and the Misericordia therefore allotted to such girls a number of dowries ranging in value from 10 to 200 lire. The principal dowry trust in the town, the Pietà, founded by the famous condottiere Bartolomeo Colleoni in the fifteenth century, preserved an existence separate from the Misericordia.[117]

In years of abundance, the officials took a number of bread-tickets and distributed them in winter to the poor of neighbouring villages and mountainous zones, increasing the ration as the year went on, and as prices rose with dwindling supplies. In famine years, they could expect the poor to come to them, and some 15–20,000 immigrants to overrun the streets of Bergamo. In 1575, the Misericordia proudly boasted that in the famine of four years before no-one had actually starved. They claimed that even under this heavy stress they carefully assessed the claims of every individual according to information supplied by the parish priest and by the elected village officials, the *sindaci*. Resources could always be temporarily increased by selling or pledging the property of the institution.

There is, therefore, sufficient evidence to suggest that by 1575 the town of Bergamo was dealing with its poor in a highly systematic and discriminating fashion, carefully deciding how best to bestow its resources. It reacted against haphazard and indiscriminate almsgiving. The ancient structure of the Misericordia was adapting itself to the methods and needs most approved by the sixteenth century. At what stage it began to apply these methods is not known—though already, in 1555, Pietro Antonio Barbarigo had written that not a single loaf of bread was ever dispensed without a carefully considered vote by the governing body of fifteen members. There is no information about any attempts to suppress begging: but the house-to-house distributions of the Misericordia were evidently designed to eliminate the need to seek charity on the streets. Through the Somaschian orphanages and through the Misericordia itself, the citizens of Bergamo recognized the possibilities of undermining the most degrading forms of poverty through the provision of vocational training and of opportunities to work.

Over the period 1540 to 1570, population pressure had created formidable incentives to introduce discriminating and systematic methods of poor relief, and to suppress begging in order to preserve both public

[117] On the Pietà, see Roncalli and Forno, *Atti di Borromeo*, I/ii, pp. 114–18; Belotti, *Storia di Bergamo*, II, pp. 79 f.

health and public order. Poor relief had attempted to surmount the problems of an expanding economy, to regulate the redistribution of population which expansion entailed. During the next decade, however, the machinery developed by private enterprise and by the state had to be set in motion to deal with the dislocation of the economy by disasters of unprecedented magnitude—by the pestilence of 1575–7, which drastically relieved the pressure of population. Epidemics called for poor relief because of the supposed connexion between poverty and liability to the disease; because quarantine regulations suspended normal economic activity, and demanded the destruction of vast quantities of supposedly infectious clothing and bedding; and because so many families lost their principal breadwinners. The problems faced in 1528–9 reappeared on a vaster scale in 1575–7, when some 30 per cent of the people of Venice died of the pestilence. Once again, public health and poor relief became as suitable a matter for state intervention as the recruiting of militias, the repair of fortifications or the equipment of a fleet. Poor relief temporarily lost its formally voluntary character: it was required of a man as part of his civic duty that he should relieve the misery of the poorer members of society—in his own interests as well as in theirs.

Inevitably, a certain tragic irony runs through any account of a medieval or early modern epidemic. With their left hands, governments created infinite distress by a partly mistaken social policy, which entailed the suspension of commerce and the paralysis of the ordinary economic activities on which thousands relied for support. With their right hands, the same governments strove to alleviate the poverty they had inflicted on their subjects to save them from sudden death. Some sixteenth-century Venetians believed that plague was transmitted by human contact, or by poisonous miasma, and that as such it could well result from filthy and insanitary conditions. Rival theories represented it as a sickness conveyed, like typhoid or cholera, by swallowing rotten food or bad water, such as salt water mixed with fresh in Venetian wells.[118] The belief that men and merchandise—especially textiles— were chiefly to be blamed for spreading the sickness was, however, mainly responsible for the disruption of the economy.[119] A century and a half later, an English physician, George Pye, was to maintain that quarantine measures were never justified in a great trading nation:

[118] See A. Canalis and P. Sepolcri, 'Prescrizioni mediche ufficiali e altri provvedimenti di governo in Venezia nella peste del 1575–6', *Annali della Sanità Pubblica*, XIX, *fascicolo* vi, November–December 1958.

[119] See the list of goods liable and not liable to infect with plague, A.S.V., *Provveditori alla Sanità, Capitolare I*, f. 101 f.; also Hirst, *Conquest of plague*, pp. 307, 381, 406 f.

> The Plague may possibly destroy a hundred thousand lives; but the Loss of Trade may starve and destroy ten times a hundred thousand.[120]

Already, by the autumn of 1575, representatives of Verona had cause to urge precisely this argument upon the Venetians. In September, alarming mortality had occurred in the parish of San Zeno in Verona —with some deaths from *petecchie* (the measle-like spots which accompanied typhus), some from *petecchie* and boils—a far more ominous sign. Consequently, the Venetian government had ordered the imposition of a general blockade on Verona, which brought woollen and silk manufacture to a complete standstill. Marc' Antonio Corfini, representing the Veronese, argued that

> An incomparably greater number of people has died purely as a result of unemployment, than of typhus or any other contagious disease. . . . These miserable people cannot hope for any assistance, because they are imprisoned in a city which is forbidden to trade with its neighbours, erected on an unfertile site, and smitten by the scourges of many tempests and floods from rivers and streams.

He maintained—an argument later to be repeated by Venetians—that there was no contagion in the air, and that such sickness as menaced Verona was a famine-fever: a disease of the poor, who lacked the victuals to sustain life. The Venetians, apparently convinced, lifted the ban; but they could not, by government fiat, immediately loose the knot that they had tied, and the neighbouring Vicentines persistently hindered or cut communications between Verona and the capital. Verona, indeed, suffered more heavily from the precautions than from plague itself.[121] Venice sustained the full impact both of high mortality and of quarantine regulations.[122]

In Venice, the government did not expressly forbid the manufacture of cloths or silks, but in mid-November 1575 the Provveditori alla Sanità attempted to put out of work all traders who handled second-hand clothing and rags, all cobblers, and all whose livelihood depended on gathering audiences (potential foci of infection). These ranged from

---

[120] *Ibid.*, p. 62.

[121] A.S.V., *Senato, Terra, filza* 67, 22 September, 10, 26 October, 1575; *filza* 68, 3, 5, 15 November 1575; reg. 1575/77, f. 29v., 26 November 1575; *filza* 69, 16 June 1576. Corfini's petitions are filed under 26 October 1575.

[122] The epidemic has been studied in great detail by Ernst Rodenwaldt in his *Pest in Venedig*, where he summarizes in chronological order the measures adopted by the Venetian government against the plague. These provisions were collected into one volume by Cornelio Morello, secretary or Scrivan to the Ufficio della Sanità, between 1577 and 1584. I have worked from the original records of the Senate and Provveditori alla Sanità, and also from the copy of Morello's work in M.C.V., Cicogna MSS. 1547, *Monumenti della peste di Venezia del 1575 raccolti da Cornelio Morello.*

charlatans, mountebanks and strolling players at one end of the spectrum to schoolmasters at the other. The ban was raised a month later, as the plague subsided during the winter, but was then reimposed on 22 June 1576.[123] In any case, periods of isolation enjoined on all plague-contacts soon spread unemployment beyond the limits of these forbidden occupations. Members of the employing classes were emigrating to their country estates, and doubtless paying off workpeople and servants as they went: the emptying of the city inevitably caused demand, consumption and employment to contract. In 1576 and 1577, the output of broadcloth disastrously slumped: since the industry had begun its sustained development earlier in the century, it had suffered only one comparable setback—during the War of Cyprus, which had severed connexions with the markets of the Levant.[124] Printing also came to a standstill.[125] Periods of compulsory quarantine imposed by the Sanità on 12 June 1576 ranged from as little as eight days to as many as forty, according to the length and intimacy of the contact with victims of the pestilence.[126]

Two lecturers in physic from Padua, Girolamo Mercuriale and Girolamo Capodivacca, now advanced the argument that the disease was not plague, because it was selecting its victims from the poor and humble, not from every social level. The inference might well be that if the roots of the lethal disease lay in poverty and malnutrition, quarantine regulations which aggravated such distress would only worsen the outbreak. Anyway, if the disease was not contagious, they were unnecessary and harmful to trade.[127] Already, in late June 1576, the Venetian government was (like Verona) struggling against subject cities which refused to admit even Venetian merchants equipped with a clean and authentic bill of health.[128]

> 'If', later wrote the official historian Andrea Morosini, 'it were noised abroad that the city was in the grip of a pestilential disease, terror would arise in every estate, customs revenue would be diminished, the traders of Europe and Asia would recoil from the city, and the enemies of the Republic would be incited to revolt.'

[123] M.C.V., Cicogna MSS., 1547, under dates 10–13 November, 17 December 1575; 22 June 1576.

[124] Sella, 'Venetian woollen industry', p. 109.

[125] See the information about the issue of copyrights in Horatio F. Brown, *The Venetian printing press* (London, 1891), pp. 238–9: though from this it appears that the slump occurred during and after 1577, with a recovery only in 1582.

[126] A.S.V., *Provveditori alla Sanità*, vol. 732, *Notatorio VIII*, ff. 149v.–150.

[127] M.C.V., Cicogna MSS. 1547, under date 20 June 1576; Andrea Morosini, *Historiae Venetae*, in *Degli istorici delle cose veneziane i quali hanno scritto per pubblico decreto*, VI (Venice, 1719), pp. 626 f.

[128] A.S.V., *Senato, Terra, filza* 69, 23 June, 2 July 1576.

The authority of the Paduan physicians earned acceptance, but only briefly, for their bold pronouncements, and their courage in ministering personally to the sick, unfortunately coincided with an abrupt seasonal increase in the fury of the disease. This, according to Professor Rodenwaldt's fragmentary data, mounted in virulence from about 20 July onwards, and reached a peak early in August 1576.[129] The Paduans did benefit Venice by modifying the policy of confining the healthy in the vermin-infested houses where plague deaths had occurred. They had at least seen a connexion between wretched living conditions and the incidence of plague, and this inspired them to stress the need for evacuation wherever possible. Their recommendations involved the Senate in an unusually ambitious scheme designed to foster the welfare of the poor. Between 9 and 13 July 1576, Mercuriale and Capodivacca suggested that, to end the epidemic,

> it would first be necessary that all the poor who, both because of their cramped dwellings and because of their urgent need of victuals, are in obvious danger of falling sick and of greatly increasing the epidemic, be immediately removed from the city and taken (with only the property most vital to them) to some country place to live in wooden sheds or other habitation. There they could easily be kept so long as they were well fed until the sickness was extinguished; and the other property left in their houses could also be saved without danger to the city and without the confusion which we witness daily in the transportation of infected and suspect property. If anyone fell sick there, he could be cured by salaried doctors if his disease were not contagious, and be sent to the Lazaretto if it were. There is no point in saying that this operation, apart from the great expense involved, would greatly damage the city by depriving it of workmen. Your Serenity should not be deterred by the expense, because, all things considered, the Venetian Republic has never had greater need to spend than this—when the property, estates and lives of every man are in danger. As for the workmen, it would be far better not be so much concerned about business and trade, which are daily falling off of their own accord: to hope to save everything, and set it in motion once more in a brief space of time, rather than wait to be forced to suspend it altogether, with greater loss and ruin.[130]

Henceforth, the Venetian government did at least hesitate to commit itself to the most drastic of all measures: the issue of a general seques-

[129] Rodenwaldt, *Pest in Venedig*, p. 177.

[130] M.C.V., Cicogna MSS. 1547, entry between 9 and 13 July 1576; see also A.S.V., *Senato, Terra, filza* 69, 30 June 1576, which refers to the death of two Jesuit fathers and the grave sickness of the barbers and of one of the servants assigned to the Paduan physicians; and *ibid.*, 13 July 1576, whereby the Senate permitted Mercuriale and Capodivacca to return to Padua, and professed themselves satisfied with the 'courage and readiness to serve which they have shown on this occasion'.

tration order which would forbid the great majority of Venetians to leave their homes for a period of perhaps fifteen days. On 31 July, the Senate officially abandoned the theory that the disease was a mere famine-fever, and concluded that association between people and the transport of goods were at the root of the worsening situation. Although (with many abstentions) they voted in favour of general sequestration, nevertheless they swung back in the opposite direction a week later. They now ascribed the plague once more to bad housing conditions, as the Paduans had taught them, and cancelled the order to freeze the whole economy.[131] For the time being, they put some faith in the evacuation of the slums as a remedy. Certainly, foul and insanitary housing would promote plague indirectly by favouring rat-infestation. Moreover, there is a strong probability that typhus was in its season combining with plague to attack the people; and typhus would be fostered by overcrowding.

By the summer of 1576, the Venetian authorities found themselves unable to maintain the principle that the poor should be supported by voluntary almsgiving, and began to resort to taxation to support their welfare activities. In March, the Provveditori alla Sanità were still relying on exhortation and persuasion by parish priests to raise funds to support 'sequestered' plague contacts:[132] later, the problem became too vast to respond to such conventional treatment. They faced, as before, the problem of what to do with potentially infected clothing and bedding from the houses of victims. The Sanità did not approve any cheap and reliable method of disinfection until late October 1576, when the people of Murano claimed to have rendered dangerous property harmless by steeping it in running saltwater.[133] The safest course was always destruction—if dumps were formed on the lagoon islands, there was always a serious risk of theft, for any watchman likely to accept the job of guarding them would probably be a criminal. The Provveditori alla Sanità were compelled to deprive the poor of a substantial part of their assets: inevitably, they felt obliged to pay compensation, rather than beggar a large section of the people. Already, on 24 February 1576, long before the epidemic reached its height, the value of infected property in the dumps stood at 18,635 ducats, including 1,460 ducats on account of goods burnt at the beginning of the outbreak. The Senate voted the Sanità a sum of 1,208 ducats to pay full compensation for all articles worth twenty ducats or more, and one of 8,714 ducats to pay for one half of the remainder only.[134]

[131] *Ibid., filza* 69, 31 July, 6 August 1576.
[132] M.C.V., Cicogna MSS. 1547, 8 March 1576.
[133] A.S.V., *Provveditori alla Sanità, Notatorio IX*, vol. 733, ff. 45–7.
[134] A.S.V., *Senato, Terra, filza* 68, 24 February 1575 Venetian style.

Taxation seemed the only answer to these various problems. In Venice itself, the Senate raised funds by three principal means, of which the first was a poor rate levied on the same principles as in 1528:[135] this time, of one *grosso* on every ducat of rent paid by a Venetian householder (4 and one-sixth per cent). Those who paid less than 15 ducats a year for their homes enjoyed exemption. Assessments were based on returns submitted in 1566 to the department which exacted the state tithe or Decima on real property. Those who owned their houses paid the *grosso* per ducat according to the valuation for tax-purposes set by the magistrates upon the property. Inmates of alms-houses were also liable to pay the *grosso* if their houses were valued at more than 15 ducats a year by a hastily appointed commission of three deputies. The money must be collected with the utmost speed: only eight days might elapse before penalties for non-payment were imposed. The Senate levied the tax on this principle on 26 June 1576, and ten days later provided that the parish priests and deputies who collected it should spend one-half in their own parishes, and send the remainder to their superior officers, Heads of the Sestieri, who could take a broad view of the needs of the entire district and thereby enable the richer parishes to relieve the poor.[136] In mid-August, the Senate then exacted a second instalment of the tax, this time levying it only on those who paid over 25 ducats a year in rent. They also designed it to penalize those who had fled from Venice in the panic, and who were neither helping to execute measures against plague nor employing workmen, servants and odd-jobbers. Such emigrés were liable to pay 3 *grossi* per ducat or $12\frac{1}{2}$ per cent on their annual rent. The exaction of such a tax would obviously be difficult, and the Senate found a useful sanction only in the third week of September, by threatening to stop the interest payments from government loan funds to all who had failed to pay their poor rate. In October, still faced with serious deficiencies, they finally appointed an Esattore, authorized to sell government securities owned by defaulting taxpayers.[137]

The government followed a superficially similar policy in dealing with the local public health offices of the nearby mainland areas—in Mestre, Castelfranco and the Padovano. On the Padovano, they imposed a land tax of 2 soldi per *campo*, but hedged it round with so many exemptions that it proved pitifully inadequate. It scarcely realized 3,000 ducats, when the daily needs of Padua consumed some 400. Even extensions of the tax can hardly have eked it out for more than a

---

[135] See above, p. 247.
[136] A.S.V., *Senato, Terra, filza* 69, 26 June, 6 July 1576.
[137] *Ibid., filza* 69, 13 August 1576; *filza* 70, 3, 18 September, 11 October 1576.

week or two. The governors of Padua claimed to have exhausted every other possible expedient before asking for taxation, from the generosity of private persons to that of religious and professional fraternities and of the Monte di Pietà.[138] The Monte di Pietà, which had started as a loan bank charging the poor very modest rates of interest, also kept funds in reserve to lend to the local authorities in such violent emergencies as famines or plagues.[139]

The Venetians themselves, who relied on the Jewish community to provide the poor with cheap loans and had no Monte di Pietà, kept no reserve fund specifically destined to aid the poor. However, since the War of Cyprus they had accumulated a deposit, fed by the direct taxes of the Decime and Tanse, theoretically to remain intact for a period of twenty years. This resolution did not prevent the government from raiding the deposit in emergencies, and eventually, in 1577, from using some of it as a sinking fund to pay off the heavy debts incurred during the war.[140] Between September and December 1576, the Senate authorized the withdrawal of some 96,000 ducats from the deposit in order to spend them on the protection of public health and the relief of the poor.[141]

The last source of funds was the *tansa*: the tax normally levied on those deriving an income from sources other than land and real estate, and engaging in some form of *industria*. The Senate imposed this tax in four instalments, and allowed it to be exacted at a much more leisurely pace. The first quarter must be paid by the end of July and the last by mid-October.[142]

Sums so raised were duly devoted to mitigating the effects of economic paralysis, and to struggling against the cramped squalor which the Paduan physicians had clearly associated with the disease. By April 1576, the normal payment to persons isolated in their houses had been 4 soldi per mouth per day:[143] the average daily wage of a builders' journeyman or *lavorante* in 1571-4 had been 24 soldi a day.[144] In view of the fact that such a journeyman would probably have to support dependants, and that he would certainly not work every day, the daily

---

[138] *Ibid., filza* 70, 20 September 1576, for Padua and the Padovano; *filza* 69, 13 July 1576 for Mestre; *filza* 70, 4 September 1576, for Castelfranco.

[139] See below, pp. 604–8.

[140] See Fabio Besta, *Bilanci generali della Repubblica di Venezia* (Milan, 1912), pp. 250–3.

[141] A.S.V., *Senato, Terra, filza* 70, 1 September, 18 September, 6 October, 18 October, 1 December 1576.

[142] A.S.V., *Senato, Terra, filza* 69, 16 July, 10 August 1576.

[143] M.C.V., Cicogna MSS. 1547, 18 April 1576.

[144] See Brian Pullan, 'Wage-earners and the Venetian economy, 1550–1630', *Economic History Review*, second series, XVI (1964), p. 426.

4 soldi seems quite a reasonable sum to be paid to each of these *seques-trati*. In August 1576, moreover, the Collegio considered raising the maximum dole to 6 soldi per head.[145] One group of workmen, employees of the Arsenal, received special consideration throughout the epidemic. The government, anxious to prevent such vital trades from decaying, had always guaranteed half pay to ship's caulkers and carpenters registered at the Arsenal, even if there was no work for them to do.[146] At the end of June, the Senate guaranteed to Arsenal workers in isolation one-half the normal Arsenal wage, whilst the Provveditori alla Sanità undertook to support their dependants at the normal rate.[147]

More ambitious still were the proposals to remove the poor from their disease-ridden parishes in the city to some comparatively distant site, where prospects of escaping the pestilence were better. On 16 July, the Senate ordered the lagoon island of Sant'Erasmo to be fitted out as a hutted camp, divided into six sestieri corresponding to the districts of Venice, with the Arsenal providing the wood and the carpenters to shape it.[148] Sant'Erasmo was successfully used as a refuge from early August to early November, when the approach of winter made it unserviceable.[149] However, it is doubtful whether the Senate ever carried out a more grandiose plan to evacuate 10,000 of the threatened poor to a site on the river Brenta above Lizza Fusina.[150] But, even if some of these proposals remained only proposals, they serve as a reminder that the government did occasionally depart from the rigid and mistaken policy of confining plague contacts in the houses whose vermin had caused the sickness.

Yet the final impression is one of heroic but hopeless struggle. The registers and files of the Senate and the Provveditori alla Sanità inevitably exaggerate governmental efficiency, and often hint only slightly at the degree of success with which its commands were enforced. The last, most important link in the chain of command was the parish deputy, and many of those appointed to act as taxing and relieving officers certainly failed to take up their posts. Between April and June 1577, the Senate accepted the excuses of nineteen noblemen who had failed to obey summonses to serve in August of the previous year. The defaulters often protested, quite plausibly, that the news of their election had never been conveyed to them in the country houses to which they

[145] M.C.V., Cicogna MSS. 1547, 3 August 1576.
[146] F. C. Lane, *Venetian ships and shipbuilders of the Renaissance* (Baltimore, 1934), pp. 217 f.
[147] A.S.V., *Senato, Terra, filza* 69, 29 June 1576.   [148] *Ibid.*, under date.
[149] M.C.V., Cicogna MSS. 1547, 3 August 1576; A.S.V., *Provveditori alla Sanità, Notatorio IX*, vol. 733, f. 57, 1 November 1576.
[150] M.C.V., Cicogna MSS. 1547, 8 August 1576.

had retreated—not, of course, for fear of plague, but to look after their estates. The remoter parts of the Trevigiano or Polesine had been inaccessible to messengers from Venice. Patricians whose own houses had been boarded up because a death had occurred therein found themselves, on returning to Venice, with no base from which to carry out parish work.[151] In the face of death, the stern devotion to the common weal which roused the admiration of foreigners showed signs of breaking down. The Senate, the Council of Ten and the Quarantie, the chief civil and criminal tribunals, continued to function throughout the epidemic. But the Great Council, the assembly of all adult nobles over twenty-five years of age, became sadly depleted. Normal attendance at its assemblies fell in the summer of 1576 from 1,300 to 300 and even less.[152] Its thinning ranks reflected emigration on the part of the governing and employing classes, and the consequent lack of lesser noblemen, and perhaps also of citizens, to execute the Senate's reverberating commands at the level where they most mattered.

The history of the great plague of 1575–7 does not depict the triumph of a highly-organized state over disease and poverty: though it does show the further recognition of a close link between the preservation of the state and the control of poverty. The plague did not, in the long run, produce any more determined effort to improve the housing conditions of the poor, and thereby defend the state against an enemy more terrible than any Turk. Nor did poor relief assume a completely rational and worldly complexion. As practical, physical measures failed to curb the epidemic, the Venetians officially turned to supernatural aid. The value of almsgiving now seemed to lie, not so much in its practical effect of saving the pauper from starvation, as in its power to appease the wrath of God, for the plague was his flail. A pastoral letter of the Patriarch Giovanni Trevisan, issued on 9 August 1576, represented the abandonment of worldly goods to almsgiving as one of a series of pious practices which might produce this desirable result—combining with confession, communion, and prayer.[153] This plague's most tangible monument is still the votive offering of September 1576, the Palladian church of the Redentore, from whose dome on the Giudecca waterfront the figure of San Rocco stands sentinel over Venice. To this vow, and not to the intervention of the state, the historian Morosini attributed the waning of the pestilence in the autumn of 1576.[154]

[151] A.S.V., *Senato, Terra, filza* 71, various entries from 9 April to 22 June 1577.
[152] A.S.V., *Maggior Consiglio, Deliberazioni.*
[153] M.C.V., Cicogna MSS. 1547, 9 August 1576.
[154] Morosini, *Historiae Venetae*, pp. 631–4.

The great plagues of 1575–7 marked the end of a distinctive period of about forty years. In those years, population pressure, exerted on food supplies available within the Venetian dominions, had created powerful incentives for the enforcement of the poor laws—formulated before this phase of expansion began. According to statistics compiled by Cornelio Morello, an official of the Provveditori alla Sanità, the plague had claimed 3,700 victims between early August 1575 and late February 1576. Its deadliest phase extended throughout the hot, dry summer of 1576, and by the end of February 1577 it had killed another 43,000 persons in Venice. Between March and July 1577, three or four thousand others died, making a total death-roll of 50–51,000, perhaps 30 per cent of the entire population of the city.[155] The surviving censuses suggest that the population of Venice never fully recovered— they placed it at 135,000 in 1581 (a figure consistent with Morello's estimate); at 150,000 in 1586; and finally, after a long silence, at 140,000 in 1624, on the eve of a second and equally savage pestilence which broke out in 1630.[156]

On the mainland, meanwhile, the plague inflicted especially heavy losses on Brescia and Padua. According to a report of Pasquale Cicogna, serving as Podestà in Padua, by 4 May 1577, 6,424 people had died 'in the city' of Padua from the plague. No exact figure was available for deaths in the pesthouses, but Cicogna guessed it would raise the total death-roll for Padua itself to approximately 10,000. He apparently had precise information on the number of deaths from plague in each village of the Padovano between April 1576 and early May 1577. This showed that losses had proved much lighter in the countryside, and the total came only to 1,731.[157] In 1571 a rough estimate had placed the population of Padua at 36,000, that of its territory at 140,000. Figures for Brescia put the city's population in 1579 at about 20,000, as compared with 38,000 in 1572, whilst that of the whole province apparently fell from 390,000 in 1553 to 320,000 in 1579.[158] Friuli had already lost considerable numbers at about the time of the War of Cyprus, when the censuses suggested a descent from 166,000 to 140,000. In 1579, a further census, conducted during a visit of the

[155] For slightly but not significantly different versions of these figures, see M.C.V., Cicogna MSS. 1547; G. B. Galicciolli, *Storie e memorie venete profane ed ecclesiastiche* (Venice, 1795), II, p. 215; Beltrami, *Storia della popolazione*, p. 57, n. 1. Morello estimated the number of dead between March and July 1577 variously at 'about three thousand' and 'about four thousand', since the necrology from which he worked in order to calculate his figures was lost for that period.

[156] Beltrami, *Storia della popolazione*, p. 59.

[157] A.S.V., *Collegio, Relazioni, busta* 33, *Miste*, vol. IV, ff. 32–5.

[158] Beltrami, *Veneziani in Terra Ferma*, Appendice al Capitolo I.

Venetian Provveditore General in Terra Ferma, counted 11,605 heads in the provincial capital, Udine, and 137,175 in the rest of Friuli, making a total of 148,780: still markedly less than during the period 1548–69. Nor is it likely that recovery followed. In 1587, representatives of the peasantry of Friuli complained of constant emigration into Germany and elsewhere because of the barrenness of their soil and the unreliability of their climate, with its 'fatal tendency to produce storms and floods, which are now assuredly covering little less than one-third of the whole country'.[159] Any movement taking place from Friuli to the capital was insufficient to enable Venice to recover its former numbers. On the other hand, of the mainland cities, Vicenza, though seriously affected, suffered comparatively lightly;[160] the returns for Verona showed 52,120 inhabitants in 1572, 51,265 in 1577, 46,992 in 1583 and 56,179 in 1593.[161]

These figures convey the general impression that the upward trend was curbed; that the expansion of population, and with it the expansion of the Venetian economy, was temporarily halted. This expansive phase had brought to the poor a complex mixture of benefits and disadvantages: expanding industry offered chances of employment, but at the same time the abundance of labour available to feed it might tend to depress wages. The uncertainty and instability of the food supply, in spite of the activities of improving landlords, was another concomitant of rising population. If expanding population could, initially, act as a stimulus to economic activity, there came a time when it threatened only to impoverish. The enforcement of the poor law formed one aspect of the general response to this complicated situation. It demanded that available resources be employed as carefully as possible, that distributions of alms be made only to the deserving, that the rich or well-to-do be made constantly aware of their moral duty to transfer a portion of their wealth to the poor. In the great natural disaster that marked the end of this phase, it became a civic duty as well. The problem of public order became increasingly acute in a city periodically troubled by famine and called upon at all times to absorb a flow of immigrants. As the balance changed between maritime and landed activities, the Venetians felt the urge to preserve the seaman's craft and the need to man their ambitious navy. Economic expediency thus ensured that the principles conceived in earlier decades, when the

[159] See above, p. 290–1, and A.S.V., *Senato, Terra, filza* 104, 31 December 1587, petition of the Sindici of the Contadinanza della Patria di Friuli, which contains a reference to the census of 1579.

[160] Rodenwaldt, *Pest in Venedig*, p. 110; Beltrami, *Veneziani in Terra Ferma*, p. 2, n. 3.

[161] See Donazzolo and Saibante, 'Sviluppo di Verona', p. 71.

causes of instability were different, would now be consistently applied in a less warlike, more expansive era. Public action was necessary to deal, not only with the problems of an expanding population, but also with the forces that cut population back: different challenges produced a similar response.

THE SUPERVISION OF CHARITIES AND THE CORRECTION OF ABUSES, 1540–1600

The efficient administration of poor relief depended, not only on innovation, but also on maintenance, preservation and resurrection. Some mechanism must be devised to ensure that the wishes of charitable testators were carried out, that hospitals and other institutions were administered with the minimum degree of corruption, and that their inmates were genuinely poor and morally deserving. In this field also, ecclesiastical and lay authorities moved in the same direction, and shared similar aims. Both were eager to ensure that the existing resources were used as effectively as possible: this was an essential facet of discriminate charity. The bishop and the board of lay charity-commissioners were both invited, during the sixteenth century, to assume this responsibility.

Much sixteenth-century ecclesiastical legislation entailed, not the formulation of new principles, but the re-enforcement of old-established canons. The Council of Vienne, meeting in 1311 under the aegis of Clement V, had issued the fundamental law in the canon 'Quia contingit'. This began with a complaint that the governors of hospitals, lazar-houses and almonries had failed to wrest the estates and rights of these institutions from the hands of usurpers; they had allowed them to be lost and their buildings to decay. The governors were themselves guilty of converting revenues to their own uses. The canon instructed them to restore order, to repair loss and damage, to prepare the hospitals for the reception of the poor. Should they fail to do so, then the bishop must intervene and compel them to take action, even if the hospital enjoyed the privileges of exemption from his immediate jurisdiction. With some qualifications, the canon laid down the principle that the wardenship of a hospital ought not to be regarded as a benefice whose only purpose was to provide revenue for some secular clergyman. It should be entrusted to a person of integrity who would carry out his duties conscientiously: in future, he must compile careful inventories of the property of the institution, and must render account of his stewardship every year to the local bishop or his deputy.[1]

[1] *Constitutiones Clementis Papae V, titulus* XI, *cap.* ii, in *Corpus Iuris Canonici*, Part II, *Decretalium collectiones*, ed. Emil Friedberg (Leipzig, 1881), coll. 1170–1. See also Tierney, *Medieval poor law*, p. 86.

Y

This constitution of the Church provided for action by the ecclesiastical authorities. In Venice, at least, lay commissions were occasionally appointed to discharge the function of supervising the administration of hospitals and charitable trusts. The Senate established such commissions in 1489 and again in 1526,[2] though these were not permanent bodies maintaining constant vigilance, and it is impossible to say how much they accomplished. Again, in 1545, when re-enforcing the poor law, the Provveditori alla Sanità had tried to establish a less fallible system for registering all bequests made to the poor and for ensuring that the testators' wishes were fulfilled. The papal nuncio added his blessing, by threatening defaulting executors with excommunication.[3]

In the middle 1540's, attempts to restore efficiency and discipline in the hospitals formed part of a wider programme for the reform of the clergy. In the past, reform of the Catholic Church had promised to come through at least three possible channels: from the Papacy itself, starting with the Roman Curia; through the spontaneous reform of individual religious houses or orders, or that of individual dioceses; or, finally, through the summoning of a General Council. During the pontificate of Paul III, these three ways were at last meeting, when the Pope ceased to reject or evade the idea of the Council.[4] The aims of the Council which opened at Trent in 1545 included the restoration of episcopal authority: much of the corruption which had infested the Catholic clergy resulted from the absence of effective supervision by the bishop. Many bishops were absent from their sees, distracted by the papal curia or by princely courts: there was little point in forcing them to reside in their dioceses unless they were equipped with adequate powers to restore order, and entitled to ignore the exemptions which had created patches of immunity from episcopal authority, in many sees.[5] Long before the Council, certain bishops, like Barozzi of Padua and later Giberti of Verona, had acted vigorously in their dioceses, applying the principles formulated by Gasparo Contarini. Giberti's activities included the visitation of hospitals, though his admiring biographer, Zini, hastened to indicate that in Verona itself the three major hospitals of the Pietà, San Giacomo and the Misericordia were so diligently administered by Veronese noblemen that the Bishop had little cause to intervene. Giberti confined himself to 'commending' the hospitals to their governors, and to providing them with 'patient, assiduous and wise' chaplains, who would visit the sick and

---

[2] See D.M.S., XLII, coll. 257–60, 28 July 1526, and above, p. 211.

[3] A.S.V., *Provveditori alla Sanità, Capitolare I*, f. 55, 57v.–58, and above, p. 299.

[4] See especially Jedin, *History of the Council of Trent*, I.

[5] *Ibid.*, especially pp. 441–2; L. Cristiani, *L'Église à l'époque du Concile de Trente* (Paris, 1948).

persuade them to make their confession and take communion before death overtook them. The Bishop intervened rather more in the affairs of the smaller hospitals of the diocese, where he seems to have been able to influence the appointment of procurators to defend the temporal interests of the hospitals. The staff of the hospital were to give an account of their administration every year to these procurators, with whom the Bishop's agents then associated themselves.[6] Giberti's own legislation, embodied in his famous constitutions, demanded that the governors of all *luochi pii*, religious and charitable foundations, should do their work 'with the knowledge and collaboration of the Archpriest or Rector, or of his deputy, and always further the interests of the church'. Again, he provided that they must render account annually in the presence of episcopal commissioners. Giberti also threatened with severe spiritual penalties anyone, whether in orders or not, who failed to execute the wishes of testators. All notaries asked to draw up wills which included legacies for religious and charitable purposes (*ad pias causas*) were now, if they lived in the city of Verona, required to register the revelant clauses with the Bishop or Vicar-General. If they lived in the country, they should inform the rector of the parish church, and send a copy of the disposition to the diocesan authorities.[7]

Individual action by at least one bishop in the Venetian Republic, during the 1530's and early 1540's, therefore preceded the legislation of the General Council—which often sought, not to innovate, but to spread, approve and publicize methods already locally employed within restricted areas. In 1546, a Frenchman, Guillaume du Prat, Bishop of Clermont, and a Spaniard, Bernal Diaz de Lugo, Bishop of Calahorra, raised at Trent the question of corruption in hospitals and of the bishop's power to take action. They were especially perturbed at the exemptions which threatened to secure corruptly administered hospitals against his intervention. The Council, however, contented itself with merely providing for the re-enforcement of the Clementine constitution of Vienne: it did not attempt to re-emphasize any particular clause of this canon.[8] Explicit legislation, clearly designed to assert the authority of the bishop, followed only in 1562 and in the later sessions of the Council of Trent. These decrees proclaimed that bishops were

[6] Zini, *Boni pastoris exemplum*, p. 282–3.

[7] Giberti, *Constitutiones*, *titulus* VIII, cap. ix–xiv, in his *Opera*, pp. 132–5.

[8] See Hubert Jedin, 'Zwei Konzilsdekrete über die Hospitaeler', *Atti del primo congresso italiano di storia ospitaliera* (Reggio Emilia, 1957), pp. 379–82; Jean Imbert, 'Les prescriptions hospitalières du Concile de Trente et leur diffusion en France', *Revue d'histoire de l'Église de France*, XLII (1956), pp. 8–9. I owe both these references to the late Mr H. O. Evennett. See also Stephanus Ehses, *Concilii Tridentini Acta*, Part II (Freiburg-im-Breisgau, 1911), pp. 841, 975, 999; Mansi, *Concilia*, XXXIII, col. 58.

executors of all 'pious dispositions'—they, at least, were always ultimately responsible for seeing them carried out. Bishops were entitled to visit hospitals, colleges, and confraternities or Scuole, except for those under the immediate protection of the King—a qualifying clause added at the instigation of the Portuguese Ambassador.[9] The bishop had jurisdiction over Monti di Pietà and Monti di Carità, even should they be under the 'care' of laymen, and even if they enjoyed the insidious privileges of exemption. His authority extended over all things designed to promote the worship of God, the salvation of souls or the maintenance of the poor. Nothing, theoretically, ought to impede his reforming zeal.

The Tridentine legislation then dealt with the question of accountability. Administrators of charitable foundations must render account annually to the ordinary (i.e. to the bishop in his capacity of ecclesiastical judge), even if they were laymen. They must do so unless there was some express provision to the contrary in the foundation statutes of the institute concerned. If it was already the custom to account to some other persons specially appointed for the purpose, then the bishop or his agents should associate themselves with these auditors: they should not replace them.[10]

Further legislation in the last sessions, in 1563, again re-enforced the canon 'Quia contingit' and forbade those who had obtained hospitals as ecclesiastical benefices to neglect their duty of dispensing hospitality. No-one might regard hospitals as mere sources of income, carrying no obligations. More radically, the law went on to destroy one of the chief pretexts for not keeping hospitality. It provided that, where hospitals had been reserved to the use of a particular class of paupers, pilgrims or sick persons, but there were few or no such persons in the neighbourhood, then they ought to be converted to another use as near as possible to the original one. Here, the decision rested with the bishop and with the two most experienced members of his chapter. Here again, however, nothing could be done if the foundation statutes explicitly provided against conversions of this kind. In view of the decline of leprosy in the later Middle Ages, leper hospitals were obviously liable to be affected by this law. Certain pilgrim-routes, moreover, had lost popularity in the late Middle Ages.[11] Finally, as a further remedy against

9 See Gabriele Paleotti, *Acta Concilii Tridentini annis 1562 et 1563 originalia*, ed. in Sebastian Merkle, *Concilia Tridentini Diaria*, III/1 (Freiburg-im-Breisgau, 1931), p. 431.
10 Stephanus Ehses, *Concilia Tridentini Acta*, Part V (Freiburg-im-Breisgau, 1919), pp. 967-8; Mansi, *Concilia*, XXXIII, coll. 136-7.
11 The Parisians, for example, found many fewer pilgrims bound for Jerusalem or St James of Compostella—see Coyecque, 'La police des pauvres à Paris', p. 116; Roger Doucet, *Les institutions de la France au XVIe siècle*, II (Paris, 1948), p. 808.

corruption, the Council of Trent laid down that no-one should be allowed to administer the same hospital for a period of more than three years—unless it was stated in the hospital's constitutions that he might do so.[12]

Church and State were fundamentally agreed about the necessity of restoring decayed charities, of eliminating corruption and of forcing hospitallers to do their duty. This identity of aim might, however, lead to conflicts of jurisdiction: who was entitled to take the lead in reforming charitable institutions? French Kings, as well as French towns, had issued laws committing the administration of hospitals to lay officers, and excluding the clergy. It was possible that the Tridentine decrees affecting charitable foundations might produce challenges to royal jurisdiction, and this constituted one of several arguments against their promulgation in France.[13] Hospitals stood in an uncertain position on the borderline between lay and ecclesiastical jurisdiction. For a hospital to be complete, and to meet all the requirements of the sick, it needed 'parochial rights': its almoner must be entitled to baptize, to hear confessions, to give extreme unction and to bury the dead. It existed to perform spiritual functions, and was, in effect, a species of church.[14] The decretal 'Quia contingit' assumed that hospitals would possess altars and be equipped with priests celebrating the sacraments and dispensing them to the poor. There was, therefore, a strong case for assuming that hospitals should ultimately be subject to the bishop. It could, on the other hand, be argued that such hospitals were founded and often staffed by laymen, and were designed to benefit communities governed by lay magistrates. Why, then, should the bishop claim final authority over them?[15]

The Venetians certainly regarded the question of taxing hospitals as delicate and uncertain, and seemed unable to reach any firm conclusion as to whether, for fiscal purposes, hospitals should be counted as clerical or as lay establishments. During a debate in June 1527, in the Senate, the Procurator Luca Tron had argued that hospitals were 'sacred things, and should pay what the Pope decides', whilst his opponent the Cavalier Alvise Mocenigo held that they consisted of 'lay property bequeathed ad pias causas'.[16] The question arose again in

[12] Stephanus Ehses, Concilii Tridentini Acta, Part VI (Freiburg-im-Breisgau, 1924), pp. 768, 1,089; Mansi, Concilia, XXXIII, col. 185.

[13] Imbert, 'Les prescriptions hospitalières', pp. 19 f.

[14] Imbert, Les hôpitaux en droit canonique, pp. 67 f.; cf. also Clay, Mediaeval hospitals, pp. xvii–xviii.   [15] See below, p. 332.

[16] D.M.S., XLV, col. 275, 6 June 1527. D.M.S., LVI, coll. 137–46, 10 April 1532, gives particulars of the Taxa fata al Clero per li VII Savii, July–October 1527—this includes seven hospitals as subject to the tax, though only three were actually obliged to contribute anything. The larger and newer hospitals were not asked to contribute.

1534–6,[17] and again it is uncertain what conclusion was reached. Rights of presentation to hospitals constituted another source of potential disagreement, and one especially bitter dispute flared up in Padua in 1544. Open conflict broke out between the Bishop, Cardinal Pisani, on the one hand, and, on the other, the civic authorities of Padua with the backing of the Venetian government. This raised, however inconclusively, the unanswerable question as to whether, for all purposes, hospitals were to be regarded as lay or as ecclesiastical institutions, and it is therefore worth examining the debate in some detail here.

The dispute probably owed some of its acrimony to the many enemies made in Venice by the Pisani family, through their voracious pursuit of ecclesiastical preferment. In the years 1520–50 or thereabouts, the Cornaro–Pisani and Grimani connexions had engrossed a disproportionately large fraction of the bishoprics and commendatory abbacies in the Italian territories of the Venetian Republic.[18] Francesco Pisani had in 1517 obtained a cardinal's hat from Leo X through the influence of his powerful father Alvise Pisani; had climbed high in curial favour; and had in 1524 been rewarded with the rich see of Padua. Subsequently, he also became Archbishop of Narbonne and administrator of the see of Cittanova in Istria. His loyalty to Clement VII earned him the Bishopric of Treviso in July 1527, and thereby brought him directly into conflict with the Venetian Senate, which had already chosen to instal another patrician, Vincenzo Querini. Debates proceeded from 1527 to 1531, without reaching any clear conclusions, and Francesco Pisani solemnly entered this diocese only in 1538.[19]

The dispute in Padua likewise arose over a question of patronage. The city authorities elected one Father Francesco Negno to take charge of the hospital of San Lazzaro or leprosary of Padua, claiming that they were merely acting in accordance with the city statutes. Cardinal Pisani simultaneously bestowed the same hospital on a member of his household, Father Hieronimo of Pavia. The Venetian Senate, supporting the city of Padua, formally declared that

> these things are not ecclesiastical benefices, but merely involve the care and government of poor lepers and of the slender revenues and alms bestowed upon them.[20]

[17] A.S.V., *Senato, Terra*, reg. 1534/35, ff. 30, 120, 19 June 1534, 9 April 1535; reg. 1536/37, f. 13, 11 April 1536. On this last occasion, the hospitals of the Ca' di Dio and San Francesco of Padua claimed exemption from the Sussidio, and the Sette Savii sopra il Clero were authorized to adjudicate their claims.

[18] See Logan, *Studies in the religious life of Venice*, pp. 178 f.

[19] See Rodolfo Gallo, 'Una famiglia patrizia: i Pisani ed i palazzi di Santo Stefano e di Stra', *Archivio Veneto*, 5th series, XXXIV–XXXV (1944), pp. 80 f.

[20] A.S.V., *Senato, Terra*, reg. 1543/44, f. 80v., 14 April 1544.

The Ambassador in Rome was instructed to negotiate with Pisani, who still resided in Rome, although he had shown some signs of concern for the welfare of his diocese,[21] and to get him to retract his claim. He must ensure that

> these elections of hospitallers be kept within our jurisdiction and that of the civic officials, so that there may be a substantial increase in alms and revenues for the benefit of the poor, and the hearts of the citizens may be inspired to do good works and help the hospitals. If the matter were dealt with otherwise, they would lose confidence, and the whole thing would go wrong, as can clearly be seen by experience.

The implication was clear—the clergy, because of their tendency to treat hospitals as mere articles of patronage, ought not to be trusted with ultimate responsibility for them. A few years earlier, in 1539, the Great Council in Venice had formally granted to the new hospital of the Incurabili protection against being treated as an ecclesiastical benefice,[22] and the direction of the new Venetian hospitals remained strictly in the hands of lay congregations of governors. Subsequent events would reveal that lay patrons were just as unscrupulous as clerics in appropriating the revenues of hospitals. But such was the official argument of the Senate in 1544. Admittedly, the Paduans had prejudiced their own case by putting a cleric in charge of San Lazzaro: but the Ambassador Francesco Venier explained to the Pope that they had done this purely as an economy measure. Revenues were insufficient to maintain both a lay governor and a chaplain; lay governors had been elected in the past.[23]

The controversy came to the Pope's attention. He, for good measure, accused the Venetians of fomenting heresy by undermining ecclesiastical jurisdiction—especially at Padua (which through its university was especially open to insidious foreign influence), but also at Treviso, Brescia and elsewhere. The Ambassador Venier courteously protested the desire of the Venetians to 'live as good Catholics'.[24] Pisani himself, when approached by Venier in Rome, showed no signs of yielding, though he earnestly affirmed his loyalty to the Republic and his eagerness to serve it by any legitimate means. He mustered evidence to support his case that this hospital—and, by implication, others as well—

---

[21] Cf. Angelo Martini, 'Tentativi di riforma a Padova prima del Concilio di Trento', *Rivista della storia della chiesa in Italia*, III (1949), pp. 67–8.

[22] A.S.V., *Maggior Consiglio, Deliberazioni, Liber Novus*, f. 39, 7 January 1538 Venetian style.

[23] A.S.V., *Archivio Proprio Roma, fascicolo* 6, ff. 52v.–53, despatch of the Ambassador Francesco Venier, 5 April 1544.

[24] *Ibid.*, f. 55.

was in fact an ecclesiastical benefice. He recalled that during the pontificate of Nicholas V the statutes of the city of Padua had been examined by ecclesiastical authority, when the Pope had threatened excommunication if they were not modified. In those days, Cardinal Colonna, acting on the Pope's mandate, had approved new statutes drawn up by the civic authorities and clergy in collaboration. He had seen that

> some were honourable and others tolerable, and had found that those relating to hospitals had been cancelled and rescinded.

Pisani claimed that the hospital had never been under lay patronage since, and that (at the instance of the late Cardinal Grimani) Pope Julius II had conferred it on Father Giovanni Battista de' Cavalli, predecessor of Hieronimo of Pavia. This was an ecclesiastical benefice, firstly because the laity had never previously objected to its being treated as ecclesiastical patronage; secondly, because a cure of souls was attached; and thirdly, because it had been subject to episcopal visitation. Pisani repeatedly assured the Ambassador that he had instructed Hieronimo of Pavia to keep hospitality, in accordance with the decree of Vienne (always supposing there was any significant demand for it). He could not eject Hieronimo, because he was no longer in his service—it subsequently transpired that he had been dismissed for pawning and otherwise 'dissipating' the contents of the Cardinal's wardrobe. Nor could Pisani do anything so prejudicial to the jurisdiction of the Church.[25]

The eventual outcome of this episode is not at all clear: the matter was probably allowed to lapse by the Venetian government. Pisani had warned the Ambassador that even if he did eject Hieronimo of Pavia the right of presentation would simply revert to the Pope himself; the Ambassador was generally reluctant to tangle with the Pope, lest his government be faced with 'a sterner adversary' than the pluralistic Cardinal. The Venetians confidently but questionably assumed that the nuncio was on their side. Pisani professed himself willing to have the case judged by him: but only because the nuncio had in fact written to Rome to say that the Paduan hospital was a piece of church preferment. Tempers ran high, and for a time the Deputies of Padua suffered excommunication. The Pope himself grew indignant at reports that the Venetian government had made 'a certain intimation' to Cardinal Pisani's nephew—presumably to the Alvise Pisani who had been granted the reversion of the see of Padua.[26] He threatened to

[25] *Ibid.*, ff. 64–65v., 3 May 1544.
[26] On Alvise Pisani, see Giuseppe Alberigo, *I vescovi italiani al Concilio di Trento (1545–7)* (Florence, 1959), pp. 61 f.

treat the offence as committed, not against the Cardinal, but against the person of His Holiness—even, he added, against Christ himself.

The conduct of the Venetian government could well be compared, or so the Pope said, if not to that of Henry VIII of England, at least to the tyrannous acts of Henry II, who had persecuted the Archbishop of Canterbury and driven his followers after him into exile in France. Pisani was conferring these benefices as if the Pope were bestowing them himself, and there could be no question of compromise on the clerical-curial side.[27]

The Pisani affair of 1544 illustrates the ambiguous and uncertain position of hospitals, poised on the frontier between lay and ecclesiastical control: a reasonable case could be made out for either, and the Venetian Republic was generally jealous of any encroachment on its jurisdiction. It could not, however, defend its claim with equal obstinacy in all parts of its dominions. The likelihood of independent episcopal action was much greater on the mainland than in Venice itself. In fifteenth-century Lombardy, the bishops had figured prominently in the foundation of the new, centralized hospitals.[28] Soon after the final sessions at Trent, the provincial synods of Borromeo encouraged them to act. For all their famous anti-clericalism, the Venetians did not cavil at the Tridentine decrees or refuse as firmly as the French to promulgate them. The Venetians objected to the clauses which provided that under no circumstances should priests be subject to the jurisdiction of lay courts. But with this reservation, they ordered the publication of the Tridentine Bull in the summer and autumn of 1564.[29] Unfortunately, it is impossible here to give any detailed or exhaustive account of the application in the dioceses of the Venetian mainland of the Tridentine decrees affecting charitable institutions. However, a few hints can be conveyed, by way of a rough indication of the possibilities.

To the west of the Venetian Terra Ferma, at least some of the Tridentine decrees were quite promptly enforced by the Bishop of Bergamo.[30] Cardinal Pisani's nephews, Alvise Pisani, Bishop of Padua, and Giorgio Cornaro, Bishop of Treviso, both brought the new legislation to their sees. Alvise Pisani summoned two diocesan synods for the purpose in 1564 and 1566, and for his work at the Council of Trent was raised to the purple by Pius IV in 1565.[31] Matteo Priuli, who had also been present at Trent, and who acquired the see of Vicenza in

---

27 A.S.V., *Archivio Proprio Roma, fascicolo* 6, f. 75v., 24 May 1544.
28 See above, pp. 203–5.
29 See Romanin, *Storia documentata di Venezia*, VI, pp. 253 f.
30 Ughelli, *Italia sacra*, IV, col. 504.
31 *Ibid.*, V, col. 570; Alberigo, *I vescovi italiani*, pp. 61 f., 83.

1565, acted similarly.[32] In Verona, Agostino Valier, admirer and biographer of Borromeo, sedulously maintained the tradition of Giberti during his long occupancy of the see, and took an intense interest in the administration of charity: he intervened in the affairs of the Monte di Pietà, about 1580, and procured the foundation of a new beggars' hospital.[33] In the vast Patriarchate of Aquileia, execution of the decrees was longer delayed, but they were enforced after 1585 through the vigorous action of Francesco di Marc'Antonio Barbaro. He conducted the first visitations of the whole diocese for a period of nearly two hundred years, and proved very diligent in upholding orthodoxy and suppressing infiltrations of heresy from German-speaking lands.[34]

It is certain that Borromeo, in his provincial synods of 1565 and 1573, issued to his bishops a number of specific directives calling upon them to ensure that charitable foundations were preserved from decay; that the wishes of their founders were strictly respected; and that charity was dispensed only to those who were economically poor and morally deserving. Hospital administrators must carry out all prescriptions of the Councils of Vienne and Trent. Bishops could not only apply ecclesiastical sanctions against those who failed to discharge their obligations, but also deprive them of office. Borromeo added one or two refinements to the conciliar decrees: no property belonging to religious and charitable institutions might be alienated, save in accordance with the holy canons and with the bishop's formal approval. These institutions were not to let their property to anyone who owed them money, and all prospective tenants must provide pledges or guarantors. Notaries must now inform the bishop if any of the legacies they recorded had been made out of ill-gotten gains: evidently, the bequests of the usurer or of any other dishonourable businessman were not to be accepted. Again, alms should be collected only in the diocese in which the institution actually stood, and only by persons of good reputation. They should do the work either gratis or in return for a fixed fee. On no account should they take a cut out of the alms themselves.

It was essential that

the revenues assigned to the poor be distributed only to the truly poor, in

---

[32] Ughelli, *Italia Sacra*, V, col. 1,067; Giuseppe Alberigo, 'Studi e problemi relativi all'applicazione del Concilio di Trento in Italia (1945–58)', *Rivista storica italiana*, LXX (1958), p. 262; Giovanni Mantese, 'Nota d'archivio sull'attuazione dei decreti tridentini a Vicenza', *Rivista della storia della chiesa in Italia*, XIV (1960).

[33] See below, pp. 363, 593–4.

[34] Ughelli, *Italia sacra*, V, coll. 136–7; Alberigo, 'Applicazione del Concilio di Trento', pp. 259–60.

accordance with the poverty of each individual, and with the wishes of the testator.

Such were the provisions of the first provincial synod.[35] The fourth synod, of 1573, issued instructions as to how almsgivers were expected to discriminate between the worthy and the unworthy. They must do so on the advice and testimony of the parish priest, who, like an overseer of the poor, was expected to know all the needs and circumstances of his flock. If necessary, the testimony of reputable lay parishioners could be used to supplement that of the priest. Almoners must inquire, not only into the needs of potential recipients, but also into their conduct and morality. They should also discover whether they knew the essentials of the Christian faith, and whether they were attending any of the schools of Christian doctrine established to teach them these.

The fourth synod added further recommendations for the efficient administration of charities. Chapters or governing bodies must rotate office among their members. There must be no self-perpetuating oligarchies, never obliged to hand over to successors likely to check on their activities. They must keep proper records, including a minute-book, and a register of all legacies and testamentary obligations laid upon the institution. They must also deposit a copy of this register with the bishop. Furthermore, in order to preserve the institution, they should set up tablets of stone or marble somewhere on the premises of the institution, recording its 'origin, establishment and title'.[36] Perhaps this tangible memorial would serve as a perpetual reproach to all who tried to convert the buildings to selfish or improper ends.

Borromeo's instructions do at least indicate that the Tridentine decrees were percolating down from the level of the General Council to that of the provincial synod, and that additional provisions were being made for their enforcement. Borromeo himself carried out visitations in Bergamo in 1575, when extensive information about the hospitals, fraternities and Misericordie of the city and diocese was in fact submitted to him. The Bishop of Bergamo had always, since the mid-fifteenth century, enjoyed some influence over the appointment of officials to the Great Hospital of San Marco, and it was scarcely surprising that Borromeo should leave instructions that

> The most reverend Bishop shall watch over the spiritual and physical care of those who are admitted to this hospital, and shall not neglect to review the accounts of its administration and to visit it frequently.[37]

[35] *Acta Ecclesiae Mediolanensis*, f. 21r.–v.
[36] *Ibid.*, ff. 86v.–87.
[37] Roncalli and Forno, *Atti di Borromeo*, I/ii, p. 159. Cf. A.S.V., *Sindici Inquisitori in Terra Ferma*, busta 63, ff. 110–12, which shows that in 1596 the Bishop, together

With the Hospital of the Maddalena for the insane, governed by the Disciplinati of Bergamo, the situation was far more ambiguous: it enjoyed exemption from episcopal authority and was immediately subject to the Apostolic See, though the bishop had in the past been invited to approve certain statutes, which had by his authority been inserted in the registers of the hospital. These statutes recognized that a diocesan official should be made responsible for seeing them enforced.[38] In any case, the Tridentine decrees were designed to restore episcopal authority, and to prevent exemptions being pleaded against the bishop. Some discussion arose over the visitation of the city's most elaborate and wealthy institution, the general almonry known as the Misericordia. On 15 October 1575, the city council considered Borromeo's suggestion that the Bishops of Bergamo ought annually to carry out visitations of the Misericordia. Diplomatically, they decided to elect four deputies to express the city's contentment at the visitation which Borromeo had in fact conducted, but also to petition that

> He should, in his ample wisdom, find some means of preserving the most ancient exemption which has been continually enjoyed by the said institution.

They could adduce a Bull of Nicholas V, which exempted the Bergamese Misericordia from the jurisdiction of papal legates as well as from that of the Archbishop of Milan and the Bishop of Bergamo. It is, however, impossible to discover at present what conclusion was reached—especially as the council expressed anxiety, in these delicate and compromising circumstances, not to enter into any written negotiations with Borromeo.[39]

In general, however, it seems reasonable to conclude that Borromeo's influence, spilling over from Milanese into Venetian territory, provided a strong incentive for intervention by ecclesiastical authorities in the affairs of lay charities and lay religious fraternities. Not all the regions annexed to the Venetian Republic shared Venice's own rigorous tradition of excluding the clergy from responsibility for the administration of charitable institutes. In Bergamo at least, the civic authorities did not proclaim, as aggressively as the Paduans and Venetians in 1544, that hospitals were lay foundations which ought to be exclusively under lay control: instead, they based such objections as they raised on documents of papal origin. The conciliar decrees theoretically entitled

with the Consiglio Minore, elected the fifteen citizens who governed the Great Hospital of San Marco, and also acted as one of the twelve governors of the Monte dell'Abbondanza.

[38] Roncalli and Forno, *Atti di Borromeo*, I/ii, pp. 134–5.
[39] *Ibid.*, I/i, pp. 368–72.

the bishops to override exemptions: but their right to do so was always liable to be questioned, at least mildly.

Moreover, Borromeo's influence was not strictly confined to the dioceses of Bergamo, Brescia and Crema within his province. By indirect means, through his admirers, it extended eastwards into the Venetian dominions.[40] Influence was not exerted only in one direction, from Milanese into Venetian territory. Borromeo was himself an earnest admirer of Giberti, the pioneering Bishop of Verona, and made fervent inquiries about his methods from those who had once worked under him. Between 1564 and 1566, Borromeo, in his own province, enlisted the aid of Nicolò Ormaneto and Alberto Lino, two former assistants of Giberti. Ormaneto, as Borromeo's Vicar-General, drafted many of the decrees of his first provincial council, whilst Lino attended especially to the visitation and reform of nunneries. Subsequently, Ormaneto held the see of Padua, from 1570 to 1577.[40a] There, his successor was Federico Cornaro, who had served as Bishop of Bergamo from 1561 to 1577, had attended Borromeo's first four provincial synods, had enforced at least some of the Tridentine decrees, and had, during the Apostolic Visitation of Bergamo in 1575, earned Borromeo's commendation for his 'vigilance'. Cornaro remained Bishop of Padua until 1590.[41] In Verona, Agostino Valier continued the tradition of Giberti, and was himself an admirer of Borromeo. He secured preferment for another imitator of Borromeo, Luigi Lollino, a noble of Cretan origins who was Bishop of Belluno from 1596 to 1625.[42] Even if no specific information can be presented here about the concern which these bishops showed for the supervision of charity, it is worth drawing attention to their connexions with Borromeo. Certainly Valier intervened in the affairs of the local Monte di Pietà as if he were obeying some of Borromeo's instructions, issued in 1569, on the subject of interest charges.[43] By about 1602, he was also concerned with the establishment of a hospital for beggars—perhaps in accordance with one of Borromeo's recommendations of 1565, whereby charity must be denied to sturdy or fraudulent beggars, but the genuinely sick or impotent should be gathered into one place, under shelter.[44]

[40] See, in general, Logan, *Studies in the religious life of Venice*, pp. 271 f.

[40a] See Enrico Cattaneo, 'Influenze veronesi nella legislazione di San Carlo Borromeo', in *Problemi di vita religiosa in Italia nel Cinquecento: Atti del Convegno di Storia della Chiesa in Italia* (Padua, 1960), pp. 125–35.

[41] Ughelli, *Italia sacra*, IV, col. 504, V, col. 460.

[42] See Luigi Alpago-Novello, 'La vita e le opere di Luigi Lollino, vescovo di Belluno (1596–1625)', *Archivio Veneto*, 5th series, XIV (1933), XV (1934): at XIV, pp. 35, 37, 41 f.

[43] See below, pp. 593–4, and *Acta Ecclesiae Mediolanensis*, f. 34v.

[44] *Ibid.*, f. 21v., and below, pp. 362–3.

It is also likely that the promise—or threat—of episcopal intervention spurred the Venetian government into itself taking action in the provinces to eliminate corruption. In the diocese of Brescia, the Bishop and the civil government appreciated the possibilities of collaboration. From 1559 to 1579, the Venetian patrician Domenico Bollani occupied the see of Brescia. He had previously followed a civilian career and had served as governor of Brescia; the Venetians had pressed strongly for his appointment by Paul IV, and they approved in general of his conduct.[45] On 20 September 1572, the governors of Brescia wrote to inform the Senate that in their province there were many institutions called Misericordie, Monti di Carità or Monti di Pietà whose revenues were maladministered because their officials were accountable to no-one, and because the money was appropriated by persons who could well afford to give alms themselves. The Bishop had made representations to the governors 'with his usual charity',

> showing us also the decrees of the holy councils which reprimand all bishops who neglect their care, and at the same time exhort lay princes to give them every aid and encouragement.

In all probability, they had seen Borromeo's decrees as well as those of the Council of Trent: the next words seemed to reflect his terminology. The governors and the Bishop joined in bringing this matter to the notice of the Venetian government,

> so that in your wisdom you may issue those orders which seem to you most appropriate, that the administration of those *luochi pii* may be set in order, by frequently examining the accounts, by ensuring that their administration is not allowed always to remain in the hands of a small number of persons, and by ensuring that alms be distributed in suitable fashion to the most needy persons, according to the wishes of the testators or founders of these pious institutions.

Early in October 1572, the Senate took the hint. It authorized the governors to inform themselves about these establishments,

> and, taking the advice and opinion of the Right Reverend Bishop, you two Rettori may together set in order the administration of the *luochi pii* in the various parts of the province committed to you, and may draw up those constitutions and ordinances concerning the administration and disposition of their revenues that you judge necessary for the complete execution of the wishes of the testators or of their founders and for the benefit of the poor. We wish any ordinances and regulations established by the two of you concerning these matters to be just as valid and to carry the same weight as if they were decreed by the Senate itself.

[45] Logan, *Studies in the religious life of Venice*, pp. 195–6.

340

The wording of this decree showed obvious appreciation of the Bishop's attitude, but carefully provided that all actual decisions must be made by the Rettori or civilian governors, acting in the name of the Senate.[46]

The Senate and governors later followed a similar procedure in Friuli and in the Bergamasco. In May 1578, the governor or Provveditore of Cividale di Friuli mentioned to his superiors in Venice that the Vicar-General of the Patriarch of Aquileia was now proposing to embark on a visitation of confraternities and charitable institutions in the area. The Senate once more hastily intervened, professing themselves

> deeply concerned that the revenues bequeathed to these fraternities and religious institutions may be properly administered and distributed according to the instructions and intentions of their founders.

Doubtless out of anxiety to forestall any ecclesiastical action which might encroach on their own jurisdiction, they told the governor to investigate the matter himself, once more taking 'the advice and opinion of the Reverend Vicar or of the ordinary', and to 'regulate and thoroughly review' the administration of fraternities.[47] The best defence against the expanding claims of the clergy was to remove the need for their intervention. Again, in Bergamo in 1590, the Senate authorized the governors to inquire into certain abuses in charitable institutions which they had themselves reported, once more taking the Bishop's advice.[48] Later, on his return to Venice in June 1591, the governor Cattarino Zeno said that the Misericordie or almonries of the Bergamasco were suffering from a grave abuse. Their revenues were partitioned among all the members of the communes they served—

> sometimes according to dignity and wealth (*per stimo*), and sometimes at so much per head, so that the rich and well-to-do have more part in them than the poor and wretched.

The governors claimed to have made it possible for many communes to support all their poor, by acting on the authority granted them by the Senate.[49] They did not, of course, permanently eliminate the corruption, and much later, in 1622, the Podestà Girolamo Bragadin complained of haphazard accounting in the Misericordie. This permitted

[46] A.S.V., *Senato, Terra, filza* 60, 7 October 1572.
[47] A.S.V., *Senato, Terra, filza* 74, 14 June 1578.
[48] A.S.V., *Senato, Terra, filza* 117, 6 October 1590.
[49] A.S.V., *Collegio, Relazioni, busta* 35, report of Cattarino Zeno, 14 June 1591. See also ff. 4v.–5 of the report of Alvise Priuli, 12 June 1593, where he describes the Misericordie as generally well governed, and as subject to surveillance by the Venetian Rettori.

corrupt administrators to convert the money to other uses, thus contravening the wishes of testators. He claimed to have restored order once more, and suggested that in the course of every *reggimento* or period of office the governors should be obliged to audit the accounts of one-third of the Misericordie.[50]

Elsewhere, there was at least one other instance of action taken by provincial Rettori, with the support of the Venetian Senate, to prevent the embezzlement of the revenues of a local charity. Don Francesco and Don Cristoforo Barati, of the small town of Schio in the province of Vicenza, left revenues to the extent of 2,000 ducats a year, to be spent partly on the establishment of a hospital and partly on erecting a trust which would dispense marriage portions of 25 ducats each to five local maidens every year. The testators committed the management of both trusts to the Archpriest and Syndic of Schio, together with a local and locally appointed Governatore. Don Francesco Barati died in July 1599, but nearly three years later the leaders of the commune of Schio had still made no attempt to dispense any of the revenues to the poor. According to Giovanni Francesco Grimani and Nicolò Pizzamano, Rettori of Vicenza, they had violated the terms of the bequest by alienating the trust's property to the value of 1,000 ducats at derisory prices, and were spending the money chiefly on lawsuits and prosecutions calculated to discomfort their own personal enemies. 125 persons of the neighbourhood, who qualified as 'poor wretches' or *persone miserabili*, had then elected an advocate to appear before the Rettori of Vicenza or before the Doge himself to try to recover their rights. The Rettori then intervened, and successfully advised the Senate against permitting the alienation on perpetual lease of a number of scattered pieces of land to the extent of about 100 *campi*.[51] They also, for a time at least, removed the administration of the trust from local hands, and appointed an Esattore and Procuratore of their own. In 1604, representatives of the commune complained in Venice that the Rettori had mistakenly punished the offices rather than the guilty men, and that they were not in fact getting the job done any better. It transpired that they had let the 100 *campi* for a somewhat lower annual rent than had the leaders of the commune. The former Rettore Pizzamano admitted the fact in a letter to the Senate, but claimed that this apparent inefficiency was the result of sabotage, and of local conspiracy to oppose and frustrate their efforts. Their Esattore and Procuratore would give place in time to a Governatore, a native or resident of Schio, who would be responsible for leasing the trust's property

[50] *Ibid.*, under date 17 March 1622.
[51] A.S.V., *Senato, Terra, filza* 165, 12 December 1602.

every five years, with the authority and consent of the Most Honourable Governors of Vicenza for the time being, and would collect the revenues, protect the property, feed the poor, and, in a word, be charged to carry out the wishes of the founders to the full.

This official would be required to give the Rettori a pledge of 1,000 ducats as a guarantee of good administration, and he would receive a salary of 60 ducats a year, plus a house. Communal representatives had objected that they had given their services free: but in fact they had taken their reward by debiting the trust for travelling expenses to Vicenza or Venice itself. In reality, they had undertaken these journeys purely for personal reasons.[52]

Clearly, in some areas, the solicitude of churchmen for the faithful administration of charity acted as a spur to intervention by lay authorities; elsewhere, laymen were sometimes capable of moving without this stimulus. In Venice, the supervision of hospitals, fraternities and other charities became wholly the responsibility of government commissions, with no obvious signs of action from the Patriarch or his underlings. Certainly, Giovanni Trevisan, who held the Patriarchate from 1560 to 1590,[53] presented little challenge to the Venetian government. Borromeo despised him for sinking to the level of a Byzantine Patriarch, of a superior state official rather than an independent authority. He condemned his failure to guide the Venetian people, who, nonetheless, remained sober and pious, if highly perverse in their attitudes to questions of jurisdiction. In 1580, one Ducal Councillor candidly confessed to the papal nuncio that

in all his activities and undertakings the Patriarch invariably comes to discuss and consult with the Doge and Signory, and he employs as his secretary one of the Secretaries of the Senate, Missier Lorenzo Massa, who has been assigned to him.[54]

In these years, 1580–1, the Venetians were faced with the prospect of an Apostolic Visitation of the diocese of Venice, perhaps on lines similar to the one conducted in Bergamo by Borromeo himself. The government resisted any suggestion that the visitors be authorized to examine nunneries, hospitals and other philanthropic establishments, Scuole, or boards of lay churchwardens (*procuratie*) in the parishes of the city. As it happened, they eventually secured the appointment by the Papacy of the nuncio Lorenzo Campeggio and of the Bishop of

---

[52] A.S.V., *Senato, Terra, filza* 173, 12 February 1604 Venetian style.
[53] H.C., III, p. 350.
[54] See Giovanni Soranzo, 'Rapporti di San Carlo Borromeo con la Repubblica Veneta', *Archivio Veneto*, 5th series, XXVII (1940), pp. 23–5, 36–7; also Logan, *Studies in the religious life of Venice*, pp. 429–30.

Z

Verona, Agostino Valier. These prelates conducted only a mild and tactful visitation, to which only secular clergy and male regulars were subject. Visitatorial zeal increased only with the accession of Lorenzo Priuli to the Patriarchate in 1591. He at least examined the church-wardens and the officers of the fraternities of the Sacrament[55]—but not, apparently, the hospitals, the Scuole Grandi or the Procuratie of St Mark's, all of which were subject to their own temporary or permanent boards of auditors and investigators.

The existence of these boards provided an excellent practical reason why the clergy should not intervene—the state was already taking action itself to root corruption out. In July 1561, the Senate had established a commission on the same lines as in 1489 and 1526. Three Senators, assisted by one notary from the Cancelleria, were to examine the state of the hospitals in Venice itself, on Murano, and in the rest of the lagoon. They must re-read the wills of all who had made bequests to the hospitals, examine their foundation statutes, and discover whether these were in fact being properly observed. They must inquire whether any portion of these goods had been alienated, and whether the hospitals now sheltered both the right sort of poor and the right number thereof.[56] They would have no authority over hospitals directly submitted to the jurisdiction of the Doge. A few years later, in 1567, this category certainly included the large hospitals of the Incurabili and Pietà. Care of the Incurabili was specially commended to the Doge in his constitutional oath. The Prioress of the Pietà sought that the revenues and expenditure of the Pietà should also be specially commended to the Doge, and that he should arrange for the accounts to be audited every six months.[57] Ducal protection saved these hospitals, not only from the local magistracy, but also (according to the Tridentine decree of 1562) from any possible threat of intervention by the ordinary.

This regional hospital board differed from its forebears only in developing into a permanent magistracy with some chance of taking effective action. The Senate appointed the first commissioners for a period of two years, instead of a mere six months, as previously, and at the end of this term elected another board. Hitherto, the magistrates had enjoyed no jurisdictional authority: they had merely been an advisory body which offered recommendations to the Collegio. Now, in October 1563, the Senate accorded them first-instance jurisdiction

[55] *Ibid.*, pp. 68–9, 100–1, 427 f.; also Pastor, *History of the Popes*, XIX, pp. 77–9.

[56] A.S.V., *Senato, Terra*, reg. 1560/61, ff. 89v.–90v., 24 July 1561.

[57] A.S.V., *Maggior Consiglio, Deliberazioni, Liber Angelus*, f. 17v., 10 November 1567; also *ibid.*, *Liber Frigerius*, f. 131, 4 August 1585, which refers to the responsibility of the Doge and Procurators for the hospital of the Pietà.

to issue decrees and sentences (*termination et sententie*) in matters concerning the regulation and abuse of hospitals and other religious institutions of this city and the Dogado, and also in those involving the misappropriation of their revenues, which has in the past been perpetrated by private individuals in an unjust and fraudulent manner.

The Senate itself would act as a court of appeal.[58] Finally, two years later, the Senate declared this a permanent magistracy: its successes in the past four years justified this step.[59] The first Venetian legislation anticipated the Tridentine decrees; both Tridentine and Venetian laws reflected the general anxiety of all authorities, clerical or lay, to exploit existing charitable resources as effectively as possible.

In general, the commissioners and the Senate tried to improve the methods by which the hospitals kept their records, and to ensure that they kept track of their own property and income, and of all wills, deeds and other legal documents pertaining to their establishments. These must be catalogued in registers known as *catastichi* or *repertorii*, of which one copy should always be sent to the hospital commissioners.[60] In particular, the commissioners conducted detailed investigations of various hospitals, inquiring with especial care into the worthiness and poverty of their current inmates.

The Hospital of Gesù Cristo di Sant'Antonio, under the management of the Procurators of St Mark's, became an inviting early target for inquiries. The state was directly responsible for its foundation, and it (together with the substantial numbers of almshouses distributed by the Procuratie and Scuole Grandi) was one of many charities designed to provide special incentives to serve the Republic in the navy or merchant marine. In 1563, the hospital commissioners drew the attention of the Procurators to the fact that thirteen out of the forty-four on the hospital's roll had only the most dubious titles to charity. At least eight of these thirteen did not live in the hospital itself, but merely received alms or other benefits from it. Six either lived in their own cheap little houses, or in the houses of noblemen as servants or almsmen:

Piero, son of Domenico, of Venice, who lives on the Giudecca in Ca' Lombardo, and pays 3 ducats' rent.

Giacomo of Venice, a young man, who lives in the house of Missier Giorgio Zorzi.

Luca, a cooper, of whom it was said that he never came near the place except to get his money. He lives in the house of Missier Marco Grimani.

[58] A.S.V., *Senato, Terra*, reg. 1562/63, f. 163, 6 October 1563.
[59] A.S.V., *Senato, Terra*, reg. 1564/65, f. 173, 20 October 1565.
[60] A.S.V., *Senato, Terra*, reg. 1562/63, ff. 109v.–110, 13 March 1563.

Bortolamio of Mestre, who lives in the house of Missier Vincenzo Grimani.

Giacomo, son of Paolo, potter, who lives at San Basegio and pays 4 ducats' rent.

Francesco of Padua, maker of hoops for barrels, who lives in Cannaregio.

Moreover, Oliviero of Murano had charge of a hospital of his own, that of the Santo Spirito on Murano, in which he lived, and Giovanni, son of Nicolò, known by the patrician surname of Barbarigo, lived in the hospital in Corte Nuova at the Misericordia in Cannaregio.

Of the remainder, four enjoyed other benefits, including the income from small profitable jobs in government employ, which were commonly awarded to ex-servicemen:

Angelo, known as the Blind Man—we understand that he has an almshouse (*casa di bando*), that he has a job at the customs-station, that he gets one *mocenigo* a day from the Arsenal, that he is one of the Poveri al Pevere, and that he is buying himself the post of watchman at the Arsenal.

Giorgio of Zara, a robust man of about forty, who has the ferry at the customs-station.

Paolo Tosi of Piove di Sacco, who has a job at the office of the Macina (*which administered the tax on the grinding of corn*), receives wages of 10 lire a month, and lives at San Gregorio.

Martino of Cherso, a ship's captain.

The hospital commission therefore recommended to the Procurators of St Mark's that these men be excluded from the benefits of the hospital, though they held that the number of inmates should be kept down from forty-four to thirty-one only during the current period of dearth and famine. Presumably they were not inviting the Procurators to reinstate the same thirteen when the famines ended.[61]

In dealing with this hospital, the chief purpose of the Venetian government was always to reserve it for those who, 'having spent their lives in the service of the state, are now reduced to impotence or decrepitude and have nowhere to go', and to eject 'persons who not only have acquired no merit, but who, in view of their age, trade or other considerations, could perfectly well earn a living by other means'. Later in the century, commissioners appointed to 'revise' the Procuratie of St Mark's also recommended legislation by the Senate on the Hospital of Sant'Antonio. The chief purpose of these laws was to reserve the benefits primarily for non-patrician officers on galleons, galleys, roundships and *marciliane*: for masters, mates, bo'suns and pilots. If there

[61] A.S.V., *Provveditori sopra gli Ospedali e Luoghi Pii, busta* 17/21, f. 7.

were not enough of these, vacancies could be filled by those who had served the state in other, lesser capacities. The Senate stipulated, in 1589, that inmates must be at least sixty years of age, unmarried, and prepared to live on the premises rather than maintain separate establishments elsewhere. The Tridentine decree of 1563 might have inspired them to add the clause which provided that the Prior must no longer be elected for life. He should serve for a term of four years only, but the Senate offered him the chance of reappointment, in the belief that this would increase the incentive to carrying out his duties conscientiously.[62]

In most of their dealings, the hospital commissioners expressly insisted that charity must go only to the truly poor, on the principle that

> It is certain that alms are the more pleasing to God the slenderer the means of the person to whom they are dispensed.

A fair test of this was the willingness of paupers actually to go and live in the hospital itself rather than merely accept outdoor relief from its managers. Six women who enjoyed the charity of the late Bernardo Pusco in the parish of San Nicolò were duly warned to move to his hospital in September 1566.[63] But beyond these economic criteria lay other moral criteria, the determination to put down lewdness and blasphemy among the poor. These considerations emerged clearly during the inquiries, in 1564 and 1574, into the Hospital of San Giobbe in the parish of San Geremia in Cannaregio.[64] In 1574, this represented a fairly elaborate organization. The hospital consisted of 120 separate almshouses, with a church, a dispensary or *spiciaria*, and wells supplied with fresh water. The foundation also provided for the distribution of bread, wine and money to a certain number of women inmates. The Prior, Giorgio Da Ponte, claimed that when he entered on office in 1568 there were only 17 such women, but the number had then been stepped up to as many as 48, and there were now 42.

The conduct of several inmates left much to be desired. In 1564, the hospital commissioners took up the complaint of the then Prior, Giovanni Marcello. Marco, a boatbuilder, had been keeping on the premises a 'betola' or 'riduto' for Jews. It was evidently a combined tavern and casino, where they met

---

[62] A.S.V., *Senato, Terra, filza* 111, 12 August 1589; *filza* 112, 14 September 1589.
[63] A.S.V., *Provveditori sopra gli Ospedali, busta* 17/21, ff. 28–9, 13 September 1566.
[64] A.S.V., *Provveditori sopra gli Ospedali, busta* 17/21, f. 16v., 27 September 1564; ff. 43–6, 28 September 1574.

to gamble, eat and drink, with little respect for our Lord God, and slight reverence for that religious institution, causing much scandal to the inhabitants of the neighbourhood.

Apart from the general unseemliness of gambling, it was an object of zealous Catholics in the Tridentine era to prevent all loose and unnecessary contact between Jews and Christians.[65] The commissioners duly gave orders to stop this abuse.

Ten years later, they conducted a full investigation into the affairs of San Giobbe and its beneficiaries. Their minute book recorded in detail the interrogation of the Prior, Giorgio Da Ponte. When asked 'What sort of people live in these houses?' he answered frankly that

There is much discontent in the neighbourhood on account of people who shock their neighbours by using foul language, and it is said that some of them lead immoral lives.

This was charged against Angela, a carpenter's wife, Lucia, a capper or capper's wife (*baretera*), Gianetta di Maria of Scutari and a lame virago known as La Padrigua. The Prior claimed to have

admonished them, and brought a blush to their cheeks, and told them that no-one ought to commit such lewd actions in that sacred place, and that they must amend, because I would inform the governors, as indeed I did on more than one occasion.
Q. And what did the governors say?
A. I brought the women to the church, and everyone assembled there, and the governors came and reprimanded the women, both the lame one and the capper, and deprived the lame one of the alms in money and the capper of the flour and wine for a term of one year.
Q. But surely this is a light punishment, in view of the offences committed by these women?
A. Well, it was the dancing that started it all.
Q. Why didn't they turn them out altogether, knowing they were leading this immoral life?
A. Well, I didn't fail to inform them, and I can only say that they imposed the penalty I just described.

Further inquiries concerned other loose and foul-mouthed women who lived in the almshouses: Giustina, daughter of the broker Alvise; Betta Codelera; Margarita, called La Bemba; and Betta Griega. There were signs of concern for children exposed to contact with prostitution—Jesuit campaigns had recently established, in 1559–61, a Casa delle Zitelle for the reception and education of imperilled girls.[66]

[65] See below, pp. 528–9, 555–60.　　　　[66] See below, pp. 385–91.

Q. Do you know one Betta Griega?

A. Yes, gentlemen. I've heard there's a certain Doctor Novara who comes to her house and stays there four or five hours, and this woman has a very beautiful daughter, and when he goes up she comes downstairs.

Some of these women had provoked complaints to the police magistracy of the Cinque alla Pace.

The morality of those who dwelt in hospitals was thus of much interest to the hospital commissioners. They also faced the problem of hospitals which were in no sense fulfilling their proper function, whose governors had simply converted them and their revenues to other, irrelevant uses. On one occasion, a cleric was partly at fault, though the lay patron shared the blame, and there seemed little justification for the Venetian government's formal, stylized assertion that the clergy were peculiarly unreliable. In 1563, the commune of Chioggia, to the south of the lagoon, elected two procurators to complain to the hospital commissioners (not to the Bishop of Chioggia) of the misuse of the property and revenues of the hospital of the Ca' di Dio near the harbour. The commune had granted land to the hospital in 1298 and 1305 to equip it to extend its premises, and had also restored the hospital when damaged in time of war. At present, the need for hospitals was acute, not only because of persistent famine, but also because of the number of sailors who died at sea or were captured by pirates, leaving helpless wives and children. A local citizen, Domenico Belhaver, had obtained from Sixtus IV the right of presentation to the chaplaincy at the altar of San Salvatore in the hospital church, for himself and his heirs and successors. His descendant Ludovico Belhaver had abused his position when, on the death of the incumbent Giovanni Tagliacozzo in 1540, he had installed Father Giacomo de' Cavalli (de Equitibus), Archpriest of Loretto, as chaplain. He had presented the Archpriest to the papal nuncio, and, by falsely representing that the revenues did not exceed 12 ducats a year, had got them all assigned to his chaplain. Ludovico Belhaver and the priest had then divided the revenues between them, 7 staia of corn a year to Ludovico and 18 to the priest. They had likewise divided up the flax and other produce yielded by land which the hospital owned at Bogion, a village in the Padovano, shared the revenues from government securities, leased the lands bestowed by the medieval commune, and let the premises once occupied by the poor as shops or stores—though occasionally some Franciscan Friar took up a tenancy. The chapel contained images of Christ and the Virgin which had once been much venerated, but the Archpriest never visited the place except for the purpose of collecting his rent. No beds, bedding or utensils remained in the hospital. The

349

procurators now asked the hospital commission to get the hospital restored and cause it to resume its functions.[67] The minutes unfortunately contain no records of action taken by the commissioners—but in 1565 the Senate, when raising the commission to the status of a permanent magistracy, observed that

> they have recovered some hospitals which had been usurped and obtained by fraudulent means by private persons from the Apostolic See.[68]

These remarks may well have referred to the Ca' di Dio at Chioggia.

In some of their other enterprises, the commissioners were less fortunate: they encountered persistent obstruction and prolonged litigation, recurring at intervals over a period of more than thirty years. In 1564 and 1567, they twice attempted to deprive Giovanni the German, a shoemaker, Prior or Padre of the Hospital of Santa Maria dell'Annunziata for the German Shoemakers in the parish of San Samuele. The premises had been gravely abused, turned into dance-halls or gambling-dens, and rooms had been let to persons of ill-fame. Moreover, there were disquieting signs of heretical iconoclasm, for images of the Madonna and saints had been defaced and 'German words' scribbled upon them. The commissioners instructed the governors of the hospital to find another Prior, to expel all the disreputable inmates from the hospital, to remove from it anyone paying rent to live there, and to introduce suitable paupers.[69] Their orders, however, produced no permanent results. In February 1592, members of a later board visited the hospital, and found it in the hands of two German shoemakers: Pietro, called 'the merchant', because he ran a thriving business at San Giovanni Grisostomo nearby, and one Tommaso Morchi, who lived there with his wife and children. They used the rest of the hospital to house their own apprentices, whom they promptly ejected if they went to work for anybody else. They lent or hired the chapel as a banqueting hall. The commissioners duly deprived the unscrupulous tradesmen, who, however, then appealed against all articles of the sentence to the Collegio, associating with them other Germans

> to whom, since they were ignorant of the language, they managed to convey the impression that the sentence we had issued for their benefit (by recovering the hospital from the two usurpers just mentioned) would instead be very prejudicial to their interests.

[67] A.S.V., *Provveditori sopra gli Ospedali*, busta 17/21, f. 12r.–v.
[68] A.S.V., *Senato, Terra*, reg. 1564/65, f. 173, 20 October 1565.
[69] A.S.V., *Provveditori sopra gli Ospedali*, busta 17/21, f. 16, 26 September 1564; also ff. 29v.–32v., 23 July 1567.

The Collegio finally upheld the sentence—in the fifth year after the original visitation. However, at this point the affair rose to the diplomatic level—since the Imperial Ambassador then intervened and had the case transferred to be judged by yet another court of appeal: the Dieci Savii del Corpo del Senato con li Quindeci Aggionti. The Senate, doubtless fearing international complications, refused to grant the request of the hospital commissioners that they should prevent these delaying tactics.[70]

Parallel to the movement for the review of the older hospitals, there developed another for the removal of abuses in the Procuratie of St Mark's. In spite of their reputation for absolute integrity, and their exalted status among Venetian magistrates, events were to show that the Procurators were not beyond criticism. They disposed of extensive resources, in the form of almshouses, marriage portions, and alms to be dispensed to the poor, both clerical and lay. In the middle of the century, and in 1565, the concern of the government to save the navy and merchant marine from erosion led them to issue regulations for the distribution of almshouses to poor mariners, carefully stipulating who, for these purposes, was to be regarded as a mariner.[71] The regulations of 1565 were framed to guarantee a constant supply of officers for warships equipped with oars, by offering them prior claims to charitable benefits in their old age or retirement. Most of these almshouses were controlled and distributed by the Procurators and by the Scuole Grandi. Only in 1569[72] and 1572, however, was there an attempt to establish commissions with comprehensive powers to 'review the testaments and ordinances which are in our Procuratie'. The war of Cyprus, with its accompanying acute demand for galley-crews and mariners, may have provided the incentive for this, but at the same time have rendered the commissions ineffective by diverting attention to more immediate needs. The Senate erected the first efficient board of investigators in 1578. This body, known as the Revisori sopra le Procuratie, was formally empowered to examine the books, cashboxes and rentrolls of the Procurators, and also to inquire into their investments in public funds, their building expenses, and their expenditure on the repairs of house property. The commissioners were to report monthly to the Collegio, and to draw up indictments against all guilty of irregularities or more serious malpractices. As if to preserve their dignity, the Senate charged the Procurators themselves (as they had

[70] A.S.V., *Senato, Terra, filza* 139, 9 April 1596.

[71] A.S.V., *Maggior Consiglio, Liber Novus,* f. 134r.–v., 25 June 1547: *Liber Rocca,* f. 151r.–v., 29 September 1565.

[72] A.S.V., *Senato, Terra, filza* 54, 12 November 1569.

previously done in 1547) to conduct diligent inquiries as to whether their almshouses and hospitals were in fact 'enjoyed' by persons with the requisite qualifications. After six months, the Revisori would become responsible for correcting abuses. These commissioners would, in the first instance, be appointed for a period of two years; afterwards, a new board must be elected every five years to carry out a similar survey.[73]

The Revisori used their authority to some effect, and in November 1579 publicly humiliated one of the Procurators, the Cavalier Giovanni Da Lezze, for abusing his position. He was accused of spending excessive sums from procuratorial funds on his own dwelling-house, and of specifically contravening the Great Council's decree of 1532, which forbade Procurators to give to their colleagues or other persons 'moneys or other things belonging to the Procuratie'. When in charge of the funds, he had lent the sum of 2,061 ducats to the late Procurator Andrea Lion. The Senate originally voted to fine Da Lezze the sum of 500 ducats, but the proposal met substantial opposition; 88 voted in favour, 33 against, and 37 abstained. Perhaps on the grounds that it had not obtained a strong enough majority, the motion was balloted again on two occasions six days later; but each time the opposition grew stronger. Compromise eventually came on 12 December, when the Senate merely condemned Da Lezze to restore the money. This, again, proved a highly controversial suggestion, and was passed by 75 votes in favour to 40 against, with 32 abstentions. The decree contained a dark reference to other Procurators having been involved,[74] and, indeed, in March 1580, a group of five Procurators, Marco Grimani, Lorenzo Correr, Andrea Da Lezze, Alvise Tiepolo and Paolo Nani, had formally to certify to the Revisori that they had reimbursed the Procuratie for various forms of irregular expenditure.[75]

Later in the year, the Senate issued other regulations, on the advice of the Revisori, designed to quell abuses in the Procuratie. A minor, but significant decree ordered them not to make advances of wages, or loans on any other account, to their paid servants or Gastaldi, for any period longer than six months. They must always obtain an adequate security.[76] The Procurators also received instructions to rearrange and classify the confused masses of records in their archives.[77] The question then arose of regulating the actual distribution of charity. The authority of the Great Council lent added weight to a comprehensive regulation

---

[73] A.S.V., *Senato, Terra, filza* 74, 19 June 1578.

[74] A.S.V., *Senato, Terra, filza* 79, 19, 25 November, 12 December 1579.

[75] A.S.V., *Senato, Terra,* reg. 1580/81, f. 3, 5 March 1580.

[76] A.S.V., *Senato, Terra, filza* 80, 20 June 1580.

[77] *Ibid., filza* 81, 19 November 1580.

issued in September 1580. This sternly declared that the Procurators were not entitled to bend the orders of deceased testators by interpreting them in their own way. They must execute them to the letter. However, a large proportion of the funds had simply been left to be dispensed at the discretion of the Procurators, and the Great Council now proceeded formally to define the charitable objects on which they could be spent. All moneys available should be pooled. Procurators must not distribute them on their own individual initiative, but should hold board meetings in each Procuratia, and decide by a two-thirds vote how to bestow their charity. The first respectable object was the provision of marriage-portions for worthy, impoverished girls. These must be carefully graded in accordance with the status of the candidates: up to 50 ducats for noblewomen, up to 40 for citizenesses, and 5 to 20 ducats for plebeians. Entrants to poor nunneries, and orphan-girls raised by hospitals, could also receive such benefits. Another object lay in freeing slaves captured by Muslim enemies and exposed to the Islamic faith, and in the release of prisoners arrested for debt. Otherwise, the Procurators should collectively dispense the moneys in the assistance of the poor. They would normally do this over the counter in their own offices off the Piazza San Marco, in doles of not more than three ducats at a time, though the law showed the usual indulgence towards *poveri vergognosi*, for whom alms could be sent to their houses. The Great Council specified that they must distribute money— not cloth or other goods. Presumably this clause was designed to avert fraud on the part of the Procurators. Finally, the new law provided that, on the vote of three-quarters of the Procurators present, some of these moneys could be used for special church festivals. Evidently, poor relief must enjoy priority over the splendours of worship.[78]

The commission of 1578–80 had obviously made a determined and intelligent attempt to put the administration of charity by the Procurators on a regular footing. They had done their best not to respect persons, and had made examples of prominent men. Another such commission took action again in 1589–90. It acted less drastically, but introduced further legislation on the management of house property, and dealt with conditions in the Hospital of Gesù Cristo di Sant' Antonio, subject to the Procurators of St Mark's.[79] The commissioners now attacked one other specific abuse—in the practice whereby certain Procurators seized the best almshouses for themselves, and gave them

[78] A.S.V., *Maggior Consiglio, Deliberazioni, Liber Frigerius*, ff. 70v.–71, 4 September 1580.

[79] A.S.V., *Senato, Terra, filza* 111, 12 August 1589; *filza* 112, 14 September 1589; *filza* 113, 13 December 1589; *filza* 115, 25, 26 July 1590; *filza* 117, 9, 12 November 1590.

to personal favourites from their own clienteles. The Senate ordered the expulsion of these occupants, and instructed the Procurators to redistribute the houses, later anticipating that there might be about 15 such dwellings.[80]

Despite the intermittent efforts of these commissions, and the vaunted integrity of the magistrates, mild corruption, irregularity and inefficiency remained endemic in the Procuratie for the rest of the century. In 1591, the future Doge Leonardo Donà, a conscientious patrician of almost pedantic integrity, was chosen Procurator of St Mark's De Citra, and occupied this position until his promotion to the supreme dignity in 1605. During his tenure of office, he kept a diary recording the activities of himself and his colleagues. This showed how little impression the board of 1588–90 had in fact made on the major financial problems. The accounts recording the dispensation of alms at the discretion of the Procurators revealed debts of 13,000 ducats incurred since 1588; those which recorded the provision of dowries for maidens, debts of 7,000 ducats. To remedy this, Donà suggested that the Procurators should only distribute alms when the moneys earmarked for the purpose had actually come in—presumably, the 13,000 and 7,000 ducats had been borrowed from other funds, and never returned. Nor should they make any distributions at Christmas 1591. On this occasion, and in the next few years, Donà resisted the practice (officially condemned in 1580) whereby the Procurators dispensed alms individually at the rate of about 50 ducats a time without having to consult or account to their colleagues. In 1598, even he relented a little—

> for the sake of peace, I said I would agree that at Christmas and Easter each Procurator should be allowed to make his own dispensations to his paupers, to the sum of twenty ducats and no more.

Donà was most forthright in his attempt to suppress altogether the practice of distributing alms over the counter. Instead, the money should be taken into the parishes, and there dispensed from house to house 'to wretched and shamefaced persons', on the advice of the parish priest and in his presence. Clearly, this method would enable them to bestow charity with far greater discrimination and better results. In 1597, he finally carried his point, and with the Procurator-Treasurer Soranzo distributed alms in Dorsoduro; later, with the parish priests and officials of the Procuratia, he dispensed them in the parishes of San Felice, Sant'Angelo, Santa Maria Zobenigo and Santa Maria Formosa. Here Donà was advancing considerably further than the official legislation, which had recognized the more casual method. His

[80] A.S.V., *Senato, Terra, filza* 115, 26 July 1590; *filza* 117, 9 November 1590.

methods resembled those adopted, from 1586 onwards, by the Scuola di San Rocco for the administration of the Dalla Vecchia trust.[80a] In 1598, indeed, Donà recorded that his colleagues seemed ready to agree to dispense alms in future to the hospitals of Santi Giovanni e Paolo, the Incurabili and the Pietà, and to the Fraternity of the Poveri Vergognosi. They would have a decree passed to this effect in the Great Council, and thereby eliminate all casual almsgiving—though he himself doubted their power to keep such a resolution.[81] His scepticism was apparently justified. Nevertheless, if the government's commissions had sometimes done no more than nibble at the problem, one of the Procurators themselves had sincerely attempted to reform the institution from within, and to press in particular for more methodical almsgiving.

The story of these government commissions may well create the impression of excellent but frustrated intentions, of inability to dig beneath the upper crusts of corruption and inefficiency. However, in the face of a severe economic challenge about 1590, which heightened public awareness of the problem of poverty and vagrancy, the Provveditori sopra gli Ospedali achieved one permanent and valuable success —in the erection of a large beggars' hospital which complemented the existing general hospitals, and brought Venice close to the total elimination of all authorized begging, even by 'impotent' persons, in its streets and churches.

From the late 1580's, the Venetian Republic, with much of the Mediterranean, faced a series of acute famines as severe as any in the sixteenth century.[82] For Venice, their immediate causes were foul weather, and inability to import grain in sufficient quantities to compensate for the destruction of home harvests. The governors of Padua had complained of poor harvests in 1585 and 1586,[83] and those of Bergamo said in 1591 that dearths had been severe over the past five years.[84] In 1587, one-third of Friuli was reported to be lying under

---

[80a] See above, pp. 182–3.

[81] For the above, see Mario Brunetti, 'Il diario di Leonardo Donà, Procuratore di San Marco de Citra (1591–1605)', *Archivio Veneto*, 5th series, XXI (1937), pp. 101–23; see also Federico Seneca, *Il Doge Leonardo Donà: la sua vita e la sua preparazione politica prima del Dogado* (Padua, 1959), pp. 196–205.

[82] For this question in general, see Fernand Braudel, *La Méditerranée et le monde méditerranéen à l'époque de Philippe II* (second edition, 2 vols., Paris, 1966), I, pp. 538 f.

[83] A.S.V., *Collegio, Relazioni, busta* 43, report of Marc'Antonio Memmo, 12 November 1587.

[84] *Ibid., busta* 35, report of Cattarino Zeno, 14 June 1591.

flood-water, a situation which caused extensive peasant emigration to Germany and elsewhere.[85] But the sharpest crisis came in 1590, through the alternation of rain and river-flooding with periods of drought occurring at the most inopportune times of year. In August 1590, for example, reports reached Venice from Treviso that not enough food remained for three months of the year in the province, through the failure of rye and bean crops which provided the staple diet of local peasants. The danger of drought was especially severe—the *biave menute* which ought normally to supplement the 'greater' crops were likely also to fail,

> because in some places it has never rained, and in others the rain has come so late that there will be little or no harvest of millet and sorghum.[86]

Likewise, in the fertile Padovano, which bore the heaviest responsibility for supplying the Venetians, the governors found that

> the many and continuous rains which have fallen throughout autumn, winter, and even spring have caused rivers to break their banks in important places, so that a large part of the abundant grain which this most fertile countryside used to produce has been lost, and to this a poisonous and evil miasma has been added, and has so ruined the countryside that little grain has been harvested, and this has been of wretchedly poor quality.[87]

From further west, the governors of Crema told the Senate how, in June or early July 1590, they had summoned the Consuls of thirty villages damaged by violent storms, and heard that, where they would normally have harvested 35,000 *some* of grain, now they could expect to reap barely 4,000—to say nothing of the loss of vines, flax and hay.[88]

In the harvest year which began in 1590, Venice drew to itself a total of only 342,000 *staia* of grain—of which 76,000, or about 22 per cent, were imported from outside the territories of the Venetian Republic. In 1586–7, 1589, and 1591–3, Venice attracted over half a million *staia*. The optimum ration of grain per head per annum was reckoned, in the second half of the sixteenth century, at about 4 *staia*, the minimum necessary to support life at 3 *staia*.[89] With a population estimated in 1586 at just below 150,000, Venice fell in 1590 hopelessly short of these requirements. The whole Mediterranean was in grave difficulties:

[85] A.S.V., *Senato, Terra, filza* 104, 31 December 1587.
[86] A.S.V., *Senato, Terra, filza* 115, 18 August 1590. For similar reports of alternating drought and rain, see *ibid.*, *filza* 116, 15 September 1590, reports from Bassano, Asolo, Uderzo and Cittadella.
[87] A.S.V., *Senato, Terra, filza* 115, 4 August 1590.
[88] *Ibid.*
[89] Aymard, *Venise et le commerce du blé*, pp. 17, 20, 112–13, 117.

behind the foul weather lay a dangerous situation in which food supplies threatened to run out, in some areas because of an over-abundant
population, in others because of rural depopulation, the expansion of
pasturage, the disproportionate growth of such towns as Naples and
Palermo.[90] The increase of the people in the Venetian Republic had at
least been checked or slowed by the epidemics of 1570–80, and plague
had broken out in Milan, Mantua and Genoa as well as in Venice.[91]
But Venice was no island entire of itself, and the foul weather, destroying local harvests, caused it to feel with rare directness the dearth and
distress of the Mediterranean as a whole. Foreign governments,
Roman, Neapolitan and Turkish, had in the past shown ominous signs
of establishing tighter controls on exports. The Venetians had ceased
to expect supplies from Egypt or Syria, and had fallen back increasingly
on grain from the Balkans after the middle of the century.[92] They
certainly realized the possibility of importing grain from central, and
(more adventurously) from northern, Europe via Danzig:[93] but they

[90] For evidence of increasing population in areas within the scope of the Mediterranean grain-market on which Venice intermittently or continuously depended, see,
for example, O. L. Barkan, 'Essai sur les données statistiques des registres de recensement dans l'Empire Ottoman aux XVe et XVIe siècles', *Journal of the Economic and
Social History of the Orient*, I (1958), pp. 26–7, 29–31. This shows an increase in the
population of 12 important towns in the Ottoman Empire, and an increase in the
population of the province of Anatolia between the periods 1520–35 and 1570–80.
Giuseppe Coniglio, *Il Viceregno di Napoli nel secolo XVII* (Rome, 1955), pp. 23–4,
suggests an increase of about 14 per cent in the population of the Viceroyalty of
Naples between 1561 and 1601. H. G. Koenigsberger, *The government of Sicily under
Philip II of Spain* (London, 1951), believes in an increase of 4·4 per cent between 1548
and 1599, a very modest increase; though Coniglio, *Il Viceregno di Napoli*, produces
figures for 1548 and 1607 which suggest an increase of nearly 20 per cent (see pp. 25–
26). On the other hand, complaints of depopulation and desertion of the land are
just as numerous: see Koenigsberger, pp. 76–9, and Coniglio, pp. 27–9. On depopulation in various regions of the Papal States in the late sixteenth century, see Jean
Delumeau, *Vie économique et sociale de Rome dans la seconde moitié du XVIe
siècle* (Paris, 1957–9), II, pp. 528 f., 540, 565. Somewhat earlier, in 1573, the retiring
Venetian Bailo at Constantinople, Marc'Antonio Barbaro, had argued that Ottoman
territories were suffering from serious depopulation: in Alberi, *Relazioni degli
ambasciatori*, III/i (Florence, 1840), pp. 313–14.

[91] In general, see K. J. Beloch, *Bevölkerungsgeschichte Italiens*, I (Berlin–Leipzig,
1937), p. 68; also Paolo Morigia, *Historia delle antichità di Milano* (Venice, 1592),
pp. 126–7, and Giuseppe Felloni, 'Per la storia della popolazione di Genova nei secoli
XVI e XVII', *Archivio Storico Italiano*, CX (1952), pp. 236–8. However, according to
Felloni, the population of Genoa rose again quite rapidly from about 48,000 inhabitants in 1581 to 62,000 in 1597 and 68,000 in 1608.

[92] For Rome, see Delumeau, *Vie économique et sociale de Rome*, II, pp. 591–2;
Coniglio, *Il Viceregno di Napoli*, pp. 43, 77; for Turkey, see Aymard, *Venise et le
commerce du blé*, pp. 46–50.

[93] See Mario Brunetti, 'Tre ambasciate annonarie veneziane', *Archivio Veneto*, 5th
series, LVIII (1956), pp. 110–15; A.S.V., *Senato, Terra*, reg. 1590, f. 134, 3 November
1590; reg. 1591, f. 4v., 7 March 1591; *Senato (Secreta), Dispacci Germania*, filza 17,
ff. 154–6, 224v., 225, 278; filza 18, ff. 52–3, 92r.–v., 196v., 229, 230r.–v., 239.

were much slower than the Tuscans to secure large supplies of northern grain.[94] Turkey unexpectedly came to the rescue in 1590, but nothing could ultimately prevent the price of wheat from rocketing to unprecedented levels.

This situation produced, on a still vaster scale, the disorder and panic which had formerly in the 1520's inspired the Venetian poor law and the philanthropy of some of the new orders and voluntary religious societies. The Venetian Francesco Da Molin described how peasants starved in the Romagna and Bolognese as well as in the subject territories of the Republic.[95] Grain had been commissioned on a large scale from Sicily, but Sicilian officials excused themselves, protesting that they had not enough for their own requirements. The Turks, fortunately, did not break faith. Grain prices touched 40 lire the *staio* in February 1591 (over the period 1589–98, the average price, if averages have any meaning at all, was about 24 lire).[96] Molin wrote that

> It seemed that an angel brandishing a sword of savage hunger was driving a wretched crowd of poor people to wander throughout all Italy.

He described the invasion of Venice by innumerable starving peasants of the Padovano and Trevigiano. Some, in this extremity, were actually poisoned by taking food; but others recovered through the Christian charity of certain Venetian citizens. The invaders lived in the squares and camped out under archways; Molin, perhaps referring to the danger of typhus, spoke of the 'filthy odour and infected air' about them.

The Venetian government acted vigorously enough on familiar lines. It issued edicts for the import of grain from the mainland to Venice, orders to frustrate the manoeuvres of speculators and would-be exporters; it assigned money to most of the mainland cities to enable them to purchase supplies wherever these could be obtained; it placed supplies of millet and other cheap crops in the granaries and bakeries, encouraging projectors to experiment with substitute foodstuffs and introduce rice into the loaf.[97] Most surprisingly, however, it discovered that, by

---

[94] See Aymard, *Venise et le commerce du blé*, pp. 156 f.—the first large northerly grain fleet reached Venice only in March 1594. For a similar conclusion, see Fernand Braudel and Ruggiero Romano, *Navires et marchandises à l'entrée du Port de Livourne (1547–1611)* (Paris, 1951), pp. 50 f.

[95] Molin, *Compendio*, B.M.V., MSS. Italiani, Cl. VII, DLIII (8812), pp. 162–4.

[96] Aymard, *Venise et le commerce du blé*, pp. 109, 120–1.

[97] See especially A.S.V., *Senato, Terra*, reg. 1590, ff. 86v.–87, 91v., 23, 31 August 1590; reg. 1591, ff. 7, 41v.–42, 45v.–48, 54v., 75v.–76, 9 March, 8, 16 June, 7 July, 10 September 1591; for grants of subsidies to mainland cities, see the numerous entries in *filze* 115–22; for the use of substitute breadstuffs, see reg. 1591, ff. 1v.–2, 3 March 1591, and reg. 1593, f. 90, 25 September 1593.

the firm application of stringent rules, it could supply itself with most of its victuals from inside its own dominions. Some provinces on the mainland would naturally depend on importing across the nearest border—but Venice itself could achieve this kind of autarky. In the regions closest to Venice, an expanding population had demanded the fuller use of land, the reclamation of marsh and the clearing of forest. Although epidemics had in certain places caused population growth to slacken and had lightened the burden on resources over the decade 1570–80, it is probable that, given the erratic behaviour of food prices and the buoyancy they showed even after the plague, there was no swift retreat from the recently reclaimed lands. The Venetians certainly thought themselves nearer to autarky. In 1591, the Senate officially announced that

Experience has shown that in our state quantities of grain and other foodstuffs can be collected, which are little less than sufficient to supply the need—since in this present year of great and almost unprecedented dearth the state has in fact supplied its needs with only a small quantity of corn and no other kind of *biave grosse* from foreign countries, from which we have always been accustomed to import great quantities. Hence, when thorough measures are taken to prevent the export of corn and other crops, and when our laws are properly enforced concerning the transport of grain at the proper time to our city (as is also the rule in other cities of our state), and when—in accordance with the decrees—a great deposit of corn and millet has been formed after the custom of our forbears, not to be touched except in case of urgent need, we shall be able to rest assured that supplies will at no time fail, that we shall not have to apply to foreign countries, and that the poor will also be relieved of the high and exorbitant prices at which they have been forced to purchase grain, especially in this present year. . . .[98]

This was not mere reassuring propaganda. Statistical evidence recently collected by M. Maurice Aymard appears to confirm the Senate's claims. In 1591, grains from outside Venetian territories accounted for only 19 per cent of all grain reaching Venice—the lowest proportion recorded at any time between 1573 and 1594. Even in 1566 and 1567, when harvests were good, such imports had accounted for as much as 69 per cent and 63 per cent of all grain reaching Venice. The proportion of imported grains rose from 19 per cent in 1591 to 45 per cent in 1592 and 41 per cent in 1593, but fell again to 24 per cent in 1594. In 1590, the proportion had been as low as 22 per cent,[99] but this reflected inability to obtain cereals from abroad rather than a capacity for doing without them.

[98] A.S.V., *Senato, Terra*, reg. 1591, ff. 45v.–48, 16 June 1591.
[99] Aymard, *Venise et le commerce du blé*, pp. 112–13, 117.

2A

The desperate circumstances of 1590 did not in fact recur during the years which followed, though the general level of wheat prices remained consistently high throughout the decade. Some of the meaning of this can be grasped, however faintly, by comparing the movement of these prices with the only money wages—those of builders working on the property of the Scuola di San Rocco—about which there is precise information. Between 1567–76 and 1589–98, average grain prices seem to have risen by about 90 per cent. Between 1566–74 and 1591–1600, the wages of master masons and carpenters rose by about 45 per cent, from 34 to 49 soldi a day; those of journeymen or *lavoranti* by some 60 per cent, from 22 to 35 soldi a day. Since the *lavorante* was less far above subsistence-level, with his modest wages, a higher proportional increase was probably necessary to keep him alive during the 1590's. It is probable that in the first few years after the plague, approximately from 1577 to 1585, increases in the money wages of builders had kept pace with rising prices—especially those of fully-fledged masters, who could defend themselves better against being diluted by willing supplies of immigrant labour from the provinces. The availability of immigrants held down the journeyman's wage in the building trades, and possibly in others also, even after the plague. The government was clearly, over these years, fixing the wages it paid to Arsenal workers and keeping them down much more arbitrarily than private employers could ever do. In any case, the soaring prices of the 1590's promised to destroy any gains made by the workers of Venice as a result of the labour shortages created by the plague. These famines could scarcely fail to intensify the problem of poverty and begging. Food prices were certainly outstripping builders' wages; though of course there is no reason to suppose that the cost of industrial products was comparably increasing.[100]

At the end of the 1580's, the government became increasingly concerned with the renewed problem of acute poverty. In December 1588, the Senate declared that

> Everywhere there are vast numbers of paupers who go through the city begging and interrupting the prayers and offices in the churches.

The Provveditori alla Sanità were overworked, and unable to cope with this problem without assistance. The Senate therefore instructed the hospital commissioners to join and confer with them, and to decide how to deal with mendicity.[101] To a large extent, their recommendations merely called for a re-enforcement of the poor laws on established

[100] See Brian Pullan, 'Wage-earners and the Venetian economy, 1550–1630', *Economic History Review*, XVI (1964); Aymard, *Venise et le commerce du blé*, p. 109.   [101] A.S.V., *Senato, Terra, filza* 109, 17 December 1588.

lines, with certain minor extensions. Reporting in January 1590, when famine was intensifying the problem, the Provveditori alla Sanità, Leonardo Loredan and Marco Capello, recommended that as usual a distinction should be made between Venetians and 'outsiders'. As usual, the term 'outsider' was applied to subjects of the Venetian state who were not natives or residents of Venice, as well as to subjects of 'alien jurisdictions'. For the time being, these outsiders should merely be sent home, and Venetian subjects be 'commended' (as in 1529) to the governors of their localities. The Venetian poor themselves, on the other hand, were duly classified as

> either sick persons, or boys and girls, or women with numerous children, or aged, crippled and incapable, or, finally, persons who have fallen from some kind of high social rank (*persone decadute da qualche condittione civile*).

The Provveditori recommended, without much originality, that the sick should be taken to hospital and cured, whilst the old and crippled should be cared for by their parishes and by such institutions as the Procuratie, the Scuole and the richer monasteries. Small children must be taken to the Pietà and other hospitals. As before, the older children of beggars should be sent to serve an apprenticeship at sea, though the Provveditori anticipated that, as the merchant marine had recently contracted in size,[101a] it might be difficult to dispose of them by this means. At their suggestion, heavy and light galleys, and also merchant galleys, were drawn into the system. The Senate provided that each galley should accept four beggar children, who were to serve the mate and *maestranze*—a term which might possibly refer to the ship's carpenters and caulkers who served with the fleet. These officers and craftsmen were bound to accept them unless they had children of their own with them whom they were training in seamanship and discipline. Hitherto, only ships with a capacity of over 400 *staia* had been obliged to accept beggar children for training as apprentices or cabin-boys (*mozzi*); the law was now extended to include smaller craft with a capacity of 350–400 *staia*. The rules which required the masters of merchant vessels and the pursers (*scrivani*) of galleys to present children at the Ufficio della Sanità at the end of the voyage remained essentially unaltered.[102]

[101a] On this, cf. Ruggiero Romano 'La marine marchande vénitienne au XVIe siècle', in *Les sources de l'histoire maritime en Europe, du Moyen Âge au XVIIIe siècle: Actes du Quatrième Colloque International d'Histoire Maritime*, ed. Michel Mollat (Paris, 1962).

[102] A.S.V., *Senato, Terra, filza* 114, 15 March 1590. For other refinements of the rules on taking cabin-boys, see A.S.V., *Provveditori alla Sanità, Capitolare II*, ff. 62v.-63v., 8 May 1593.

The Senate would probably have liked to adopt the recommendation about the expulsion of foreign beggars—the Provveditori had seen the spectacle they presented as deeply piteous, but had also declared that

> the number of vagabonds and foreign beggars has increased, and this city has become almost the sole receptacle for all these wretches, who are either useless or supremely idle.

The object was always 'to provide for the needs and to curb the insolence of the beggars'. However, on 7 June 1591, perhaps a fortnight before the normal harvest-time, the Senate had to make 1,000 ducats over to the Provveditori alla Sanità for distribution to the peasants starving in the streets of Venice. Nor did the harvest of 1591 settle the matter: a further 600 ducats went to support peasant immigrants on 17 August, and on 28 December 1591 the Provveditori received a further grant of 100 ducats to place some of the immigrants in hospital —perhaps intended as a seasonal gesture of good will.[103] To eschew all responsibility for the unhappy immigrants was scarcely possible. Some phrases in the report of the Provveditori alla Sanità in March 1590 indicate that they were already thinking in terms of a new hospital, and felt that this hospital ought to do something for foreigners, rather than merely shelter behind the principle that each locality ought to care for its own poor. Whatever happened, Venice would always be a transit-station 'for poor pilgrims, soldiers and other foreigners'. She ought not to lag behind other cities in showing 'an exemplary charity towards foreigners'. It seemed that previous boards of Provveditori alla Sanità and Provveditori sopra gli Ospedali (perhaps as a result of the conferences enjoined on them in 1588) had recommended the erection of a new hospital—but nothing had come of it.

As it happened, there was a new wave of hospital foundations in Italy in the last quarter of the sixteenth century. These hospitals of the Mendicanti formed a standardized, exportable type of institution, which in this somewhat resembled the Incurabili of earlier days. How, exactly, the institutions were disseminated must remain uncertain: but the Venetians, as appears from the remarks quoted above, always retained a certain sense of competing with other towns, and were anxious not to let their amenities seem inadequate. Borromeo had, in 1565, suggested the establishment of beggars' hospitals,[104] and Brescia, within his province, had acquired such a hospital in the aftermath of plague in 1577.[105] Crema also built one at some time between 1584 and

103 A.S.V., *Senato, Terra*, reg. 1591, ff. 38v., 66v., 131r.–v.

104 *Acta Ecclesiae Mediolanensis*, f. 21v.

105 A.S.V., *Sindici Inquisitori in Terra Ferma*, busta 64, f. 61; *Senato, Terra, filza* 232, 19 February 1618 Venetian style.

1633,[106] whilst Michele Priuli, Bishop of Vicenza, attached a beggars' hospital to the church of San Valentino there in 1584.[107] The city of Verona also acted in 1602–4, likewise on some prompting from the Bishop, Agostino Valier: the retiring governor in 1604 described the Mendicanti as a symptom of the city's 'zealous respect for divine worship', adding that the citizens had 'followed the papers drawn up by the most illustrious and reverend Cardinal and by Monsignor his most reverend Coadjutor'.[108] Abroad, the Senate knew that Turin had such a hospital by 1584.[109] Under the auspices of Gregory XIII and Sixtus V, the Romans experimented with a beggars' hospital, though not with any permanent success.[110] The immediate model for the Venetians was the hospital at Bologna—to judge by a somewhat later report of the combined commissioners, which declared in March 1594 that the only final solution to the question of beggars was 'to shut them up in a hospital, as many Italian cities have done, especially Bologna'.[111]

The magistrates discovered the solution in converting an old-established and decayed hospital to new uses which corresponded with contemporary demands. The internationally circulated treatise of Vives on poor relief,[112] and later the Tridentine decree of 1563, had both recommended such conversions. In 1591, the Senate ordered the hospital commissioners to undertake a general inquiry in execution of the powers granted them in 1561 and 1563.[113] Shortly afterwards, they acceded to a series of requests from the then board of Provveditori, who bitterly complained that their work had been hindered by obstructions and cross-appeals, and that they had no lawyers—*avvocati* or *defensori*—to present their case in the lawsuits in which they were constantly getting involved. To expedite procedure, they asked that another Senate commission, the Collegio dei Dieci Savii Ordinarii dell'Eccellentissimo Senato, should act as court of appeal, but that litigants must give notice of appeal from the sentences of the hospital

[106] See A.S.V., *Collegio, Relazioni, busta* 40—the report of Zaccaria Balbi, of 24 April 1633, mentions a Hospital of the Mendicanti; there is no mention of this in the earlier report of Pietro Zane, 28 May 1584, although this deals with the hospitals of the city.

[107] Ughelli, *Italia sacra*, V, col. 1,067.

[108] A.S.V., *Senato, Terra, filza* 162, 25 May 1602; *Collegio, Relazioni, busta* 50, 1 April 1604, report of Daniele Dolfin.

[109] A.S.V., *Senato, Terra, filza* 90, 18 April 1584—whereby the Senate approved an offer of 50 ducats made by its Ambassador to the Hospital of the Mendicanti in Turin.

[110] Delumeau, *Vie économique et sociale de Rome*, I, pp. 412 f.

[111] A.S.V., *Senato, Terra, filza* 131, 26 May 1594.

[112] Vives, *Il modo del sovvenire a poveri*, ff. 51v.–52.

[113] A.S.V., *Senato, Terra, reg.* 1591, ff. 143v.–144, 144v.–145, 2, 30 January 1591 Venetian style.

commissioners within eight days and bring their suit to a conclusion within two months. They also asked for Advocates Fiscal (who normally represented government departments) to be briefed to defend the rights of hospitals wherever possible, and for guarantees of immediate access to any relevant documents they might demand to see. The Senate granted them all these requests.[114] The new procedure came too late to prevent the German shoemakers from using delaying tactics for a period of four years. But the hospital commissioners were able within a year or two to draw public attention to abuses in the hospital of San Lazzaro, on a lagoon island.

This, as its name suggested, was a leprosary. Its origins were obscure, and it had been founded at some remote date in the past. The presumption, as it was in the lagoon and therefore situated inside the Dogado, was that a past Doge had been its founder. He must have either been its patron, or have made a gift of the hospital to the lepers. The island was a fair size, with a 'very suitable' church and excellent houses for the chaplain, prior and 'patrons'. But the dwellings reserved for the lepers themselves had fallen into decay, and there was no-one to occupy them. Some regular clergy, perhaps devoted to the care of lepers, had once lived on the island, and the lepers and clergy between them had elected a Prior, who was responsible for governing the hospital and for disposing of its revenues, the fruit of Christian bequests, which now amounted to about 1,000 ducats a year. Formerly, the Patriarch or 'Bishop of Castello' had confirmed the election of the Prior, and the Prior had accounted to him annually for his administration. However, three noblemen of the city, whose present descendants were Ottaviano di Michele Pisani, Francesco di Daniele Vitturi and Pietro di Giovanni Battista Bembo, had exceeded their authority as procurators. The normal duties of procurators merely entailed defending the temporal interests of hospitals or monasteries, but these patricians had asserted a bogus claim to choose the Prior and to instal only those few paupers that seemed good to them, whether or not they suffered from leprosy. They had reduced the community of religious to a single chaplain, and eventually decided to dispense with the Prior altogether. These patricians now claimed that their ancestors had built the hospital, and that it was in their gift: but, when challenged, they were unable to support their claims except by asserting 'ancient possession'. The procurators simply wasted the revenues on 'superfluous expenditure' and on the salary of a nominal Prior who did not even live on the island. The hospital commissioners then appealed to the Senate to take action, and to deal with the case itself, without delegating it to any other

[114] A.S.V., Senato, Terra, filza 122, 30 January 1591 Venetian style.

magistracy.[115] This the Senate agreed to do; and eventually, after eighteen months, it solemnly declared that Vitturi, Pisani and Bembo were not entitled to claim any rights whatever over the Hospital of San Lazzaro. In May 1594 it sternly required them to hand over to the hospital commissioners all the books, deeds, other documents and moneys belonging to the hospital.[116]

The question now arose of what to do with the premises and revenues of San Lazzaro, and the two government commissions felt little doubt about the answer. In March 1594, they couched their joint recommendations in terminology appropriate to the post-Tridentine era. Their phrases, in fact, resembled those of the Bull *Quamvis infirma*, in which Sixtus V had recently ordered the establishment of a beggars' hospital in Rome.[117] Begging constituted, not only an offence against public order, but an offence to God: it was a religious, as well as a secular problem. They fulminated against

> the immense gravity of the sins committed by night in public streets and other public places by certain beggars; the poverty of many others, which eventually brings them to die on the streets like dumb brutes in the sight of everyone and without the sacraments of Holy Church; and their mis-behaviour, especially in churches, which disturbs the prayers of the devout to the grave scandal of everyone.

The soul of the beggar was at stake, as well as public and ecclesiastical decency. The only possible measure was to lock beggars up in a hospital. The commissioners said that they were already receiving substantial sums every week from monks and friars in the city for the support of the poor—perhaps in Venice, as in Verona and Bergamo,[118] monasteries had been discouraged from conducting some of their own haphazard dispensations of alms, and invited to channel them through expert hands. Surely this, together with the charity of the Procurators of St Mark's and of the Venetians in general, could be used to supplement the revenues of San Lazzaro (now optimistically reckoned at about 1,500 ducats a year). San Lazzaro could be transformed into a beggars' hospital, keeping one or two places for the rare surviving lepers. No-one should be discouraged by the enormous numbers of the poor beggars, since there were various well-tried methods of reducing them to a manageable level. One counter-proposal came, in the course of the debate, from the Cavalier Pietro Duodo, a member of the

[115] A.S.V., *Senato, Terra, filza* 124, 17 October 1592.
[116] A.S.V., *Senato, Terra,* reg. 1594, f. 11v., 15 March 1594; *filza* 131, 26 May 1594.
[117] Sixtus V, 'Quamvis infirma', 11 May 1587, B.R., VIII, pp. 847–53; Delumeau, *Vie économique et sociale de Rome,* I, pp. 404–5.
[118] See above, pp. 277, 312–13.

Collegio and a Savio di Terra Ferma: this was merely that the revenues be applied to providing training in the navy, merchant marine or Arsenal trades for foundling-children who had emerged from the hospital of the Pietà, and who, because of inadequate after-care, were drifting into vagabondage. The present system of drafting children on shipboard only catered for those who were already vagabonds. But the Senate, on 26 May 1594, resolved without opposition that

> the balance of the revenues of the hospital of San Lazzaro shall, after first providing for the needs and benefit of poor lepers, be applied to the poor beggars of this city.

The two government commissions were placed in charge of the restoration of the hospital on its island.[119]

Progress at first was slow. The commissioners had simply envisaged restoring the buildings on the island, and retaining the hospital there. But it transpired that the hospital would depend for support to a great extent on voluntary contributions from persons who actually visited the site: perhaps to avail themselves of indulgences granted to those who visited the church and gave alms there. By December 1595, the number of inmates had, however, increased to 42. Revenues were now estimated at 1,200 ducats per annum, and the governors had spent over 700 ducats that year on equipping the hospital and clothing the poor. Without timely help, further expansion would be impossible, and the need could not be met.[120] Already, a decree of the Great Council had tentatively authorized negotiations to find a site for the hospital in Venice itself—particularly on the grounds that this would inevitably bring more alms.[121] A commission of Delegates in charge of the building of the new hospital had been appointed, and in 1596 this consisted of six noblemen, the first four being Senators—Nicolò Querini, Domenico Contarini, Marco Gradenigo, Alvise Morosini, Francesco Correr and Federico Dandolo. Another nobleman, Girolamo Salamon, had made a bequest to the new hospital. However, the proposal to re-establish the hospital in Venice itself encountered tough opposition, particularly from two hospital commissioners, the Procurator Federico Contarini and Pietro Basadonna. They held that the Senate and Great Council had been misled by the Delegates into sanctioning an over-ambitious building project for which there was no real need. The best way to proceed was rigorously to apply all the provisions of the poor law, so as to reduce the crowd of beggars to those aged persons, widows

[119] A.S.V., *Senato, Terra, filza* 131, 26 May 1594.
[120] A.S.V., *Senato, Terra, filza* 138, 9 December 1595.
[121] A.S.V., *Maggior Consiglio, Deliberazioni, Liber Surianus*, f. 101r.–v., 27 September 1595.

and children of both sexes who could only be dealt with by a hospital, and to eliminate those who could earn a living without begging. There was no need for the hospital itself, or so they implied, to act as a work-house: the authorities should

> expel the foreigners, set the healthy to work, put disobedient vagabonds on the galleys at half pay, send the children to serve as cabin-boys on the roundships and other vessels, and finally deal with the poor in the parishes in the most skilful manner possible.

Once this had been done, the Venetians would only need to finance a comparatively modest institution. Describing the present project as a 'confused and ill-considered undertaking', Contarini and Basadonna passed on to criticizing the choice of site. It was expensive, there were better sites available, it was off the main streets and screened from the public by the great monastery and church of Santi Giovanni e Paolo (the Doges' mausoleum). Moreover, it was too near the long-established hospital of Santi Giovanni e Paolo, the Derelitti, the product of the earlier famines of 1527–9. Presumably Contarini and Basadonna meant that these popular rivals would be competing for a share in the available funds of alms. They thought it all too likely that the Delegates would squander on the building funds that ought to go directly to the support of the poor.

On this point, the Provveditori alla Sanità diverged from their colleagues. They pointed out that the Delegates did not propose to use the revenues of San Lazzaro or the bequest of Salamon to finance the building. Instead, they wished to raise a loan of 6,000 ducats at 5–6 per cent, and to pledge, not the hospital's property, but their own as security. The hospital's treasurer would be responsible for paying off the interest, and perhaps part of the capital, in instalments of up to 500 ducats a year. These payments would not be made out of the revenues of San Lazzaro, but out of the earnings of the paupers, and out of any donations that might be made with no strings attached. The first buildings, like those of Santi Giovanni e Paolo and the Incurabili, should be of wood: halls of stone would only come later.

Despite these arguments, the suspicion excited by Contarini and Basadonna delayed the project, which failed four times to pass the Senate between 29 August and 1 September 1597.[122] About fifteen months later, it appeared that some of the jealously guarded revenues of San Lazzaro were in fact going to support a house in Venice itself, at San Lorenzo in Castello, for beggar girls: but they were receiving too gentle treatment, as 'zitelle' rather than 'mendicante', and this was making no impression on the problem of begging. The Senate un-

[122] A.S.V., *Senato, Terra, filza* 144, 1 September 1597.

sympathetically ordered this establishment to be disbanded, and its inmates to be sent, where appropriate, to the Zitelle (a house of Jesuit foundation for the care of poor girls), but otherwise to be distributed among the hospitals 'so that they do not go to the bad'.[123]

In spite of persistent differences of opinion about the site, the governors of the hospital eventually, in August 1600, succeeded in purchasing the land coveted at least since 1596. The vendors were the magistracy of the Collegio delle Acque, responsible for the waters of the Venetian lagoon. The governors believed that the nearness of Santi Giovanni e Paolo would be a positive advantage, and pointed out that the hospital was on the way to both San Marco and Rialto, where there were always crowds of people. The site covered 2,294 square yards (*passa quadri*), and the governors offered six ducats per square yard, making a total of some 13,800 ducats. Of this, they proposed to pay 6,000 in advance, and the rest in instalments of 500 ducats a year. Their petition to the Collegio alle Acque gave no hint as to whence the money was coming for the purchase, but it sounded as though the proposals made in 1596 by the Delegates would in fact be carried through.[124] Generous private charity may also have helped. Within the next few years, a Brescian mercer, Bortolomio Bontempelli (known, from his shop-sign, as Bortolomio dal Calice), gave the sum of 36,000 ducats to building permanent premises of stone. On his death, he bequeathed 100,000 ducats to the hospital, which his brother invested on its behalf in the Mint at 4 per cent, in 1616.[125]

The Senate at once approved the purchase of land at Santi Giovanni e Paolo,[126] and the hospital began operations in earnest. The statutes published in 1619 give some indication of the principles on which it operated.[127] It worked under the supervision of a governing body of nobles, citizens and merchants. In December 1600, this board consisted of 20 noblemen and 20 citizens and merchants. At any given time, half of these were on active duty, whilst half formed a reserve. By way of respecting the original statutes of San Lazzaro, the governors were bound to give priority to lepers (should any be found) and to sufferers from skin diseases (*rogna*—a term which may have excluded syphilis). This apart, the hospital was designed for those who had no fixed residence and could not earn a living,

[123] A.S.V., *Senato, Terra, filza* 148, 26 November 1598.
[124] Bembo, *Istituzioni di beneficenza in Venezia*, pp. 222–3.
[125] See *Capitoli della veneranda congregatione dell'hospitale di Santo Lazaro et Mendicanti della Città di Venetia* (Venice, 1619), pp. 7–8.
[126] A.S.V., *Senato, Terra, filza* 155, 9 August 1600.
[127] See the *Capitoli* cited above, especially pp. 48 f. on the type of poor to be admitted, and on the suppression of begging; pp. 36–8 on conditions of work.

either because of their tender age, or because they know no trade, or because of personal incapacity, or on account of old age and decrepitude.

The hospital was designed to complete a system within which hospitals and other houses specialized in accommodating particular categories of poor. Santi Giovanni e Paolo and the Incurabili dealt with disease and with orphans; the Pietà specifically with foundlings rather than orphans in general; the Poveri Vergognosi with the house poor; the houses of the Zitelle and Soccorso with children threatened with prostitution and women who had actually engaged in it. The object of the Mendicanti was to eliminate virtually all begging: earlier in the century, the Provveditori alla Sanità had always envisaged the presence of a certain number of licensed beggars, not accommodated in any hospital.[128] At any given time, six of the forty governors of the Mendicanti would be responsible for suppressing all begging in the city and its churches, with the aid of members of the hospital staff. If necessary, they could apply for support to the Provveditori alla Sanità. Only the blind were allowed to continue begging: they must be natives of Venice, and might beg only at the doors of churches—not venture in and interrupt the services. Those who merely begged out of roguery or 'furfantaria' should be placed at half pay on board galleys or merchant vessels, if they had no fixed domicile. Outsiders—in the sense of non-Venetians— were liable to expulsion. In the immediate past, as in March 1590, suggestions had sometimes been made that the Venetians should show charity towards foreigners as well as natives, and indeed in 1595 the hospital of Santi Giovanni e Paolo had accommodated several hundred wounded and wretched soldiers of the Papal States trudging back from the recent wars in Hungary. Even then, however, the Provveditori alla Sanità had hastened, whilst giving alms, to speed them on their way.[129] By the early seventeenth century, the conservative principle was uppermost: the Mendicanti was strictly for Venetians, and each locality must look after its own poor.

The hospital would do its best to employ the women and children entrusted to its care, and to teach them to work. The women were trained in spinning, the girls also in making 'peroli et cordele'. The proceeds of their work would be sold to support the hospital. A majority of women and children should be put to work outside, but the governors and staff must take care not to apprentice or dispose of anyone who could usefully serve the hospital itself. Prospective employers were not to choose employees themselves: let the matron select them to their requirements. Should a former inmate break off his contract with

128 See above, p. 298.
129 A.S.V., *Senato, Terra*, reg. 1595, ff. 166–7, 19 December 1595.

an employer found for him by the hospital, the governing congregation must inquire into the circumstances and decide whether to receive the pauper back into the hospital. Should it do so, it would protect his interests, by recovering any property he had left behind and any wages due to him. Girls who had been 'contaminated or violated' must not be received back, so that 'fear of punishment shall be an effective restraint upon them, and they shall always live with due propriety'. All girls who had been found work would be visited twice a year, to ensure that they were well treated and that their virtue was not endangered. An important function of the hospital was, therefore, to act as a kind of paternalistic employment agency, carefully keeping track of all whom it had benefited. It found its women and children employment as apprentices or in domestic service. It is possible that employment in the city was at last being regarded as preferable to the rigours of service at sea. In their petition of 1600 to the Collegio alle Acque, the governors of the Mendicanti had promised, not only to improve the morals of the beggars generally, but also to

> prevent the infidels from continuing to steal and kidnap many boys and children.[130]

This was a hazard of the mariner's life of which the Provveditori alla Sanità had shown a certain uneasy awareness.[131]

The hospital worked on a fairly large scale on these principles. At the end of 1601, the governors reported that they had in the course of the year dealt with about 800 paupers, and disposed of more than half of them through apprenticeship or domestic service, through forcible recruitment to the navy, or by returning 'foreigners' with 'passports' to their native places. This left about 370 inmates, old people and small children, lepers and sick persons.[132] In 1605, and 1618, the Mendicanti was again described as having about 400 inmates.[133]

The establishment of the Mendicanti as a going concern marked the last stage in the government's campaign against the acute and abject poverty which threatened public order and public decency. In the second half of the sixteenth century, ecclesiastical and lay authorities had continued to work towards essentially similar ends. The pursuit of these had occasionally provoked conflict over jurisdiction and patronage, but had aroused little or no dispute over policy towards the poor.

[130] Bembo, *Istituzioni di beneficenza*, p. 223.
[131] See above, pp. 307–8.
[132] A.S.V., *Senato, Terra, filza* 163, 22 June 1602.
[133] A.S.V., *Senato, Terra, filza* 175, 11 August 1605; *filza* 230, 4 September 1618.

In the 1560's and the 1590's, economic pressure and food crises had created urgent needs, not only for the efficient enforcement of the poor law, not only for the erection of additional accommodation to extend indoor relief, but also for the full exploitation of existing and old-established facilities. The principles embodied in the Tridentine decrees, from 1547 to 1563, were applied in Venice, though not necessarily enforced by clerical authority—including the radical suggestions of 1563, for the conversion of obsolete foundations to up-to-date uses. The Tridentine decrees were not innovations, so much as symptoms of a general desire to provide more extensive hospital accommodation. Borromeo's influence, and the memory and example of Giberti, probably provoked more independent and vigorous clerical action, which sometimes had the effect of inspiring the civil government to intervene in order to uphold its own jurisdictional claims. In Venice, a lay commission did most of the work.

Commissions of inquiry into the management of hospitals and other charities generally defended the principle that relief ought to go only to the truly poor and worthy: that people's economic and moral titles to alms ought to be carefully scrutinized. Venice had a reasonable share of the endemic abuses in the smaller hospitals against which the canon of Vienne was originally directed; both clergy and laity were sometimes guilty of misappropriating revenue and neglecting hospitality. The mechanism of these commissions was probably not sufficient to uproot corruption, and left too many chances of obstructionism to the recalcitrant: but there were some solid achievements. A decayed leper colony became the basis for a new enterprise which almost totally eliminated begging. A large part of the function of the hospital of the Mendicanti was to provide work. In the late sixteenth century, neither churchmen nor magistrates showed signs of deviating from the earlier principles, stated afresh in pre-Tridentine years, that beggars should be regarded with icy suspicion. Idleness must be eliminated, if necessary through penal measures, but also through education and the provision of opportunities to work. These provided self-discipline and the way to self-support and self-respect; they might incidentally benefit the economy, especially in sectors like the merchant marine where supplies of skilled labour showed signs of flagging. Begging was a religious as well as a secular problem: the beggar, apart from disturbing order in church, was outside the system of parochial supervision, discipline and instruction which could teach him the way to save his soul. Often he died without the sacraments. No evidence suggests that Venetian authorities thought begging desirable, or even tolerable, and none looked upon it with sentimental indulgence.

371

6

EDUCATIONAL CHARITY AND MORAL
REFORM, 1540–1620

The years 1520–40, crucial in the development of Venetian philanthropy, had seen the foundation of the hospitals of the Incurabili and Santi Giovanni e Paolo, and of the Fraternity of the Poveri Vergognosi. These formed the nucleus of an expanding group of charities which aimed at offering the children of the poor a Christian education of some practical value, and at affording them protection against moral corruption in infidel ignorance. Partially at least, these charities were designed to do rescue-work, and to save souls from the special temptations which poverty created, especially by its tendency to drive women into prostitution. Convention portrayed women as helpless creatures in constant need of protection, and therefore especially deserving of charity. Moreover, the figure of the Magdalen, the harlot who earned forgiveness by repentance, shone with especial brilliance before the eyes of religious reformers as a symbol of the power of penitence to earn salvation.[1] Some of these charities ventured beyond the pale of respectability, to approach and reclaim the outcasts of society with a mixture of spiritual and corporal charity. In this they were consciously following the steps of Christ himself by brushing with the fringes of the underworld and ignoring the censures of the Pharisees. Here again, the organization of charity depended on the introduction of certain institutions of a standardized type—often started or revived in Rome itself, and often spread by the energies of the Jesuits, who had placed themselves under the Pope's command. These sixteenth-century charities taught elementary Christian doctrine through a network of Sunday schools, and unceasingly worked to convey to their pupils the value of the sacraments of communion and confession. Towards the end of the century at least, they attempted to conquer the prisons as well as the brothels, to bring to their inmates spiritual consolation and the hope of release. The visitation of prisoners had long been one of the traditional works of mercy commended in the Gospel, but at the end of the sixteenth century a new society began to

[1] Émile Mâle, *L'art réligieux de la fin du XVIe siècle, du XVIIe siècle et du XVIIIe siècle* (2nd edition, Paris, 1951), pp. 65–70, shows how she emerged in the religious art of the seventeenth century as a symbol of effective repentance. Before that time, several nunneries of penitents or Convertite had been dedicated to her.

specialize in this form of charity, and to promote it with method and system.

The Society for the Poveri Vergognosi, founded in 1537, continued to function throughout the century, and to collaborate at intervals with the Provveditori alla Sanità. This fraternity, together with the whole system of parish outdoor relief, helped to undermine begging by making it unnecessary. In April 1570, for example, the Provveditori alla Sanità, in the face of the typhus epidemics which followed the severe famine, attempted to organize medical care for the poor throughout the city, using the pharmacy from which the fraternity dispensed its medicines. It called on the two Colleges of physicians and barber-surgeons to provide free medical aid within the parishes, issuing prescriptions which (countersigned by the parish priests) were then made up at the dispensary of Sant'Antonino. Significantly, the Provveditore Hieronimo Vendramin, deputed by his colleagues to arrange this, went to confer with the governors of the fraternity at the Priory of the Trinità, in the presence of Andrea Lippomano—who was evidently still connected with its affairs.[2]

In its narrowest sense, the term Poveri Vergognosi was used to describe persons of gentle birth, or at least of 'citizen' rank, who had suffered reverses of fortune which plunged them into a poverty doubly painful because they were unused to it, ashamed to beg, and ill-equipped to do manual work. Used in a broader sense, the term could refer to anyone, whatever his social rank, who was ashamed to beg, and who might therefore be in greater need than someone who openly, perhaps obstreperously, demanded alms. Clearly, by the end of the century the Fraternity of the Poveri Vergognosi had extended their activities to include artisans, and were discharging most of the varied functions assigned to Giberti's Compagnie della Carità in Verona. 'The poor families of noblemen, citizens and merchants, who have sunk into poverty because of the misfortunes of the world' still stood high among their priorities in 1595. But they were also aware of the misery caused by a temporary recession in the textile trades, both wool and silk:[3] the output of woollens had reached a high peak, with 26,018 cloths in 1591 and 27,299 in 1592, but had then fallen steeply during the next two years, to 23,941 cloths in 1593 and 18,294 in 1594.[4] Early

---

[2] A.S.V., *Provveditori alla Sanità, Capitolare I*, ff. 151v.–153.

[3] Petition of the governors of the confraternity, of 16 March 1595, in A.S.V., *Senato, Terra, filza* 139, 9 April 1596.

[4] Sella, 'Venetian woollen industry', p. 109.

in 1608, representatives of the fraternity again described how many wool- and silk-workers had applied to them for relief during the bitter winter which had paralysed their trades, and how they had also relieved many disbanded galleots.[5] Again, the official statistics for the Venetian output of broadcloth confirm that there was a slackening of production in 1607, though less marked than on the previous occasion.[6] The fraternity distributed food, fuel, clothing and medicines, through twelve governors who went out daily, two to each sestiere, to visit the sick and other deserving cases. At all times, they accompanied their alms with improving advice—

> reminding everyone to give thanks to God, to pray for their benefactors (and especially for the Venetian state), to bear their misfortunes with patience, to take care that their children go and learn Christian doctrine and that big girls do not stray into error, to live as good Christians, to engage in frequent devotions, and to apply themselves to some virtuous employment. . . .[7]

This summed up many of the preoccupations of sixteenth-century charity.

Meanwhile, throughout the century, the general hospitals continued to expand and to act both as institutions for the care of the sick and as orphanages for the upbringing, education and after-care of children. Their inmates often numbered several hundred, greatly increasing during epidemics or periods of war. In March 1556, the hospital of Santi Giovanni e Paolo had only 130 inmates;[8] but in 1565 the numbers (which included sick patients, orphans and galleots) had reached 450.[9] In 1572, in the state of emergency created by the War of Cyprus, soldiers and galleots brought the total to nearly 600.[10] In April 1584, the hospitals of Santi Giovanni e Paolo and of the Incurabili, together with the older institute of the Pietà and the recently founded house of the Zitelle, claimed to be supporting about 3,000 children or *creature* between them, and to be providing marriage portions or conventual dowries every year for about 300 girls passing out of their hands.[11] The Incurabili worked on a scale similar to that of Santi Giovanni e

[5] A.S.V., *Senato, Terra, filza* 185, 29 February 1607 Venetian style: petition of the governors, dated 7 February 1607 Venetian style.

[6] Dr Sella's figures show the total output of the industry as being 20,010 cloths in 1605, 20,833 in 1606, 18,778 in 1607, 23,318 in 1608, 18,318 in 1609, and 17,129 in 1610. The industry had passed its peak, and was gently going downhill.

[7] See n. 3 above.

[8] A.S.V., *Senato, Terra, filza* 23, 30 March 1556.

[9] A.S.V., *Senato, Terra, filza* 45, 11 December 1565.

[10] A.S.V., *Senato, Terra, filza* 59, 31 March 1572.

[11] A.S.V., *Senato, Terra, filza* 90, 18 April 1584.

Paolo. It claimed to have 350–400 inmates in 1565, rising to 450 in 1567.[12] By 1583 it accommodated 250 sick persons, with 200 virgins and orphans: in 1588, over 100 girls and as many boys, with over 400 patients 'when the waters are given'.[13] This phrase may have described some therapeutic ritual which tended to increase the numbers to an abnormally high level. At the beginning of the seventeenth century, the hospital of the Mendicanti, with a normal quota of about 400 inmates, added still further to the available resources for indoor relief. These claims—usually made by the governors of the hospitals themselves—suggest that the total number of persons either in hospital or dependent on hospitals was in fact far greater than the official censuses indicated. The censuses estimated the numbers of the 'hospital poor' as follows:

	1552	1563	1586	1593	1642
Hospital poor	741	1,479	1,111	1,290	1,945
Total pop.	158,069	168,627	148,637	139,459	120,307[14]

Some of the discrepancy might be explained by the possibility that the census-takers did not count as inmates those who were boarded out by the hospitals, but kept under hospital supervision: such as the hundreds of foundlings farmed out by the Pietà to wetnurses in the town. They were probably counted as part of the households of their foster-parents. The other general hospitals may have also boarded some of their orphans out, rather than keep them all under a single, vast roof. The apparently sharp increase in the hospital poor between 1552 and 1563 was probably due, not only to actual increases among the inmates, but also to the government's more accurate knowledge of the resources of the city. Surveys conducted by the Provveditori sopra gli Ospedali, after 1561, may well have improved this. The foundation of the Mendicanti at least partially explains the increase of 50 per cent in the hospital poor recorded between 1593 and 1642, in spite of the reduction of the total population by the plague of 1630–1.

As well as increasing in size, the hospital of the Incurabili put forth branches. Concern for the control of syphilis, from which the hospitals had originally started, led naturally into a desire to control prostitution, or at least to mitigate its evil spiritual consequences. Here again, there was an essential sympathy between the aims of religious societies and those of the state: members of these societies may well have influenced the legislation issued, in increasing volume after 1539, for the control of prostitution—when it became the specific concern of the

[12] A.S.V., *Senato, Terra, filza* 44, 22 September 1565; *filza* 48, 28 February 1566 Venetian style.   [13] A.S.V., *Senato, Terra, filza* 107, 27 August 1588.
[14] Beloch, 'Popolazione di Venezia', p. 27. The figure for the total population in 1593 is not apparently accepted by Professor Beltrami (see p. 59).

2B

Provveditori alla Sanità. Prostitution, endemic in all monogamous societies and all which encourage sexual frustration, flourished conspicuously in Venice, as one of the largest ports in Europe, as a centre of tourism, and as a point of departure for pilgrims. It was an article of faith among philanthropists that young women must, where possible, be guided either into marriage or the cloister, which would afford them the necessary protection against the loss of their virtue. Hence the paramount importance of dowries in the minds of pious testators. The courtesans of Venice, who had reached the upper levels of their profession, became as proverbial as the wine of Vicenza, the bread of Padua or the tripes of Treviso.[15] There were strong incentives, both spiritual and material, to control prostitution: the danger of disease, the threat to public order and decency from brothels and from prostitutes plying their trade in churches, the determination of religious reformers to improve the moral climate, and their concern with reclaiming the souls of sinners. Hopeless poverty threatened the prostitute whose beauty departed, and her downfall provided material for moralistic poems. In 1532, a Venetian press published the boasts and laments of a Ferrarese courtesan in Rome—probably fictitious, but certainly symbolic. These were embodied in ominous verses which traced the descent of a harlot, ruined by disease and age, to keeping a lodging-house, acting as a procuress, washing clothes and cooking in a tavern, with the disease advancing inexorably.[16] More terrible was the *Mattinata*, an obscenely vindictive poem which rejoiced in the misery awaiting an offensive prostitute who had achieved the dignity of an upper-floor house and a kitchen full of majolica-ware. Before next April she would be reduced to begging on the bridges, or lying on a mat near the churches with faggots for a pillow, festooned in *bollettini* or licences to beg, grotesquely clad in odd garments, a prey to the desires and curiosity of paupers and boys. The hospital of the Incurabili became the symbol of ruin: 'the hospital is calling you from a thousand miles away'.[17]

The circles of reformers round the hospitals of the Incurabili were at first mainly concerned with providing opportunities to withdraw from prostitution, to expunge by a life of repentance the sins commit-

---

[15] Thomas Coryat, *Coryat's crudities* (reprint of the edition of 1611, 2 vols., Glasgow, 1905), II, p. 14.

[16] *El vanto della cortigiana ferrarese qual narra le bellezza sua*, reprinted as Appendice A to Arturo Graf, 'Una cortigiana fra mille: Veronica Franco', in his *Attraverso il Cinquecento* (Turin, 1888), at pp. 355–61.

[17] *Ibid.*, Appendice B, pp. 362–6. Venice is clearly the setting for this poem, which contains many Venetian dialect words. There are some local allusions—e.g. to the Carampane, the red-light district of Venice (see Tassini, *Curiosità venezione*, pp. 135–136).

ted. They did not try to rehabilitate prostitutes in the context of worldly society, but to allow them to withdraw from the world by a voluntary act of self-sacrifice, to remove themselves from its temptations and insecurity. Asceticism would surely compensate for past licentiousness. Roman institutions, known to members of the Compagnie del Divino Amore, provided a model. The theory behind the spiritual conquest of prostitution appeared in the Bull of 1520 by which Leo X confirmed the establishment of the nunnery of the Convertite in Rome:

> Our saviour Jesus Christ, the son of God, when he took on human form, came, as he himself said, to save the sheep which had strayed. Hence, when the Pharisees and the publicans complained that he associated with sinners, he chose to recite the parable (now in the Gospel of St Luke) of the sheep which had strayed and was afterwards found, so that he might show, as the same evangelist bears witness, that there is more joy in heaven over one sinner that repents, than over ninety-nine righteous people who have no need to repent. And he so far commended the sacrament of penitence that when St Peter, the chief of the apostles, in whose place we (although unworthy) rule upon earth, asked him how many times sinners should be forgiven, he replied 'Not seven times only, but seventy times seven'....[18]

In Venice, a patent of the Patriarch, issued in 1525, mentioned 'sinful women converted to God' among the inmates of the Incurabili.[19] Likewise, in 1531, Averoldo di Averoldi, papal nuncio and Bishop of Pola, made a separate bequest of 600 ducats to the Convertite.[20] They formed a recognized branch or department of the hospital, but were not physically detached from it until a few years later. According to the official account attached to the statutes first printed in 1719, the Pope authorized the erection of 'A nunnery of the Convertite, either on the Giudecca or at the hospital of the Incurabili', before 1530. The Convertite acquired houses on the Giudecca between 1530 and 1534, but only between 1542 and 1548 did they move into a specially designed building on the Giudecca. Before 1551, sisters of the Convertite did not take the veil, but underwent probation in a house at San Marcilian, and were then solemnly escorted to the parish church of Santa Eufemia. Here the ceremony of cutting off their hair marked their entry on a new life of rigid austerity, far removed from their previous loose existence. Thence they processed to the nunnery itself.[21] In 1551, the Venetian

---

[18] Leo X, 'Salvator noster', 19 May 1520, M.B.R., V, pp. 743–8.
[19] Cicogna, *Inscrizioni veneziane*, V, p. 310.
[20] D.M.S., LV, coll. 112–13, 5 November 1531.
[21] For this see *Capitoli et ordini per il buon governo della congregatione del monasterio di Santa Maria Maddalena delle Convertite della Giudecca* (Venice, 1719), pp. 7–12.

Cardinal Francesco Pisani, a member of the congregation which governed the house of penitent women in Rome,[22] persuaded Pope Julius III to authorize the Convertite of Venice to adopt the Rule of St Augustine. In this, they followed the precedent of the Roman Convertite. Finally, in 1562, the Venetian sisters reached the last phase in their development, by becoming a cloistered order severed from unnecessary worldly contacts.

The numbers of the Convertite grew with surprising rapidity: the institution was obviously popular and fulfilled what was, in some proportions, both a social and a spiritual need. The Jesuits, soon after the establishment of their colleges in Venice itself and in Padua, began to commend the nunnery as part of their campaign to promote frequent confession and sincere repentance, though sometimes they merely consigned imperilled girls to the care of respectable and benevolent citizens. In 1553, the Convertite numbered about 220, rising to 300 in 1556, 310 in 1557, 340 in 1559, and 400 'including our lay sisters (*con le nostre converse insieme*)' in 1560.[23] Numbers then fell sharply, whether from lack of financial resources or from the failure of many entrants to persevere, to 231 in 1564, rising again to 266 in 1586 and to almost 300 in 1596–7.[24] In 1620, their numbers stood at 376.[25] The purpose and scope of the community may, of course, have changed with the years, and it may have admitted women who were not, strictly speaking, reformed prostitutes; it may have provided a refuge for poor women who could not afford the dowry required by more respectable or fashionable convents. However, a certain stigma still clung to membership in the late sixteenth century: in 1597, Suora Clementia, the Prioress, wrote that

> we find ourselves without relatives and friends, for we have abandoned them all in order to serve God and save our souls, and they disdain to

---

[22] See Tacchi Venturi, *Storia della Compagnia di Gesù*, I/ii, doc. 80, p. 296. On Cardinal Pisani see also above, pp. 332–5.

[23] A.S.V., *Senato, Terra, filza* 17, 18 March 1553; *filza* 18, 20 November 1553; *filza* 24, 11 September 1556; *filza* 26, 17 September 1557; *filza* 28, 21 January 1558 Venetian style; *filza* 31, 22 August 1560. A Flemish Jesuit, whose name was italianized as Giovanni Gambero, estimated the numbers in 1553 at about 250—see his letter to Loyola of 2 September 1553, in M.H.S.J., *Litterae Quadrimestres*, II, p. 384.

[24] A.S.V., *Senato, Terra, filza* 40, 12 August 1564; *Consiglio dei Dieci, Parti Comuni, filza* 165, 23 December 1586; *Senato, Terra, filza* 141, 27 February 1596 Venetian style.

[25] Petition of Suora Maria Benedetti, Prioress of the Convertite, on or before 5 October 1620, in A.S.V., *Senato, Terra, filza* 243, 17 December 1620. For the rescue operation designed to save the Convertite from dispersal in 1601, see A.S.V., *Collegio, Notatorio*, reg. 63, f. 20v., and *Senato, Terra*, reg. 1601, f. 25v.

come and visit the nunnery of the Convertite, for they do not like anyone to know that their sisters or other relatives are in there.[26]

But Fynes Moryson, the English traveller, writing in the early seventeenth century, tersely described one plausible reason for the popularity of the Convertite. Of the courtesans of Venice he remarked that

The richer sort dwell in fayre hired howses, and have their owne servants, but the Common sort lodge with Baudes called Ruffians, to whome in Venice they pay of their gayne the fifth parte, as foure Solz in twenty, paying besydes for their bed, linnen and feasting, and when they are past gayning much, they are turned out to begg or turne baudes or servants. And for releife of this misery, they have Nonneryes, where many of them are admitted, and called the converted sisters.[27]

This remark may merely reflect the cynicism of Moryson's Venetian informant. But on the other hand it may genuinely imply that the original aims of the Convertite had been perverted, even while the nunnery became more useful in curbing begging and bawdry.

Other nunneries for Convertite sprang up in the mainland cities of the Venetian dominions, especially in those most open to the new currents of evangelism. Giberti, with financial support from the ex-Bishop of Bayeux, Ludovico di Canossa, founded a community in Verona, based on a nucleus of about thirty penitents. He provided them with suitable premises, and placed them under the direction of a woman of mature years who first showed them how to put off their immodest dresses and assume others, 'not the habits of nuns, but no less modest'. These converts were taught how to read, to sew and weave, to attend to their devotions and to sing the psalms. They, too, were cut off from the world, seeing only their physician and confessor. Some, who proved unable to persevere in this austere vocation, were either placed in service or married off.[28] Vicenza had a community of Convertite by 1537.[29] Likewise, during the 1550's, the first Jesuits in Padua expressed hope that one of these communities would soon be established there, as in Rome.[30] Indeed, in 1558, the Jesuit Benedetto Palmio, a successful and inspiring preacher, did procure the establishment in Padua of a religious house designed to help women escape

[26] A.S.V., *Senato, Terra, filza* 141, 27 February 1596 Venetian style.
[27] Fynes Moryson, *Shakespeare's Europe* (previously unpublished chapters of his *Itinerary*), ed. Charles Hughes (London, 1903), pp. 411–12.
[28] See Zini, *Boni pastoris exemplum*, pp. 284 f.; Ballerini, *Vita Giberti*, in *Opera*, pp. xxi–xxii; Dalla Corte, *Istorie di Verona*, III, pp. 321–2.
[29] See below, p. 383.
[30] See especially the letter of Elpidio Ugoletti to Ignatius Loyola from Padua, April 1552, in M.H.S.J., *Litterae Quadrimestres*, I, pp. 615–16.

from prostitution.[31] Treviso had acquired a community of Convertite by 1559.[32] By the turn of the century, the Lombard provinces certainly had their Convertite, though not in such numbers as in Venice. An official survey of Bergamo in 1596 recorded that in the 'church and convent of the Maddalena of the Convertite' there were 44 young women, who lived by alms.[33] In 1611, there were 15 women in the 'Chiesa della Carità delle povere Convertite' in Brescia.[34] In 1607–8, Filippo Bon, governor of Crema, described how about two years previously a small group of young women 'formerly of disreputable life' had now assembled 'in a small house to lead a withdrawn and exemplary life, living confined in that place and serving God'. He later added that there were eight 'women of the people' governed within the community by two of citizen rank. They received protection from three lay citizens nominated as governors or procurators by the hospital of the Misericordia in Crema, and were visited and supervised by a group of four gentlewomen.[35] The idea of the Convertite was still appreciated, since new foundations were arising at this late date.

From 1539 onwards, legislation and government action in Venice itself began to press in the same direction as organizations founded by private initiative. In 1539, the Council of Ten extended the competence of the Provveditori alla Sanità to include the control of prostitution: making an award of additional powers to mark their success in repelling foreign vagrants from Venetian territory.[36] Broadly speaking, government action forked in two directions. It aimed, not at eliminating, but at curbing prostitution, by attaching a stigma to it and by formally separating prostitutes from reputable society. Again, it began to adopt preventive measures against the corruption of young girls whose poverty and insecurity might easily decoy them into prostitution. Legislation, in 1539 and 1572, attempted to expel all prostitutes who had entered the city in the past two years and in the past five years respectively. Wartime conditions inevitably encouraged prostitution, and in any case a state was well advised to court divine favour during a war against infidels. The Provveditori alla Sanità also attempted to drive 'all public and infamous prostitutes' within eight days into 'the

---

[31] See Francesco Sacchini, *Historiae Societatis Iesu*, Part II (Antwerp, 1620), pp. 52–3. But this probably resembled more closely the type of institution known as the Casa di Santa Marta in Rome and as the Soccorso in Venice—see below, pp. 391–3, and Tacchi Venturi, *Storia della Compagnia di Gesù*, I/i, p. 385.

[32] A.S.V., *Senato, Terra*, reg. 1559/60, f. 31, 30 June 1559.

[33] A.S.V., *Sindici Inquisitori in Terra Ferma*, busta 63, f. 68v.

[34] *Ibid.*, busta 64, f. 23v.

[35] Letters of the Podestà, dated 30 October 1607 and 8 April 1608, in A.S.V., *Senato, Terra*, filza 187, 12 June 1608.

[36] Orford, *Leggi e memorie venete sulla prostituzione*, doc. 98, p. 100.

brothels and public places assigned to their trade'. Common prostitutes must be driven into their own ghetto.[37] The decree of the Provveditori to save churches from desecration by prostitutes, originally formulated in 1539, was, if not the most consistently applied, at least the most repeatedly re-enforced of measures against prostitution: it reappeared in 1571, 1582 and 1613. The gist of the law was that

> The said courtesans or prostitutes may not go into any church on the day of its principal festival or celebration, so that with their many lascivious words, deeds and actions they may not be a bad example to the men and women who go to these churches for a good purpose, to the shame of this city, the dishonour and defilement of holy places, and the offence of God's majesty. On other days, when they go into any church, they may not stand, kneel or sit upon the benches to which our noblewomen and citizenesses of good and respectable rank betake themselves. They must remain apart from them and afar off, taking care not to give offence to other good persons. They may not go to confession at any time save between Nones and Vespers, so as not to contaminate those who come to church for a good purpose.[38]

The magistrate thus recognized his duty to guarantee decent conditions for public worship.

At the same time, the Provveditori alla Sanità introduced a number of measures designed for the protection of young people; occasionally, at least, householders were actually prosecuted under these laws. No women under the age of thirty might be kept as servants in brothels.[39] In 1559, there were at least two prosecutions of persons charged with keeping young girls in houses which lodged foreigners. On 14 March, the Provveditori received information against

> ser Alvise, shoemaker at the Golden Head in Calle de' Botteri, for lodging foreigners in his house and employing as maids young girls aged about 14 and 17, contrary to orders issued by our office. One of these is in the hospital of the Incurabili suffering from the French pox, and the other has also caught the disease. The order that those who lodge foreigners may not keep such girls in their houses was made so that they should not be shamed or plagued with disease. . .[40]

In 1539, again, the Council of Ten had expressed anxiety for the welfare of servant girls changing employment, and had instructed the Provveditori alla Sanità to ensure that in each parish there was one house of good reputation open, so that they should not be driven into

---

[37] *Ibid.*, docs. 98–9, pp. 100–2; doc. 115, p. 120.
[38] *Ibid.*, docs. 114, 122, 137, pp. 119, 125–6, 136–7.
[39] *Ibid.*, doc. 99, p. 102, and, for examples of prosecutions, doc. 110, p. 282.
[40] *Ibid.*, doc. 115, p. 287.

brothels.[41] On very similar lines, the Provveditori alla Sanità also, in 1542, condemned the machinations of bawds who ensnared unemployed, unwary and unprotected girls:

> There is no doubt that there is nothing more gracious in the sight of God than the elimination of the first cause of the abuses committed. For we see clearly every day that there are diabolical persons who at the instigation of the devil are continually watching to seduce and lead astray poor orphans and girls who are forced to beg for their living in the city, or even poor servant girls who are on their way to lodge with our nobles and citizens, by offering to clothe them and be their mistresses, with many other blandishments. Once they have fallen into the hands of these bawds (*rufiane*), they hire them chemises, headdress, stockings, shoes, dresses, cloaks and capes, and by means of this the bawds keep them at their mercy and live off the earnings of their girls, who can never free themselves and are constrained of necessity to commit wicked sins and become accustomed to these meretricious vices. This is a most potent reason for the infinite number of such disreputable prostitutes now in the city and increasing daily.[42]

Under the order which followed, a certain Isabetta Vanzaga twice suffered prosecution, in 1550 and 1553, for corrupting girls who could never otherwise have afforded to dress in the style appropriate to a harlot.[43]

In the early 1540's, the law had plainly stated the need for prevention. But the official condemnation of bawdry and occasional prosecutions were not enough. Private action was needed to supplement the law. In the next twenty years, religious reformers and philanthropists extended their aims from merely providing chances for repentance to trying to cut at the roots of the corruption. The original suggestion for establishing an institution for this purpose seems to have come from the circle surrounding the Regular Clerks of St Paul at the hospital of Santi Giovanni e Paolo. This congregation, later and better known as the Barnabites, had been founded in Milan before 1530 by Antonio Maria Zaccaria, Giacomo Antonio Morigia and Bartolomeo Ferrari. Lodovica Torelli, Countess of Guastalla, whom Zaccaria served as chaplain, had from the beginning taken a close interest in the congregation. In the early 1530's, a congregation of women, known as the Angeliche, had sprung up parallel to the Clerks of St Paul. The broad purpose of these organizations was to reform both clergy and laity, and to raise their moral standards.[44] After their introduction into

---

[41] *Ibid.*, doc. 98, p. 100. [42] *Ibid.*, doc. 101, p. 105.
[43] *Ibid.*, doc. 110, p. 283; for other examples, *ibid.*, docs. 107–8, pp. 280–1.
[44] See O. M. Premoli, *Storia dei Barnabiti nel Cinquecento* (Rome, 1913), pp. 1 f.

Venetian territory, they formed a specific connexion with hospitals and other social institutions. Bishops on the Venetian mainland had first seen the possibility of employing the Paulines and Angeliche: Nicolò Ridolfi of Vicenza invited them to his diocese in 1537, where, among other things, they tried to prevent the relaxation of discipline in the Convertite. Giberti, always alive to new possibilities, invited them, the following year, to start a mission in Verona, where they concentrated especially on the hospitals of the Misericordia and the Pietà for orphans, sick and foundlings.[45] Perhaps inspired by this precedent, representatives of the Venetian hospital of Santi Giovanni e Paolo appealed to Milan in 1544. The headquarters of the new congregation sent them, in response, two fathers, Dionisio da Sesto, and Girolamo Marta (a native of Castelfranco in Venetian territory), together with certain Angeliche. In Venice, they rapidly attracted circles of patricians and noblewomen who devoted themselves enthusiastically to good works and religious observances under Pauline direction. These disciples enjoyed the wealth, the influence and the leisure to conduct a successful charitable campaign. Women from certain leading Venetian families—including the Cornaro, Contarini, Marin, Loredan, Grimani, Priuli and Bembo—offered to collaborate with Father Marta in assembling a number of poor orphan children in a house called the Conservatorio delle Zitelle Periclitanti.[46]

However, an unfortunate scandal cut short the development of the project; it culminated in the expulsion of the Paulines from all the territories of the Venetian Republic early in 1551. One cause of the misunderstanding was the connexion of the Paulines with the potentially hostile state of Milan, now under Spanish control, and the known friendship of the Countess of Guastalla with the Milanese governor Ferrante Gonzaga. More immediately, trouble was provoked by the arrogance of the Angelica Paola Antonia Negri, who, during her time in the diocese of Padua, had inspired veneration as a saint. She arrived in Venice about 1548, where, however, she succeeded in bitterly offending one patrician in particular and in alienating all or most of the governors of Santi Giovanni e Paolo. Their complaints, presented to the Senate, procured the expulsion of the Paulines and Angeliche, on the grounds of the excessive deference paid to Paola Antonia Negri, of the close contact between the men and women of the parallel congregations, of suspicions of abusing the confessional in order to probe state secrets, and of other charges.[47] The Paulines or Barnabites several times investigated the possibility of returning to the Venetian Republic,

[45] *Ibid.*, pp. 38–9, 57–8.   [46] *Ibid.*, pp. 66–7, 71–2.   [47] *Ibid.*, pp. 92–104.

but did not in fact do so until the early seventeenth century.[48] The foundation of a house for 'imperilled virgins' was in fact left to the Jesuits, though former disciples of the Paulines undoubtedly took part in the campaign, and sent letters to inform the Pauline Girolamo Marta of its progress.[49] The hospital of Santi Giovanni e Paolo, deserted by the Paulines, eventually—by the late 1580's—formed a bond with the Somaschians,[50] the congregation founded by Girolamo Miani, one of its own early supporters.

Negotiations for the introduction of a Jesuit colony into Venice had begun soon after the official incorporation of the Society of Jesus in 1540. The Venetian government, through letters to its Ambassador in Rome, first expressed a wish to receive Jesuit preachers in 1542, and Laynez, the future general of that Order, was sent in response.[51] During this decade Andrea Lippomano, Prior of Holy Trinity and supporter of the new religious and charitable movements, determined to endow Jesuit colleges in Padua and in Venice itself. Although houses of professed Jesuits proposed to live on voluntary contributions alone, fixed revenues were necessary to the support of student members of the Society. Negotiations for the establishment of these colleges were eventually completed in 1548, when Lippomano held out against substantial opposition from his own family, who felt no desire to renounce the revenues from his profitable commendams.[52] The first Jesuit colony reached Venice itself early in 1550,[53] there to fit into the social framework under Lippomano's cautious paternal guidance. The general purpose of the Jesuits, as defined in 1551–2 by Loyola's secretary Juan Alonso Polanco, was

to devote all their cares and energies, by the grace of God, to helping themselves and their neighbours in things relevant to salvation, to the service and glory of God.

The means employed to this ultimate end are normally preaching the word of God, reading the Holy Scriptures on all Sundays and festivals, generally teaching Christian doctrine, assiduously hearing confessions,

---

[48] *Ibid.*, pp. 170–1; 248–9 and doc. 39, pp. 551–2; 338–40, 377–9.

[49] See below, p. 386.

[50] See a letter to the Somaschians in Pavia, from the Presidenti della Camera dell'Ospedale di Santi Giovanni e Paolo, dated 3 April 1587: in a *Registro di lettere* in A.S.V., *Ospedali e Luoghi Pii*, busta 910, *fascicolo* 1. The Presidenti had recently written to ask the Somaschians to 'confermar in questa casa' one Father Battista Perego, and now asked them to do the same for Missier Giovanni Maria Scaramuccia, who was in charge of the orphanage.

[51] Tacchi Venturi, *Storia della Compagnia di Gesù*, II/2, pp. 211 f.

[52] *Ibid.*, pp. 372–8, 664–8, 672–9, 680–4; M.H.S.J., Polanco, *Historia Societatis Jesu*, I, pp. 147–8, 272–5.

[53] M.H.S.J., Polanco, *Historia Societatis Jesu*, I, pp. 404–5, II, pp. 60–1

and attending to various good works and spiritual exercises; and, that they may the more surely persevere in these activities, they take the three vows of chastity, poverty and obedience, with a special vow to obey the Holy Apostolic See even to the extent of going to Turkey or the Indies or any other part of the world to which they may be sent.[54]

Schemes for the reclamation of prostitutes or for the prevention of corruption among young people accorded very well with the aims and methods of the Jesuits. They were concerned with the salvation of souls, with Christian and moral education, and, through the confessional, with asserting the value of penitence. They quickly resumed their connexion with the hospital of the Incurabili, collaborating with the society for teaching Christian doctrine whose headquarters were established there, and which occasionally sent recruits to the Jesuits.[55] At least from 1552, they occasionally steered penitent sinners into the Convertite.[56] Their close connexions with Rome would probably guarantee them some knowledge of two institutions founded on Loyola's instigation during the 1540's: the Casa di Santa Marta, and the institution of the Vergini Miserabili. These, like so many Roman institutions of the early sixteenth century, proved to be exportable, and to meet the requirements of other societies. Loyola's Vergini Miserabili, founded by 1546, may have inspired the projected Conservatorio delle Zitelle Periclitanti conceived by the Paulines in Venice, though there is no proof of this. Its object was to wean the daughters of prostitutes forcibly from their mothers' care. It took them between the ages of nine and twelve—after which they were regarded as irredeemably corrupt—and educated them in Christian knowledge and conduct. Finally it provided them with dowries either to marry or enter the religious life.[57]

In the late 1550's, an able Jesuit preacher, Benedetto Palmio, first Provincial of Lombardy, revived the scheme in Venice itself. Palmio, an early Italian recruit to the Society of Jesus, had developed a forceful

---

[54] From a *Breve informatione circa l'instituto della Compagnia chiamata di Giesù*, in M.H.S.J., *Polanci complementa*, I, pp. 65–8.

[55] M.H.S.J., *Litterae Quadrimestres*, I, pp. 328–9, III, pp. 18–19—letters of Cesare Helmi to Loyola from Venice, 23 May 1551, 9 June 1554; Polanco, *Historia Societatis Jesu*, II, p. 212, IV, pp. 124–5.

[56] M.H.S.J., *Litterae Quadrimestres*, I, pp. 519–20, 531, 615–16, 695, 707, II, p. 384: letters of Giovanni Gambero to Loyola from Padua and Venice respectively, 15, 23 January 1552; of Elpidio Ugoletti to Loyola from Padua, April 1552; of Andrea Frusio from Venice, 29 June, 2 July 1552; of Giovanni Gambero from Venice, 2 September 1553. See also M.H.S.J., Polanco, *Historia Societatis Jesu*, II, p. 472, III, pp. 116–17.

[57] See Tacchi Venturi, *Storia della Compagnia di Gesù*, I/ii, doc. 84, pp. 314–20, II/ii, pp. 183 f.; Delumeau, *Vie économique et sociale de Rome*, I, pp. 429–32.

style of pulpit-oratory designed to give an immediate, practical guide to conduct and to ignore theological subtleties.[58] His campaign began in Padua in 1558, where—as if in response to a need earlier stated by the local superior, Elpidio Ugoletti—his preaching inspired the foundation of a refuge for female penitents. He also established a Compagnia della Pietà, which discharged many of the usual functions of Giberti's Compagnie della Carità or of the fraternities of the Poveri Vergognosi.[59] In Venice, he spoke from the pulpit of the Incurabili, and from that of the Santi Apostoli on the other side of the Grand Canal. His sermons quickly drew generous gifts, to the tune of 1,500–2,000 ducats, from rich merchants and from at least one nobleman, Hieronimo Surian.[60] He was certainly able to build on the foundations laid by the Paulines, and to use the helpers whom they had inspired. In July 1560, Adriana Contarini and her sisters, members of this group, described the foundation of the Zitelle to their former confessor Girolamo Marta:

1560 letter to Girolamo Marta

> We have now been urged by the Lord to set in motion an activity some time ago implanted in our minds by him. At his desire, we started work four months ago, and there are now thirty girls all dragged from the grasp of the Devil. We have brought them all together in one house and are ready to buy them a site any day now. The money we have accumulated now amounts to 5,000 ducats, and we want to raise a good deal more, in view of the terrible distress of these poor children who are sold by their own mothers at the age of twelve or thirteen or even less, and who come of every social rank—nobility, citizenry or workers. . . .

They wrote to ask advice about the appointment of a suitable matron or counsellor: as yet they had found no satisfactory candidate. However, nearly two years later, another correspondent, Isabella Grimani, was able to tell Marta that Maria Bernardo and Isabella Contarini had taken charge of the rescued girls.[61]

There seems, as yet, to be no means of discovering the content of Palmio's original sermons, or the methods by which the house of the

[58] See Tacchi Venturi, *Storia della Compagnia di Gesù*, I/i, p. 304.

[59] *Ibid.*, I/i, pp. 385, 403–4; Sacchini, *Historiae Societatis Jesu*, Part II, pp. 52–3.

[60] See the letters of Cesare Helmi to Loyola, in M.H.S.J., *Litterae Quadrimestres*, VI, pp. 43–4, 889–90—dated 13 January 1559 and 28 September 1560; also the account of the early history of the institution in *Constitutioni et regole della Casa delle Cittelle di Venetia eretta e fondata sotto il titolo della Presentatione della Madonna* (Venice, 1701), pp. 3–6.

[61] Letter of Adriana Contarini and her sisters to Girolamo Marta, from Venice, 5 July 1560; and of Isabella, wife of Antonio Grimani, then serving as Capitano in Verona, 18 January 1562. Isabella Grimani described how she had made contact with former devotees of the Paulines in Verona. See Premoli, *Storia dei Barnabiti*, doc. 28, pp. 532–4.

Zitelle was originally governed when the preliminary arrangements were completed and the Zitelle set up house on the Giudecca. However, in 1588, Palmio returned to Venice to deliver exhortations to the governors of the Zitelle and to issue them a new set of statutes. Both the preliminary sermon and the statutes of 1588 were printed in 1701, and these give some idea of the theory of charity which inspired the Zitelle, and of the methods it employed.[62] Palmio's is perhaps the only Venetian charity-sermon both to have survived and come to light in this century. It expressed many of the ideals implied in the statutes of pious organizations and in the preambles of government legislation, exalting, as the highest form of charity, the conquest and rescue of souls from damnation. The sermon insisted that charity conferred merit only if performed out of the pure love of God: implying that charity directed towards purely social ends had no value.

> It is not enough to proffer aid to the needy: it is vital that this transaction, this relief which is extended to them, should proceed from the true sentiment of the love of God, for, if we bestirred ourselves to help our neighbour from any other motive, the service we did him would be unacceptable to God.[63]

Palmio dilated on the supreme merit of soul-saving, with several scriptural examples, and demanded rhetorically,

> What merit, then, will you acquire in the sight of God, for your efforts are devoted, not to saving a single man or woman sinner, but to saving a great multitude of young virgins from being seized by the most cruel lion, 'qui circuit semper quaerens, quem devoret', and from being seduced by the depravation of the world, and to keeping them pure and immaculate for God who created them...? God, whilst he hates the ugliness and dishonour of the carnal, earthly and sensual life, yet wonderfully rejoices in the immaculate purity of virginity and modesty, which, by the mercy and grace of the Holy Spirit, is so well preserved and guarded in this house.

On the rôle of good works in the accumulation of merit, Palmio argued that their value derived from the willingness of God to accept them: God had no need of human assistance, but men had a need to serve God, to become 'collaborators of Jesus Christ Our Lord in procuring the salvation of so many souls'.[64] In this sense, good works certainly bestowed merit: but meritorious works were acts of genuine mercy and compassion, not mechanical rituals. The heart of the sermon lay in

[62] See Palmio's address 'Alle congregationi delli magnifici Signori Governatori et delle magnifice Signore Governatrici della Casa delle Cittelle di Venetia nella Zuecca', printed with the *Constitutioni et regole delle Cittelle*, cited above.
[63] *Ibid.*, pp. 11–12.   [64] *Ibid.*, pp. 7–8.

phrases which recalled Leo X's Bull for the erection of the Convertite in Rome in 1520:

> God himself has very clearly demonstrated the excellence of mercy, preferring it to sacrifice and to victims, saying, in the sixth chapter of Hosea, 'I desire mercy and not sacrifice'. . . . Now those who strive for the conversion and salvation of sinners are greatly favoured by Jesus Christ Our Lord, who, on the authority of this sentence of Hosea, weightily—as we read in the ninth and twelfth chapters of St Matthew—reproved the arrogance and hauteur of the Pharisees, who, glorying in the external ceremony of sacrifices and victims, yet performed few acts of mercy. And although they professed to be very holy, and to have a perfect knowledge of the law, he clearly convinced them that they were very far from possessing such knowledge. For, contrary to the commandment of God, they thought more highly of sacrifices than of works of mercy. Hence it happened that they censured him because he conversed and ate with sinners. . . . But 'Go,' he said to them, 'learn what this means: "I will have mercy, and not sacrifice". You want the people to honour you as Doctors and Masters of the Law, but in fact you do not understand it. . . . If I eat and converse with sinners, don't you see that my associating with them is an act of great mercy, for I eat and live with publicans and sinners, to teach them, to enlighten them, and to lead them to the observance of the law of God. . . ?'[65]

The message of Erasmus, and of the pre-Tridentine Catholic reformers, had survived into the late sixteenth century. Formal religious observances were not enough: what mattered was the spirit of mercy or charity permeating all Christian conduct. The third part of the constitutions instructed the Governors, of both sexes,

> not to be content with attending the Most Holy Sacraments in the belief that that is everything. With the aid of God's mercy, they must succeed in gathering the fruit claimed of the sacraments—that is, an increase in their accustomed virtues, diligence in carrying out their duties, and abundance of all the good works appropriate to a true Christian according to the rank and condition of every person.[66]

The statutes of the Zitelle were designed to preserve the specialized character of the institution, and to maintain a division of labour between Venetian charities. The girls must be over nine or ten years old, must be both beautiful and healthy, and must, on account of their beauty, the misconduct of their parents or guardians, or the harsh pressure of poverty, be in imminent danger of losing their virtue. It was

[65] *Ibid.*, pp. 18–19.
[66] See the *Constitutioni delle Cittelle*, paginated separately from Palmio's address, Part III, ch. iv, p. 16.

388

not enough that a girl should be poor or an orphan: there were institutes to take care of these problems already.[67] The two congregations of Governatori and Governatrici (at least twenty men and twelve women) were responsible for selecting inmates. The Presidente and Deputati chosen from among the governors would deliver them a list of cases to be visited. Each girl would be visited by two pairs of Governatori, calling on the assistance of brothers of the Fraternity for the Poveri Vergognosi. The Governatrici were sent to discover details, especially about the girl's health, with which it was proper for only women to concern themselves. Both congregations would then vote on the claims of the candidate, and anyone who obtained more than half the available votes in each congregation would be admitted. If the danger were very great, the procedure could be drastically abridged, on the authority of at least two-thirds of each of the congregations.[68]

Under the protection of the house, girls received an upbringing designed to fit them for their future life as housewives or as nuns, and to educate them in Christian knowledge and conduct. They were trained to do useful handwork—probably lacemaking or embroidery— which could be used to pay for their keep. The older girls were expected to produce work worth about 10 soldi every day, the younger about half as much. If they succeeded in producing more than this quota, the surplus became theirs. The older girls were therefore expected to earn about $2\frac{1}{2}$ ducats a month apiece. The matron consigned, out of this sum, one ducat a month on behalf of each girl to the treasurer, for her keep. The remaining $1\frac{1}{2}$ ducats were then assigned to the ordinary domestic needs of the house, to providing clothes and linen, and to paying for a part of the dowries it would eventually furnish. Should a girl pass the 10-soldi mark, the extra money was placed in a common chest in a small bag with her name on it. If she needed anything special, her private store of money was raided, and a note entered on a book designed for the purpose.[69]

The girls normally underwent a period of five to six years' instruction in devotion (especially to the Virgin Mary), in the Christian virtues of humility, obedience, purity and charity, and in the examination of conscience.[70] The course was varied by disputations in Christian doctrine at Carnival time, by occasionally devising tableaux-vivants depicting sacred subjects, and by singing or versifying the psalms.[71] Then the time arrived for the Casa to launch its protégés into the cloister or the

[67] Ibid., Part IV, ch. iii and iv, pp. 20–1.
[68] Ibid., Part IV, ch. v–ix, xxxii, pp. 21–3, 32.
[69] Ibid., Part V, ch. lxvi–lxxi, pp. 52–3.
[70] Ibid., Part IV, ch. xv, p. 27; Part V, ch. lii, p. 49.
[71] Ibid., Part V, ch. lvi, pp. 49–50; ch. lxxii, pp. 53–55.

world. Four Protettrici, chosen from among the female congregation of governors, found husbands or arranged for the admission of girls into nunneries, with the assistance of two male Protettori. They were instructed to look for the following qualities in prospective husbands:

> first, they shall be born of a good father; secondly, be modest and god-fearing; thirdly, be healthy and well-disposed; fourthly, they shall be happy to associate with godfearing persons of a good life; fifthly, they shall be well-launched on some good employment, and shall be well-known, and shall attend very diligently to their shops and trades. The more good qualities they have, the better for the girls they have to marry. One must always take care that the contracts are appropriate to the rank of the girls.[72]

On its own account, the Casa offered a dowry of 100 ducats, 50 in money and 50 in clothing. But the statutes suggested that the Scuole and Procuratie should be asked to assist, to help to obtain a more impressive husband and secure entry to a higher-grade nunnery. The obligations of the institution did not, however, stop at this point, since it was expected to provide some after-care. The Governatrici were bound to visit former inmates, in their houses or cloisters, every four months, and to inform the congregations of any action necessary on behalf of the girls. The house also had two Sollicitatori, responsible, should a girl be widowed, for disentangling her dowry from the estate of her husband. It would be vital to her future after his death. The after-care was justified on the grounds that '*Qui cum dilexisset suos usque in finem dilexit eos*', and perhaps also by the practical reason that girls brought up in so rarefied an atmosphere would scarcely be equipped to face the perils of the world.[73]

The Casa delle Zitelle probably owed much to the recommendations made in the past by Girolamo Miani, and now worked out to a certain extent in the female orphanage at Santi Giovanni e Paolo. Provisions that the work should, as far as possible, be self-supporting may have increased its chances of success. This institution formed part of a general scheme being slowly promoted, by different religious groups reacting on one another, for the conquest of sin and ignorance among the poor. Palmio and his disciples were not attempting mere hand-to-mouth charity, by the temporary relief of physical needs: instead, they aimed at a take-over bid, at establishing an institution which would, in the interests of the soul, assume all the functions of a zealous and exacting parent. The Casa developed into a fairly large institution. In

72 *Ibid.*, Part IV, ch. xviii–xix, p. 28, wrongly numbered 24.
73 *Ibid.*, Part IV, ch. xxxi, pp. 31–2; Part V, ch. lxxiv, pp. 56–7. On the duties of the Sollicitatori, see Part I, ch. xi, p. 5.

Questa è la real sala del Collegio, dove ogni giorno si riduce la mattina il
Serenissimo Prencipe con la Signoria per dare udienza ai Legati del Pontefice,
e a gli Ambasciatori di Re e d'altri Prencipi grandi, e si trattano molte cose
importanti intorno al governo dello Stato Serenissimo

Secretari

THE COLLEGIO AT WORK

Here the Collegio, with the Doge presiding, is seen receiving ambassadors. Notice the Secretaries—
leading citizens of Venice—at the tables in the foreground.

facing p. 390

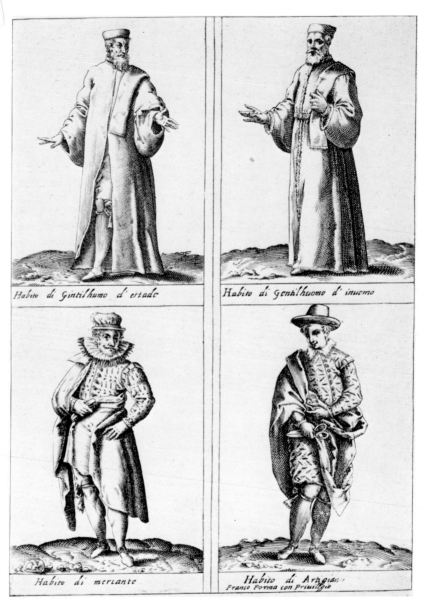

Habito di Gintilhuomo d'estade

Habito di Gentilhuomo d'inuemo

Habito di mercante

Habito di Artigian
Franco Forma con Priuillgio

VENETIAN SOCIAL TYPES

This print—first published in the early seventeenth century—shows a nobleman in winter and in summer dress; a non-noble merchant; and an artisan—representatives of three 'estates' of respectable Venetian society.

facing p. 391

1567, it had 90 girls, rising to 150 in 1580 and 180 in 1582, when its governors hoped to increase the numbers by the admission of another 80 recruits.[74] However, about 1620, the official Jesuit historian, Sacchini, thought that in his time the numbers were only about 140.[75]

About 1577, Venice acquired another institution, eventually known as the Casa del Soccorso, which complemented the Incurabili, Convertite and Zitelle: the last side of the square, to make all complete. The original inspiration for this was probably the Casa di Santa Marta in Rome. In 1543, Paul III had issued the Bull which approved the Compagnia della Grazia a Santa Marta. The Roman fraternity was to administer a species of half-way house. This would provide an immediate refuge, chiefly for women who in their husbands' absence had 'loosed the reins of modesty and continence'; and also for any other kind of woman guilty of the sin of adultery. Those entering the house were simply required to take a vow never to leave it until they were either reconciled with their husbands, equipped with a marriage-contract, or prepared to enter the Convertite.[76]

A certain Venetian tradition ascribes the foundation of the Soccorso to a famous literary courtesan, Veronica Franco[77]—although, as Croce pointed out in his edition of her letters, her association with the house cannot be convincingly proved.[78] However, Veronica Franco undoubtedly showed much interest in the means by which girls and

[74] A.S.V., *Senato, Terra, filza* 50, 13 September 1567; *filza* 80, 29 March 1580; *filza* 84, 25 June 1584—this last petition from the Governors mentions the fact that the staff of the Zitelle brought the total numbers to about 200. A further petition, dated on or before 22 November 1588, mentions over 200 inmates—see *filza* 110, 18 March 1589.

[75] Sacchini, *Historiae Societatis Jesu*, Part II, pp. 52–3.

[76] Tacchi Venturi, *Storia della Compagnia di Gesù in Italia*, I/ii, doc. 77, 78, pp. 284–94; II/ii, pp. 160 f.

[77] This tradition is ultimately based on a collection of documents made in 1761 by the governor Angelo Malipiero, *Notizie istoriche della Pia Casa di Santa Maria del Soccorso*, now M.C.V., Cicogna MSS., vol. 3690. Most of the important documents in this collection were printed in Cicogna, *Inscrizioni veneziane*, V, pp. 414–17, 420. Malipiero produced copies of a petition from Veronica Franco, offering to reveal to the Signoria an invaluable method of providing revenue for the support of a new pious institution to offer shelter to repentant prostitutes; and of another petition from the governors of the Soccorso, proposing to raise revenue by a means which Malipiero assumed to be the one at which Veronica Franco was hinting. They merely invited the Signoria to copy Pope Pius V, who had decreed that in Bologna the property of all prostitutes who died intestate in the city and without legitimate and natural children should be applied to the maintenance of a similar institution. There is no evidence that these proposals were in fact the same. The date of foundation suggested by Malipiero—1577—was, however, about right: a petition of the governors of the Soccorso, in A.S.V., *Senato, Terra, filza* 131, 31 March 1594, describes the house as having been in existence for about sixteen years.

[78] Veronica Franco, *Lettere: dall'unica edizione del MDLXXX*, ed. Benedetto Croce (Naples, 1949), pp. XIII–XIV, 76–7.

2c

women could be diverted from prostitution. She was determined, in the letters published in 1580, to strip the glamour from the courtesan's profession. She addressed one letter to a mother in the process of training her daughter to dress immodestly in order to become a courtesan or '*femina del mondo*':

> To pledge one's body and one's energies to this slavery, the very thought of which makes one shudder, is an experience altogether too unhappy and too repugnant to human feelings. To offer oneself as a prey to so many, at the risk of being stripped, robbed, killed or deprived in a single day of all that you have earned in so many, with so many other risks of injury or of contagious and revolting diseases; to eat with the mouth and sleep with the eyes of another, to move at another's desire, always heading plainly towards the shipwreck of one's life and possessions: what greater misery could there be? What riches, pleasure or luxury can compensate for so heavy a burden?

Veronica Franco claimed to have suggested that the girl be admitted to the Zitelle. The mother had listened gratefully at first, but had afterwards backslid.[79]

This letter belonged to that order of correspondence which is strictly designed for publication. But there is no reason to doubt its writer's sincerity, or her knowledge—based on experience—of the prostitute's problems. In a petition to the Senate, which she drafted (even if she did not actually present it) before 1577, Veronica Franco lucidly stated the need for a new institution to supplement the existing ones:

> There are many women who, out of poverty or sensuality or for some other reason, lead a dishonourable life, but who are sometimes moved by the Holy Spirit to think of the miserable end, both in body and soul, to which for the most part they come by this means. They could easily withdraw from ill-doing if they had some reputable place to repair to, where they might maintain themselves and their children. For they are not allowed to enter among the Zitelle or Convertite if they have mothers, children, husbands, or other necessary responsibilities. It is, moreover, difficult for them to persuade themselves to pass, in a moment, from such a licentious existence to so strict and austere a way of life as that of the Convertite. Because there is no provision for such cases, they persist in wrongdoing, and in this abominable crime among others: that women in need sell the virginity of their own innocent daughters, and launch them on the same sinful path that they themselves have walked, to the loss of so many souls, the scandal of the world, and the grave offence of the Majesty of God.[80]

[79] *Ibid.*, pp. 36–9.
[80] See Cicogna, *Inscrizioni veneziane*, V, pp. 414–16. Cf. also the account of Veronica Franco's testament of November 1570, in Giuseppe Tassini, *Veronica Franco* (Venice, 1888), pp. 77–8.

As it happened, the Casa del Soccorso may well have been founded on Jesuit inspiration, or by the circles to whom the Jesuits acted as confessors. At first, its penitents led the usual hand-to-mouth existence common to religious institutions which could not escape the mortmain laws, and therefore had no regular income from investments in real property. They lived solely on an irregular supply of alms, in a house in the parish of Santi Gervasio e Protasio, able to accommodate up to thirty members of the community. Soon after 1590, the women moved to new premises at San Raffaele which could take up to fifty inmates. To some extent, sales of work supplemented the flow of alms. Any property owned by the women who entered was put aside, and was reserved to provide dowries for them when they left the house: if it did not suffice, it would be supplemented by the funds of the house itself, such as they were. A gentlewoman served as Prioress of the community, with an assistant, a 'mistress' and a portress. The foundation paid salaries to the usual adjuncts of all religious and charitable institutions —to a chaplain, and to a man employed to go round the town collecting for the Casa. A large congregation of gentlewomen met at the Casa once a week and visited its inmates. They, 'being set upon the way of salvation', 'attending the Most Holy Sacraments, live an angelic life without putting on the garments of a religious'.[81]

The institutions found in Venice were of a highly exportable type, appropriate to many communities: houses similar to that of Santa Marta in Rome were especially popular. In 1546, Cosimo de' Medici contemplated the foundation of such a house either at Florence or at Pisa. A modern Jesuit historian, Tacchi Venturi, has claimed that the houses for female penitents at Florence, Bologna, Modena, Trapani, Agrigento, Messina and Palermo were exact reproductions rather than mere rough imitations of the house at Santa Marta, springing up in the decade immediately before Loyola's death in 1556.[82] The system of complementary institutions for the reduction of prostitution also appeared in some of the cities of the Venetian mainland. Brescia, for example, had one or more houses for Zitelle, and a Soccorso as well as a Convertite and Incurabili: though it was assumed, in the early seventeenth century, that inmates of the Soccorso would always move on to the Convertite.[83] In Vicenza, in 1600, there was already a Soccorso,

[81] A.S.V., *Senato, Terra, filza* 131, 31 March 1594. The statutes were printed as *Capitoli et ordini per il buon governo della Pia Casa del Soccorso di Venetia* (Venice, 1701): but it is impossible to discover which were the original statutes, and which were later additions.

[82] Tacchi Venturi, *Storia della Compagnia di Gesù in Italia*, I/i, p. 385, II/ii, p. 174.

[83] A.S.V., *Sindici Inquisitori in Terra Ferma, busta* 64, ff. 59–60.

and a Zitelle was being established in a separate building, using the same church.[84]

Moreover, in Brescia, similar ideals were shared by the Company of St Ursula, founded during the 1530's by Angela Merici. Its purpose, however, was both to afford protection to young women and to enable them to lead a useful and virtuous life, devoted to good works, outside the confines of a cloister, or, indeed, those of a lay institution like that of the Zitelle. By 1566, according to Francesco Landini, a Tuscan priest and a member of the Congregazione della Pace, the Compagnia di Sant'Orsola in Brescia comprised 130 virgins, in addition to the widows responsible for their supervision. It was designed, he explained, to

> assist and edify many young virgins, both rich and poor, who, even though they feel a deep respect for the religious way of life, are nevertheless disinclined to shut themselves up within the narrow walls of cloisters, or bind themselves by vows; or who, again, cannot enter nunneries because of poverty, or do not wish to do so for other good reasons.

Members of this Company, he added, had worked extensively in all the hospitals of Brescia and in the schools of Christian doctrine. They had also served God by the conversion of souls, and by attracting into his service members of the households in which they continued to live.[85] This organization, which, through Borromeo's interest, spread to the diocese of Milan after 1566, had strong affinities with the old institution of the Franciscan Tertiaries, of whom its foundress was one. However, towards the close of the century, distrust of the idea of an uncloistered order of women threatened to divert the organization from its original path.[86]

Besides prostitutes, another category of outcasts claimed the attention of private philanthropists in sixteenth-century Venice: prisoners arrested for debt, and criminals awaiting trial in the city's jails. The rigours, the delays and the sheer inefficiency of the law needed to be curbed by charitable action, though the state itself made certain well-meaning attempts to safeguard the interests of prisoners. It is possible

---

[84] A.S.V., *Senato, Terra, filza* 156, 4 October 1600.

[85] From a letter of Father Francesco Landini, 'che sta nel Monte vicino a Brescia', to Friar Franceschino, 'Visdomini dell'Ordine de Minori', 21 December 1566, in *Acta Ecclesiae Mediolanensis*, ff. 338v.–339. On Landini, see Cistellini, *Figure della riforma pretridentina*, p. 145.

[86] See Mary Monica, *Angela Merici and her teaching idea (1474–1540)* (New York, 1927), pp. 306 f.

that the Jewish loan-banks in Venice itself, and the Monti di Pietà outside it, reduced the risk of being arrested for petty debts—since they enabled the poor to realize their assets more quickly, and at less risk of losing them outright or incurring heavy interest payments.[87] However, for the unfortunate, Venice maintained six district lock-ups, one in each sestiere, known as the Casoni. Debtors could also be confined in certain of the prisons at San Marco and Rialto. By 1551, it was already the rule that persons imprisoned in the Casoni could not, while they were inside, be taxed with, and rearrested for, any further debt. This rule did not, however, apply to the prison known as the Leona at San Marco: its inmates enjoyed no such protection, and consequently many of them, charged with a series of debts, never emerged from confinement. In 1551, the Great Council removed the anomaly, and put the Leona on an equal footing with other debtors' prisons.[88] Again, debtors for sums of less than 50 ducats were immune from being arrested in their own homes, though this rule often produced a kind of self-imposed house-arrest scarcely less paralysing than formal imprisonment. Debtors were allowed to emerge for a brief period twice a year without the risk of arrest, a provision theoretically designed to enable them to take communion and go to confession. In 1557, however, a government decree insisted that these periods be reduced to eight days only. The magistracy of the Auditori Vecchi had allowed the period of immunity to creep up to as much as one month.[89]

The system of arresting for debt was doubtless justified as a form of duress, a turn of the screw designed to force a man's relatives or dependants to raise money for his release. It may occasionally have acted as a deterrent to the unscrupulous. But it was often open to the charge of inhumanity and inefficiency, since it prevented the victims from working to repair their own misfortunes. The Auditori Vecchi had authority to take steps to release poor prisoners at Christmas and Easter, either by arrangement with their creditors or by paying off their debts out of charitable funds. Early in 1535, the Great Council assumed the existence of a number of wills containing bequests to poor prisoners, and decreed that all notaries drawing up wills in which prisoners received benefits must take the relevant clauses and show them to the Auditori Vecchi. Likewise, all trustees or executors responsible for the enforcement of wills containing legacies to poor prisoners must produce them to the Auditori Vecchi within six months. On more than one occasion, however, the Auditori were accused of neglect of duty in this

[87] See below, Part III.
[88] A.S.V., *Compilazione delle Leggi*, busta 309, f. 216r.–v., 19 March 1551.
[89] A.S.V., *Maggior Consiglio, Deliberazioni, Liber Rocca*, f. 58r.–v., 4 April 1557.

matter.[90] Sometimes, legislation aimed at procuring more humane treatment of the debtor's property: in 1570, a law attempted to protect the beds and bedding of poor debtors from seizure. These, in any case, tended to fetch very low prices at auctions, since potential purchasers often feared that they might be contagious.[91]

Towards those accused of criminal offences, the chief responsibility of government and society was to guarantee, not only justice, but reasonably expeditious justice as well. The state recognized the principle of setting up a poor persons' defence scheme, but was hardly generous towards it, in terms either of men or of money. Laws of 1441 and 1475 had first appointed an Avvocato dei Pregionieri to represent the interests of poor prisoners, and the Great Council made a second such appointment in 1535. The prisons of San Marco and Rialto, and the cells or *camarotti* of the Signori di Notte (a minor police magistracy), were then full to overflowing. Each Avvocato, however, received a salary of only 10 ducats a month,[92] and very likely he was tempted to devote much of his time to more lucrative private practice: even supposing that two Avvocati could ever have sufficed to deal with all the poor culprits in Venice. Occasionally, other resolutions of the Council of Ten reminded such lesser magistrates as the Giudici di Proprio and the Signori di Notte of their duty to press the Quarantia al Criminal (the supreme criminal court) for the rapid expedition of prisoners against whom they had no intention of proceeding further.[93] In at least one year—the year of spectacular Christian victory, 1571— the state piously issued an amnesty to certain classes of prisoner.[94]

Again, the sixteenth century did witness at least one attempt to improve the state of accommodation in prisons. Serious outbreaks of typhus in the jails at San Marco in September 1563 created the incentive to do so, in view of the risk to public health. The Council of Ten ordered the prisons to be cleaned out and fumigated. Infirmaries should be established in the prisons, and the prisoners themselves should keep them clean. The College of Physicians was to detail certain of its members to attend these sickbays, and the Avvocati must visit them regularly to see if they were in good order. The Ten then issued further

[90] A.S.V., *Maggior Consiglio, Deliberazioni, Liber Diana*, ff. 175–6, 17 January 1534 Venetian style; cf. also A.S.V., *Senato, Terra, filza* 205, 2 April 1613.

[91] A.S.V., *Maggior Consiglio, Deliberazioni, Liber Angelus*, ff. 52v.–53, 5 November 1570.

[92] A.S.V., *Maggior Consiglio, Deliberazioni, Liber Diana*, f. 188r.–v., 17 October 1535.

[93] A.S.V., *Compilazione delle Leggi, busta* 309, f. 218, 11 December 1558, ff. 241– 242v., 8 March 1578.

[94] A.S.V., *Maggior Consiglio, Deliberazioni, Liber Angelus*, ff. 69v.–70, 23 October 1571.

orders for the enlargement of certain cells in the Rialto prisons: several of these should be merged into one, for at present many people fell sick and died because of overcrowding in these black holes. Balconies should also be built at the Leona and other jails, to afford the inmates some relief in the terrible heat of summer. It is impossible to say how conscientiously these orders were carried out: but at least they record humane intentions on the part of the government.[95]

Organized private action was necessary in order to supplement official concern. The Scuole Grandi had done a little in the past to administer bequests to prisoners, though at the close of the sixteenth century the Scuola di San Rocco, for example, was bestowing only about 1½ per cent of its charity upon their relief.[96] In their early years in Venice, the Jesuits had formed some acquaintance with 'most honourable and noble matrons' who, at their confessors' suggestion, bestowed alms on various kinds of poor, including imprisoned debtors.[97] But a society which specialized in the relief of such debtors, on the model of the Compagnie del Divino Amore or the Fraternities of the Poveri Vergognosi, did not emerge until the 1590's. It was, like the Casa delle Zitelle, the product of sermons preached from the pulpit of the Incurabili: not by a Jesuit, but by an Observant Franciscan, Giovanni Battista Calzo da Pesaro.[98]

The Compagnia della Carità del Crocefisso began in 1591 as a small devotional society confined to a maximum of fifteen members—a limit removed by the Patriarch two years later. Domenico Scrova, parish priest of San Lio, also helped to assemble the society. Its purpose was to contemplate Christ's passion and his redemption of the world, 'and thereby be more earnestly inspired to do holy works of charity to the honour and glory of God and the Blessed Virgin Mary'. It also strove to practise all the Pauline doctrine of charity, which opened 'the way of salvation in a few lines'. Some time after its foundation, the brothers of the society determined to apply themselves specifically to the aid of imprisoned debtors (as in the statutes of 1594), and later—according to rules drawn up and confirmed by the Patriarch in 1597—to the assistance of criminals and of those accused of criminal offences.[99] The essential machinery, erected in 1594 and expanded three years later, appointed visitors to repair to the jails and collect information about the prisoners, which they then reported to the governing congregation.

[95] A.S.V., *Consiglio dei Dieci, Parti Comuni, filza* 90, 7 April 1564.

[96] See above, pp. 164–6.

[97] M.H.S.J., Polanco, *Historia Societatis Jesu*, V, p. 166, *anno* 1555.

[98] M.C.V., Cicogna MSS., *busta* 3118, *fascicolo* 6, *Constitutioni et ordini della Compagnia della Carità del Crocefisso per li carcerati di Venetia.*

[99] *Ibid.*, ff. 1v.–8.

They took the opinion of the prisoners' parish priests and of their jailers; they also spoke with their creditors. Having carefully selected the cases deserving of help, the congregation sent out chosen deputies (known, from 1597, as Assunti) to negotiate with the creditors. Between 1594 and 1597, the force of officials expanded with the growing scope of the society: from two visitors and two Assunti in 1594 to twelve visitors and four Assunti in 1597.[100]

Adopting the usual tone of the sixteenth century, the statutes of 1597 prescribed that the deputies should attend to the spiritual consolation of prisoners, that they 'might be released, not only from the jails, but also from the sins which hold them bound'. To raise the moral tone, they should ensure that the sexes were segregated and that women did not associate freely with male turnkeys. To curb homosexual practices, young men, wherever possible, should be assigned to separate cells. Prison visitors should confer with the judges in an attempt to ensure that the inmates could hear Mass every festival and take communion (after confession) on high festivals and at other appropriate times. The society proposed to appoint two or three suitable persons to collect alms in each sestiere for the purpose of financing Masses in the prisons.[101] These later statutes also laid down more specific rules for the guidance of visitors listing deserving cases. They should establish the 'social rank, conduct, poverty and other relevant circumstances of the prisoners, not only by means of certificates from their parish priests and jailers, but also by any other means deemed expedient'. Priority must go to those who had been in prison longest and suffered most, and to the morally deserving. But persons 'of ill-repute (*in mala opinione*)' must not be altogether neglected. 'To prevent fraud', the rules of the society also provided that no-one should be bailed out of prison on more than one occasion. The society deputed some of its brothers to attend the sessions at which the Auditori Vecchi liberated debtors, equipped with funds from the congregation to help deserving cases who had spent twenty or more days in prison.[102]

The statutes of 1594 certainly envisaged the possibility of helping those accused of crimes to obtain swift justice,[103] but this became a major concern of the society only after 1597. Criminals had their Avvocati, appointed by the state, but 'men of goodwill (*persone di cuore*)' were vital to remind the overworked public defenders of the existence of some of the oppressed. As it was, there were many prisoners due for trial by the Quarantia al Criminal or the Capi del Consiglio dei Dieci who had merely been forgotten, and could often be

100 *Ibid.*, f. 11r.–v., 18v.–21v.   101 *Ibid.*, ff. 23v.–24.
102 *Ibid.*, ff. 27v.–29v.   103 *Ibid.*, f. 11v.

immediately released if somebody bothered to remind the courts of their existence. The Signori di Notte were normally very quick, but even they allowed queues of accused persons to accumulate in their cells. Other magistracies wielding some powers of criminal jurisdiction —the Provveditori alla Sanità, Collegio alle Acque, Esecutori alla Bestemmia, Avogadori di Commun and Censori—had failed to expedite criminals. One clause in the statutes declared that this work was 'much more charitable' than that of releasing 'civil' prisoners, 'since by this means we shall be executing the wishes of those who formulated the laws'. These words seem to reflect a shift in the aims of the society.

The Compagnia della Carità also recognized, and proposed to work for, a number of prisoners who had been dealt with by the courts but not released. Some had contracted debts to the state while in prison— presumably for board and lodging—and this prevented their being either released outright or sent on from prison to the galley-service to which criminals were frequently condemned. The Compagnia proposed to obtain their release by securing an act of the Senate which cancelled the debt. Other prisoners languished in jail out of inability to pay the fines imposed on them, especially by one of the police magistracies, the Cinque alla Pace. Here, the society hoped to procure the application of a law whereby a determinate sum was remitted from the fine for every month the delinquent spent in prison. Alternatively, they could make arrangements for him to provide a security, and then to pay a certain amount every month. People left in prison because the proceedings had forced them to incur heavy legal costs or other debts to private persons should be helped, like civil debtors, by alms or by negotiations with their creditors.

To care for accused persons and convicts, the society now appointed six lay and six clerical visitors: each pair of visitors took one prison— from the Galleotta, Valiera, Giustiniana, Preggione Forte, Leona and Rialto—and repaired there every week. Laymen should see that the prisoners were provided with bedding, mattresses and similar comforts. Clergymen ought to guarantee supplies of spiritual books, of rosaries both for communal and private use, of images of Christ, the Madonna and the saints. They should suppress gambling and blasphemy, which were common outlets for the prisoners' energies, and generally take an interest in the prisoners. Finally, the society proposed to send visitors, both lay and clerical, to visit sick galleots in the hospital at Sant' Antonio.[104] Convicts serving on the galleys were vulnerable to most of the forms of oppression practised in Venetian prisons, and especially

104 *Ibid.*, ff. 30–5.

to the kind of debt-slavery mentioned in the statutes of the Compagnia della Carità del Crocefisso.[105]

At first, the society seems to have depended for support on subscriptions placed by its members in a collection-box.[106] Later, it probably attracted bequests, or acquired control of moneys previously directed by testators towards prisoners. On at least one occasion, it attempted to secure the rights of prisoners by questioning the administration of an ancient bequest. In 1398, one Lorenzo di Tomasi had made an elaborate legacy to the Scuola Grande della Misericordia. Half the revenue from certain property should be devoted to the marriage of poor maids, a quarter to the poor of the Scuola, and a quarter to extricating poor debtors from the jails. At the turn of the fifteenth century, the property (in the Merceria) was rebuilt with the aid of moneys provided by the Scuola, and all additional revenue yielded by the property after its improvement was appropriated to the Scuola itself. In 1614, the total revenue of the Tomasi trust was 1,480 ducats a year, of which 1,174 were appropriated to building and 60 to taxation. Most of the rest went on marriage portions (120 ducats), freeing prisoners (58 ducats) and alms to the poor (also 58 ducats). This total of 236 ducats was alleged to be equivalent to the revenues of the trust in 1504. On this occasion, the Compagnia della Carità got the administration of the trust reformed through action of the Council of Ten,[107] and in 1627 the Misericordia was retaining only 690 ducats for its own purposes and dispensing 750 ducats in equal proportions to prisoners, maidens and paupers.[108] According to a petition submitted by the Compagnia della Carità to the Council of Ten, on 16 December 1614 the Guardian Grande of the Misericordia received orders to 'subscribe all the warrants sent to him by the governors of the congregation for releasing prisoners according to his conscience'. The Compagnia provided the information, the Scuola the funds.

The surviving statutes of this prisoners' aid society contain familiar features: the combination of spiritual preoccupations with corporal; the anxiety to formulate, in minute detail, criteria for the selection of the deserving poor; careful attention to the general problem and its ramifications; a preference for collective, rather than individual action. The constitution of the society was far nearer to that of the Compagnie

---

[105] See Alberto Tenenti, *Piracy and the decline of Venice, 1580–1615*, trans. Janet and Brian Pullan (London, 1967), p. 114.

[106] *Constitutioni dell Compagnia della Carità del Crocefisso*, ff. 11v.–12.

[107] For papers relating to the case, see A.S.V., *Consiglio dei Dieci, Parti Comuni, filza* 302, 17 August 1615; see also above, p. 129.

[108] Statement submitted by the Scuola della Misericordia, in A.S.V., *Milizia da Mar, fascicolo* 706.

del Divino Amore than to that of the Scuole Grandi. It was outward-looking, in that it provided chiefly for the needs of poor persons who were not members of the society. It specialized in one particular form of relief. Its tone was evangelical. It made far greater use of the clergy in its deliberations and in the actual relief-work, and was more careful to court the approval of ecclesiastical authorities: the Patriarch Priuli approved the foundation itself in 1593, and also confirmed the statutes of 1594 and 1597.

A prominent feature of sixteenth-century philanthropy in England, after the break with Rome, was the increasing preoccupation of testators with the endowment of grammar schools, and their concern to promote secondary education, rather than university education in theology. It is hard to find anything exactly comparable in sixteenth-century Venice. The efforts of Miani and his followers, of the Paulines and of the Jesuits, had provided extensively for the education of orphans and of those whose parents had failed them: education in Christian doctrine and conduct, education in trades, handicrafts or other skills that would increase their independence and reduce their poverty. The poor law, with its rough-and-ready condemnation of vagabond children to apprenticeship at sea, had moved approximately in the same direction. There is less sign, however, of any general attempt to provide secondary education of a more intellectual nature to children still living with their own families. Certainly the Jesuits achieved little success with the school they tried to start in the 1550's. Probably the more well-to-do families either employed private tutors or, as the Jesuits complained, appreciated only a very practical education. However, Venice (like other parts of Italy) did establish an extensive Sunday-school movement, which aimed at raising the general level of literacy, because literacy was the key to Christian knowledge. Ostensibly, this movement catered for children from all social ranks, though it probably drew more heavily on the poor than on the genteel.

Verona, under Giberti's guidance, formed a network of such schools, probably well before Venice itself did so. According to Giberti's biographer, fifteen churches in the city of Verona were assigned to the new schools of Christian doctrine. Each school was equipped with one lay and one clerical Prior, a staff of four or five members of the clergy or laity, and two officers to maintain discipline. The curriculum hinged on a printed Dialogue or Catechism, in which a teacher and pupil discussed the elements of the Christian faith and the essential principles of good conduct. The pupils learnt this by heart, and asked one another

questions about 'matters which concern every Christian'—including
the Lord's prayer, the twelve articles of faith, the Ten Commandments,
the prescribed works of mercy, and others. They were encouraged to
go to confession every month.[109] Moreover, the teaching of Christian
doctrine became a major concern of the Jesuits, from the time that
Laynez conducted his early visits to Venice and the Veneto in the
1540's.[110]

The organization created in Venice for the teaching of Christian
doctrine centred on the hospital of the Incurabili, and worked in conjunction both with the Jesuits and with the Theatines still established
at San Nicolò di Tolentino. In 1551, one of the Venetian Jesuits,
Cesare Helmi, told Loyola how

> Certain good men have established a congregation for the purpose of
> reforming their own lives and winning souls for Christ, and have under-
> taken the task of teaching children Christian doctrine.

They had implored the Superior, André des Freux, to visit them on
Sundays and holidays to observe and criticize their methods: since he
was too busy, Helmi had taken on the job himself.[111] A Theatine,
Giovanni Paolo da Como, codified the regulations governing the
Sunday-school movement in 1568. These statutes impart valuable
information about the professed objects of the organization, and about
how the work was conceived.[112]

In foundation statutes of this nature, it was usual to represent the
work undertaken as being a supremely, even uniquely, valuable form
of charity. True to form, the constitutions proclaimed the absolute
superiority of the soul to the body, and therefore the superiority of
spiritual to corporal charity.

> What greater charity or mercy can there be than to have mercy on the
> soul rather than on the body? For the soul is worthier than the body as
> light than darkness, gold than dross, or heaven than earth. Consequently,
> mercy and charity towards the soul of one's neighbour (by instructing

[109] Zini, *Boni pastoris exemplum*, p. 292; Giberti, *Constitutiones, titulus* iv, ch. xx,
in his *Opera*, pp. 63–4.

[110] See the letter of Laynez to Paschase Broët, from Padua, 11 December 1543,
M.H.S.J., *Lainii Monumenta*, I, p. 30; letter of Quiros de Rivera to Ignatius Loyola
from Padua, 26 June 1546, *ibid.*, *Epistolae Mixtae*, I, p. 294.

[111] M.H.S.J., *Litterae Quadrimestres*, I, pp. 329–30, letter of 23 May 1551. See also
ibid., I, p. 390, II, pp. 551–2, III, p. 17—letters of Andrea Frusio (André des Freux)
of 1 September 1551, and of Cesare Helmi of 20 January and 9 June 1554.

[112] *Ordini et Capitoli della Compagnia dell'Oratorio il quale è nell'Hospitale de gli
Incurabili in Venetia, circa il governo delle Schole de Putti, che sono in detta Citta;
nelle quali s'insegna la dottrina Christiana a' figliuoli il giorno della Festa doppo il
disnare. Raccolti dal Reverendo Padre Don Giovan Paolo da Como, Preposito delli
Reverendi Padri Clerici Regolari di San Nicola* (Venice, 1568).

these children in the way of God, out of love and honour towards him) are far more worthy, precious and excellent than charity and mercy performed only for the body, since one single soul is worth more than all the world put together.[113]

Schools for this purpose had been erected, not only in Venice itself and in Padua, but also in other cities of Lombardy and Italy, and especially in Rome.[114] In Venice, the central organization responsible was a spiritual fraternity known as the Society of the Oratory (Compagnia dell'Oratorio), which met in the hospital of the Incurabili, and included among its devotions the recitation of the Office of the Madonna and the taking of frequent communion. This fraternity elected thirteen 'principal brothers', on the model of Christ and his twelve apostles, to hold office for life, and either to summon general congregations or to hold 'particular' ones amongst themselves. Below them were twelve assistants or Coadjutors. From the 'principal brothers', the congregation elected, in rotation, one to serve as Prior and another to be Superior of the whole organization. Each of the separate schools of Christian doctrine run by this body possessed its own hierarchy of officials, headed by a priest as Prior and by a layman as Subprior. The priest should, where possible, be one of the thirteen heads of the congregation, or at least a member of the Society of the Oratory, or, failing that, somebody well-disposed towards the work. The lay Subprior of each separate school must be one of the principal brothers or one of the Coadjutors. Below these officers were two Counsellors, two or more Correttori, a secretary or Scrivano (always with a successor under instruction by his side), two sacristans, two or more doorkeepers, an infirmarian, and any appropriate number of teachers to instruct the children who attended. Teachers were recruited from the members of the Society, and, where necessary, supplemented by the older and more responsible pupils in the schools themselves. The Counsellors in each school would occasionally act as Masters of Novices, instructing in their duties young men and older persons who offered their services as teachers.[115]

The purpose of the organization was to drive back ignorance and perhaps also to throw up defences against heresy. The teachers received detailed instructions as to what to teach the children. They began with simple devotional practices. They should teach them to say 'Thanks be to God' or 'Praise the Lord', and show them how to make the sign of the Cross. All must learn the Lord's prayer, Hail Mary and Creed, together with the Ten Commandments. Sober and submissive conduct

---

[113] *Ibid.*, p. 12.   [114] *Ibid.*, p. 3.
[115] *Ibid.*, pp. 10–11, 13–15, 30–2.

was also essential. Children must be taught to respect their elders and to defer, especially, to the priesthood. At home they should pray, 'bless the table' before meals, and say grace afterwards. Cursing, blaspheming and fighting were strictly proscribed. The brothers must set the example by taking communion every month, or at least on 'the appointed festivals', sometimes doing so in a body in their parish churches. They should make 'all the larger children, who are capable of mischief' go to confession at least three or four times a year.[116]

Here, as in Giberti's Verona, the pivot on which all instruction turned was an Interrogatorio or Catechism. Pupils, after being taught to read a little and becoming acquainted with less difficult books, eventually graduated to the study of this work, and to conducting discussions or 'disputations' on the lines which it suggested. Only the 'head children', or Putti Capi, conducted these disputations. Sessions of the schools were held between dinner and Vespers on Sundays and other festivals and holidays. After studying their books, the children 'recited' the contents, were then questioned about the Ten Commandments, and, finally, processed in a body to a local church—if possible, singing hymns on the way. In the church, the 'head children' duly disputed, 'with reverence and respect towards God, little and well'. On Sundays, the children recited the form of prayer laid down in the Catechism, 'for all the States of the Church, both temporal and spiritual, general and particular'; on saints' days, the Litanies.[117]

This society, evidently an offshoot of the Incurabili, and one of the group of charities associated with the Jesuits and Theatines, offered, as a form of spiritual benevolence, to extend Christian knowledge and raise standards of conduct. The society embodied an organized effort to improve primary education and to increase literacy. More advanced educational programmes probably had less success. It is difficult, however, to be certain of this, since the educational history of Venice remains to be written, and this study is able to focus only on institutions specifically designed to cater for some sector of the poor. In the early seventeenth century, there was an attempt—which eventually proved successful—to establish a college for the specific purpose of catering for poor noblemen, and to provide education at pre-university level. The original series of proposals, made in the Senate in 1609, came from the Procurator Federico Contarini.[118] Contarini had always sympathized with the aims and ideals of the Jesuits, and in 1593 the

116 *Ibid.*, pp. 34–5, 42–3.
117 *Ibid.*, pp. 44–7.
118 For Contarini's speech, see Luigi Zenoni, *Per la storia della cultura in Venezia dal 1500 al 1797: l'Accademia dei Nobili in Giudecca* (Venice, 1916), doc. I, pp. 159–161.

papal nuncio Taverana had described him as 'always inclined to further the interests of the Church (*sempre favorevole alle cose ecclesiastiche*)'. He had served in the 1590's as one of the Provveditori sopra gli Ospedali, showing himself markedly ill-disposed towards the expensive project for the establishment of the Mendicanti. But he was especially interested in the education of young people, and was sufficiently involved with the Casa delle Zitelle to have himself buried there, to erect in its church a marble altar with a votive picture, to establish there a perpetual chaplaincy and a dowry trust for the benefit of ten poor girls. His proposals may, in a sense, have been the legacy of the Jesuits, and, in their evident concern for the relief of impoverished noble houses, have owed some inspiration to the Fraternity of the Poveri Vergognosi. The anti-clericalism and hostility to things connected with the Jesuits which followed the Interdict may, indeed, have been responsible for the original failure of Contarini's project. This was not realized until 1619, four years after his death.[119]

In fact, even the 1550's had witnessed two parallel attempts to offer pre-university education to the public at large: one made by the Jesuits, the other by the state itself. Soon after their arrival, the Jesuits had with high hopes devoted themselves to the erection in Venice itself of a college to instruct both budding members of their own Society and pupils recruited from the city. It would teach grammar and the humanities, and possibly also scriptural knowledge, scholastic theology and even a little mathematics.[120] In June 1552, when there were eleven Jesuits in Venice, the number of scholars (divided into four classes) was about 145; but it dropped a year later to 103 in the middle of summer and to only about 80 in September. Thereafter, down to the year 1556, the numbers fluctuated between about fifty and about eighty. The Jesuits blamed the Venetians' disappointing response on their philistinism—their determination to send their children, at the earliest possible opportunity, to train for a business career. The site of the school, too, was remote and uninviting, and attracted few pupils.[121] In mid-June 1556, the school was forced to close because of plague, and, although the Jesuit Cesare Helmi was eager to reopen it the following winter, the patron of the Society in Venice, Andrea Lippomano,

[119] For the above, see Gaetano Cozzi, 'Federico Contarini: un antiquario veneziano tra Rinascimento e Controriforma', *Bollettino dell'Istituto di Storia e dello Stato Veneziano*, III (1961), pp. 195–205.

[120] M.H.S.J., Polanco, *Historiae Societatis Jesu*, II, p. 209.

[121] M.H.S.J., *Litterae Quadrimestres*, I, pp. 692, 703–4, letters of Andrea Frusio to Loyola from Venice, 29 June, 2 July 1552; *Epistolae Mixtae*, III, p. 342, Cesare Helmi to Loyola, 10 June 1553; *Litterae Quadrimestres*, II, pp. 386–7, Giovanni Gambero to Ignatius Loyola, 2 September 1553; Polanco, *Historia Societatis Jesu*, IV, pp. 124, 127, 129; V, pp. 167, 171; VI, p. 226.

thought this inadvisable.[122] Reports from Venice to the General Laynez in 1561 showed that the Jesuits were then maintaining only a *casa dei professi*, with five priests, and not a college.[123] This state of affairs became formal in 1570. Jesuit colleges remained only in Padua and in Brescia, to which the course in the liberal arts was moved in 1570.[124] A further Jesuit college, however, arose in Verona on Valier's instigation in 1578, and at the time of the Jesuit withdrawal from the Venetian state in 1606 another foundation was in the offing at Vicenza.[125]

The Jesuit school at Padua suffered other misfortunes. A serious quarrel with the University broke out in the late sixteenth century, and the government ordered the school to be closed. However, several leading noblemen, including the Doge Marino Grimani and the Procurator Jacopo Foscarini, were anxious to see it reopened, and even the University consented to this on condition that its curriculum was carefully circumscribed.[126] In 1604, the Jesuits opened a college for noblemen in Brescia.[127] However, the events of the Interdict prevented the school at Padua from ever opening. The proposals made by Contarini may have been intended to provide a substitute for Jesuitical education, though his college would doubtless have been in clerical hands.

In the 1550's, the state had also tried to extend public educational facilities. It already employed a public lecturer in philosophy, who on Fridays and Saturdays taught the 'moral philosophy'—i.e., the *Ethics*, *Economics* and *Politics* of Aristotle—so that men might learn to 'control themselves and at the same time to govern their own households and the commonwealth'.[128] There were also one or two lecturers in the humanities, but they taught only at San Marco, and their school (as a Jesuit testified in 1551) was little attended.[128a] In 1551, the Senate proposed to add to the machinery for free education by providing one lecturer in the humanities and one teacher of grammar to function in a publicly maintained school in each of the sestieri. The humanists

---

[122] *Ibid.*, VI, p. 229.

[123] M.H.S.J., *Litterae Quadrimestres*, VII, p. 137—Flaminio Ricchieri to Laynez, 30 January 1561.

[124] M.H.S.J., *Polanci Complementa*, II, p. 716—from the *Commentariola Polanciana* for 1570; Francesco Sacchini, *Historiae Societatis Jesu*, Part III (Rome, 1649), p. 278.

[125] *Ibid.*, Part IV (Rome, 1652), p. 175; Joseph Jouvancy, *Historiae Societatis Jesu*, Part V (Rome, 1710), p. 98.

[126] Cozzi, 'Federico Contarini', pp. 199–202.

[127] Jouvancy, *Historiae Societatis Jesu*, Part V, p. 298.

[128] A.S.V., *Senato, Terra*, reg. 1553/54, f. 56r.–v., 14 October 1553; *filza* 57, 8 March 1571. The first of these entries records the death of the lecturer Sebastiano Foscarini, the second that of the lecturer Francesco Da Ponte.

[128a] M.H.S.J., *Epistolae Mixtae*, V, p. 737: Andrea Frusio to Loyola from Venice, 14 October 1551.

MARY MAGDALEN

For the significance of the Magdalen, as a symbol of effective repentance and as patroness of the Convertite, see above, p. 372 and Part II Chapter 6.

facing p. 406

PORTRAIT OF A NOBLEMAN

facing p. 407

should receive salaries of 200 ducats each, the grammarians of 60.[128b] However, the financial provisions—out of newly imposed and earmarked taxes—proved to be inadequate, and in 1567 the government came down to earth and introduced a less ambitious scheme. It now proposed to offer the public only four humanists and four grammarians. The grammarians, paid 80 ducats each, provided free instruction based on the works of Donatus, 'the rules of Guarinus', and so forth. The more exalted humanists received 150 ducats by way of stipend, and gave two lectures every day except on Sundays and holidays. In the morning they expounded some book of Cicero, and in the evening concentrated on Virgil, Terence or Horace. Every week they gave two prose exercises.[129] This system, in a modified form, was still a going concern in 1608, though its finances were obviously precarious: the salaries of all involved cost the state over 900 ducats a year, whereas the taxes supposed to pay them rarely averaged more than 700. By this time, the four humanists and four grammarians had been joined by another lecturer, who offered instruction in law and in the all-important profession of the notary.[130]

Some free public instruction was, then, available at about the time when Contarini spoke in 1609. But mere attendance at free public lectures would hardly provide members of the poorer nobility with the intensive discipline and supervision which they required, and which only some form of boarding-establishment was likely to provide. In the early seventeenth century, several critics complained bitterly of the indiscipline of younger members of the patriciate, and sometimes specifically of the misconduct of the poor. For example, in 1619, Ottaviano Bon wrote to Luigi Lollino, Bishop of Belluno, in terms which recalled Federico Contarini's:

One of the most serious defects of our government is the number of very poor noblemen, who, from their lack of fortune, remain without instruction or education—as a result of which they become the prey of their carnal instincts, and behave like animals rather than men. In their public and private responsibilities, both in the city and outside it, they commit those acts of robbery, arrogance and crime which are daily revealed, because they are concerned with their own personal advantage and not with the good of the state. Hence the people are badly governed, and they protest and complain, to the detriment of the state's reputation, and hence even good men suffer resentment and displeasure. . . .[131]

128b Printed in Besta, *Bilanci generali*, pp. 219–21.
129 A.S.V., *Senato, Terra*, reg. 1566/67, f. 172v., 4 November 1567.
130 A.S.V., *Senato, Terra, filza* 188, 2 September 1608.
131 Zenoni, *Per la storia della cultura*, p. 4.

At about this time, the problem of the poor nobility was passing through one of its more acute phases, and awareness of it was sharp. The Spanish Ambassador, Bedmar, drew attention to it in his reports on Venice: these reports were highly tendentious, but contained passages in which the abuse and criticism became more specific and discriminating, as if it were founded on genuine knowledge. At one point, Bedmar wrote that the Venetian nobility—or at least those of modest fortune who made their living out of legal office in the judiciary—were nine-tenths illiterate. They were seriously ignorant of legal procedure, and far too liable, in the courts, to be swayed by the eloquence of the last speaker. This interfered with the proper dispensation of justice, and the results of several lawsuits had been (to put it mildly) surprising.[132] The Venetian government itself clearly felt the need to raise the standards of its administrators, as well as to produce a disciplined and submissive attitude on the part of the poorer towards the richer nobles. Before and after 1620, the poorer nobility rose in protest against the rich on more than one occasion. In 1617, Alvise di Vicenzo Da Riva, one of the Heads of the Quarantia al Criminal, led an attack on the expensive management of the current war with the Habsburgs, in which he accused the established members of the Collegio and Senate of graft and profiteering. The Council of Ten—the instrument and vehicle of the older, richer patricians—arrested Da Riva, whereupon the Great Council refused to vote into the Senate many of the Senate's habitual members.[133] Again, in 1620, the Ten prosecuted a group of noblemen for conspiracy: they had attempted to break the rich patricians' monopoly of higher office by equipping themselves with extra quantities of voting-pellets for use in elections in the Great Council. These would enable them to vote into office themselves, their friends, or others willing to bribe them.[134] Finally, in 1627–8, arose Renier Zeno, a flamboyant demagogue of great panache, who exploited the discontent of the poorer nobility successfully in order to focus attention on the deficiencies of the Council of Ten and of the justice it administered.[135]

The Venetian Establishment saw its salvation, not in keeping the

---

[132] Bedmar, *Relatione universa delle cose di Venetia fatta da Don Alonso della Cueva, Ambasciadore di Spagna, hoggi Cardinale*, British Museum, Additional MSS. 5471, ff. 150v.–151.

[133] Gian Carlo Sivos, *Libro Quarto delli Dosi di Venetia*, B.M.V., MSS. Italiani, Cl. VII, no. 122 (8863), ff. 71v.–72.

[134] *Ibid.*, ff. 191–2v.; see also A.S.V., *Consiglio dei Dieci, Registro criminale 1620*, f. 54 f.

[135] On the Zeno movement, see the account in Gaetano Cozzi, *Il Doge Nicolò Contarini: ricerche sul patriziato veneziano agli inizi del Seicento* (Venice–Rome, 1958), ch. vi.

lesser noblemen poor and ignorant, but in increasing their knowledge and their sense of duty towards the state. Nicolò di Giovanni Battista Contarini opened the successful campaign for the foundation of an Accademia dei Nobili in 1618, speaking on the same lines as Ottaviano Bon.[136] The arrangements drawn up in 1619 prescribed that the school should cater for boys whose parents paid, between them, less than 20 ducats in tithe or *decima* (the standard direct tax on real property), and nothing in the way of *tansa* (the global tax which took account of income from other sources). The general purpose of the Academy was to instruct its charges in reading, writing and calculating. Moreover, in addition to godliness and good conduct, they were to be fitted for careers in government or in the navy, by instruction in the use of maps for navigation and in the humanities. A list of the Academy's requirements compiled in 1623 included 'Thirty books of Christian doctrine and twenty copies of Cicero's *De officiis*'.[137] The books of Christian doctrine may have been the Catechisms or Interrogatorii used by the Sunday-school movement formerly under Jesuit surveillance. Certainly by 1641 it was clear that the next stage for pupils of the Academy ought, ideally, to be either the University of Padua or the beginnings of a naval career: bounties were offered to all who would take up either of these careers.[138]

The Venetian Academy was established on the Giudecca, and the state originally proposed that it should cater for about forty scholars, who would need 100 ducats per head per annum to support them. A second such Academy was erected—with less success—in Padua in 1635. Some of its ideals, and perhaps those of the Venetian Academy, are reflected in an oration written upon its establishment by Baldassare Bonifaccio, an archdeacon of Treviso. He had also had connexions with the Venetian Academy, and had served as its Rector until his dismissal in mysterious circumstances in 1623.[139] Bonifaccio preached heroic and undiscriminating patriotism, self-abnegation like that of the Admiral Vettore Pisani who had suffered with such fortitude the injustice done him in the name of his country. He emphasized, in the following terms, the virtues of obedience and of submitting to the direction of social inferiors during the period of instruction at the Academy:

It is true that you are born to command: but nobody who does not know how to obey is capable of commanding, and, as Solon says, no government which has not first experienced subjection is capable of acquiring an

[136] Zenoni, *Per la storia della cultura*, doc. II, p. 162.
[137] *Ibid.*, doc. III, pp. 163–4, and p. 14, n. 2.
[138] *Ibid.*, p. 16.   [139] *Ibid.*, pp. 12, 17.

empire. Only the common virtues are required of the people: but heroic virtues are demanded of you, who are the sons of heroes. Everyone knows how to submit to those who are their masters by nature or at least by fortune. But for some time you will have to submit your wills to those who, even though inferior to you in social rank, are nevertheless your superiors by virtue of the office they hold. You may then, after bearing patiently with the government of others, with the magnanimity which belongs to noble hearts, govern your country with grace and accomplishment. Every man owes everything to his country, but you are bound to it by especially strong ties, since the grace of God has placed you in the most perfect condition of freedom that can be enjoyed in the world today, by creating you, not merely sons, but fathers of your fatherland.[140]

These words seem to reflect the current preoccupation with the indiscipline of the nobility and with their disregard of lesser men's rights and feelings.

As it happened, the Academy in Padua petered out comparatively rapidly. In 1641, Pietro Correr, Capitano of Padua, said that although this Academy had been founded to take forty boys aged up to sixteen to 'study the humanities' its numbers had now fallen to only twenty-two, many of whom were aged eighteen or nineteen and on the point of leaving.[141] By 1642 the school was closed. But the Academy on the Giudecca in Venice itself survived till the end of the Republic.

In the second decade of the century, the Venetian government had shown increasing eagerness to encourage members of the nobility to attend the University of Padua, especially by resuscitating the charitable foundations which would enable them to do so. Another measure consisted of enforcing the laws which forbade Venetian noblemen to study at foreign universities. In 1614, the governor Giovanni Battista Foscarini said that there were—or ought to be—thirteen colleges in Padua for the support of students attending the University, and that some of these were reserved to Venetian nobles. Many abuses had, however, corrupted their administration, and some were occupied by dissolute criminals. Foscarini had tried to restore order to the Collegio da Rio, and the Senate had then instructed the Rettori of Padua to draw up new regulations for all the colleges. The governors also tackled the Collegio di Ravenna, but complained of not receiving prompt approval from the Senate for their new statutes.[142] Three years later,

---

[140] For the text of the oration, see M.C.V., Cicogna MSS., *busta* 2999, *fascicolo* 22, *La Nova Accademia de' Nobili Veneti*.

[141] See his report of 9 July 1641, in A.S.V., *Collegio, Relazioni, busta* 43.

[142] Report of 16 September 1614, *ibid.*; cf. also A.S.V., *Senato, Terra, filza* 207, 21 September 1613.

another Podestà of Padua, Giovanni Dandolo, again complained of this abuse, and declared that

> there are many nobles in this state who are poor or of slender means, but who, if they were given the opportunity of living in Padua and attending the University, would undoubtedly emerge in time as excellent Senators, and very well fitted for government.[143]

Meanwhile, the Capitano Vitale Lando had argued that the number of nobles attending at Padua had fallen because so many people sent their sons out of the country to acquire an education, and hence the numbers had descended from about sixty to no more than seven or eight.[144]

In the years which followed, one governor, in 1626, claimed success for the re-enforced laws which prohibited Venetians from going to study elsewhere.[145] But the governors Andrea Vendramin and Pietro Correr, reporting in 1640–1, were still unsatisfied with the state of the colleges at the University, and especially with the Collegio Amulio, which kept not a single student. Correr claimed that there were fifteen colleges at Padua, several for Venetian nobles, and that if every college did its duty in accordance with the wishes of the founders it would be possible to maintain another 160 students at Padua. The best remedy would be greater diligence in seeking out neglected legacies.[146]

The early seventeenth century seems to reveal heightened concern with education, particularly with the education of those whose birth fitted them to be public servants. It is possible that the departure of the Jesuits had created a vacuum which needed to be filled by some alternative institution—although the Venetians themselves had signally failed to appreciate the efforts of the Jesuits in the mid-sixteenth century. The inefficiency and indiscipline of the poorer nobility was, in seventeenth-century Venice, a grave threat to the reputation of the patriciate as a whole, and to the peace of mind of its richer members. This provided another, perhaps more immediate, incentive to the establishment of new academies. In the mainland cities, there were several contemporaneous attempts to excite in the minds of the local nobles a sense of their duty towards the state—especially in serving as cavalry-officers. Military academies, or 'riding academies' (*accademie cavalleresche*), promised to perform this desirable task, though they were not specifically designed for the poor. One of the earlier academies was that of Verona, founded in 1565–6 partly by the voluntary association of a

[143] Report of 28 November 1617, A.S.V., *Collegio, Relazioni, busta* 43.
[144] Report of 21 May, 1616, *ibid.*
[145] Report of the Podestà Giulio Giustinian, 30 April 1626, *ibid.*; the measure was recommended by the Capitano Nicolò Vendramin in his report of April 1618—*ibid.*
[146] Reports of 20 March 1640 and 9 July 1641, *ibid.*

group of 'honourable gentlemen', and partly on the inspiration of Astorre Baglioni, then serving as governor of the local militia at Verona.[147] However, a series of such foundations came only in the early seventeenth century—at Padua, Udine, Treviso, and Vicenza, whilst the academy at Verona was restored in 1610.[148] In the words of an official report, the academy at Padua, founded by the Cavalier Pietro Duodo in 1608–9, was equipped with

> not only a riding master at a large salary, but also with a master who drills them in the use of weapons; and they have recently engaged a lecturer in mathematics; and with these most noble occupations they preserve mutual love; and in any case they will be able to be employed in the service of Your Serenity.[149]

However, it is doubtful whether any of these academies achieved any permanent and lasting success. The Paduan academy became far more attractive to German visitors than to the locals.[150] The disgusted governor of Treviso, in 1612, could only conclude that the local citizens had not the slightest aptitude for cavalry manoeuvres;[151] and in Verona in 1629 the military academy enjoyed none of the popularity of the civilian Accademia Filarmonica.[152]

Hitherto, the discussion has dealt only with the aims and organization of the hospitals, voluntary societies and other charities of Venice. Little, unfortunately, can be said at present about the finances or the economic problems of these establishments. However, the scanty information which has both survived and come to light suggests two tentative conclusions. The larger hospitals, both in Venice itself and in at least one of its subject cities, depended to a very large extent on voluntary contributions and on other 'irregular' sources of income in order to meet the demands made upon them. They did not meet a very large proportion of their expenditure by drawing on investment income. Again, in Venice, at least one of the newer institutions—the Incurabili —came to rely far less on fixed and regular sources of income than did such older foundations as the Pietà and San Giobbe.

[147] Reports of Alvise Grimani and Marc'Antonio Morosini, in A.S.V., *Collegio, Relazioni, busta* 33, *Miste,* ff. 66v.–67, 72.

[148] See Pullan, 'Service to the Venetian state', p. 109.

[149] Report of the Capitano Francesco Morosini, 1 July 1610, in A.S.V., *Collegio, Relazioni, busta* 43.

[150] Reports of Francesco Pisani, July 1633, Girolamo Ciuran, 2 May 1634, and Alvise Priuli, 8 November 1634, *ibid.*

[151] Report of Vincenzo Pisani, 10 May 1612, A.S.V., *Collegio, Relazioni, busta* 48.

[152] Report of Lorenzo Surian, 7 December 1629, A.S.V., *Collegio, Relazioni, busta* 50.

Most of the information relates to the late sixteenth or early seventeenth century. Early in 1603, the governors of the Pietà informed the Senate that their total annual expenditure was 24,000 ducats. Their regular income was normally only 8,000 ducats, and this year had fallen below that level, because of the liquidation of government consolidated loan funds then in progress: their holdings in the Monte Nuovissimo and Sussidio had been returned to them, and had yielded no income over the past year.[153] Comparable with the Pietà was the Bergamese general hospital of San Marco, whose regular income in 1627 stood at 12,000 ducats, its total expenditure at 28,000.[154] The Pietà, therefore normally expected to meet about one-third of its commitments out of regular income, the hospital in Bergamo 40–45 per cent. However, the situation of more recently erected hospitals in Venice was much more precarious. The regular income of the Incurabili in the 1580's—sixty years after its foundation—covered less than 10 per cent of its expenditure. In 1583, its fixed income was only 600 ducats, its expenditure over 7,000. In 1588, its governors claimed that expenditure had reached 10,000 ducats, with no accompanying rise in regular income.[155] Likewise, in 1601, the governors of the Mendicanti claimed to have spent 20,000 ducats in the past year, where during the previous decade government commissions had estimated the revenues of the nascent institution at 1,000 to 1,500 ducats only. However, this figure of 20,000 ducats did include some expenditure on setting up the buildings, and the substantial bequest of Bortolomio Bontempelli (invested in the Mint at 4 per cent in 1616) would certainly increase, perhaps even double, the regular revenue.[156]

The hospitals showed much less tendency to acquire real property in Venice itself than did the Scuole Grandi. Almost certainly, the provisions of the mortmain law of 1536 applied to them, in view of their ambiguous position as dubiously lay and possibly clerical institutions.[157] The fiscal survey of 1661 showed that the hospital of Santi Giovanni e Paolo derived an income of 1,475 ducats a year from real property in Venice, the Incurabili one of 784 ducats, and San Lazzaro e Mendicanti one of 959 ducats. For older hospitals, the corresponding figures were: the Pietà, 1,450 ducats; Santi Pietro e Paolo, 1,160; the Ca di Dio, 297; the German shoemakers, 146.[158] It may be that most of this

---

[153] A.S.V., *Senato, Terra, filza* 165, 15 February 1602 Venetian style.
[154] Report of Nicolò Donà, 22/27 November 1627, in A.S.V., *Collegio, Relazioni, busta* 36.
[155] A.S.V., *Senato, Terra, filza* 89, 13 December 1583; *filza* 107, 27 August 1588.
[156] A.S.V., *Senato, Terra, filza* 163, 22 June 1602, and above, p. 368.
[157] See above, p. 136.
[158] Beltrami, *Storia della popolazione*, Appendice, Tavola 24.

property was acquired before 1536; or that the government applied the mortmain law of 1536 in such a way as to limit rather than to prevent altogether the acquisition of Venetian real estate. Between 1536 and 1605, the hospitals, like other *luochi pii*, were entitled to invest in, or to retain legacies of, real property situated on the mainland. However, there were disadvantages here, since properties left to charitable institutions by numerous testators were most unlikely to be concentrated within a conveniently small area, and the difficulties of supervising and efficiently exploiting them might be very great indeed. Admittedly, at least one hospital on the mainland—that of Santi Giacomo e Lazzaro in Verona—made a determined effort to concentrate its holdings through sales and exchanges in the course of the sixteenth and early seventeenth century.[159] But to do this required time and skill, and these properties were not such convenient investments as Venetian houses and shops. Again, it may be that some of the ideals of the Theatines seeped through to the hospitals with which they were connected, and that the governors came to believe that they should not consume their time in the administration of estates, rather than in urgent evangelical work. Investment in government loan funds offered an alternative to investment in city or country properties. But in an inflationary period, like the second half of the sixteenth century, such investments possessed few advantages, since the debtor would benefit rather than the creditor. Finally, the hospitals, unlike the Scuole Grandi, were dealing with urgent needs, with sick persons and orphans demanding immediate relief or protection, and not with chronic poverty. They may, in consequence, have been far more eager to put their funds to instant use, rather than invest them and thereby guarantee a regular income in the future. These considerations may explain the failure of the Incurabili, in particular, to secure a substantial regular income.

The larger Venetian hospitals derived their 'casual' revenues from various sources. Miani's doctrines had emphasized the importance of children learning to support themselves, and many of the orphans at Santi Giovanni e Paolo and later at the Mendicanti were obviously expected to do this—as witness a measure of 1549, whereby all girls in the hospital of Santi Giovanni e Paolo must be found work outside it as soon as possible.[160] Other resolutions of 1565 and 1567 provided that girls should be sent out to their prospective employers to serve them on approval for one month. After this, the hospital must ensure

---

[159] See below, pp. 420–1.
[160] *Coppia tratta del Libro delle Parte et Ordini dell'Hospedal de S. Zuane Polo pertinenti al buon governo delle fie*, in A.S.V., *Ospedali e Luoghi Pii*, busta 910, fascicolo 2, f. 1, 18 October 1549.

that a contract for a definite period was drafted. No-one could break it without good reason. Employers must come and pay the girls' wages at the hospital every year.[161] By 1575, the girls were already raising funds by singing in public, and the hospital's governors decided to devote half the proceeds of these concerts to providing the children with dowries when the time came for them to marry.[162] The early statutes of the Mendicanti suggest that it proceeded on very similar lines. The inmates of hospitals and other institutions also produced handwork which they subsequently sold: the Zitelle and the women of the Mendicanti certainly did so. In 1553, again, the procurators of the nunnery of the Convertite petitioned on behalf of the 200-odd women penitents that they be allowed to establish a 'spinning-mill (*molino de filatogio*)' in order to supplement the meagre supply of alms for their support. The Provveditori di Commun duly considered the possibility that this might infringe the rights of those enrolled in the crafts of the textile industries, but eventually recommended that the Convertite should be allowed to establish such a 'mill'. The Senate agreed that they should be regarded as the equivalent of two normal spinners' establishments. In the course of the negotiations, the procurators expressly argued that the Convertite had no hope of acquiring property of their own, because to do so would have infringed the state's law.[163]

Much of the casual income of the hospitals and other institutions almost certainly came from outright cash gifts made by testators duly prompted, in accordance with the law, by their notaries. Only a thorough statistical survey, based on a sampling of the notarial archives, would establish the extent to which these gifts were made. The will of a certain Battista Ferro, drawn up in 1584, provides a fair specimen of such gifts:

> I leave to the Scuola of the Most Blessed Sacrament in the church of San Polo 25 ducats
>
> To the Hospital of Santi Giovanni e Paolo 10 ducats
>
> To the Hospital of the Incurabili 10 ducats
>
> To the Catecumeni 10 ducats
>
> To the Hospital of the Pietà 100 ducats
>
> To the Convertite 100 ducats

[161] *Ibid.*, f. 1v., 2v., 18 December 1565, 4 February 1567 Venetian style.
[162] *Ibid.*, f. 2v., 4 April 1575. On the subsequent development of music in Venetian hospitals, see Denis Arnold, 'Orphans and ladies: the Venetian conservatoires (1680–1790)', *Proceedings of the Royal Musical Association*, 59th session (1962/63); Denis Arnold, 'Instruments and instrumental teaching in the early Italian conservatoires', *The Galpin Society Journal*, XVII.
[163] A.S.V., *Senato, Terra, filza* 17, 18 March 1553; *filza* 18, 20 November 1553.

I wish 25 ducats to be dispensed after my death to the poor of the parish of San Polo

I wish 10 ducats to be dispensed to the *poveri vergognosi* of the city

I wish 10 ducats to be dispensed to poor prisoners.[164]

It is probable—though this needs confirmation through prolonged research—that the system whereby notaries drew testators' attention to the existence of these establishments had the effect of guaranteeing them a substantial casual income, rather than of producing a large number of trusts in their favour.

Hospitals, to meet their obligations, also needed a flow of gifts from persons who visited the place itself or its church, and gave alms there: sometimes allured by the promise of an indulgence granted by the Pope. The choice of a site was of paramount importance: hence the prolonged debate over the location of the Mendicanti in the 1590's.[165] Likewise, in 1564, the Convertite, complaining of acute poverty, said that their worst misfortune was 'that we are situated at the far end of the Giudecca, where nobody ever comes who may be moved to help us on seeing our wants and necessities'.[166] The Incurabili, on the other hand, may have gained substantially from its fashionable pulpit, from the eloquence of such preachers as Benedetto Palmio or Giovanni Battista Calzo da Pesaro, and from forming the centre of the movement for the erection of Sunday schools. All these things would help to attract people to the hospital, and all visitors were potential almsgivers.

The state itself would offer various forms of aid, in a somewhat haphazard and piecemeal fashion, to the hospitals and other institutes. In 1489, it had made a characteristic resolution to assist the Pietà by allowing it 200 *staia* of flour and 200 loads of firewood every year, whilst the Arsenal was expected to provide one amphora of wine every month. Official policy favoured special grants of this kind to individual hospitals, rather than any comprehensive treatment of them all. Moreover, the Senate also agreed to write to Rome and ask for 1,000 ducats of revenue from ecclesiastical benefices to be assigned to the hospital and thereby increase its regular income:[167] the government had no objection to the hospitals enriching themselves by means of clerical, as distinct from lay, property. However, the indult granted by Innocent VIII had still not taken full effect some eighty years later: for in 1571 the hospital was receiving only 242 ducats of revenue from the annexed benefices, 200 from an abbey in the Trevigiano, and the rest from the

---

[164] A.S.V., *Scuola Grande di San Rocco, Libro dei Testamenti*, f. 236, in *prima consegna, busta* 438.   [165] See above, pp. 366–7.

[166] A.S.V., *Senato, Terra, filza* 40, 12 August 1564.

[167] Malipiero, *Annali veneti*, p. 685, 6 July 1489.

chaplaincy or *Chiericado* of Santa Eufemia in Venice itself. The Roman curia was also pestering it for the dues payable when benefices were transferred to it.[168]

Again, in 1525, the Senate once more attempted to restore the fortunes of the Pietà. It should have the right to sell or hire out one of the boats in each of the Venetian ferry-stations, and to send out a band of musicians with a standard or *penello* to collect alms throughout the city. Let the Venetian ambassador in Rome ask the Pope for an indulgence benefiting all who gave alms to the hospital. Finally, the Pietà should receive a certain proportion of the revenue from judicial fines imposed by Venetian magistracies.[169] Direct taxation on property was not a popular method of raising funds, but indirect taxation on crime served the needs of several institutions. The Senate also extended this favour to the Convertite at their request in 1564: a further 2 soldi would be added to every lira of the fine imposed, and duly made over to their nunnery.[170] Both the Pietà (in 1532) and the Convertite (in 1586) had to apply separately to the Council of Ten for similar grants, since the Ten did not regard such decisions of the Senate as binding on them.[171] Both institutions complained to the Ten in 1588–9 that their revenues from this source were reduced by ingenious evasions. Criminals argued that the obligation to pay an additional 2 soldi per lira to each of these institutions prevented their making satisfaction to the parties they had injured; that it would bring loss to their heirs or diminish the sacrosanct dowries destined for their daughters. If they bought their way out of sentences of banishment by payments to the Arsenal or other favoured establishments, then the *luochi pii* got nothing. At the request of the two institutions, the Ten attempted to make it clear that any condemnation, under any form of words, would carry the obligation to make over a percentage of the fine imposed to the Convertite and the Pietà.[172]

In the early seventeenth century, the device of the judicial fine was again used in order to finance the Accademia dei Nobili on the Giudecca. This patrician school received an exceptionally high proportion of state aid on its foundation in 1619. At least 4,000 ducats would be necessary for the maintenance of the first forty scholars for one year,

[168] A.S.V., *Senato, Terra, filza* 57, 25 August 1571. According to D.M.S., XLI, col. 160, 9 April 1526, the Pietà had by 1526 received only 40 ducats of annual revenue under the terms of the indult of Innocent VIII.

[169] D.M.S., XXXIX, col. 300, 11 August 1525; see also D.M.S., LVIII, col. 465, 22 July 1533, for examples of condemnations under the sumptuary laws benefiting the Pietà.

[170] A.S.V., *Senato, Terra, filza* 40, 12 August 1564.

[171] A.S.V., *Consiglio dei Dieci, Parti Comuni, filza* 165, 23 December 1586.

[172] A.S.V., *Consiglio dei Dieci, Parti Comuni, filza* 176, 28 February 1588 Venetian style.

of which private donors guaranteed only 550 ducats. The fiscal magistracy of the Camerlenghi di Commun received instructions to subsidize the Accademia to the tune of 3,000 ducats a year until a similar sum became available from another source. Soon afterwards, the Accademia received further assignments of revenue from the proceeds of the sale of contraband and confiscated goods, and from the income of the expelled Jesuits of Padua.[173] The legacy of Andrea Lippomano was used, at last, to provide a substitute for the Jesuits he had supported.

Some of the hospitals on the mainland which did possess extensive estates appear to have exploited them with moderate efficiency during the late sixteenth and early seventeenth century. Much would depend on how far the governors, over the inflationary years, insisted that revenues should be paid to them in kind rather than in cash, or on how far they leased their lands on short-term contracts which could be revised in accordance with the rising cost of living. If these conditions were fulfilled, land should theoretically have been a profitable investment, at a time of population pressure and buoyant food prices, and revenue from land should have greatly helped the hospitals to meet the demands upon them. The rough estimates made by the governors of Bergamo suggest that the general hospital of San Marco had an income of about 3,000 ducats in 1555, rising to 12,000 ducats in 1627:[174] an increase probably effected both by new donations and acquisitions, and by the appreciation of lands and revenues already possessed in the mid-sixteenth century. Occasionally, the hospital met deficits in its budget by selling or pledging some of its land as security. Thus, in 1573, the total receipts of the hospital, both from regular income and from alms, amounted to 48,292 lire, its expenditure to 69,869 lire: leaving a deficit of 21,577 lire. The hospital solved its problem by selling property to the value of 24,999 lire. The following year, 1574, the deficit was only 6,642 lire, when total receipts were 55,139 lire and expenses 61,781 lire.[175] Such methods may always have been necessary in order to surmount crises which produced exceptional demands on the hospital, whilst at the same time making almsgivers—concerned for themselves and their families—more tight-fisted. Venetian hospitals, with their smaller reserves of property, could not use this device so freely.

[173] Zenoni, *Per la storia della cultura*, docs. III–IV, pp. 162–7.

[174] A.S.V., *Collegio, Relazioni, busta* 35, report of Piero Antonio Barbarigo, 10 May 1555, and *busta* 36, report of Nicolò Donà, 22/27 November 1627. In 1596, the hospital's income was estimated at 10,000 golden crowns—A.S.V., *Sindici Inquisitori in Terra Ferma, busta* 63, f. 110r.–v.

[175] See Roncalli and Forno, *Atti di Borromeo*, I/ii, pp. 251–5. See above, pp. 311–12, for the use of similar methods by the Misericordia of Bergamo.

The great hospital of Santa Maria dei Battuti at Treviso, which received its rents in kind, also increased its income fairly substantially in the late sixteenth century. In 1564, its annual income consisted of 400 butts of wine and 4,000 *staia* of wheat, whilst it also received house-rents to the value of 3,600 ducats a year.[176] In 1578, its income was 18–20,000 ducats or more, 'according to the value of the goods';[177] from 1595 onwards, the governors of Treviso usually estimated the revenue at about 30,000 ducats, or (as in 1607) at 25–30,000.[178] If anything, the proportion of revenue received in the form of wheat increased over these years, whilst cash rents diminished: in 1609, the hospital apparently received 4,500 *staia* of wheat, 400 butts of wine, and about 1,000 ducats in cash rents every year.[179] Venetian governors complained bitterly of corruption in the hospital, whose accounts they could never examine in detail; they thought that the hospital never did enough to force tenants to pay economic rents, or to collect them efficiently. The hospital's attitude towards tenants was not merely indulgent, but actively corrupt.[180] However, the hospital was in a strong position, since a large proportion of its income would automatically keep pace with rising prices.

There is no comparable information yet available about any Venetian hospital: though it is certain that one of the older establishments, the hospital of San Giobbe in Cannaregio, also received much income in kind. In 1574, its dues amounted to $297\frac{1}{2}$ *staia* of grain, Motta measure, and 285 *mastelli* of wine, Motta measure, with relatively insignificant sums from investments at the Mint (52 ducats a year) and from a *livello* (20 ducats) paid by one Viviano di Viviani at Creo, in the region of Mestre. The hospital also received 'presents of pigs (or pork)' at Christmas. Some of the grain and wine was dispensed directly to the occupants of the hospital's 120 almshouses: each received half a *staio* of flour (Venetian measure), one *quarta* of wine and a number of *regaliere*, gifts or presents. The Prior of the hospital received an allowance of 20 *staia* of grain and 20 *mastelli* of wine (Motta measure), with eight ducats a year for fuel, and a bonus of 20 ducats for his own good work at the hospital. The book-keeper received 4 *staia* of flour for his pains. The rest of the produce was probably sold to meet the hospital's

---

[176] Report of Pietro Pizzamano, 6 June 1564, A.S.V., *Collegio, Relazioni, busta* 48.
[177] Report of Giovanni Michiel, 18 June 1578, *ibid.*
[178] Reports of Stefano Viaro, 6 December 1595, Antonio Mocenigo, 9 February 1605 Venetian style, Francesco Tiepolo, 4 September 1607, Almorò Dolfin, 3 June 1625, *ibid.*
[179] Report of Alvise Moro, 17 March 1609, *ibid.*
[180] Reports of Vincenzo Pisani, 10 May 1612, Almorò Dolfin, 3 June 1625, Antonio Zeno, 4 April 1628, and Paolo Querini, 1 July 1639, *ibid.*

various cash requirements: income taxes for the state (53 ducats in *decima* and 10 in *tansa*); duties paid when the produce was transported from the fields of the mainland to Venice itself; repairs to the houses, and to the Prior's dwelling; fresh water for the wells; medicines for the pharmacy or *spiciaria*. Moreover, some of the inmates received alms in cash: in 1574, the prior dispensed 10 soldi every Saturday, making a total of 168 ducats a year, to 42 women pensioners.[181] Here again, a hospital disposing of extensive revenue in kind should have been in a strong position in an inflationary period: though its administrative problems in supervising its estates and keeping its tenants in order were certain to be far greater than those of institutions like the Incurabili. Corruption may, almost inevitably, have weighed like an impost on revenues derived from these sources.

One hospital on the mainland, that of Santi Giacomo e Lazzaro in Verona, made impressive progress in its techniques of management in the sixteenth and early seventeenth centuries. The hospital was originally a lazar-house, and the first documentary evidence of its existence dates from 1146. In 1223, it had absorbed the other leper-hospitals in the city.[182] In the early seventeenth century, this was the richest hospital in Verona, though, since much of its revenue went to the support of a pesthouse or *lazzaretto*, its services were only occasionally called upon. The surplus revenue was deposited in the Monte di Pietà, and in 1612 the deposit held about 30,000 crowns. The city used 20,000 crowns as a reserve fund to purchase grains in years of shortage. The remaining 10,000 were treated as a loan to the Monte di Pietà: it paid interest at the rate of 5 per cent per annum, which was used to maintain the hospital of the Misericordia, the poorest in Verona. The Venetian Rettori professed themselves dissatisfied with the administration of the revenues.[183] But (however dispensed) they seem to have been managed with a fair degree of acumen. In the mid-fourteenth century, according to a detailed study by Professor Lecce, the hospital had owned substantial landed property—but this was broken up into many fragments. Its 897 *campi* were divided up into 576 separate parcels. Fragmentation persisted into the early sixteenth century: in 1522, the hospital or its tenants cultivated wheat on 274 *campi* divided into 67 parcels of land. However, by 1643 the property of the hospital had expanded, and covered 1,875 *campi*—compared with 897 in 1346. But most striking was the relative concentration of the property, now held in

---

[181] A.S.V., *Provveditori sopra gli Ospedali e Luoghi Pii, busta* 17/21, ff. 43–6. See also above, pp. 347–9.

[182] See Michele Lecce, 'I beni terrieri di un antico istituto ospitaliero veronese (secoli XII–XVIII)', *Studi in onore di Amintore Fanfani*, III (Milan, 1962), p. 53.

[183] A.S.V., *Collegio, Relazioni, busta* 50, report of Girolamo Cornaro, 5 May 1612.

only 194 parcels, grouped round farmsteads large enough to support peasant households. In 1346, the hospital had held land in as many as 61 different localities; but by 1643 the number of separate localities had fallen to only 10. By the late sixteenth century, where the hospital received rents in cash, it entered into short-term contracts, usually for periods of five years only. At the same time, it made sharecropping *agreements, but tended to abandon these in the early seventeenth century. Little trace remained of the older system of perpetual leases, which would have proved disastrous in a period of rising prices.[184]

The scanty available evidence suggests that at least one of the large junior hospitals of sixteenth-century Venice—that of the Incurabili—possessed a financial structure which differed from that of the Scuole Grandi and of the older hospitals, both in Venice itself and on the mainland. It depended very heavily on 'casual', as distinct from 'regular', revenue. It lacked one of the chief assets open to some Venetian charities, in the right to acquire real property in an accessible place where it could easily be supervised, and where the governors could reduce the risk of loss through dilapidation or defaulting tenants. Population pressure might well increase poverty and drive up food prices: but it should also have had the effect of increasing property values and rents—so long as the property was managed with reasonable efficiency. Charity could thus increase at the same time as poverty, if not at the same rate. On the other hand, the managers of the Incurabili were spared much time-consuming administrative responsibility, and the hospital had the satisfaction of immediately applying the contributions it received to meeting the urgent needs of the poor. The application of the mortmain laws probably cramped the development of Venetian hospitals: but their own governors may have preferred not to waste time on investment and administration.

The group of voluntary charities discussed in this chapter aimed at evangelism and education for the ultimate purpose of saving souls. They showed a strong concern with the care and discipline of the young, but also offered the chance of repentance to the more mature. These charities divided between them the labour of caring for the poor, and specialized in particular tasks, so as to build up a comprehensive system. Their statutes attempted to lay down standardized procedures, so as to reduce—but not to eliminate—the area of individual discretion. The transplanting of tried institutions from one community to another helped to speed up the development of charitable organiza-

[184] Lecce, 'I beni terrieri', pp. 62 f., 72 f., 85, 117 f., 127 f.

tion. Sixteenth-century charities worked for the reclamation of the outsider: they were not concerned merely with relieving the respectable, but plumbed the lower depths of the social and moral hierarchies. They did not intend to condone immorality, but to approach the outsiders and to treat them if they showed signs of repentance. This was a vital part of the imitation of Christ.

These organizations owed much to the influence of priests, exerted from the pulpit or the confessional—an influence sometimes regarded by the state as sinister and potentially subversive. Much of the work, however, depended on members of the laity—often on members of the leisured classes who had the time to devote to charitable labours. The clergy staffed the hospitals and administered the sacraments, acting as spiritual directors to inmates and governors alike. Final responsibility for the management of the temporal affairs of the institutions rested, however, with boards of lay governors. These charities always claimed that their ultimate ends were spiritual. But their preoccupation with instilling the principles of good conduct, with communicating Christian knowledge, and with advertising the sacraments did not deflect them from an apparently realistic and well-informed appraisal of urgent social needs—of the evil aspects of prostitution, of the paralysing consequences of arrest for debt, of the helplessness of forgotten prisoners in the jails. A Christian education (combined, at secondary level, with a classical) helped to preserve the social order, as it was conceived by orthodox members of the Venetian patriciate. It taught the young to avoid idleness, to support themselves, to submit respectfully to superiors. It promised to instil into members of the patriciate—made disreputable by poverty and ignorance—a greater sense of duty and of devotion to the common weal.

APPENDIX TO PART II

Venetian Hospitals of Medieval Origin

The hospitals listed below were all either certainly or probably founded before the beginning of the sixteenth century: there is no record of their foundation in the sixteenth-century papers which I have examined. Unless otherwise stated in the footnotes, the source for the information in the first four columns is a list of Venetian hospitals, *luoghi pii* and other charitable foundations contained in M.C.V., Cicogna MSS., *busta* 2987/2988, *fascicolo* 19, *Ospitali e Case date da abitare per carità.* This is marked on the flyleaf 'circa 1560', and certainly belongs to the period between 1561 and *c.* 1600. It mentions (f. 24) the Casa delle Zitelle, whose foundation was completed in 1561; and makes no mention of the very important hospital of San Lazzaro dei Mendicanti, which was reorganized and finally moved into Venice from a lagoon island about 1600. The list may well have been compiled by an official of the new magistracy of the Provveditori sopra gli Ospedali e Luoghi Pii, founded by Senatorial decree on 24 July 1561 (A.S.V., *Senato, Terra,* reg. 1560–1, ff. 89v.–90), to examine the state of existing charities in Venice.

Unless otherwise stated, the figures in the column headed 'No. of inmates' refer to the number of inmates of the hospitals in the second half of the sixteenth century, at the time when the above document was drawn up.

PILGRIM HOSPITALS

Hospital	Parish	Sestiere	No. of inmates	Origins
Pellegrini	S. Pietro	Castello		

ISOLATION HOSPITALS

S. Lazzaro (for lepers)		Lagoon	5 in 1528([1])	Founded 1262, possibly by a certain Leone Paolino. Appropriated in 16th century by members of Bembo, Vitturi and Pisani families on grounds that their ancestors had founded it.([2])

[1] D.M.S., XLIX, coll. 110, 115, for 29 and 31 October 1528.
[2] See Samuele Romanin, *Storia documentata di Venezia* (reprint, 10 vols., 1912–21), II, p. 398; Tassini, *Curiosità veneziane,* p. 421; report of the Provveditori sopra gli Ospedali, A.S.V., *Senato, Terra, filza* 124, 17 October 1592.

423

2E

Hospital	Parish	Sestiere	No. of inmates	Origins
Lazzaretto (for plague victims)		Lagoon		Resolved in 1467 to build 100 rooms (*camere*) at the Lazzaretto Nuovo to 'keep the city free of plague'[3]

HOSPITALS FOR FOUNDLINGS AND OTHER ORPHANS

Hospital	Parish	Sestiere	No. of inmates	Origins
Pietà	S. Giovanni in Bragora	Castello	800 in 1551; 1200 in 1559[4]	Founded 1346–48 by a Franciscan, Pietro of Assisi[5]
S.ta Agnese	S. Barnabà	Dorsoduro	6 in 1526[6]	Probably in existence by 1383[7]

HOSPITALS FOR EX-SERVICEMEN

Hospital	Parish	Sestiere	No. of inmates	Origins
Gesù Cristo di S. Antonio	S. Pietro	Castello	30 in 1503; 30–45 in 1563[8]	Founded by state action, 1471–1503.[9]

HOSPITALS FOR WOMEN

(a) Hospitals administered by the Procuratori di San Marco

Hospital	Parish	Sestiere	No. of inmates	Origins
Ca Bandi	S. Canciano	Cannaregio	17	Founded in 1421 by Francesco Bandi, a Lucchese silk merchant[10]
S. Pietro	S. Eufemia	Dorsoduro		Founded in 1316 by Pietro Brustolado; reserved for women by decree of the Procuratori de Supra, 1 July 1589[11]
S. Boldo	S. Boldo	S. Polo	12	Founded in 1395 by Tommaso and Lorenza de Matteo of Florence[12]

[3] Domenico Malipiero, *Annali veneti dall'anno 1457 al 1500*, ed. Agostino Sagredo in *Archivio Storico Italiano*, VII (1843–4), p. 655.

[4] A.S.V., *Senato, Terra*, reg. 1550/51, f. 89v., 31 January 1550 Venetian style; reg. 1557/58, ff. 169v.–170, 18 February 1558 Venetian style.

[5] Bembo, *Delle istituzioni di beneficenza*, pp. 3–4.

[6] D.M.S., XXXVII, coll. 670–1, 27 February 1525; XL, coll. 696–7, 21 January 1526.

[7] Tassini, *Curiosità veneziane*, p. 8.

[8] D.M.S., IV, coll. 810–12, 12 March 1503; A.S.V., *Provveditori sopra Ospitali e Luoghi Pii*, busta 17/21, *Atti e Terminazioni 1561–1575*, f. 7, 3 February 1562 Venetian style.

[9] See above, pp. 212–15.   [10] Tassini, *Curiosità veneziane*, p. 467.

[11] *Ibid.*, p. 484.   [12] *Ibid.*, p. 86.

(b) *Other hospitals*

Hospital	Parish	Sestiere	No. of inmates	Origins
S. Bortolamio	S. Pietro	Castello		
Ca Caretto	S. Pietro	Castello		Founded in 1438 by Nicolò and Maddalena Caretto[13]
Marchi	S. Pietro	Castello		
Ca' di Dio	S. Martino	Castello		Founded by Friar Lorenzo in 1272; house property donated by a furrier, Maggio Trevisan. Originally used to accommodate pilgrims, but later converted to the use of 50 poor widows of good reputation[14]
S. Leonardo	S. Leonardo	Castello	3	Founded by Cecilia, widow of Alvise Pisani [15]
Crosecchieri	SS. Apostoli	Cannaregio	12	Founded during 13th century; endowed by Bertold, Patriarch of Aquileia, and by Doge Renier Zeno. Reserved to women from mid-15th century[16]
Maddalena	S. Margarita	Dorsoduro	10	
Trinità	S. Raffaele	Dorsoduro		
Maddalena	S. Raffaele	Dorsoduro		Founded in 1361 by the brothers Gabriele and Luciano Prior; further endowed by will of Luciano Prior, 1376[17]
Marin	S. Agnese	Dorsoduro		Founded by Franceschina di Nicolò Marin, widow of Bartolomeo della Torre, 1432[18]
Pusco	S. Nicolò	Dorsoduro	4	Founded by Bernardo Pusco[19]
Ca Badoer (S. Giovanni Evangelista)	S. Stin	S. Polo	12	Founded before the early 14th century by the Badoer family[20]

[13] *Ibid.*, p. 585.   [14] *Ibid.*, p. 107; Bembo, *Istituzioni di beneficenza*, p. 273.
[15] A. S. De Kiriaki, G. Gozzi, G. Malamocco, T. Mozzoni and G. Berchet, *La beneficenza veneziana* (Venice, 1900), pp. 136–9.
[16] Tassini, *Curiosità veneziane*, p. 294.   [17] *Ibid.*, p. 372.
[18] De Kiriaki, *La beneficenza*, pp. 136–9.   [19] *Ibid.*
[20] Tassini, *Curiosità veneziane*, p. 612.

INSTITUTIONS FOR PIZZOCARE OR FEMALE TERTIARIES

(a) *Institutions specifically described as hospitals*

Hospital	Parish	Sestiere	No. of inmates	Origins
Santa Giustina (Franciscan)	S. Giustina	Castello	32	
S. Canciano	S. Canciano	Cannaregio	5	Unknown; administered by the Scuola Grande di S. Giovanni Evangelista
S. Maria dei Carmeni	S. Barnabà	Dorsoduro	23	

(b) *Other institutions for Tertiaries*

S. Domenico (Dominican)	S. Pietro	Castello		
S. Martino (Dominican)	S. Martino	Castello		
Corte delle Pizzocare	S. Moisè	S. Marco	8	
S. Marcuola (Servites)	S. Marcuola	Cannaregio	28	
SS. Apostoli (Dominican)	SS. Apostoli	Cannaregio		
S. Raffaele (Franciscan)	S. Raffaele	Dorsoduro		Founded during the 13th century[21]

HOSPITALS ATTACHED TO PROFESSIONAL ASSOCIATIONS

Bakers' Guild (Scuola dei Forneri)	S. Marciliano	Cannaregio	
Tailors' Guild (Arte dei Sartori)	SS. Apostoli	Cannaregio	Hospital building bears the date 1511[22]
Silkworkers' Guild (Scuola dei Samiteri)	S. Croce	S. Croce	

HOSPITALS ADMINISTERED BY THE SCUOLE GRANDI

San Geremia	S. Geremia	Cannaregio	Administered by the Scuola di San Giovanni Evangelista
Misericordia	S. Marciliano	Cannaregio	Administered by the Scuola della Misericordia; founded before 1390[23]
San Marco	S. Maria Nuova	Cannaregio	Administered by the Scuola di San Marco

[21] *Ibid.*, pp. 530–1.   [22] *Ibid.*, pp. 601–2.   [23] See above, p. 65.

Hospital	Parish	Sestiere	No. of inmates	Origins
Carità	S. Trovaso	Dorsoduro	11	Administered by the Scuola della Carità
S. Giovanni Evangelista	S. Stin	S. Polo	4	Administered by the Scuola di San Giovanni Evangelista; founded in 1330([24])

HOSPITALS ATTACHED TO FOREIGN COMMUNITIES

Sick Germans (Tedeschi Infermi)	S. Samuele	S. Marco		Probably founded in 1433 by German bakers working in Venice ([25])
German Shoe-makers (Callegheri Tedeschi)	S. Samuele	S. Marco		Built during the 14th century, enlarged in 1482([26])
Southern Germans (Tedeschi di Alemagna Alta)	S. Croce	S. Croce		
Poor Armen-ians (Poveri Armeni)	S. Giuliano	S. Marco		Said to form part of the legacy of Doge Ziani (12th century), adminis-tered by Procuratori of San Marco

OTHER HOSPITALS

(a) *Administered by the Procuratori of San Marco*

S. Trinità	S. Trinità	Castello	20	
Veriseli	SS. Apostoli	Cannaregio	4	May have been the hos-pital founded in 1332 by Giovanni Varicelli([27])
Ca Pesaro	S. Giacomo dell'Orio	S. Croce	14	Founded in 1361 by Angelo da Pesaro; pas-sed to the Procuratia de Supra in 1517([28])

(b) *Administered by other trustees*

S. Pietro e S. Paolo	S. Pietro	Castello		
Lorenzi	S. Pietro	Castello		
S. Giovanni Battista	S. Martino	Castello		

[24] See above, pp. 64–5. [25] Tassini, *Curiosità veneziane*, pp. 672–3.
[26] *Ibid.*, p. 506. [27] De Kiriaki, *La beneficenza*, pp. 136–9.
[28] A.S.V., *Senato, Terra, filza* 117, 12 November 1590.

Hospital	Parish	Sestiere	No. of inmates	Origins
S. Giobbe	S. Geremia	Cannaregio	120 alms-houses in 1574; 40–50 pen-sioners in 1574	Founded in 1378 by Giovanni Contarini[29]
Misericordia	S. Marciliano	Cannaregio		
Ca Contarini	SS. Apostoli	Cannaregio	8	
Annunziata	S. Vio	Dorsoduro	10	Founded by Marco dalla Frasca, 1320[30]

[29] Tassini, *Curiosità veneziane*, pp. 482–3; see also above, p. 347.
[30] De Kiriaki, *La beneficenza*, pp. 136–9.

PART III: VENETIAN JEWRY AND THE MONTI DI PIETÀ

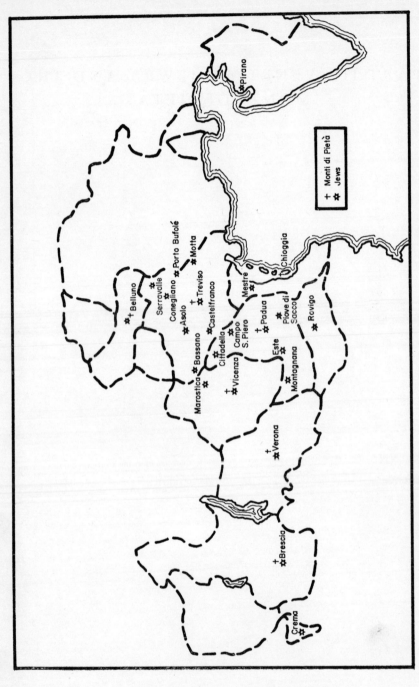

JEWISH COMMUNITIES AND MONTI DI PIETÀ ON THE MAINLAND, C. 1500

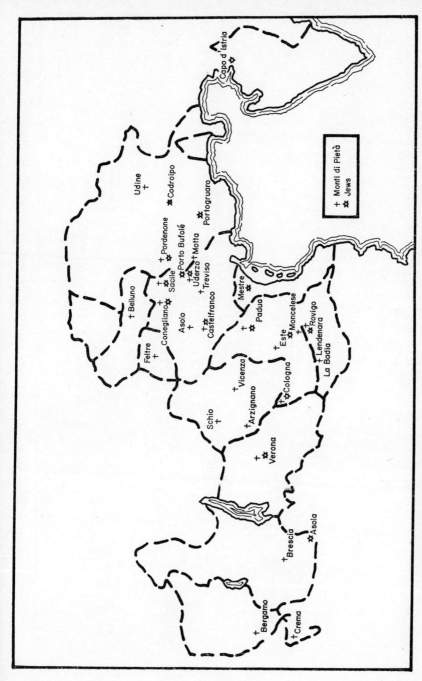

JEWISH COMMUNITIES AND MONTI DI PIETÀ ON THE MAINLAND, C. 1600

Legend:
+ Monti di Pietà
✿ Jews

Labels on map:
Capo d'Istria ✿
Udine +
Codroipo ✿
Pordenone ✿
Porto Bufolé ✿
Portogruaro ✿
Sacile +
Uderzo + Motta +
Treviso +
Belluno +
Conegliano ✿
Asolo +
Castelfranco + ✿
Feltre +
Mestre ✿
Padua +
Moncelese +
Rovigo ✿
Este +
Lendenara ✿
La Badia +
Vicenza +
Cologna ✿
Arzignano +
Schio +
Verona +
Brescia +
Asola ✿
Bergamo +
Crema +

INTRODUCTION:
THE LEGAL POSITION OF MONEYLENDERS

Hitherto, this book has dealt only with the various forms of outright charity or poor relief practised by the Venetians and their subjects—with methods of philanthropy or poor relief which entailed handing money or goods to a person with no expectation that they should ever be returned, or otherwise supporting, educating or benefiting him without the hope of any material repayment. But, to complete the system of poor relief in many communities of medieval and early modern Europe, it was vital to provide some access to cheap credit. Poverty was not alleviated only by the outright charity of fraternities or of individual donors, by the discipline of poor laws and beggars' hospitals, by the limited security which the guilds afforded, or by the anxiety of the devout for the salvation of souls. The poor urgently needed some means of riding out the crises and uncertainties of their ordinary existence: the bad harvests, the fluctuating food prices, the seasonal stoppages of work, the tax demands which ignored the realities of the economic situation. If the poor could not save cash, they needed the opportunity to borrow, to convert what goods they did possess into ready money without the threat of irredeemable loss or of sinking into debt. For a government or civic authority to control poverty, it must control indebtedness, and indebtedness could not be checked merely by fiat: by merely passing laws to curb the rate of interest charged by the professional lender. The authorities must strive to ensure that funds were available for small loans on modest securities, and that these funds were abundant enough to equip the public loan bank to undercut the more voracious private lenders who inevitably sprang up to meet the constant demand for credit.

In the high and later Middle Ages, three major courses of action gradually presented themselves, each with its own perils for those anxious to observe the divine law as interpreted by the Church. Princes, republics and cities could tolerate and connive at the lending of money by private entrepreneurs—doing little, except at long intervals, to restrain its abuses. Alternatively, they could license such lending by

431

publicly contracting with moneylenders, whether these were nominal Christians (at least theoretically of Lombard or Tuscan origin), or whether they were Jews. Issuing licences would almost certainly enable the state to draw financial advantages from the moneylender's trade. It might help it to impose more rigorous discipline on the loan business. The man with an assured monopoly of moneylending in a given district might be able to charge lower rates of interest because of the greater volume of his transactions—provided the fiscal demands made upon him were not so high as to force the rate up again. The final possibility was first realized on a large scale in fifteenth-century Italy, though it had been anticipated in France and England. This lay in the creation of public loan banks which would lend small sums, either gratuitously or at very low rates, to poor persons, largely for the purposes of consumption. Such was the original end of the institutions called Monti di Pietà, though they did not throughout their career confine themselves to this, and their scope was soon widened. According to certain contemporary theories, the poor themselves owned the Monti di Pietà. They were not merely supervised, but actually administered by the communes under whose jurisdiction they were established—or, at least outside the Venetian Republic, by a combination of municipal officials and representatives of local churches. The Monti di Pietà, at first promoted and spread by Observant Franciscan preachers, set out not only to fulfil an urgent social need, but also to free the Christian poor from economic dependence on the Jews, and to eliminate the sin of usury committed by nominal Christians.

There is room for much doubt as to whether the canons on usury seriously hindered the development of trade, industry or capitalistic agriculture by creating misgivings about the lawfulness of investment for profit. In the twelfth and thirteenth centuries, general Councils of the Church and lawyer Popes like Innocent IV had attacked the practice of lending money at interest partly on the grounds that moneylending was a devouring trade. It threatened to divert attention from more productive forms of economic activity; in particular, it threatened to ruin agriculture, and thus created a danger of famine. But so long as an investment obviously entailed some degree of risk to the investor, legal experts were usually willing to regard it as a partnership, and partnerships were not condemned as sinful.[1] However, one form of

---

[1] III Lateran, c. 25 (1179); II Lyons, c. 26 (1274)—Mansi, *Concilia*, XXII, col. 231, XXIV, coll. 99–100. Cf. T. P. McLaughlin, 'The teaching of the canonists on usury (XII, XIII and XIV centuries)', *Mediaeval Studies*, I–II (1939–40), I, pp. 110–11; J. T. Noonan, Jr., *The scholastic analysis of usury* (Cambridge, Mass., 1957), pp. 13, 49; F. C. Lane, 'Investment and usury in medieval Venice', *Explorations in Entrepreneurial History*, new series, II (1964).

economic activity unmistakably attacked by the canon law was the small-loan business—the practice of lending upon a fixed rate of interest, theoretically without risk, to relieve a need. The sin of taking usury was especially liable to arise out of contracts for the loan of money, or victuals, or other commodities which could be used only by being consumed.[2] If, in such contracts, the creditor asked for anything back in excess of the principal, then (according to texts incorporated in Gratian's *Decretum*) this excess was usury. In terminology borrowed from Roman law, a loan of such commodities was, if freely given, a *mutuum*; should a charge be made, it became a *foenus*. The *mutuum* was distinguished from the *commodatum*, a loan of a different type. A *commodatum* was a loan in which the lender retained ownership of the thing lent, such as a house, a horse or a cloak, and would normally expect the same object eventually to be restored to him by the borrower. A *commodatum* for which some charge was made became a *locatio*, a contract of bail, lease or hire. Contracts of *locatio* were deemed legitimate by the canonists in so far as the lender undertook to bear the consequences of the object lent naturally deteriorating in value. If, however, a man lent consumer goods, such as money or wheat or oil, he could retain no ownership in them, because they were consumed as soon as used. He was, therefore, not entitled to charge for the use of something which was no longer his. Such was the theoretical justification for condemning the practice of charging for loans of money or consumer goods. The essence of the *mutuum* was that it involved the transfer of ownership from the lender to the borrower; it was the process whereby *meum* became *tuum*, 'mine' became 'thine'. Christ himself had enjoined 'Mutuum date, nihil inde sperantes'—'Make your loans freely, and do not hope for anything out of them'.[3] The decretal *Consuluit*, derived from a letter of Pope Urban III (1185–7), had used this precept to justify the condemnation of taking interest on loans of money or victuals.

However, by the early fifteenth century, certain 'titles' to receiving in such loans something in excess of the principal had won fairly wide recognition. These included the related titles known as *damnum*

[2] For what follows, see McLaughlin, 'Canonists on usury', I, 95, 101–2; Noonan, *Scholastic analysis*, 19–20, 30, 39–41, 53–4, 71–2; A. E. Trugenberger, *San Bernardino da Siena: considerazioni sullo sviluppo dell'etica economica cristiana nel primo Rinascimento* (Bern, 1951), p. 84 f. The thirteenth-century canonist Hostiensis (Henry of Segusio, Cardinal-Bishop of Ostia and Velletri, d. 1271) elaborated the distinction between *mutuum* and *commodatum*. By the beginning of the fifteenth century, the Tuscan preacher Bernardino of Siena was treating with a certain suspicion the argument that ownership passed from lender to borrower in a *mutuum*, but he had not altogether rejected it, and there was no doubt of his opposition to usury in general.
[3] Luke, vi, 35.

emergens (loss arising) and *lucrum cessans* (profit ceasing). *Damnum emergens* entitled the lender to receive something in addition to the principal if he had suffered a loss on account of the loan. *Lucrum cessans* was justified by the argument that one who, on account of the loan he made, missed a legitimate opportunity of making a profit, was as much entitled to compensation as somebody who had incurred actual expenses through a loan. The case of *lucrum cessans*, though more popular with civil lawyers than with canonists, was accepted in the thirteenth century by Hostiensis, and in the fifteenth by the Sicilian canonist Panormitanus (Nicolò de' Tudeschi, Archbishop of Palermo).[4] Again, these titles were discussed and justified by the great Tuscan preacher of the fifteenth century, Bernardino of Siena, in his forty-second Lenten sermon. Under the heading of *lucrum cessans*, Bernardino discussed the case of the merchant who, by lending 'out of charity', deprived himself of a chance of lawful gain. Here, he argued, 'the receiver of the money not only deprives the owner of his money, but also of the use and fruit of exercising his industry in it and through it'.[5] Bernardino, an outspoken and powerful enemy of the corruption of usury, thus defended the taking of interest on loans made from a charitable motive. Theories based on the title of *lucrum cessans* would, in the future, prove very relevant to the development of the Monti di Pietà, institutions furthered by members of Bernardino's Order.

Since the first half of the twelfth century, oecumenical Councils had legislated against the taking of usury as a sin condemned by both Old and New Testament. The Lateran Councils of 1139 and 1179 demanded that usurers be denied all the consolations of Church membership, that they be excluded from communion and Christian burial, that the Church reject their offerings.[6] In the late thirteenth and early fourteenth century, the Councils focused attention on corporations and other public bodies which deliberately licensed public moneylenders, as distinct from merely tolerating them. This hostile lawmaking culminated in the fifteenth canon of the Council of Vienne, soon afterwards added to the main body of canon law in the Constitutions issued by Pope Clement V in 1317.[7] The canon announced that some corporations were, 'by statutes of theirs which are sometimes concluded by oaths', contracting with public moneylenders, and knowingly enforcing

[4] McLaughlin, 'Canonists on usury', I, 145–6.

[5] Noonan, *Scholastic analysis*, pp. 126–7.

[6] II Lateran, c. 13 (1139); III Lateran, c. 25 (1179)—Mansi, *Concilia*, XXI, coll. 529–530, XXII, col. 231.

[7] II Lyons, c. 26—Mansi, *Concilia*, XXIV, coll. 99–100; *Clementis Papae V Constitutiones*, Bk. V, tit. 5, 'De usuris', in *Corpus Iuris Canonici*, Part II, *Decretalium collectiones*, ed. Emil Friedberg (Leipzig, 1881), col. 1184.

the payment of usurious debts owed to them. It proceeded to impose sentence of excommunication on all public authorities which failed to erase such statutes from their books within three months. It also excommunicated magistrates who enforced the payment of usuries, and those who prevented usuries from being fully restored by persons who had once received them. Ecclesiastical censure should be used to compel suspected moneylenders to submit their books for inspection whenever the question of usury was raised. Moreover, all who maintained that no sin lay in taking usury would incur the penalties of heresy; and inquisitors were authorized to proceed against such persons as if they were suspected of heresy. In the following century this canon, *Ex gravi*, was to trouble the consciences of public authorities which had licensed Jewish lenders. Claims would be made, on behalf of Franciscans who preached against the Jews, that they freed cities from the excommunication under which they lay.[8] A Paduan doctor was to cite the Clementine Constitutions in the Venetian debate on the Jews in 1520.[9] By this reckoning, authorities which licensed the usurer in the hope of controlling him were worse situated than those that made no attempt to intervene.

The fact that general Councils of the Church had condemned public contracts with moneylenders did not mean that their decrees were universally enforced, or that all usurers felt a sense of intolerable guilt. Several French cities, for example, contracted on similar terms with Lombard and Jewish moneylenders in the late fourteenth century.[10] Some businessmen, however, in centres of intense lending like Lombardy and Tuscany, took the law of usury seriously enough to make large-scale restitution by their wills, even as late as the early 1500's.[11] By 1254, the Venetian government was beginning to legislate against usury on its own account, and to add the law of the limited state to the

[8] E.g. by Giacomo Vanucci, Bishop of Perugia, in 1462, on behalf of Michele Carcano of Milan—see Heribert Holzapfel, *Die Anfänge de Montes Pietatis (1462–1515)* (Munich, 1903), p. 36.

[9] D.M.S., XXVIII, coll. 321–2, 3 March 1520: 'then came Sier Nicolò Michiel the Doctor, formerly Avogadore di Commun, citing texts, and had two texts read from the *Decretum* and the Clementine Constitutions, and spoke well against retaining the Jews'.

[10] Cf. James Parkes, *The Jew in the medieval community: a study of his political and economic situation* (London, 1938), pp. 316 f.

[11] In general see B. N. Nelson, 'The usurer and the merchant prince: Italian businessmen and the ecclesiastical law of restitution, 1100–1550', *Journal of Economic History*, VII (1947), Supplement VII. For particular examples, Armando Sapori, 'L'interesse del denaro a Firenze nel Trecento (dal testamento di un usuraio)', in his *Studi di storia economica medievale* (Florence, 1946), p. 96; Florence Edler de Roover, 'Restitution in Renaissance Florence', *Studi in onore di Armando Sapori*, II (Milan, 1957).

law of the Universal Church. No Venetian might lend upon usury, either within Venice or outside it, either in person or through an agent. The Great Council was already associating usury with heresy more than forty years before the issue of the canon *Ex gravi*, for in 1270 it fused into one body magistracies dealing with usury and with heresy. In 1281, the Great Council recognized the menace of certain Tuscan usurers operating from the mainland, in the region of Mestre, then still subject to the civic authorities of Treviso. The Venetians proposed to make every effort to persuade the Trevisans to remove the moneylenders. Should they fail to do so, proclamations must be made to restrain Venetians from crossing the lagoon to borrow money on the mainland.[12] Evidently the Venetian government was not merely afraid for its own position in the face of the usury law recently passed by the Second Council of Lyons: it genuinely feared the insidious effects of moneylending in impoverishing its subjects. Venetian policy did not, however, try to prohibit all lending upon interest: it was largely concerned to stamp out petty loans at interest, and to prevent recourse to professional lenders. Another law, of 1333, forbade the lending at interest of small sums, of less than 100 *lire di piccoli*. Where larger amounts were involved, the government simply stipulated that it should exercise control over the sale of pledges. In these matters, attention had shifted from the question of whether interest could be accepted at all to that of the amount of interest permissible.[13]

Absolute vetoes on the acceptance of interest on petty loans, however pious and correct, did not solve the problem of how the poor were to obtain the necessary credit. In the legislation of Church Councils, there remained a significant ambiguity. These prohibitions might conceivably apply only to nominal Christian moneylenders, and it might be legitimate to license a Jewish banker in the interests of the poor. There was always the argument that the canon law was not binding on the Jews. As certain burghers of Brescia phrased it, with succinct brutality, in 1441, the Jews were 'assuredly damned', whereas Christians bore 'the Holy Cross upon their foreheads, stamped by the precious blood of the immaculate Lamb'.[14] To contract with Jewish usurers did not, therefore, imply the sacrifice of souls to perdition. It was possible to interpret a certain canon of the Fourth Lateran Council of 1215, which had met under the presidency of Innocent III, as implying that Jews could

[12] *Deliberazioni del Maggior Consiglio di Venezia*, ed. Roberto Cessi, II (Bologna, 1931), pp. 222, 224.

[13] Gino Luzzatto, 'Tasso d'interesse e usura a Venezia nei secoli XIII–XV', *Miscellanea in onore di Roberto Cessi*, I (Rome, 1958); Lane, 'Investment and usury', loc. cit.

[14] Agostino Zanelli, 'Predicatori a Brescia nel Quattrocento', *Archivio Storico Lombardo, serie terza*, vol. XV, *anno* XXVIII (1901), p. 90.

be licensed to lend at controlled rates of interest. The canon *Quanto amplius* ran as follows:

> The more that Christians are restrained from the exaction of usury, the more does the treachery of the Jews increase in this matter, so that in a brief interval they consume the property of Christians. Wishing, therefore, to protect Christians in this region from monstrous oppression by the Jews, we ordain by decree of this Council that if from henceforth the Jews extort heavy and immediate usuries from Christians, Christian property shall be removed from them until they make sufficient amends for their immoderate oppression.[15]

Of the Council's hostility to the Jews there was no doubt. But the canon seemed to some of its interpreters to allow the Jews to lend at moderate rates; and the subsequent canons of Lyons and Vienne made no specific mention of the Jews. On the other hand, *Quanto amplius* suggested to other authorities that all usury must be condemned as 'heavy and immoderate'.[16]

The authority of Scripture—or at least of certain verses in Deuteronomy—also promised to justify the taking of usury from persons of an alien faith, as a method of weakening or damaging them. The words of Deuteronomy, xxiii, 19–20, refused to allow anyone to take interest from his brother, but permitted lending at interest to a foreigner.[17] During the first Christian millennium, Jewish rabbis and scholars had forbidden usurious transactions, but their prohibitions had very likely applied only to inter-Jewish loans. They did, however, impose restrictions on loans to aliens, holding especially that a Jew might lend to a non-Jew only if it was economically necessary. He might do so to earn a living, but not purely for the accumulation of riches. He must, as far as possible, safeguard himself from contamination by unnecessary contact with the devotees of an alien faith.[18] After the millennium, economic necessity did draw the Jews into moneylending, as a result of their exclusion, especially in England, France and Germany, from other methods of earning a living. They were gradually ousted from land ownership, from engaging in oriental trade, and even from guild

---

[15] IV Lateran (1215), c. 67—Mansi, *Concilia*, XXII, 1054–5.

[16] McLaughlin, 'Canonists on usury', I, p. 99; B. N. Nelson, *The idea of usury: from tribal brotherhood to universal otherhood* (Princeton, 1949), pp. 16–18.

[17] 'You shall not lend upon interest to your brother, interest on money, interest on victuals, interest on anything that is lent for interest. To a foreigner you may lend upon interest, but to your brother you shall not lend upon interest; that the Lord your God may bless you in all that you undertake in the land which you are entering to take possession of it.'

[18] Siegfried Stein, 'The development of the Jewish law on interest from the Biblical period to the expulsion of the Jews from England', *Historia Judaica*, XVII (1955), p. 4 f.; cf. also Parkes, *Jew in medieval community*, pp. 340–1.

2F

membership. From Alexander III's pontificate onwards, the official policy of the Catholic Church began to demand that Jews pay tithes on real property acquired from Christians, lest the Church be deprived of revenue. Since they were compelled also to pay taxes as Jews to royal treasuries, this acted as a form of double taxation severe enough to damage their economic interests as landowners, and provided an incentive to sell out. The acquisition of a fief by a Jew presented difficulties, since entry into a feudal tenure demanded that a Christian oath be sworn. For a Jew to acquire lordship over Christian vassals, serfs or villeins was deemed undesirable. The development of powerful Christian cities, such as Genoa, Pisa and Venice, which traded on their own account with the Levant, resulted in Jewish exclusion from oriental trade: though centuries later Venice, Ancona and Leghorn were again to demand their services to trade with the Turk. The Jews themselves were not wholly reluctant to enter the profession of moneylending, if only because it offered the means of earning a living whilst enjoying ample leisure for study. Cash from land sales often afforded them initial supplies of liquid capital for the purpose.[19] Where they faced the risk of expulsion, there was a strong incentive to keep their assets liquid.

By the twelfth and thirteenth centuries, prominent Jewish rabbis had begun to approve the acceptance of interest on the grounds that the Jews could live no other way, that royal taxation was heavy, and that it was no longer possible to avoid business dealings with Gentiles. In the twelfth century, Jewish moneylenders sprang up in England, northern France and the Rhineland, parallel to the Lombards and Cahorsins, nominal Christians of southern origin, often recruited from such Lombard cities as Asti and Chieri. From the Rhineland, they spread into other regions of Germany.[20] Northern Italy, hitherto served by its own indigenous lenders, began to inherit them from the close of the thirteenth century.[21] By the mid-fourteenth century, the *Meissener Rechtsbuch*, a law treatise widely current in eastern Germany, was advancing the view that although the Jews were restrained by the divine law from taking usury, yet they were forced by economic and social necessity into doing so under the conditions of the present day. No

[19] S. W. Baron, *A social and religious history of the Jews* (8 vols. and Index, New York, 1952–60), IV, pp. 153 f., 186, 202 f., 223–4; Stein, 'Jewish law', p. 19; cf. also Léon Poliakov, *Les banquiers juifs et le Saint-Siège du XIIIe au XVIIe siècle* (Paris, 1967), pp. 36–7.

[20] Parkes, *Jew in medieval community*, pp. 316 f., 340 f.; L. Rabinowitz, *The social life of the Jews of northern France in the XII–XIV centuries as reflected in the rabbinical literature of the period* (London, 1938), pp. 45–6; Stein, 'Jewish law', pp. 23 f.

[21] Attilio Milano, *Storia degli ebrei in Italia* (Turin, 1963), pp. 109 f.

other occupations remained open to them.[22] In northern Italy, as in the German Empire, late medieval Jewry remained in this ambiguous theoretical position: forced by economic pressures into an activity condemned by the law of God. In territory which was, or became, Venetian, the exclusion of the Jews from other activities—or at least from industry—was not absolute or universal. There was probably much Jewish capital behind the woollen industry of Rovigo in the fifteenth century—but, on the other hand, in Verona in 1443 Jewish newcomers were forbidden to engage in any economic activity other than banking.[23]

Among theologians and jurisconsults, opinion on the propriety of contracting with Jews was uncertain and divided. Arguments based on Deuteronomy had not found wide acceptance among prominent churchmen, for they were met with the thesis that the Old Testament permission to the Jews to lend upon usury to aliens had been a temporary concession which had since expired.[24] The canonist Alessandro of Nevo, in four *Consilia* drawn up at Padua between 1440 and 1455, held that the Church had no right to authorize the Jews to commit any mortal sin, and that the acceptance of usury was such a sin. On the other hand, such thinkers as Pietro of Ancarano, Paolo di Castro and Alessandro Tartagni of Imola believed that the Jews should be fully authorized to lend money—whilst Giovanni of Imola, expounding the canon *Ex gravi* of 1311 in the Clementine Constitutions, maintained that, since it did not expressly mention the Jews, its prohibitions on public authorities contracting with moneylenders did not apply to agreements concluded with Jews.[24a]

The territories which in the course of the fourteenth and fifteenth centuries came to form the mainland possessions of the Venetian Republic marked the point of convergence of two currents of Jewish immigration. The Jews came southwards from Germany and northwards from central and southern Italy. In northern Italy the Jews did not, as in medieval Spain, simply constitute one of several alien elements in a mixed and varied population.[25] Instead, they formed peculiar communities introduced into particular cities or states because of the economic and fiscal advantages which the authorities hoped to extract

[22] Guido Kisch, *The Jews in medieval Germany: a study of their legal and social status* (Chicago, 1949), pp. 192–4.
[23] Cecil Roth, *History of the Jews of Italy* (Philadelphia, 1946), pp. 129–30.
[24] Nelson, *Idea of usury*, pp. 12 f.
[24a] Poliakov, *Les banquiers juifs*, pp. 41–50, 75; cf. also below, pp. 495–6.
[25] For what follows see S. W. Baron, *The Jewish community: its history and structure to the American Revolution* (3 vols., Philadelphia, 1948), I, pp. 214–16, 242–5, 274–6, 282; S. W. Baron, 'The Jewish factor in medieval civilization', *Proceedings of the American Academy for Jewish Research*, XII (1942), pp. 35–7, 42–4.

from them. These communities enjoyed a certain degree of autonomy: the powers of their own Jewish councils were increased by the government's interest in levying taxation. The sum to be contributed by the Jews for the privilege of residence in a given country was agreed with the local authorities, but apportioned and levied by the Jewish leaders themselves. An agreement or *condotta* lasting perhaps three to seven years, negotiated with the local government, defined the rights and duties of the Jewish community during its sojourn. The Jews lived within a country on the principle that the law of the state in which they found themselves was law, so long as it did not conflict with the divine law as seen and interpreted by their rabbis. They were aliens without protectors, other than the government which had issued the *condotta*. In the late Middle Ages no other state was willing to make diplomatic representations on their behalf, though in the sixteenth century the Turkish government of Suleiman the Magnificent, strongly influenced by distinguished Jewish immigrants, began to exercise an unofficial protectorate over Italian Jews in Venice and the Papal States.[26] In Italy at least, the Jews were aliens on account of their voluntary decision to associate themselves in adhering to a faith which differed from that of their hosts. In theory the border between Christianity and Judaism could easily be crossed by accepting baptism. However, in states equipped with a powerful Inquisition, complications were easily created by the suspicion that new converts might backslide, and they found themselves in a vulnerable position, unable to shake off a Jewish past. Racial considerations coloured the Spanish attitude to the Jews; but there was no legislation in the Venetian Republic comparable with the Spanish statutes on purity of blood.[27]

For all their usefulness to the poor and to the fisc, the Jews were regarded by the Christian majority surrounding them with a peculiar mixture of resentment, distrust and occasional hatred. In northern Italy this could scarcely be explained as resentment at the economic power of the Jews. The most advanced areas of the peninsula had never been in Jewish tutelage. Cities like fifteenth-century Brescia had considered introducing the Jews for the purpose of undercutting exorbitant Christian lenders—these had long preceded them. The official policy of the Church demanded that Jews and Judaism be preserved, but at the same time be humiliated and publicly reduced to an inferior status. The policy which the Papacy followed, in its capacity of head of all

[26] Cf. Cecil Roth, *The House of Nasi: Doña Gracia* (Philadelphia, 1947), p. 147.
[27] Baron, 'Jewish factor', pp. 17–18, 40–1, argues for the racial and nationalistic connotations of medieval antisemitism. Kisch, *Jew in medieval Germany*, pp. 310 f., holds with special reference to Germany that the antisemitism of the late Middle Ages was purely religious in origin.

churches and in that of an Italian temporal prince, was latent in some words of Innocent III's Bull *Sicut Judaeis* of 1199—'Although Jewish perfidy is in many ways worthy of reprobation, nevertheless, because through them our own Faith is truthfully confirmed, they are not to be severely oppressed by the faithful'. The Jews received protection against violence, forced baptism and the desecration of their festivals and cemeteries, on condition—a significant rider—that they had in no way attempted to subvert the Christian faith.[28]

The attitude of Catholic Christians to the Jews in their midst was influenced by the belief that this nation was rejected and cursed by God for its wilful refusal to recognize Jesus as the Saviour foretold by the prophets, and for his crucifixion, the murder of God. Certainly, by the twelfth century, theologians such as Anselm of Aosta, Peter Abailard, and even Abailard's opponent Bernard of Clairvaux had modified the harsh patristic tradition, by which, if the Jews were ignorant of the divinity of Jesus, their ignorance was *affectata*, 'studied', and therefore culpable. Abailard went furthest in arguing that the Jews implicated in the crucifixion had committed no sin at all, because they believed themselves to be executing the will of God. Aquinas, however, later chose to attribute to the Jews a formidable measure of guilt for the crucifixion of Christ, though he did distinguish between the leaders of the Jewish people and the lesser Jews whom they had cozened into believing Jesus an impostor. In his interpretation of conflicting biblical texts on the subject of Jewish guilt, he admitted that the leaders of the Jews had not fully grasped 'the mystery of his [Jesus's] divinity'. He concluded severely that

> studied ignorance does not exonerate from blame, but seems rather to increase it: for it shows that a man is so bent upon sinning that he wishes to incur ignorance rather than avoid the sin. And so the Jews have sinned as the crucifiers, not merely of Christ the man, but even of Christ the God.

The guilt of the Jews was hereditary and collective, and justified their inferior status as perpetual serfs of the Church.[29]

Resentment at the Jews was peculiarly virulent on account of the belief that they had no reasonable excuse for not acknowledging the truth of the Scripture. They had access to the Scriptures and lived

[28] Cf. Baron, *Jewish community*, I, pp. 216 f.; Léon Poliakov, *Histoire de l'antisémitisme*, II (Paris, 1961), pp. 303–21.

[29] Cf. George La Piana, 'The Church and the Jews', *Historia Judaica*, XI (1949), pp. 117, 124 f.; Thomas Aquinas, *Summa Theologica*, Part III, *quaestio* xlvii, *articulus* 5–6, in *Opera omnia iussu impensaque Leonis XIII Pontificis Maximi edita*, XI (Rome, 1903), pp. 459–61.

among Christians; yet they persisted obdurately in their wrong interpretation of them. Popular medieval legends supplemented the teachings of the higher clergy in portraying the Jews as deliberate unbelievers. They explained Jewish obstinacy by depicting the Jews as the inhuman allies of the Devil, his fellow-conspirators against the Christian faith. Hence the Jews might be deemed capable of grandiose plots for the poisoning of wells, of obtaining Christian blood for use in Passover rites, of enacting gruesome parodies of the crucifixion of Christ by the sacrifice of kidnapped Christian boys.[30] Preachers eager to discredit the Jews and to eliminate Jewish moneylending from Italian cities could easily exploit this deep-seated suspicion and distrust of the insecure, deliberately abased minority in the midst of Christian communities.

The employment of Jewish moneylenders was a profitable, perhaps even a legitimate, alternative to conniving at Christian usury. At the same time it meant settling in one's city or state a group of defenceless aliens whose relationship with the Christian majority was permanently uneasy. The right of the Jews to lend at interest in a Christian community could never go unquestioned for long—especially when the Franciscans began to offer a practical alternative to Jewish loan banks. Accumulated legend and the official policy of the Church demanded that the Jews be humiliated and kept apart from Christians, prevented from acquiring any power over them; that Christians beware of the contaminating presence of the Jewish faith. In the years from about 1450 to 1600, by a slow and complex process within the Venetian Republic, Jewish loan banking was to become concentrated in the capital itself and otherwise confined to rural areas. On the mainland, large urban Jewish communities were to survive only in Padua and Verona. Apart from the capital itself, the large cities of the Venetian Republic were officially to be served by Monti di Pietà. These chapters set out to describe the process; to examine the relationship, formed by religious attitudes, economic necessity and reason of state, between the Venetian government, its people and the Jews; and to discuss the function and development of the Monti di Pietà designed to replace them and to free communities of the scourge of usurious lending.

---

[30] Cf. Cecil Roth, 'The mediaeval conception of the Jew: a new interpretation', *Essays and studies in memory of Linda R. Miller* (New York, 1938); Joshua Trachtenberg, *The Devil and the Jews: the medieval conception of the Jew and its relation to modern antisemitism* (New Haven, 1943); Norman Cohn, *The pursuit of the Millennium* (London, 1957), pp. 60 f.

1

THE EARLY JEWISH BANKERS AND THE
FIRST MONTI DI PIETÀ

The Jews who acted as loan bankers in the Venetian Republic began to migrate from Germany and from central and southern Italy in the middle and late thirteenth century. A high proportion later concentrated in Venice itself, after the invasion of the Veneto by French and imperial troops during the war of the League of Cambrai in 1509. There they formed the 'German nation' within Venetian Jewry, chiefly concerned with moneylending and dealing in second-hand goods. Emigrants from Spain and Portugal became prominent in Venice by 1496. But they found no favour in the sight of the government, and could not settle confidently and in large numbers before the last quarter of the sixteenth century. Iberian Jews were dedicated, not to loan banking, but to international trade, though from the late sixteenth century they helped to finance the banking business, and contributed to the taxes paid by the Jewish nation as a whole.

The status of the Jews in Germany was fast deteriorating, at least by the height of the thirteenth century. They had suffered large-scale violence in the Rhineland from the popular movements involved in the First Crusade.[1] From the Land Peace of Mainz in 1103 to the enactments of 1236 imperial policy had extended greater protection to the Jews, and had made them a special group on a par with women, children and clerics, at the same time depriving them of the right to bear arms in their own defence. The effect of this, however, was to emphasize their servile and dependent status: a status depressed by the influence of canon law and of a Roman law more harshly interpreted in Germany than Italy.[2] Before 1300, pogroms and massacres were falling on many communities in Franconia, Bavaria and Austria. Anti-Jewish violence was heightened by rumours of a Jewish conspiracy against Christendom, of a foul combination of Jews and lepers to poison the wells and 'anoint' the houses of prospective victims— rumours which spread from France into Germany during the great

[1] Cf. H. Liebeschütz, 'The Crusading movement and Jewry', *Journal of Jewish Studies*, X (1959).
[2] For this see Kisch, *Jews in medieval Germany*, pp. 305–64. On Roman law and the Jews in Italy, cf. A. T. Sheedy, *Bartolus on social conditions in the fourteenth century* (New York, 1942), pp. 230 f.

epidemics of 1348–9. In Italy itself, Rome was the largest centre for the diffusion of Jewish lending to other parts of the peninsula. At the same time, opportunities for the Jewish banker were opening in northern Italy through the upgrading of certain Christian firms which were moving into the finance of industry or international trade, or extending credit to kings and princes.[3]

The Venetian government seems to have made its first contract with Jewish leaders in 1298, for the purpose of undercutting nominal Christian lenders like the Tuscans of the Mestre region.[4] During much of the next two centuries, the Jews were theoretically settled in Mestre, and not in Venice itself. For the Venetians, like other contemporary governments, occasionally tried to segregate undesirable but ineradicable elements of the population—beggars, prostitutes or Jews—in the hope of controlling them and reducing contamination. Confining the Jews to Mestre might make access to them more difficult. However, the Jews were allowed to reside in Venice during the years 1366–95.[5] They were then relegated to Mestre, but allowed to return to Venice for periods of fifteen days at a time. Only in 1496 did the Venetians seek to enforce this provision more rigorously, by enacting that Jews might spend only fifteen days a year in Venice. Even then it was necessary to relax the provision a little in favour of Jewish bankers, since sales of unredeemed pledges were held in Venice itself under the supervision of a magistracy with which Jewish bankers constantly had dealings.[6]

The large Jewish communities of Padua and Verona were formed in the late fourteenth and early fifteenth centuries, shortly before and soon after the Venetian conquest of these formerly sovereign and independent cities. During the fourteenth century, Padua had enjoyed an unsavoury reputation for usurious dealings, not only because it possessed a small group of professional lenders or *campsores* (nominal Christians, often of Tuscan origins), but also because a very high proportion of the citizens lent money on the side as a part-time occupation to supplement their income from other sources. Theirs were consumption loans, rather than investments designed to finance commercial ventures.[7] With its international university and a big population of chronically penniless students, Padua created a substantial demand for the services of moneylenders, and Jews eventually came to contribute

[3] Milano, *Storia degli Ebrei*, pp. 112–14, 118 f., 129–30; Trachtenberg, *The Devil and the Jews*, pp. 102 f.

[4] Roth, *History of the Jews of Italy*, p. 123.

[5] Cecil Roth, *The history of the Jews of Venice* (Philadelphia, 1930), pp. 17–20.

[6] D.M.S., I, col. 81 (26 March 1496).

[7] See J. K. Hyde, *Padua in the age of Dante* (Manchester, 1966), pp. 40–2, 181–90.

to them. From 1369 onwards, Jews from the Papal States, from Rimini and Ancona, were engaged in trade and moneylending in Padua, from which they spread outwards to the townships of Montagnana, Este, Piove di Sacco, and, at some stage, Camposampiero.[7a] By 1432, Jews were maintaining seven lending establishments in Padua, though some of these may have been subsidiary branches of large concerns rather than independent banks.[8] During the 1430's and 1440's, the Jews of Padua and of its territory contributed to the smoother operation of the fiscal system, both by paying substantial forced loans themselves, and by advancing money to citizens to enable them to pay their taxes.[8a]

The Veronese invited German Jews to their town in 1408, apparently hoping thereby to reduce the extortionate charges of Christian lenders.[9] As for Vicenza, some Jews from central Italy probably arrived in the town in the second half of the fourteenth century. Small traders seem to have preceded bankers, but in 1425 and again in 1435 the commune contracted with Jewish lenders who came, ultimately, from Ancona and Modena. In the agreement of 1435, one of the bankers, Jacob, son of Moses of Ancona, was described as 'moneylender at Padua'—for Padua was evidently colonizing its neighbour towns.[10] Further west, the Lombard city of Brescia, acquired by the Venetians during the contest with Visconti Milan in 1426, proceeded with greater caution and uncertainty. One party in the city councils clearly favoured contracting with the Jews, both to relieve Christians of the necessity of committing mortal sins, and to lower their exorbitant charges. The councils debated the matter without any clear result in 1434, 1441 and 1444; Christian interest rates in Brescia were estimated at 60–80 per cent,[11] whereas Paduan Jews at this time were lending at only 20–25 per cent.[12] There were evidently some Jewish banks in Brescia or its district by 1463, since the Council of Ten in Venice then confirmed certain concessions

---

[7a] Antonio Ciscato, *Gli ebrei in Padova (1300–1800)* (Padua, 1901), pp. 19–23 and docs. I–II, pp. 229–36. On Piove di Sacco and Camposampiero, see also Luke Wadding, *Annales minorum, seu trium ordinum a S. Francisco institutorum*, XIV–XV (Rome, 1735–6), XIV, p. 514; XV, p. 7; also D.M.S., I, col. 653.

[8] Ciscato, *Ebrei in Padova*, p. 44.

[8a] A. Pino-Branca, 'Il comune di Padova sotto la Dominante nel secolo XV (rapporti amministrativi e finanziari)', *Atti del Reale Istituto Veneto di Scienze, Lettere ed Arti*, XCIII (1933–4), pp. 1,270–1, 1,302.

[9] Girolamo Dalla Corte, *Istorie della città di Verona* (3 vols., Venice, 1744), III, p. 6; D. Fortis, 'Gli ebrei di Verona: cenni storici', *L'Educatore Israelita*, XI–XII (1863–4), XI, pp. 200–1. Dalla Corte's account was written in 1592.

[10] Daniele Carpi, 'Alcune notizie sugli ebrei a Vicenza (secoli XIV–XVIII)', *Archivio Veneto*, serie v, LXVIII (1961), pp. 18–19; Giovanni Mantese, *Memorie storiche della Chiesa Vicentina*, III/2 (Vicenza, 1964), pp. 652–3.

[11] Zanelli, 'Predicatori in Brescia', pp. 90–1, 100.

[12] See below, pp. 446–7.

made to them.[13] However, the hesitations of certain Brescians do provide evidence that conciliar laws genuinely aroused many doubts and scruples about the practice of deliberately contracting with money-lenders—even where it could be argued that they were outside the pale of canon law.

To the north and north-east of Venice, Treviso, about 1400, had four or five Jewish loan banks, and there were Jewish lenders, also, in Conegliano and Serravalle.[14] Jewish lenders had appeared sporadically in Friuli, Istria and Dalmatia during the thirteenth century. But probably Tuscans—often Ghibelline exiles—were more popular till the close of the fourteenth, when Jewish settlement became widespread.[15] In the Polesine, the low-lying region to the south-west, Jews had been established at least since 1391, in Rovigo.[16] Records of Jewish migrations to Venice during the invasions of 1509 imply that there must also have been Jewish communities at Bassano, Castelfranco, Asolo and Cittadella. At the same time, Jews from Belluno were reported to have migrated to Feltre 'to make terms'.[17]

Information about the conditions on which the Jews lent money during the fifteenth century suggests that they could at least contemplate lowering their rates to as little as 12 per cent—the Jews of Treviso seem to have made such an offer in 1398. Rates in Treviso were still moderate in the mid-fifteenth century—for in 1446 the Venetian representatives in the town contracted with Aberlino, son of Marco, of Vicenza, who proposed to keep available for loans a capital sum of at least 4,000 ducats, and to lend at 15 per cent.[17a] But the interest charged in Padua was substantially higher, and attempts to depress the level proved ineffectual. Here, in 1408, Jews lent at 20 per cent on pledges and at 25 per cent on the less secure guarantee of written bonds. In February 1415, the Venetian government tried to cut this to 12 per cent on loans of over 25 lire, and 15 per cent on smaller loans. But in Padua the Jews commanded a strong bargaining position. The demand for their services was strong, and as yet there was no cheap and workable alternative to retaining them. The Jews closed their banks, and the university protested against the measure in unison with the commune

[13] Zanelli, 'Predicatori in Brescia', p. 109.
[14] Luigi Bailo, *L'istituzione del Monte di Pietà in Treviso, 1496* (Treviso, 1885), p. 7; Roth, *History of the Jews of Italy*, p. 124.
[15] *Ibid.*, pp. 116–17; Milano, *Storia degli ebrei*, pp. 132–3; Antonio Ive, 'Banques juives et Monts-de-Piété en Istrie: les *Capitoli* des juifs de Pirano', *Revue des Études Juives*, II (1881), pp. 176–7.
[16] Roth, *History of the Jews of Italy*, p. 129.
[17] D.M.S., VIII, coll. 305, 340, 344, 355–6, 376, 393, 410, 418, 548, 550.
[17a] Bailo, *Monte di Pietà in Treviso*, pp. 7–9.

of Padua. The Venetian Senate was forced to allow lending to continue at the old rates.[18]

An agreement concluded with a firm of Jewish bankers in Istria indicates the relatively liberal terms which a small town in an obscure and backward region was prepared to offer to obtain credit for its citizens. The commune of Pirano, seat of a Venetian Podestà, struck this bargain (after one false start) in 1484, with the Jew Joseph and his partners, Moses and Jacob Sacerdote, and Abraham and Aaron Stella.[19] The essence of the agreement was that the Jewish bankers undertook to make a total sum of 1,500 ducats available for loans to inhabitants of the administrative district of Pirano. On one month's notice, they must be prepared to increase the amount to 2,000 ducats. The rate of interest chargeable by the Jews to inhabitants of the district was fixed at 20 per cent. A higher rate of 30 per cent became lawful in loan contracts with outsiders, no doubt to ensure that the Piranese would enjoy priority, and to compensate the lenders for the greater risk in advancing money to persons who could less easily be compelled to honour their obligations. The Jewish firm would enjoy the monopoly of all legal moneylending in the district, and nobody might lend at interest without their permission. The regulations on banking showed remarkable determination to indemnify the Jews against all possibility of loss in their transactions. Normally, they would lend on the security of pledges, for an initial period of two years, and might accept pledges of any kind except church furnishings and other properties, which must not be allowed to pass into Jewish hands—as if from fear of desecration. Should they wish to do so, they might extend the loan beyond the normal two-year limit. If the borrower failed to pay the interest due, the banker could auction the pledge after one year had elapsed.

Auctions of pledges were to be held four times yearly and conducted by a judge of the district, together with the town-clerk of Pirano. They were bound to auction a second time all pledges which, at their first sale, had failed to produce a sum sufficient to cover the sum lent, the interest due upon it, and the expenses incurred—presumably by the banker in storing the pledge, in looking after it properly, and keeping the books which recorded the transaction. Theoretically, the Jew ran no risk, for should the sale still produce too little the borrower was bound to compensate the lender and indemnify him against all loss. However, any profit on the sale was restored to the former owner of the

[18] Ciscato, *Ebrei in Padova*, pp. 40–2.
[19] The articles of this agreement are printed in Ive, 'Banques juives en Istrie', pp. 189–95.

447

pledge, not claimed by the Jewish banker. Another clause which favoured the bankers protected them from being held responsible for the deterioration of pledges in their care, or for pledges stolen or burnt. Jews were not bound to lend on the security of written promises unless they themselves chose to do so. The establishment of a fixed rate of interest and the elimination (in theory) of any risk to the Jew from the transaction made the bargain frankly usurious by the criteria of ecclesiastical law. The Jewish firm enjoyed greater liberty in lending to 'foreigners' from outside the Podestaria of Pirano, for they were entitled to make their own arrangements for the buying, selling and auctioning of all pledges belonging to such outsiders. They were also empowered to send out agents into other parts of Istria where no loan banks had been erected by the local communes, there 'to give and lend money upon interest to outsiders'.

The Jewish bankers of Pirano were still largely free of restrictions on other forms of economic activity. These *capitoli* expressly permitted them to engage in trade, to buy and sell any kind of goods, and to be 'treated in all respects like the citizens of Pirano'. Whether such clauses entitled them to manufacture goods is uncertain. However, they were in one respect outwardly differentiated from Christian citizens, in being compelled to wear the distinctive badge which the Fourth Lateran Council had prescribed for the purpose of separating Jews from Christians—especially to control sexual relations between devotees of the two faiths.[20] This took the form of an 'O' on the outside of their clothing. However, the 'O' was compulsory only for male Jews above the age of thirteen, never for women or girls, and even the men were not bound to wear the badge on journeys. Moreover, the Jews obtained a number of guarantees for the protection of their faith and religious observances. They were authorized to establish a synagogue and cemetery in Pirano. Butchers would supply them with meat prepared in accordance with the Jewish laws. No-one should force the Jews of Pirano to lend on the Sabbath or other Jewish festivals. Finally, the contract with Joseph and his partners obviously saw them as the nucleus of a future Jewish community, for they were entitled to bring in Jewish schoolteachers to instruct their children, and to invite to Pirano 'any other Jews that they see fit'.

The *capitoli* thus concluded with the Jews of Pirano were to remain in force for ten years. Thereafter, they would be automatically renewed for another five, unless the authorities expressly resolved to get rid of the Jews. In 1484, as in 1508 and 1520,[21] the Venetian government was

---

[20] IV Lateran (1215), c. 68—Mansi, *Concilia*, XXII, col. 1,055.
[21] The *capitoli* of 3 August 1508, repeated in 1520, provided that the Jews 'may

evidently allowing individual local authorities to strike their own bargains with the Jews, at least with respect to their banking activities, and not attempting to standardize their practices. Local initiative decided whether to contract with the Jews, and sometimes when to expel them, whilst the Venetian government merely confirmed, modified or rejected proposals submitted to it.

The Pirano agreement reflected the citizens' obvious eagerness to obtain the services of Jewish lenders. Pirano, however, lay far from the main centres of the anti-Jewish agitation which had developed during the fifteenth century. The Papacy, as M. Poliakov suggests, has acted throughout most of its history as a 'regulator' of the fortunes of the Jews, turning against them in their moments of comparative prosperity, but protecting them from the most savage violence.[22] Towards the middle of the century, under the influence of the Observant Franciscan leaders, in response to the demands of the King of Castile, Eugenius IV issued the Bull *Dudum ad nostram*. Previously, communities of Italian Jews had banded together with moderate success to exert pressure on his predecessor, Martin V.[23] But the Papacy was not deaf to the demands of Bernardino of Siena and Giovanni of Capistrano, the first Vicars-General of the Observant movement within the Franciscan Order. Bernardino, whose influence had spread beyond Tuscany after 1417, had eloquently attacked usury as the denial of all Christian charity, a corrupting disease which infected all the members of a community which acquiesced in it.[24] His canonisation in 1450, six years after his death, bore witness to his favour with the Papacy. The Bull which Eugenius issued in 1442 was designed to produce the greatest possible degree of separation between Christians and all outside the faith, whether Jews or Saracens, as if to protect Christianity from insidious contamination. It rigorously banned all forms of social intercourse between Christians, Jews and Saracens, and forbade Jews and Saracens to be preferred to Christians in elections to civic office. Nor could they act as physicians or midwives, be tenants, stewards, agents, servants, marriage-brokers, or members of the same guilds. Nor might Christians serve Jews, even by performing small household tasks for them on the Jewish Sabbath. The Bull reiterated the old provision that Jews must pay tithes on all landed property acquired from Christians. It added legal disabilities to economic restrictions, by enacting that in

lend at the rates which are customary in the various localities, both to local inhabitants and to foreigners'—printed in M. Lattes, 'Documents et notices sur l'histoire politique et littéraire des juifs en Italie', *Revue des Études Juives*, V (1882), p. 229.

[22] Poliakov, *Histoire de l'antisémitisme*, II, p. 303.
[23] Baron, *Jewish community*, I, pp. 319–21.
[24] Noonan, *Scholastic analysis of usury*, pp. 71 f.

lawsuits Christians might testify against Jews, whilst Jews were barred from witness against Christians. Finally, it prohibited the taking of usury by Jewish moneylenders, and demanded that they make restitution for usuries accepted in the past. As issued by Eugenius, the Bull was clearly a response to the complaints of the King of Castile against the abuse of privileges by Spanish Jews.[25] Nicholas V reissued it in 1451 after a lenient interval at the start of his pontificate,[26] and it was then repeated in 1456 by Calixtus III: this time with explicit reference to abuses committed by Jews resident in Italy.[27] There could now be no doubt that the Pope intended this policy of segregating and debasing the Jews to be applied in Italy as well as in Spain.

Nevertheless, despite these general vetoes on contracting with Jewish bankers, it remained possible for Christian rulers to apply to the Holy See for special concessions entitling them to make agreements with the Jews, and absolving them and their officials from ecclesiastical censures. Hence, for example, in 1456 Francesco Sforza, Duke of Milan, applied to the Pope, asking that 'for the peace of his conscience' the Holy See might approve his current bargain with the Jews. He apparently got satisfaction, even though Calixtus III had renewed the anti-Jewish Bull of Nicholas V. Papal Bulls did not prove to be the deadly enemies to Jewish loan-banking that they seemed, and by the end of the century the curia had developed a regular system of issuing patents to Jewish financiers—though the Venetian Republic never found it necessary to quieten its official conscience by inviting papal pronouncements on these matters.[27a]

The attacks of Observant Franciscan preachers convinced of the heinousness of lending at interest; the collaboration they obtained from bishops and certain civic authorities; the malicious propaganda they disseminated against the Jews: these were far more menacing. The Observants, with their Christian loan banks or Monti di Pietà, were prepared to offer a viable alternative to the Jewish lender. Unless he were eliminated, the Jews would inevitably retain economic power over Christians, and the total isolation or removal of the Jews would never become feasible. The Franciscan campaign against the Jews was to continue long after the Popes had abandoned obvious animosity against them. This would revive only in the days of the Caraffa Pope, Paul IV, in the early days of the Counter Reformation.[28] In a famous thesis pro-

[25] Eugenius IV, 'Dudum ad nostram', B.R., V, pp. 68–70.
[26] Odoricus Raynaldus, *Annales ecclesiastici ab anno MCXCVIII*, ed. J. D. Mansi, IX (Lucca, 1752), pp. 510, 570–1.
[27] The Bull of 28 May 1456 refers to 'the aforesaid Jews and Saracens who dwell amongst Christians both in Italy and in other parts of the world'—B.R., V, pp. 127–30.
[27a] Poliakov, *Les banquiers juifs*, pp. 94–104, 236.   [28] See below, pp. 517–18, 528–9.

pounded in 1875, the German historian Wilhelm Roscher interpreted outbreaks of anti-semitism as the struggles of nations which had developed indigenous merchant classes to break loose of the economic tutelage of the Jews.[29] Clearly, this cannot explain Italian anti-semitism in the fifteenth century, since the Italians had never depended solely on the Jews, even in the small-loan business (let alone in international trade), and since Lombard and Tuscan lenders had preceded Jewish. However, it is true that an effective anti-Jewish movement could develop only when institutions had been devised to provide credit still cheaper than any the Jews could offer. It was public institutions, not private merchants, that made the real difference.

A very serviceable definition of the term Monte di Pietà, as this was generally used, came in 1749 from Francis-Xavier Zech, a learned German Jesuit and controversialist. He described it as 'a certain fund of money (or of other consumable goods) collected together for the assistance of the poor, to be lent to them on the security of pledges'.[30] In the fourteenth century, certain bishops and burghers in England and France had already tried to accumulate funds designed to lend at low rates or without interest at all, to save Christians from impoverishment at the hands of usurers. The Bishop of Mende had made such a proposal in 1326, the Bishop of London in 1361; so had a group of burghers at Salins, in Franche-Comté. But they had not reserved these funds exclusively to the use of the poor, and the Bishop of London had in his will provided for a series of loans graded according to the social status of the borrower.[31] Certainly, there was no sign of any wide campaign, traversing the boundaries of many cities and dioceses, for the systematic replacement of Jewish by Christian loan banks. Such a movement arose only in Italy in the mid-fifteenth century, where it was spread by the vigorous evangelism of Observant Franciscan preachers.[32]

---

[29] Roscher's essay is translated in part as 'The status of the Jews in the Middle Ages considered from the standpoint of commercial policy', in *Historia Judaica*, VI (1944), with an introductory essay by Guido Kisch. Cf. also Kisch, *Jew in medieval Germany*, pp. 320 f.

[30] Francis-Xavier Zech, *Rigor moderatus doctrinae pontificiae circa usuras, Dissertatio II* (Ingolstadt, 1749), p. 151.

[31] Holzapfel, *Die Anfänge der Montes Pietatis*, pp. 29–30. Other accounts of the institution at Salins appear in G. B. Depping, *Les juifs dans le moyen âge: essai historique sur leur état civil, commercial et littéraire* (Paris, 1834), p. 289; J. Morey, 'Les juifs en Franche-Comté au XIVe siècle', *Revue des Études Juives*, VII (1883), pp. 33–4. According to Morey, the 'Mont de Salins' lent at 7 per cent on the security of real property and chattels.

[32] Much information about the early history of the Monti di Pietà is scattered through vols. XIV and XV of the encyclopaedic history of the Franciscan Order, the *Annales Minorum* compiled between the 1620's and the 1650's by the Irish Franciscan Luke Wadding (cf. Canice Mooney, 'The writings of Father Luke Wadding,

Some of these, like Michele Carcano of Milan, revealed wider interests in the systematic organization of other forms of charity and poor relief, and did not specialize only in the extension of credit to the poor.[33]

In all probability, the first Monte di Pietà which conformed to Zech's description was that established in Perugia in 1462. Admittedly, an institution called a Monte di Pietà was erected at Ascoli Piceno in 1458, inspired by the sermons of a Franciscan, Domenico of Leonessa. But there is nothing in any known document to suggest that this was a loan bank giving credit to the poor on the security of pledges—more likely, it was a general charitable fund, designed especially for *poveri vergognosi*.[34] Perugia was an important city of the Papal States, in which a papal legate shared authority with the civic magistrates. Once, in 1260, it had been the seed-plot of the great flagellant movement, and it was now to provide the model for social institutions just as significant as the Scuole dei Battuti.[34a] From 1310, Perugian authorities had recognized the Jews as useful to the commune and to private persons for their activities as moneylenders. But in 1425 the sermons and later the 'statutes' of Bernardino of Siena, designed to stiffen morality and secure public decency in Perugia, had attacked usurers in general and had discriminated against Jews with refined ferocity.[34b] Such blows, however, fell lightly and ineffectively—because Bernardino failed to offer any alternative solution to the problem of providing cheap credit. This came only in 1462. The idea may have originated with Barnabà Manassei, Vicar of the Umbrian province of the Observance, and have

O.F.M.', *Franciscan Studies*, XVIII, 1958). Most modern accounts owe much to Wadding, and this one is no exception. It should be said, however, that Wadding sometimes drew his information from local histories not contemporary with the events they describe. A standard modern account is Heribert Holzapfel, *Die Anfänge der Montes Pietatis* (Munich, 1903). Giuseppe Garrani, *Il carattere bancario e l'evoluzione strutturale dei primigenii Monti di Pietà: riflessi della tecnica bancaria antica su quella moderna* (Milan, 1957) provides a vast quantity of information, arranged on a comparative basis, about the early constitutions of the Monti di Pietà. Briefer introductions to the subject are Anscar Parsons, 'Bernardine of Feltre and the *Montes Pietatis*', *Franciscan Studies*, new series, I, no. 1 (1941); and Henri Lapeyre, 'Banque et crédit en Italie du XVIème au XVIIIème siècle', *Revue d'histoire moderne et contemporaine*, VIII (1961). Anscar Parsons, 'The economic significance of the *Montes Pietatis*', *Franciscan Studies*, new series, I, no. 3 (1941), carries the story of the institution outside Italy—cf. also Zech's *Dissertatio*, cited above, n. 30, Section VII, pp. 150 f. Giuseppe Coniglio, art. 'Monti di Pietà', *Enciclopedia Cattolica*, VIII, provides a useful bibliography.

[33] See above, p. 206.

[34] See Stanislao Majarelli and Ugolino Nicolini, *Il Monte dei Poveri di Perugia: periodo delle origini (1462–1474)* (Perugia, 1962), pp. 122–32.

[34a] See above, pp. 34–5.

[34b] Majarelli and Nicolini, *Il Monte di Perugia*, pp. 70–86, 91–2; Antonio Fantozzi, 'Documenta Perusina de S. Bernardino Senensi', *Archivum Franciscanum Historicum*, XV (1922), pp. 119–25.

been cast into a workable form by his fellow-Observant, the jurist Fortunato Coppoli. These two Franciscans probably conveyed their proposals to Ermolao Barbaro, Bishop of Verona, a Venetian prelate who had governed Perugia as legate for rather more than a year. Barbaro chose the Observant Michele Carcano to preach a course of Lenten sermons, in which he pronounced that 'the city of Perugia is excommunicate on account of the agreements it has made with the Jews to encourage the poisonous crime of usury, and will remain so until these concessions are rescinded and annulled'. The supreme council of Perugia then assumed responsibility both for repudiating its agreement with the Jews, and, at the end of April 1462, for establishing a Monte di Pietà. Other foundations soon followed, at Orvieto and Gubbio, and the Perugian Monte di Pietà provided the pattern and inspiration to many others. The Perugians themselves took intense pride in their pioneer work. In 1464, a Perugian council declared that 'This Monte is justly called the Perugian Monte, for it was first established in this city, like a chandelier which throws out light, and deserves to be copied by all the faithful'. Over a century later, the citizens maintained the tradition, when in 1571 they inscribed over the entrance to its premises the claim that 'This was the first Monte di Pietà in the world'.[34c]

The Franciscans made their first foundations in the zones of Central Italy which lay between the Apennines and the Adriatic: in Umbria, the traditional focus of their activities, and in the Marches. Within ten years they had inspired about twenty such establishments in these regions.[35] Statutes formulated by Marco of Montegallo acquired a kind of official authority, and were widely imitated, so that the Monte could spread in a standardized form.[36] Fortunato Coppoli earned a reputation as defender of the Monti di Pietà against opponents who claimed that their small interest charges were usurious. Once exported from the Papal States, the institution certainly provoked opposition, and Dominican preachers protested from the pulpits of Florence in 1473. After a public disputation, the Vicar-General pronounced in favour of the Franciscans. But these indecently open arguments had discredited the cause of the Monti in Florence for the time being, and the city had to wait for Savonarola (an unconventional Dominican) to establish its

---

[34c] For the fullest and most recent account of the foundation of the Monte di Pietà, see Majarelli and Nicolini, *Il Monte di Perugia*, pp. 101–14, 133 f.; also Wadding, *Annales Minorum*, XIV, pp. 93–5; Holzapfel, *Die Anfänge*, pp. 33 f.; Paolo Sevesi, 'Il Beato Michele Carcano di Milano, O.F.M.', *Archivum Franciscanum Historicum*, III–IV (1910–11), III, pp. 648–53; Parsons, 'Bernardine of Feltre', pp. 18–20.

[35] Holzapfel, *Die Anfänge*, pp. 33 f.

[36] *Ibid.*, p. 59.

2G

first Monte di Pietà in the 1490's.[37] Nevertheless, other Tuscan cities—including Siena, Pistoia and Prato—did acquire Monti di Pietà in the 1470's. Still wider dissemination came in the 1480's, when the Monti di Pietà found acceptance in Liguria, Lombardy and the territories of the Venetian Republic.[38] However, their legality in the face of the canon law was still open to doubt—as was the Franciscans' claim that to contract with Jewish usurers was unlawful. The Popes had early begun to approve and confirm the statutes of individual Monti di Pietà—starting with Orvieto in 1464 and Perugia in 1467[39]—but they had issued no general pronouncement to justify the principles on which these were based. The battle had to be fought afresh in many individual towns or bishoprics.[40] Dominican arguments provided theoretical ammunition for those who were sceptical about the success of the Monti or who objected for other reasons. It was possible to hold that papal Bulls of confirmation were invalid if they conflicted with the divine law or with the existing canons of the Church.

The anti-Jewish agitations which accompanied or coincided with the spread of the Monti di Pietà caused the Venetian government certain misgivings. However, the Venetians obtained reassurance in 1463 from the Papal Legate, John Bessarion, Cardinal of Nicea, who was then visiting Venice in connexion with the negotiations for Pius II's proposed crusade against the expanding might of Ottoman Turkey. His letter, addressed to Doge Cristoforo Moro on 18 December 1463, was to be cited in argument as much as sixty years later by those who favoured retaining the Jews in Venice itself.[41] Bessarion recorded that the Venetian government and subject authorities had in the past frequently contracted with Jews, with great benefit to all concerned 'and for the sake of greater economy (*pro minori dispendio*)'. He was clearly referring to the lower rates of interest charged by Jewish lenders. Certain persons, however, had recently disputed the validity of such contracts, maintaining that these were void and there was no obligation to

[37] *Ibid.*, pp. 60–1; Marino Ciardini, *I banchieri ebrei in Firenze nel secolo XV e il Monte di Pietà fondato da Girolamo Savonarola* (Borgo San Lorenzo, 1907), doc. XVI, pp. lii–liii, and pp. 63–7; F. R. Salter, 'The Jews in fifteenth-century Florence and Savonarola's establishment of a *Mons Pietatis*', *Cambridge Historical Journal*, V (1936), pp. 202–3; Alberto Ghinato, 'Un propagatore dei Monti di Pietà del '400: Padre Fortunato Coppoli da Perugia, O.F.M.', *Rivista di Storia della Chiesa in Italia*, X (1956).

[38] Holzapfel, *Die Anfänge*, pp. 63 f.

[39] *Ibid.*, pp. 10–12.

[40] Wadding describes several such disputes—at Mantua (1485), Parma (1488), Lucca (1489), Ticino (1493): see *Annales Minorum*, XIV, pp. 397, 445, 464–6, XV, p. 37.

[41] Bessarion's letter is printed in Ludwig Mohler, *Kardinal Bessarion als Theologe, Humanist und Staatsmann*, III (Paderborn, 1942), pp. 529–30. For the use made of it in the debates of 1519–20, see D.M.S., XXVIII, coll. 63–4.

observe them. In reply, Bessarion, without expressly mentioning the delicate matter of usury, first inquired whether it was permissible to retain a Jewish community next to a Christian at all. He said that the main purpose of his legation was to render the Christian people more acceptable to God. But he often thought of the salvation of those who had strayed from the path, especially if Christians could somehow profit by associating with them. Hence,

> following in the steps of the Bishops of Rome, we permit Jews to live among Christians, so that if they wish to they may some time happily mend their ways (commode resipiscere); but if they do not want to reform they will be unable to find any excuse before a rigorous judge for their obstinacy.

Bessarion thus justified the retention of the Jews on the grounds that living among Christians might lead to their conversion. By virtue of his apostolic authority, he then pronounced that all agreements with Jews must be strictly observed, 'and that Jews shall be permitted to live, dwell, trade and associate freely with them (Christians) in peace and harmony'. The Papal Legate was departing from the harsher policy suggested by the legislation of Calixtus III. He further added that all authorities who had entered into agreements with the Jews were freed from any sentences of excommunication they might have incurred on that account.

In the years which followed, the Venetian Republic showed itself favourable to the establishment of Monti di Pietà on subject territory, and occasionally to the expulsion of Jews from particular districts. But it continued to protect them from the mob violence provoked by at least one popular Franciscan preacher, Bernardino Tomitano of Feltre, and there is no evidence that it favoured the repudiation of agreements with the Jews that had not expired in the course of time.

Michele Carcano of Milan, whose sermons had contributed to the foundation of the original Monte di Pietà in Perugia, seems to have made the first attempt to introduce this institution to a Venetian subject city. In 1469, he arrived in Padua and exhorted the citizens to establish a Christian loan fund. His proposals won the enthusiastic approval of the Venetian government, but the scheme suddenly collapsed after a promising start, and no more was heard of it in Padua till 1490.[42] Only in the 1480's were Monti di Pietà generally established in the great cities of the Venetian dominion on the mainland of Italy. One possible reason for the failure of Carcano's scheme in Padua lay in the fact that the Paduans had recently tried the experiment of expelling Jewish

[42] Sevesi, 'Michele Carcano', III, pp. 661–3.

moneylenders from the city itself, and the results had not been fortunate. The Jews had simply removed to the villages of the Padovano and had used the privileges they still enjoyed there, which entitled them to exact interest at 30 per cent from 'outsiders' who did not inhabit a given village. Paduans and university students had to apply to them there, paying travel costs and higher rates. Meanwhile, the Jewish traders left in Padua lent secretly to the Paduans and got the tickets signed by the village bankers; they were said to charge as much as 40 per cent by this means. The regrettable experiment had lasted from 1455 to 1467, when the Venetian government again authorized Jewish bankers to lend in Padua itself three days a week. It was, therefore, understandable that the Paduans, having so recently reintroduced the Jews, should treat with caution proposals that might make them emigrate, and which could not guarantee that equal supplies of capital would be made available.[43]

The greatest single influence on the early Monti di Pietà in the territories of the Venetian Republic stemmed from the work of a powerful, bigoted and courageous Franciscan, Bernardino Tomitano, a native of the subject city of Feltre. In the course of his career, this formidable friar procured the foundation, reform or expansion of about thirty Monti di Pietà, in Lombardy, Liguria, the Veneto, and central Italy, and at Aquila in the Kingdom of Naples.[44] His first years of intense activity in the Venetian Republic ran from 1477 to 1483, when with his brethren he was forced to leave Venetian territory in response to the Interdict pronounced by Sixtus IV during the war of Ferrara.[45] He returned in 1490, to spend much of the last four years of his life campaigning against the Jews and in favour of the Monti di Pietà in Venetian subject towns and villages, though not, in these last years, in Venice itself.

Bernardino's attacks on usury and on the corrupting presence of the Jews formed part of his wider campaign for the preservation of faith, morals and public decency; for the relief of the poor; and for their protection against lax or oppressive government. In his first years in the Veneto he seemed little concerned with the Monti di Pietà. A main activity was to censure the particular abuses for which individual cities had become notorious—blasphemy, promiscuity, incest or the immodest dresses of women. At Venice in 1481 he preached his Lenten sermons on the theme 'Blessed art thou among women', adding the words 'and blessed are all women that put off vain things'—by which

[43] Ciscato, Ebrei in Padova, pp. 52–5.
[44] Holzapfel, Die Anfänge, pp. 66 f.
[45] Wadding, Annales Minorum, XIV, pp. 328–9, 352–3.

he meant vain female ornaments. At Vicenza in 1492 and at Padua the following year he organized great 'bonfires of vanities'. In his own city of Feltre he set up as a general censor of public morals and pornographic literature. The victims of his puritanism there included a certain humanist who was ordered not to acquaint his pupils with the Epigrams of Martial, the erotic poetry of Ovid, or the works of Catullus and Petronius. In Brescia he demanded the establishment of separate prisons for women.[46]

Beyond this, Bernardino of Feltre, by his personal example and his organizing ability, showed a deep concern for the welfare of the poor. He championed them in the midst of natural disaster and against misgovernment. During the plague epidemic in Padua in 1478 he worked bravely for the poor, strengthened by the words of Bernardino of Siena that all who died through doing works of charity in a plague season ought to be regarded as martyrs. He refused to heed the harsh government admonition not to entertain in his friary 'guests from unknown places that may be infected' with plague. He insisted on collecting funds for the relief of the sick himself, refusing to delegate the task to others; on washing the feet of guests; and on personally performing menial tasks in the friary. Typically, he also ignored government prohibitions on public preaching which would assemble crowds and so spread infection. The citizens ought to recover their health through abstaining from immorality, not from neglecting to hear the healing word of God.[47] Some years later, in Vicenza, he founded permanent institutions for the care of beggars in general, and of paupers of gentle birth in particular. In Vicenza, too, he obtained from the local Council and later from the Venetian Senate the repeal of an inhuman law whereby men and women who could produce the heads of outlawed relatives were themselves to be pardoned for all crimes they had committed.[48] During his exile in Mantua in 1484 he had proved to be an outspoken critic of the Marquess's government, and had rebuked the ruler for his arbitrary treatment of the law, his failure to show mercy to widows, paupers and orphans, his neglecting to control the pillaging of the soldiery and to prevent violations of ecclesiastical property.[49]

Bernardino, then, was in a broad sense a promoter of charity and an energetic critic of social behaviour. The question of usury and of possible remedies against it was by no means his only preoccupation. This, however, bulked increasingly large in his work after 1484, when he procured the foundation of a Monte di Pietà in Mantua[50] and soon

[46] *Ibid.*, XIV, pp. 175–6, 229, 267, XV, pp. 6, 7, 9, 37, 45, 63–6, 67–8.
[47] *Ibid.*, XIV, pp. 195–6.   [48] *Ibid.*, XV, pp. 13, 63.
[49] *Ibid.*, XIV, pp. 382–4.   [50] *Ibid.*

afterwards moved into central Italy and Lombardy. But his prejudice against the Jews was then no novelty. His actions contributed to the spread of irrational anti-Jewish sentiment, based on ugly and slanderous myths, in the Veneto after 1475. His colleague, Michele Carcano, was also implicated. In 1475 Bernardino of Feltre preached the Lenten sermons at Trent, on Austrian territory. There he attacked the influence of the Jews and their free association with Christians, especially that of the physician Tobias and of Brunetta, 'a most subtle woman of that people', who was probably a midwife. Accused of slandering the Jews, the preacher responded by prophesying that before Easter Sunday they would 'give a worthy proof of their goodness'. His 'prophecies', not surprisingly, were made to come true; the body of a small child named Simon was found during Holy Week, and his death was ascribed to ritual murder by the Jews. Despite papal condemnation, the legends that the Jews either use Christian blood in their Passover rites or re-enact the passion of Christ on the bodies of Christian children have always proved hardy and persistent. The cult of the martyred child began to spread in spite of the active discouragement of Pope Sixtus IV —the Bishop of Trent, Johann Hinderbach, was passionately eager for its promotion.[51] It can hardly have been a mere coincidence that similar accusations were levelled at the Jews of Padua within a month. The Venetian government proved sceptical, unwilling to believe the charges, and a ducal letter issued on 22 April 1475 in the name of Doge Pietro Mocenigo declared that 'We surely believe that the rumour of a boy being murdered is a mere fabrication and falsehood'. It reproved the Capitano of Padua—perhaps too late—for his action against the Jews.[52] On Venetian territory, Michele Carcano publicized the martyrdom of Simon of Trent. His correspondence with the Bishop of Trent reveals that the movement had found sympathizers within the Venetian patriciate, including a certain Francesco Tron and 'many other Venetian noblemen'.[53] In all probability, the irresponsible conduct of

[51] *Ibid.*, XIV, pp. 132–3; H. L. Strack, *The Jew and human sacrifice* (*human blood and Jewish ritual*): *an historical and social inquiry*, trans. H. Blanchamp (London, 1909), pp. 193 f.; Trachtenberg, *Devil and Jews*, pp. 132 f. Sixtus V officially recognized the cult of Simon of Trent—but only in 1588. Confessions were exacted from the Jews of Trent by torture and there were grave inconsistencies in the evidence.

[52] Cecil Roth, *The ritual murder libel and the Jew: the report by Cardinal Lorenzo Ganganelli* (*Pope Clement XIV*) (London, 1934), pp. 48–9. Ganganelli's investigation was conducted after 1758, when the Jewish communities of Poland attempted to defend themselves against charges of ritual murder by applying to Rome. Benedict XIV referred the question to the Holy Office of the Inquisition, which designated its *consultor* Ganganelli to investigate it.

[53] Paolo Sevesi, 'Beato Michele Carcano, O.F.M. Obs., 1427–84 (Documenti inediti)', *Archivum Franciscanum Historicum*, XXXIII–XXXIV (1940–1), XXXIII, pp. 385–404.

Bernardino of Feltre, his determination at all costs to discredit the supposed enemies of the Christian faith, and the publicity spread by Carcano, helped to rouse credulous suspicion and fear of the Jews in the towns and villages of the Veneto.

By its action in Padua in 1475, and by its humane treatment in 1603 of a similar accusation launched against a Jew named Joseph in Verona, the Signory of Venice earned the praise of the eighteenth-century Franciscan, Lorenzo Ganganelli (later Pope Clement XIV), in his fair and balanced investigation of the ritual murder libel. Whatever the conduct of Venetian governors in the provinces, the central government in Venice never acted precipitately to condemn the Jews. However, when investigating accusations of this type, it did not always reject them. Other cases followed the episodes in Trent and Padua—at Porto Bufolè and Motta in 1480; at Marostica, near Vicenza, in 1485.[54] Only the case at Porto Bufolè, however, seems to be described by contemporary evidence. The Venetian annalist Domenico Malipiero told how, in 1480, Andrea, son of Giacomo Dolfin, Podestà of Porto Bufolè, had passed savage death-sentences on a small group of Jews supposed on Holy Thursday to have kidnapped and murdered an Albanian beggar-boy. The Venetian government, disturbed at the severity of the sentence, sent out an Avogadore to examine the proceedings. It may have intended to use this as a test case to establish the plausibility of the accusation in general. A solemn trial was held, and the accused were defended (allegedly at great financial profit) by Giovanni Antonio Minio and by certain Doctors of Law from the University of Padua. Eventually, all three Jews were condemned to be burnt alive.[55] Despite the central government's relative caution and fairness, Venetian judges had now shown themselves prepared to credit at least one charge of ritual murder levelled against the Jews. No action, however, was taken

[54] Dalla Corte in his *Istorie di Verona*, III, p. 106, refers to a case similar to those of Trent and of Porto Bufolè occurring at Motta in 1480. Motta and Porto Bufolè, on the borders of Friuli and the Trevigiano, are not far from one another, and Dalla Corte may have been referring to the incident described by Malipiero, not to a separate event. Ganganelli refers to a dissertation by one Father Benedetto da Cavalesio on the martyrdom of Simon of Trent, published in 1747. This 'mentions Lorenzino, a child bled to death by the Jews in 1485 at Marostica in the province of Vicenza, and in proof of this the author cites a certificate of the episcopal court of Padua': as well as the fact that the child was locally recognized as a martyr. See Roth, *Ritual murder libel*, p. 55. Dr Giovanni Mantese points out that from the beginning of 1479 there had been several pilgrimages from Vicenza to the 'basilica' of Simon of Trent, and that the acts of a pastoral visitation conducted in October 1488 by Pietro Barozzi, Bishop of Padua, mention the cult at Marostica of a child allegedly murdered by the Jews. See Mantese, *Memorie storiche della Chiesa Vicentina*, III/2, pp. 481–2, 651.

[55] Domenico Malipiero, *Annali veneti dall'anno 1457 al 1500*, ed. Agostino Sagredo in *Archivio Storico Italiano*, VII (1843–4), p. 671.

on an accusation later made in Venice itself, in 1514, by a fanatical Carmelite.[56]

Anti-Jewish prejudice, resting on such foundations, may have helped the preachers who, after 1485, promoted the Monti di Pietà in the Veneto, and there may have been links between the Marostica affair, the strictly enforced decrees which expelled the Jews from Vicenza in 1486, and the foundation in the city of a Monte di Pietà.[56a] Elsewhere, however, preachers seldom succeeded in procuring the immediate expulsion of the Jews, for their Christian loan banks needed time to establish themselves and to raise adequate funds. Where such expulsions were obtained—as at Brescia in 1494 or at Verona in 1499—they do not seem to have eliminated the Jews permanently, for there were still Jews in those cities in 1509.[57]

In 1490, Bernardino of Feltre resumed his spectacular career in the Veneto. Since 1484, he had founded, resuscitated or otherwise furthered the interests of Monti di Pietà at Mantua, Perugia, Assisi, Gubbio, Parma, Aquila, Chieti, Rieti, Terni, San Gimignano and Lucca.[58] The arguments used to inspire his hearers to give to the Monti di Pietà may well have foreshadowed those later presented in his surviving sermon, delivered in 1493, in favour of erecting a Monte di Pietà at Pavia. He then maintained that the more persons a donor helped with alms, and the more effectively he gave assistance, the larger the store of merit which would be amassed thereby. Gifts to a Monte di Pietà would never be consumed or worn out, in the same way as gifts of bread, wine or footwear to the poor. Indeed, they would be used in perpetuity, benefiting three or four persons every year. Such gifts offered the means of performing all the seven works of physical mercy, because the pauper could use loans made by the Monte di Pietà to buy bread, wine, clothing or medicine, or any other such necessities (the assumption being that these were the legitimate purposes to which moneys from a Monte di Pietà could be applied). 'Give to the Monte and you have given everything.'[58a]

At Genoa, in 1490, Bernardino received a letter from his intimate friend Pietro Barozzi, the energetic and pious Bishop of Padua, describ-

---

[56] D.M.S., XVIII, col. 144.

[56a] Cf. Carpi, 'Ebrei a Vicenza', pp. 17, 20–1; Mantese, *Memorie storiche della Chiesa Vicentina*, III/2, pp. 482, 654–7.

[57] Wadding, *Annales Minorum*, XV, p. 68; Dalla Corte, *Istorie di Verona*, III, pp. 122–3; Fortis, 'Ebrei di Verona', XI, p. 202; D.M.S., VIII, coll. 305, 344.

[58] Wadding, *Annales Minorum*, XIV, pp. 383–4, 396–8, 409, 434, 445, 451–2, 462–3, 464–6.

[58a] For extensive quotations from this sermon, see Gino Barbieri, *Il Beato Bernardino da Feltre nella storia sociale del Rinascimento* (Milan, 1962). See pp. 58–9 for the remarks described above.

ing how plans were already afoot to found a Monte di Pietà to curb the influence of Jewish usurers in Padua and the surrounding territory. Barozzi informed him that

> Public opinion, in the city and suburbs and in the countryside, has never more unanimously favoured such a project. However, just as not all the Israelites wished to be freed from slavery in Egypt, even so certain persons among us are complaining against our proposals, preferring to leave banking in the hands of the Jews. . . . Hence we beg you to come and visit us as soon as possible. . . . The Lord will enable you to bring to a happy completion the work which has already been undertaken.

Bernardino reached Padua in October 1490, and, in Barozzi's absence, at first met with a disappointing reception. But after the Bishop's return that December, the citizens warmed to the evangelist summoned to destroy with his rhetoric the defences of Paduan Jewry and of its supporters. The Monte di Pietà of Padua was finally erected with Venetian approval in May 1491[59]—though for more than half a century it was to coexist with Jewish lenders, except at the times when they had voluntarily taken refuge in Venice.[60] After Bernardino's departure, the Conservators of the new Monte di Pietà were able to inform him that many peasants from the surrounding region were fervently contributing to the Monte di Pietà. The new foundation had brought two especial benefits to the people. To serve its needs, larger quantities of small coins had been newly minted, and this had very greatly benefited the poor.[61] Presumably it did so by making it much easier to conduct all kinds of petty transaction—easier for the poor to buy victuals in small quantities, easier to employ poor men for odd jobs, perhaps also easier to give alms in the streets or elsewhere.[62] Moreover, the Monte di Pietà was now making advances of seed corn to the people, which the peasants could repay at harvest-time, either in kind or at the current market price. Previously, usurers had been

---

[59] Wadding, *Annales Minorum*, XIV, pp. 481–2, 512–13; Jacopo Moro, *Il Monte di Pietà di Padova, 1469–1923* (Padua, 1923), pp. 12 f.; Pietro Mattei, *Cenni storici sui banchi di pegno e i Monti di Pietà: il Monte di Pietà a Padova* (Padua, 1953), pp. 27 f.

[60] See below, pp. 478–81.

[61] See Barbieri, *Bernardino da Feltre*, pp. 55–6.

[62] The words of Fynes Moryson, written in the early seventeenth century on the small coinage of Italy, may also be applied to the late fifteenth: 'These small moneys, the aboundance of people in a narrow land, and the common peoples poverty, but most of all their innated pride, such as they had rather starve for want, then beg, these things make them doe any service for a stranger for a small reward, and make the passages of rivers, or channells (as at Venice), and all necessaries, to be afforded for a small piece of money. Neither is it a small commoditie of these little brass moneys, that it makes the meaner sort more ready to give alms. . . .' See Fynes Moryson, *Itinerary* (4 vols, Glasgow, 1907—reprint of the original edition of 1617), IV, pp. 95–6.

accustomed to exact either one-third or one-half of the entire harvest by way of interest on their loans.[63] Evidently, the loans made by the Monte di Pietà were not merely consumption loans in the narrowest sense. They were not intended to further commercial ventures, but could be used to support agriculture.

From 1491, Bernardino's reputation as a preacher flourished in the Veneto, and municipal authorities competed with enthusiasm for the honour of his presence and the stimulus of his eloquence. At Camposampiero in 1492, representatives of at least five small towns besieged him with requests to preach in their pulpits.[64] The Venetian government, however, viewed his rabble-rousing tendencies with caution and disapproval, and on reaching Crema in that year he found himself banned from preaching by order of the Signory. Allegedly, however, the governor of Crema failed to enforce this Venetian command because the people rioted on hearing that Bernardino had secretly withdrawn; and he had to be recalled to pacify them.[65] The government was probably concerned for the safety of the Jews not only from humanitarian motives and from a general desire to preserve public order; it was easy to reflect that the Jews held as pledges much property of Christian citizens. Pogroms would inevitably cause Christians damage and loss. At this stage, moreover, relatively few authorities were wholly convinced that the Monti di Pietà could act as a complete substitute for Jewish loan-banking. At Crema, Bernardino of Feltre justified himself by saying that

> If I have to speak of the Jews, I shall say what I say in every other city—that no-one who holds his soul dear may harm the Jews, in their persons, their property, or in any other thing. For justice, Christian charity and love must be shown to the Jews also, for they too partake of our human nature. I have always said so in every city, and now I say it in Crema and demand to be heard: for this is meet and right, such is the commandment of the Supreme Pontiffs, so does Christian charity demand of us. But it is true that the canon laws expressly bar us from habitual and frequent association with Jews, from employing Jewish doctors, and from attending their feasts.
>
> How can I be a preacher of the truth, and yet gloss over these offences to God and the canon laws? Jewish usuries are not only immoderate, but so unbridled that they cut the throats of the poor and tear out their hearts; and I, who live off alms and eat the bread of the poor, shall I be a dumb dog in this place of truth?[66]

[63] Barbieri, *Bernardino da Feltre*, pp. 55–6. M. Poliakov believes that in general there is little evidence of Jews lending seed-corn, but finds an instance of this in the Veneto in the late fifteenth century: *Les banquiers juifs*, pp. 117–18.

[64] Wadding, *Annales Minorum*, XV, pp. 7–9.

[65] *Ibid.*, XV, p. 12.   [66] Quoted in Holzapfel, *Die Anfänge*, pp. 86–7.

This medley of arguments in the mouth of the self-styled champion of the poor and defender of the canon laws ought, if taken literally by its hearers, to have produced a distinction between the Jews as usurers and the Jews as human beings. It should have preserved them from violence. In the past, however, Bernardino's sermons had often roused popular sentiment against the Jews, and in the Trent affair it is hard to believe that he did not intend to produce this result. Not only the Venetian, but also the Florentine and Milanese governments regarded him with distrust.[67] Jewish communities sometimes managed to forestall him by the use of ducal letters of protection. They probably kept these letters by them, and brought them up to date as the need arose. A ducal letter to the governors of Verona, ostensibly issued on 15 May 1492, ordered these magistrates to summon Friar Bernardino and warn him to say nothing from the pulpit that might rouse the people to violence against the Jews—'Let him merely castigate other abuses, and not mention the Jews themselves nor speak ill of them'. This letter included a clear statement of policy, compatible with Bessarion's opinion, saying that 'we wish the Jews to be able to reside and lend at interest in all parts of our dominion according to the content of their *capitoli*'.[68]

However, these restrictions on Bernardino did not apply to the whole Venetian dominion, but only to particular places within it—to Crema, Verona, Brescia and the smaller town of Montagnana, at various times between 1492 and 1494.[69] According to the traditions of Franciscan historical writing, Bernardino was himself being persecuted by the machinations of the Jews, of a sinister and treacherous power conspiring against him by 'false insinuations'. But he enjoyed support at Venice from one of its most distinguished noblemen, Leonardo Loredan, the future Doge, and in the provinces from Antonio Bernardo, ex-governor of Vicenza, who helped him to eject a Jewish moneylender from Camposampiero and to establish a Monte di Pietà.[70] Bernardino was responsible for exporting the Monte from the larger centres like Padua and into smaller towns and villages. His initiative helped to establish Christian loan banks in Piove di Sacco, Camposampiero, Monselice and possibly Montagnana, outposts of Paduan Jewry; in his native town of Feltre, where visitors from Bassano heard

---

[67] Wadding, *Annales Minorum*, XIV, pp. 243–4, 446–7; Salter, 'Jews in Florence', pp. 205–6.
[68] Wadding, *Annales Minorum*, XV, pp. 67–8; Alberto Ghinato, 'Ebrei e predicatori francescani in Verona nel secolo XV', *Archivum Franciscanum Historicum*, L (1957).
[69] Wadding, *Annales Minorum*, XV, pp. 12, 66–9.
[70] *Ibid.*, XV, pp. 7–9.

him and tried to apply his system in their own city; and at Crema, in spite of restrictions on the matter of his sermons.[71] Apart from this, he effected the reorganization of the existing Monti di Pietà in the large centres of Vicenza, Verona and Brescia, in such a way as to make their survival much more certain.

From their early days, the Monti di Pietà had provoked opposition by making a small interest charge to cover administrative expenses on all loans. The Christian banks required an income for the rent and upkeep of their premises, on which loans were made and pledges stored in conditions of reasonable security; and above all they needed to pay the salaries of their officials. The fact that their charges were lower than those of private Christian or Jewish usurers was largely irrelevant: the whole principle of interest-taking was at stake here. The early Monti of Perugia, Orvieto and Gubbio accepted interest, Gubbio charging 12 per cent in 1463 but reducing the level to 8 per cent the following year.[72] At Perugia, the rate of interest was not to be constant, but to be adjusted annually. It was fixed at 10 per cent in 1463, but by 1468 had descended to 6 per cent.[73] Giacomo Vannucci, Bishop of Perugia, justified the interest charges on the grounds that they were intended to cover the rent of the premises of the Monte and to reward the labours of its staff. One jurisconsult, Benedetto dei Benedetti, pointed out that the commune which had placed money at the disposal of the needy was not itself making any charge for its loans. It was merely that the clerks and other employees of the Monte di Pietà—who had lent nothing on their own account—were exacting a wage for their labours and recouping their expenses. There was, therefore, no usurious contract between the lenders (the commune) and the borrowers (the poor who paid the interest).[74] But after a few years certain Friars, including Marco of Montegallo, tried to organize Monti di Pietà which would lend gratis, making no charge on the borrower on any pretext. Marco of Montegallo introduced this system to the Veneto in 1486, when he founded the Monte di Pietà at Vicenza.[75] This was possibly the first Monte actually to be erected in a large Venetian subject city, and it inspired the establishment of another on essentially similar principles in Brescia three years later. The Brescian statutes provided that the officials of the Monte di Pietà were to lend sums of up to three ducats per household on adequate pledges which must be worth at least one-third more than the sum lent on their security. The officials were to

[71] *Ibid.*, XIV, pp. 514–15, XV, pp. 7–9, 12, 37, 66–7.
[72] Holzapfel, *Die Anfänge*, pp. 45–7.
[73] Majarelli and Nicolini, *Il Monte di Perugia*, pp. 148–9, 166–7, 304, 323–4.
[74] *Ibid.*, pp. 196 f., 323–4.
[75] Holzapfel, *Die Anfänge*, pp. 59, 82.

lend 'for periods of six months, gratis and without any payment', and to receive back 'only the principal lent'. Any profit made in auctioning unredeemed pledges must be returned to their former owners. The Monte was not self-financing: the Commune of Brescia assumed the responsibility for paying the officials.[76] Shortly afterwards, a Ligurian Friar, Michele of Acqui, who had preached in Brescia during the Lent of 1490, founded a Monte di Pietà in Verona in August of that year. The Monte di Pietà in Verona was, again, designed to lend on pledges but without charging interest.[77]

A genuine difference of opinion was developing, both among the Observant Franciscans and within the Veneto itself. The Monte di Pietà at Padua, the creation of Barozzi and Bernardino of Feltre, from the start proposed to charge interest at the rate of 5 per cent.[78] Bernardino set out to impose his own scheme at Vicenza, Verona and Brescia, where the existing Monti showed signs of flagging or becoming extinct. At Vicenza borrowers were not legally charged interest, but they were expected to make some donation out of gratitude to the funds of the Monte. The result, not surprisingly, was that from embarrassment, or fear of not being accommodated in the future, borrowers habitually made presents of sums equivalent to four times the 5 per cent charge suggested by Bernardino. It could be argued that only technical considerations differentiated this from a compulsory interest charge, and that the effect on the poor man's pocket was considerably worse. Two sermons from Bernardino, however, persuaded the Bishop and city council of Vicenza to adopt his methods.[79] In 1493, Michele of Acqui and Bernardino of Feltre discussed the question in principle at a formal debate in the Franciscan Chapter-General, where Bernardino seems to have advocated the interest charge essentially on the grounds of administrative necessity. He admitted that it would be 'more attractive

[76] Zanelli 'Predicatori a Brescia', docs. VII, VIII and X, pp. 138–44; also Elia Cavriolo, *Dell'istorie della città di Brescia libri XIV* (Venice, 1744—originally written in 1585?), p. 211, and Wadding, *Annales Minorum*, XV, p. 68.

[77] Dalla Corte, *Istorie di Verona*, III, pp. 116–18.

[78] Mattei, *Il Monte di Pietà a Padova*, p. 37; Garrani, *Carattere dei Monti di Pietà*, pp. 24–5.

[79] Wadding, *Annales Minorum*, XV, p. 6. The case of 'gratis dans' was one of the titles to receiving something over and above the principal recognized in the thirteenth century by the canonist Hostiensis. Innocent III in a letter of 1206 had declared that what the debtor offered freely in excess of the capital was not to be considered usury. It was later specified that the creditor must make no actual demand, and that there must be no express or tacit agreement that such a gift would be made. Cf. McLaughlin, 'Canonists on usury', I, pp. 125, 143–4. Philippe de Maizières, a councillor to Charles VI of France, had in 1389 proposed the foundation of a loan bank which would charge no interest. Its funds might be increased if all who had made claims on the services of the loan bank offered out of gratitude a gift equivalent to perhaps 10 per cent of the loan received—Holzapfel, *Die Anfänge*, pp. 30–1.

and more Christian' (*speciosius et religiosius*) if loans could be made without interest charges. But no institutions that did so were likely to survive for very long. Officials and servants of the Monti di Pietà would never undertake the work without payment, and they must not be remunerated out of the capital of the Monte itself or from any moneys deposited with it. By this time, Bernardino was able to cite in his favour a large corpus of precedent. Many of his brethren—apparently including Marco of Montegallo—had founded loan banks charging interest; Popes from Pius II to Innocent VIII had approved the foundation of such institutions; and the Universities of Perugia, Siena, Bologna and Pavia had allegedly justified them also. The decision of the Chapter-General favoured the arguments of Bernardino. A later Chapter-General, held in 1498, stipulated that in future Franciscans should not propose the establishment of Monti di Pietà unless they exacted interest for the support of staff and officials, as Bernardino of Feltre had recommended. 'For experience had shown that Monti of this type could not survive without something of the kind.' Franciscan preachers had, moreover, a duty to ensure that in future all Monti di Pietà should conform to this rule.[80]

By 1500, therefore, the Monti di Pietà had become an institution widely accepted and approved in central and northern Italy. The principle that interest charges were not only legitimate but compulsory had been officially established within the Franciscan Order. In the Venetian Republic, further foundations had followed the death of Bernardino of Feltre, with the erection of Monti di Pietà at Chioggia in 1495, Treviso in 1496, and Belluno in 1501–3.[81] Rarely if ever were these able to replace the Jewish bankers completely. Thus, in 1497, the Trevisans obtained from the Venetian government authority to expel their Jews, allowing them to lend in future only in the smaller centres. But the following year Venetian Avogadori di Commun modified this by providing that Jews might remain in the city, but not lend at interest. Nevertheless, there were still Jewish bankers in Treviso in 1509.[82] Only the invasions of that year prevented the Jews from continuing to lend at Padua.

Again, the Monti di Pietà were gradually acquiring theoretical as well as practical justifications for their activities and interest charges, winning a recognized place in the sight of ecclesiastical lawyers. Fortunato Coppoli, during the debate with the Dominicans in Florence in

[80] Wadding, *Annales Minorum*, XV, pp. 41, 152.

[81] Holzapfel, *Die Anfänge*, pp. 101–2; for Belluno, A.S.V., *Collegio, Relazioni*, b. 34, reports of Francesco Soranzo, 23 September 1592, and Angelo Contarini, 14 January 1614.

[82] D.M.S., I, coll. 779, 985; VIII, col. 425.

1473, had produced an elaborate defence of the interest charge. This he supported on the grounds that loans made by a Monte di Pietà could be broken down into four elements. They involved a contract of loan, or *mutuum*; a 'contract of pledge'; a 'contract of placing work'; and a 'contract of commission'. The first two contracts were concluded between the community which had established the loan bank and the borrowers themselves. They were made through the agency of the clerks who issued the loans and received the pledges. But the third and fourth contract came into being between the borrowers and the officials of the Monte di Pietà, the officials acting, not as representatives of the commune, but as private persons. As such, they were entitled to receive a salary for their work at the counter and in the storeroom. Moreover, they personally risked being held responsible for the loss or deterioration of the goods pledged and left in their keeping under the fourth contract of *mandatum*.[83] In this, the officials were much worse situated than the Jews of, say, Pirano, who were indemnified against loss to a much greater degree.[84] The officials and the commune, therefore, were not selling time and the use of money in the way condemned by medieval usury laws. The officials were demanding a fee for their labour, and compensation for the risk which they took. The element of labour and the element of risk, both of which could justify the acceptance of a sum over and above the principal lent, were therefore both present in contracts between the Monte di Pietà and its clients.

The Franciscans had won the argument in Florence but failed to establish their bank. Twenty years later, when the attempt to establish interest-free banks was fading out, polemic was still lively, opposition stemming from Dominican and Augustinian theologians. The treatment of the question in 1498 by the Dominican Thomas da Vio, otherwise Cajetanus, revealed that two main lines of argument were being used by the defenders of the Monti di Pietà. One of these portrayed the poor who borrowed from the Monte as its true owners, who were bound to pay for its upkeep. The fairest means of distributing the burden was surely to make those who received the greatest benefits from the Monte di Pietà offer the largest contributions to their maintenance. Cajetanus did not object to the existence of an institution dedicated

---

[83] Ciardini, *Banchieri ebrei*, pp. 63–5, Ghinato, 'Fortunato Coppoli', pp. 209–11. Coppoli's distinction between the commune and the Monte on the one hand, and the officials of the Monte on the other, seems to be repeated in Innocent VIII's Bull in favour of the Monte di Pietà in Mantua (1486), and in Leo X's Bull 'Inter multiplices' of 1515. The Bull of 1486 justifies payments made to Mantuan officials on the strength of the 'trouble and risk' which they took. See below, pp. 469, 472.

[84] See above, pp. 447–8.

to lending; nor did he deny its right to charge for its services. He merely objected to the principle on which interest charges were distributed among the borrowers: he who borrowed most was the neediest, and therefore ought to be charged least. With a certain logic, Cajetanus further argued that most of the services performed by officials of the Monti di Pietà were in fact performed for the benefit of the lenders rather than the borrowers: they were designed to ensure that the lenders obtained their due. There was therefore no good reason why the borrowers should pay for these services. Moreover, it was unjust to charge in proportion to the amount and time of each loan, because the work involved did not vary in proportion to the size and length of the loan. Surely the case would be met if individual borrowers were charged for the trouble of taking care of especially perishable pledges. Otherwise, or so Cajetanus implied, a flat rate, rather than a proportional interest charge, would be the only acceptable means of compensating the officials for their trouble.

Thus, by the close of the century, the Dominican Cajetanus was not seeking to overturn the whole structure of the Monti di Pietà. He was questioning the principle of charging interest, but not that of demanding fees for the service of public lending to the poor.[85] Finally, in 1515, a Bull of Leo X, issued with the approval of the fathers assembled at the Fifth Lateran Council, officially silenced the critics of the Monti di Pietà. This was the first general statement of principle, as distinct from the mere approval and confirmation by the Papacy of the statutes of individual Monti di Pietà. After the issue of the Bull, Domiñgo Soto of Salamanca, chaplain to Charles V and conservative opponent also of the poor laws, was the only major theologian to continue the Dominican tradition of opposing the interest charges of Christian loan banks.[86]

Leo X's Bull *Inter multiplices*, of 4 May 1515, began by reciting the conservative arguments, based on well-established medieval traditions, of the opponents of the Monti di Pietà.

Certain masters and doctors have maintained that those Monti are illegal in which something in addition to the principal, proportionate to the sum lent, is exacted by the officials of the Monte, after a certain length of time, from the poor to whom a loan has been given, so that they cannot be guiltless of the crime of usury, of injustice, or of some kind of evil. For Our Lord, as St Luke bears witness, expressly commanded us not to hope

---

[85] Noonan, *Scholastic analysis of usury*, pp. 296–9, for this exposition of Cajetanus's arguments. The Augustinian Nicolò Bariani had produced his *De monte impietatis* in 1494, and the Monti di Pietà were defended in 1497 by Bernardo de' Busti. Cajetanus's treatise was written in reply to Bernardo.

[86] Noonan, *Scholastic analysis*, p. 300; cf. also Parsons, 'Economic significance', p. 21. For Soto's views on the poor laws, see above, pp. 282–5.

for anything out of a loan in addition to the principal lent. For usury is correctly held to arise whenever an attempt is made to obtain a profit and interest payment without labour, expense or risk out of the use of a thing which is unfruitful.

However, the arguments of these masters and doctors were not merely theoretical: they seemed to be hinting at corrupt administration and misappropriation of funds.

They have further sought to prove that expenses for the maintenance of these Monti, which should (or so they say) be paid by other persons, are in fact extorted only from the poor to whom the loans are given; and they imply that something over and above the necessary and moderate expenses is being offered to certain other persons, not without some semblance of evil and incentive to crime.

This enigmatic phrase might imply corruption on the part of the officials in charge of the Monti. Or it might simply be an objection to the possible fact that the Monti di Pietà were already raising a proportion of their capital by inviting deposits as well as donations and bequests, and were prepared to pay interest for the sake of attracting depositors.

The text of the Bull then described the defence of the Monti. This was based on the familiar argument that nothing was sought or even hoped for out of the loan itself. The poor were required to pay only for the services of the officials, and they—it was argued in a manner reminiscent of Fortunato Coppoli—ought to be distinguished from the Monte itself, which was strictly non-profitmaking. The payments to officials were moderate and necessary, and were offered by those who benefited from the loans made by the officials out of the Monte. The essential justification for the interest payments was the principle that 'He who enjoys the benefit should also shoulder the burden' (*qui commodum sentit, onus quoque sentire debeat*).

Leo X, praising the zeal of both parties to the dispute, now pronounced in favour of the Monti di Pietà. He declared that a Monte di Pietà in which moderate interest rates were exacted to pay the salaries of officials and maintain the Monte, and in which the Monte itself made no profit, was in no sense evil. Such an institution would create no incentive to the commission of sin. The Monti di Pietà were not usurious, and the Pope issued a formal declaration that it was lawful for preachers to commend them as charitable works—perhaps with the aid of indulgences granted for the purpose by the Apostolic See. Pope and Council, however, still maintained the principle admitted by Bernardino of Feltre at the Franciscan Chapter-General of 1493—that it would be 'much more perfect and holy' if the Monti made no charge

2H

at all. Ideally, the founders of Monti di Pietà ought to establish *census*, annuities or rent-charges, and so provide a permanent income for the payment of officials independently of the interest paid by the poor. Finally, the Pope determined to enforce his judgment by threatening with excommunication all who preached against the content of the Bull. His pronouncement won the approval of all the Council, with the single exception of Hieronimo, Archbishop of Trani, who persisted in the opinion, based on his personal experience, that 'the said Monti did more harm than good'. In spite of such misgivings, sometimes based on a stiff-necked conservatism, sometimes on genuine distrust of the administrative soundness and general viability of the Monti di Pietà, these institutions had at last won the protection of a general law of the Church.[87]

At this point a more detailed examination can usefully be made of the early statutes of some of the Monti di Pietà in the Venetian Republic, and of the principles on which they were governed. Clearly, the Christian loan banks of Padua (1491) and Treviso (1496) were run on lines essentially similar to those approved by Innocent VIII in 1486, in his Bull confirming the Monte di Pietà founded at Mantua through the exhortations of Bernardino of Feltre.[88] Between 1486 and 1496, a standard type of Monte di Pietà, apologetically resigned to charging the poor for its loans, was evidently emerging. The familiar combination of bishop, governor and wandering Observant preacher, first seen at Perugia and since often repeated, produced the Monte di Pietà at Treviso.[89] The statutes formulated in the name of the city councils found confirmation and approval from the Venetian government.

The Monti di Pietà offered small loans to people who lived in the cities and districts in which they were established—persons who were genuinely poor, and who did not intend to put the money to any 'vicious or disreputable purpose'. The founders of these institutions bound their officials to inquire both into the origin of the pledge and into the

[87] Wadding, *Annales Minorum*, XV, pp. 470–1; Mansi, *Concilia*, XXXII, coll. 905–907; B.R., V, pp. 621–3.

[88] For the Bull 'Ad sacram' of Innocent VIII, see Wadding, *Annales Minorum*, XIV, pp. 411–15. The statutes of Treviso (1496) are printed in full in Garrani, *Carattere dei Monti di Pietà*, pp. 315–25. Those of Padua are described in the monographs by Moro and Mattei, already cited.

[89] According to the statutes of Treviso, the city council had been persuaded to take action by Bishop Nicolò Franco, by the governor Hieronimo Orio, and by Domenico Ponzone of the Order of Observant Franciscans.

use to which the money might be put. In this, the Monti di Pietà contrasted with the less inquisitorial Jewish banks. Innocent VIII's Bull, no doubt reflecting the aspirations of Bernardino of Feltre, threw the heaviest stress on the moral purpose of the foundation. It distinguished between the poor who were forced to borrow out of genuine need, and those who determined to borrow deliberately for dissolute or immoral ends. The *depositarius* of the Mantuan Monte was not allowed to lend either for business purposes or to satisfy gamblers. The Italian Monti di Pietà did not, like the loan institutions which later appeared in England and Germany,[90] lend to small artisans or shopkeepers to help them start up in business. They sometimes (as the example of Padua suggests) advanced seed-corn to peasants, but otherwise concentrated on the temporary relief of poverty by loans for the purpose of consumption. The officials at Treviso were not bound actually to inquire into the circumstances of prospective borrowers—but only to exact an oath that they were genuinely in need, and would not apply the money to any disreputable use.

Loans at Padua were restricted to three ducats per household at any given time, at Treviso to two. The statutes permitted the officials to lend only for short periods—six months at Treviso, a year at Mantua—which compared unfavourably with the longer-term loans permitted to Jewish lenders, as at Pirano. They did, however, save the borrowers from suffocation through accumulated interest: obligations to a Jewish banker could increase indefinitely. At Treviso, pledges made of gold, silver or some other imperishable substance must be worth one-third more than any sum lent on their security. If they were clothes, textiles or other goods liable to deteriorate, they must be worth at least fifty per cent more than the sum lent. If a pledge were unredeemed at the end of the loan period specified in the constitution of the Monte, then it must be sold by public auction. If, at the third time of asking, a pledge still failed to produce enough to cover the interest due on it, then the official who had accepted it was bound to compensate the Monte out of his own pocket. Any surplus realized at the sale went, not to the official or the Monte, but to the former owner of the pledge. In this respect, the borrower was theoretically better off if he dealt with a Monte di Pietà, rather than a Jewish banker: the risk of the pledge not covering the interest was borne by the official and not by the borrower. The risk borne by the officials, through loss, deterioration or under-

[90] Zech, *Rigor moderatus*, pp. 213–14; Parsons, 'Economic significance', p. 8; R. D. Richards, *The early history of banking in England* (London, 1929), p. 94; F. G. James, 'Charity endowments as sources of local credit in seventeenth- and eighteenth-century England', *Journal of Economic History*, VIII (1948); W. K. Jordan, *Philanthropy in England, 1480–1660* (London, 1959), pp. 42–6.

valuing of the pledge, was specifically invoked by Innocent VIII to justify interest charges at Mantua. However, these different regulations might well induce the Jewish banker to value the pledge much more highly than the Massaro of the Monte di Pietà.

Interest payments, calculated by the month, were rated at 10 per cent per annum in Mantua, but at only 5 per cent in Padua and Treviso. They were due, as Innocent VIII carefully specified, not to the Monte itself, but to its officials. The Trevisan statutes couched their demand for interest in remarkably diffident and apologetic phrases, shaped to disarm their critics:

> Again, it is necessary for the maintenance of the said Monte to have in some fit and proper place secure premises, cashboxes, counters, and books, and to meet many expenses, and to satisfy the *massaro*, the bookkeeper and their servants with the salary which has been fixed for them, so that they may act in good faith and not shun hard work but rather recognize their duty to God, and devote all their loyalty, energy and vigilance to the increase of the Holy Monte. In the belief that at present there is no other means of satisfying the aforesaid needs without reducing the capital of the Monte, be it enacted that until some other method is discovered

every borrower using the services of the Monte should be bound to pay a 5 per cent interest charge.

In Mantua, the commune, the Church and the Marquess's government were charged with supervising the administration of the Monti di Pietà. But the Venetians followed their usual principles by entrusting the management of charitable funds—as with the hospitals and lay fraternities—to laymen only and not to clerics. Despite the initiative of bishops and friars in the foundation of Monti, their function was confined to commending the institution to the public. In the Venetian commonwealth, the Monti di Pietà were the responsibility and property of the whole commune. Representatives drawn from several social levels should therefore share in their government, though, not surprisingly, the upper and middle classes enjoyed much heavier representation than the artisans. In Verona, the Council of the Monte was least democratic. The city councils of the Twelve and the Fifty elected twelve persons of different families to serve without payment as governors of the Monte. Three should be of noble or gentle birth (Cavalieri, Marchesi or Conti, in the style of Verona). Three should be university graduates: such persons enjoyed a special right to representation. Finally, there must be three merchants, and three other citizens.[91]

[91] Garrani, *Carattere dei Monti di Pietà*, p. 83.

Treviso proposed to organize its governing body—called Conservatori —on similar principles, but with a rather wider social sweep. Here, notaries and guildsmen or artisans also held places on the board. The Paduan system, however, proved the most complicated. In its first fifty years, Padua acquired a large Consiglio del Monte which—controlling the city's main financial organ—formed a kind of parallel to the older city councils, and developed into an object of small-town power politics. Originally, however, the Consiglio del Monte simply consisted of the civil and military governors; of four members of the executive council known as the Deputati ad utilia; of four members of the magistracy in charge of ecclesiastical affairs in the city and district (the Deputati alle chiese); and of twelve Conservatori proper. These Conservatori included eight prominent citizens 'of whatever rank may seem appropriate to the Council, and two merchants of good character and reputation'. The remaining seats on the board were filled by one representative from the principal religious fraternity of Padua, the Fraglia della Carità e Misericordia; and by a notary chosen by his own professional body or Collegio. Later revisions of the statutes, however, increased the full complement of the governing body, by 1535, to 118.

The Trevisan statutes carefully specified the functions of the Conservatori. They controlled the funds of the Monte; a simple device ensured that all should share in this. The two chests or cashboxes containing the capital of the Monte each had five locks, and each Conservatore held one key to one of the locks. One Conservatore acted as treasurer, and removed funds from the chest, fifty ducats at a time, under the eye of his colleagues, to be sent below and dispensed from the counter by the paid official of the Monte known as the Massaro. This Massaro, elected by the city council, must be a native of Treviso, hold no other office, and provide a security of at least 500 ducats as proof of good faith. The Massaro took charge of all lending operations, always with one of the Conservatori present to check him. A second paid official was the clerk or Quadernier, who recorded in his ledgers all transfers of money from the Conservatori to the Massaro. He also made a duplicate copy of all pawntickets written out and issued to borrowers by the Massaro who received their pledges.

In their early days, the Monti di Pietà depended for funds chiefly on charitable donations and bequests. The eloquence of such preachers as Bernardino of Feltre and Michele of Acqui, combined with solemn and elaborate public processions through the streets of the city, often raised enough to give the first impetus to the Monte di Pietà. A later historian recorded that a procession in Verona on 29 August 1490 raised the sum of 2,017 ducats for the Monte di Pietà, a pious show for the sake of charity. Established fraternities, like the Fraglia della Carità, recognized the Monti as good works to which their members could enthusiastically contribute. Michele of Acqui distinguished himself by organizing new fraternities whose main object was to contribute to the maintenance of the local Monte. His Fraternity of San Bernardino, founded at Verona in 1490, at once enrolled some 18,000 members, and its membership rose within a year to about 70,000, drawn from the city and the surrounding countryside. Alexander VI's Bull of confirmation, granting indulgences to this fraternity in 1491, described it as a mixed society consisting of clerks, religious and laity of both sexes. Michele of Acqui erected similar fraternities at Brescia, Cremona and Genoa during the 1490's.[92] Padua adopted similar measures in 1492, by recruiting a special Fraglia del Monte whose members pledged themselves to contribute the sum of one soldo per month to the upkeep of the Monte di Pietà. In Treviso, notaries incurred a statutory obligation to ask all testators if they wished to bequeath anything to the local Monte di Pietà—catching them at a psychological moment, when it might be hard to refuse and reject the suggestion.

As a non-profitmaking concern, the Monte depended heavily on voluntary aid. Pietro Barozzi, however, had tried to use other methods, and in 1490 had obtained the imposition of a tax known as a *dadia* for the support of the Monte. But this promptly aroused such opposition that it had to be revoked. At some stage the Monti di Pietà began to raise capital for the use of the poor by acting as deposit or savings banks. Their strongrooms could safely preserve sums left for safekeeping with them. There was no risk, as with other banks, that they might use them in commercial speculations. At some stage also, the Monti di Pietà set out to attract deposits of this kind by allowing them to be treated as investments on which a modest rate of interest should be paid—justified by the title of *lucrum cessans*. The emphasis thus shifted from the service done by the Monte in safely storing the money, to the service done by the depositor in making his money available to the poor. When these practices began is uncertain, and discussion of their development must be deferred. But it does appear that the Monte di Pietà in Vicenza acted from an early stage as a deposit bank. The Monti di Pietà did not remain exclusively charitable institutions, either in their methods of raising funds or in the uses to which they devoted them.[93]

[92] Dalla Corte, *Istorie di Verona*, III, pp. 116–18; Wadding, *Annales Minorum*, XIV, pp. 517–19; XV, pp. 20, 139.

[93] For Vicenza, see Garrani, *Carattere dei Monti di Pietà*, p. 159. Garrani has argued, indeed overstated, the thesis that from the start of their career the Monti di Pietà were banks rather than charitable institutions.

By the end of the fifteenth century, the Monti di Pietà had earned wide acceptance in large and small towns of central and northern Italy. They were Christian loan banks inspired by Franciscan eloquence and episcopal action, administered, at least in the Veneto, by officials of the communes. For the first time, the law of the Church was approving institutions whose chief function was to lend money, not for commercial purposes, but for poor relief; institutions which did not do so gratuitously. They existed to relieve the poor by tiding them over periods of economic difficulty, and to guard morality by refusing to lend for frivolous or wastrel uses. They were also designed to free Christians from subjection to Jewish moneylenders: to reduce all necessary contacts between Christian and Jew, to further the ecclesiastical policy of segregating different faiths, to deprive of all power over Christians a people which must be allowed to survive only in a condition of ignominious apartness. However, the Monti di Pietà had not entirely achieved their aims. Jewish banks still coexisted with them in the mainland territories of the Venetian Republic. Venice itself, unvisited by Bernardino of Feltre in his later days, had shown no signs of introducing such a Monte. Jewish banks still retained certain advantages for the borrower. They were less inquisitorial; they lent for longer periods; they may have valued pledges more generously; they could lend on the security of written bonds as distinct from pledges, and, in the countryside, on the security of future harvests. Moreover, they required no proof of poverty as a prelude to lending money.[94] Monti di Pietà which, like that of Savona on Genoese territory, lent to the rich as well as the poor on low interest rates, existed in some places: but they were not as yet very widely established.[95] Again, the state could raise funds for the purposes of defence by laying heavy taxes upon the Jews. It could not, with so clear a conscience, divert to this end funds given for charitable purposes. All these considerations combined to keep the Jewish banks in existence—quite apart from the ineptitude or maladministration of some of the officials of the Monti di Pietà. However, during and after the War of the League of Cambrai, the Jewish population of the Venetian Republic was partially resettled, so as to produce a heavy concentration of Jews in Venice itself, and to leave the mainland to the Monti di Pietà.

[94] Attilio Milano, 'Considerazioni sulla lotta dei Monti di Pietà contro il prestito ebraico', *Scritti in memoria di Sally Mayer: saggi sull'ebraismo italiano* (Jerusalem, 1956), pp. 216–17.

[95] Holzapfel, *Die Anfänge*, pp. 63–5; Garrani, *Carattere dei Monti di Pietà*, pp. 126–8. The Monte di Pietà in Rome was founded on principles similar to those of Savona—but only in 1539.

2

FOUNDATIONS OF THE GHETTO, 1509–1537

On 3 August 1508, the Venetian Senate, which was heavily taxing the Jews of the mainland (doubtless to finance its wars), responded to their pleas that it regularize their uncertain position.[1a] They seem to have felt two main causes for anxiety—the first, in the indefinite extent of the outright taxation or forced loans they were liable to pay; the second, in doubts as to the validity of some of the concessions authorizing Jews to set up banks in particular areas of the mainland. In May 1508, the Senate had rescinded an agreement made by subjects of the territory of Conegliano authorizing Simon the Jew to open a bank in the district—on the grounds that these *capitoli* had been ratified only by ducal letters of 22 January 1507, and had not been thoroughly debated by the Senate[1b] However, in August 1508, the Senate declared that even Jews who were lending 'only on the strength of ducal letters' should be authorized to continue living and lending in Venetian territory for the next five years. It then specified the general conditions on which Jews were to live in Venetian territory, allowing some room for local variation, especially in determining the level of interest chargeable by the Jews for their loans.[1c]

The clauses approved by the Senate entitled the Jews to live and keep banks in the usual places on the mainland, lending to Christians at the rates customary in particular localities, both on pledges and on written bonds—indeed, on everything except sacred objects, and weapons or armour.[1d] Jews were free to lend to one another at whatever rates they chose. Only in 1520 was the Senate to impose a general limit on the rates of interest chargeable to Christians on the mainland— some Senators professing to be shocked that the Jews had been entitled to exact as much as 30 per cent interest on loans secured only by the

---

[1a] A.S.V., *Senato, Deliberazioni (Secreta), registro 1507/09*, f. 120v.

[1b] A.S.V., *Senato, Terra, registro 1508–1509*, f. 8.

[1c] *Ibid.*, ff. 25v.–26v.

[1d] If Jews lent on the security of sacred objects, they could be compelled to restore them without any payment at all—presumably not even of the sum lent. They could not be compelled 'to restore pledges to anyone, soldier or civilian, unless they receive their capital and interest, unless they have been lending on weapons or armour'. No doubt this was mainly designed to stop the military from incapacitating itself for war and other duties.

written bond of the borrower.[1e] In many respects the general *capitoli* of 1508 resembled the *capitoli* of the locality of Pirano in 1484[1f]—the Jews were still protected against being held responsible for the loss of pledges through fire, theft or sack, though if they mislaid pledges they were bound to pay for them. However, the normal duration of a loan was now to be fifteen months and not two years, as at Pirano; nor was there any clause obliging the borrower to compensate the Jew, should an auctioned pledge fail to realize enough to cover the principal lent, the interest due upon it, and the banker's expenses. The clauses assumed that the Jews would rent, not own, their houses. They could 'purchase and maintain' enough land to bury their dead, making cemeteries 'such as they used to have on the Lido', with adjacent houses for their sextons. Each Jewish community could also 'maintain' a synagogue, and an inn to accommodate 'Jewish strangers, in the usual manner'. Butchers were—as in the Pirano agreement—bound to provide meat prepared in accordance with Jewish requirements. As if for their own protection, as well as to preserve due reverence on Christian festivals, Jews were legally required to stay in their houses from Holy Thursday to Easter Sunday, whilst at the same time the local authorities were bound to issue proclamations threatening to punish anyone who molested the Jews. Insults and violence towards Jews, and accusations of ritual murder, were particularly liable to occur at this season. Also for their own protection, the Jews were dispensed from the obligation to wear the distinctive yellow cap on journeys from one place to another.

These were the general conditions on which the Senate proposed to tolerate the Jews of the Venetian dominions. It did not, in this document, define their obligations to the treasury. However, the invasion of the Veneto the following year drastically changed the situation by redistributing the Jewish communities, by producing a large concentration of Jews in Venice itself, and by calling for the payment of increasingly heavy taxes on the part of Jewish bankers and of their co-religionists. For the Venetians, the Jews assumed a new importance, both as taxpayers and as lenders to the poor and financially embarrassed, as servants of the poor and of the state. These functions were

[1e] Cf. the proposal of Pietro da Ca' da Pesaro, 4 June 1519: 'because the Jews who lend on the mainland are accustomed to lend on written bonds at the rate of 30 per cent per annum, which is excessively high interest and the ruination of the poor, let it be resolved that the said Jews who lend upon written bonds on the mainland may not in future charge more than 20 per cent per annum....' (A.S.V., *Senato, Deliberazioni Secreta, registro 1519/21*, f. 92); repeated by Antonio Grimani and others, 10 February 1519 Venetian style, *ibid.*, f. 96; finally incorporated in the *capitoli* first proposed on 2 March 1520 and passed on 16 March 1520—*ibid.*, f. 98v., 102. See also below, p. 497.

[1f] See above, pp. 447–9.

complementary—for the Jews, constantly handling coin and forbidden to invest in real property, kept their assets liquid and easily taxable.

In the late spring and early summer of 1509, the fatal collision between the ambitions of the Venetian Republic in the Romagna, and Pope Julius II's determination to reconstitute the States of the Church, brought in its train the War of the League of Cambrai. Habsburg and Valois joined the Pope in conspiring to dismember the empire of the Venetian Republic. The loyalty of many higher-ranking citizens in the great cities of the Terra Ferma failed to withstand the test of invasion, and they capitulated with a readiness that gravely shook Venetian self-confidence. In May 1509 the Venetians suffered the demoralizing defeat on the field of battle at Agnadello. Though some of the conquered cities, such as Padua, were recovered from enemy occupation within a few weeks, the struggle for the recovery of Venetian territory and for security from invasion lasted at least eight years.

During the invasions, Jewish refugees fled to Venice from over a wide area to seek government protection. In a time of such insecurity, they had good reason to fear violence and accusations of treachery from their neighbours, as well as the looting of enemy troops. A defenceless alien minority might well be blamed for the approaching disaster.[1g] Venice itself absorbed for the time being at least a substantial part of the Jewish communities of Mestre and Padua, and it may have sheltered other displaced Jews in large numbers. Anxious for the protection of goods deposited as pledges with the Jewish bankers of Mestre, the government authorized the official removal of Jewish banks into the city of Venice itself.[2] The Jews and their banks were a form of government asset far too valuable to be hazarded in wartime. No source of taxation or forced loans could wisely be neglected. The Jews, especially through involvement in banking and the small-loan business, attracted and concentrated money and property in a readily taxable form, and paid special taxes disproportionate to their modest numbers. The heavy taxes levied by the government, coinciding with the cessation of trade, created an urgent need for the services of bankers to lend, not only to the poor, but also to persons on higher social levels. For these reasons, as well as from common humanity, the Venetian government began to tolerate in the capital itself the presence of resident Jewish bankers and of a substantial Jewish community in the years after 1509. The Venetians occasionally tried to rid the capital of a proportion of the Jews, but did not attempt to remove Jewish bankers.

[1g] Cf. the brief reference to the sacking of the Jews by the Veronese on 31 May 1509, after their decision to surrender to Maximilian: D.M.S., VIII, col. 344.

[2] D.M.S., VIII, coll. 305, 340, 355–6, 406.

In April 1511, perhaps inspired by Franciscan preachers launching their seasonal assault on the crimes and hereditary guilt of Jewry, the government gave Jews resident in Venice notice to quit within a month —but some were privileged to remain, including bankers who had immigrated to Venice for security. Sanuto reported that there were then about five hundred Jews of both sexes in Venice itself.[3] There is no sign, however, that the Jewish community of Venice dwindled in the years which followed. In 1516, during a debate on the establishment of a separate Jewish quarter, it was said that about 700 Jewish *men* alone were living in Venice.[4] The enforced concentration of Jews within the narrow, overcrowded space of the Venetian Ghetto after 1516 may have caused many to emigrate,[5] and the greater security achieved on the mainland a year or two later would probably produce the same result. The reliability of these estimates is open to doubt, and the means used in arriving at them are unknown. But one can speak confidently of an extensive Jewish community of several hundred persons resident in Venice itself. Not all Jews in the Venetian Republic had sought the capital, however. Austrian invaders had offered protection to Jews in Bassano, Castelfranco, Asolo and Cittadella, promising them the status of 'court Jews' under the tutelage of the Emperor Maximilian.[6] Such offers may well have reduced the incentive to flee before the invaders. A decree levying a tax of 5,000 ducats on Jewish subjects in October 1511 proposed that two-thirds be paid by Jewish bankers and by others domiciled in Venice; the remainder by 'outsiders' or *forestieri*.[7] This, too, suggests that a large proportion of the Jews were still outside the capital: but that the greater part of their wealth had now become concentrated within it.

This concentration was strengthened by the removal to Venice of a banking family which had formerly had ramifications at Padua and Mestre. For the next twenty years, Asher Meshullam of Mestre, whose name was italianized as 'Anselmo del Banco', headed the Jewish community of Venice. In February 1510, Anselmo became responsible for choosing two other Jews and with them taxing the Jewish community resident in Venice itself.[7a] His brother was Chaim or Hayyim Meshullam, italianized as Vita or Vivian, also for some years a banker in Venice. Asher and Chaim Meshullam were the sons of Salamon of Camposampiero, a township of the Padovano, who may have been the Jew disturbed there by the visitation of Bernardino of Feltre in 1492.

[3] D.M.S., XII, coll. 110–11.
[4] D.M.S., XXII, coll. 108–9.
[5] See below, pp. 487–8.
[6] D.M.S., VIII, col. 376.
[7] D.M.S., XIII, coll. 105–6.
[7a] A.S.V., *Senato, Terra, registro 1508/09*, f. 161v., 21 February 1509 Venetian style.

THE FAMILY OF ASHER MESHULLAM, KNOWN AS ANSELMO DEL BANCO

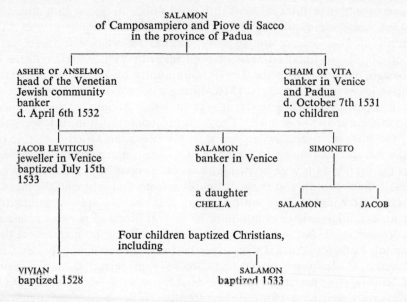

SALAMON
of Camposampiero and Piove di Sacco
in the province of Padua

ASHER or ANSELMO
head of the Venetian
Jewish community
banker
d. April 6th 1532

CHAIM or VITA
banker in Venice
and Padua
d. October 7th 1531
no children

JACOB LEVITICUS
jeweller in Venice
baptized July 15th
1533

SALAMON
banker in Venice

SIMONETO

a daughter
CHELLA

SALAMON   JACOB

Four children baptized Christians,
including

VIVIAN
baptized 1528

SALAMON
baptized 1533

Chaim Meshullam, a man famous for his generosity and charity to-wards fellow-Jews, also kept a bank at Crema at some stage in his career.[8] The recovery of Padua at the end of June 1509, after only forty-two days of imperial occupation, brought with it the sack of the Jewish bank run by 'Vita'—possibly Chaim—and Cervo.[9] In Venetian as well as imperial hands Padua was unsafe for Jews. By 1517, Chaim Meshullam was keeping two loan banks, probably both in Venice itself, and was then refused permission to open a third.[10] He returned to lend in Padua only in or shortly before April 1520. The previous summer he had been sentenced to three years' exile from Venice and district, after being charged with bringing false accusations of murder with intent to rob against a fellow-Jew, the physician Chalò.[11] Chaim Meshullam died in Padua on 7 October 1531; but his brother Asher

[8] For the identification of Asher Meshullam with Anselmo del Banco and of Chaim Meshullam with Vivian, see N. Porgès, 'Élie Capsali et sa chronique de Venise', *Revue des études juives*, LXXVII–LXXIX (1923–4), pp. 31–3, 38, LXXVII. This deals with the chronicle of a Cretan Jew, composed in 1517. Further details of the family appear from the resumé of the will of Chaim Meshullam of 4 October 1531, in D.M.S., LV, coll. 30–4. On Bernardino's visit to Camposampiero, see Wadding, *Annales minorum*, XV, p. 7.

[9] D.M.S., VIII, col. 523; cf. also Porgès, 'Capsali', LXXVIII, pp. 16–18.

[10] D.M.S., XXIV, coll. 470, 474.

[11] D.M.S., XXVII, col. 463; XXVIII, col. 460.

480

Meshullam, 'Anselmo del Banco', remained in Venice till his death, after some years of senile incapacity, in April 1532.[12] Anselmo was succeeded as head of the banking firm by his son Salamon before his death. Another son, Jacob Leviticus, followed a spectacular and dangerous career as a jeweller, which exposed him to several nearly disastrous encounters with Venetian law.[13]

Apart from the concerns of Asher and Chaim Meshullam, there stood, in the early years, a second substantial Jewish bank in Venice—that of Abram, son of Fricele, and his close relatives. Whether they also formed part of the family of Meshullam it is impossible to say.

In 1510, the Jews of Venice protested that the damage inflicted on them by the war made it impossible to continue paying taxes at the current rate—which seems to have been as high as 14,000 ducats a year. Their annual basic tax was now reduced to 5,000 ducats—a concession symptomatic of the losses they must have suffered and of the disturbance to their financial activities. In addition to this, they paid a further 850 ducats a year to retain in Padua premises on which it might later be possible to open banks.[14] In 1512, however, the Senate began squeezing additional taxation from them, to the tune of some 10,000 ducats, on the grounds that their numbers and wealth had greatly increased since 1510.[15] The Jews failed to meet these additional obligations, protesting that their only assets consisted of pledges and not of liquid capital. Brusque bargaining proceeded, in which the government turned the screw by the simple expedient of imprisoning the heads of the Jewish community: Asher and Chaim Meshullam, the physician Marco Emmanuele, a certain Mendlin (italianized as 'Mandolin Grando'), and, a week later, two bankers formerly of Montagnana, another part of the Paduan Jewish complex.[16] The Jews used their only weapon, a threat to close their banks, though the diarist Sanuto doubted whether they really intended to do so.[17]

Indeed, the relationship between Jews and the Venetian government did not end at this point. In July 1513, on the expiry of the Capitoli of 1508, Asher Meshullam negotiated new terms with the Council of Ten—which seems to have exercised over the Jews a jurisdiction parallel to that of the Senate. Meshullam now proposed that his own firm should pay 2,000 ducats annually, and that of Abram, son of

[12] D.M.S., LV, coll. 30–4; LVI, col. 33.
[13] See below, p. 483.
[14] A.S.V., *Senato, Terra, registro 1508/09*, f. 161v., 21 February 1509 Venetian style; cf. also D.M.S., XI, col. 404; XIII, coll. 105–6; XIV, coll. 258, 304, 388.
[15] A.S.V., *Senato, Terra, registro 1512/14*, ff. 7v.–8, 21; 20 April, 9 June 1512.
[16] D.M.S., XIV, coll. 255, 258, 291.
[17] D.M.S., XV, col. 270.

Fricele, another 2,000. Should this arrangement be acceptable both to the Council and to Abram, Asher Meshullam would then accept responsibility for taxes to be paid by the rest of the Jewish corporation—so long as these did not exceed 2,500 ducats in all. Alternatively, Abram and his family business partners could choose to pay their taxes with the rest of the Jewish corporation, instead of being separately assessed —in which case he and they would have to produce 4,500 ducats between them, including 850 ducats' rent for the banks of Padua. The Council of Ten then contented themselves with renewing the *condotta* for a period of five years, on condition that Asher Meshullam, Abram and the rest of the Jewish community paid between them an annual tax of 6,500 ducats. Asher Meshullam thus, apparently, played a dual rôle, as chief tax-payer and as tax-collector: he acted as guarantor for the payment of taxation, and was authorized by the Ten to exact payment from individual Jews.[18] This agreement merely established the fundamental or minimum obligations of the Jews to the Venetian fisc, and did not protect them against the levying of additional forced loans.

Certainly, official demands for advance payments of taxation and forced loans continued to multiply, though in exchange for some of their loans the Jews did obtain concessions. In the summer of 1515, on payment of a loan of 5,000 ducats to the government, to be restored three years later, the Jews were formally confirmed in their right to establish shops dealing in second-hand goods in Venice itself. The government licensed nine such shops, and a few months later added a tenth on payment of 100 ducats outright and on receipt of a further loan of 400.[19] The Jews had very likely engaged in the trade before receiving this concession: but it was a regular fiscal device to make tacitly recognized activities depend on the purchase of government licences.

Again, several members of the rich family of Meshullam became entangled in judicial proceedings, and extricated themselves only on payment of substantial sums to the state. Their insecurity and the suspicion they automatically roused may have made them exceptionally vulnerable to charges of malpractice—though it is impossible to know anything about the truth or otherwise of the accusations made against them. Some of these came, indeed, from within the Jewish community itself. Jacob, son of the banker Anselm, accused his uncle Chaim of keeping an unauthorized bank, and the bitterness within the family

[18] A.S.V., *Consiglio dei Dieci, Parti Miste, filza* 31, *fascicolo* 182, 15 July 1513.
[19] D.M.S., XX, coll. 339, 342, 354, 360; XXII, col. 38. In December 1516, proposals were made for a Jewish loan of 10,000 ducats, which was eventually granted in return for some minor concessions and for six months' exemption from the ordinary taxation (8,000 ducats per annum)—D.M.S., XXIII, coll. 329–30, 338, 360.

survived to appear in the clauses of Chaim Meshullam's will fourteen years later. Chaim Meshullam was 'absolved' by the Venetian court on condition that he lent the Signory 3,000 ducats for a term of eighteen months. His accuser, too, had good reason to regret the lawsuit, for he faced charges of suborning witnesses, and obtained his release from prison only on offering a similar loan of 2,000 ducats for eighteen months.[20] The demands of fiscalism were evidently causing the government to relax its standards of justice. It was not levying fines on men proved guilty, so much as blackmailing the vulnerable into making extraordinary loans. Jacob's profession as a jeweller threw him more than once into the teeth of the law. One case involved a sapphire, deposited in his father's bank, which he claimed to have won gambling with the nobleman Pietro di Andrea Bragadin at cards, on premises owned by Giovanni Lando, Archbishop of Crete. In 1519, at least eight years after this affair, he was accused of inducing a poor nobleman, Bernardo di Hieronimo Zane of San Polo, to bear false witness in the matter.[21] Again, in 1522–4, Jacob was charged with misappropriating a diamond acquired from a Polish Jew—a stone which apparently belonged to the Count Palatine of Cracow, Captain and Grand Chancellor of Poland. The court sentenced him to restore the diamond and to be blinded publicly. This, again, may have been intended as blackmail, since he managed to buy himself out of the sentence by handing the sum of 2,000 ducats to his father, presumably for the government.[22] Forced loans and the profits of dubious justice supplemented ordinary Jewish taxation. Since Chaim Meshullam was also accused of suborning witnesses in a case against the Jewish physician Chalò,[23] bribery may have been regarded as the Jewish crime *par excellence*, gaining plausibility from popular belief in Jewish treachery, in the Jews as a sinister agency which got its way by the improper use of money. Jewish litigants might, indeed, have been forgiven for believing that even justice could not be obtained without money. The government's attitude could well have encouraged such thoughts.

[20] D.M.S., XXIV, coll. 460–1, 470, 474, 505.

[21] D.M.S., XXI, col. 114; XXVI, coll. 339–41. Jacob incriminated the Archbishop of Crete by accusing him of coining false moneys, and the Archbishop was sent to the Pope for trial (D.M.S., XXVII, coll. 87, 139–40, 157).

[22] D.M.S., XXXIV, coll. 229, 339; XXXV, coll. 246, 253, 437, 443; XXXVI, coll. 245, 493, 496, 571, 598–9, 611.

[23] D.M.S., XXV, col. 229; XXVII, col. 463. In 1516, Asher Meshullam had paid 1,000 ducats and lent the government 2,000 for the liberation of two of his brothers banished for criminal offences (D.M.S., XXI, coll. 499, 503). In 1524, Salamon, second son of Asher Meshullam, was sentenced to six months' imprisonment and three years' banishment from Venice for mocking the Avogadore di Commun during Jacob's trial. He too was allowed to buy himself out with the sum of 600 gold ducats (D.M.S., XXXVII, coll. 310, 316).

During their first years in Venice, the Jews faced seasonal attacks during Lent and Passiontide from visiting preachers. These demanded their spoliation or expulsion, and warned the state of their corrupting and dangerous influence, of the risk of incurring divine displeasure by continuing to tolerate them at crucial moments in the development of the Italian wars. Franciscans, a fanatical Carmelite and one or two renegade Jews equipped with papal briefs all broadcast this message from fashionable pulpits like that of the Frari. Anti-Jewish measures were among the acts of purification which the state must perform if God were to prosper it. In the first quarter of the sixteenth century, both Florentines and Venetians seriously believed in the effective power of divine intervention and in its relevance to the worldly struggles in which they were engaged.[24] In the summer of 1509, the Venetian diarist Girolamo Priuli discoursed on the moral corruption which had brought on the Venetians the divine chastisement of the defeat at Agnadello and the collapse of the mainland dominions. The delay and sale of justice, the violation of oaths, electoral intrigues, immorality in nunneries, the toleration and practice of sodomy, the mercenary pursuit of ecclesiastical benefices: all these had invited the penalty of military defeat.[25] Preachers, counselling the Republic and censuring these abuses in the tradition of Bernardino of Feltre, spoke in a similar strain, and added the Jews to their catalogues of evils. The government occasionally restrained their excesses.

Friar Ruffino Lovato (or Volpato), of Padua, preached in Venice in Lent and Easter week in 1509, 1511 and 1516. On Good Friday 1509, at the Madonna dell'Orto, he declared it lawful to deprive the Jews of all their money 'and leave them nothing to live on'. The Republic should also issue an edict against blaspheming in the field. These simple measures would surely lead to victory. Two years later, he preached in Campo San Polo, a vast square in the centre of the district most heavily inhabited by immigrant Jews, and on 2 April 1511 incited the Venetians to sack them. Complaints from the Jewish community caused the government to admonish him and at least one other Franciscan preacher; but on Good Friday, 18 April, he was still attacking the Jews as the murderers of Christ and attempting to provoke a pogrom.[26] On 31 March 1516, a preacher in St Mark's itself demanded that the recent decree of the segregation of the Jews should not be revoked in response to Jewish bribery. He insisted on the need for justice, for the

---

[24] Cf. Felix Gilbert, 'Florentine political assumptions in the period of Savonarola and Soderini', *Journal of the Warburg and Courtauld Institutes*, XX (1957), pp. 206 f.

[25] Girolamo Priuli, *Diarii*, IV, ed. Roberto Cessi (Bologna, 1938), pp. 29 f.

[26] D.M.S., VIII, coll. 70–1, 79, 88; XII, 98–9, 121; XXII, col. 65.

elimination of blasphemy, sacrilege and sodomy, 'vehemently declaring that if provision were made for these things, God would prosper this Republic against its enemies'.[27] In April 1519, Giovanni d'Agnolina, a Florentine by birth and then a Franciscan Superior or Guardian at Ferrara, preached on Palm Sunday against the Jewish faith before an audience which included about fifteen Jews. On Good Friday, before the assembled Collegio, he attacked prostitution and criticized the prevailing laxity in Venetian nunneries. Inevitably, he extended his invective to the Jews now segregated in the Ghetto, 'urging the state to force them to hand over the money which really belongs to us, and not to treat them as they have been treated in the past'. The Jews, as usurers, must be forced to restore their illicit gains. Parading his own incorruptibility, the preacher described with sententious relish how the Jews of Venice had tried to bribe him to keep silence.[28]

Occasionally, visiting preachers tried to counter the influence of individual Jews. In 1515, Giovanni Maria of Arezzo warned the congregation in the Frari against the sinister influence of a popular Jewish physician, Master Lazarus.[29] Physicians were always open to the charge of exploiting their intimate relationship with Christian patients in order to infect them with the Jewish faith. Jewish bankers formed an equally obvious target. In April 1514, the renegade Jew Francesco of Lucca arrived in Venice with a papal brief which entitled him to proceed against his former co-religionists 'with the aid of the secular arm'. He procured the arrest of the banker Chaim, but the Avogadore di Commun, Giovanni Capello, promptly intervened and secured the banker's release. Francesco of Lucca had obtained the Patriarch's permission to act in this way, but had not applied to the Signory, and the Avogadore probably resented the violation of lay jurisdiction as much as the interference with a person so useful to the fisc. Summoned to justify himself, the apostate poured out his slander to the Collegio. He accused the Jews of constant intrigue against Christians, of defiling public images of the Madonna, of devouring the substance of Christians by the taking of usury, of kidnapping a Christian child with intent to martyr him.[30] The Collegio apparently took no action on any of these stylized charges.

On at least one occasion, the committee of public safety decisively attempted to silence an antisemitic Friar. In 1520, the Heads of the Ten dealt severely with Friar Albertino of the Venetian convent of San Giacomo di Paludo, said to enjoy the support of the Venetian nobleman Antonio Condulmer. Friar Albertino had preached in Padua

[27] D.M.S., XXII, coll. 97–8.   [28] D.M.S., XXVII, coll. 182, 193.
[29] D.M.S., XX, col. 98.   [30] D.M.S., XVIII, col. 144.

21

during Holy Week and had tried to provoke attacks on the Jews. The Paduans then proposed sending orators to Venice to demand the expulsion of the Jews from their city. But the Heads of the Ten forbade the Friar to preach either in Venice itself or in Padua. The Jewish *condotta* had recently been renewed after prolonged debate, and the Venetian authorities were not enthusiastic about seeing the question reopened. Though supported by Daniele Renier, a member of the Collegio, the Paduans received no encouragement, and Jewish lending, under the auspices of Chaim, was re-established in Padua.[31]

Pulpit-ranting against the Jews, licensed with reservations by the Signory at one particular season of the year, contributed to producing one tangible result: the segregation, though not the expulsion, of the Jewish community. Sanuto, himself level-headed and no fanatic, was shocked by the freedom at first permitted to the Jews. In April 1515, they were living in the roughly adjacent parishes of San Cassiano, Sant'Agostino, San Polo and Santa Maria Mater Domini, on the Frari side of the Grand Canal. These formed an unofficial area of Jewish residence, where Jews mingled with Christians. Worst of all, the Jews openly showed themselves during Holy Week, in a manner contrary to their previous habit of lying low from Palm Sunday till after Easter.[32] In the past, both papal legislation and the terms of *condotte* had imposed similar curfews on them, perhaps in their own interests.[33] The banker Chaim had done the Jewish reputation little good on his arrival in Venice by renting the great palace of the Casa Bernardo, in the region of Campo San Polo.[34] Such ostentation hardly suggested that the Jews were being kept in their properly subordinate state.

The practice of establishing Jewish quarters separated from Christian dwellings by actual physical barriers was not without medieval precedents. At least one Polish diocese had introduced such measures before the close of the twelfth century, on the grounds that Polish Christianity was too tender and immature to be exposed to the hostile and insidious influence of Jewry.[35] But it fell to the Venetians in 1516 to contribute the word Ghetto to the vocabulary of persecution. The previous year, the Savio Giorgio Emo had proposed that the Jews be moved to the Giudecca, but the bankers Asher and Chaim protested that this would expose them to violence at the hands of troops, who were perhaps billeted on that island. They expressed a preference for

---

[31] D.M.S., XXVIII, coll. 460, 500; XL, col. 672.
[32] D.M.S., XX, col. 98.
[33] E.g. Eugenius IV, 'Dudum ad nostram', 1442, B.R., V, pp. 68–70; Ive, 'Capitoli de Pirano', p. 194.
[34] Porgès, 'Élie Capsali', LXXVIII, pp. 15, 18.
[35] Cf. Baron, *Jewish community*, I, p. 225.

Murano.[36] A solution—no more acceptable to the Jewish leaders—appeared in the following Lent. Zaccaria Dolfin, a member of the Collegio, referred on 26 March 1516 to Franciscan warnings about the 'corruption of the state (*perversità del Stado*)' which would inevitably ensue if Jews were still entertained in the city. He suggested that they be enclosed in the area which was already—before Jewish occupation —known as the Ghetto Nuovo, the 'new foundry' in Venetian dialect.[36a] This was 'like a fortress', with a single entrance that could be guarded at night by boats belonging to the police force controlled by the Council of Ten. It could therefore perform the double function of protecting the Jews from violence and plunder, and of enabling an effective curfew to be imposed upon them. This combined fortress and concentration camp could symbolize the separation of Venetian Jews from their Christian neighbours, and, with its overcrowded squalor, stress their inferiority. The banker, Asher Meshullam, promptly protested to the Collegio that the Jews would be far more exposed to pillage if they no longer lived 'in the midst of noblemen and other Christians'. To compel all the Jews to move even their business premises into the Ghetto was to break faith with the dealers in second-hand goods who had recently paid substantial sums for the licensed shops at Rialto. This would result in large-scale emigration, and the banker would have no-one from whom to collect the taxes he had promised the Venetian government in advance. Surely, he pleaded, such measures should be adopted only when Venetian possessions on the mainland had been fully recovered, and when Jews were able to return in peace and security to their homes. There were certainly no houses left for them in Mestre.[37]

Unmoved by this eloquence, Zaccaria Dolfin persisted, and brought his proposals before the Senate. On 29 March, with some promptitude, the decree appeared. The preamble recalled that the Jews had been admitted to Venice for the preservation of Christian property in their hands. But nobody had intended that they should be licensed to go where they pleased by day and night, mingling with Christians and living in their houses. The voice of the preacher echoed in vague accusations of Jewish atrocities and acts of indecency or blasphemy. The decree itself provided that all Jews should move into the Ghetto. Proprietors of houses in this quarter had made difficulties, and as if to placate them the Jews were ordered to pay rents at one-third more

[36] D.M.S., XX, col. 138.

[36a] On the origins of the name Ghetto, see Giuseppe Tassini, *Curiosità veneziane, ovvero origini delle denominazioni stradali* (new edition, ed. Lino Moretti, Venice, no date), pp. 295, 296.

[37] D.M.S., XXII, coll. 72–3; cf. also coll. 108–9.

than the current rate. Moreover, owners of these houses were exempted from the obligation to pay the normal secular tithe or *decima* upon them. Christian watchmen were to guard the gates of the Ghetto and enforce the curfew, with two police boats for security. Jews caught outside the Ghetto at night were liable to fines and imprisonment. There should be no synagogue in Venice—only at Mestre.[38] On 1 April, proclamations ordered all Jews into the Ghetto within ten days. Second-hand dealers and bankers held out against the order for a little longer, and the banks obtained a temporary stay of execution. But by the end of July 1516, even Asher Meshullam had been forced to enter the Ghetto, there to join the physicians and the traders of Rialto.[39] The curfew was relaxed only in favour of Jewish physicians, who were allowed to leave the Ghetto at night to attend sick patients—provided they accounted for their movements to the watchmen on duty. A sentence in a decree of 29 July 1516, fixing the wages of Christian watchmen, implied that the narrowness of the Ghetto had—as Asher Meshullam predicted—forced many Jews to return to their homes.[40] The government may have intended to produce this effect, while shrinking from a direct expulsion order. The segregation of the Jews by the Ghetto wall was supplemented by the segregation of the yellow badge, the portable sign of inferior status. In March 1517—again a Lenten measure—the government issued a decree that all Jews must wear yellow hats. The respected physicians, including Master Lazarus, Master Chalò and the astrologer Master Moses, were forced to abandon their black hats.[41] A month or two later, they also lost the right to wear the uniform of the professional man with the wide 'ducal sleeves' or *manege dogal*.[42] The Jewish community was still indispensable to the warring state of Venice. But its apartness and inferiority, expressed in these tangible signs, now stood forth clearly.

Thus, after a few years of unaccustomed freedom in the extraordinary circumstances of the war on Venetian territory, the Jews were forced back into a position of subordination. The government had, partly in response to the fervent demands of the preachers, introduced formal safeguards against the infection and desecration of Christianity by the enforced presence of the Jews. Not surprisingly, the whole question of their retention reopened in the summer of 1519, on the expiry of the *condotta* issued six years before. Between June 1519 and March

---

[38] D.M.S., XXII, coll. 85–8.   [39] D.M.S., XXII, coll. 100, 162, 375.

[40] D.M.S., XXII, coll. 390–2.

[41] D.M.S., XXIV, 50–1, 59. In 1529–30, various privileges were issued entitling individual Jewish physicians to wear the black hat: D.M.S., L, coll. 67, 474; LI, 32; LIII, 177.

[42] D.M.S., XXIV, coll. 298–9.

1520, their affairs periodically entangled the Senate in prolonged and heated debates.[42a] The recovery of the mainland dominions had removed one of the strongest arguments for the retention of a Jewish community in Venice itself. In July 1519, the Heads of the Ten closed the Jewish shops dealing in second-hand goods, and the bankers Anselm and Abram issued formal notice of their intention to shut down their banks within the next six months.[43] For the time being, the Jews remained in uneasy suspense whilst the question of their future was hammered out. Sanuto remarked, in his commentary on one discussion, that the only question which could sensibly be debated was that of the terms on which the Republic could contract with the Jews; there could be no serious possibility of expelling them altogether,

> because, once and for all, the Jews are necessary for the sake of the poor, since there is no Monte di Pietà here as there is in the other cities, and one can only discuss whether to keep them here or in Mestre, and whether the *capitoli* are suitable or not. But one cannot attack the Jews themselves, since even the Pope retains them in Rome—though it is true that they are not allowed to lend.[44]

Nevertheless, several prominent magistrates of Collegio rank demanded the total suspension of all contracts which would have retained the Jews in Venice itself or its environs. Their arguments were based specifically on the canons of the Church and the divine law, which overrode even the pronouncements of individual Popes on the matter. Beyond this lay the more general argument that good fortune and prosperity (in a literal and material sense) would surely result from the expulsion of the Jews, even though this appeared at first to involve fiscal and economic inconvenience and sacrifice. Even though he favoured the retention of the Jews in the Ghetto, with permission to lend at 15 per cent in Venice itself and 20 per cent on the mainland, the Savio Pietro da Ca' da Pesaro still added that

> it would be good to expel them from the whole world, and God would prosper this Republic as he did the King of Portugal, who, on expelling them, discovered the new route to India, and God made him the King of Gold. Even so did the King of Spain permit such great wealth to depart from his country, for the sake of exiling these devourers of Christians and enemies of Christ.[45]

Zaccaria Dolfin, formerly responsible for the relegation of the Jews to the Ghetto, spoke in November 1519 in favour of returning them to

[42a] For the text of the various proposals made during these debates, see A.S.V., *Senato, Deliberazioni (Secreta), registro 1519/21*, ff. 91–102.
[43] D.M.S., XXVII, col. 467.   [44] D.M.S., XXVIII, col. 62.
[45] D.M.S., XXVII, coll. 358–9.

Mestre and of increasing their basic fiscal obligations to the level of 10,000 ducats a year. He too 'made a great show (*grande ypocrexia*) of not wanting them', and added likewise that

> if we keep them we must beware of the wrath of God, and that there are no Jews in France or Spain, and God prospers those kingdoms.

The Cavalier Gabriele Moro, another participant in the November discussion, exploited this simple argument still further with the aid of recent evidence.

> Spain expelled the Jews from its dominions, they went to Naples, and King Alfonso lost his kingdom. The Duke of Milan, because he favoured and retained Jews, was expelled from his state. . . .

However, the thesis that there was some direct and obvious correlation between the presence of the Jews and the misfortunes of the rulers responsible for tolerating them at last encountered the opposition it deserved from a group of Senators who, in Sanuto's opinion, 'had the welfare of the poor in mind'. They countered Dolfin and Moro on their chosen premises by pointing out that

> the Jews were driven from Spain and exported great wealth therefrom. They then went to Constantinople and the Sultan Selim conquered both Syria and Egypt.

Perhaps, in this connexion, Jewish wealth was more immediately potent than Divine Providence.[46]

Arguments founded on divine and canon law were less easily assailable on grounds of simple logic. Antonio Condulmer, the patrician supporter of the antisemitic Friar Albertino of San Giacomo di Paludo, declared that under no circumstances should the Republic contract with the Jews, for to do so was contrary to the sacred canons and the teaching of the saints. Not even the Pope, cried Gabriele Moro, could grant that the Jews might lend upon usury.[47] Graduates, Doctors of the University of Padua, which had previously declared itself strongly in favour of the Paduan Monte di Pietà, combined persuasively to present the canonistic argument, and followed one another to the rostrum in the later debates at the beginning of 1520. Lorenzo Venier, Giovanni Basadonna, Sebastiano Foscarini, Giovanni Badoer, Hieronimo Badoer and Nicolò Michiel formed this articulate and learned pressure group. Among them, Nicolò Michiel was a former Avogadore di Commun. Sebastiano Foscarini, a Senator, Doctor of Laws, and public lecturer in philosophy, maintained that the Pope could not without transgressing the divine law grant that the Jews might lend upon usury,

[46] D.M.S., XXVIII, coll. 61–4.   [47] *Ibid.*

for this is contrary to the words of the commandment of God, who says *non foenerabis fratrem tuum*, etc.

He was evidently impervious to the argument that the Christian was not the Jew's brother. The Pope could not openly and deliberately license anyone to commit a sin, 'though it is true that once a sin or wrong has been committed the Pope can grant absolution'. Bessarion's pronouncement of 1463 had been cited in defence of the Jews at an earlier session. But 'the Cardinal of Nicea could not grant' that the Jews should lend upon interest. It was certainly true that Bessarion's letter contained no explicit mention of usury. Foscarini himself finally concluded that it would be better to expel the Jews altogether.[48]

However, the powerful argument of economic and fiscal convenience, if not actual necessity, still resisted the tirades of the Doctors and the Savii. There was still no Monte di Pietà in Venice, which had not been visited by Bernardino of Feltre in his later years, and might not indeed have welcomed him with enthusiasm.[49] The anti-semitic Friars and others who had attacked the Jews in Lent and at Easter had not— according to Sanuto's terse notes of their sermons—made any constructive suggestions about substitutes for Jewish moneylending. With taxation so heavy and the fisc so demanding as in the years 1509–19, attempts to raise funds for a charitable Monte would have been unlikely to succeed. Only the Jews could fulfil the triple function of paying taxes, lending to the state, and lending to the poor at reasonable rates: though these, of course, were at least three times as high as the rate now usual with a Monte di Pietà. Only the Jews could enable the state to profit from the moneylender's activity. But in the debates of 1519–20, the Monte di Pietà at last found an advocate in the eminent figure of the Procurator Antonio Tron, then serving as a member of the Collegio.

Tron, a veteran magistrate born in April 1439,[50] had returned to public life in January 1520 after some years of retirement. On accepting the office of Savio del Consiglio, he had remarked to Doge Leonardo Loredan

that he saw the city in a state of great disorder, and one could not do justice for fear of intrigue; but he wanted to attend to his soul as he had done for some time past.[51]

[48] D.M.S., XXVIII, coll. 250–1, 319–20, 321–2, 355–6. For Foscarini's post, see also D.M.S., XXXI, col. 198. He was quoting the familiar words of Deuteronomy, xxiii, 19–20—see above, p. 437.

[49] Though according to Wadding, Bernardino received an invitation to preach in Venice in 1491: having no permission from his superior, he was forced to refuse— Wadding, *Annales Minorum*, XIV, p. 514.

[50] D.M.S., XXXV, coll. 314–15.   [51] D.M.S., XXVIII, coll. 151–2.

In the first half of 1520, he attacked with legislation a variety of social, fiscal and administrative abuses.[52] His concern for poor relief showed, not only in his proposals for the establishment of a Monte di Pietà, but also in his demands for the improved administration of the Procuratie of St Mark's.[53] His personal austerity and integrity, and his generosity in 'giving much charity to the poor, but not to the gentry', earned him at his death in 1524 the reputation of 'an excellent patrician (*optimo patricio*)'. He was an honorary member of the Scuola Grande della Misericordia and of six smaller Scuole.[54] On two occasions, in 1521 and 1523, he was to miss very narrowly election to the office of Doge, for which he refused to canvass or intrigue: and in 1523 he was certainly the most widely-favoured candidate.[55]

Tron's interest in charity, finance and efficient administration may have inspired him to take up the cause of the Monte di Pietà. On 10 February 1520, he suggested that the Jewish *capitoli* should be confirmed for one year only, and that during this breathing-space capital for a Monte di Pietà should be raised by the diversion of certain indirect taxes to this use.[56] The taxes he singled out were the wine-excise, and the duty of 4 soldi per *staio* introduced in 1513 on the grinding of corn, and known as the *dazio della macina*.[57] It is not clear whether he wanted the entire yield from these taxes devoted to the Monte di Pietà. If so, this would indeed have been a drastic measure, since the wine-excise alone had in 1500 accounted for some 12 per cent of the total revenue raised by the Signory from within the city of Venice itself. Between 1500 and 1512, the government had farmed this excise to contractors in return for sums which averaged between 70,000 and

[52] Antonio Tron carried a measure to the effect that those who had misappropriated public moneys should not be able to plead benefit of clergy and escape punishment by taking holy orders after their condemnation (25 February 1520, D.M.S., XXVIII, coll. 273, 281–2). Against considerable opposition in the Senate, he procured the passage of a decree limiting the size of the followings of noblemen who accompanied Venetian governors on their way to take up their posts; and also carried a poposal limiting the number of persons eligible for election to the post of Savio del Consiglio (5 May 1520, D.M.S., XXVIII, coll. 490–1, 509, 523–4). Later he pleaded successfully for the appointment of a commission to review tax assessments in the city of Venice itself, taking account of assets not in the form of real property (10 August 1521, D.M.S., XXXI, coll. 206, 207, 209).

[53] A measure of 2–4 March 1520, proposed by Antonio Tron, was designed to secure the fairer distribution and better maintenance of almshouses (D.M.S., XXVIII, coll. 319, 325). On 30 June 1522, on the election of Pietro da Ca' da Pesaro as Procurator, he campaigned for measures which would have made the Procurators regularly give some account of their administration (D.M.S., XXXIII, coll. 331–2).

[54] D.M.S., XXXV, 324–5, 330.

[55] D.M.S., XXX, coll. 385, 389, 393, 480; XXXIV, coll. 128, 133, 156–7, 159; XXXV, 324–5.

[56] D.M.S., XXVIII, coll. 250–1.

[57] Fabio Besta, *Bilanci generali della Repubblica di Venezia* (Venice, 1912), p. cxix.

80,000 ducats annually.[58] By March 1520, Antonio Tron had gained support from the three Heads of the Quarantia al Criminal, Gabriele Barbaro, Lorenzo Vitturi and Giovanni Antonio Memmo, who probably belonged to the order of relatively poor noblemen who sought judicial posts.[59] The text of the proposals unsuccessfully advanced by Tron and his allies made it clear that their ultimate purpose was, not merely to forbid Jewish moneylending, but to free the Venetians of any need whatever for contact with the Jews—on the grounds that the toleration of Jews in Venice itself was a thing contrary to the long-standing traditions of Venetian government. 'Even though the holy canons permit some contact between Jews and Christians, nonetheless our most wise ancestors, bearing in mind how pernicious are the activities of the Jews, decreed by law at various times that they must not settle in our city'. It was more than time for Venice to follow the example of its own subject cities, and to establish a Monte di Pietà for the relief of the poor.[59a]

However, Andrea Trevisan, another member of the Collegio, criticized the proposals on the grounds that he distrusted the institution of the Monte di Pietà. It would be exploited by the wrong people—it is uncertain whether he meant corrupt administrators as well as borrowers of dubious morals. The funds would be used 'for corrupt intrigues and by evil-livers (*per broio e marioli*), and not by those who have need'.[60] Trevisan evidently felt no confidence in those statutes of many Monti di Pietà which were designed to ensure that the money they lent was not used for improper purposes. Beyond this, there probably lay the fact that proposals for the diversion of taxation from military, naval and administrative uses were, given the present political and military situation, most unlikely to command sympathy.

During the discussions, the Jews had found one formidable defender in the octogenarian Procurator Antonio Grimani, serving in November 1519 as Savio del Consiglio. He had declared that

> the Jews are necessary to aid the poor, and it makes no difference whether they remain in the Ghetto or go to live in Mestre. It is necessary that their *capitoli* be confirmed, together with those loans that they made to our noblemen up to the time of the war of . . . . . . ; and there is no need for all this pious rubbish (*pizocharie*), and we should allow the Jews to lend at interest because they have no other livelihood, but amend the *capitoli* as the Collegio have done; and whilst they were at Mestre, Mestre was

---

[58] *Ibid.*, pp. 171–3, 181.

[59] D.M.S., XXVIII, coll. 319–20.

[59a] A.S.V., Senato, *Deliberazioni (Secreta), registro 1519/21*, f. 97r.–v., 10 February 1519 Venetian style; ff. 99v.–100, 2 March 1520.

[60] D.M.S., XXVIII, coll. 250–1.

burned by the enemy, but when they came to this city we recovered our dominions. And in this war they have assisted us with large sums of money.[61]

On the subject of loans to the state, and of government ingratitude towards its servants, he had acquired painful personal experience. His mind wandered, as he spoke, back to the summer of 1499, when fortune had plunged him from the summit of worldly success into depths of unpopularity and humiliation. A self-made merchant of undistinguished family, he had won an enviable reputation for good luck, business acumen and skill as a naval commander. In the face of the Turkish threat, the Venetians had pinned all their hopes of deliverance on Antonio Grimani, elected Capitano Generale in April 1499.[62] He had lent generously to the state and had disbursed from his own private fortune sums of 16,000 and 4,000 ducats to enable Venetian warships to depart promptly from Venice itself and from Crete.[63] But his fleet—allegedly vastly superior—had failed to engage the Turks, Lepanto was lost to the Venetians, and he himself was charged and convicted of dereliction of duty.[64] His pains, as he put it in 1519, had earned him imprisonment at the hands of the state he had served. It was, perhaps, out of a certain fellow-feeling that he defended the Jews from expulsion. In fact, his expedition had been partially financed by a considerable Jewish loan in May 1499. The Collegio had approached 'the Jews Anselmo and Salamonsin of Piove di Sacco'—almost certainly Asher Meshullam and his father—and had obtained from them a loan of 15,000 ducats.[65] The memory of this—though there is no record of an explicit reference to it in his speech—may have influenced his championship of the Jews, and of the traditional policy of contracting with

[61] D.M.S., XXVIII, coll. 62–3.

[62] Cf. especially Girolamo Priuli, *Diarii*, ed. Arturo Segre, I (Città di Castello, 1912), pp. 167, 220–1. On this famous incident and on Grimani's career in general, see Samuele Romanin, *Storia documentata di Venezia* (reprint, Venice, 1912–21), V, pp. 133 f., 338 f., 383–4.

[63] Malipiero, *Annali veneti*, p. 163; Priuli, *Diarii*, I, pp. 129–30; D.M.S., II, coll. 621, 631, 650.

[64] Priuli, *Diarii*, I, pp. 326–32; D.M.S., III, coll. 6–7, 387–90, 393. Antonio Grimani was sentenced to exile on the Dalmatian islands of Cherso and Ossaro, from which he escaped in 1502. He made his way to Rome, where his son Domenico, Patriarch of Aquileia, was a cardinal. He did much to further the interests of his country at the court of Pope Julius II. In 1509 he was recalled from exile and in recognition of his services restored to the office of Procurator, of which he had been deprived on his conviction in 1500. On the death of Leonardo Loredan, he was elected Doge on 6 July 1521—see D.M.S., XXX, coll. 479–90, especially the sketch of his life at col. 483. Antonio Grimani died of old age on 7 May 1523—D.M.S., XXXIV, col. 127.

[65] D.M.S., II, coll. 742, 745, 754; Priuli, *Diarii*, I, p. 121. Acording to Priuli, the Jews made the loan on the security of government salt revenues, which they sold at a loss of 20–25 per cent.

them. This policy was sanctioned by the letter of Cardinal Bessarion, which Grimani now caused to be read.[66]

Sanuto himself shared the conservative and commonsense approach of Antonio Grimani, to whom, as it happened, he was related by marriage.[67] Excluded that year from the Senate proper and its Zonta barred from participating in the official discussion, he privately drafted notes for the speech he would have liked to make in the debate of 10 November 1519. He concentrated mainly on down-to-earth arguments from the current economic situation, and presented his judicious opinion as follows:

> Had I, Marino Sanuto, been a member of the Senate as I was last year, I would have spoken, though not to speak for the Jews, because I could describe many sharp practices of theirs in connexion with their loans. I would have spoken on the *capitoli* and had them amended, proving that Jews are even more necessary to a city than bakers are (*dimostrando è necessarii più hebrei e pistori in una terra*), and especially to this one, for the sake of the general welfare. I would have referred to laws, and to what our ancestors have always done, and to the opinion of the Doctors Alessandro of Imola, Pietro of Ancarano, Baldus and others, who advise us that Jews can be kept to lend upon interest. And thus I would have spoken on the question at issue. It is true that I would not have wished them to keep shops dealing in second-hand goods, so as not to deprive Christians of a living, even though if they kept them goods could be sold very profitably (*ancora che a tenirli sia gran beneficio di le robe si vol vender*). Our countrymen have never wanted Jews to keep shops to trade in this city, but to buy and sell and go away again. But there should be none of this humbug in our State about expelling the Jews when there is no Monte di Pietà. The treasuries of the Monte Vecchio and Nuovo are not paying interest, and the Monte Nuovissimo is doing so only with very great difficulty. There is very little trade in the city. Shopkeepers are complaining that they are not selling their goods, and it will not be forgotten that a man can on his property borrow from the Jews at 15 per cent in order to fulfil his own needs and feed and maintain his family. And I would have enlarged greatly upon this point, but God has not willed it so.[68]

[66] See above, pp. 454–5.
[67] D.M.S., XXX, coll. 479–80, 484; XXXI, col. 7.
[68] D.M.S., XXVIII, col. 63. Pietro of Ancarano (1333–1416) had declared that Jews ought to be fully authorized to lend, on being asked by the ruler of Mantua whether he ought to compel Christians to repay debts contracted with the Jews. Alessandro Tartagni of Imola (1424–77) argued, like the Brescians in the 1440's, that the Jews were damned in any case, so that the Pope, by allowing them to lend upon usury, was not encouraging them to commit any mortal sin (see Poliakov, *Les banquiers juifs*, pp. 43–5, and above, p. 436). See also Alessandro's *Consilia* (7 vols., Frankfurt-on-Main, 1575), VI, *consilium* xcix, ff. 48v.–49v.; VII, *consilium* xiii, ff. 10v.–11v. These opinions, given in cases of Jews having illicit sexual relations with Christian

Sanuto thus professed to entertain no illusions about the Jews, but to justify their retention on conservative and legalistic grounds, and more especially on those of economic necessity: the lower level of commercial activity, and the failure of government funds to pay interest, created an urgent need for credit and for the services of moneylenders to tide the Venetians over this period of stagnation. As his remarks implied, difficulties had arisen, not only over the question of licensing Jews as moneylenders, but also over concessions to keep shops dealing in second-hand goods. The second-hand trade complemented that of the banker, not because pawnbrokers were allowed to sell unredeemed pledges themselves, but because the Jews were probably already excluded from occupations which entailed the manufacture of goods, for which membership of Christian guilds was a vital qualification. In June 1519, Antonio Balbi of the Quarantia al Criminale had upheld the Jewish second-hand trade, on the grounds that it afforded the best means of disposing of deceased persons' effects at good prices. In any case, the right to keep the shops could be sold to the Jews for the sum of 1,000 ducats a year.[69] In the past, this concession had produced valuable loans from them.

Sanuto regarded the Jews as a well-tested economic tool which the city of Venice was wholly unequipped to throw away. He suspected the motives of the Jews' opponents sufficiently to say, at one point, that much of their righteousness was sheer hypocrisy on the part of men who would have liked to lend at 40–50 per cent or more, 'as is the usual practice on Rialto', and not at the modest rates of 15 20 per cent charged by the Jews.[70] Eventually, the argument of fiscal necessity— and perhaps also arguments of the type privately set forth by Sanuto— won the contest, and defeated the eloquence of the Doctors by a narrow margin.

On 16 March 1520, the Senate, by 93 votes in favour to 66 against, with 15 abstentions, agreed to renew the *capitoli* of 3 August 1508, with a number of emendations originally proposed a fortnight earlier in an unsuccessful resolution suggested by Andrea Foscarini and by the Doctor Marino Zorzi. The principal motive of this decision—as the preamble to the decree expressly stated—was the need to provide money for the Arsenal and for the fleet.[71] The Procurator Tron, champion of the Monte di Pietà, had suggested raising these funds through

women, state for example that 'the statutes of a locality must be observed in dealing with Jews', and that 'it is lawful for us to associate and have dealings with Jews'. Cf. also Sheedy, *Bartolus on social conditions*, pp. 230 f.

69 D.M.S., XXVII, coll. 358–9.

70 D.M.S., XXVIII, col. 63.

71 A.S.V., *Senato, Deliberazioni (Secreta), registro 1519/21*, ff. 98–9, 102.

the imposition of a full *decima*, the direct tax on real property.[72] But Venetian Senators, themselves not exempt from this tax, preferred instead to levy the money from the Jews. The annual Jewish tax was now raised from 6,500 ducats (as in 1513) to 10,000. The increase, however, was not as steep as it appeared on the surface, because, in return for this tax, the Jews were expressly authorized to keep in the Ghetto shops dealing in second-hand goods. In 1515, they had had to pay separately for the privilege of keeping such shops, which was not covered by the agreement of 1513 negotiated by Asher Meshullam with the Council of Ten. Of this total of 10,000 ducats, 4,500 were earmarked for the loan fund of the Monte Nuovo—probably to contribute to the interest payments made to government bondholders. 850 ducats, as before, were required as rent for the banks at Padua, and another 300 as rent for three banks at Mestre. This left a total of 4,360 ducats, to be paid on account of each year's residence, half of which would go directly to the navy, the other half to the Arsenal. Moreover, the Jews were required to make an advance payment of 4,000 ducats, again half to the Arsenal and half to the navy, to be spent on ropes or canvas and ironwork (*canevi et ferramenti*). This advance payment was to be deducted, in four annual instalments, of 1,000 ducats each, from the four annual payments, of 10,000 ducats each, expected to be made by the Jews under this agreement. Since the *condotta* covered banking arrangements on the mainland dominions of the Republic, presumably the tax was to be paid both by the Jews of Venice and by all Jews resident in Venetian subject cities on the mainland. The Jews were not—in 1520 any more than in 1513—protected from further forced loans or other fiscal demands.

In return for these payments, the Jews of Venice were to be entitled to lend, both to Venetians and to foreigners, at 15 per cent. There was probably no change here, for Sanuto had written in November 1519 of men borrowing from the Jews at that rate. On the mainland, however, the highest legal rate of interest was now fixed at 15 per cent on pledges and at 20 per cent on written promises to pay. No new Jewish banks were to be established—the Senate proposed to return to the situation before the invasions and diaspora of 1509. Apart from this, conditions altered little. The Jews were given protection against being held responsible for the deterioration of pledges left in their care, provided they had taken reasonable precautions to keep them properly. They were forbidden to lend on the security, not only of sacred objects, but also of various types of 'cloth of silk and gold from abroad', which had become illegal—whether through governmental protectionist measures,

[72] D.M.S., XXVIII, coll. 321–2, 355–6.

or as a result of sumptuary laws. The new *capitoli* envisaged the possibility of another Jewish migration into Venice, since one clause permitted bankers on the mainland to bring their pledges to the capital for safe keeping in case of war, and to do so without paying customs duties either on the outward or on the return journey.

The banker Asher Meshullam, as head of the Jewish community, personally responsible for the payment of a high proportion of the taxes, protested to the Collegio that the Jews lacked the resources to meet the state's demands. But his aphorism 'When the will and the means are in conflict, it is the means that count in the end (*Quando il voler col poder combate, il poder sta de sora*)' failed to carry conviction. On 2 May 1520, the Jews accepted the terms which the Senate offered,[73] and the Venetian Ghetto survived for the time being. From the spring of 1520, Jewish banking re-established itself on the mainland in most of the important centres it had occupied before the war—with the exception of Brescia and Treviso and their surrounding districts. The Venetian government denied the Jews entry to these cities on the grounds of alleged misconduct in or after the invasions of 1509—though Jewish communities and Jewish bankers did return to Asolo, in the province of Treviso, and in the Bresciano Jewish lenders did eventually reappear, at some time during the next fifty years, in zones where local lords enjoyed immunities and seigneurial jurisdictions.[74] By 1520, Jewish bankers were active in the large cities of Verona and Crema, and Chaim Meshullam was reopening his premises in Padua, where, by the beginning of 1526, he kept several branches. Smaller centres of Jewish lending on the mainland, in addition to Asolo, were Portogruaro in Friuli, Porto Bufolè on the Friulian border, Conegliano in the province of Treviso, and Cittadella and Montagnana in the Padovano.[75]

For the time being, fiscal and economic necessity had garanteed the continued presence of the Jews, both in Venice itself and in the mainland provinces to its north and west. Little dispute arose over the renewal of the Jewish *condotta* in September 1523, and, if anything, the terms granted to the Jews on the mainland became more generous in the next few years. In October 1523, the Jews received permission to colonize new ground by opening banks in places where they were not yet established—so long as the local Venetian governors were prepared to write in support of their claims.[76] In 1525, moreover, the Jews were

[73] D.M.S., XXVIII, col. 363, 481. [74] See below, pp. 541–2.
[75] For Padua, see D.M.S., XXVIII, col. 460, XL, col. 672; for the rest, D.M.S., XXVIII, coll. 363, 460. On Asolo, see also Lattes, 'Documents et notices'.
[76] D.M.S., XXXIV, col. 392; XXXV, col. 45; A.S.V., *Senato, Terra, registro 1523/24*, f. 38r.–v., 45.

authorized to raise from 15 per cent to 20 per cent their interest on loans on the security of pledges—though they were not allowed to return to the higher rate of 30 per cent on written bonds usual before 1520.[77]

However, the fact that such concessions were made in 1523 did not imply surrender on the part of the anti-Jewish juntas in Venice. Fresh efforts were made to procure the foundation of a Monte di Pietà. There seems to be no evidence yet available that the plan now proposed was either inspired by Franciscan agitations, connected with the Procurator Antonio Tron, or formulated by those who had attacked the Jews during the debates of 1519–20. It issued, instead, from persons associated with the Compagnia del Divino Amore, who (after the foundation of the hospital of the Incurabili for syphilitic patients)[78] extended their activities to include the foundation of a Monte di Pietà as well. The Senate considered the question again at the end of March 1523, on the basis of a petition submitted by the procurators, or governing congregation, of the hospital of the Incurabili. The petitioners used noticeably different tactics from their predecessors—in that they abstained from directly attacking the Jews, or from suggesting that the purpose of erecting a Monte di Pietà in Venice would be to get rid of the Jews altogether. Elsewhere, Monti di Pietà—like those of Padua and Verona—were coexisting with Jewish banks, and had not yet replaced them. Moves which threatened to provoke the Jews into closing down their banks and leaving Venice temporarily without provision were likely to prove unpopular with a large section of senatorial opinion. The petitioners seemed chiefly anxious to dissolve conservative prejudice against the Monti di Pietà by fervently pointing out how the Monti di Pietà had proved themselves highly beneficial to all communities that had started them, and by maintaining that they depended on 'charitable and voluntary subsidies, without burdening or damaging anyone'. They were probably trying, here, to allay the suspicion that taxation might be levied to raise funds for such a Monte. Now that poverty and misery were so profound, it was doubly urgent to provide such facilities. This altered approach to the problem achieved an important initial success: the Senate approved in principle the establishment of a Monte di Pietà, proposing to settle the details of its constitution later.[79]

About a year later, in April 1524, the thirteen procurators of the

---

[77] D.M.S., XXXIX, col. 55; cf. also A.S.V., *Consiglio dei Dieci, Registro Comune 1528*, ff. 86v.–87.
[78] See above, pp. 235–8.
[79] A.S.V., *Senato, Terra, registro 1523/24*, f. 7r.–v., 27 March 1523.

Incurabili brought their proposals to the Collegio. Eleven of this company were noblemen, headed by Vincenzo, the devout son of the late Doge Antonio Grimani. Vincenzo's views on these matters evidently differed from those of his father. Only one of the eleven—the Doctor Nicolò di Francesco Michiel—can tentatively be identified with one of the opponents of the Jews in the earlier debate, four years previously. The remaining two procurators were textile merchants, who signed themselves 'Domenego Honoradi da le telle' and 'Francesco de Zuane da la seda'. In many respects, the proposed statutes superficially resembled in principle those of the Monti di Pietà at Mantua, Verona, Padua and Treviso, already discussed. Ultimate control of the Monte di Pietà would have been vested in a board of governors centring round the thirteen procurators, whose hospital, the Incurabili, would become the headquarters of the new Monte. The governors would meet on its premises, and all operations connected with moneylending would also be transacted there. To make the enterprise 'more universal', the procurators suggested associating with themselves one citizen from each of the five Scuole Grandi of the city. Such citizens must be chosen by the chapters of their Scuole Grandi, and must have served as Guardiani Grandi or at least as Vicars. By this means the procurators hoped to retain the services of men highly experienced in the administration of public charity. The governing body would therefore, at the outset, consist of eleven noblemen and seven citizens, and it would, moreover, be empowered to co-opt a number of nobles, citizens and 'well qualified persons' likewise prepared to interest themselves in the Monte di Pietà. The governors would be required to serve as Presidenti, in rotation—at all times, there would be five Presidenti (three nobles and two citizens) supervising the Monte's affairs in detail, on duty for periods of three months at a time. The governors were also to provide three Sindici to review the administration of the Monte at the end of every year.

The governors were to elect Cassieri (the equivalent of Massari elsewhere) to carry out the actual operations of lending on pledges and of collecting the capital and interest when the loans expired. Every Cassiere must be a *cittadino originario* of Venice. Lending operations were to be conducted on principles very similar to those followed at Treviso and elsewhere in the late fifteenth century, with a 5 per cent per annum interest charge similarly justified on the familiar grounds that 'it is meet and proper that workers should be paid for their trouble, and only just that he who has been served should make satisfaction'. Here there was nothing unusual.

However, one prominent and unfamiliar feature of the proposed Venetian statutes was the extent to which they envisaged the capital

Monte de Pietà, Vicenza

facing p. 500

JEWISH MERCHANT FROM PADUA

facing p. 501

being raised, not from charitable gifts or bequests, but through loans or deposits which could be restored to the persons making them. Each of the thirteen procurators offered to act as guarantor, to the tune of 1,000 ducats, 'for the restitution of money placed at the disposal of the said Monte'. All members of the governing body were supposed to offer similar guarantees—representatives of the Scuole Grandi would be allowed either to make guarantees personally, or to do so in the name of their Scuola Grande. Moreover, the statutes later provided that

> No money lent to the Monte by any person or office may be sequestrated, and for this reason the names of the lenders shall be kept secret, and one-quarter of the money must always be kept in reserve in the cash-box to be restored to those who make loans, so that everybody may know that whenever he wants his money it will be restored to him.[80]

But the procurators did not discuss the conditions on which such loans or deposits were to be made—were they to be made purely out of charitable motives, by persons who would not charge the Monte for the use of their money, or was any kind of interest to be paid upon them? Since the governors were expressly required only to guarantee 'restitution', and not to guarantee interest payments, it seems most likely that the deposits envisaged would have been purely charitable loans.

However, the Council of Ten suddenly exercised its prerogative of intervening for the protection of the public interest, and cut short the progress of the scheme. On 19–20 April 1524, the Ten decisively crushed the new project, with a decree which instructed the Heads of the Ten to send for the noblemen who had recently presented the statutes to the Collegio,

> and they shall charge them in stern, severe and well-chosen words that on pain of their lives and of the displeasure of this Council they shall no further propose or speak of this matter.
>
> And be it also resolved that from henceforth no one may propose or speak of this matter of the Monte di Pictà without the express permission and decree of this Council assembled to the full number of seventeen, and no such decree or resolution shall be considered to have passed unless it has received all seventeen votes.

Moreover, the noblemen concerned were never to reveal that they had received any admonition from the Heads of the Ten, but were quietly to drop the project, and Bortolomio Comin, Secretary to the Collegio, received orders to hand over the offending Capitoli to the Council of

---

[80] A.S.V., *Consiglio dei Dieci, Parti Miste, filza* 53, *fascicolo* 68, 20 April 1524.

2K

Ten—in whose files they remain to this day. The noblemen responsible seem to have submitted meekly enough—whether from fear or because they were genuinely convinced by the Ten's arguments—and to have made no attempt to reopen the matter. Indeed, five of them were said to have declared themselves 'very ready to obey this command'.[81]

To justify its drastic action, the Council referred to certain 'most important causes and well-considered reasons spoken and declared here', but did not record what they were. The diarist Sanuto, in his cryptic note of the affair,[82] gave no hint of them, and only conjectures can be offered here. There were still many doubts—of the kind voiced by Andrea Trevisan in 1520—about the viability of Monti di Pietà, and about their tendency to corruption and maladministration. Jewish bankers, in business on their own account, could scarcely be corrupt in the same sense, for they were not handling public money raised by charitable subscription. To the end of the 1520's, Venice was intermittently involved in the power struggle for Italian territory, and her navy still depended on Jewish contributions for its upkeep. It was all too likely that any proposal to establish a Monte di Pietà, even if not cast in the form of a direct attack on the Jews, would evoke a counter-threat from the Jews to close their banks and emigrate. The Council of Ten might reasonably doubt the wisdom of throwing the poor on to an institution which itself depended on voluntary contributions or loans: this was hardly the most propitious time either to propose new taxes or to divert old ones to the ends of social welfare. Again, a Monte di Pietà would fail to discharge many of the valuable functions performed by Jewish banks.[83] It would not, as the Jews did, accommodate persons who were not in the ordinary sense poor, but who nevertheless needed credit on reasonable terms to relieve them of financial embarrassment. The Cassier, under the proposed statutes, would have been bound to lend only to 'needy persons living in this city', and in the first year of the Monte's existence he would not have been permitted to lend a total of more than 3 ducats to any one household at any given time. Admittedly, this maximum would have been increased, had the Monte prospered, after its first year—but only to 5 ducats. In the past, Jews in the Padovano had lent far larger sums to persons of some social standing. The method of proceeding in a Monte di Pietà was always condescending and frankly charitable—in Venice, as elsewhere, borrowers would

---

[81] A.S.V., *Consiglio dei Dieci, Miste, registro 1524*, ff. 20v.–21.

[82] D.M.S., XXXVI, col. 237: in which Sanuto simply states that the project 'fo mandà a monte per i Cai di X'.

[83] On this theme in general, see the very illuminating remarks of Milano, 'Considerazioni sulla lotta dei Monti di Pietà', and of Poliakov, *Les banquiers juifs*, pp. 188–91.

have had to suffer the humiliation of swearing that they did not want the money 'for any immoral and dishonest reason'. The fact that the Monte di Pietà would have been based in a pox hospital would scarcely have relieved the embarrassment of the genteel borrower. Had the Jews consented to remain, all could have been well: but they might have refused to do so, had the Monte di Pietà threatened to deprive them of a large slice of their business.

Again, it would have been far less easy for the state to convert to its own uses the moneys of the Monte di Pietà than to tax or otherwise exploit the Jews. It is worth recalling here that at the end of June 1509 the leading citizens of Padua had, during the imperial occupation, considered using funds from the Monte di Pietà for the purpose of paying German infantry then stationed at Bassano. But they had encountered strong resistance, and the Deputies of the Monte di Pietà had opposed the project with the contention that 'the Monte is made for the poor, and there are no Jews now lending in Padua'.[84] Raids or *intacchi* on the funds of these Monti were by no means unknown in the sixteenth and early seventeenth century—but they were far less ethical than the taxing of the Jews. Monti di Pietà, in fact, lacked the Jews' double capacity for extending credit both to the poor and to the state, and, with their relatively high interest rates, for accommodating the claims of both.

Again, M. Léon Poliakov has advanced an interesting hypothesis to explain the action of the Council of Ten. He suggests that the Monte di Pietà planned in 1524 'threatened to become an autonomous financial power, capable of influencing the conduct of public affairs'. He brings forward no contemporary evidence for this, but cites the remark of the seventeenth-century Venetian rabbi Simone Luzzatto that the Venetian government wanted nobody but 'the subject and feeble nation' of the Jews, which had no seditious thoughts, to assume the task of lending to the needy.[85] It seems a far cry from the conduct of pawnbroking to becoming the kind of financial authority M. Poliakov describes—but there may be some truth in his remarks. Control of charity implies power—those who dispense charity thereby acquire authority over the poor—and, in that sense, any charitable person or institution is potentially subversive to the authority of the state. In the past, however, the Venetian government (as the history of the Scuole Grandi shows) had been conspicuously successful in containing

---

[84] D.M.S., VIII, col. 442.

[85] Poliakov, *Les banquiers juifs*, pp. 238–9; Simone Luzzatto, *Discorso circa il stato de gl'Hebrei, et in particolar dimoranti nell'inclita Citta di Venetia* (Venice, 1638), f. 33v.

religious and charitable institutions and in adapting them to its own purposes. But the suggestions of the procurators in 1524 might well have disproportionately enhanced the authority over the poor wielded both by the Incurabili and by the Scuole Grandi. Again, the governing council of the Monte would not have consisted of persons appointed directly by the Senate, Council of Ten or Great Council—it would have been a self-appointed, and perhaps self-perpetuating, oligarchy, based on a nucleus of powerful families, expanding and renewing its ranks by co-optation. One final reason for the Ten's decision may have lain in the consequences anticipated from the acceptance of loans by the Monte di Pietà. If these were originally intended to be gratuitous and purely charitable loans, how long could they have remained so? The question of whether Monti di Pietà could legitimately pay interest on loans made to them was later to form the subject of much intricate theological discussion—even after the issue of the Bull *Inter multiplices* of 1515 the Monti di Pietà had one other theoretical barrier to crash, and the question was not to be properly settled for at least thirty years.[86] The Ten, in the 1520's, might have been forgiven for preferring to dodge the issue. It is also possible that the Monte di Pietà might have provided opportunities for tax evasion, since deposits in its coffers were not to be sequestrated, and since the names of depositors were to be concealed.

Quite probably, objections to this particular set of proposals for a Monte di Pietà gave welcome ammunition to those who distrusted the institution in general, and who preferred to stick to the Jews, as the devil they knew and as the most versatile and least patronizing lenders available. The veto of the Council of Ten smothered the pious project, and did so permanently. The Ten's decree was to be cited again in 1573, when the Senate next seriously considered the wholesale expulsion of the Jews from the dominions of Venice.[87]

For the moment, the Jews faced no official rivalry in the small-loan business in Venice itself. But prejudice and fiscalism created continual uncertainty for them. In 1526, further attempts to secure advance or additional payments for the support of the navy raised the possibility of the Jews terminating their current agreement with the Signory, or at least of their not renewing it when it next expired.[88] Then, in March 1527, the Cavalier Gabriele Moro, who had been one of the Jews' opponents in 1519–20, succeeded in squeezing through the Senate a controversial proposal that the Jews should be forced to return to Mestre on conditions similar to the ones imposed in 1394 and 1496. Henceforth, no loan banks should transact business in Venice itself,

[86] See below, pp. 524–5, 589 f.   [87] See below, p. 539.   [88] D.M.S., XLI, col. 83.

and no Jew would be entitled to spend more than fifteen days a year in the city. Two Jews from each bank would be permitted to attend the auctions of unredeemed pledges held in Venice itself by the magistracy of the Sopraconsoli. This proposal seemed designed to get the worst of every world—it would have controlled Jewish lending merely by making it more costly and inconvenient to resort to a Jew; and it would have provided no alternative source of supply for the loan-seeker. Nevertheless, in return for these discomforts the city of Venice itself would have been freed of the contaminating presence of the Jews. The preamble of the decree recorded as an official belief the familiar argument that Venice had always prospered when there were no Jewish lenders in the city, and that when there were the contrary had always been observed. At the third vote, the Senate passed Moro's retrograde resolution by the narrow margin of 105 votes in favour to 95 against, with four abstentions recorded.[89]

It is, however, doubtful whether this decree was actually enforced. The soaring grain prices and the plague and typhus outbreaks of the years 1527–9 forcefully drew attention to the problem of the poor and resulted in the first official legislation for the general control of begging.[90] The removal of the banks to Mestre would simply have increased the burden on the borrower by the addition of travel costs to interest rates. The need of the poor for credit probably became more acute than at any time since the famines of 1504. By October 1527, the Jewish banks in Venice were already closed for fear of another forced loan of 10,000 ducats. Sanuto remarked on the inconvenience this caused at a time of rising grain prices.[91] The proceeds of the loan would, as usual, have been destined for the Arsenal and for the navy—for provisions, hemp, ropes, and so forth.[92] Some time had still to elapse before the expiry of the terms granted, in September 1523, for a period of five years, with one year of grace. On 31 July 1528, the second-hand dealers of Venetian Jewry received permission to remain in Venice even if their co-religionists departed.[93] A few months later, the dualism of Senate and Council of Ten, or perhaps the ultimate sovereignty claimed by the Ten in all matters affecting the Jews, again preserved the Venetian community. The Ten, having quashed the Monte di Pietà in 1524, again showed a stronger tendency than the Senate to favour the traditional method of securing moneylenders by contracting with the Jews. In September 1528, the Council confirmed what Sanuto tersely described as 'the old *capitoli*' of the Jews, and this

[89] D.M.S., XLIV, coll. 285, 299, 303–6.
[90] See above, pp. 240–54.
[91] D.M.S., XLVI, col. 153.
[92] D.M.S., XLVI, coll. 177–8.
[93] D.M.S., XLVIII, col. 324.

almost certainly had the effect of overruling the Senate and of preventing the enforcement of the Moro decree of March 1527. The Jews, on this occasion, asked to be allowed to remain in the Ghetto, and for 'Anselm' (i.e. Asher Meshullam) and his heirs and agents to be permitted to continue banking there—whilst other Jews of Venice should be entitled, not only to ply the second-hand trade, but also to make or sell veils and coifs ('*fare . . . l'arte di vellami et scuffie*'). The Council of Ten raised no objection to these demands.[94] There were still Jews in Venice in 1532, for in March of that year the Collegio summoned the Jews 'of this city', headed by Consiglio, a second-hand trader, and demanded a loan of 10,000 ducats—telling the Jews that if they wished to refuse they must go and live elsewhere.[95] Despite such threats, the Council of Ten and Zonta again took control of Jewish affairs in 1533 and renewed the *condotta* for a further period of five years; then, in 1537, the Jews were eventually granted terms for another ten.[96]

These agreements with the Jews made no alterations in the terms on which they were to be allowed to lend: only their tax liabilities varied. In this, in 1528, 1533 and 1537, there were three elements: firstly, the basic annual tax, fixed at only 5,000 ducats in 1528, but raised in 1533 to 5,850 and kept at that level in 1537. The rent payable at Padua and Mestre remained constant—at 850 ducats for banks in Padua, and 300 for those of Mestre. Most complicated and variable, however, was the third element, which consisted of various forms of block payment to be made within a month or two of agreement being reached. It could include (a) outright gifts, and (b) advance payments of taxation which were subsequently deducted in instalments from the basic annual tax. In 1528, the Council of Ten required an advance payment of 10,000 ducats, to be subtracted in four instalments from the basic annual taxes for the first four years. In 1533, however, it preferred, instead, to demand an outright gift of 3,000 ducats, to be sent to buy hemp at Montagnana, ultimately destined to supply the Cretan fleet. Under the agreement finally reached in March 1537, the Jews were required both to make an outright gift of 6,000 ducats and to advance a further 6,750 ducats to the government, to be deducted from the first five instalments of the basic annual tax. On this occasion, the *condotta* was to last for ten years, and not merely for the usual five. After making the advance payment of 6,750 ducats, the Jews would, for the first five years, in fact

---

[94] A.S.V., *Consiglio dei Dieci, Registro Comune 1528*, ff. 86v.–87v.; D.M.S., XLVIII, col. 450.

[95] D.M.S., LV, col. 656.

[96] For the text of these agreements, see A.S.V., *Consiglio dei Dieci, Registro Comune 1533*, f. 107r.–v.; *Registro Comune 1535/36*, ff. 197v.–198; *Registro Comune 1537/38*, ff. 2v.–3.

be paying only 4,500 ducats annually instead of 5,850, and these 4,500 ducats were to go to the Monte Nuovo—this time, to contribute to its liquidation and the repayment of its creditors. The Council of Ten also specified in detail what was to be done with the block payment disbursed by the Jews, and its decision shows that the Venetian government continued to use Jewish money to finance its navy and to equip its eastern bases with provisions. The block payment—gift and advance —amounted to 12,750 ducats, of which 5,000 were to finance 'artillery' and 4,550 to be sent to Corfù to equip galleys. The remaining 3,200 ducats were designed to meet the needs of the naval base of Nauplia, to buy corn and to make biscuits for naval provisions—2,000 must be sent to Nauplia directly, the other 1,200 to Constantinople, there to reward Ayas Pasha for a consignment of grain exported from Turkish dominions to Nauplia.

Government treatment of the Jews had not become markedly harsher: if anything, it was alleviated during the 1530's. But in 1537 the Jews complained convincingly of the depletion of their fortunes, and particularly of that of the family of Meshullam.[97] Asher's fortune had now devolved on his son Jacob, who, after so many tribulations at the hands of Venetian judges, had been baptized a Christian at a magnificent ceremony held in the Frari on the festival of the Madonna, 15 July 1533. The Venetians had borne him so little grudge for his alleged crimes in the past that the Doge had created him a Cavalier di San Marco, an honour described by Sanuto as totally without precedent, and he had taken the name of Marco Paradiso.[98] A brief of Pope Clement VII, issued at the request of Jacob's sons, had authorized him to keep his wealth and property after his conversion to Christianity, provided he restored all usurious gains—where possible by making repayment to the injured parties themselves, but otherwise by donations to religious and charitable uses.[99] Moreover, Chaim Meshullam of Padua was said to have reduced the wealth of Jews in the Venetian Republic by marrying his daughters to persons domiciled in other states, thus exporting their dowries. Many other Jews were said to have migrated and to have

[97] A.S.V., *Consiglio dei Dieci, Parti Comuni, filza* 21, 6 March 1537.
[98] D.M.S., LVIII, coll. 563–9. Concerned with this baptism were several persons associated either with anti-Jewish measures or with the proposals for a Monte di Pietà. Before the ceremony, Jacob and his son Salamon (baptized at the same time, with the name of Francesco) lived in the house of Vincenzo Grimani. Among the godfathers were Sebastiano Giustinian, one of the procurators of the Incurabili in 1524, and the Cavalier Gabriele Moro, who had nearly succeeded in getting the Jews relegated to Mestre in 1527.
[99] For the brief, *ibid.*, coll. 567–9. On this method of restitution, see Nelson, 'The usurer and the merchant prince'. Two of Jacob's sons had been converted to Christianity before he himself was, and had taken the names of Paolo and Pietro.

died abroad. The Council of Ten did in fact grant them easier terms, and agreed to extend their *condotta* from five years to ten.

By the early 1530's, the city of Venice itself had accepted the Jews as residents, though it had walled them into the fortress of the Ghetto and had set them apart by the use of the yellow badge which emphasized their servitude. The atmosphere of tolerance which had permitted Chaim to rent the Bernardo palace, and Jacob to gamble with nobles in the house of the Archbishop of Crete, was gone forever. But, on the other hand, economic, social and fiscal necessity had resisted, if not allayed, the superstitious uneasiness of the pious; it had parried the arguments of the doctors learned in the canon law and armed with the Clementine Constitutions. To retain the Jews was less righteous than to establish a Monte di Pietà. But the range and versatility of the Jews, as bankers to the poor, taxpayers, lenders to the state and to persons who were not technically paupers, was far greater than that of a Christian loan bank. Through the Jews, the state at a crucial moment could share in the profits of the moneylender's trade. In all probability, the Jewish tax at its most extortionate accounted for less than 1 per cent of the gross revenue of the Venetian Republic from the city of Venice itself, and from its mainland and 'maritime' possessions. It was worth perhaps half the tithe levied on the clergy of the city itself and half as much as the taxes levied on the meat trade in Venice; about an eighth as much as the principal wine excise. But it was equivalent to something like 6 per cent of the total sum realized by direct taxation from sources within the city of Venice itself. The Jews were probably by far the heaviest payers of direct taxation in the Venetian dominion.[100] Such taxes came as a most welcome supplement to the revenue of the state, which could not afford to neglect a single exploitable source of income. In any case forced loans and 'profits of justice' substantially increased the Jewish contribution to the state. The fact that the Jewish *tansa* was earmarked for the Arsenal and the navy during the 1520's heightened its importance; so did the substantial advance payments made by the Jews. The Jews, moreover, performed in times of economic hardship a service of whose social value Sanuto for one was acutely aware. The unsentimental, unfanatical and calculating element in the Venetian Senate which regarded the Jews as economic tools for the benefit of the poor and the state triumphed at last in 1520. The decisive action of the Council of Ten

---

[100] Cf. the figures for the yield of these taxes in 1500 in Besta, *Bilanci generali*, pp. 171–3. In 1500, the total gross revenue of the Venetian Republic was 1,145,580 ducats, of which 615,750 came from within the city of Venice. Direct taxation on Venetians accounted for 154,000 ducats.

cut short the experiment of the Monte di Pietà, and committed the Venetians, in contrast to their mainland possessions, to relying on Jewish bankers. The Jews remained in Venice as a segregated minority enjoying government protection, tolerated for its economic utility, dependent for support on loan banking and the second-hand trade.

3

THE TURN OF THE SCREW, 1541–1571

Before the late 1540's, little change occurred in the situation of the German Jewish or Italian Jewish communities of Venice and the Venetian dominion. However, in the first half of the sixteenth century, the Venetian government, like other Italian states, faced the problem of Jewish immigration from another quarter. With the dispersal and resettlement of the great communities of the Iberian peninsula, the face of European Jewry and the distribution of Jewish wealth, talent and manpower were now undergoing radical change. The displaced Jews were of two kinds—professed Jews expelled en masse by the decree of the dual monarchy of Castile and Aragon after the conquest of Granada in 1492; and crypto-Jews opprobriously known as Marranos, who were often illegal emigrants from Portugal. Marranos were the product of forced conversion, conforming outwardly to Christianity, but secretly handing on from one generation to the next a clandestine Judaic religion. Widespread massacres and pogroms in Castile and Aragon in 1391, and the violent campaigns of such preachers as Vicente Ferrer, had generously contributed to the spread of Marranism. After the expulsion decree of Spain in 1492, many exiles had simply crossed the frontier into Portugal, whose ruler, John II, had received the richer Jews on terms advantageous to his fisc. But the Spanish government had projected its anti-Jewish policy, the logical climax of the Reconquista, beyond its own frontiers. In 1496, as a condition of the marriage of the new King of Portugal, Manuel the Fortunate, to the daughter of Ferdinand and Isabella, the Spaniards had demanded the expulsion of all professed Jews from Portugal. Reluctant to lose such profitable subjects, Manuel had resorted to the expedient of forcing baptism on many of their number. Baptism enabled these New Christians to penetrate into new spheres of activity—in the fifteenth century, into the financial administration of Castile, and, in the sixteenth, into the spectacular and lucrative colonial trade of Portugal, whose spices passed to northern Europe through the medium of the Antwerp staple. On the other hand, the fact that they had once outwardly accepted Christianity, even under duress, exposed them to the Inquisitor's investigations and penalties. The suspicion—often justified

510

—that they had lapsed into Jewish practices became the pretext for relentless persecution, and a strong incentive to emigrate.[1]

No prolonged settlement of Jewish exiles proved possible in southern Italy. The Spanish monarchy rapidly enforced its expulsion orders in the Aragonese possessions of Sicily and Sardinia. Naples for a time offered shelter, but in 1504 this Kingdom fell irrevocably under Spanish domination. Anti-Jewish measures, against both professed and crypto-Jews, though delayed for a few years, came into force in 1510 and 1514–15. A remnant of rich families was at first allowed to stay, but in 1541 the expulsion became total and unqualified.[2] However, in central and northern Italy, official attitudes were markedly different. Many of the exiles had found toleration and acceptance in the Muslim territories which surrounded the Mediterranean, and especially in the lands later absorbed by the Ottoman Turkish Empire. Their knowledge and skills enriched the Turkish economy. Large Jewish communities arose in Istanbul and Salonica, whilst the importance of Galilee, and especially of Safed, increased both as an economic centre and as one of Jewish scholarship.[3] For states of central and northern Italy deeply interested in Levantine trade, the Levantine Jews became a sought-after prize— and so, occasionally, did Marranos direct from Portugal. The Papacy acquired direct dominion over the port of Ancona during the pontificate of Clement VII, and, eager to promote its trade with the east, encouraged Portuguese Marranos to settle there by granting them safeguards against inquisitorial prosecutions for apostasy.[4] Later, in 1551, Cosimo I de' Medici, the mercantilist Duke of Tuscany, bent on reviving Tuscan trade with the Levant, invited Jews with other Levantine peoples to dwell in his state.[5]

The official Venetian attitude to professed Jews from the Levant (though not to crypto-Jews from Portugal) harmonized with that of the Pope and the Duke. The Venetian government then—as later in the

---

[1] Cf. Cecil Roth, *A history of the Marranos* (Philadelphia, 1932); I. S. Révah, 'Les Marranes', *Revue des études juives*, série iii, vol. I (1959); I. S. Révah, 'Pour l'histoire des Marranes à Anvers', *ibid.*, série iv, vol. II (1963); J. H. Elliott, *Imperial Spain, 1460–1716* (London, 1963), pp. 94–9; Henry Kamen, *The Spanish Inquisition* (London, 1965).

[2] Milano, *Storia degli ebrei*, pp. 216–33; cf. also Roth, *Marranos*, pp. 196–8.

[3] Cf. Cecil Roth, *The House of Nasi: Doña Gracia* (Philadelphia, 1947), pp. 90–7; Simon Schwarzfuchs, 'Les marchands juifs dans la Méditerranée orientale au XVIème siècle', *Annales: Économies, Sociétés, Civilisations*, XII (1957), pp. 117–18; Itzhak Ben-Zvi, 'Eretz Yisrael under Ottoman rule, 1517–1917', in Louis Finkelstein, ed. *The Jews: their history, culture and religion* (2 vols., London, 1961), I, pp. 603, 621– 628; Milano, *Storia degli ebrei*, p. 235.

[4] Roth, *Marranos*, pp. 205–6; Roth, *Doña Gracia*, pp. 134–7.

[5] Umberto Cassuto, *Gli ebrei a Firenze nell'età del Rinascimento* (Florence, 1918), pp. 89–90, 173–5.

century—valued the Jews highly for their experience and skill in handling the trade which converged on the Balkan peninsula. In 1541, as part of a general scheme for the revival of commerce, the Senate determined to provide better conditions for 'itinerant Levantine Jewish merchants (*hebrei mercadanti levantini viandanti*)'—on the grounds that they were handling the greater part of all trade between Venice and the Balkan peninsula. The government's concern for Balkan trade in general appeared from its decision, at the same time, to remove customs duties for the next two years on all goods originating in the Balkans and brought to Venice—except for fats, wines and grains.[6] The concession would probably have affected wool, hides and wax, among other things. Foreign merchants were now to be relieved of many inconveniences and minor irritations which discouraged them from doing business in the city. Levantine Jewish merchants had complained to the board of trade, the Cinque Savii alla Mercanzia, that they had no space in which to live comfortably within the narrow circuit of the Ghetto Nuovo. The Senate therefore agreed to accommodate them, instead, in the Ghetto Vecchio, a small square or *campadello* which lay between the Ghetto Nuovo and the wide canal of Cannaregio. In no way, however, did it abandon the principle that the living quarters of these Jews must be sealed off from those of Christians. The Collegio gave orders to build a wall across the entrance to the square and to block up the doors of three houses which gave on to the outside of the Ghetto Vecchio. The noble proprietor of the Ghetto Vecchio, Leonardo Minotto, was ordered to evict his current tenants, and was promised that the Jews would pay him rents higher by a third than the present ones.[6a] In this he received the same treatment as the owners of the Ghetto Nuovo—but the Senate refused to absolve him, as it had absolved them in 1516, from the obligation to pay taxes on the property.[6b]

The Levantine Jews enjoyed the status of resident aliens; they were not Venetian subjects but Turkish, and had not, like their co-religionists of German or Italian origin, made any formal contract with the Venetian government. They were forbidden to engage in banking or in the second-hand trade, or in any form of economic activity other than 'simplice mercantia'—transporting and exchanging goods. At first the Senate intended to allow them only four months' continuous residence

---

[6] A.S.V., *Senato, Mar, registro 1541/42*, ff. 26v.–28, 2 June 1541. The concession did not extend to silks, spices or other merchandise from Syria, Egypt or Persia arriving in Venice by way of the Balkans. Cf. also L. A. Schiavi, 'Gli ebrei in Venezia e nelle sue colonie', *Nuova Antologia, serie* iii, vol. XLVIII (1893), p. 493.

[6a] A.S.V., *Collegio, Notatorio, registro 1539/42*, f. 120, 155v.–156v., 20 July 1541.

[6b] A.S.V., *Senato, Terra, registro 1540/41*, ff. 134v.–135, 20 July 1541.

at a stretch, but soon increased this to two years,[6c] and they may, later in the century, have obtained still more lenient terms. They certainly became entitled to rent houses in the Ghetto Vecchio for long stretches of time, whether or not they resided there continuously. Thus, in 1585, a Levantine Jew, Judah Passo, could describe how his father David Passo had lived for seventeen years at Number One in the Ghetto Vecchio, a house on two floors, with his wife and children.[6d] Levantine Jews had at first been forbidden to bring their families to Venice.

By 1541, therefore, the government was officially recognizing a second Jewish community, springing up beside the old and performing distinctive economic functions for the benefit of Venice. The Levantine and German Jewish communities did not remain as physically separated from one another as was at first intended—for the Levantine Jews did not wish to occupy all the Minotto houses, and some Jews from the Ghetto Nuovo moved into the Ghetto Vecchio.[6e] For the time being, trade with the Levant had nothing to do with moneylending—but, later in the century, the profits of this commerce were to be enlisted to help finance the loan banks kept by the German Jews for the benefit of the poor of Venice.

To crypto-Jews, and Jews direct from Spain, Portugal and Antwerp, the Venetian attitude was markedly hostile, and did not obviously relent till the last two decades of the sixteenth century. Twice—in 1497 and 1550—the government issued orders for their expulsion. Some Marranos came early to Venice, and their removal was provoked by the alleged malpractices of a small group of rich Spanish–Jewish corn-merchants, including Juan Xanches, Rafael Besalù and Juan Beltrame. Despite their recent expulsion from Sicily, the centre of the grain-trade in the Western Mediterranean, they evidently retained business connexions there, and in March 1497 handled a consignment of 50,000 *staia*. For this they obtained payment at the rate of $7\frac{1}{2}$ lire per *staio*, together with the bounty promised to all who imported corn to Venice before May of that year. This deal proved unprofitable to the Venetian government, which was forced to sell the corn to the public at substantially lower prices. In August, it rejected further proposals by the Spanish merchants on the grounds that the Jews were refusing to offer the Signory 'honest prices'. Resentment and suspicion grew when rumours of Jewish misconduct reached Venice from Sicily, and the Jews were accused of trying to corner the market in exported Sicilian

---

[6c] A.S.V., *Senato, Mar, registro 1541/42*, ff. 46v.–47, 10 September 1541.

[6d] A.S.V., *Ufficiali al Cattaver, busta 243, registro 3*, f. 45—petition dated 18 October 1585, dealt with on 1 March 1586.

[6e] See the remarks of Francesco Morosini and Andrea Basadonna, Ufficiali al Cattaver, 13 June 1586—*ibid.*, ff. 53v.–54.

grain in order to sell it in Venice at exorbitant rates. The truth of the matter is hard to know—but it is possible that the Viceroy of Sicily was making some malicious attempt to incriminate the Jews. The contemporary annalist, Domenico Malipiero, referred to a further import of grain by the Jews which was refused by the Signory as being of too poor quality, but was nevertheless sold by the Jews at high prices on account of the prevailing shortages. Distrust of the Jews for this specific reason arose at a time when Venice was collaborating with Spain in recovering the Neapolitan territories overrun by the French in the invasion of 1494–5. The Venetians could, without much pain, adopt an anti-Jewish attitude superficially consonant with that of their ally, and on 13 November 1497 the Venetian government gave the Marranos settled in Venice itself six months' notice to quit. From Venetian subject territories, including the Apulian cities then under Venetian dominion, many of the Marranos were forced to depart immediately.[7] However, the term Marrano was difficult to define, unless a government were prepared to describe members of all recently converted families as Marranos, on the assumption that they must be reverting to Jewish practices. Such a policy was probably repugnant to the Venetians, who pompously celebrated any Jewish conversions which took place on their own soil. As it happened, both Rafael Besalù and Juan Beltrame lived to die in Venice; both were buried in the Frari, within a few months of each other, in 1514, Beltrame's corpse clothed in a friar's habit; and both were described at the time of their death as rich Marranos.[7a]

Moreover, by the 1540's, Italy had developed into a form of transit-station for outwardly Christianized Jews, often departing illegally from Portugal by way of Flanders, and often headed for the lands of the Turkish Empire, where they might revert unmolested to the Jewish faith. After prolonged delays, the Portuguese had at last introduced an Inquisition on the Spanish model into their country in 1536. In 1539–1540, it had begun activity in earnest, and it acquired unlimited powers in 1547.[8] During the 1530's, certain prominent Jewish entrepreneurs, including Diogo Mendes, a spice-merchant and financier of Antwerp, had devised underground organizations designed to help transcontinental escapes into Turkey. One such organization was run from Venice by Daniel Bomberg, formerly of Antwerp. The Venetian attitude to the Marranos, uncertain for a time, worsened again about 1550. The incident of the Mendes family, in the 1540's, did not improve it by

[7] D.M.S., I, coll. 535, 733, 819; Malipiero, *Annali veneti*, p. 708.
[7a] D.M.S., XVII, coll. 541–2; XIX, col. 25.
[8] Roth, *Marranos*, pp. 66–71; Révah, 'Les Marranes', pp. 36–41.

provoking the unwelcome threat of Turkish interference in the domestic affairs of the Venetians. Gracia, widow of Francisco Mendes, and her sister Brianda, widow of the spice-merchant Diogo Mendes, had left Antwerp in 1544 and headed for Venice. They were the heirs, and Gracia the administrator, of the vast and coveted Mendes fortune. The Venetian government saw a chance to confiscate this when Brianda denounced Gracia as a judaizer. However, it being correctly rumoured that the sisters, like so many other exiles, were headed for Turkey, the Sultan Suleiman also registered interest in the Mendes fortune, and by 1549 there arose the possibility of Turkish intervention to obtain the release of Gracia Mendes. In 1549, she and her sister were allowed to emigrate under safe-conduct to the state of Ferrara, which received them as professing Jews and not as New Christians.[9] Now knowing some of the hazards of exploiting the Marranos, the Venetian government soon afterwards resolved to sever all connexion with them.

On 8 July 1550, the Senate re-enacted the decree of 1497 for the expulsion of the Marranos, described as an 'infectious species of men' and as 'a heathen people, without religion, enemies of the Lord God'. Venetian noblemen, citizens and subjects who had entered into any form of association or understanding with Marranos were ordered to sever all links with them.[9a] The papal nuncio, Ludovico Beccadelli, greeting the decree with delight, reported to Rome that there were supposedly about 10,000 Marranos in Venice at this time, and that they were a menace both to religion and (because of the 'bad contracts they conclude') to trade.[9b] Venetian merchants in general, however, are not likely to have pressed for the July decree, for within a few weeks a group of Rialto businessmen protested to the Doge at the confusion it created. They declared that, to import wool into Venice, most of them depended on companies of Spanish, Catalan and Portuguese merchants active in Florence, who were importing by way of Leghorn and then redistributing wool to the rest of Italy. They, too, controlled supplies of silk, sugar and pepper from the Iberian peninsula, and the Venetians depended on them to send money to Lyons, Flanders and elsewhere. There were other Spanish and Portuguese merchants in Flanders, Lyons, Rome, Naples and Sicily; New Christians in Apulia sent oil, wine and fruit to be sold in Venice, and used the proceeds to purchase cloth there. No doubt some of these merchants were Marranos. If the Venetian merchants played safe, so as to run no risk of incurring the

[9] Roth, *Doña Gracia*, pp. 30 f., 52–64.

[9a] A.S.V., *Senato, Terra, filza* 11, 8 July 1550.

[9b] See Pio Paschini, *Venezia e l'Inquisizione Romana da Giulio III a Pio IV* (Padua, 1959), pp. 40–1.

penalties prescribed by the Senate for those who persisted in dealing with Marranos, they would overturn the existing structure of international trade. 'We do not know what stock men come from, how they live, or what they believe or do not believe.' In response, the Senate, for the protection of Venetian commerce, clarified its law by saying that its intention had never been to prohibit traffic with Marranos resident in foreign countries, but merely to prevent them from settling in Venice or its subject lands. There were limits—at least in Venetian eyes—to the lengths to which any policy of segregation could suitably be pushed. The Senate further resolved to set up machinery to 'make diligent inquisition of those who are called Marranos'—entrusting the investigations to a board consisting of the Censori and of the recently-established Inquisition.[90] With what success they proceeded is not yet known—though Venice's extensive trading connexions made it certain that the process of eliminating the Marranos without damaging commerce would always be an extremely complicated and delicate one.

Jealousy and suspicion of their commercial activities, resentment and frustration at the possibility of Turkish intervention on their behalf, cannot, however, fully explain the attitude of the Venetian government to the Marranos. The expulsion order of 1550 coincided with a period of marked deterioration in the status and prosperity of the Jews of Venice and the Venetian dominions. From 1547 onwards, several subject cities and towns raised apparently spontaneous demands for the total suppression of moneylending by the Jews, and for the curtailment of their other economic activities, especially of the manufacture and sale of textiles. The Venetian government acceded willingly enough to these requests, and at the same time pursued an unmistakable policy of increasing the burdens of the Jews by stepping up taxation and reducing the legal rate at which Jewish bankers were permitted to lend. Understandably, this policy provoked—as perhaps was intended—extensive Jewish emigration; and—a less calculated, and from all points of view a less desirable result—produced grave instability in the Jewish banks in Venice itself. A necessary complement to this was the foundation of Monti di Pietà in areas (especially the Polesine di Rovigo and parts of the Trevigiano) which had not previously known them, or where earlier foundations had collapsed through corruption, inefficiency or sheer lack of charitable funds.

One clear explanation for this revival of hostility towards the Jews lies in the hardening of religious attitudes which had become very visible in the 1540's at Rome and elsewhere. There was an increasing

[90] A.S.V., *Senato, Terra, filza* 11, 22 August 1550; *registro* 1550/51, ff. 43v.–44, 29 August 1550.

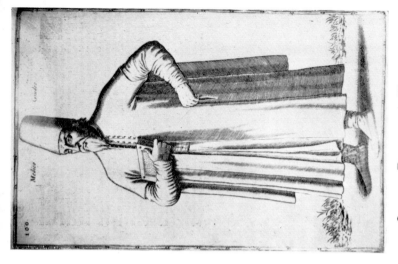

JEWISH DOCTOR IN TURKEY

For the influence of Jews (including Jewish physicians) at the court of the Ottoman Sultan, see below, pp. 538–9.

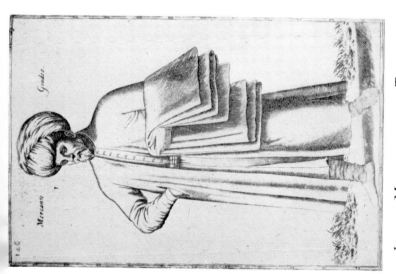

JEWISH MERCHANT FROM TURKEY

'Levantine' Jews in Venice, who were Turkish subjects, probably looked like this.

facing p. 516

JEWISH WEDDING *and* LIGHTING THE LIGHTS

facing p. 517

determination to define, protect and extend Catholic orthodoxy by systematic campaigns both of repression and of evangelism. The 1540's saw papal confirmation and acceptance of the Jesuit Order; the gradual eclipse of the moderates at Rome, and the growing prominence of reformers as rigorous as Giovanni Pietro Caraffa, the future Pope Paul IV, who after 1542 assumed, with Juan Alvarez de Toledo, Cardinal of Burgos, the direction of the revived Roman Inquisition; the first sessions of the Council of Trent; the outbreak of open warfare between the Emperor Charles V and the Protestant princes of Germany. Venetian policy towards the Jews bore some relation to that newly adopted in the Papal States, especially during the pontificate of Paul IV (1555–9). In the 1540's, the Roman Inquisition was reintroduced into Venice. The Venetians, as if to guard against violations of their jealously guarded temporal jurisdiction, insisted that a commission of three noblemen known as Tre Savii sopra l'Eresia should sit as part of the tribunal.[10] But the effect of this, as the nuncio Beccadelli himself bore witness, was to lend added authority to the Inquisition, rather than to limit its scope.[10a] The government, in the nuncio's view, often proved itself eager to co-operate in repressing heresy in its dominions, and in resisting the infection of alien faiths.[10b] Jews who had never embraced Christianity were not, like the Marranos, subject to the Inquisition. But a war on heresy could easily hinge over into campaigns against the Jew and the infidel. Cardinal Verallo, of the Inquisition at Rome, protested vehemently to the Venetian ambassador in December 1550 that 800 copies of the Talmud were in the press at Venice, that these were 'the most pestilential Jewish attacks on the Christian religion that could ever be found, and the whole of Jewry only has six or seven copies, and because of their scarcity there used to be very few Jews who knew anything of their own law—but now, with so many available, they will put their children to study them as soon as they emerge from the womb'.[10c] Accusations of laxity towards heretics were thus accompanied by accusations of indulgence towards Jews. Indeed, two Venetian noblemen, Marco Antonio Giustinian and Alvise Bragadin, had within the past five years established rival presses for the production of Jewish books—since the Jews were officially forbidden to do any printing themselves. However, in 1553, Beccadelli, acting on

[10] Pastor, *History of the Popes*, XII, pp. 503–6, 510–11; XIII, pp. 210–11.

[10a] Cf. Beccadelli's description of the tribunal, in a letter of 23 September 1551, in Paschini, *Venezia e l'Inquisizione*, pp. 79–80.

[10b] *Ibid.*, pp. 37–8, 112–13. Cf. also Edouard Pommier, 'La société vénitienne et la Réforme protestante au XVIe siècle', *Bollettino dell'Istituto di Storia della Società e dello Stato Veneziano*, I (1959), pp. 4–6.

[10c] Paschini, *Venezia e l'Inquisizione*, pp. 65–6.

2L

instructions from Rome, eventually succeeded in getting all known copies of the Talmud, whether owned by the Jews or still on Gius-tinian's premises, publicly burnt at San Marco and Rialto.[10d]

In addition to these direct attacks, the Venetian government, by no means out of sympathy with Roman aims, began to apply economic and fiscal pressure to the Jews—often in response to representations from particular centres on the mainland. Attacks on the Jews in the next two decades were probably designed, not merely to secure still better terms for the poor in the small-loan business, but also to restore the Jews to their proper position of subordination and prevent them from acquiring and exercising economic power over Christians. This motive was declared in the notorious anti-Jewish Bull, 'Cum nimis absurdum', issued in 1555 by Paul IV, and there are hints of it in Venetian policy. However, the correspondence between Venetian and Roman policy need not imply that Venice was merely responding obediently to Roman pressure. It is very likely that spontaneous public and official opinion in Venice favoured an anti-Jewish policy, with which the Papacy later concurred. The petitions of subject towns against the Jews antedated the legislation of Paul IV by several years, though they did not anticipate the revival of the Inquisition; and Paul IV's policy of segregation added relatively little to that adopted by the Venetians in 1516. Likewise, the Venetian attack on the Marranos in 1550 preceded by five years the treacherous act of Paul IV, when, violating the guarantees given by his predecessors Paul III and Julius III, he sent commissioners to investigate the orthodoxy of Portuguese Jewish settlers in Ancona.[11]

In November 1547, representatives of Crema, formerly one of Chaim Meshullam's spheres of interest, drew attention to a privilege of 1499, which had forbidden Jews to lend in the city without first obtaining the consent of a two-thirds majority within the local Council. The Venetian Senate, on being informed that the local Monte di Pietà would be able to meet all demands for credit likely to be made upon it, agreed to order that the 'privilege' should be observed—which, in effect, meant prohibiting Jewish lending.[12] About a month later, a deputation from Verona requested that on the expiration of the current *condotta* in October 1548 the local Jews should be forbidden to lend upon usury either in the city itself or in its surrounding territory. The Senate then forbade the Jews to lend, either in Verona or in Conegliano. On

---

[10d] *Ibid.*, pp. 108–11.

[11] Pastor, *History of the Popes*, XIV, pp. 271 f.; and especially Roth, *Doña Gracia*, ch. VII, pp. 134–75.

[12] A.S.V., *Senato, Terra, filza* 6, 5 November 1547.

17 December 1547, the Senate agreed to a similar petition from Padua
—perhaps the greatest centre of Jewish banking in the Republic, outside the capital itself.[13] Jewish lending had rapidly expanded in Padua
after its re-establishment there before or during the 1520's. It obviously
fulfilled an urgent local need, especially among the University students,
and opinion in Padua was divided. The Faculty of Law, or Università
dei Legisti, made unsuccessful representations that the Jews should not
be forbidden to lend to students—a demand which they repeated in
1548 and 1563.[14] On the other hand, demands that Jewish lending be
suppressed—at least from Verona[15]—were not without precedents. But
they had never permanently choked Jewish banking, which now seems
to have been effectively suspended in these cities, and not to have
revived at any time during the period under review. All the communes
concerned professed to be able to rely for small loans on their well-
endowed and firmly-established Monti di Pietà. The Paduans stated in
1547 that the capital of their Monte now stood at over 60,000 ducats,
whilst a more detailed statistic, submitted in October 1554 by the
governor Marc'Antonio Grimani, estimated the total working capital
of this Monte at 99,900 ducats.[16]

Anti-Jewish sentiment was by no means confined to the larger towns
endowed with substantial Monti di Pietà—nor did it express itself
solely through constitutional channels. Two pogroms occurred in the
little town of Asolo in the Trevigiano in 1544 and again in 1547.
According to the Jews, the peasants of the *contado* round Asolo,
rather than the townspeople, were their most savage enemies. Thirty-
nine peasants received sentences of banishment in 1544 after an attack
on the Jews. Some returned from exile in August 1547, whereupon the
Council of Ten wrote to the authorities of Treviso and Asolo exhorting
them to protect the Jews. But the governors failed to prevent a fresh
outbreak of violence on 22 November 1547, when 14 Jews were murdered and others wounded in a 'savage and bloody slaughter', and
when the peasants sacked the possessions of Jews and the pledges they
were holding in their banks. The following year, since popular resentment was obviously running so high against the Jews, the Senate
agreed to forbid Jewish banking in Asolo as well. One petition from
the commune of Asolo shrugged off the pogroms with the words 'if, in
the 36 villages of our territory, some persons among so great a number
have transgressed the limits of reason, they have suffered the punish-

---

[13] A.S.V., *Senato, Terra, registro 1547/48*, ff. 87v.–88, 94r.–v.
[14] Ciscato, *Ebrei in Padova*, pp. 61–3.
[15] See above, p. 460, and Fortis, 'Ebrei di Verona', XI, p. 301.
[16] See his report in A.S.V., *Collegio, Relazioni, busta* 43, at ff. 6v.–7.

ment which justice required'. The Asolans—following what was now becoming the standard procedure—sent in a certificate from the Podestà to prove that their Monte di Pietà (endowed with a modest capital of 3,000 lire) was in a thriving state, and promised to maintain it in good working order. The Jews pointed out that their banking activities could not possibly harm the Monte di Pietà, because its rates were lower than theirs, and 'anyone not totally devoid of sense will pay the lower interest rate rather than the higher'. No doubt they hoped to carry on business because of the inadequate capital of the Monte, and because they followed somewhat different rules in making their loans. Evidently they were prepared to risk further outbreaks of violence. But their arguments availed them nothing. The Senate eventually determined that the Jews should be permitted to remain in Asolo and to exercise all trades permitted by the *condotta*—other than moneylending. They should also be entitled to exact old debts, due to them on account of their past operations.[17]

In view of the declared hostility to the Jews in many localities on the mainland, it was scarcely surprising that the Venetian Senate should choose (in December 1548) to impose far harsher terms on the Jews at the next *condotta*. During the debate in Venice itself, two members of the Collegio, Tommaso Mocenigo and Hieronimo Polani, proposed that, since the acceptance of usury was utterly prohibited, the Jews should be forbidden to make loans in any part of the Venetian dominions—but should be allowed to continue with their other traditional activities. This experiment should be tried for a period of one year, in which the Jews should pay taxes at the lowered rate of 5,000 ducats per annum. However, such suggestions were too radical, and the Senate chose instead to increase the taxation paid by the Jews whilst at the same time cutting their interest charges. The initial proposal was to increase the tax to 12,000 ducats a year, all included—an advance of over 70 per cent on the earlier basic tax of 5,850 ducats plus 1,150 in rent for the banks of Mestre and Padua.[18] However, under this proposal, Jewish interest rates would have been allowed to continue at their former level. Eventually, however, the Senate amended the *capitoli*, so as to compel the Jews to pay taxes at the rate of 10,000 ducats a year, and to prevent them from exacting more than 12 per cent interest on any loan. This was a severe blow, especially to mainland bankers, who had been accustomed to charge 20 per cent; in Venice

[17] A.S.V., *Senato, Terra, filza* 8, 24 September 1548. The authority quoted in Milano, *Storia degli ebrei*, p. 285, says that the community in November 1547 consisted of 37 Jews, and that the peasant bands killed ten and seriously injured another eight.

[18] See above, p. 506.

520

itself, the highest permitted rate had been 15 per cent. These increases in taxation could not be justified on the grounds that Venice was engaged in war. Rather, it was as if the Jews had now enjoyed their appointed term of liberty, and as if their accumulated wealth was now to be wrung from them. Apart from this, there were relatively few significant changes in the conditions on which the Jews were to be allowed to work and live under the Republic's protection. In Venice, they could still (as in 1528)[19] engage in the second-hand trade, and make or sell veils and coifs; they were expressly forbidden to act as tailors or furriers, or to sell new materials. On the mainland, in areas not forbidden to them by decree of the legislative councils of Venice, they could not only lend at interest (*fenerare*), but also engage in trade (*mercadantare*). However, they were now forbidden to print or publish books, though they were still entitled to buy and sell them, and to finish those works they had already begun to produce. They were to pay only the general tax or *tansa* imposed on all Jews by the *condotta*, would not be liable for local taxation, and were expressly exempted from any obligation to billet soldiers in their rented houses.[20]

Moreover, to enforce its decrees, the Senate conferred additional powers on the governors of mainland territories in October 1551, by authorizing them to condemn to galley service, imprisonment or heavy fines all Jews caught lending at interest in areas barred to them by recent enactments.[21] It also found the need to provide—in 1553—that Christians should not purchase Jewish credits, and exact the debts owing to Jewish lenders, molesting communes and imprisoning private men for debt. This, or so the words of the decree claimed, destroyed the entire purpose of the government's former contracts with the Jews, since

> this Council has permitted the Jews to dwell in our dominions for the sole purpose of preventing Christians from lending upon usury in violation both of the divine and of the civil laws.[22]

By such practices, Christians would make themselves accomplices in the sin of usury.

From the late 1540's, it became increasingly difficult, even for communities which wished to tolerate the Jews, to contract with them as moneylenders. The proposition that a Jew should lend at only 12 per cent seemed at this time to be totally uneconomic: perhaps such low

---

[19] See above, p. 506.
[20] A.S.V., *Senato, Deliberazioni (Secreta)*, reg. 1548/49, ff. 54v.–57, 19 December 1548.
[21] A.S.V., *Senato, Terra*, reg. 1551–2, f. 22, 17 October 1551.
[22] A.S.V., *Senato, Terra*, reg. 1553–4, f. 19v., 9 May 1553.

rates, combined with such high taxation, had never been tried. Contracts with Jews did not apparently run concurrently in all individual localities, and the *condotta* with the Jewish banker of Rovigo, capital of the low-lying Polesine, was not due to expire until the end of 1550. Nicolò Nani, governor of Rovigo, sent to Venice for approval the proposed agreement with a Jew who was willing to lend—but at 20 per cent. The Venetian government stuck to its prescribed policy, and demanded that he lower the rate of interest to 12 per cent only. The only practicable possibility lay in a Monte di Pietà. The governor Nani claimed that the Jew had been the ruin of the local poor, lending money at fully 25 per cent, though it transpired that he was perfectly entitled to do this under the terms of his agreement with the municipal authorities. In one of his letters to the Senate, the governor expressed a preference for either the erection of a new Monte di Pietà or the re-establishment of a 'feeble' one, founded some years before with a capital of 500–600 ducats only, by the then governor, Giovanni Alvise, son of Zaccaria Grimani. The Venetian Senate, as if well satisfied, authorized the establishment of a new Monte di Pietà in Rovigo on 27 June 1551. The Polesine was a province in an especially precarious condition, since it was liable to flooding, and was also one which absorbed much Venetian capital in the effort to reclaim land and partially solve the insistent population problem. The governors of Rovigo expected the Monte to be especially beneficial in tiding the poor over the years when the waters destroyed the harvests, and in enabling them to pay their taxes.[23]

Rovigo was not the only town in the Polesine to acquire a Monte di Pietà at this time: the neighbouring communes of La Badia and Lendenara, which lay to the south of the Adige, likewise did so in 1550–4. There, however, the project failed to command the approval of the local Venetian governor, who thought it improvident and premature. In June 1552, the Podestà of La Badia, one of the family of Tron, wrote as follows on the economics of establishing a Monte di Pietà in a small town or village:

> I say that when the commune finds itself disposing of at least 1,500 ducats for the purpose of establishing a Monte di Pietà, it will be a thing of great profit and benefit to this place and to the welfare of its poor inhabitants. But as there are only 500 ducats which belong to a local confraternity that is offering them of its own free will, it does not seem to me that they should be allowed to establish the Monte on the basis of so small a sum.

[23] A.S.V., *Senato, Terra*, reg. 1550–1, ff. 146v.–147; correspondence with the governor Nicolò Nani and the former governor Giovanni Alvise di Zaccaria Grimani, *ibid.*, *filza* 13, 27 June 1551.

If a Monte were erected, it would be necessary for the Jewish bankers who reside here and dispense plenty of funds to everyone to remove themselves.

If only the aforesaid 500 ducats remain, they will be adequate to satisfy barely one-third of those who have need of some assistance by this means.

In spite of this warning, the Senate overrode the Podestà and authorized the establishment of a local Monte di Pietà.[24] Nevertheless, the attempt to eliminate Jewish lending in the Polesine proved, in the years which followed, much less successful than in Padua, Verona or Crema. From its early years the Rovigo Monte suffered from an imperfect, if not actually chaotic, system of accounting which made it exceptionally easy for its administrators to perpetrate frauds. Inefficiency and active corruption consumed a large fraction of its available funds, especially through the misconduct and peculation of its Massari at the turn of the century. Even in the 1570's, the decade when hatred and distrust of the Jews mounted to its disagreeable climax, the area surrounding Rovigo depended on Jewish loans to supplement the inadequate supplies of the Christian bank.[25]

In this period of population pressure and recurrent famine, the expulsion of Jewish bankers would surely have been impracticable had not the system of Monti di Pietà been extended. Several new foundations were made in the course of the next twenty years, including one at Bergamo in 1557.[26] Bergamo was possibly the only subject city of over 10,000 inhabitants not to possess a Monte di Pietà before the middle of the century. Although the Bergamasco was a poor and naturally barren area, from which extensive emigration took place, the urgency of establishing a Monte di Pietà there had been greatly reduced by the existence of well-endowed hospitals of medieval origin, and still more by the widespread network of charitable fraternities or Misericordie, both in Bergamo itself and in the countryside. More typical, and perhaps more urgent, were the foundations of Monti in smaller towns near the border between the province of Treviso and the Patria di Friuli: at Uderzo in 1565, at Sacile in 1566, and at Motta in 1575.[27] In the last quarter of the century, when plague had cut back the population of Venice and certain parts of the Veneto, and when religious ardour against the Jews was cooling, the Senate records reveal no new foundations of Monti di Pietà.

[24] A.S.V., *Senato, Terra, filza* 16, 6 October 1552, *filza* 19, 24 April 1554.
[25] A.S.V., *Collegio, Relazioni*, b. 46, reports of Francesco Moro, 17 April 1564, and Pietro Marcello, 28 May 1574; cf. below, pp. 537 f.
[26] A.S.V., *Senato, Terra, filza* 25, 13 July 1557.
[27] A.S.V., *Senato, Terra*, reg. 1564–5, ff. 48v., 193–8, *filza* 45, 9 December 1565; reg. 1566–7, ff. 57–63, *filza* 46, 31 August 1566; *filza* 66, 28 June 1575.

At this time, Monti di Pietà were not merely being extended into new areas. They were beginning to discover new sources of working capital, and thereby enlarging the sums available to the poor and to other borrowers. The original foundations of the late fifteenth century had raised funds mainly through the generosity of charitable donors— but their early statutes had sometimes visualized the possibility of 'deposits' of money being made on the premises of the Monte. Such deposits did not become the property of the Monte in the same sense as moneys left or given to it outright by the charitable. But the Monte was entitled to use such sums for the benefit of the poor of the district, and to lend them on pledge, so long as it was always prepared to restore the depositor's money on receiving due notice. Some or all of these early deposits were made without the depositor receiving any interest on the money he had made available to the Monte: the Monte, by keeping it safe in its coffers within stout walls, was serving the depositor, and not the other way about. However, during the first half of the sixteenth century, two fresh demands began to be heard. The Monte di Pietà itself wished to provide new incentives to the depositor by offering him a modest rate of interest on his capital. To take a typical example, by borrowing from investors at 4 per cent, and lending at 6 per cent, the Monte di Pietà might be able to transact business on a much larger scale, and could even extend its activity—like the Jewish banks—to include loans to non-paupers who needed ready cash. At the same time, the general public welcomed any increase in investment opportunities, and especially perhaps in the kind of safe opening which the Monte di Pietà appeared to offer. In theory, it was unethical to invest in a Monte di Pietà and receive interest on one's capital simply out of a desire to lock it up in a safe security: but it is difficult not to believe that this motive in fact weighed heavily with many investors.

It seems impossible to say exactly when the Italian Monti di Pietà began to act as deposit banks in this sense. But in all probability, the Monte di Pietà in Florence, its funds exhausted during the prolonged siege of the last Florentine Republic in 1529–30, was subsequently reconstituted largely through the acceptance of interest-bearing deposits of this kind.[28] Certainly, by the 1540's and '50's, the highest authority in the Catholic Church was beginning to recognize the practice as legitimate, subject to certain conditions. In 1542, Paul III, on the intercession of Cardinal Giacomo Sadoleto, had granted the governing body

---

[28] According to Thomaso Buoninsegni, *Trattato de' traffichi giusti et ordinarii*, translated from the Latin by Vitale Zuccoli (Venice, 1588), f. 145r.–v. Buoninsegni, a Dominican from Siena, was described on the title-page of this work as a lecturer in theology at the University of Florence. On this theme in general, see Garrani, *Carattere dei Monti di Pietà*, and Lapeyre, 'Banque et crédit en Italie'.

of the Monte di Pietà in Modena permission to pay interest on deposits at the rate of 5 per cent, for the purpose of increasing the funds available for the Monte to lend to the local inhabitants.[29] This practice soon spread to the Veneto—or, at least, soon obtained recognition there. In 1547, the city council of Vicenza passed a decree to the effect that deposits of money could now be made in the Monte and recorded in a special book kept for this purpose by its officials, and that depositors should be entitled to receive interest at the rate of 4 per cent. All such deposits could be withdrawn on one month's notice. The Vicentines justified this step on the grounds that the Monte di Pietà had found its moneys hopelessly insufficient to deal with the increase in population and hence in the number of paupers. Formerly capable of lending sums of five ducats at a time, it had now been compelled to reduce the maximum loan to one ducat only. The Vicentines obtained confirmation of their decree from Rome some years later, in Julius III's brief 'Salvator noster' of 8 January 1555.[30] This brief developed into a well-known precedent, and was used, for example, as the authority for re-establishing a system of interest-bearing deposits when the decayed Monte di Pietà of Rovigo was resuscitated in 1608.[31] However, it was not apparently the first such concession made to a Venetian city. According to Julius III's brief, the people of Vicenza had acted in the knowledge that the Veronese had already received an apostolic indult authorizing them to adopt measures of this kind. Indeed, in 1544 the citizens of Verona had obtained permission from Venice to enlarge the scope and activity of their Monte 'by issuing orders to lend any sum of money to any kind of person on the security of pledges of equivalent value'.[32]

This growth (potential or actual) in the resources of some of the Monti, and this broadening of their activities, made the attack on the economic functions of the Jews practicable. With this new stage in their development, the Monti were capable of providing a more complete substitute for the Jews: especially if, as in Verona, they were prepared to lend to 'any kind of person'. Conceivably, the problem of population pressure had led, by some tortuous and indirect process, to a greater anxiety on the part of authority to make funds available for the relief of the poor, coupled with the sense that existing funds were

[29] Pietro Ballerini, *De jure divino et naturali circa usuram* (2 vols., Bologna, 1747), prints this brief of Paul III, 'Charitatis opera', from copies in the statute book of the Monte itself and in the Registers of Paul III in the Vatican. See vol. II, pp. 239–40.

[30] This appears from the text of the brief, printed, *ibid.*, II, pp. 243–5. Cf. also Zech, *Rigor moderatus*, pp. 198–9; Buoninsegni, *Trattato*, f. 144v.

[31] A.S.V., *Senato, Terra, filza* 188, 13 October 1608.

[32] A.S.V., *Senato, Terra, filza* 14, 2 December 1551.

inadequate. The increase of poverty may have made the relatively high interest charges of the Jews seem positively outrageous, and have provoked incidents like the pogroms at Asolo. Through the Monti di Pietà, a replacement for Jewish lending was now at hand, and the citizens of Verona, Padua, Crema, Conegliano and Asolo felt able to rely on them completely. Unfortunately, not much evidence is available about the extent of interest-bearing deposits in the Venetian Monti di Pietà in the middle of the sixteenth century. But it is possible to say, from a governor's report of 1554, that deposits of one kind or another constituted as much as 55 per cent of the working capital of the Monte di Pietà in Padua at this time, whereas only 33 per cent of the capital originated in charitable gifts or bequests. The statistic, however, fails to indicate how large a proportion of the deposits bore interest.[33] Rather better figures have survived for the new Monte di Pietà at Rovigo. In October 1554, the Monte's own capital—given to it outright by the charitably-minded—amounted to some 4,000 ducats. Deposits at 6 per cent added another 2,600 ducats to this, and thus constituted about 40 per cent of the total working capital. Whether the Monte continued to lend at 5 per cent, when so high a proportion of its capital came from 6 per cent deposits, or whether it increased the rates charged on at least some of its loans, is not yet known. In the next ten years, the proportions changed significantly; charitable funds increased very little, whereas deposits (not necessarily all at 6 per cent) rose by 150 per cent or more. In April 1564, charitable funds owned by the Monte stood at 4,379 ducats, whereas deposits of all kinds amounted to a total of 6,813 ducats.[34]

Religious and economic causes, together with innovations in banking techniques, were combining against the Jews. Demands for their outright expulsion, common in the fifteenth century, were, however, very rare, and seem to have issued only from the city of Udine, the capital of Friuli. In the summer of 1556, the Senate ratified articles drawn up at the request of the inhabitants by Giacomo, brother of the Luogotenente Domenico Bollani: these articles gave the Jews six months to leave Udine.[35] Local anti-semitism had probably been inflamed by the epidemic of plague which broke out in the mid-1550's, and the ejection of the Jews may have been intended as the expulsion of ill-luck, as a

[33] The report of Marc'Antonio Grimani, 3 August 1554, ff. 6v.–7, in A.S.V., *Collegio, Relazioni*, b. 43, shows that the capital of the Monte itself, in the form of *elemosine*, stood at 33,500 ducats; deposits amounted to 54,000 ducats, and the total working capital to 99,000 ducats. For the other elements in this, see below, p. 585.

[34] Reports of Giovanni Francesco Salamon, 27 October 1554, and Francesco Moro, 17 April 1564, A.S.V., *Collegio, Relazioni*, b. 46.

[35] A.S.V., *Senato, Terra, filza* 23, 6 June 1556.

means of assuaging the wrath of God, or as a pious act of thanksgiving for the passing of the scourge.

More common were attacks on the Jews in their capacity of usurers, and objections to their engaging in activities which ought theoretically to have been the monopoly of Christian guildsmen. In the first half of the century, Jews had, in Venice itself, been restricted mainly to money-lending and the second-hand trade. But such regulations did not generally operate on the mainland possessions of the Venetian Republic, where Jews, if forbidden to own land or real property, were entitled to engage in 'commerce' (*mercadantar*) of all kinds. Already, by 1545, the City Council of Padua was attempting to confine the Jews to *strazzaria*, the trade in second-hand clothing, and to prevent them from selling gold and silver objects, new cloth, and materials such as silk, velvets and brocades.[36] A few years later, in the small town of Castelfranco, to the west of Treviso, the Podestà Marc'Antonio Bembo proceeded to investigate the activities of the Jew Solomon, who had until recently kept a loan bank in the town. After examining wool-carders who worked in the Jew's house, and tailors who bought cloth of various qualities from him, the Podestà concluded that

> he alone among these Jews engages in the wholesale trade in cheap and fine cloth of every kind.

Solomon, a versatile entrepreneur, was also engaged in the second-hand trade. The Venetian Senate, now eager to curtail activities other than moneylending among the Jews, acted on the report by ordaining that all Jews who were manufacturing goods on their own account should register with the governors under whose jurisdiction they lived within the next eight days. Within one month, they must cease all activity of this kind. This was a general veto which applied to the entire Venetian mainland, and not merely to Castelfranco.[37]

The prohibition on manufacturing was not, however, equivalent to a total veto on engaging in any form of traffic in new, as distinct from second-hand, goods. The Jewish *condotta* issued in 1558 brought, for the first and indeed the only time, a comprehensive restriction of this kind which set out to confine the Jews of the mainland to the second-hand trade. They, like the Venetian Jews, were to deal only in *strazzaria*, and not to sell new goods of any kind. The term *strazzaria* was not to include certain kinds of 'knitted' or 'woollen' goods. The Jews were never to act as tailors, furriers or printers: these professions the Senate again, as in 1548, expressly closed to them. Pressure from guilds-

---

[36] Ciscato, *Ebrei in Padova*, pp. 98–9.
[37] A.S.V., *Senato, Terra, filza* 19, 28 May 1554.

men and mercers, through town councils on the mainland, contributed to this measure—though the attitude of consumers to Jewish trading tended to differ considerably from that of merchants or manufacturers who believed their livelihood to be threatened by it. The University of Padua saw the Jews as welcome competitors to the Christian guilds, which could otherwise, as unchallenged monopolists, have demanded what prices they liked of the unfortunate student body. After the issue of the *condotta* in 1558, the Faculty of Law, and even (by a narrow majority) the city council itself, resolved to support the Jews of Padua in their attempts to get the prohibition revoked. For this, as it happened, they waited in vain for the next eight years, until the issue of the new *condotta*.[38]

Venetian policy towards the Jews coincided in all essentials, at this time, with that of the reigning pontiff, Paul IV. His Bull, 'Cum nimis absurdum', issued on 14 July 1555, had declared that his purpose was to destroy the prosperity of the Jews in the Papal States. The Jews had taken advantage of the toleration extended to them by Christians; they had exploited their licence to mingle with them in order to abandon their servile status and claim 'mastery' or *dominatum* over Christians. They lived among Christians without any distinction of dress; they dwelt near churches, and bought houses in the more fashionable and prosperous quarters of the cities in which they lived. They employed Christian nurses, maids and other servants. But the Jews, so long as they persisted in their error, must acknowledge themselves slaves, whilst Christians had been freed by the sacrifice of their Redeemer. The relationship between Jew and Christian must find outward, visible and material expression, through the physical humiliation of the Jew and his segregation from the Christian. In prescribing separate Jewish quarters and distinctive badges, in prohibiting the ownership of real property, Paul IV was going no further than the Venetian Republic had already gone, at least in the capital itself.[39] Already, in 1547, the Council of Padua had resolved to petition the Senate in Venice to confine the Paduan Jews in a ghetto, not only to prevent sexual intercourse between persons of different religious persuasions, but also to eliminate the scandal that the Corpus Christi procession should have

---

[38] For the text of the Venetian *condotta*, see A.S.V., *Senato, Terra, filza* 28, 16 November 1558; for its effect, see papers submitted by the Jews of Venice, *ibid.*, *filza* 44, 6 August 1565, and by the Jew Simeon on behalf of the Jews of Padua in the course of a later dispute, in *ibid.*, *filza* 96, 31 December 1585. Simeon asserted that the *condotte* of 1491, 1520, 1529 and 1548 had permitted the Jews to sell and deal in new goods rather than *strazzaria*. Only the *condotta* of 1558 had deprived them of this right, which the Senate restored in 1566. Cf. also Ciscato, *Ebrei in Padova*, pp. 111 f.

[39] Paul IV, 'Cum nimis absurdum', B.R., VI, pp. 498–500.

to pass 'through streets which the false Jews inhabit, for they have the richest and most beautiful houses in all the streets of Padua'.[40] Paul IV's prohibition on Jews employing Christian servants was echoed in Venice a few years later by decree of the Patriarch Giovanni Trevisan.[41] The most striking coincidence, however, lay in the determination, both of the Pope in 1555, and of the Venetian government in 1554–8, to restrict all forms of Jewish trade, except in second-hand goods. Paul IV likewise attempted to confine the Jews to moneylending and *strazzaria* only, and specifically forbade them to deal in corn, barley or any other form of victuals. Venice's preoccupations focused mainly on the textile industry and the marketing of cloth.

In the late 1550's and the following decade, the leaders of the Jewish community of Venice itself submitted memoranda to government offices, and also to the Senate, which starkly revealed the deterioration in the strength and prosperity of Venetian and mainland Jewry. These were, of course, the pleas of a party interested in the reduction of taxation and the lightening of its own distress—but there is no reason to rule them out of court. The Jews wasted little time on pathetic eloquence, but concentrated on a number of bald, factual statements, which the Senate could presumably have verified quite easily. Between 1548 and 1556–8, or so the Jews claimed, taxpayers responsible for producing 4,346 of the 10,000 ducats levied annually on the Jewish community from 1548 onwards had either emigrated or gone bankrupt. All the Jews of Crema—responsible for taxes of 800 ducats a year— had emigrated, together with the smaller communities of Montagnana and Castelfranco, and with some Jews of Padua. At the time when the Jews prepared the first of these memorials, the community of Udine had not yet suffered expulsion, though the plague epidemic had damaged their fortunes and the sanitary authorities had burned much of their property as being liable to convey infection. The Jews of Udine were, however, assessed at some 450 ducats, so that their removal would have brought the loss of tax-capacity up to a total of 4,800 ducats. A list of emigrants submitted with the memorandum included the names of Volpino, Simon, Prospero and Abram of Crema; Isachino and Leon of Verona; Lazzarino of Bergamo; Lazarus of Padua; 'The Widow (*la vedoa*)' of Cittadella; Joseph and Vita of Montagnana; Esdras of Rovigo; Joseph of Treviso; Jacob of Castelfranco; Zaccaria of Conegliano; Mendlin of Udine; Armelina of Cividale; and Dolce of

[40] Ciscato, *Ebrei in Padova*, pp. 75–7.

[41] M.C.V., Cicogna MSS. 2583, 'Variorum ad Venetam Ecclesiam atque ipsius Veneti cleri spectantia', vol. II, f. 95v. By this the Patriarch ordered all parish priests and curates to admonish their flocks not to perform domestic services for the Jews or to suckle or take care of their children.

Pola. In the years which followed, the roll-call of the departed continued to lengthen, as did the list of Jewish banking failures.[42]

In 1565, the Venetian Jewish Council submitted a list of eleven firms which had lent money under the terms of the *condotte* of 1548 and 1558, some, if not all of them, in Venice itself. In 1558, there were basically three banks in existence simultaneously in the Venetian Ghetto, though the bankers were entitled to extend their concessions to others, and this and later *condotte* referred to 'quelli che hanno causa da loro'. The eleven firms listed were as follows:

> Mendlin, son of Angelo.
> The brothers Mendlin and Jacob, sons of Consiglio.
> The brothers Salamoncino and Cervo, sons of Solomon.
> Simon, son of Caliman.
> Caliman, son of Grassino.
> Leon Luzzatto, son of Moses.
> Abram Luzzatto, son of Moses.
> Jacob of Serravalle.
> The nephews of Jacob of Serravalle.
> The brothers Marco and Benedetto of Cividale, sons of Raphael.
> Anselmino and Nasimbene, the nephews of Simon, son of Caliman.

In 1565, the Jewish Council represented that the last four years had seen the disastrous bankruptcy of Mendlin, son of Angelo, assessed for taxation at 500 ducats, and of 'other Jews who had deposited money with him', assessed at another 200. One Jew, liable for 250 ducats, had departed to bank under the more benign conditions offered by the Duchy of Mantua, and two other residents of Padua had also departed, thereby disposing of a further 250 ducats in taxes. Worst of all, the loan bank of Mendlin and Jacob, the sons of Consiglio, was said with perfect accuracy to be tottering on the verge of collapse. Its creditors, who had fatally lost confidence in the bank, referred with agitation to its 'titubatione' and to their own fear of a second Jewish failure for a total sum of over 150,000 ducats.[43] Mendlin, son of Consiglio, paid taxes at the rate of 780 ducats a year. The last two banks on the list were also described as having 'come to grief (*venuti al manco*)', and

---

[42] Papers submitted by the Venetian Jewish community, in A.S.V., *Senato, Terra, filza* 44, 6 August 1565, and *filza* 46, 16 March 1566. The list referred to here is not expressly described as a list of emigrants—but it seems legitimate to deduce from its context and contents that that is what it is.

[43] Petition of these creditors, A.S.V., *Senato, Terra, filza* 44, 6 August 1565; cf. also the later petition of the creditors of Salamoncino and Cervo, *ibid.*, *filza* 50, 27 September 1567.

as unlikely to continue to lend. Banking had now become a heavy and dangerous burden, not a source of profit, and in 1565 the Jews begged the Senate not to assign them the responsibility of deciding who was to lend. If the figures submitted by the Jewish Council were accurate and truthful—and they themselves were responsible for the apportionment of the fiscal burden determined overall by the *condotta*—then the tax-paying capacity of the Jews of Venice and its dominions had fallen since 1548 by some 68 per cent. This may have reflected a comparable diminution in the wealth of the Jews, due partly to export and partly to outright loss.

The Venetian government believed the Jews' story sufficiently to reduce the *tansa* demanded of them under the terms of the *condotte*, though it did not reduce this tax in proportion to the losses allegedly suffered by the Jews. The *condotta* of 1558 fixed the tax at 8,000 ducats. Before 1565, it may have been reduced still further, to 6,000, and the next *condotta*, in 1566, undoubtedly fixed the tax at 5,000 ducats only. Thus, a 50 per cent reduction in taxes appeared against an alleged loss of 70 per cent in taxpaying capacity among the Jews of Venice and the Veneto. However, the Senate turned the screw still further in 1566 both by reducing the legitimate rate of interest to 10 per cent only and by decreeing important changes in the structure of Jewish banking.[44]

Jewish banks were undoubtedly showing grave instability at this time—a fault they shared with Christian firms, which, in the thirty years which separated the Priuli failure of 1552 from the Pisani–Tiepolo crash of 1584, were inflicting grave losses on their investors and depositors.[45] The most obvious reason for Jewish failures was the highly unfavourable conditions under which the *condotte* forced the Jews to transact business from 1548 onwards. In 1558, the three or more banks of the Ghetto were to lend at the rate of 12 per cent only, under rigorous supervision. To guard against fraud, a clerk or Scrivan, chosen by the Collegio and receiving a salary of 100 ducats a year, sat in a booth in the Ghetto on all days when pawnbroking was in progress. His duty was to prepare statements of account on request for all the borrowers, indicating how large a sum they had received from the bankers and how much interest was payable on it. The clauses of the *condotta* clearly visualized the possibility that the Jews would lend to persons other than the poor of the city, and merely stipulated that persons borrowing sums of five ducats or less should somehow enjoy

---

[44] For the *condotte*, A.S.V., *Senato, Terra, filza* 28, 16 November 1558; *filza* 46, 16 March 1566.

[45] On this question, see the remarks in the Introduction to Brian Pullan, ed. *Crisis and Change in the Venetian economy* (London, 1968), pp. 16 f.

priority over all others. The Jews were obliged to keep all pledges, if unredeemed, for fifteen to eighteen months before these were sold by public auction under the supervision of the magistracy of the Sopra-consoli. Pledges were not to be sold without the Jewish lender's consent for a sum insufficient to cover the capital lent, the interest due on it, and the expenses of keeping the pledge and recording the loan (*cavedal, utile et spese*). On the other hand, should any profit be realized on the sale, the magistrates must restore it to the former owner of the pledge, or, if no claimant appeared, send it to the Procuratia of St Mark's. The Jews must bear the loss on an overvalued pledge; they could not, by way of compensation, benefit by undervaluing.

The Jews themselves maintained unavailingly in 1565 that the rate of 12 per cent was wholly uneconomic, and substantially lower than the rates permitted everywhere else in Italy—including the Papal States —where Jewish communities still survived. They argued that

> Lending at 12 per cent only yields very small profits, especially in small loans, as we have need of just as many assistants, and high rents to pay, and expenses are high, so that it would be better to keep the money in the cashbox rather than to lend it.

They drew attention to the relatively indulgent attitude of the present Pope, Pius IV, to the Jews. The Papacy as an institution was inclined to regulate Jewish wealth rather than to persecute relentlessly over several generations; and Pius IV had, from 1562, permitted the Jews of the Papal States to lend at 20 per cent and to engage in every kind of trade. 'In all the rest of Italy, still more is allowed to them'.[46]

It is highly probable that the knowledge that Jewish bankers, with heavy taxes and a low return on their loans, could not reasonably expect to make a profit by their activities, resulted in a grave loss of confidence and caused nominally Christian investors to withdraw their capital from Jewish banks. The general atmosphere of suspicion and distrust of the Jews, and the possibility that the *condotta* might be withdrawn altogether and the Jews expelled, scarcely encouraged investment in this quarter. The *condotta* of 16 November 1558 had passed the Senate with some difficulty, and had only obtained the required majority at the third ballot: though it is, admittedly, hard to say whether this delay was caused by difficulties over the *condotta* as a whole, or objections to some of its particular clauses, especially that defining *strazzaria*. The *condotta* officially extended for five years, followed by a grace period ('di rispetto') of another two, so that the *condotta* proper expired in November 1563. The Jews remained in

---

[46] A.S.V., *Senato, Terra, filza* 44, 6 August 1565.

suspense for the next two years, and on 6 August 1565 the Senate rejected the proposed *condotta*, with 72 votes in favour to 107 against, and 14 'neutral'. In mid-September, the Jews were officially granted a further period of one year in which to wind up their affairs, during which time they would be entitled neither to lend at interest nor to engage in the second-hand trade.[47] However, a few months later the Senate relented, and on 16 March 1566 passed a decree allowing the Jews of Venice to remain in the Ghetto for a period of five years followed by the usual interval of grace. But the long uncertainty, lasting two years and four months, may well have been fatal to the Jewish banks.

At this time, Christians had invested substantially in Jewish banks in Venice. Such a practice had been common enough in some fifteenth-century states—it was recognized, for example, in agreements with the Jews concluded at Florence and Siena in 1457, and was mentioned by Francesco Sforza in correspondence with Pius II a few years later. Creditors of Jews could feel free of the reproach of having taken interest from fellow-Christians, for the Jew screened the depositor from the poor or other Christian borrowers who eventually used the money.[47a] Christian took interest from Jew, Jew from Christian: and this made the practice, by some standards, technically legitimate if not morally defensible. Clearly the habit had persisted in Venice, well into the sixteenth century. Petitions from the Jews' Christian creditors came before the Senate in 1565. Those of the loan bank of Mendlin and Jacob, the sons of Consiglio, demanded new guarantees in the next *condotta* to protect them against loss. The Jewish community should be made collectively responsible for any future failure on the part of their co-religionists, and the *condotta* should not be renewed unless the heads of the Jewish nation 'guarantee to your lordships that the affairs of these brothers are in a sound condition'. This was a vicious circle: distrust of the Jewish bankers delayed the passage of the *condotta*, and the uncertainty of the Jews' future probably created some sort of 'dry' run on their banks, a steady and prolonged withdrawal of capital, if not an actual panic. Creditors of the bank of Salamoncino and Cervo, prepared to take a more reasonable attitude, later recalled that Mendlin, son of Consiglio, had in fact failed to meet his obligations, and that the importunity of his creditors had forced him to withdraw from business: whereas, given time, he could have paid everyone concerned.[48]

[47] A.S.V., *Senato, Terra, filza* 44, 14/15 September 1565.
[47a] See Poliakov, *Les banquiers juifs*, pp. 84–8.
[48] A.S.V., *Senato, Terra, filza* 44, 6 August 1565; *ibid., filza* 50, 27 September 1567.

2M

Information about the bank of Salamoncino and Cervo, which has survived among the Senate's papers, gives some idea of the scale of Jewish banking at this time, and of the extent of Christian investment in it. In October 1564, Francesco Manenti, an official of the Sopraconsoli, testified that he had seen the firm's books and from them had ascertained that between 1 March 1562 and 28 February 1563 the bank had handled some 39,260 pledges, each valued at 10 ducats or less. The proportion of pledges which their creditors failed to redeem was evidently pretty low, and perhaps in the region of $2\frac{1}{2}$ per cent, for in the same period the Sopraconsoli supervised the sale of 912 unredeemed pledges.[49] The figure for the total number of pledges suggests that the bank—one of at least three Jewish banks in Venice—was handling about a quarter as much business as the Monte di Pietà in Padua in the early 1550's. Padua's was one of the three largest Monti di Pietà in the Venetian dominions on the mainland of Italy, and it probably supplied much of the surrounding territory as well as the city of Padua itself. This Monte had, according to the governor of the city, handled 167,736 pledges in 1551–2, and 131,465 in 1552–3.[50] No precise conclusion can emerge from such rough comparisons: but one can tentatively suggest that the combined Jewish banks of Venice may have transacted business on a scale comparable with that of the largest Monti di Pietà. After the suspension of the *condotta*, in September 1565, the Senate ordered 'all the papers and deeds of credit of Cervo and the late Salamoncino his brother' to be consigned to the office of the Sopraconsoli, and the process of winding up the firm began. A petition to the Senate drawn up in 1567 revealed that Cervo's Christian creditors represented a sum of 41,182 ducats. These creditors expressed a certain confidence in Cervo's ultimate ability to meet his obligations —up to 31 December 1566, Cervo had succeeded in exacting debts owed to him to a total sum of 46,797 ducats, which he then used to pay off his own debts. His creditors believed that Cervo's total assets or credits amounted to 108,000 ducats, and his debts to no more than 60,000. The process of liquidation continued at least until 1573.[51]

The relative calm and certainty shown by the creditors of Cervo was not, however, universal. In the 1560's, the feeling grew that to invest in a Jewish bank was highly undesirable. Already, in July 1563, the Senate, troubled by 'complaints of usurious contracts made by various persons with Mendlin the Jew', was committing the Advocates Fiscal

49 A.S.V., *Senato, Terra, filza* 46, 16 March 1566.
50 Report of Marc'Antonio Grimani, 3 August 1554, ff. 6v.–7, in A.S.V., *Collegio, Relazioni,* b. 43.
51 A.S.V., *Senato, Terra, filza* 44, 14/15 September 1565; *filza* 50, 27 September 1567; *filza* 61, 20 June 1573.

and the Giudici del Piovego to conduct inquiries.[52] This probably referred to the fact that Christians were depositing money in Jewish banks and receiving interest on their capital. Such bargains, contracted with a Jew, could not be justified on the same grounds as deposits in a Monte di Pietà. Quite apart from such ethical or legal considerations, the creditors of the same Mendlin had made it all too clear that they did not consider their money to be safe. The Jewish *condotta* of the spring of 1566 did at least alleviate the Jewish burden by reducing taxation and by restoring the right to engage in trade on the mainland. On the other hand, it stipulated that there must be at least five bankers in the Ghetto (who could extend their concession to another five persons), and that they must lend at 10 per cent only. The Senate then added a very significant clause to the effect that none of these bankers must be in debt to Christians, either as principals or as pledges for other persons. The logical effect of this provision should have been to make the banks wholly dependent on deposits and investments by other Jews, and indeed there is some evidence surviving from the late sixteenth and early seventeenth centuries that the banks were from henceforth supported entirely by Jewish subscriptions, investments or levies.[53] By 1566, then, the Venetian Republic had reached a new stage in the curtailment of Jewish economic power, and in the process of setting the Jew apart from the Christian. The Jew was not entitled to receive and control Christian money, to use it either in commercial speculation or in loans to the poor. Funds for such purposes must come exclusively from Jewish sources.

In the next seven years, Jewish fortunes sank to their nadir, not only in the Venetian Republic, but in central and northern Italy as a whole. These were the years of the pontificate of Michele Ghislieri, Pope Pius V, and of the outbreak of war with the Ottoman Empire, in which the Venetian Republic, through the Turkish attack on Cyprus, was instantly and directly involved. Shortly after his accession, Pius V expressly repudiated the milder policy of his predecessor towards the Jews of the Papal States, and reverted to the rigorous measures of the Caraffa Pope, Paul IV. It may be significant that the Venetian *condotta* of 1566 was safely concluded before Pius V issued the first of his Bulls, 'Romanus pontifex', on 19 April 1566. The Pope was undoubtedly designing his policy for dissemination abroad, since he charged bishops to publish and enforce the letter, and exhorted secular princes to afford them every assistance.[54] Three years later, he carried the persecution of

---

[52] A.S.V., *Senato, Terra*, reg. 1562–3, f. 145.   [53] See below, p. 567.
[54] Pius V, 'Romanus pontifex', 19 April 1566, and 'Cum nos nuper', 19 January 1567, in B.R., VII, pp. 438–40, 514–16.

the Jews within the Papal States to new lengths. The Bull 'Hebraeorum gens', first reciting the misdeeds of the obstinate, treacherous and profoundly ungrateful Jewish nation, declared with brutal cynicism that the Jews, apart from a certain number of Levantines required for the maintenance of commercial links between Ancona and the Ottoman Empire, were now no longer useful to the States of the Church. They should therefore be totally expelled from the Pope's dominions, except for a remnant consisting of those Jews who already dwelt in Rome and Ancona.[55] The total expulsion of the Jews from Rome remained unthinkable; some must stay, to bear witness by their serfdom to the truth of the Christian religion.

Pius V found a response beyond his own territorial frontiers. In the Spanish Viceroyalty of Milan, the influence of the zealous and powerful Archbishop Carlo Borromeo procured the introduction of the yellow hat for the Jews, together with prohibitions on Jewish loans at interest. Borromeo's provincial synod of 1565 had passed a resolution obliging bishops to devote themselves to the establishment of a Monte di Pietà 'in every city, and in the more important towns': there was, at least, some hope that such a campaign would provide the necessary alternative to Jewish lending. The Genoese, having expelled the Jews from their capital in 1550, extended the order to their subject territory in 1567. Moreover, this new upsurge of anti-Jewish legislation did not occur only within territory under the direct dominion of Spain and the Pope, or, like Genoa, bound closely to Spain by economic bonds. The Medici Duke of Tuscany had not previously fallen into line with papal treatment of the Jews, though he had acquiesced in the burning of Talmudic books ordered by Julius III. Towards Pius V, however, he now showed himself more complaisant, in his new anxiety to obtain from the Pope the title of Grand Duke of Tuscany, valuable for diplomatic ends and especially for the purpose of disconcerting the Spaniards. His devotion to the Church could well be demonstrated at the expense of the Jews. Hence, in 1567–71, his government introduced the distinctive yellow badge for Jews and prohibited all Jewish moneylending. It cancelled existing contracts on the score that the Jews had infringed the terms of their *condotte*. Finally, it attempted to force all Tuscan Jewry to live within the confines of the ghettoes of Florence and Siena.[56]

The Venetian government made, for the time being, no attempt to

[55] B.R., VII, pp. 740–2.

[56] Cassuto, *Ebrei a Firenze*, pp. 91–117. On Borromeo and the Monti di Pietà, see Wadding, *Annales minorum*, XV, pp. 471–2; *Acta Ecclesiae Mediolanensis* (Milan, 1583), f. 21v.

repudiate its agreement with the Jews. But the Jewish *condotta* next came up for review in the year when the Christian victory at Lepanto was swiftly followed by the loss of Cyprus to the Turk—in the year of a crusade, and crusades against the infidel abroad had never boded well for the Jew, the vulnerable infidel at home. As an act partly of revenge, partly of thanksgiving, on 18 December 1571, the Senate resolved to expel the Jews both from the capital itself and from the entire Venetian dominion. The preamble explained the purpose of the act in the following terms:

> Since the Majesty of the Lord God has granted to all Christendom and especially to this Republic the favour of so fortunate and glorious a victory over the Turk by the disruption of his fleet, it is appropriate to show some sign of gratitude towards Jesus Christ our blessed defender and protector by making a demonstration against those who are enemies of his holy faith, as are the Jews, against whom our devoted forefathers have clearly declared in the laws, and especially in that adopted in this Council on 18 March 1527. These were its words: 'That it should above all be noted that whenever steps have been taken to expel the Jews, both the state and private individuals have been seen to prosper, and whenever contracts have been made with them, the contrary has clearly appeared.' On account of this admonition by our ancestors and of the benefits we have received from the Majesty of God, we must not fail at the present time, as aforesaid, to make some demonstration against this depraved race, which if ever it has treated the poor with fraud, extortion, deceit and dishonesty, and if ever it has betrayed and rebelled against the state, is assuredly doing so at the present time, as is very well known to this Council.[57]

It seemed at last as though the Venetian government had abandoned its attack on the Jews through economic restriction and fiscal pressure, and was at last frankly, as an act of piety and devotion, proceeding to disband Venetian Jewry. Expulsion seemed ready to follow segregation, under the stimulus of this last crusade, as the act of a Catholic government vindictive in its triumph.

[57] A.S.V., *Senato, Terra, filza* 58, 18 December 1571. The decree of 1527, quoted in this preamble, was the unenforceable resolution, proposed by the Cavaliere Moro, to relegate the Jews to Mestre—see above, pp. 504–5.

4

THE JEWISH ECONOMY, 1571–1618

The resolution of the Venetian Senate to expel the Jews in December 1571 was, in one of its aspects, the culmination of the anti-Jewish policy it had systematically and cruelly pursued during the last quarter century. But it was more than this, and more than a crusader's act of petty revenge. Rumours were abroad that the rape of Cyprus was an act inspired by the flamboyant and plutocratic leader of the Jewish nation in the Ottoman Empire, Don Joseph Nasi, favourite of the Sultan Selim, opponent of the Vizier Mehemet Sokolli, and since 1566 Duke of Naxos and the Archipelago.[1] As one of the Portuguese family of Mendes, Joseph Nasi had little reason to love or respect the Venetian Republic. His numerous interests comprised a kind of proto-Zionism: he strove for the creation of a semi-autonomous Jewish community, a refuge from persecution and insecurity, in the dominions of the Ottoman Empire. It is possible that in the mid-sixteenth century he had hoped to establish such a community among the Mediterranean islands of the Venetian Republic. Disappointed in this aspiration, he had found a site for his project at Tiberias in Galilee: but by the end of the 1560's rumours circulated that Nasi was now aspiring to the rank of King of Cyprus, should this be conquered from the Venetians. Contemporary historians assigned Joseph Nasi heavy responsibility for the outbreak of the war, and accused him of trying to foment a pro-Turkish rebellion in Cyprus in 1568, or of exploiting the news of the great Arsenal fire in Venice in 1569 to convince the Sultan that his enemy's fleet had been hopelessly crippled, and that now was the moment to attack.[2]

Perhaps, then, the Senate's decision was an act of revenge on Nasi and his people, and the suggestion that the Jews were committing treason against the state, if still as untrue, was somewhat less vague and tritely conventional than usual. But the Venetians could not, or dared not, carry out their vengeance on the Jews. In the next year or two circumstances forced them into peace negotiations with the Ottoman

---

[1] For what follows, see mainly Cecil Roth, *The House of Nasi: the Duke of Naxos* (Philadelphia, 1948); also Romanin, *Storia documentata*, VI, pp. 270 f.; Schiavi, 'Ebrei in Venezia', p. 494; Roth, *Jews of Venice*, pp. 88–93; Sir George Hill, *A history of Cyprus*, III (Cambridge, 1948), pp. 842–3, 879–80, 883.

[2] Roth, *Duke of Naxos*, pp. 105 f., 140 f.

Turks, and revived their concern for Levantine trade. This made a general act of vengeance on the whole Jewish nation inadvisable. If, after the Turkish defeat at Lepanto, Nasi suffered discredit, Jewish influence in general at Selim's court lost little of its strength. In healing relations with Venice, the Vizier Mehemet Sokolli collaborated with Solomon Ashkenazi, a Jew born a Venetian subject in Udine in 1520. Educated in medicine at Padua, he had served as a physician in Poland and settled in Constantinople in 1564. Ten years later, he was sent to Venice as the Sultan's emissary. Very probably, the reprieve of the Jews was a necessary condition of peace with Turkey.[3] The German Jewish nation was too impoverished for the Sultan to wish to attract it to his own dominions; and some Jews at his court were internationally-minded enough to show concern for the fate of their co-religionists. Moreover, the Venetians were reluctant to make, or incapable of making, alternative suggestions as to how the interests of the poor could be preserved and loans be guaranteed them. They cited the decision of the Council of Ten which had quashed the proposal for a Monte di Pietà in 1524, and this may have provided a convenient excuse for not expelling the Jews, rather than a genuine deterrent against establishing a Monte in Venice.[4] Apart from possible indolence or prejudice on its part, the Senate already had reason to know of corruption and maladministration in some of the Monti on the main-land,[5] and, at this crucial moment, to doubt the wisdom of expelling the Jews.

The Venetian government now adopted a curious compromise, possibly unique in Italy if not in Europe. Whilst retaining the Jews, it forced them to lend to the poor under similar conditions and at the same rates as a Monte di Pietà—and this new dispensation was to prevail at least for the next sixty or seventy years. A kind of equilibrium, an appropriate form of co-existence, was now reached between the Venetian Republic and its Jews. Under the terms of the new *condotta*, issued by the Venetian Republic in the summer of 1573, the Jews Marcuzzo Fricele and Samson Pescaruol of Venice, as representatives of the Jewish communities, bound themselves to make a total sum of up to 50,000 ducats available to lend to the poor of Venice on pledges in instalments of two or three ducats at a time. These Jewish

[3] *Ibid.*, pp. 150–60.
[4] A copy of this decree appears in A.S.V., *Senato, Terra, filza* 61, 29 June 1573. The decree of 18 December 1571 was expressly revoked on the grounds that it conflicted with the earlier decision of the Council of Ten.
[5] Cf. the report of Giovanni Battista Contarini, 1 May 1566, on the Monte di Pietà at Padua—A.S.V., *Collegio, Relazioni*, b. 43; and the letter of Piero Gritti, Podestà of Vicenza, of 5 October 1571, in A.S.V., *Senato, Terra, filza* 58, 9 November 1571.

banks were subjected to the close supervision of the magistracy of the Cattaveri, who were instructed to ensure that this sum was being employed for the proper purpose. Pledges should be kept for a maximum of twelve months only, instead of the limit of fifteen to eighteen months permitted by the *condotta* of 1558, and then, if still unredeemed, sold as before under the auspices of the Sopraconsoli. From henceforth, interest charged by the Jews was drastically lowered from 10 per cent to 5 per cent per annum only—expressed, in terms reminiscent of the statutes of the Monti di Pietà, as 'one bagatino per lira a month to cover expenses'.[6] Jewish banks should remain, but changed out of recognition: not only should they be starved of Christian capital, but they should also cease to be self-supporting and profit-making institutions. They should operate like Monti di Pietà fed, not by Christian charity, but by Jewish taxation, and existing to benefit the devotees of an alien faith. By 1573, all the older banks had probably disappeared.

After 1573, proposals for the expulsion of the Jews were only once seriously debated by the Senate during the period now under review—when, in 1580, Giacomo da Ca da Pesaro, one of the Heads of the Quarantia, accused them in the usual stereotyped, vague and unspecific language of plotting for the ruin of the poor and bringing them no benefits. His proposal commanded a fair following in the Senate, but after three ballots failed to obtain the necessary majority; and the Senate—again after three votes—eventually chose to contract once more with the Jews.[7] During the 1580's, the atmosphere perceptibly lightened.

In the year of Lepanto, Christian loan banking had triumphed on the mainland, and the Jews no longer plied this trade in any large city, with the possible exception of Rovigo. Udine, Brescia and Crema were all free of Jews, and they survived only as traders in Verona and Padua. Jews banked only in townships, villages and rural areas, and the process of harrying them still continued here, especially in Friuli and the Bresciano. In November 1571, even before the Venetians issued their decision, the city council of Cividale in Friuli resolved to ask the Venetian Senate to remove the Jews from their town, even if the Venetian *condotta* were renewed in the near future. The local Provveditore, Marco Cornaro, asked to report and make recommendations on this matter, resorted for information to a somewhat biased source: the records of criminal proceedings against the Jews. Not surprisingly, he discovered plenty of evidence of their alleged malpractices. The pres-

[6] A.S.V., *Senato, Terra, filza* 61, 11 July 1573; reg. 1572–3, ff. 136v.–141v.
[7] A.S.V., *Senato, Terra, filza* 80, 24 May 1580.

ence of the Jews round Cividale was, he asserted, wholly pernicious. They refused to lend to all comers, as their *capitoli* obliged them, but in fact dispensed loans in a highly selective manner to their clients. They produced only one-third of their loans in the form of money, rendering the rest in grain, which they grossly overvalued. They did not lend at the prescribed rate of 10 per cent only, but at 25, 30 and even 40 per cent, adding the interest to the capital. Again, Jews in this region dealt in corn, wine, cloth, fats and other goods, which they sold fraudulently on credit at twice their rightful value, treating their debtors with the utmost harshness. For good measure, in tones suspiciously echoing the phrases of Pius V's recent Bull 'Hebraeorum gens', the Provveditore threw in a general charge of keeping thieves' kitchens and receiving stolen goods. As far as the Venetians, as well as the Council of Cividale, were concerned, he had returned an acceptable answer. The Senate gave the Jews of Cividale notice to depart within three months.[8]

The Bishop of Brescia may have inspired the action taken by the governors of Brescia in 1572. Since 1517, the Venetian government had denied the Jews entry to the province of Brescia on the grounds of their supposed misconduct during the French occupation after 1509. The Rettori testified that no Jews had in fact been admitted to this region, except on to the lands of the Martinengo lords and the Counts of Gambara, local potentates who enjoyed privileged seigneurial juris- dictions. As the Jews themselves later explained, these lands consisted of the villages of Gabiano, Pavone, Oriano, Orzi Vecchi and Verola, where they kept a total of five banks, two of relatively 'ancient' founda- tion. The Jews constituted, not only an economic, but also a spiritual danger, and the governors warned the Senate that if they were allowed to extend their activities

> harm will be done, not only to property, but also (as the Right Reverend Bishop has warned us) to souls, since the Jews are so freely associating with these poor and simple peasants, and it is impossible in villages to make them live in places set apart from Christians, as is usual in towns.

In August 1572, the Rettori of Brescia felt able to write that these feudal lords had admitted that they really enjoyed no privilege entitling them to admit Jews on their own initiative when public policy was against this. As if to preserve the Christian faith from insidious con- tamination, and the poor from consumption by usury, the Senate authorized the Rettori, in the usual fashion, to give the Jews notice to quit within three months. The Jews might claim that no complaints had ever been lodged against them, and that in the recent famines they

[8] A.S.V., *Senato, Terra, filza* 60, 4 September 1572.

had procured large and valuable imports of grain. They had lent both on pledges and on written bonds, and had saved the poor from having to borrow at the rate of 30 per cent in 'foreign places' (*terre aliene*)— possibly across the Mantuan border. All they gained, however, in this atmosphere of religious ardour, was a respite until September 1573.[9]

Nevertheless, such hostility towards the Jews did not persist in all small towns and country districts after 1573 and the renewal of the Venetian *condotta*. Between 1573 and 1588, the Senate granted several requests to small-town and village authorities eager to contract with Jews. Mestre, Castelfranco, Asola, Cologna, Pordenone, Portogruaro, Sacile, Porto Bufolè, Uderzo, Conegliano, Capo d'Istria and Moncelese all contracted or re-contracted with Jews during this period, so that at least twelve centres of Jewish lending, outside the Polesine, survived the era of the harshest oppression.[10] In December 1594, a list of Jews from the mainland who attended the Jewish council in Venice ran as follows:

> Consiglio, son of Jacob, son of Consiglio, of Rovigo
> Abram, son of Grassin Scaramella, of Codroipo
> Lazzaro, son of Mendlin, son of Consiglio, of Rovigo
> Simon, son of Leone, of Padua
> Manuel, son of Zaccaria, of Conegliano
> The sons of the late Salamoncin, of Rovigo
> The sons of the late Abram of Serravalle, of Cologna
> Mendlin, son of Marcaria, of Capo d'Istria
> The bankers of Asola, in the Bresciano
> Cervo, banker at Capo d'Istria
> Volpino, son of Marcaria, of Capo d'Istria.[11]

This list cannot serve as a guide to all the existing Jewish banks, since some bankers may have felt it not worth their while to attend the council in Venice for the apportionment of taxation and for the transaction of other business. The list did not, for example, include any representative from Mestre, where there was still a Jewish community in the early seventeenth century, and where Joseph Gallindo and

---

[9] *Ibid.*, and *filza* 61, 6 March 1573.

[10] For Mestre, A.S.V., *Senato, Terra, filza* 62, 21 November 1573; Castelfranco, *filza* 63, 6 April 1574; Asola, *filza* 63, 6 April 1574; Cologna, *filza* 65, 27 January 1574 Venetian style; Pordenone, *filza* 66, 19 March 1575; Portogruaro, *filza* 69, 7 April 1576, mentioning a Jewish moneylender at Sacile; Porto Bufolè, *filza* 81, 19 November 1580, which includes a letter from the Podestà-Capitano, Piero Gritti, mentioning that Portogruaro, Capo d'Istria, Uderzo, Conegliano, Mestre and Asolo or Asola had already contracted with Jews; Moncelese, *filza* 106, 22 March 1588.

[11] A.S.V., *Ufficialli al Cattaver, busta* 244, reg. 5, 133.

Abram Gibre acted as bankers in 1607.[12] Not everybody on the list was a banker—there had officially been no Jewish banking in Padua since 1548, yet the name of 'Simon, son of Leone, of Padua', appeared on the list. But it does suggest that Rovigo was then an important centre of Jewish activity—as it remained in the 1620's.[13] It also appears that Codroipo, near Udine, in Friuli, was a Jewish centre: in 1617, Abram Scaramella was described as 'the Jewish banker at Codroipo'. Jewish banking continued at Cologna into the early seventeenth century, when (in 1605) it was conducted by 'Menechin and his son Jacob, of Serravalle'[14]—probably the same persons as those who attended the council in 1594.

From 1591 onwards, the Venetian Jews became responsible for supplying replacements to the mainland. A clause in the new *condotta* of that year prescribed that when a Jew on the mainland departed or was dismissed, the community he had served would be entitled to apply to the Venetian Ghetto to furnish them with another banker on similar terms.[15] The official rate of interest charged by Jewish bankers now varied from a minimum of 10 per cent (at Mestre and Castelfranco in 1573–4, at Moncelese in 1588) to a maximum of 15 per cent (found only at Sacile in 1576—possibly under the terms of a contract concluded some years earlier). Rates of 12 per cent or $12\frac{1}{2}$ per cent—as in the Venetian *condotte* of 1548 and 1558—were often approved. The people of Mestre in 1585 failed to discover any Jew who would lend at less than $12\frac{1}{2}$ per cent.[16] Naturally, these facts are chiefly valuable as an index to public policy and official aims: one cannot confidently assume that the Jews in fact stayed within the official limits, or indeed that they could practicably do so. The charges brought against Joseph Levi of Asola in 1615 raise doubts of this kind. They suggest (though they by no means prove) that the Jews of Asola had lent at illicit rates from the 1570's onwards.[17] Likewise, in 1576, the people of Portogruaro were said to be applying to lenders—whether Jews or Christians was not stated—in the neighbouring Friulian villages of San Vido, Belgrado and Latisana, there to borrow at the exorbitant rate of 30 per cent. The Venetian government had not approved any such rates since 1520.[18] However, circumstances apparently made it possible for the Venetian Jewish banks to lend at 5 per cent only.

---

[12] *Ibid.*, *busta* 246, reg. 7, ff. 191v.–192, 200v.–201v., 212, 244.
[13] See below, pp. 559–60.
[14] A.S.V., *Ufficiali al Cattaver*, *busta* 245, reg. 6. ff. 285v.–286.
[15] Chapter 5 of the *condotta*, in A.S.V., *Senato, Terra, filza* 122, 7 December 1591.
[16] A.S.V., *Senato, Terra, filza* 94, 27 June 1585.
[17] See below, pp. 563–4.
[18] A.S.V., *Senato, Terra, filza* 69, 7 April 1576.

Little communities obviously found paying a higher rate of interest on small loans more practicable than the process of accumulating capital, through either charity or taxation, to found a local Monte di Pietà or augment an existing one. Admittedly, the commune of Asola, which lay to the south-east of Brescia and not far from the disputed jurisdictions of Gambara and Martinengo, professed the praiseworthy intention of founding a Monte di Pietà some time in the future, even while it contracted with a Jew in the present. There were then three Jewish banks in the region of Asola, but they lay beyond the Mantuan and Milanese borders, at Caneto, Castel Giuffredo and Isola (on this point, the statement of the commune of Asola accords with some remarks of the threatened Jews of the privileged jurisdictions). These banks lent, at least to outsiders, at 30 per cent, and Asola needed to undercut them. The Provveditore Pietro Maria Contarini predicted that the introduction of a Jewish banker would frustrate many local usurers who, as a sideline, also oppressed the poor by engrossing grain. One of the purposes of contracting with the Jew was to enable the commune to pay off its arrears of taxation. Contarini now suggested that the commune should borrow from the Jew the sum of 2,000 ducats, 1,000 at 7 per cent interest, the other thousand without interest for a period of three years. Of these, 1,500 ducats would be devoted to freeing the commune of its debts to the Venetian treasury, the remaining 500 to 'establishing a holy Monte for the benefit of all concerned'. However, the Senate, whilst permitting the commune to contract with a Jew to lend at 12 per cent, made no mention of Contarini's other proposals, and Asola probably had to wait for its Monte di Pietà until 1615.[19]

Other areas which possessed Monti di Pietà found them inadequate to meet the needs of the local population. The huge Monti di Pietà of Padua, Verona and Udine served wide stretches of territory outside their own cities, with an annual turnover, in the early seventeenth century, of two or three hundred thousand ducats each.[20] But the distribution of charitable resources throughout the Venetian dominion remained uneven, and left several communes without sufficient provision. Moncelese, in the province of Padua, had been endowed with a Monte since the early sixteenth century—perhaps continuously since the visitation of Bernardino of Feltre in the 1490's. But this was a dwarf bank, whose capital in 1519 stood at 386 lire, or about 62 ducats. In 1554, it had reached 674 lire or 109 ducats. In 1588, Giorgio Contarini and the future Doge Marino Grimani, then serving as Rettori of

[19] A.S.V., *Senato, Terra, filza* 63, 6 April 1574.
[20] See below, pp. 624–5.

Padua, described to the Venetian Senate how the capital of the Monte proper, derived from charitable gifts, amounted to approximately 300 ducats, and deposits to about 1,000—but there was some kind of run on the bank, many persons were demanding the restoration of their deposits, and the Massaro had reported that this entire sum had now been lent out on pledge. The disastrous weather and scanty harvests of 1586 and 1587 had plunged the region into poverty and the commune into heavy debts, incurred in the effort to raise supplies of grain. In the first famine year it had raised 3,700 ducats on the security of its own property to buy grain, and in the second another 4,000. The territory of Moncelese supported a population of 8,000, and its credit arrangements, its barriers against uncontrollable indebtedness, were puny and frail indeed. In 1588, the Venetian Senate acceded to the pleas of the commune and the recommendations of the Rettori by granting them permission to contract with a Jew to lend at the low rate of 10 per cent.[21] Moncelese may have been an extreme case: but the governors even of certain quite populous cities—especially Treviso—complained of the inadequate funds of the local Monte di Pietà,[22] and on one occasion, Benedetto Correr, Podestà of Vicenza, wrote in 1598 that the lack of funds in the city Monte drove the locals, at great expense, into the arms of the Jews of Cologna.[23]

After 1575, enthusiasm for the foundation of new Monti di Pietà had evidently waned, though it revived a little in the early seventeenth century with new establishments at Pordenone in Friuli and at Asola in the Bresciano.[24] The Venetian government and its provincial representatives also moved at this time to investigate maladministration in the Monti, and concentrated on preserving or reconstituting the existing funds. At least from the 1580's onwards, the policy of the Papacy, both as a territorial prince and as head of the Catholic Church, inclined more favourably towards the Jews as economic servants of the Christian community. Admittedly, Gregory XIII, in 1581, had tried to re-enforce previous decrees restraining Jewish or infidel physicians from attending Christian patients, on the grounds that they endangered the souls of the sick and dying. Moreover, in a decree which, according to Sarpi,

[21] A.S.V., *Senato, Terra, filza* 106, 22 March 1588.
[22] A.S.V., *Collegio, Relazioni*, b. 48: especially reports of Vincenzo Pisani, 10 May 1612, and Antonio Bragadin, 27 July 1622.
[23] A.S.V., *Collegio, Relazioni*, b. 51: report of 20 October 1598. According to the report of Nicolò Pizzamano, 8 October 1603, *ibid.*, Monti di Pietà existed in two small towns of the Vicentino, Arzignano and Schio, as well as in Vicenza itself. Cologna itself possessed a Monte di Pietà in 1601—*Senato, Terra, filza* 160, 3 November 1601.
[24] A.S.V., *Senato, Terra, filza* 160, 17/28 October 1601; *filza* 215, 25 September 1615.

545

was not widely received or published by Catholic states, he had tried to extend the authority of the Inquisition to cover offences like blasphemy or impiety committed by Jews.[25] But Sixtus V, acceding to the papal throne in 1585, reversed the policy of Paul IV and Pius V by inviting Jews to settle extensively once more in the States of the Church, and to perform the functions, not merely of Levantine traders, but also of bankers. Statistics compiled by modern historians have indicated that between 1587 and 1609 the Camera Apostolica granted over three hundred Jewish banking patents to Italian states other than the Venetian Republic. It made 148 such grants to Jews in Rome, Ancona and the rest of the Papal States. Elsewhere in Italy, duchies and principalities independent of Spain—Savoy–Piedmont, Mantua and the outlying Mantuan fief of Monferrato—applied most extensively for patents. Milan, Genoa and Savona proved much more sparing.[26] Sixtus V's Bull 'Christiana pietas' of October 1586 had authorized Jews to engage in every kind of trade, including victualling, and to employ Christian wage-earners at proper rates, though never as domestic servants.[27] The Venetians did not consider it necessary to obtain Roman permission to license Jewish lenders, and the Senate made several concessions before 1586–7. It may be that Venice's action reflected a general softening of attitude towards the Jews in Italian non-Spanish societies, and that the Papacy subsequently took account of this, responding to, rather than creating, opinion.

The argument of economic necessity or at least of economic advantage weighed heavily enough to ensure the survival or even spread of Jewish communities in the Veneto, even though prominent churchmen still expressed misgivings about the contamination of Judaism and insisted on an official attitude of ill-natured suspicion. A Venetian census of 1586 estimated the numbers resident in the Venetian Ghetto at 1,694[28]—about half as many as in contemporary Rome, which now

[25] Gregory XIII, 'Alias piae memoriae', 30 May 1581, B.R., VIII, pp. 371–3; 'Antiqua iudaeorum improbitas', 1 July 1581, ibid., pp. 378–80; Paolo Sarpi, Discorso della origine, forma, leggi ed uso dell'Ufficio della Inquisizione nella città e dominio di Venezia, in his Opere (Helmstat, 1761–8), IV, pp. 41–3.

[26] Cf. E. Loevinson, 'La concession de banques de prêts aux juifs par les papes des seizième et dix-septième siècles: contribution à l'histoire des finances d'Italie', Revue des études juives, 92–5 (1932–3); Milano, 'Considerazioni sulla lotta dei Monti di Pietà', pp. 218–20. Cf. also Jean Delumeau, 'Les dettes à Rome au XVIe siècle', Revue d'histoire moderne et contemporaine, IV (1957), pp. 25–8.

[27] B.R., VIII, pp. 786–9.

[28] Julius Beloch, 'La popolazione di Venezia nei secoli XVI e XVII', Nuovo Archivio Veneto, nuova serie, III (1902), pp. 13–14; Daniele Beltrami, Storia della popolazione di Venezia dalla fine del secolo XVI alla caduta della Repubblica (Padua, 1954), p. 79. This census estimated the total population of Venice at over 148,600.

boasted some 3,500.[29] Communities of 200-odd remained in Padua and Verona at about the same time. In 1585, the Rettori of Padua, Andrea Bernardo and Lorenzo Donà, reported that about 280 Jews were then living in Padua.[30] Similarly, the Rettori of Verona in 1589 calculated that their city contained twenty-six Jewish households or 'case', comprising on average eight or nine persons in each, and bringing the total Jewish population to some 225, mostly very poor, though some did a little trading.[31] No figures apparently survive for the Jewish population of Rovigo, whose continued activities were to cause grave offence to the pious in the new century. After 1589, the number of Jews in Venice almost certainly increased substantially through the reception of Spanish Jews recently excluded from Ferrara, and, about 1640, even a few years after a catastrophic epidemic, was at least 2,600.[32] Estimates for the Jewish population of Verona, though they become considerably vaguer, also suggest an increase. The Rettori in 1599 believed in the existence of 33 Jewish households and about 300 Jews in Verona, an estimate quite consonant with that of 1589.[33] Their successors in 1600, however, offered the estimate of 400 Jewish persons in 60 households,[34] which may have been produced by guesswork only. Figures for the Jews of Padua are markedly higher in the early seventeenth century. In 1615, the Jews numbered 665, just under 2 per cent of the whole population, then estimated at 35,463. On the eve of the plague of 1630, they were variously counted as 593 and (by the physician and Rabbi Abraham Catelan) as 721. Catelan held that the plague reduced them

[29] Cf. Léon Poliakov, 'La communauté juive à Rome aux XVIe et XVIIe siècles', *Annales: Économies, Sociétés, Civilisations*, XII (1957), pp. 119–20.

[30] A.S.V., *Senato, Terra, filza* 96, 31 December 1585.

[31] A.S.V., *Senato, Terra, filza* 111, 3 June 1589.

[32] Schiavi, 'Ebrei in Venezia', p. 507, refers to an estimate by Simone Luzzatto, c. 1639, of the Jewish population at about 2,650—including 1,078 women and 491 children. However, in his work *Discorso circa il stato de gl'Hebrei, et in particolar dimoranti nell'inclita Citta di Venetia* (Venice, 1638), Luzzatto had somewhat vaguely estimated the whole Jewish population of Venice at 6,000 (f. 28), and the total Jewish population of Italy at some 25,000 (f. 91). Beltrami, *Storia della popolazione*, gives the figure of 2,671 for 1642 (p. 79). Beloch, 'La popolazione', p. 20, quotes a census of 1642 which mentions 549 heads of Jewish households. The census takers claimed to have found an average of just under 5 persons per household in Venice as a whole— 24,462 households to a total population of 120,439. However, as the Rettori of Verona suggested, Jewish households may well have been larger units than Christian, and it is best to treat the figures of 2,600 as minimum estimates. There must have been considerable room for ambiguity in the taking of censuses—e.g. over the question of including non-resident Levantine merchants.

[33] A.S.V., *Senato, Terra, filza* 149, 13 February 1598 Venetian style.

[34] A.S.V., *Senato, Terra, filza* 156, 29 September 1600; repeated by the Podestà Giulio Contarini, 25 November 1608, who also says about 60 families (*ibid., filza* 192, 22 October 1609).

to 300.[35] Probably, in the countryside, miniature communities grew round the dozen or more centres of Jewish lending. In 1609, the governor of the small town of Conegliano, to the north-east of Treviso, informed the Senate that the town had 35 Jews in a population of 3,740.[36] It is plausible that in the late sixteenth century the total Jewish population of the Venetian Republic was no more than 3,000, in a state of over 1½ million inhabitants. But the peculiar position of the Jewish people, the mixture of toleration and opprobrium it encountered, and the highly specialized economic functions it discharged, threw the Jews into peculiar and somewhat unwelcome prominence.

The Jews' most conspicuous function was always moneylending. Communes and Rettori, using the argument best calculated to appeal to Venetian fiscalism, declared that credit was vital to enable their citizens to pay their taxes. They stressed the argument that if no such facilities existed in a given commune, its citizens would go and find them elsewhere, suffering in their purses, wasting their time, and where practicable crossing the Mantuan border in order to do so. It is possible that Jews were usually allowed to lend at much higher rates to persons who did not reside in their own territory, and that this increased the inducement to particular villages or townships to contract with Jews of their own.

The big Jewish banks of the early sixteenth century, such as the Meshullam concerns, had been profit-making private enterprises running on their own impetus, and handling Christian capital entrusted to them. But the banks of the late sixteenth century were public services, and were, or became, the responsibility of the whole Jewish community under Venetian rule. They were financed by taxation levied by the Jewish council in Venice. Banking, owing to the far lower rates of interest now chargeable, must have become a less profitable pursuit in itself, and the operation of the banks therefore depended on the Jews engaging in other economic activities which increased their taxpaying capacity. It is now necessary to examine these, and so incidentally to discover something about the other social and economic functions of the Jews.

In Venice itself, the 'German' Jews rendered their chief service to the Christian community by keeping loan banks for the poor, whilst their chief form of profit-making activity lay in the second-hand trade. It may be that, within the Ghetto, an élite of second-hand traders was beginning to replace the old élite of bankers. In 1594, a group of

[35] Ciscato, *Ebrei in Padova*, pp. 98–9; Ciro Ferrari, *L'Ufficio di Sanità in Padova nella prima metà del secolo XVII* (Venice, 1910), p. 169.
[36] Report of Marco Magno, 1 August 1609, A.S.V., *Collegio, Relazioni*, b. 40.

strazzaruoli described themselves as 'all of us merchants transacting much business', and said that their houses were 'frequently visited by noblemen and by the most prominent men in the Republic', in search of tapestries, hangings and similar commodities which they wanted to buy or hire. The Ufficiali al Cattaver, the Venetian magistrates in charge of Jewish affairs, recognized that these businessmen—the brothers Abraham, Benedetto and Nascimben Calimani, their cousin Isaac Luzzatto, Iseppo dalla Baldosa, Orso dalla Man, the Sorzetti, and Anselmo, son of Salamon Scocco—were indeed 'merchants with a good name and a high reputation', and that no complaints had ever been received about them.[37] About a year later, five of these petitioners— Orso dalla Man, Abram and Benedetto Calimani, Isaac Luzzatto and Iseppo dalla Baldosa—were serving as the Heads of the Jewish corporation, the Università degli Hebrei.[38] A number of *strazzaruoli* enjoyed the use of wharves or quays (*rive*) on the outside of the Ghetto, on which the customers could see the goods displayed without the embarrassment of having to enter the Ghetto itself. Christian watchmen, however, kept the keys to these wharves, which were opened or locked on the instructions of the Christian magistrates.[39] The *strazzaruoli* lent hangings and other properties to Venetian magistracies, such as the Rason Vecchie, for ceremonial purposes—this seems to have been an obligation accepted by the Jewish corporation as a whole, and assigned to particular *strazzaruoli* in return for a payment from communal funds. Hence, in 1616, Caliman Calimani recalled how, some years ago, he and his brother Nascimben had agreed to furnish out the Doge's palace on festival days, and, among other things, to supply decorations for Holy Thursday and for the festival of the Bucintoro, at which the Doge wedded the sea. The heads of the Jewish corporation had promised to pay the Calimani 90 ducats a year for performing this service.[40]

This extensive second-hand trade gave rise to a subsidiary profession —that of broker or *sanser* in the Ghetto. These middlemen accompanied would-be purchasers of goods into the Ghetto, guided them to a Jewish shop, perhaps gave them advice about the transaction, and saw fair play: in return for which they received a commission, probably paid by the Jew rather than by the Christian customer. The right to act as broker constituted an office of profit, which the state used to reward deserving persons. In the 1560's and in the 1580's there were 16 official

[37] A.S.V., *Ufficiali al Cattaver, busta* 244, reg. 5, f. 128–9, 27 October 1594.
[38] *Ibid.*, f. 165, 19 December 1595.
[39] See also the list of those who had the use of the 11 *rive*, ibid., ff. 121v.–122, 27 July 1594.
[40] *Ibid., busta* 245, reg. 6. f. 218, 6 April 1616.

2N

sanseri in the Ghetto, to whom the law tried to guarantee a monopoly. Twelve were Christians, the other four Jews.[41] Ducal letters issued in 1567, in the name of Doge Hieronimo Priuli, rewarded the services of a Jewish physician, Joseph de Datolis, who, during recent periods when plague seemed to threaten Venice, had done much, without regard for his own life, to extinguish the disease. The Signory therefore granted him the reversion of two *sansarie*, the next ones to fall vacant, to be registered in the names of his two sons Moses and Simon: they would be entitled to act personally as brokers, or to perform the office through substitutes approved by the Ufficiali al Cattaver.[42] Such a reward was deemed good enough for a Jewish physician. Among Christians, the grant of two *sansarie in Ghetto* was the kind of favour which the Doge could appropriately bestow on Pietro Antonio, beadle, tipstaff or *commandador* at the entrance to the Collegio, on the occasion of a daughter's marriage, in recognition of twenty-two years' service without a wage.[43] Christian middlemen evidently, being more numerous, extracted more of the side-profits from the second-hand trade, thereby throwing an additional burden on the Jews.

In theory, a broker ought to have been present at all transactions, but in 1586 the Christian brokers complained in a body that the Jews had invented a new ruse to avoid paying brokage. Instead of confining themselves to the Ghetto, they were hawking their wares round the houses and inns of the remoter parishes on the perimeter of the city— in San Domenico, Quintavalle, the Giudecca, San Nicolò and Santa Maria Maggiore—where no brokers could possibly attend. Not only did they sell much shoddy rubbish to unprotected widows and orphans —but they might also, on the pretext of selling goods in their houses, have sexual intercourse with poor women and prostitutes, in a manner contrary to Venetian law. Shocked at this appalling possibility, the brokers demanded measures to prevent it. In accordance with their suggestions, the Ufficiali al Cattaver issued a new regulation to the effect that nobody other than the proprietors of second-hand shops in person might carry materials out of the Ghetto to sell them in the Christian city, and even they were allowed to enter only the houses of noblemen, citizens and merchants.[44] The brokers and the magistrates evidently presumed that persons of exalted rank could be trusted to

[41] *Ibid., busta* 242, reg. 1—proclamations regulating the profession of broker in the Ghetto at ff. 2–3, 11v.–12, 19v.–20, etc., 3 May 1565, 9 September 1567, 9 November 1568; for the number of brokers, *ibid.*, f. 12v., 9 September 1567, and ff. 99v., 100, September 1585. This register is entirely devoted to matters connected with the broker's profession.

[42] *Ibid.*, f. 13r.–v., 27 June 1567.

[43] *Ibid.*, f. 15r.–v., 21 August 1568.

[44] *Ibid.*, f. 104, 24 May 1586.

observe the rules of Christian decency where the unwary or defenceless poor could not.

The Jews, as second-hand traders, performed one other useful function—they frustrated conspiracies by Christian dealers, old-clothiers and junk merchants. In 1597, the Sopraconsoli in Venice called attention to the existence of price-fixing rings among Christian bidders attending the auctions of pledges at Rialto, and said that they caused the poor severe losses by holding prices down. They therefore recommended that Jews be permitted to bid at auctions on the same terms as Christians. Hitherto, a special clause in the *condotte* had apparently discouraged Jews from bidding. This prescribed that, should the auctioneer knock down a pledge to a Jew, it must be held for another eight days to give the Christian owner a further chance to redeem it—as if it were doubly shocking that any Christian property should pass to a Jew. On the suggestion of the Sopraconsoli, the Senate now rescinded the clause.[45]

The restriction of the Jews to *strazzaria* in Venice was not complete: the government modified some of the regulations imposed in 1558. Originally, these forbade them to act as furriers or to work with new furs: but in 1584 they received permission to deal in certain kinds of fur imported from the Levant, perhaps through their co-religionists— 'i.e. *agneline*, *boldroni* and other varieties of new furs'.[46] But in general, they were not supposed to produce goods even for their own consumption. The Jews in Venice were not permitted to infringe the monopoly of manufacturing enjoyed by the Christian guilds—though elsewhere, and especially in Padua, they were believed to provide valuable competition to Christian artisans who could otherwise have held the people to ransom. As the Rabbi Simone Luzzatto pointed out years later, in the 1630's, the Jews were supposed to provide employment for Christians by consuming their products in Venice.[47] In 1597, for example, the Venetian guild of tailors, the Arte dei Sartori, demanded the imposition of more explicit restrictions upon the Jews in order to protect their own monopoly and their livelihood. In the presence of the Collegio, representatives of the Jews of Venice agreed to stipulations that

'no Jew may work as a tailor, either on his own account or for an employer, either as a cutter or as a stitcher, even in the Ghetto';

[45] Chapter 17 of the *condotta* of 1597, A.S.V., *Senato, Terra, filza* 141, 31 January 1596 Venetian style.

[46] A.S.V., *Senato, Terra, filza* 91, 19 June 1584.

[47] Luzzatto, *Discorso*, ff. 28v.–29. He guessed that some 4,000 artisans were necessary to serve the needs of the 6,000 Jews.

'no Jew may import new clothes of any kind into this city';
'no Jew may give tailor's work to anyone, either in the Ghetto or outside it, who is not a properly qualified master in the tailors' guild'. [48]

Behind these regulations, though it was never expressly acknowledged,
there probably lay the desire to deny the Jews the satisfaction of
creative work, and to thrust them into a position in which they appeared
to be social parasites—dealers, middlemen and moneylenders, never
producers. Anti-semitism itself foists upon the Jews the characteristics
it later ascribes to their innate depravity.

Nevertheless, some other occupations remained open to the Jews,
from that of the physician downwards. For obvious reasons, they
needed their own butchers and slaughterers, whom the corporation of
Jews living in the Venetian Ghetto subjected to communal control and
taxation.[49] Fruiterers bearing the Jewish names of Scaramella and
Pugliese occasionally appear in the registers of the Ufficiali al Cattaver,
but it also seems that Christians sold fruit and vegetables to Jews in
the Ghetto.[50] Hence, in September 1617, 'Bortolo, son of Rimondo
Rimondi, fruiterer in the Ghetto Vecchio, and Hieronimo and Paolo,
greengrocers in the same place' received instructions to shut down
their shops and leave the Ghetto Vecchio every Friday evening 'at the
sound of the third trumpet' 'and not to sell any more to any Jew'.[51]
In 1613, the Jewess Fidela Scaramella owned a greengrocery business
in the Ghetto, but Giovanni Ceriol, who seems to have been a Christian,
was running it for her and paying her a rent or *affitto*.[52]

The books of the Cattaveri also mention a Jewish hatter, Ser
Angelino, and a Jewish carver (*intagliador*), Consiglio, son of Gras-
sino.[53] The ban on Jews printing or publishing books, imposed in
1548, seems to have been enforced less rigorously at the close of the
century, when Jews occasionally obtained copyrights for works they
had printed. Jewish printers may possibly have been allowed to work
only on presses owned by Christians in Venice, the magistrates
occasionally, as in 1590 and 1594, granted permission to small groups
of Jews to stay out of the Ghetto beyond the normal curfew to assist in
the printing and correction of works in Hebrew.[54] In 1594, Israel, his

[48] Chapter 11 of the *condotta* of 1597, A.S.V., *Senato, Terra, filza* 141, 31 January
1596 Venetian style.
[49] A.S.V., *Ufficiali al Cattaver, busta* 246, reg. 8, f. 129v.; *busta* 258, reg. 35, 2 May
1602, 30 May 1602, 29 July 1604; *busta* 245, reg. 6, f. 52v., 93v., 217, 291v., 314v.
[50] *Ibid., busta* 246, reg. 7, f. 10v., 22 October 1604; *busta* 243, reg. 3, f. 58,
18 August 1586.
[51] *Ibid., busta* 245, reg. 6, f. 320.   [52] *Ibid.,* ff. 53, 56, 79v.
[53] *Ibid., busta* 258, reg. 36, 18 June 1602, 9 November 1598.
[54] *Ibid., busta* 243, reg. 3, f. 190v.; *busta* 244, reg. 5, f. 101v., 127v.

son Elisama and Rabbi Nessim were proposing to attend for this purpose at the printing press of Missier Giovanni a Gara. There were Jewish printers called Esdra in 1593 and Israel in 1607.[55] Bookselling had not been prohibited, and booksellers also bound books.[56] Moreover, at the turn of the century, Jewish dancing masters, musicians and players were obviously sought-after by Christian pupils and audiences —as witness a licence prepared in September 1585 to authorize a Jew to enter the houses of eleven noblemen and five other persons 'to teach their children to sing, dance and play musical instruments, freely and without restraint'.[57] Don Livio of Ferrara, a Jew resident in the Venetian Ghetto, received permission in the Carnival season to take his pupils or 'company' to dance in the houses of noblemen during the Carnivals of 1594 and 1595.[58] Iseppo, with two fellow lute-players, was entitled to visit the houses of noblemen during Carnival until 'the sixth hour of the night'.[59] In November 1590, a company of fourteen Jewish players obtained a licence to go out of the Ghetto during the Carnival 'to try out and perform *una opera premeditada*'.[60] Generally speaking, the Jews could buy, sell, display their talents and exercise the skill of a physician—but they could not market the products of their own hands, and all contacts with the world outside the Ghetto's walls were strictly regulated by government licences.

On the mainland, Venetian authorities sometimes recognized the social and economic importance of the Jews' function as second-hand dealers. Thus, Alvise Antonio Bondumier, governor of Porto Bufolè, a centre of Jewish residence and activity at least since the late fifteenth century, explained in 1580 that it was the local custom for persons indebted to the fisc or to private individuals to be '*pegnorati*'. Execution was levied on their goods or chattels, which were removed to the local depôt known as the Camera dei Pegni, and if necessary auctioned to defray the debt. Sheer lack of purchasers made it acutely difficult to dispose of these goods, and they were often sold for far less than their true value.[61] The governor Bondumier told the Senate that the Jews were important purchasers of *pegni* or pledges in Uderzo, Motta and other neighbouring regions, 'under the conditions laid down by the ordinances of Your Serenity'. Uderzo and Motta, incidentally, were equipped with recently-erected Monti di Pietà, and Bondumier may

---

[55] *Ibid.*, *busta* 244, reg. 5, f. 84v.; *busta* 246, reg. 7, f. 192.
[56] *Ibid.*, *busta* 243, reg. 3, f. 47, 49, 83v.; *busta* 246, reg. 7, f. 97, 6 March 1606.
[57] *Ibid.*, *busta* 243, reg. 3, f. 35v.
[58] *Ibid.*, *busta* 244, reg. 5, f. 101, 137v.
[59] *Ibid.*, f. 192v., 4 January 1596 Venetian style.
[60] *Ibid.*, *busta* 243, reg. 3, f. 191.
[61] A.S.V., *Senato, Terra, filza* 81, 19 November 1580.

have been referring to their auctions as well as to those of Camere dei Pegni.[62] The governors of Verona in 1589 likewise stated that their Jews, forbidden to lend at interest, acted mainly as *strazzaruoli*, and bought goods second-hand at the sales of the Monte di Pietà and Camera dei Pegni.[63]

In Padua, and even in Verona, the Jews fulfilled an urgent need by providing competition to Christian traders, inducing them to lower their prices, and saving consumers from the ill-effects of monopolies enjoyed by Christian guilds. In 1589, the Veronese Rettori conveyed the impression that Jewish trade in their city was seriously restricted and handicapped by prejudice and distrust on the part of Christian traders. They refused to allow goods on credit to Jewish merchants whose financial soundness they could not easily assess. Only one outstanding merchant family remained—the heirs of one Abram Bas, who had enjoyed special privileges from the Venetian government.[64] But in 1600 other Rettori bore witness to there being no complaints against the Jews, and to their providing valuable competition to the other merchants of the city.[65]

The economic importance of the Jews of Padua, and the value set upon them by local consumers, are much clearer. The *condotta* of 1558, which had forbidden the Jews to trade in newly-manufactured goods on the mainland, though it had ceased to apply in 1566, had created ambiguities and uncertainties of which the local weavers, mercers and tailors were determined to take advantage. The Jews, they claimed in 1585, in one of a series of disputes on this question, must be prevented from selling new goods, especially silken cloth. The Jews themselves replied that mere *strazzaria* was sufficient to support life only in Venice itself, and that 'the second-hand shop of a Venetian Jew is worth more than all those of the Terra Ferma put together'. Such trade in Padua consisted only of a few oddments, and they must not be confined to it. On the other hand, they fulfilled a real need by enabling university students to exchange old garments for new stuffs and silken cloth—a thing impossible in a Christian mercer's shop. The Paduan magistracy of the Deputati ad Utilia freely confirmed this, and added that the Jews provided the students of the University and the soldiers of the garrison with 'everything indispensable to their studies and to furnishing and decorating their rooms'.

The Deputati were fully prepared, on this occasion, to accept the Jews' argument that their competition was anchoring the price of silk

[62] A.S.V., *Senato, Terra*, reg. 1564/65, ff. 193 f.; *ibid.*, *filza* 66, 28 June 1575.
[63] A.S.V., *Senato, Terra*, *filza* 111, 3 June 1589.   [64] *Ibid.*
[65] A.S.V., *Senato, Terra*, *filza* 156, 29 September 1600.

to a reasonable level. The Jews contended that, in the period when Jews had not traded, the mercers had enriched themselves at the expense of the poor, whereas between 1566 and 1585 the Jews had lowered the price of such merchandise by 12–15 per cent (despite the fact that the general movement of prices was almost certainly upwards rather than down). The Deputati extolled the prosperity of the Paduan textile trade. It was especially important for its brides' trousseaux, which could now be manufactured within the Venetian dominion. The demands of contemporary luxury and ostentation, the increasing splendour of weddings which accompanied the inflation of marriage portions, had evidently forced Venetians to go abroad for supplies in the past. The Deputati claimed that because of the flourishing state of the market there were now at least a hundred looms producing silk in Padua, and that the activities of Jewish mercers were substantially responsible for this. Both the Jews and the Deputati claimed that the cheapness of Jewish goods resulted from the special restrictions on Jewish investment and from the fact that the Jew could never hope to indulge in personal ostentation or social climbing—this made him content with very modest profits. The Jews pointed out that Christian mercers could hold on to their goods much longer, waiting for large profits, because they had other forms of wealth and sources of income to support them meanwhile. The Deputati likewise remarked that

> under this government the Jew is forbidden to invest his money in anything other than merchandise, and so long as he knows that trade is progressing and multiplying he is content with smaller gains than the Christian, who wishes to invest his money in estates, houses and other real property, and is not content with a little, but develops a voracious desire for gain. Christian mercers used to rise remarkably in Padua, where in our own day we have seen a mercer's apprentice suddenly making a fortune of 25,000 ducats or more.

These arguments, impressive testimony to the economic utility of the Jews in spheres other than banking, eventually convinced an adequate majority in the Venetian Senate—though opposition was quite substantial. In 1585, by 104 votes in favour to 52 against and 20 'neutral', the Senate chose to grant the Jews of Padua a *ricondotta*, letting them 'engage in business in the way they have done in the past, without, however, being permitted to lend at interest or ply the tailor's trade'.[66]

During these years, the state continued to regard the Jews with

---

[66] A.S.V., *Senato, Terra, filza* 96, 31 December 1585. Luzzatto in his *Discorso*, published in 1638, constantly stresses the importance of the fact that the Jews were forced, unlike Christians, to confine themselves to trade, because they could never lawfully invest in real property.

suspicion and to hold them apart from the surrounding Christian world: in Venice regulating all contacts between the Ghetto and the city, in the provinces creating new ghettoes where none had previously existed. In Venice, Jews were allowed to employ Christian servants or porters on carefully prescribed conditions. The magistrates usually granted them permission to work in the Ghetto in terms similar to the following:

> Licence is given to Donna Antonia di Valentina, a Slovene, to serve in the Ghetto in the houses of Jews on condition that she does not drink, eat or sleep in the Ghetto . . . it being understood that she is over 60 years of age.

Other licences almost invariably mentioned the age of the prospective porter or woman servant, the magistrates having established that he or she was elderly or at least of mature years; such persons could be better trusted, and, being less physically attractive, were less likely to sleep with the Jews (always one of the preoccupations of those who wished to keep them in their proper state of serfdom and apartness). On 9 September 1585, licences went to Leonardo, son of Marco Fari, aged about 45; to Laura, a widow, aged 50; to Daniele, son of Bortolomio, a Friulian, aged 50; to Betta of Bassano, aged 44; to Matteo, a 'Friulian from Poland', aged 38; to Julia of Treviso, aged about 42. Others granted licences on 13 September were somewhat younger—aged between 28 and 36.[67] A relatively rich Jew like Caliman Calimani, of the family of prosperous *strazzaruoli*, could afford to employ two porters for four nights in his house to carry lights and move heavy objects on the occasion of a wedding, in November 1585.[68] But, for the most part, Jews required Christians to serve them chiefly on the sabbath, and in March 1589 they protested in alarm against a recent proclamation which forbade these servants to do anything more than bring them water and fuel. They asked that porters be allowed to lay fires for them and to perform other vital services, and that they be permitted to employ them on Fridays 'up to the fourth hour of the night'. The Ufficiali al Cattaver acceded to the request, but refused to allow porters to do this during Lent, and insisted, as usual, that they must never take anything to eat in Jewish houses.[69] Their regulations were designed to reduce intimate contacts, and to curb any form of association that might imply friendliness or equality, or, on the other hand, provide opportunities for mutual outrages between Jew and Christian at the approach of the Passover and of Passiontide. In March 1590, the magistrates declared expressly that during Lent nobody other than their own officers (*fanti*), the official brokers (*sanseri*), or the Christian

---

[67] A.S.V., *Ufficiali al Cattaver, busta* 243, reg. 3, ff. 33–5.
[68] *Ibid.*, f. 40.   [69] *Ibid.*, f. 127.

watchmen of the Ghetto were to enter the houses of Jews. Certainly, no porters or boatmen might ever go into them at that season.[70] The general assumption was that young people, and the poor and ignorant, must be protected at all times from the Jews, and prevented from consorting with them. There was less risk that noblemen, citizens and merchants, or even poor persons of mature years, would be corrupted or harmed by the Jews, and contact could be permitted under stringent regulations.

High dignitaries of the Church, in Venice and its provinces, sometimes pressed for more rigorous measures to protect Christians from the insidious presence of Jewry. In Venice, Lorenzo Priuli, a more energetic and independent Patriarch than his predecessor Giovanni Trevisan, submitted in 1596–7 a memorandum which, though totally unoriginal, is interesting for its regurgitation of traditional charges against the Jews and for its demands for the enforcement of Gregory XIII's decrees about them. The Counter Reformation had evidently rejuvenated much malicious medieval gossip.

> The fraudulent treachery of the Jews must be feared all the more because these are domestic enemies who can associate with every simple and unwary person.

These words set the tone of the document. The misdemeanours of the Jews, it seemed, included entering Christian houses when only women were at home on the pretext of peddling goods, and committing various crimes there. Especially,

> it happens that if any woman bears a child they steal the newly-born infant, take it to the Ghetto and bring up the children of Christian women, some of them already baptized, in the Jewish faith.

Hence, in the future, the Jews must be prevented from admitting Christians to their schools and synagogues or presenting them with unleavened bread or other ritual foods. They must wear yellow caps which would immediately betray the fact that they were Jews; they must not keep Christian servants, use Christian nurses, or employ Christian workmen. All Jews must sleep in the Ghetto. They must not take in Christians to eat with them; Christians must not remain in the Ghetto by night. Jews must not

> receive any neophyte [i.e. any Jew newly converted to Christianity] in their houses upon any pretext, since they have by their deceit caused many poor wretches to prevaricate, even though they were well set upon the way of salvation.

[70] *Ibid.*, f. 163.

Jews must not emerge from their houses on Good Friday, when they must keep the doors and windows shut. Nor must they mock at processions bearing the Holy Sacrament, if they happened to meet one in the street, but retire modestly up some convenient side alley—instead of remaining to shrug their shoulders with eloquent contempt at the Eucharist. Nor should Jewish physicians be allowed to attend Christian patients,

> because if they do attend Christians they cause them to incur excommunication, and if the patients die they cannot have Christian burial, and this practice was prohibited by the Bull of Pope Gregory XIII of blessed memory, of 30 March 1581, for the safety of the souls of the poor and sick.

The Patriarch also asked the government to give orders that Jews should duly attend the conversion sermons or lectures prescribed for them by order of Gregory XIII in 1584.[71]

The Patriarch's requests did not find their way into the *condotta*, and it is uncertain whether the Venetian government considered it its duty to grant them. Some such measures were, however, eventually enforced in Padua and Verona in the early years of the new century. Since the 1570's, the Jews of these cities had been threatened with confinement in ghettos on the Venetian model. In 1574, the Venetian Senate had permitted the Jews of Verona to remain only on condition that they moved into a separate Jewish quarter: the Bishop and many gentry entertained plans to establish a ghetto. Later contracts repeated this provision with monotonous regularity, even stipulating in 1584 that if the Rettori failed to find 'the place separated from the Christians' within two months the concession to the Jews would become null and void.[72] This clause was not enforced, and the place was not found. Federico Cornaro, Bishop of Padua, pressed for the introduction of a ghetto in his own city, as did Agostino Valier, Bishop of Verona.[73] Administrative difficulties blocked both projects until 1600. The Rettori of Verona eventually explained in 1600 that some of the sites pre-

---

[71] A.S.V., *Senato, Terra, filza* 141, 31 January 1596 Venetian style. For the decrees of Gregory XIII, see B.R., VIII, pp. 371–3, 487–9. The Patriarch, however, did not mention Gregory XIII's Bull on the Inquisition and the Jews.

[72] A.S.V., *Senato, Terra, filza* 65, 28 December 1574; *filza* 79, 6 December 1579; *filza* 93, 12 January 1584 Venetian style; *filza* 111, 3 June 1589.

[73] For Padua, see A.S.V., *Senato, Terra, filza* 82, 3 March 1581; *filza* 96, 31 December 1585. From *filza* 108, 5 September 1588, it appears that Cardinal Cornaro had offered to make good the expenses of erecting a ghetto in Padua. For Cardinal Valier's part in inspiring the erection of the Veronese ghetto, see for example the memorandum of Cattarino Zeno and Piero Morosini, *filza* 156, 29 September 1600.

viously contemplated were in the middle of the town and therefore too
near to government offices, to the principal public buildings (*palazzi
publici*), and to monasteries and convents. They felt bound to preserve
some semblance of taking the Jews' own wishes into account, and had
allowed them to refuse remoter sites on the edge of the town, on the
grounds that these were too insecure and that not enough business
would come their way. At last, however, it had been possible to discover a place between the Via Nuova and the Strada dei Pellizzari,
called 'Sotto i Tetti', about which the Jews were said (by the Rettori)
to be positively enthusiastic. This area contained 23 'very good' houses
and plenty of shops, which could easily be enclosed, and the owners of
the houses, having previously let to artisans, were now willing to accept
the Jews as tenants.[74] The Jews' supposed enthusiasm, if it ever really
existed, may well have been dampened by the fact that they then incurred heavy expenses in enclosing the area and in repairing and renewing some of the dwellings. The city allowed them to use its own
communal property as security, to raise a loan of some 15,000 ducats
at 6 per cent for this purpose.[75] Similarly, in 1602, the Paduans took
the first steps towards establishing a ghetto, again at the Jews' expense.
They received an advance out of certain funds deposited in the Monte
di Pietà, the sum of 3,000 ducats to buy 'the land on which the main
square of the Ghetto and the entrance to it will stand'. They must repay
the money over the next six years, and were to enjoy the use of the
land only, never becoming its owners even when the loan was repaid.[76]
Neither Padua nor Verona was equipped with a ready-made fortress
like the Venetian Ghetto: lack of similar opportunities had delayed
the segregation of Jewish dwellings for nearly thirty years. But even in
these cities the ghetto arrived at last.

Finally, the Jews of Rovigo attracted the authorities' attention. The
disorganization of the Monte di Pietà was such that even in 1624 three
Jewish banks survived in the city, lending to locals at 12 per cent and
to outsiders from La Badia and Lendenara at 15 per cent. Jews not
only acted as mercers, but also sold salted meats and other victuals, and
their shops, on the same *piazze*, were indistinguishable from those of
Christians. The governor Girolamo Correr claimed that he had urged
the foundation of a ghetto, and this proposal had been favourably
received by the local magistracy of the Regolatori. But they had done
nothing about it. However, four years later, another Podestà-Capitano,

[74] A.S.V., *Senato, Terra, filza* 149, 13 February 1598 Venetian style.
[75] A.S.V., *Senato, Terra, filza* 156, 29 September 1600.
[76] A.S.V., *Senato, Terra, filza* 164, 19 October 1602.

Marino Zane, felt able to congratulate himself on getting the Jews of Rovigo penned into a ghetto, to the great satisfaction, it seemed, of all concerned.[77]

Nevertheless, a corollary to this segregation into which they were forced, to the condition of degraded apartness in which they lived, was the relative autonomy of the Jewish communities in the Venetian dominion. They formed a corporation with clearly defined rights and duties, though the definition was subject to periodic adjustment. If the *condotta* determined the total tax liability of the whole Jewish community, the Jews themselves were responsible for apportioning the burden. In an alien, potentially hostile land which exploited their wealth and services whilst confining them to rented slums, the Jews nevertheless enjoyed the right to pursue a way of life distinctively their own.

The sovereign body which controlled the affairs of all Jews of Italian or ultimately German origin resident in Venice or in its mainland possessions was the Jewish council, chapter or Capitolo meeting in Venice itself. It was this council which levied taxation for the support of the Jewish banks. Not all Jewish taxpayers—not even all the taxpayers of Venice—attended the chapter. In 1594, the chapter consisted of between 60 and 70 Jews from within Venice itself, of six officials serving as Heads or agents of the Jewish community, and of eleven Jews from the mainland—representing some, but by no means all, of the provincial settlements.[78] In 1589 the number of taxpayers in Venice alone had been in the region of 200,[79] where the total Jewish population was about 1,700. Quite probably—to judge by a phrase used in 1610—*persone mecaniche* were excluded from the chapter:[80] they were very likely odd-job men, handymen and menials of all kinds, rather than artisans. Agents of the Jewish corporation in Venice levied taxes on the mainland communities as well as on the Venetian, where necessary getting the Ufficiali al Cattaver to back them up. Thus, in 1601, Isaac Soncino, as Cassier of the Jewish corporation, asked for letters

---

[77] A.S.V., *Senato, Terra, filza* 188, 13 October 1608 (letter of Alvise Querini, dated 18 March 1608); *Collegio, Relazioni*, b. 46, reports of Pietro Gradenigo, 2 August 1612; Girolamo Correr, 6 March 1624; Francesco Trevisan, 5 August 1625; Marino Zane, 10 May 1628.

[78] A.S.V., *Ufficiali al Cattaver, busta* 244, reg. 5, ff. 132–3.

[79] *Ibid.*, reg. 3, *busta* 243, ff. 133–4v.

[80] *Ibid.*, *busta* 246, reg. 8, f. 120v., 10 July 1610; it was intimated to 'the Jew Ser Giacomo de Datole that by this morning at the time when cases are heard he must have nominated ten *giudici confidenti* in place of the ones rejected by their lordships, and that these must not be Levantines or Ponentines or *persone mecaniche*, but men who attend the great chapter'.

to be sent to the governor of Capo d'Istria instructing him to compel the heirs of the late Mendlin Macaria to pay their taxes.[81]

The principal officers of the Jewish corporation in Venice were the so-called Capi or Heads. Their number varied according to resolutions passed from time to time by the chapter. In 1585, for example, the chapter determined to reduce the number of the principal officers from twelve to six: two of the six should be called Deputati e Capi, and all the six officers together should form a council known as the *congregazione piccola*, which was smaller and more manageable than the chapter. The Capi were entitled to summon both the small congregation and the chapter and to propose resolutions to them; any two members of the small congregation, acting in concert, could summon either the small congregation or the chapter to deliberate. The small congregation, probably handling most routine business, made all its decisions by the votes of two-thirds majorities.[82] The term Capi, however, seems often to have been used loosely to denote all members of the small congregation. Its numbers fluctuated; in 1615, for example, there were 'eleven Heads of the Ghetto', judging a dispute between two Jews.[83]

At least in the 1580's, offices in the principal Jewish councils were regarded as burdens rather than as sought-after positions of power. Since the Heads of the Jewish corporation were responsible (among other things) for negotiating the *condotta*, they were uncomfortably placed on the frontier between the Jewish world and the Christian state, and exposed to the opprobrium of both. In 1585, some prominent Jews went to great lengths to avoid incurring these duties, threatening to emigrate if the office were imposed upon them, and putting down substantial pledges—in money—that they would carry these threats out.[84] Three years later, the Heads spoke epigrammatically 'of the long time we have been like the target at shooting-practice in the service of this corporation (*del longo tempo che siamo statti come il bersaglio alla frezza alla servitù della università*)'.[85]

The Venetian government also allowed the Jews much autonomy in the settlement of civil disputes between themselves, allowing them—and sometimes ordering them—to elect their own arbitrators, known as *giudici confidenti* or *giudici arbitri*.[86] The authority of the synagogue

---

[81] *Ibid.*, busta 258, reg. 36, 26 November 1601; for other examples, *ibid.*, busta 246, reg. 7, f. 50, 118, etc.

[82] *Ibid.*, busta 243, reg. 3, f. 26r.–v.   [83] *Ibid.*, busta 245, reg. 6, f. 167.

[84] *Ibid.*, busta 243, reg. 3, ff. 23v.–25v.

[85] *Ibid.*, f. 96r.–v., 17 April 1588.

[86] For various instances, *ibid.*, busta 246, reg. 7, f. 105, 107r.–v., 161, 184, 186v., 197, 197v.

stood beside that of the chapter, often acting as a kind of police-force and wielding its power to excommunicate with the permission of the Ufficiali al Cattaver or on their instructions. The Cattaveri commonly called on the rabbis to use their power in order to track down stolen goods which might be pledged at the Jewish banks or sold to Jewish dealers. Hints occur here that the second-hand trade was expected to include jewellery as well as clothing or other materials. A typical decree of the Cattaveri might run as follows:

> On the orders of the most noble Signori Cattaveri, you, the rabbis of the Ghetto and the beadle, are instructed to pronounce excommunication in your synagogues in the manner of the Jews upon all who have received as pledges or purchased since yesterday linen, or medallions of gold, silver and bronze, or house furnishings: and those who have bought or accepted such things as pledges must come and immediately notify the office of the most noble Signori Cattaveri, because they may belong to the most noble Signor Lorenzo Bernardo and his brother, sons of the most noble Signor Andrea, or to the most noble Signor Francesco di Zaccaria Bernardo, and must be restored to them. . . .'[87]

Another such decree listed materials, including velvets and the type of silken fabric known as *ormesini*, which had apparently been stolen from Antonio Venturini, a Christian *strazzaruol* at the Ponte della Beccaria.[88]

At one point, indeed, a member of the Cattaveri, Hieronimo Barbarigo, objected to the power of the rabbis. In July 1618, he complained to the Senate of the Jews freely interpreting the words of the current *condotta* which entitled them to live according to their own rites ('*viver col ritto loro*'). Allegedly, they took the phrase to mean that they were not only entitled to keep their own synagogues, but also to compel Jews to bring all civil and criminal lawsuits before Jewish judges, and through these courts to form a species of state within a state. Barbarigo argued that the Jews should not in future be entitled to wield the sanction of excommunication without the permission of the Cattaveri.[89] But the Senate did not—at least, not immediately—incorporate his suggestions in the *condotta* or expressly interfere with the existing degree of Jewish autonomy. The state itself had frequently exploited the authority of the rabbis, and was probably not anxious to curtail it.

Apart from managing its own judicial and fiscal arrangements under the surveillance of the Cattaveri, the Ghetto also maintained a number

[87] *Ibid.*, *busta* 244, reg. 5, f. 146v., 14 July 1595.
[88] *Ibid.*, f. 102, 9 February 1593 Venetian style.
[89] A.S.V., *Senato, Terra, filza* 231, 14 December 1618.

of charities and educational establishments for its own poor, helping in this way to build up a more self-contained and self-reliant world. The Jews had almsgiving fraternities (*fraterna dell'elemosina, fraterna della misericordia*);[90] a fraternity for clothing the poor;[91] another for lodging foreigners on their travels;[92] another for procuring the release of prisoners;[93] another for providing marriage portions for Jewish maidens.[94] Many of the preoccupations of Jewish charity resembled those of Christian. Another fraternity ran a children's school,[95] and there was also a Jewish 'academy'.[96]

Formal suspicion of the Jews as conspirators against Christianity and treacherous proselytizers accompanied a shrewd appreciation of their economic utility. In the period under review, the Senate's records reveal only one obvious instance of economic, as distinct from religious, anti-semitism—one in which the misconduct allegedly committed by a Jewish moneylender served as a pretext for getting rid of him. In 1614–1615, Antonio Priuli, the future Doge, then serving as Provveditore Generale in Terra Ferma, helped the commune of Asola in the Bresciano to repudiate its debts to the Jew Joseph Levi. The story told by the Provveditore Generale and by the citizens of Asola accused the Jews of persistent misconduct in the area since 1574, for which they now proposed to hold Joseph Levi responsible—conveniently ignoring the fact that, as he pointed out, his father had lent money in the district only from 1597 onwards, and he himself only since 1610. Though licensed to lend at 12 per cent, the first Jewish banker had presented to the town council terms so outrageous that they had rejected them. Nonetheless, the Jew had persisted in lending according to these rejected and iniquitous *capitoli*, never seen or approved by the Venetian government, and in doing so at rates of 15 per cent, 20 per cent or even 30 per cent. Why the citizens had so long permitted him to do this is by no means clear. But it may be that it was generally recognized that Jewish lenders in small country towns could not make a living unless they exceeded the official rate of 12 per cent, and that they were tacitly allowed to do so until it became convenient to treat this practice as a crime, and to use it against the Jew involved. The citizens of Asola

[90] A.S.V., *Ufficiali al Cattaver*, busta 243, reg. 3, ff. 10v., 24; busta 246, reg. 7, f. 207, 252.

[91] *Ibid.*, busta 246, reg. 7, f. 27; reg. 8, f. 173v., 186; busta 258, reg. 36, 4 December 1603, 26/29 March 1604.

[92] *Ibid.*, busta 246, reg. 7, f. 252; reg. 8, f. 72v.; busta 258, reg. 36, 18 January 1601 Venetian style.

[93] *Ibid.*, busta 245, reg. 6, f. 202v., 207v.

[94] *Ibid.*, busta 244, reg. 5, f. 1, 122v.; busta 246, reg. 7, f. 187v.

[95] *Ibid.*, busta 246, reg. 7, f. 74.

[96] *Ibid.*, busta 258, reg. 36, 3 July 1602, 8 July 1602, 18 April 1603.

further complained that when clients brought bundles of goods to Joseph, he would never write down the details, but would simply record that so-and-so had pledged a bundle. On redeeming this object, the borrower would find it stuffed with 'rags of no value whatsoever'. Priuli then estimated the damage inflicted by the Jew on the district of Asola. The commune owed him 10,000 ducats or more, private individuals over 22,000 ducats, and he had lent a total of 13,000 on pledges in addition to this. The Jew had obtained possession of land and real property; he had taken payment in the form of crops, and given these out on credit at excessive prices. Priuli now pleaded that the heavily indebted town and district of Asola would suffer total ruin and lapse utterly into the power of the Jews if the Signory failed to take action. He added that, since the Levi family had partners or associates in the Duchy of Mantua, a high proportion of the wealth of a group of Venetian subjects was being exported and lost to the Venetian treasury. He therefore asked the Senate to confirm the sentence passed on Joseph Levi—a fine of 10,000 ducats, 5,000 of which must be used to establish a Monte di Pietà. The Senate seeing no reason to interfere with the sentence, the Monte di Pietà was indeed founded.[97]

The truth behind this case cannot be discovered with any certainty. Should a commune choose to repudiate its debts, a Jewish banker was peculiarly vulnerable—much more so than a feudal lord advancing money to his peasants and villagers. Charges of misconduct would be readily believed by somebody in authority. Even if a commune tacitly acquiesced in a Jew lending at more than the permitted rate, it could always turn this into a weapon against him at an appropriate moment. This kind of repudiation was a welcome means of cutting many knots —or so it seemed at first. It only remains to add that the new Monte di Pietà did not flourish, and by 1621 was on the verge of collapse.[98]

However, the question which most needs answering is that of how Venice succeeded in forcing its Jewish community to lend money at the uniquely low interest rate of 5 per cent per annum. In the past the Jews had, as in 1565, complained that even rates of 12 per cent had yielded very small profits.[99] Theoretically, rates of 5 per cent could have been more than enough to cover the rents and administrative costs of the banks. Some Monti di Pietà in the late sixteenth and early seventeenth century managed to lower their charges to 4 per cent, 3 per cent or even $2\frac{1}{2}$ per cent per annum[100]—though they may have had to pay

[97] A.S.V., *Senato, Terra, filza* 215, 25 September 1615.

[98] A.S.V., *Senato, Dispacci, Provveditori da terra e da mar, filza* 270, despatches of Donato Morosini, Leonardo Moro and Marco Giustinian, Sindici Inquisitori in Terra Ferma, 10 May and 5 June 1621.

[99] See above, p. 532.   [100] See below, pp. 579–80.

lower rents for their premises than did the Jews of Venice. But there is no doubt that Venetian rates were and remained very low indeed compared with those charged by Jews elsewhere in Italy. Throughout the sixteenth century, the Popes had systematically depressed the rates chargeable in the Papal States by Jewish pawnbrokers—but they had never succeeded, for more than a few years, in reducing them to less than 18 per cent.[101]

One explanation for this Venetian feat almost certainly lies in alterations in the state's fiscal demands—to which the interest charged by the Jews had always been intimately related: higher taxation demanded higher interest rates, except at times when the state was deliberately trying to impose intolerable conditions upon the Jews. At least for a time after 1573, contributions to the non-profitmaking loan banks of Venice seem to have become the principal form of taxation paid by the Jews. Instead of paying the Venetian treasury sums subsequently applied to the Arsenal and the navy, the Jews of Venice and the mainland paid to their own officials and tax-collectors dues applied to the non-profitmaking banks of Venice. From 1573 onwards, the *condotte* of the Venetian Jews ceased to stipulate that they should pay to the treasury a regular annual basic tax or *tansa*; and from 1591 they prescribed that all Jews resident in Venice and on the mainland should contribute to the Venetian banks, and that the Jews should elect their own tax-assessors (*tansadori*) to apportion the burdens.[102] In this way too, the Jewish communities were becoming more self-contained. The state, perhaps out of a pious reluctance to draw on the profits of usury, was foregoing the contributions it had formerly received directly from the Jews, in order to enable them to serve the poor at more reasonable rates. However, other forms of taxation were not totally abandoned. The Jews of Padua and Verona paid small sums, of a few hundred ducats a year, directly to the Venetian government. The tax liability of the Jews of Verona was fixed at 250 ducats a year in 1574–84, rising to 300 in 1584–1609.[103] In 1585, the Rettori of Padua said that the tax paid

[101] Delumeau, 'Les dettes à Rome', pp. 25–8, cites an edict of Gregory XIII, issued in 1575, which declares that Leo X had tolerated lending at 60 per cent, Paul III at 48 per cent, Pius IV at 14 per cent and Pius V at 12 per cent only. But Gregory XIII compromised by tolerating a maximum rate of 18 per cent, a provision which remained in force for the rest of the century. Luzzatto, *Discorso*, f. 33, writes that elsewhere in Italy Jews lent at up to 18 per cent, and the 5 per cent interest charge was peculiar to Venice.

[102] Chapters 4 and 6 of the *condotta* of 1591, A.S.V., *Senato, Terra, filza* 122, 7 December 1591.

[103] A.S.V., *Senato, Terra, filza* 65, 28 December 1574; *filza* 79, 6 December 1579; *filza* 93, 12 January 1584 Venetian style; *filza* 111, 3 June 1589; *filza* 156, 29 September 1600; *filza* 192, 22 October 1609.

20

by the 280 Jews of the city was at present 200 ducats, and recommended that it be increased to 400. In 1607, the Jews of Padua were also paying a local rate of 300 ducats, for the upkeep of public streets in the city.[104] Jewish money also continued, on occasion, to finance the Venetian navy—but, as far as one can tell, it did not do so on a comparable scale. Venetian Jews seem to have been assessed for the galleots' tax like other corporations; in 1607, they were required to produce 1,250 ducats for galleots. This contribution, however onerous at the time, was very slight compared with the sums which the Jews had disbursed at the beginning of the sixteenth century.[105]

However, the situation seems to have changed by the 1630's. In 1638, the rabbi Simone Luzzatto drew attention to the profits which Jews brought to the fisc: though these consisted mainly of indirect taxes, and of customs duties paid by Jewish merchants. The Jews had again paid substantial sums in direct taxes recently, though these resulted from extraordinary, rather than from regular levies. Of such levies, the most burdensome was the recent *tansa straordinaria*, of 1636, which had raised 11,000 ducats from the Jews, and a levy of another 6,000 assessed according to house-rents, which Luzzatto regarded as especially burdensome to the Jewish tenants of the Ghetto. By the 1630's, too, the Jews had apparently incurred a very onerous obligation to pay for the expense of lodging visiting princes and ambassadors, 'and when the state paid for this it used to disburse at the rate of 800 ducats a month'.[106] It would be difficult to prove that in the decade 1630–40 the Jews were being lightly taxed apart from their contributions to loan banks: but it is possible that even then these taxes were temporary and extraordinary. In any case, the situation may have changed very substantially between the 1570's and the 1630's, and in the 1570's the state may have foregone taxation to enable the Jewish banks to establish themselves. A long interval of peace made it practicable to do this. In the 1630's, the taxpaying capacity of the Jews had probably increased through the expansion of Levantine trade, and the demands of war finance were then greater.

During the negotiations for the *condotta* of 1607, the heads of the Venetian community provided some valuable, if all too scanty information about the financing of the Venetian banks. In 1573, their total liability had been limited, in the first instance, to 50,000 ducats: they were not obliged to lend beyond that sum. However, at the next *con-*

[104] A.S.V., *Senato, Terra, filza* 96, 31 December 1585; *filza* 142, 11 March 1597; *filza* 183, 4 August 1607.
[105] A.S.V., *Senato, Terra, filza* 184, 5 October 1607.
[106] Luzzatto, *Discorso*, ff. 28–31.

dotta (in 1580) the ceiling was removed, and the Jews claimed in 1607 that they were called upon to lend about 100,000 ducats a year to the general public. Most of all, they dreaded a stoppage or failure in the textile trades, 'and consequently in all other trades', which would create an impossible demand upon them to tide the poor over the crisis.[107] In 1618, the Jews represented to the Senate that the sum they lent annually had now increased to as much as 200,000 ducats a year, though on this occasion the Senate did agree to limit their total obligation in the immediate future to 100,000 ducats only.[108] The Jews were evidently transacting business on a scale roughly comparable to that of the third largest Monte di Pietà in the Venetian dominion—that of Udine. In 1607, the Venetian Jews explained that to meet their obligations they were forced to raise capital of 80,000 ducats, with another 10,000 for emergency use; and on this they paid interest at the rate of $8\frac{1}{2}$ per cent, which cost them some 8,000 ducats a year. It is probable that the Jewish community as a whole borrowed this sum from a number of rich Jewish individuals. Whether they could lawfully have borrowed from Christians is extremely doubtful. Moreover, from 1591 onwards, Venetian Jewry itself had been responsible for maintaining the supply of bankers to all mainland communities. In 1607, the Sopraconsoli justified permitting the Jews to lend at usury to one another, saying that

> In the past, it has always been permitted that the Jews should supply one another with loans at interest, especially as the Jews of Venice are obliged to support both the banks of Venice itself and those of the Terra Ferma, as in chapter 5 of the *condotta*. The banker does not usually have enough money of his own to sustain the business transacted by the bank, but is supplied and assisted by other Jews who invest their money at interest, saying that this is not forbidden to them by their law. Moreover, by chapter 8 of the *condotta*, Jewish bankers are for good reason forbidden to be supplied with money by Christians. . .

The provision that Jewish bankers could never be in debt to Christians had been introduced after the Jewish bankruptcies in mid-century, and incorporated in the *condotta* of 1566.[109]

How, then, did individual Jews raise the capital, and the Jewish community as a whole the taxes, necessary to the support of the subsidized, non-profitmaking loan banks of Venice? They may, of course, have been able to borrow some of the capital from abroad, from Ottoman Jews or from co-religionists in Mantua. It is conceivable that

[107] A.S.V., *Senato, Terra, filza* 184, 5 October 1607.
[108] A.S.V., *Senato, Terra, filza* 231, 14 December 1618.
[109] See above, p. 535.

some Jewish bankers on the mainland raised profits—as Joseph Levi of Asola supposedly did—by lending at substantially more than the permitted rates of 10–12½ per cent. Silk merchants in Padua, mercers and victuallers in Rovigo, also prospered to some extent. The Venetian trade in second-hand goods excited much envy from mainland Jews like the Paduans who could not hope to rival it: though in 1618 the Venetian Jews claimed that their *strazzaria* had suffered heavily through the operation of sumptuary laws. These affected not only private persons, but also Rettori on their way to take up posts in the mainland cities. Such restrictions on fashion and display naturally reduced the turnover in discarded clothing, and the dealers had closed many of their shops in the Ghetto.[110]

The most substantial profits made by the Jews in the late sixteenth and early seventeenth century probably derived from Levantine trade. After 1580, 'Ponentine' Jews, ultimately of Spanish or Portuguese origin and since resident in Italy, began to migrate to Venice and to form a third group or category, one concerned with Levantine trade, by the side of the 'German Jews' and of the 'itinerant' merchants who were Turkish subjects. Since the mid-sixteenth century, when the Venetian government had registered such suspicion and hostility towards the Marranos, they had found shelter chiefly in the Este state of Ferrara. Now, in 1578–81, Alfonso II d'Este responded to threats and pressure from the Papacy, inspired by Spain, which procured the dispersal of the Jews from his Duchy.[111] During the next decade, the Venetian attitude to them palpably changed. The constitutional crisis of 1582–3 had brought the anti-Spanish party of the *giovani*, strong in the Senate, into greater prominence and power. To prove any direct connexion between this and the admission of the Spanish–Italian Jews to Venice would be difficult: but it may have commended itself as a minor anti-Spanish gesture. Meanwhile, the Jew Daniel Rodriguez was urging upon the Venetian government the advantages of developing Levantine trade through a new centre, the Dalmatian port of Spalato, where the Jews enjoyed extensive business connexions. In the mid-sixteenth century, Venice had done little to develop the Dalmatian possessions of Zara, Sebenico and Spalato, which conducted trade between the Turkish frontier lands and the Italian ports of the Adriatic, or through them to offer serious competition to Ragusa. But after the war of Cyprus, Jewish merchants and Turkish authorities began hatch-

---

[110] A.S.V., *Senato, Terra, filza* 231, 14 December 1618.
[111] Roth, 'Les marranes à Venise', pp. 205–6; *Jews of Venice*, pp. 65–7; Cecil Roth, 'La ricondotta degli ebrei ponentini, Venezia, 1647', *Studi in onore di Gino Luzzatto*, II (Milan, 1950), p. 239.

ing schemes to by-pass Ragusa; economic activity was developing in some Turkish Balkan provinces, especially in Bosnia, and the authorities wanted a more direct link with Italian markets.[112] After 1580, sea-routes to the Levant were becoming increasingly hazardous, increasingly threatened by piracy: and the development of overland routes into the Turkish Empire had much to recommend it. Moreover, Venice was soon to face heavy competition from the development, especially in the 1590's, of the free port of Leghorn under the Grand Dukes of Tuscany. Rodriguez, foreseeing this, encouraged the Venetians to divert Jewish settlers from Leghorn, and stressed the service they could render the Republic, not only as traders, but also by indirectly financing loan banks.

In a paper submitted on or before 16 May 1591, Daniel Rodriguez wrote that the Grand Duke

is making every effort to develop the port of Pisa[113] with Levantine trade, and is negotiating with the Grand Chancellor of Poland to direct the trade of that nation to Tuscany by way of Hamburg and Danzig, and also with other Christian princes. And just as one cannot make war without soldiers or a port without merchants, or trade with the Turks, a most rapacious nation, without expense, even so I shall be unable to do anything by myself or fulfil the promise I have made to Your Serenity, without the aid of Your Serenity and that of the Levantine and Ponentine Jewish nations.

My proposal is this: that Your Serenity should issue a general *condotta* embracing all Jews without discrimination, except for travelling Levantine Jews who reside in this city for periods of six months or less. All the rest of the Jews who reside in this city at a given time shall be obliged to contribute to the establishment of at least two banks in the Ghetto bound to serve the poor with sums of three ducats or less at the rate of 5 per cent in the normal way. At the same time, these bankers, and five or six others, or as many as Your Serenity sees fit, shall be licensed to lend, at 12 per cent per annum, sums of over 3 ducats; and all these Jews shall be *condotti* for a period of ten years for certain and a grace period of another two, supposing they are not *ricondotti* during that time. . . .[114]

[112] On the economic development of Spalato, see especially Jorjo Tadić, 'Le commerce en Dalmatie et à Raguse et la décadence économique de Venise au XVIIème siècle', *Aspetti e cause della decadenza economica veneziana nel secolo XVII* (Venice–Rome, 1961), pp. 241 f., 255 f.

[113] For the close relationship between Pisa and Leghorn, and for its development through the grain trade in the 1590's, see the study of Fernand Braudel and Ruggiero Romano, *Navires et marchandises à l'entrée du port de Livourne (1547–1611)* (Paris, 1951).

[114] A.S.V., *Senato, Terra, filza* 122, 7 December 1591. For further information about Rodriguez, see Cecil Roth, 'Immanuel Aboab's proselytization of the Marranos', *Jewish Quarterly Review*, new series, XXXII (1932–3), pp. 139–41; Schiavi, 'Ebrei in Venezia', pp. 509–10.

The proposal that a separate bank be established to lend larger sums at higher rates, although repeated at intervals throughout the years from 1580 to 1618 (and not only by Rodriguez), found no favour. But the new *condotta* of 1591 did incorporate a new arrangement whereby all Jews in the Venetian dominion were in future bound to contribute to the upkeep of the loan banks in Venice itself. The Jews of Padua and Verona, as well as (by implication) the new Ponentine immigrants, must begin contributing when their present contracts had expired. The Levantine merchants specifically objected to the arrangement a few years later, when in 1596 they protested against 'German' Jews molesting them for taxes and contributions. They 'happened to be here solely for the purposes of trade', and did not enjoy the same benefits as their 'German' colleagues. Hence, the new *condotta* carefully differentiated between 'Levantine Jews who actually have houses and live with their families in Venice (*che loco et foco habiterano con le famiglie loro in questa città*)', and, on the other hand, 'itinerant Levantine merchants who are Turkish subjects, and Corfiot Jews who enjoy special privileges'. The first group were bound to contribute to the banks, the second exempted from so doing.[115]

Clearly, then, the profits of Levantine trade began to contribute to the upkeep of Venetian banks for the benefit of the poor and others. Jewish traders permanently resident in Venice received special *condotte* in 1598 and 1611. That of 1598, granted for a period of ten years, as Rodriguez had suggested, authorized

> any Levantine or Ponentine Jewish merchant to come and live in this city with his family and remain and freely make a living here, wearing the *sessa*, i.e. the yellow hat of the Jews, and dwelling in the Ghetto Nuovo.

Jewish merchants were entitled to 'trade freely by sea (*navigar liberamente*)' as at present. The terms of their agreement protected them against arbitrary increases of excise duties or taxation, and guaranteed them equal treatment in this respect with Venetian subjects, save that 'Levantine' and 'Ponentine' Jews were bound to join the corporation of 'German' Jews in supporting the loan banks for the poor. Nonresident Turkish subjects remained exempt.[116] In or before 1611, the trading Jews again pressed for exemption from the contribution, but again the Senate decided that they must pay this special form of tax.[117]

The extensive and voluntary withdrawal of many Venetian mer-

---

[115] Communication of the Levantine Jewish merchants formally addressed to the German Jews, dated on or before 4 December 1596, in A.S.V., *Senato, Terra, filza* 141, 31 January 1596 Venetian style. On the Corfiot community, cf. David Kaufmann, 'Contribution à l'histoire des juifs de Corfou', *Revue des études juives*, XXXII–XXXIII (1896). [116] A.S.V., *Senato, Terra, filza* 148, 6 October 1598. [117] A.S.V., *Senato, Terra, filza* 199, 29 June 1611.

chants from trade in the early seventeenth century, and their increasing
tendency to invest heavily in estates on the mainland, opened opportunities to the Jews, though they never monopolized Levantine commerce. Indeed, in 1611 or 1612 the community of German Jews began
pressing for the privilege of being permitted to trade with the Levant
on the same terms as their co-religionists: but the Board of Trade
(Cinque Savii alla Mercanzia) did not see fit to recommend any adjustment to the arrangements.[118] Literary and other evidence suggests that
at least before 1640 Jewish traders contributed mainly to commerce
within the Adriatic and with the Dalmatian ports. They were much less
given to embarking their goods on long sea-voyages. Jewish merchandise was especially exposed to the attacks of such pious pirates as the
Uskoks of Segna and the Knights of St John of Malta.[119]

The researches of Professor Alberto Tenenti have furnished much
information about ships and cargoes connected with Venice which
were wrecked or sunk in the Mediterranean between 1592 and 1609.
These ships and cargoes may well represent a fair cross-section of
Venetian trade as a whole in these years.[120] On the basis of this information, M. Blumenkranz has now pointed out that a fair number of
Spanish or 'Ponentine' Jews, bearing names like Albelda, Castiel,
Faro, Gaon and Pardo, were engaged in trade with the east from
Venice in these years. Jews formed 3–4 per cent of the total of over
2,000 merchants listed as having shares in ships wrecked at sea. They
handled some 10 per cent of all merchandise passing between Venice
and Constantinople, but, more strikingly, enjoyed a near monopoly of
all Venetian trade with the Dalmatian port of Valona, and with the
island of Corfù, where a specially privileged Jewish community resided.
The Jews owned shares in cargoes, but practically never in ships, and
the records reveal only one case of a Jewish shipowner, who belonged
to the Corfiot family of Mozza.[121] Jews may, of course, have registered
their ships in the names of men of straw, who disguised the real owners.

The situation which Simone Luzzatto described in 1638 was essentially similar. Writing partly to refute the charge that the Jews had
forced their way into Venetian trade and ousted the citizenry,[122] he

[118] A.S.V., *Senato, Terra, filza* 207, 3 September 1613; *filza* 231, 14 December 1618.
[119] Cf. Alberto Tenenti, *Piracy and the decline of Venice,* trans. Janet and Brian
Pullan (London, 1967), pp. 48–9, 178–9.
[120] Alberto Tenenti, *Naufrages, corsaires et assurances maritimes à Venise (1592–
1609)* (Paris, 1959).
[121] Bernard Blumenkranz, 'Les juifs dans le commerce maritime de Venise, 1592–
1609', *Revue des études juives, série iii,* vol. II (1961).
[122] The title page describes Luzzatto's *Discorso* as an 'appendice al Trattato
dell'openioni e Dogmi de gl'Hebrei dall'universal non dissonanti, e de Riti loro piu
principali'.

pointed out that their principal function was to attract to Venice goods despatched by their co-religionists from northern and western Europe, and to trade with centres within the Ottoman Empire where the Venetians enjoyed no official representation. He drew attention to the melancholy fact that ships from the west called at Genoa, Leghorn, Civita Vecchia, Naples, Messina, Ragusa and Ancona. Thence they distributed their goods into Italy through Lombardy, Piedmont, the Romagna and the Marches; and none of this, or very little, found its way to Venice. However,

> the business destined for the Jews of Italy beyond Leghorn by their friends and co-religionists cannot go anywhere other than to Venice, since the Jews have not attempted to establish themselves or to reside in any of the places mentioned above, and Leghorn itself has to a large extent been abandoned by the Jews since the heavy losses which occurred in the grain trade in the past few years. The trade handled by the Jews must not be underestimated, since many Jews in foreign countries remit a large part of their goods to the inhabitants of this city, as for various reasons they cannot themselves repair to Venice.

Luzzatto was probably referring to goods embarked by Jews in the United Provinces and especially, perhaps, in Amsterdam: for promises of toleration had allured many Jews to the Northern Netherlands during the prolonged revolt of the late sixteenth century.[123]

The work of Rodriguez had survived. It was excellent that the port of Spalato and its trade should be in Jewish, rather than Turkish hands, 'on account of the disadvantages suffered by Venetian subjects in doing business with Turks'. The Jews, however, were not well placed in trade with Syria and Alexandria (nor had they been in 1592–1609). But they did send cash and merchandise principally to

> all that stretch of land that lies between Dalmatia and Constantinople, and to other parts of the Turkish Empire where there is no Venetian consul resident (as in other parts of the Levant where Venice has official representatives), places where it would be unwise for Venetians to send their capital to the Turks or to their Greek subjects, or even to their own correspondents, because of the danger and the discrimination which would arise against them in such places if they had no protector to defend them from outrage. But the Jews, spurred on by the need to make a living, or having other Jews, indeed the greater part of their nation, subject to the Turks, eagerly go there in person and remit their moneys and assets thither. . . .

[123] Cf. H. I. Bloom, *The economic activities of the Jews of Amsterdam* (Williamsport, Pennsylvania, 1937), pp. 1–32, 97–9; Violet Barbour, *Capitalism in Amsterdam in the seventeenth century* (Baltimore, Maryland, 1950), pp. 25, 58, 116.

Luzzatto added that the Jews

> are almost entirely without ships of their own, though in Amsterdam, Rotterdam and Hamburg there are some who have a share in ships.[124]

In this way, in the late sixteenth and early seventeenth century, the Jews served the Venetian state by filling the void left by nobles and citizens retreating from the risks of trade. The profits of international commerce—western as well as eastern—helped to maintain non-profitmaking banks in Venice itself, where banking was no longer a self-supporting profession.

Few Venetian institutions existed solely for the care and relief of the poor; and few loan banks, whether Jewish or Christian, succeeded throughout their career in confining their services to poor men. Poverty was impossible to define. The law could only introduce a kind of crude means-test by prescribing that loans at 5 per cent should not exceed the sum of two or three ducats each, and that no one pawnticket could be issued for more than that amount. But it was all too possible for someone determined to extort larger loans to take out a great number of pawntickets, thus completely frustrating the aims of those who had drafted the *condotte*. The remedy for which the Jews pleaded at intervals after 1580 was the introduction of separate banks authorized to lend larger sums at higher rates. The Senate first rejected such a proposal, designed to 'provide for every other kind of person who has need', in September 1580.[125]

The Jews repeated their pleas in 1591. They were bound to serve all comers, not only from Venice itself, but also from neighbouring towns. Again,

> much of this service is extended to many, many persons who are not poor, and who wish to be accommodated with sums of 40 or 50 ducats at a time, by dividing pledges up under several accounts (*partide*) and among several banks, so that many persons have pledges in all the banks, to the value of many hundreds of ducats. We cannot refuse them, because our obligations are indeterminate and unlimited, whereas in the *condotta* which expired in 1580 our obligations were restricted to 50,000 ducats and no more.

Two boards of Cattaveri examined the Jews' claims before the Senate made its decision. The first of them sympathized to a certain extent, and spoke of the prodigal wastage of time caused by persons 'of honourable condition' who insisted on being served first, forced the Jews to make out ten or twenty tickets, and committed a further

[124] Luzzatto, *Discorso*, ff. 16–20.
[125] A.S.V., *Senato, Terra, filza* 81, 22 September 1580.

nuisance by sending everybody out of the room so as not to be seen in the shameful act of borrowing. Caustically, the Cattaveri also suggested that the Jews themselves should not slow down the process of lending by making their loans in coins of very small denomination which took hours to count into the borrower's palm. These coins were of dubious value anyway. However, this board did recommend that the Senate should authorize the Jews to lend sums of over 3 ducats at 12 per cent to persons of any social condition whatsoever: proposals which Daniel Rodriguez was also putting forth. Nevertheless, a new board of Cattaveri opposed the suggestion, and carried the day.[126]

In 1618, the Jews did at least cause the Senate to vote on a proposal to establish another three loan banks lending under different conditions. The sums they were obliged to lend annually had apparently doubled, rising from 100,000 to 200,000 ducats, in the past eleven years.

> But Your Serenity ought to know that this immoderate increase does not result from there being a greater abundance of poor persons, but is produced by people of higher standing (*persone grandi*), who want large sums of money lent upon pledges, and by a detestable abuse introduced by merchants and shopkeepers, who pledge entire articles of merchandise, such as *grograni*, camelots and other things. In summer they obtain from the banks money on the security of their winter stock, and in the winter money on the security of their summer stock, and we are not entitled to refuse them, and they make pledges of three ducats at a time. We cannot refuse to lend even to them, because they use force and violence towards us, and though we have many times repaired to the supreme courts our misery has found no relief.

Evidently some of the funds the Jews were required to place at the poor's disposal were finding their way into a species of commercial loan, and helping merchants, as well as 'honourable' debtors, to survive and transact business. The Jews argued that even 10 per cent loan banks would not be self-supporting: the Jewish community had been forced to subsidize them before 1573; but they would at least remove some of the pressure on the 5 per cent banks. Of the various boards which reported on the matter, only one—that of the Cattaveri—opposed the suggestion. A retiring member of the board, Hieronimo Barbarigo, had objected that such a measure would simply destroy all incentive to lend sums of less than three ducats. Every Jewish banker, he predicted,

[126] A.S.V., *Senato, Terra, filza* 122, 7 December 1591, reports of the Cattaveri: (a) from Marino Barbaro, Vettore Dolfin and Zaccaria da Molin; (b) from Hieronimo Tron, Marc'Antonio Sanuto and Andrea Marcello, who objected to the Jews' proposals.

would value every pledge at slightly more than three ducats, to be able to charge the higher rate. The new banks would tempt the well-to-do, and especially the young, to borrow at a ruinous rate. The Cattaveri, however, were unusually suspicious of the Jews: neither the Cinque Savii alla Mercanzia nor the Sopraconsoli shared their opinion, and the Sopraconsoli recommended the erection of two separate banks lending sums of up to 60,000 ducats each, on tickets of up to 30 ducats, at the rate of 10 per cent.

At the same time the Jews asked for relief by resuscitating an old proposal entitling them to charge one soldo for each pawnticket they made out—an insensible burden on the borrower, but, cumulatively, able to bring them great relief. The Sopraconsoli, however, objected to this on the grounds that the poor would lose very heavily by it. They were in the habit of making pledges to the value of 4–8 lire at a time, and of pledging the same goods three or four times over in the course of a year. The Sopraconsoli shared an objection already voiced by the Cattaveri—that the Jew would be tempted to increase the number of tickets issued on any one pledge:

> for example, supposing a poor person, in order to obtain a loan of 10–12 lire, makes a pledge which includes a copper bucket, two pewter plates, two shirts and a pair of breeches, the bankers will want the pauper to take out two pawntickets, one for the goods of copper and pewter, and the other for the clothing, because they are made of different materials, and the poor man will feel the burden of this.

In the end, the Senate saw fit to introduce no change in the arrangements for borrowing and lending in Venice. Proposals for loan banks at higher rates of interest failed to obtain the required majority in 1618. The Senate, however, did limit to a total of 100,000 ducats the Jews' obligation to lend for the time being. It did also introduce an ambiguous provision, whereby the Council of Ten must authorize its subcommittee, the Esecutori contro alla Bestemmia, to punish all who attempted to extort sums of over three ducats *per pawnticket* from Jewish bankers. It apparently did nothing to prevent borrowers from demanding great numbers of pawntickets for themselves, sometimes to cover a large loan on the same indivisible object.[127]

Five per cent loan banking thus continued, essentially unchanged, from 1573 to 1618 in the city of Venice itself. Naturally, it could not fulfil all demands for credit, although it went far beyond the original intentions of those who had devised the *condotte* with the poor in mind. Occasionally, malpractices were alleged. The Sopraconsoli, in

[127] A.S.V., *Senato, Terra, filza* 231, 14 December 1618.

1613, believed the Jews to be successfully dodging the laws against usury, lending at interest outside the banks, 'pretending to buy goods with an agreement that they may be recovered after so much time has lapsed' and so disguising interest charges. They were also, it seemed, profiting by fluctuations in the exchange rates, juggling with ducats and crowns, and thus making effective gains of 12 per cent or more.[128] Comparable charges were made against the mainland banker Joseph Levi, a year or two later. However, the Sopraconsoli objected just as categorically to the growth of a large, disreputable gang of Christians who loitered at the gates of the Ghetto and round the banks, offering to get the business of the poor transacted immediately. Time was always a most important consideration in the small-loan business. These uncouth brokers received 'profits three times as great as the interest charged by the bankers', threatened and offended poor Jews, and defrauded poor Christians. They were quite capable of forging pawntickets and the banker's writing. Again, the Jewish banks clearly failed to eliminate usurious lending—whether by Jews or Christians— at much higher rates. In 1618, the Cinque Savii alla Mercanzia favoured the proposal for 10 per cent banks on the grounds that it would eliminate much unlawful lending at the rate of 25 per cent, which was evidently quite common.[129]

Clearly the Jewish banks in Venice suffered from many disadvantages, especially through the diversion of funds to richer borrowers and into semi-commercial loans, and through the obstinate conservatism and suspicion which prevented the foundation of separate establishments to lend larger sums. The harsh conditions under which the Jews were forced to lend may, almost inevitably, have forced them into minor frauds and malpractices. But, as the next chapters attempt to show, the Monti di Pietà on the mainland generally shared these defects, sometimes in a far more acute form, and sometimes proved far more unstable than the Jewish banks of Venice.

During the century or so from 1509 to 1618, Venetian Jewry had passed through at least three distinctive phases in its history: in all of which Venetian society and the state had tolerated and exploited the Jews for their utility to the fisc, the economy and the poor. In all of them they had granted the Jews a separate and distinctive way of life, under conditions of apartness and symbolic degradation. The first was

[128] A.S.V., *Senato, Terra, filza* 207, 3 September 1613, report dated 4 January 1612 Venetian style.
[129] A.S.V., *Senato, Terra, filza* 231, 14 December 1618; report dated 21 March 1618.

the phase of uneasy settlement, when the invasion of the Veneto concentrated the Jews in unprecedented numbers in the capital itself, and at last, in response to the insistent voices of the Friars, the government created the Ghetto of Venice. During these years the Jews were bankers and taxpayers, financing the Arsenal and the navy in awkward moments and times of urgent need. Their banking activities filled the gap left by the government's failure—out of conservatism, apathy, suspicion or justifiable misgivings—to establish a Monte di Pietà in Venice itself. The Jews seem to have been no mere pawnbrokers, but business entrepreneurs to whom Christian investors would entrust their capital. In the years after 1548, however, a second phase of outright hostility to the Jews set in, anticipating by a few years the overt acts of the Papacy. The Venetian government seemed bent on destroying the prosperity allowed to the Jews in the last decades, on restoring by economic and fiscal pressure the correct order of things, in which the Jew, as a serf, could acquire no power or mastery over the Christian. The communities of Venice and the Veneto shrank through emigration, whilst bankruptcies bore witness to the decline of Jewish fortunes. The process of degradation, stemming from religious motives and carried through by economic restrictions, resulted in a crisis of confidence and discredited the Jews as bankers qualified to handle Christian money and assets. The Jews were driven back on their own resources, in this field, too, cut off from the non-Jewish world. The Venetian dominions had reached the point where, by the war of Lepanto and Cyprus, they were almost prepared to dispense with the services of now impoverished Jews.

But neither in the Papal States nor in the Venetian Republic did the Counter Reformation procure the unlimited persecution or the outright expulsion of the Jews. A third phase began after Lepanto, in which the Venetian Jews paradoxically performed the functions of a Monte di Pietà, by maintaining a non-profitmaking loan bank for the devotees of an alien faith. They were forced to erect an institution of a type originally designed to destroy the older forms of Jewish lending. The modest share of Levantine and Ponentine Jews in Venice's waning international trade helped to subsidize the 5 per cent banks of Venice itself, and to equip the Jews of Venice to provide a pool from which mainland bankers could be drawn. Whilst the importance of Jews as traders increased, their importance as direct taxpayers almost certainly diminished. The state ceased to take a share directly in the profits of the moneylender's trade, foregoing this in the interest of cheap loans. The Jews remained bankers, but in Venice at least their banks rested on different foundations. Venice had desired a peculiar form of financial structure, imitating and complementing without reproducing the Monti di Pietà. The key to it may lie ultimately in Spain's expulsion of her Jews, in their migration to the lands of the Ottoman Empire, and in Venice's constant interest in eastern trade and peace with Turkey. Even after Lepanto, Venice compromised with its Jews, and they continued to render their services to the poor, the people and the state.

5

THE EXTENSION OF THE MONTI DI PIETÀ
1550–1620

In their constitutions, the Monti di Pietà founded within the Italian territories of the Venetian Republic after 1550 essentially resembled their predecessors of the late fifteenth century.[1] Significant developments, however, occurred in their financial structure—at least in the larger cities. Throughout their career, the Monti preserved their character as low-interest loan banks, publicly owned and communally administered, on the basis of standardized statutes usually ratified by the Venetian government. These statutes prescribed the exact conditions under which they should lend limited sums, for moral purposes (which did not include gambling),[2] on the security of portable pledges of cloth or metal (clothes, household utensils, trinkets, ornaments or jewellery). They specified the period after which unredeemed pledges were to be sold, and usually fixed it at just over a year: though in its early stages a Monte, like that of Bergamo, might be prepared to lend for six months only. The rate of interest charged was normally 5 per cent per annum—expressed as 1 *bagatino* or denier per lira per month: though certain Monti di Pietà proved able to lower the rate of interest in the course of time. At least from 1599 onwards, the Monte at Udine lent at 4 per cent only,[3] whilst the Monte di Pietà in Bergamo charged only 3 per cent: Sixtus V authorized Bergamo to add to its capital any profits made out of charging interest to borrowers, provided the interest rate was dropped to this level.[4] In 1582, and again in 1633, Rettori of

[1] These remarks are based on the statutes of the following Monti di Pietà, presented to and approved by the Venetian Senate and/or Collegio: La Badia-Lendenara (A.S.V., *Senato, Terra, filza* 19, 24 April 1554); Bergamo (*ibid., filza* 25, 13 July 1557); Uderzo (reg. 1564–5, ff. 193–8); Sacile (*filza* 46, 31 August 1566); Motta (*filza* 66, 28 June 1575); Pordenone (*filza* 160, 17/28 October 1601).

[2] The statutes of Bergamo introduced a new refinement, by prescribing that Massari were not to accept as pledges the clothing of married women, 'because sometimes their evil-living husbands find it easy to deprive them of their clothing for the sake of gambling or other such depraved pursuits'. However, the Conservatore on duty at the time could exercise some discretion about this, 'having considered according to his conscience the quality and condition of the person pledging the goods'.

[3] A.S.V., *Collegio, Relazioni*, b. 49, reports of Stefano Viaro, 4 November 1599, Vincenzo Capello, 12 June 1615, and Girolamo Ciuran, 11 December 1626.

[4] Zech, *Rigor moderatus*, pp. 222–3; A.S.V., *Sindici Inquisitori in Terra Ferma*, b. 63, f. 112.

Crema informed the Senate that the local Monte di Pietà lent upon pledges at the rate of 2½ per cent only.[5] The Monte di Pietà at Verona had, by 1576, adopted a system of lending sums of up to 4 *mocenighi* (about 5 lire) gratis, and of charging 6 per cent interest on larger loans.[6] Where the Monti di Pietà chose to raise their interest rates, they usually did so to equip themselves to borrow from the general public, and thereby, through interest-bearing deposits, to increase the capital available for loans.

In these matters, the statutes introduced refinements, rather than innovations; changes in degree or detail, rather than in kind. The administrative structure of the institution had hardened, and had become widely accepted and regularly used. The sources used give little or no indication that Franciscans or other travelling evangelists had much to do with these foundations: the reports and correspondence of the Rettori contain no references to ecclesiastical initiative, though the Monte di Pietà at Feltre retained a close connexion with the local Franciscans.[7] The Rettori sometimes claimed the credit for the foundations themselves, and at Rovigo in the 1540's, at Asola in 1615, they established Monti di Pietà by fining Jewish bankers or forcing them to make restitution.[8] At La Badia–Lendenara, at Uderzo, and at Pordenone local confraternities of laymen were apparently responsible for establishing the Monti di Pietà, or at least for subscribing the funds which formed the nucleus of the capital to be lent to the poor. At La Badia–Lendenara, the confraternities of the Body of Christ and of the Virgin Mary offered to start their Christian loan bank, against the Rettore's better judgment, with an initial capital of 500 ducats from pious subscribers.[9] These may have been religious societies of comparatively recent foundation; at Pordenone, the local Scuola di Santa Maria dei Battuti, almost certainly descended from the same ancestors as the Scuole Grandi of Venice, turned from its old practice of simply distributing charity grain to the poor, and took up the cause of a local Monte di Pietà. At least one Monte di Pietà owed its existence to a private

[5] A.S.V., *Collegio, Relazioni*, b. 40, reports of Pietro Capello, 28 November 1582, and Zaccaria Balbi, 24 April 1633.

[6] A.S.V., *Collegio, Relazioni*, b. 50, report of Michele Bon, 1576. Girolamo Cornaro, 5 May 1612, *ibid.*, shows that the same system was in force in the early seventeenth century. According to Nicolò Papadopoli-Aldobrandini, *Le monete di Venezia descritte ed illustrate*, II (Venice, 1907), p. 270, n. 3, the *mocenigo* was valued at 24 soldi from 1525 onwards.

[7] See below, p. 581.

[8] A.S.V., *Senato, Terra*, filza 13, 27 June 1551; filza 215, 25 September 1615; above, pp. 522, 563–4.

[9] A.S.V., *Senato, Terra*, filza 16, 6 October 1552; filza 19, 24 April 1554; above, pp. 522–3.

benefactor. In 1542, Andrea Crico of Feltre left the sum of 1,000 ducats to establish a Christian loan bank under conditions set forth in the clauses of his will[10]—perhaps to fill a gap left by the collapse of the original foundation inspired by the sermons of Bernardino of Feltre. It was as if the Friars had established the standard formula, and had earned it recognition and respectability. In the middle and later sixteenth century, their intervention became less conspicuous. In any case, they had always envisaged that laymen would perform many, if not all, of the supervisory and administrative functions necessary to the Monti di Pietà.

In most cities and towns of the Venetian Republic, the sovereign council of citizens was, for normal purposes, the ultimate authority in the government of the Monte. The Rettori, however, enjoyed a right of intervention to check abuses—one which, in the late sixteenth and early seventeenth century, they exercised with increased zeal and energy. Statutes were usually formulated subject to Venetian approval. They often provided that the citizen council should elect a special Council of the Monte, which in its turn appointed and supervised the officials. The arrangement introduced at Pordenone in 1601, whereby the governing council of the Scuola dei Battuti was to nominate all officials of the Monte di Pietà, was not a typical one. In small townships, the citizens sometimes found it unnecessary to elect a Council of the Monte, and the citizen council chose the officials directly. With only one known exception, the Monti di Pietà all remained, like the hospitals and Scuole, under exclusively lay management. The exception lay in Feltre, where Andrea Crico had provided in his will that, to preserve it from the corruption rife in the town council, his Monte di Pietà should be managed by *popolari*—non-citizens—alone. He further provided that these *popolari* should be chosen by the Vicar of the diocese, by the Guardian of the local Observant Franciscans, and by one of the oldest Friars of the same convent. The Rettori of Feltre occasionally drew attention to these facts, but did not comment adversely on them until 1643. In that year, the governor Girolamo Bragadin observed that the ecclesiastical electors were not in fact doing their job properly, and were choosing corrupt administrators. 'By laws of Your Serenity, it is laid down that clergymen are not entitled to participate in the management of charitable institutions. . . .'[11] Thus, somewhat belatedly, the Rettore recollected one of the fundamental

---

[10] According to the later report of Francesco Da Mosto, 7 April 1611, A.S.V., *Collegio, Relazioni*, b. 41.

[11] *Ibid.*: see also the reports of Marc'Antonio Memmo, 14 July 1628, and Girolamo Bragadin, 1643.

2P

principles of Venetian government—a rule strictly observed in all the statutes approved by the Senate or Collegio after 1550. However, if excluded from the practical tasks of administration, a bishop could always offer advice, and sometimes see it accepted—as witness certain elaborate suggestions of Agostino Valier in 1580-1 for reorganizing the local Monte di Pietà in Verona, and for preserving its investors from the sin of usury.[12]

Since the Monti di Pietà existed to serve poor and ordinary people, and came to serve all ranks of the community, the statutes generally laid down that members of the Council of the Monte should be drawn from different estates. They did not always penetrate far down the social hierarchy, and it is probable that neither at Verona nor at Bergamo did anyone less than a 'merchant' enjoy representation.[13] But most statutes prescribed that the Council of the Monte should not be monopolized by town councillors, and that it should, socially, be a slightly wider and more open body than the town council. It may even have compensated the permanent Outs of the cities for their exclusion from policymaking, and have provided a welcome additional source of influence and patronage. It may have given lesser men a sense of involvement in the affairs and institutions of the commune. 'Popular' pressure, demands from the non-citizens, produced the most elaborate arrangement of this kind in Padua in 1535. This, an extension of earlier provisions, attempted to guarantee to the *artefici*—members of the professional and religious corporations of the city—adequate control over the affairs of the Monte. It recalled, at least faintly, the old type of struggle in the cities of thirteenth or fourteenth century Italy, when power and patronage was so carefully and nicely apportioned between *nobili* and *popolo*, greater and lesser guilds, or *popolo grasso* and *popolo minuto*. The new statute of 1535 provided for a Council of the Monte of 118 members, under the presidency of at least one of the Rettori. One half of the Council consisted of citizens, headed by the current Deputati ad Utilia and by their immediate predecessors (to the number of 32 in all); by the 24 Conservatori of the Monte; and by three of its other officials, known as Sindici. Non-citizens were represented by the 35 elected heads or Gastaldi of the professional associations or Fraglie Temporali; and by the 23 Guardiani of the Fraglie Spirituali. The fifty-ninth representative of the people was an official

---

[12] See below, pp. 593–4.
[13] At Bergamo, two *cavalieri*, two *gentiluomini*, two *dottori* (i.e. University graduates) and two *mercanti* were to participate in the Council of the Monte. Nicolò Donà, a governor of Verona, wrote on 21 June 1635 that the Monte di Pietà was governed by a Prior and 16 citizens: four *titolati* or noblemen; four *Dottori*; four other laymen; and four merchants (A.S.V., *Collegio, Relazioni*, b. 50).

elected by the Council of the Monte itself, known as the Inquisitore delle Arti.[14] Membership of the guilds and other fraternities thus conferred the franchise—the right to influence, however indirectly, the administration of the most important financial organ built for the benefit of the people and citizens of Padua. Later, in 1609, a Rettore of Padua wrote that the *popolo* and the Arti, 'who feel an ancient and natural hatred for the citizens', always showed a very high degree of unity. They were also 'masters of the deliberations of the Council of the Monte, in spite of being only equal to the citizens in numbers'—for the last twenty years it had become clearly apparent that the citizens were deeply divided into two factions which vied to control the city council and dispense patronage.[15] The unity of the *artefici*, set against the factious divisions of the citizen body, had made the Monte di Pietà almost into a democratically governed institution: in the very restricted sense in which such words can legitimately be used in this context.

Few organizations went as far as that of the Paduans—but similar principles were, for example, painstakingly observed in the small towns of La Badia–Lendenara. These were governed by a council of 24 'of the best and most perfect (*de li piu megliori et perfetti*)'—perhaps in a social rather than a moral sense. These councillors should elect twelve of their own number, and twelve of the *popolo* outside their ranks, to deal with the affairs of the Monte. Finally, 'so that all conditions of men may participate in this council', each of the villages in the jurisdiction of the Podestariate should send two representatives to form a *gionta* of six men, entitled to be present at all deliberations of the council without casting a vote. Generally, in towns where the community was too small to need a special Council of the Monte, the statutes normally prescribed that some of the officials of the Monte itself must be *popolari*.

The Council of a Monte would normally nominate its officials, who held their posts for restricted periods. The swift rotation of office, common to so many Italian communes and civic organizations, was probably designed, not merely to distribute the burden evenly, but also to obviate fraud or detect it quickly. All statutes provided for the election of a body of directors, known as Conservatori, Presidenti or Cassieri, who were ultimately responsible for the care of funds, which they dispensed from the coffers to the Massaro in charge of loans, in small instalments as the need arose. Some constitutions obliged at least

[14] A.S.V., *Senato, Terra*, reg. 1534–35, ff. 164v.–165, 27 August 1535. On this theme, see also Angelo Ventura, *Nobiltà e popolo nella società veneta del '400 e '500* (Bari, 1964), pp. 421–39.

[15] A.S.V., *Collegio, Relazioni*, b. 43, report of Tommaso Contarini, Cavalier Conte del Zaffo.

one of the Conservatori to attend when the Massaro lent on pledge— thus providing one of several checks on his activities. The Conservatori were always, unlike the Massaro, members of the Council of the Monte. The Massaro, though of lower status in the hierarchy, was the key figure who made all the difference to the running of the Monte. Accounts of embezzlement and maladministration in the Monti imply either that the Conservatori constituted an extraordinarily ineffective safeguard against a dishonest Massaro; or that there was usually a high degree of collusion between the Massari, who were almost invariably blamed for any frauds that might be committed, and the Conservatori, whose names were kept out of the prosecutions and inquiries instituted by the governors. Each Monte di Pietà had at least one notary or accountant, who recorded all transactions independently of the Massaro. Usually, some persons were commissioned to act as Sindici, with the specific task of auditing accounts and guarding against abuses. At La Badia–Lendenara, the Sindici performed both these functions, hailing offenders before the Venetian governor, and undertook the additional task of requesting preachers to commend the Monte and take collections for its benefit. The Sindici brought the contents of church collection-boxes to the headquarters of the Monte, recorded the sums in the books, and deposited them in the coffers. In this way, a standardized hierarchy of councillors and officials, directors and executives, served each Monte di Pietà. Some were concerned with the ultimate control of funds, some with their dispensation, others with the enforcement of the statutes and the detection of fraud and abuse.

Monti di Pietà, as non-profitmaking organizations, could expand only slightly by virtue of their own inner strength. They needed fresh injections of capital from outside in order to increase: in the Veneto at least, there is no sign that—like the Florentine Monte di Pietà—they engaged in any form of commercial speculation.[16] The original statutes for the Monte di Pietà of Bergamo, drawn up in 1557, ordained that if the 5 per cent interest charge turned out to be more than enough to cover administrative costs, then the surplus must on no account be added to the capital of the Monte. The officials must dispense to the poor any surplus not claimed by those who had paid it, or else employ it in other pious works. Sixtus V, however, allowed the Monte to add such a surplus to its capital provided the interest-charge was lowered to 3 per cent. Profits from this source were not likely to prove abundant.[17]

16 Thus Buoninsegni, *Trattato*, ff. 145 f.

17 See above, n. 4. However, the governor Vincenzo Barozzi, in a report dated 3 April 1610, expressed the view that the practice of adding *utili* to capital had in fact enabled the Monte to increase quite substantially: A.S.V., *Collegio, Relazioni*, b. 35.

584

Otherwise, the Monte's capital could be increased if an unredeemed pledge were sold by auction and fetched a sum more than sufficient to cover the sum lent and the interest due on that sum. Should the former owner of the pledge fail to claim the surplus, it could be added to the capital of the Monte. Over a long period, surpluses or 'sopravanzi' of this kind could amount to quite a substantial total. In 1554, in Padua, such surpluses amounted to 3,800 ducats, whilst the proceeds of unclaimed pledges sold at the time when the Jews were in Padua provided the Monte with another 7,750 ducats. Finally, the profits from unclaimed pledges sold at the Camera dei Pegni came to 850 ducats. This total of 12,400 ducats accounted for some $12\frac{1}{2}$ per cent of the working capital of the Monte di Pietà. By 1606, however, the proportion was no more than 7 per cent—15,200 ducats in a total of 221,670.[18] This source of gain proved useful to the Monti, but was not a really substantial cause of their increase.

The organizers and prospective founders of the Monti di Pietà never lost faith in the traditional methods of money-raising—the charity sermon, and the gorgeous procession on one of the great festivals of the Church—at Easter, Pentecost or the festival of the Blessed Virgin in September. In the early seventeenth century, processions of this kind promised to restore the now somewhat precarious fortunes of the Monti at Rovigo and Bergamo.[19] All the clergy of Santa Maria Maggiore at Bergamo were to take part in the ceremony devised in 1617. All the convents, religious confraternities and professional bodies which attended at Corpus Christi must send their officials and other representatives with funds collected for the Monte di Pietà, which, in the course of the procession, they disbursed publicly at a table in front of the Monte's premises. Here the Rettori sat, with the Prior and Conservatori of the Monte beside them. This was evidently conceived as an attempt to play on the rivalries which surely existed between the various fraternities and associations. In most towns, also, notaries were obliged to remind testators of the existence of the local Monte di Pietà.

Local taxation seems to have been used comparatively seldom as a means of expanding, replenishing or maintaining a Monte di Pietà. In its early stages, however, the Monte newly founded at Rovigo in 1551 gained from the diversion of the revenue derived from the rent of pitches at a fair held in the main piazza. Since 1501, this rent had been earmarked for a fund hitherto used for paving the muddy streets of the

[18] Reports of Marc'Antonio Grimani, 3 August 1554, and Stefano Viaro, 24 January 1605 Venetian style, A.S.V., *Collegio, Relazioni*, b. 43.
[19] For Rovigo, A.S.V., *Senato, Terra, filza* 188, 13 October 1608; for Bergamo, *ibid., filza* 226, 20 September 1617.

low-lying city, but often diverted temporarily to other public works. The Venetian Senate authorized the commune of Rovigo to employ 200 ducats from the annual rent of the fair for the needs of the Monte di Pietà for a period of 20 years, and also to devote to the same purposes 100 ducats a year raised by direct taxation.[20] Such provisions, however, were rare: funds came, much more frequently, from voluntary subscriptions, and often from members of local Scuole, as at La Badia–Lendenara, Uderzo and Pordenone.

For a Monte to enjoy a regular income from any source was also comparatively rare. Hospitals on the mainland, and Scuole everywhere, usually invested in or received donations of real property—at least until 1605, when controversial legislation forbade this practice. But Monti di Pietà did not, before 1605, follow any general rule. The Bergamo statutes of 1557 prescribed that real property left to the Monte di Pietà unconditionally must be sold within two years by public auction, and the proceeds converted into cash to be dispensed in loans. A large lump sum was obviously more immediately valuable to institutions of this type than a safe investment yielding a low return. However, the Monti at Crema and Vicenza either made or received investments in real property, and continued to enjoy the income therefrom in the early seventeenth century. At Vicenza in 1598, the Monte, in addition to possessing working capital of 80,000 ducats, received an income of some 800 ducats from real property, rising to 900 in 1618. The capital invested in this security amounted to some 20,000 ducats.[21] Crema's Monte, in 1633, received an even larger income from real property, which the Rettore estimated at 1,500 ducats a year.[22] This revenue, if properly administered and dispensed in loans on suitable securities, ought in theory to have steadily increased the working capital of the Monte di Pietà. It was not consumed annually like the income from ordinary charitable trusts.

Some of the Monti di Pietà did, therefore, possess some internal mechanisms which should have enabled them to expand from year to year, and so partially keep pace with increases in the population or compensate for losses in the purchasing power of money. Otherwise they relied partly on the generosity of the citizens, their spontaneous goodwill, or their response to the promptings of the preacher, the

[20] A.S.V., Senato, Terra, filza 13, 27 June 1551.

[21] A.S.V., Collegio, Relazioni, b. 51, reports of Benedetto Correr, 20 October 1598, and Zaccaria Grimani, 10 January 1618. According to Grimani, the income was derived from landed property of about 150 campi, yielding rent of about 500 ducats; from shops, which gave a rent of 300; and from other property rented at about 100 ducats.

[22] A.S.V., Collegio, Relazioni, b. 40, report of Zaccaria Balbi, 24 April 1633.

notary and the procession. But partly also they depended on depositors —on persons who made money available to the Monte di Pietà without giving or bequeathing it outright. They might do so in a variety of ways —voluntarily, or under some form of legal compulsion; gratis, or in return for a modest interest payment. Most of the larger Monti di Pietà owed their expansion in the course of the sixteenth century, not to charity in the conventional sense, but to an increase in deposits. Certainly at Padua, Rovigo, Udine and Verona, from the second half of the century onwards, deposits came to contribute more than did charitable gifts or bequests to the working capital of the Monte di Pietà. The Monti themselves began to discharge a double function, by acting as savings banks which provided a safe security for investors who could not or would not employ their money in more enterprising pursuits, and by acting as cheap loan banks serving all classes and social estates.[23] Recognition, however uneasy at first, of the right to pay interest on deposits theoretically made in a spirit of charity with the Monte di Pietà, enabled the Monti to extend their activities, and to lend to the comparatively rich as well as to the poor.

Many deposits were made with the Monti di Pietà for legal purposes. The parties to several forms of legal transaction, and to certain if not all kinds of litigation, had been obliged to make deposits with notaries as proof of good faith. At some time during the sixteenth century—if no earlier—the subject cities of the Venetian dominion began to introduce legislation to the effect that all deposits of this kind must now be made in the Monte di Pietà, which, for the time being, would enjoy the use of the money.[24] About the propriety of such deposits little dispute was likely to arise. From its inception, the Monte di Pietà at Bergamo prepared to accept deposits 'per causa di litigio', of which the Treasurer took care. But the statutes significantly declared that 'The Monte is not to pay interest of any kind on moneys lent to it, which it must accept gratis and not otherwise'. Plans for the reconstitution of the Rovigo Monte di Pietà, passed by the Senate in 1608, also stipulated that legal deposits should be made in the Monte. With greater originality, however, they also proposed that the moneys of the chief charitable institutions in Rovigo should, instead of merely lying idle in the cashbox, always be made available for loan to the poor. The Sindicato dei Poveri, the Hospital of the Misericordia and the pesthouse or Lazzar-

---

[23] Cf. Garrani, *Il carattere dei Monti di Pietà, passim.*
[24] Cf. with the legislation of Gregory XIII, 'Inter multiplices', 1 October 1584: by which all Roman judges were to order that, in all civil and criminal cases pending before them in which there was occasion to make a deposit of over 5 crowns, the money should be placed, not with notaries, but with the Monte di Pietà in Rome. See B.R., VIII, pp. 491–3.

etto must deposit their funds in the Monte di Pietà, from which they could withdraw them on request should they be needed for building or similar purposes, or to pay priests and staff. Money derived by the commune from the fair was also to be deposited with the Monte.[25] During the sixteenth century, social legislators were showing a certain ingenuity in seeking out idle moneys and insisting that they be put to productive uses: to benefit the poor, if not to profit the owner of the funds.

The reports of the Rettori contain all too little information about the extent of these non-interest-bearing deposits, and frequently fail to distinguish between them and the other forms of deposit. However, from information submitted to Borromeo on his visitations of Bergamo in 1575, it emerges that deposits made for legal purposes ('*depositi litigiosi*') accounted for as much as 46·2 per cent of the capital of the Monte di Pietà whereas outright gifts or legacies only amounted to 32·5 per cent.[25a] The proportion of legal deposits to the whole was perhaps exceptionally high in Bergamo, because the Monte di Pietà was still not paying interest on any deposits. Borromeo's influence was strong in this region, and he had in 1569 decreed that nobody might under any circumstances accept interest for any loan or deposit made with a Monte di Pietà without being treated as a usurer.[25b] Evidently, he was still unimpressed by recent theological debates which had concluded that such charges might be legitimate. Again, deposits on which no interest was paid accounted for about one-third of the working capital of the Monte di Pietà in Vicenza in 1598. In Udine, in 1635, the proportion was lower—in the region of 10 per cent[26]—but still substantial. It is possible that compulsory deposits for legal or other purposes were supplemented by non-interest-bearing deposits from persons who did not wish to surrender their money altogether, but were quite willing to make it available to the poor for the time being. This could easily have happened in Vicenza, where, in 1598, the Monte paid no interest on any deposits, and where the local inhabitants may have been happy to use the strongrooms of the Monte to protect their fortunes from robbery. At Udine, depositors could receive interest, and perhaps usually chose to do so when offered the chance.

[25] A.S.V., *Senato, Terra, filza* 188, 13 October 1608. At Verona, the net income of the Hospital of San Giacomo, after deducting administrative expenses, was deposited in the Monte di Pietà—report of Girolamo Cornaro, 5 May 1612, A.S.V., *Collegio, Relazioni*, b. 50.

[25a] See A. G. Roncalli and Pietro Forno, *Gli atti della visita apostolica di San Carlo Borromeo a Bergamo, 1575* (2 vols. in 5, Florence, 1936–57), I/ii, pp. 287–8, 298–9.

[25b] *Acta Ecclesiae Mediolanensis*, f. 34v.

[26] See below, Appendix, p. 624.

Monti di Pietà which undertook to pay interest on deposits faced the complications raised by the doctrines of the Church on usury. There was no question of the Monte itself committing the sin of usury, but some risk that the depositors might do so, and the Monte connive at this. Learned theorists—the Dominican Buoninsegni in the sixteenth century, the Jesuit Zech in the eighteenth—pointed out that Monti di Pietà differed in two essentials from the secular Monti where the acceptance of interest was undoubtedly lawful. Secular Monti, like those of the Venetian Republic, were consolidated loan funds, and investors could never demand their capital back from the government (though the government might choose to liquidate the Monte). They could only transfer the bonds they held to other persons. They therefore deserved some compensation, in the form of an interest payment, for alienating their capital in this way. The Monti di Pietà, however, were offering to restore capital to the depositor whenever he gave due notice,[27] and, since he had never lost control of his capital, he could not on these grounds claim compensation. Again, those who purchased government stock received compensation out of 'fixed and certain revenues' of the state, whereas in the Monti di Pietà depositors were compensated by those who had borrowed from the Monte.[28]

The principal justification for receiving interest on loans to a Monte di Pietà—at least, the one most popular in the Venetian dominion—lay in the related extrinsic titles of *lucrum cessans* and *damnum emergens*. If a man possessed capital and was in a position to invest it in land, house property, agriculture, commerce or some other form of perfectly legitimate activity, but still deliberately chose out of charity to place it in a Monte di Pietà, he was entitled to some compensation for this act of self-sacrifice. It must be only partial and not full compensation. The papal briefs granted in favour of Modena in 1542 and Vicenza in 1555 expressly stipulated that their Monti di Pietà could pay interest to such depositors, provided that this rate of interest was substantially less than the return on commercial, agrarian or other lawful investment in the district concerned. In Modena the rate to be paid by the Monte was 5 per cent, in Vicenza 4 per cent.[29] Two reasons, one theological, the other economic, almost certainly underlay these papal decisions. One was that in these circumstances there were only

---

[27] Though by 1612 Verona had introduced a system whereby lenders could receive 5 per cent on their money if they chose to forego the right to withdraw it on giving due notice—see below, p. 594.

[28] Cf. Buoninsegni, *Trattato*, f. 144v.; Zech, *Rigor moderatus*, pp. 197 f.

[29] Paul III, 'Charitatis opera', 22 June 1542, and Julius III, 'Salvator noster', 8 January 1555, both printed in Ballerini, *De jure circa usuram*, II, pp. 239–40, 243–5. Cf. also Noonan, *Scholastic analysis of usury*, p. 258.

three ways for an investor to escape the sin of usury—by the formal acceptance of risk, by working for his money, or by performing an act of charity. The investor took no risk, in theory, since in most Monti di Pietà the commune guaranteed that depositors should receive their money on giving due notice.[30] Nor did he do any work: the officials of the Monte did everything necessary. There remained only charity, and there could be no charity without self-sacrifice: therefore the investor must accept a low return on his money. Probably, too, sound economic reasoning, whether explicitly declared or not, contributed to the legislation on the matter of deposits. It was undesirable that purely financial transactions—in this case loans for the purposes of consumption—should yield a higher return than investment for the sake of production or for the promotion of trade. The Church had always condemned usury as the devouring trade which tempted the greedy or ambitious away from constructive activity which would benefit the community as a whole.

The principles applied in the Venetian Republic from the mid-sixteenth century onwards seem to have been those approved by Julius III for Vicenza in 1555. In 1598, Benedetto Correr, governor of Vicenza, lucidly summarized them—he was writing at a time when Vicenza had evidently repaid all its interest-bearing deposits, but was contemplating re-establishing this system in view of the persistent demand from the people of the city and territory.

'At other times', he wrote, 'a large sum used to be taken from and given by many rich noblemen at 4 per cent interest, and thus the needs of all were supplied—but this cannot be done without burdening the conscience and the soul, unless the Holy and Apostolic See first issues a dispensation. Everyone desires this, since (as the Monte cannot meet everyone's needs) many inhabitants of the city and territory have to repair to Cologna and other places where there are Jews, and try to obtain assistance from them at great expense and exorbitant rates. I think that depositors would be content with a return of 3 per cent, which is half what can be obtained through contracts of *livello* or *censo*. There should not be great difficulty about this, even though the Monte has no funds to make the interest payments on the money it would be necessary to raise. This is where all difficulties are likely to lie—but the city of Udine has obtained the right to pay interest at $3\frac{1}{2}$ per cent, which is half the 7 per cent permitted in that part of the country, although it has no funds on which the interest could be secured.'[31]

The *censi* and *livelli* at 6 per cent to which Correr referred were loans

[30] See below, p. 591.
[31] A.S.V., *Collegio, Relazioni*, b. 51, report of Benedetto Correr, 20 October 1598.

deemed legitimate because the annual return on them was paid from 'fruitful' property.[32] In this passage he may have been pointing out that, since the Monte di Pietà could not make its interest payments to depositors out of such funds, the depositors could not justify themselves on the conventional grounds that they were taking out *censi*. There is another possible explanation of his remarks, in that it was quite usual, if not obligatory, for a commune to guarantee the repayment of all deposits made in the Monte di Pietà, and it may have been necessary for it to guarantee interest payments also. Such a clause appears, for example, in the statutes of the Monte di Pietà founded at Uderzo in 1565.

> Again, to give everyone cause that he may freely and confidently deposit money in and lend it to the said Monte, be it resolved that if (which God forbid) it should ever happen that there be not enough capital in the Monte to satisfy those who have lent or deposited money in it, then the commune of Uderzo shall be bound to satisfy and pay in full anyone who has for the benefit of the said Monte lent to or deposited in it his money, considering that this is done for the honour, benefit and profit of the people of the city.[33]

Again, in 1622, the commune of Crema and its Venetian governors proposed to establish a new Monte beside the old one—one which would borrow at $4\frac{1}{2}$ per cent and lend at $5\frac{1}{2}$ per cent, dispensing any sum requested on a pledge of equivalent value. Some difficulties arose because it was desirable, if not essential, that deposits made by private persons be secured on 'some estate or revenue of the commune', and the people of Crema had no 'real property to act as security (*stabile per l'assicuratione*)' like the communes of Brescia, Verona and Padua.[34]

It was, therefore, important that the commune should provide the investor with reliable guarantees that he would recover his capital and receive his interest. Normally, of course, the Monte would pay investors by lending at a rather higher rate than it borrowed at: but it might suffer from bad debtors, value their pledges incorrectly, or be unable to sell them; the demand for loans might suddenly flag (which actually happened in Verona after the great plague of 1630–1), and the interest on loans become inadequate to meet the lawful demands of depositors.[35] To guard against these dangers, and to eliminate as much risk as possible from the transaction, it was desirable that the commune should point to some property or some revenue which, in an emergency, could

[32] Cf. Noonan, *Scholastic analysis of usury*, p. 155.
[33] A.S.V., *Senato, Terra*, reg. 1564–5, f. 197.
[34] A.S.V., *Collegio, Relazioni*, b. 40, report of Marco Zeno, 3 March 1622.
[35] See below, pp. 618–19.

provide compensation to the disappointed, or ensure that they got their money back promptly. A theoretically riskless transaction, however, smelt of usury; and the Vicentines at least believed that a papal dispensation would be valuable in soothing the uneasy conscience of the rentier-depositor. Other communes, like that of Rovigo in 1608, probably supposed that the concession of Julius III to Vicenza in 1555 generally authorized the practice of paying interest on deposits of this nature.[36]

The title of 'loss of gain', or *lucrum cessans*, in the Venetian Republic provided the justification for paying interest on some of the deposits which swelled the funds of the Monti di Pietà. A logical consequence of this was the doctrine that nobody ought to use the Monte di Pietà as an outlet for moneys that would otherwise have 'lain idle', and still expect to receive interest upon them. The Monte di Pietà's deposit funds must be composed of moneys diverted from trade or agriculture into the loan business, with charitable intentions. In the eighteenth century, the Veronese clergyman Pietro Ballerini, in his treatise on usury, described how, after the Vicentines had obtained their concession from Julius III in 1555, Veronese preachers realized that obtaining interest on 'idle moneys' was to be condemned, and the commune passed a decree to the effect that only those who suffered 'loss of gain' were entitled to receive interest on their loans to the Monte. They obtained confirmation of this decree from Pope Pius IV, who committed further investigations of the matter to Cardinal Navagero, administrator of the see of Verona from 1562, who attended the Council of Trent as Apostolic Legate. Navagero proceeded to consult the fathers and theologians assembled at Trent upon the matter—but they did not see fit to recognize any title to interest other than *lucrum cessans*.[37]

The highly developed system of interest-bearing deposits at Verona

[36] The new regulations drafted by the Podestà-Capitano Alvise Querini stipulated that 'having seen the resolution adopted in the Council of Vicenza in the year 1547 and its confirmation by His Holiness Pope Julius III in 1555, inviting all those who have money which they can invest or employ in trade to deposit it with the Holy Monte to serve the poor, be it ordained that all who (in this city) make deposits of money may receive interest of 3 per cent per annum, which deposits they may withdraw at their pleasure on giving one month's prior notice to the Cassiero, so that he can get the money ready. . . .' See A.S.V., *Senato, Terra, filza* 188, 13 October 1608.

[37] Ballerini, *De jure circa usuram*, II, pp. 96–7; Noonan, *Scholastic analysis of usury*, p. 258. At some stage in the history of the Monti di Pietà, the rumour got about that Paul III in 1549 had authorized the practice of paying interest on moneys deposited in a Monte di Pietà which would otherwise not have been invested. But the Bull supposedly issued by Paul III in favour of the Monte di Pietà at Ferrara was dismissed by Ballerini, and its authenticity questioned, as a document 'which conflicts with all tradition and with the doctrine which the See of Rome has always maintained'. He also pointed out that no trace of the papal concession was to be found in the archives of Ferrara, or in those of Bologna and Modena, which were alleged by the text of the

created a certain uneasiness among the ecclesiastical authorities. Agostino Valier, Navagero's nephew, who reigned as Bishop of Verona from 1565 to 1606,[38] intervened in the affairs of the Monte di Pietà in 1581 in an effort to save the citizens from the sin of usury. He had discovered that the precepts of the Tridentine fathers were not being observed. The Veronese had in fact established a new loan fund, to lend unlimited sums of money on pledges of equivalent value, as early as 1544, and at some point had begun financing it out of deposits at 4 per cent.[39] They had tried to protect the interests of the poor by separating this from the funds which existed for the purpose of making small loans. According to a decree issued by Valier in 1581, a third Monte di Pietà was subsequently established out of sheer administrative necessity, to lighten the burden on the Monte of 1544. Two Venetian governors of Verona, Michele Bon and Domenico Priuli, writing in 1576 and 1578 respectively, told the Venetian Senate that the two more recently founded Monti lent between them a total of over 200,000 ducats a year, charging 6 per cent interest, payable in cash by borrowers in six-monthly instalments. To finance these operations, the Monti borrowed at 4 per cent. From the difference between the 6 per cent and the 4 per cent emerged a sum of about 2,000 ducats annually, most of which was consumed by salaries and expenses. The Monte di Pietà which was specifically concerned with the poor possessed a working capital of only 35,000 ducats, from which, however, it lent to the poor of the city and territory sums of up to 4 *mocenighi* without charging interest.[40] Valier was chiefly concerned to continue the work begun by Navagero, and to prevent people from obtaining 4 per cent on moneys which would otherwise have lain idle. He fully realized that the only feasible way to do this was to provide other investment opportunities. He therefore devised an ingenious and tortuous procedure whereby the city sold a certain fraction of its communal goods, and then (as previously agreed) leased them from the purchasers, paying an annual rent of 5 per cent. The cash proceeds of the sale were deposited in the

document to have received similar concessions. (See Ballerini, *De jure circa usuram*, II, pp. 103–6; followed by Zech, *Rigor moderatus*, pp. 199–201, 204–5). Buoninsegni uses a different justification of the payment of interest on deposits, invoking the theory of the triple contract or Contractus Germanicus to justify the payment of interest to widows, orphans and others unable to trade on their own account. This, however, seems to have been written with special reference to Florence, where the Monte di Pietà engaged in commercial activity (Cf. Buoninsegni, *Trattato*, ff. 149–55; Lapeyre, 'Banque et crédit', p. 221; and Noonan, *Scholastic analysis of usury*, pp. 202 f.)

[38] *Hierarchia Catholica*, III, p. 352.

[39] A.S.V., *Senato, Terra, filza* 14, 2 December 1551; Valier's decree of 13 February 1581, printed in Ballerini, *De jure circa usuram*, II, pp. 245–50.

[40] Reports in A.S.V., *Collegio, Relazioni*, b. 50.

Monte di Pietà. All who borrowed from this fund were then obliged to pay the city 5 per cent interest on their loans, to recompense it for the loss it had incurred by acting out of charity in their interests. This was a mere 'restauratio damni', an indemnity against loss, and as such perfectly legitimate. Meanwhile, the moneyed persons who would otherwise have lent to the Monte were able—quite lawfully—to purchase the city's property, lease it back to the city, and receive 5 per cent on their capital by way of rent. They would thus make their gains, not out of money itself, which was sterile and could not breed money, but 'out of a fruitful thing' such as land. Provided investors genuinely looked on this transaction as a purchase of real property which they intended to let, they would not be committing the sin of usury.[41]

The adoption of this procedure by the Veronese—for the Councils of Fifty and Seventy-Five apparently ordered the property of the commune to be sold in accordance with Valier's recommendation—bore witness to the genuine uneasiness which influential clergymen still felt at this new phase in the development of the Monti di Pietà. Valier, however, had appreciated the need to provide opportunities for legitimate investment. Whatever the means used—and the reports of the Rettori did not mention any attempt to repeat the procedure by further sales of communal land—the interest-bearing deposit funds of the Veronese Monte continued to expand. In 1612, the governor Girolamo Cornaro estimated the turnover of the larger loan bank or banks at over half a million gold ducats a year. The annual turnover of the bank would certainly have been considerably higher than its total working capital. This bank received some deposits gratis, and also raised funds at two different rates: 4 per cent and 5 per cent. A depositor at 5 per cent was not entitled to have his money back—he was in the same position as one who invested in a government Monte, and could only transfer his bonds to another investor. One who received only 4 per cent interest was entitled to recover his money on giving six months' notice. The larger funds lent on pledges at 6 per cent. Meanwhile, the smaller Monte di Pietà specifically dedicated to the poor continued to lend small sums gratis. In 1612, it apparently lent about 60,000 ducats a year, and in 1621 its working capital was estimated at some 50,000.[42]

The larger Monti di Pietà in Verona were now providing a very extensive personal loan service, which had nothing essentially to do with charity. They had, however, been created by an extension of the

[41] Ballerini, De jure circa usuram, II, pp. 107–9, 245–56; Noonan, Scholastic analysis of usury, p. 307.

[42] Report of Girolamo Cornaro, 5 May 1612, A.S.V., Collegio, Relazioni, b. 50; A.S.V., Senato, Dispacci, Provveditori da terra e da mar, filza 270, f. 24, letter of Leonardo Moro and Marco Giustinian, 9 August 1621.

principles originally formulated when the Monti di Pietà were first established for the benefit of the poor. The borrowers, if financially embarrassed or merely anxious to turn their possessions into ready cash, were seldom in the conventional sense paupers. The rates of interest charged to borrowers were still moderate. Funds came, not from charitable gifts, but from interest-bearing deposits: though to justify the acceptance of interest it was still necessary to plead charitable intentions, and to invoke the title of *lucrum cessans*. Pledges were often jewels, objects of gold and silver, rather than copper utensils or bundles of used clothing. The range of the Monti was wider, and both in Verona and in Udine they lent to foreigners across the Austrian and Mantuan borders. The growth and extent of this service, reaching its peak in Verona in the early seventeenth century, enabled the Monti to act as a complete substitute for the older Jewish banks.

Veronese banking activities provoked severe criticism from representatives of the Venetian government, not on the grounds that they were usurious, but on the grounds that they were unwise and doubtfully sound. In 1621, Leonardo Moro and Marco Giustinian, serving as Sindici Inquisitori in Terra Ferma, roving commissioners concerned with the correction of abuses, reported on the Monte di Pietà of Verona. The larger Monte lent some 500,000 ducats a year: up to 300,000 on the security of jewels, the rest on gold, silver and other chattels. Not more than 50 ducats might be lent on any pledge of this second type, and not more than 500 ducats on any piece of jewellery, though it was easy to circumvent the regulations by dividing necklaces, strings of pearls or girdles into their component parts, and borrowing on each of these. The Sindici warned the governors of the Monte of the dangers inherent in these practices—of the possibility of fraud in committing false jewellery to the Monte, of the difficulty of selling pledges left unredeemed. They also complained that these transactions were not benefiting Venetian subjects, but foreign princes. The Monte in Verona was in fact receiving substantial quantities of jewellery, from the Duke of Mantua especially.

'In the Monte of Verona', wrote the Sindici Inquisitori, 'there is this disorder, which is contrary to the intentions of the government and a violation of its own statutes—that the Monte receives vast quantities of jewellery from foreigners and from Princes, especially from the Duke of Mantua, who in the name of certain Veronese noblemen much favoured and beloved of His Highness is accustomed to obtain a sum of up to 200,000 ducats from the Monte. Modena, too, has a certain sum of money.'[43]

[43] *Ibid.*

Whether these predictions and censures of the Sindici Inquisitori were justified should appear from the next chapter. Their remarks are mentioned here in order to show how the expansion of the Monti through the acceptance of interest-bearing deposits accompanied, in some cases, a significant change in the nature of their activities.

During the years now under examination, most of the larger Monti di Pietà on the Venetian mainland at least contemplated increasing their capital and extending their scope by offering to pay interest on deposits. Some of them followed Verona's example by establishing separate Monti—one based on charity alone, and lending small sums, theoretically only to the poor; the other financed by interest-bearing deposits, and making personal loans of any amount to all conditions of men. But it is not certain that these funds were in all cities clearly distinguished from one another, and there may have been some cross-fertilization between the two different funds. It is quite probable that poor persons frequently took advantage of the new funds which lent at slightly higher rates: they could, after all, obtain much larger loans from them if necessary. One fund was reserved to the poor; the other served the poor among others.

Vicenza had followed Verona in the mid-sixteenth century, raising funds by interest-bearing deposits in order to deal with the problem of poverty and of an expanding population. At some stage between 1555 and 1598, it obviously liquidated these loan funds, and came to rely on 'gratuitous' deposits only. The proportion of deposits to the whole working capital of the Monte had increased sharply by 1614—presumably through the reintroduction of interest-bearing deposits, which the governor Benedetto Correr had contemplated in 1598. In 1627, a Venetian Rettore wrote that the noble governors of the Monte di Pietà were borrowing extensively to meet the needs of the poor, and that the loans they had raised amounted to 200,000 ducats. This included 30,000 ducats recently borrowed from private individuals at 4 per cent.[44] The Vicentines thus still maintained that they were borrowing for the benefit of the poor—in 1627 as in 1547. Their interest-bearing deposit funds did not expand constantly—they were apparently liquidated at least once. Liquidation might prove necessary if the Monte failed to lend enough to repay investors—if the relationship between the borrowing and lending operations of the Monte became unbalanced.

Unfortunately, no figures are available to indicate the total of interest-bearing, as distinct from other deposits, in the Monte di Pietà in Padua. One can only say that in 1554, 1606 and 1625 deposits of

---

[44] A.S.V., *Collegio, Relazioni*, b. 51, reports of Benedetto Correr, 20 October 1598; Pietro Giustinian, 10 October 1614; Girolamo Dolfin, 9 April 1627.

some sort constituted between 49 per cent and 54 per cent of the total working capital of the Monte.[45] The Monte di Pietà newly founded in Rovigo in 1551 immediately adopted the deposit system, and at the start paid 6 per cent to attract investment—an unusually high rate; by 1564, deposits of some sort accounted for some 60 per cent of the total available working capital.[46] The relatively small Monte di Pietà at Treviso was paying 4 per cent on deposits by 1578; its own capital, bestowed on it outright by charitable gifts, stood at 12,000 ducats, but additional deposits enabled it to lend 40–50,000 ducats a year.[47] Again, the great Monte at Udine, the third largest in the Venetian dominion, attained its impressive dimensions by heavy borrowing at interest, paying investors 3 per cent or $3\frac{1}{2}$ per cent. In the three years for which figures were submitted to the Senate by the Rettori—1621, 1626 and 1635—deposits of some sort accounted for 64–72 per cent of the total available working capital of the Monte. In 1635, interest-bearing deposits contributed 59 per cent of the capital, and non-interest-bearing deposits 10 per cent.[48] Full details are set out in the accompanying table.

DEPOSITS AND WORKING CAPITAL IN THE MONTI DI PIETÀ
OF PADUA AND UDINE

In this table, the column headed 'Monte's capital' shows the total sum given or bequeathed outright to the Monte di Pietà by a particular date. The column headed 'Deposits' includes both interest-bearing and non-interest-bearing deposits. All figures are given in ducats of account.

	Monte's capital	Deposits	Other moneys	Working capital
Padua				
1554	33,500 ($33\frac{1}{2}$%)	54,000 (54%)	12,400 ($12\frac{1}{2}$%)	99,900 (100%)
1606	75,500 (34%)	108,500 (49%)	37,670 (17%)	221,670 (100%)
1625	75,800 (32%)	124,650 ($52\frac{1}{2}$%)	36,620 ($15\frac{1}{2}$%)	237,070 (100%)
Udine				
1621	32,000 (28%)	82,000 (72%)	—	114,000 (100%)
1626	40,000 (36%)	71,000 (64%)	—	111,000 (100%)
1635	45,000 (31%)	101,000 (69%)*	—	146,000 (100%)

* Interest-bearing deposits then amounted to 86,000 ducats, or 59 per cent of working capital.

[45] A.S.V., *Collegio, Relazioni*, b. 43, reports of Marc'Antonio Grimani, 3 August 1554; Stefano Viaro, 24 January 1605 Venetian style; Alvise Dolfin, 21 May 1625.
[46] A.S.V., *Collegio, Relazioni*, b. 46, reports of Giovanni Francesco Salamon, 27 October 1554, and Francesco Moro, 17 April 1564.
[47] A.S.V., *Collegio, Relazioni*, b. 48, report of Giovanni Michiel, 18 June 1578.
[48] A.S.V., *Collegio, Relazioni*, b. 49, reports of Pietro Sagredo, 2 April 1621; Girolamo Ciuran, 11 December 1626; Federico Sanuto, 15 March 1635.

Generally, the larger cities to the extreme west of the Venetian dominion—Brescia, Bergamo and Crema—seem to have been rather slower to adopt the system of interest-bearing deposits. Admittedly, the Brescians discussed the possibility in 1553, but it was not until 1587 that they actually established a new Monte Grande, separate from the original Monte di Pietà, which borrowed at 5 per cent and lent at 7 per cent.[49] Once erected, it did, however, expand considerably and lend heavily under special terms to the commune of Brescia. In 1645, the Monte Nuovo, either the same thing as the Monte Grande or its successor, theoretically had a capital of 189,859 ducats, though only 83,470 ducats were in effect available for loan. The city had contributed to this situation by borrowing as much as 74,000 ducats from the Monte Grande.[50] Bergamo, on the other hand, seems to have relied on 'gratuitous' or 'legal' deposits until about 1622, when the governor Girolamo Bragadin wrote that the inadequacy of the Monte di Pietà was driving the poor on to fraudulent loans from merchants and other private lenders. He therefore persuaded the sovereign citizen Council to decree that henceforth funds should be raised by paying 4 per cent to depositors, and that the Monte di Pietà should henceforth lend at 6 per cent.[51] Possibly the fact that Bergamo was equipped with well-endowed charitable organizations of a different type had hitherto made such a step unnecessary: the Monte did not occupy the same crucial position as in Padua, Verona or Udine. Finally, Crema contemplated taking similar measures in the same year, 1622—there may have been some collaboration between the two cities. However, certain difficulties arose, and the proposal may never have been translated into action. The governor Marco Zeno recommended the project on the grounds that convents, monasteries and private persons in the city had deposited large sums of money at banks in Rome or at that of Sant'Ambrogio in Milan.[52] It is possible that the stricter, though by no means wholly successful, enforcement of the mortmain laws on the Venetian mainland in the early seventeenth century had left these institutions with funds which they needed to invest in safe securities, but could not lock up in land. The introduction of interest-bearing deposits to Crema would, according to Zeno, bring them many benefits, and would keep in the dominion much capital 'which could provide supplies whenever the need arose'.

[49] Agostino Zanelli, *Delle condizioni interne di Brescia dal 1426 al 1644 e del moto della borghesia contro la nobiltà nel 1644* (Brescia, 1898), pp. 108–9; A.S.V., *Sindici Inquisitori in Terra Ferma*, b. 64, f. 62r.–v.

[50] A.S.V., *Collegio, Relazioni*, b. 37, report of Bernardino Renier, 12 April 1645.

[51] A.S.V., *Collegio, Relazioni*, b. 35, report dated 17 March 1622.

[52] A.S.V., *Collegio, Relazioni*, b. 40, report of 3 March 1622.

Inevitably, this chapter has raised more questions than it has answered. Clearly, the character of the Monti di Pietà subtly developed and transformed itself in the sixteenth and early seventeenth century, although their constitutional structure and avowed principles remained essentially similar. Their economic functions and the range of their activities were greatly broadened; the capital of which they disposed grew substantially in face value, though it is impossible to translate this into real terms. The increase took place even though, as banks dealing in cash, they were handling a commodity which (over the inflationary late sixteenth century) was losing its purchasing power. Personal loans, whether to the poor or to men of other conditions, ceased to be financed merely by charitable subscription in the straight-forward sense of the term. In the great Monti di Pietà of Padua and Udine, moneys of charitable origin, given outright to the Monte, accounted for one-third or even less of the available working capital. Nevertheless, the principle seems to have survived, in theory at least, that the receipt of interest on money lent to a Monte di Pietà was only justifiable on the grounds that the lender's motives were charitable, and that he had lent at some cost to himself.

The larger Monti di Pietà performed the double function, not merely of systematically organizing a personal loan service, but also of acting as savings banks, of guarding cash against theft, and of providing opportunities for safe investment with a very modest return on the capital. Those indifferent to the fate which threatened usurers, or insensitive to the doctrine of *lucrum cessans*, could illicitly use the Monte di Pietà as a receptacle for moneys which would otherwise have brought them no profit, and merely have lain idle. The Monti di Pietà developed their activities as deposit banks during a period in which, in Italy in general, private banks were showing marked instability, and in which there was an increasing demand for public banks which enjoyed guarantees from governments or from municipal authorities. The first of these was the Bank of Palermo, in the early 1550's—but foundations began to multiply in the 1580's: when the Casa di San Giorgio in Genoa resumed banking activity in 1586, when the public banks of Messina and Venice rose in 1587, when the Banco di Sant'Ambrogio of Milan followed in 1593, together with somewhat similar foundations in Rome and Naples.[53] It may be that the Monti di Pietà of the Venetian Republic were in certain respects the more modest provincial equivalents of these great concerns. Nothing can at present be said about the history of private banking on the Venetian mainland—but it is certain that

[53] Cf. Fernand Braudel, *La Méditerranée et le monde méditerranéen à l'époque de Philippe II* (2nd edition, Paris, 1966), I, pp. 481–3.

private banks in the capital passed through a phase of extreme instability between the early 1550's and 1584. An early sign of malaise was the failure of a bank run by the Procurator Antonio Priuli, in 1551.[54] During the 1560's, private banks became unpopular because they were accused of driving up the price of the gold ducat or *zecchino*, the most stable Venetian currency, so that the lira of account (pegged to the silver lira) commanded fewer *zecchini*. In January 1569, the Senate then decreed that the existing private banks—those of the Dolfin, of the Pisani and Tiepolo, of the Correr and of Angelo Sanuto —should dissolve.[55] Of these, only one, the Correr bank, actually paid all its creditors in full.[55a] The Sanuto and Dolfin crashed at about the time of the war of Cyprus;[56] the Pisani and Tiepolo were permitted by Senatorial decree to continue, until they too collapsed in 1584[57]—at which time theirs was officially the only private banking firm left in Venice.

Behind some of these failures lay the hazards of commerce, for the banks lent extensively to merchants, or else their proprietors, making no rigid distinction between the capital of the bank and their own, engaged in commercial enterprises on their own account. They tied up overmuch capital in distant mercantile ventures, or in other assets not quickly or easily realized. Crises of confidence occurred when some of these ventures failed, or when reports arrived of the bankruptcy of clients with whom the Venetian establishment had extensive dealings— as the failure of a Florentine businessman, Andrea dell'Oste, brought down the Pisani and Tiepolo. The threat of impending war in 1569–70 almost certainly undermined the Sanuto bank, which had acquired substantial interests in Constantinople and in Cyprus,[58] and undoubtedly contributed to the wreck of the Dolfin concern. The outbreak of war also started runs on banks when clients began to transfer their money (voluntarily or otherwise) into loans to the government. This process, described in Professor Lane's account of Venetian banking in

[54] A.S.V., *Senato, Terra, filza* 14, 26 September 1551; reg. 1551/52, ff. 12v.–13, 16v.–17v., 18v., 81v.–82, 101v.–111v. For this and for the following remarks, see also the introduction to Pullan, *Crisis and change in the Venetian economy*, pp. 16 f.

[55] A.S.V., *Senato, Terra, filza* 52, 2 December 1568, 24 January 1568 Venetian style.

[55a] *Cronaca Agostini*, vol. II (M.C.V., Cicogna MSS. 2853), f. 168v.

[56] A.S.V., *Senato, Terra, filza* 54, 8 February 1569 Venetian style; *filza* 55, 9 August 1570; *Cronaca Savina*, Biblioteca Marciana, Venice, MSS. Italiani, Classe VII, CXXXIV (8035), ff. 331v.–332.

[57] A.S.V., *Senato, Terra, filza* 58, 5 January 1571 Venetian style; *filza* 75, 2 September 1578; *filza* 90, 17 May 1584.

[58] See A. Magnocavallo, 'Proposta di riforma bancaria del banchiere veneziano Angelo Sanudo (secolo XVI)', *Atti del Congresso Internazionale di Scienze Storiche*, IX (Rome, 1904), pp. 413–17.

the early sixteenth century,[59] helped to overthrow the Dolfin in 1570. When these runs started, the banks were found to have insufficient reserves of liquid capital available. When such things were happening in Venice, it seems unlikely that private banking on the mainland can have remained wholly immune from these hazards.

Between 1584 and 1587, Venice dispensed with the services of private banks. But in 1587 the government created the Banco della Piazza di Rialto, a bank which discharged only very limited functions, and was designed chiefly to keep money safe and to enable business-men and others to make payments by simple transfers on the books, rather than by counting out quantities of coin. At first, it did not engage in activities enabling it to pay interest on deposits.[60] Venice in the late sixteenth century therefore commanded the services of two public banks—the Bank of Rialto and the Jewish loan banks of the Ghetto—whose functions were discharged in provincial cities by Monti di Pietà. These Monti both lent on pledge to people of all conditions and kept money safely; moreover, they paid interest on deposits. Whether hold-ings in the Monti di Pietà were used as a form of currency, or whether the habit developed of making payments through transfers on their books, is not yet known. The Monti di Pietà were supposed to lend only on tangible pledges, on easily saleable assets (such, at least was the theory), and some of them secured their depositors' capital and interest on communal revenue or real property. In a period of inflation, such as the second half of the sixteenth century, the balance was loaded against all banks, since depositors had every incentive to remove their money and to put it into goods which would not depreciate. But in spite of this, deposit banking with the Monti di Pietà survived the second half of the sixteenth century.

Probably the Monti di Pietà were also favoured by the contraction of other safe opportunities for the small investor who did not dispose of enough capital to acquire land or house property. The actions of the Venetian government very substantially reduced such opportunities between the late 1570's and about 1620—first, between 1577 and 1584, by liquidating the debt of 5·7 million ducats incurred during the war of 1570-3, and then, between 1596 and 1620, by extinguishing the older consolidated state loan funds.[61] Some Venetians at least entrusted their capital, through Genoese intermediaries, to the Spanish government:

[59] F. C. Lane, 'Venetian bankers, 1496–1533', in *Venice and history: the collected papers of Frederic C. Lane* (Baltimore, Maryland, 1966), pp. 78–80.
[60] C. F. Dunbar, 'The Bank of Venice', *Quarterly Journal of Economics*, VI (1892); Gino Luzzatto, 'Les banques publiques de Venise—siècles XVIe–XVIIIe', in *History of the principal public banks*, ed. J. G. van Dillen (The Hague, 1934).
[61] See above, pp. 138–40.

but Philip II's stoppage of payments in 1596 produced repercussions in Venice, and contributed to a bitter reaction against this type of lending.[62] At present, one does not know to what extent mainlanders had been in the habit of investing in Venetian loan funds, or, conversely, how far Venetians made deposits in provincial Monti di Pietà. But, with the economic penetration of the Venetians into the mainland, the relationship between the capital and the subject provinces was becoming more intimate: and it is worth drawing attention to the probable connexions between the survival of the Monti di Pietà and the extinction of Venetian government loan funds.

The Monti di Pietà could be charged with encouraging sterile investment in loans for the purposes of consumption, rather than for productive ends. However, the nature of the sixteenth-century economy was such that it urgently required some mechanism for tiding wage-earners, artisans, labourers, paupers and all without cash reserves over temporary but acute crises. No investment in such machinery can be dismissed as altogether unproductive. It is true that in theory the Monti di Pietà were supposed to act as a distraction from trade, industry or agriculture, and not as repositories for otherwise unemployed funds. No-one was in theory entitled to receive interest from a Monte di Pietà unless he had seriously intended to invest at higher rates in agriculture or commerce, and had deliberately rejected the idea out of charitable motives. However, the low rates, seldom if ever more than 3–4 per cent, paid to depositors by the Monti di Pietà in the early seventeenth century are most unlikely to have offered a higher return than commercial or landed investment, and they were considerably less lucrative than other forms of loan, such as *livelli* or *censi*. They could hardly have distracted from productive investment in the same way as the *censos* and *juros* of Spain, of which Spanish writers so eloquently complained in the early seventeenth century.[63] The Monti di Pietà probably appealed to the genuinely charitable; to religious institutions, like those of Crema, which could not invest their capital in land and needed a safe security; to those who had lost the taste or the nerve for more adventurous speculations, or did not possess the knowledge, imagination or connexions to employ their money in active enterprises. However, until much more is known about investment in the Monti di Pietà, no definite statement can be made about this. It is quite possible that merchants and shopkeepers used the Venetian Monti di Pietà to raise

[62] Nicolò Contarini, *Istorie veneziane*, in Gaetano Cozzi, *Il Doge Nicolò Contarini: ricerche sul patriziato veneziano agli inizi del Seicento* (Venice–Rome, 1958), pp. 346 f.

[63] Cf. J. H. Elliott, 'The decline of Spain', *Past and Present*, no. 20 (November, 1961), p. 67.

money on pledge, and that this helped them in their businesses. The Jews of Venice complained in 1618 that merchants constantly borrowed from them on the security of their goods, and the Monti di Pietà may well have been exposed to similar demands. They may not, in fact, have made all their loans for the purpose of consumption: though there is no evidence as yet of systematic commercial, industrial or agricultural investment on their part.

However, the benefits conferred by a Monte di Pietà on the community in which it stood depended ultimately on the integrity with which its funds were administered and on the rigour with which the officials observed the statutes. The next chapter will discuss the broader services performed by the Monti di Pietà at their best, and the commoner abuses which impaired their usefulness or even led to near-extinction.

6

THE USES AND ABUSES OF MONTI DI PIETÀ

During the sixteenth and early seventeenth century, the Monti di Pietà served the communities which had established them in other ways than through the conduct of the personal loan business. Forbidden, except in Bergamo and possibly in Crema, to add to their capital any profits made from interest charges, they often dispensed these profits annually in pious or charitable works. They also provided the commune with reserve funds on which it could draw to relieve poverty in years of famine or pestilence, when bread prices soared, quarantine regulations paralysed economic activity, and disease incapacitated wage-earners and breadwinners for work. Occasionally, the larger cities drew on the funds of their Monti di Pietà to raise troops during national emergencies. The Monti thus acted as banks specially appointed to lend to the local governments in times of extraordinary need. Their funds were thus employed in the general interest of the poor, or of the community as a whole, rather than in that of a series of needy individuals. The extent to which a Monte di Pietà would exercise these functions in a particular community naturally varied according to the nature, wealth and efficiency of its other charitable or social institutions. In the course of the sixteenth century, many communities established public granaries and warehouses designed to accumulate reserve stocks, and so tide their people over disasters caused by foul weather or population pressure. These institutions, usually called Monti di Carità, Monti dell'Abbondanza, or Fonteghi, complemented the Monti di Pietà. Nevertheless, at least in Padua, Brescia and Bergamo, the Monti di Pietà continued to discharge very varied social functions. This statement can well be illustrated by examining the activities of the Paduan Monte, one of the three largest in the Venetian dominion.

This Monte di Pietà traced its descent from the original foundation of Pietro Barozzi and Bernardino of Feltre in 1491. In the mid-sixteenth century, it served a University and garrison town of some 36,000 inhabitants, including many textile workers, the capital of a prosperous agricultural province with a population of about 120,000.[1] How many of the people were eligible to take advantage of its services is uncertain;

[1] Cf. Domenico dall'Abaco, *Stato di Padova e suo territorio nel 1552–53*, ed. E. A. Cicogna (Venice, 1850), pp. 9–11.

in the townships of the Padovano small Monti di Pietà existed and some Jewish banking survived. From 1548, although a Jewish community remained in Padua, the Monte di Pietà enjoyed the monopoly of all lawful lending at interest. In 1554, its working capital stood at just under 100,000 ducats. Over the half-century of the price rise, its capital rather more than doubled in face value, partly through further charitable donations, partly through the acceptance of deposits. This increase of 120 per cent compares favourably with the increase of 73 per cent in the face value of charity dispensed in Venice by the Scuola Grande of San Rocco between 1561-70 and 1601-10.[2] It is difficult, however, to believe that all this capital found its way into loans to the poor. In 1554, the Monte di Pietà in Padua lent about 140,000 ducats a year; in 1551-2, it handled a total of 167,736 pledges, and in 1552-3 a total of 131,465.[3] Theoretically, the Monte di Pietà was obliged to accommodate students and soldiers before anyone else.[4] The demand on its services probably varied substantially from year to year, as the figures for the handling of pledges suggest.

Throughout the period reviewed here, the Monte di Pietà lent on pledges at the rate of 5 per cent, which proved to be more than enough to cover administrative costs. The officials of the Monte therefore dispensed the surplus annually, partly in providing dowries to poor maids (a favourite form of charity in Venice and the Venetian Republic) and partly in alms to poor monasteries and convents. The Rettori of Padua gave the following figures in ducats—perhaps very approximate estimates—which suggest the extent of this activity:

	1554	1606	1625	1638
Total interest		11,000		11,000
Less expenses	3,075	6,000		5,000
Dispensed to *donzelle* and *luochi pii*		5,000	2–3,000	6,000[5]

By the middle of the sixteenth century, a fraction of the capital of the Monte di Pietà had on several occasions found its way into large purchases of grain in lean years. In 1554, the Rettore Marc'Antonio Grimani told the Senate that in the past the officials had sometimes spent as much as 18,000 ducats in one year for this purpose.[6] The weight of the expanding population on the land, coupled with growing

[2] See above, p. 170.
[3] A.S.V., *Collegio, Relazioni*, b. 43, report of Marc'Antonio Grimani, 3 August 1554, ff. 6v.–7; and of Stefano Viaro, 24 January 1605 Venetian style.
[4] A.S.V., *Senato, Terra*, reg. 1547–8, f. 94v.
[5] A.S.V., *Collegio, Relazioni*, b. 43, under date.
[6] *Ibid.*, report of Marc'Antonio Grimani, 3 August 1554.

Venetian demand, was reducing the safety margin, and making the people uncomfortably dependent on the vagaries of the weather. In 1559, the Rettori resolved to take action by establishing a separate charitable fund to purchase grain abroad in bulk during the months of July and August, and by selling it at less than the current market rates the following May.[7] The fund, known as the Monte di Carità, was duly established, but it suffered heavily as a result of famine in the mid-1560's. Although it was reconstituted on this occasion largely through charitable gifts, there are signs that by the early 1580's it had foundered altogether, partly through maladministration.[8] Thereafter, the Monte di Pietà once more became largely responsible for providing funds to purchase grain during emergencies.

The city had always borrowed heavily from the Monte di Pietà in seasons of pestilence. Padua possessed a large plague hospital or Lazzaretto outside its walls, but this was poorly endowed, with regular revenues which in the 1580's amounted to only 400 ducats a year. During a severe epidemic, public expenditure might well run into tens of thousands. In 1528 and 1555, the Lazzaretto incurred heavy debts to the Monte di Pietà, and the visitation of plague in 1576 caused the commune to make still greater demands.[9] This epidemic wiped out perhaps 25 per cent of the population of Padua: the governor Pasquale Cicogna, a future Doge, estimated the number of deaths at about 10,000. Between April 1576 and March 1577, 6,424 deaths occurred in Padua itself, others in the Lazzaretto. To meet the expenditure caused by this disaster, the commune raised some 40,000 ducats, of which it borrowed 26,000 from the Monte di Pietà. Much of the rest came from the land-tax or *campadego* of 2 soldi per *campo* authorized by the Venetian government.[10] A decree of April 1577 attempted to provide for the future, and it established reserve funds in the Monte di Pietà which in the following years were applied, not only to epidemics of plague, but also to the famines which appeared to cause them. For the next twenty years, all persons borrowing sums of 4 lire or more from the Monte di Pietà were obliged to pay 2 *bagatini* per lira—a tax of 0·8 per cent—every time they deposited or collected a pledge.[10a] The fund so accumulated would be touched only in time of pestilence.

By 1590, the deposit amounted to 8,000 ducats. In this notorious

[7] A.S.V., *Senato, Terra, filza* 29, 14 July 1559.

[8] A.S.V., *Collegio, Relazioni*, b. 43, report of Giovanni Battista Contarini, 1 May 1566; *Senato, Terra, filza* 86, 26 February 1582 Venetian style, *filza* 87, 5 March 1583.

[9] A.S.V., *Senato, Terra, filza* 89, 21 January 1583 Venetian style.

[10] A.S.V., *Collegio, Relazioni*, b. 33, *Relazioni Miste*, vol. IV, ff. 32v.–33v. Report read in May 1577.

[10a] Cf. Ventura, *Nobiltà e popolo*, pp. 432 f.

year of acute famine, the Rettori obtained permission from the Senate to use the deposit to buy grain. They proposed to stretch the regulations on the grounds that they would be warding off the pestilence which would surely result from the famine—'for famine seldom occurs without the contagion following'.[11] From then onwards, they regularly received permission to borrow sums of 8,000, and later 10,000 ducats, from this source in order to purchase grain. They did so on the strict understanding that the money must be restored to the Monte di Pietà by some date in the following year, by the end of July, or in September. The governors sometimes borrowed 'on the express understanding that the grains which are purchased must not be sold for less than what they cost—all expenses included'. Since the seasonal fluctuations in the price of grain were so marked, the Rettori could sell the grains they had purchased abroad in late summer or autumn in the spring of the following year at cost price or at a small profit. When they did so, they could still lower the current price of grain, and thereby perform a valuable service to the poor. The Venetian government authorized the community or the Rettori to carry out this operation in 1590, 1591 and 1592; and again in 1596, 1597, 1600 and 1605.[12]

Contemporary statistics for the capital of the Monte di Pietà in Padua in the early seventeenth century sometimes distinguished between two special funds kept in reserve in the Monte, one for the use of the local department of public health, the Collegio di Sanità, and the other specifically designed for the Lazzaretto. These funds together constituted between 6 per cent and 10 per cent of the total working capital of the bank:

	1606	1619	1625
Collegio di Sanità	22,470	5,163	14,840
Lazzaretto		9,531	3,226
Total capital	221,670	223,259	237,070[13]

The figures probably fluctuated according to whether or not the deposits had just been raided to buy grain or for some other purpose.

In 1607, the Paduans obtained permission to draw 12,000 ducats from the deposit of the Collegio di Sanità to pay the hundred cuirassiers offered to the Venetian government during the Interdict, when it

[11] A.S.V., *Senato, Terra, filza* 115, 4 August 1590.

[12] A.S.V., *Senato, Terra, filza* 122, 5 December 1591; *filza* 124, 19 September 1592; *filza* 140, 18 July 1596; *filza* 143, 9 August 1597; *filza* 156, 1 September 1600 and 29 September 1600; *filza* 175, 28 July 1605; cf. also A.S.V., *Collegio, Relazioni*, b. 43, report of Tommaso Contarini, Cavalier Conte del Zaffo, 24 September 1609.

[13] A.S.V., *Collegio, Relazioni*, b. 43, under date; cf. also Ferrari, *L'Ufficio della Sanità in Padova*, pp. 35–6, 39–41.

faced a serious risk of invasion by Spain acting in support of the Pope. Again, in 1618, the Senate approved a resolution of the Council of Padua to raise 5,000 ducats from the Monte di Pietà to honour other promises of military aid to the Republic during the current war.[14] A century before, such proposals had evoked indignant protests from the Paduans: if they objected now, they did so to no purpose.[15] These deposits in the Monte di Pietà had developed into a fund for general use in emergencies, and were not devoted strictly to the welfare of the poor. The Monte di Pietà, however, helped once more to finance relief measures undertaken during the most savage of epidemics in 1630–1. Plague then reduced the population of Padua from over 30,000 to 12,122, with (in addition) about 1,600 *claustrali*, inmates of monasteries, convents and friaries. On this occasion, the cost of maintaining the Lazzaretto and relieving the poor touched 57,000 ducats, most of this sum being borrowed by the city from the Monte di Pietà. To repay it, the city proceeded to borrow some 25,000 ducats on the security of communal property, and it received permission for the next twenty-five years to levy an extra tax of two *bagatini* per lira on every pledge on which more than 6 lire was lent.[16] By 1638 this familiar measure was raising about 1,800 ducats a year.[17]

This Monte di Pietà, therefore, provided a measure of security and relief, not only in cases of individual and personal misfortune, but in years of widespread and general disaster. It greatly increased the resources available to a government confronted with the problem of organizing rescue work and of somehow reducing the suffering and death which plague and famine brought to its city. The bank of the poor could lend the commune large sums for their collective relief. In Padua, the commune was careful to pay its debts, and always made some effort to reconstitute the funds of the Monte di Pietà, apparently through small taxes on the borrowers and their pledges. Brescia, however, managed its affairs less providently, and loans to the commune seriously reduced the working capital of one of its Monti di Pietà, especially after the great plague of 1630. Here, a second loan fund, the Monte Grande or Monte Nuovo, had arisen in and after 1587, largely

[14] A.S.V., *Senato, Terra, filza* 181, 11 January 1606 Venetian style; *filza* 229, 7 July 1618. According to Ferrari, *L'Ufficio della Sanità*, pp. 40–1, loans by the Collegio di Sanità for the purpose of raising troops amounted in 1616–18 to 111,600 lire or about 18,500 ducats. This sum was not refunded promptly, but was reduced by 1629 to 33,466 lire or some 5,500 ducats.

[15] (See above, p. 503.

[16] A.S.V., *Collegio, Relazioni*, b. 43, report of Vincenzo Capello, 7 January 1631 Venetian style; cf. also Ferrari, *L'Ufficio della Sanità*, ch. iv, pp. 117–75, with further details of population losses at pp. 168–9.

[17] A.S.V., *Collegio, Relazioni*, b. 43, report of Giovanni Pisani, 9 November 1638.

if not exclusively financed by deposits at 5 per cent. In the early seventeenth century, the Monte di Pietà lent heavily to the city of Brescia for much the same purposes as the Monte di Pietà of Padua: to pay for corn-supplies, to raise funds for infantry offered to Venice in 1616 during the war in Friuli, to contribute to the vast expenses of rescue work in the great plague.[18] In 1630, Brescia did not depend so heavily as Padua on the Monte di Pietà—it defrayed only about one-sixth of its expenditure by loans from the Monte, and for the rest relied mainly on taxation or loans from private persons.[19] Nevertheless, in 1645 the Podestà Bernardo Renier reported that the city's borrowings, to the tune of 74,000 ducats, had seriously depleted the Monte di Pietà. Theoretically, the capital of the Monte Nuovo stood at 189,860 ducats: but of these only 83,470 were actually available to make personal loans. Expenses now far outstripped the proceeds of the interest charge to borrowers, and, according to an ominous balance-sheet drawn up by a local accountant for the Rettori, the Monte would at the present rate be exhausted by 1657.[20]

The history of the Monti di Pietà, however, is far from being a record of blameless and uncorrupt service to the communities of the Venetian Republic. In Venice in the early sixteenth century, the institution had excited mistrust, not on the worn pretext that it infringed the canon law, but on the quite different grounds that the funds of these institutions would be fraudulently converted or directed into the wrong hands.[21] Who, in other words, could possibly be trusted to administer them? The Jewish banker, so long as he remained a private entrepreneur, had a close personal interest in preserving and increasing his own capital. He, as well as the poor, would suffer by its dissipation: but the same would not apply to the rich citizens charged with administering the Monti di Pietà. They must be motivated by a spirit of charity or a strong sense of public obligation, and disaster would overtake the Monte di Pietà if their sense of duty flagged. None of the Monti di Pietà in the larger cities of the Venetian dominions on the mainland of Italy completely escaped charges of corruption, unwisdom or incompetence, levelled by the Rettori at their administrators. The Rettori, armed at least from 1605 onwards with special powers conceded by the Council of Ten,[22] became particularly conscious of abuses in the Monti

---

[18] Zanelli, *Delle condizioni interne di Brescia*, pp. 108–9.

[19] *Ibid.*, doc. IX, p. 234.

[20] A.S.V., *Collegio, Relazioni*, b. 37, report of 12 April 1645.

[21] See above, p. 493.

[22] Cf. the reference by Antonio Mocenigo, Rettore of Treviso, to the special powers conceded to Rettori by the Council of Ten—in his report of 9 February 1605, A.S.V., *Collegio, Relazioni*, b. 48.

di Pietà in the early seventeenth century—though some of them had already acted forthrightly enough in preceding decades.

In some Venetian cities, tight little oligarchies had arisen and had established a control of office and patronage, and sometimes of local policy, which proved almost indestructible. A well-organized faction could ensure that the principal offices within the Monti di Pietà were rotated only among their own members, who never demanded of one another accounts of their stewardship, and who willingly joined in a conspiracy of silence to conceal longstanding frauds and peculation. Collusion between Conservatori and Massari must have been necessary to allow the Massari to commit the crimes of embezzlement of which they were accused with monotonous regularity. Before such conspiracies, the elaborate system of double-checking prescribed in the statutes of the Monti di Pietà was powerless and ineffective. In small towns like Este, close networks of this kind were easy to establish, though they did eventually provoke those excluded from them into protesting to the Venetian government. A petition from the people of Este, read in the Collegio in the summer of 1614, declared that a certain group of citizens had managed to obtain control of public revenues to a total of over 14,000 ducats a year, and also of the funds and deposits of the Monte di Pietà. The local Council consisted of 48 persons all closely related to one another, with groups of four or five men drawn from the same immediate family circle. These councillors were elected to serve for life, and passed municipal offices from one to the other without keeping written accounts. They had embezzled over 20,000 lire from the Monte di Pietà's charitable funds, with another 7–8,000 lire out of deposits left in the Monte, which they had distributed among themselves. They refused to restore the sum of 1,400 ducats deposited by private persons for the support of unmarriageable daughters who had entered the local convent as nuns.[23]

In Padua, there were at least certain constitutional safeguards against the development of a situation like this: half the Council of the Monte consisted of members of the Arti and Fraglie, who with their relative solidarity confronted the divided citizen body. Among the citizens, two factions engaged in the pursuit of office, each seeking to exclude the other from participation in the spoils of local government. In 1618, these factions were led by the families of Dotta and Buzzacarina, and were generally known as the Medagini and Medagioni.[24] However, the

[23] A.S.V., *Senato, Terra, filza* 210, 23 August 1614.

[24] A.S.V., *Collegio, Relazioni*, b. 43, report of Nicolò Vendramin, April 1618 (?), and of Andrea Vendramin, 20 March 1640. According to Maria Borgherini-Scarabellin, *La vita privata a Padova nel secolo XVII* (Venice, 1917), p. 14, the division into Medag(l)ini and Medag(l)ioni dated from 1592.

fact that by 1609 one of these factions had managed to hold its mono-poly of office for fifteen years boded ill for the administration of the Monte di Pietà. In 1609 and 1611, Venetian Podestà lapsed into defeatism when confronted with such a situation. Tommaso Contarini, Cavalier Conte del Zaffo, prophesied that no Rettore would ever, in his short term of office, successfully cut at the root of the trouble. His successor Angelo Correr claimed to have taken vigorous action against misappropriators of funds and longstanding debtors, and to have exploited the powers conferred by the Council of Ten: it was generally agreed that there was much embezzlement and many disorders, but

> although I have devoted much energy to auditing the accounts, it is, as far as I can see, impossible to detect these abuses, because the affairs of the Council have for some years been dominated by one single faction, and as there is an excellent understanding amongst them they are able to adjust the records to suit themselves.[25]

Malpractices of this kind offended against all the principles which the Venetian government held most ostentatiously sacred. The Vene-tians had always devised elaborate machinery for checking the corrup-tion of oligarchy, in their own councils and institutions, and had always been remarkably free from prolonged control by any one ruling faction. Now, in 1613, the City Council of Padua, doubtless prompted or driven by a scandalized Rettore, passed new measures designed to ensure that

> every honourable citizen may the more easily participate in the distribu-tion of offices and charges, and that no-one may hold a perpetual seat in the Councils to the exclusion of another, a thing which results in ill-feeling between individuals. . . .

Old recipes were tried again—increasing the numbers of the City Council from 100 to 120, not more than three from any one family; a compulsory rest period (*contumacia*) for the 60 members of the Council who retired every year; some electoral procedures designed to secure fairer elections to the Council of the Monte di Pietà.[26] But paper con-stitutions of this kind made little impact if the will to observe them was totally lacking. The competing citizen factions survived, and in 1640 were still striving to control the vital offices of Massaro and Cassiero in the Monte di Pietà.[27] Finally, in 1650, the Rettore Nicolò Mocenigo threw up despairing hands and produced a graphic account

[25] A.S.V., *Collegio, Relazioni*, b. 43, reports of 24 September 1609 and 8 March 1611.
[26] A.S.V., *Senato, Terra, filza* 208, 10 January 1613 Venetian style.
[27] A.S.V., *Collegio, Relazioni*, b. 43, report of Andrea Vendramin, 20 March 1640.

of the prevailing corruption which epitomizes most of the commonest recorded abuses to which the Monti di Pietà were liable.

He described with resentment a group of sixteen citizens who engrossed all the offices to which the City Council elected. They arranged all business between themselves outside the open debates in the Council chamber, and acted as a pressure-group which confronted the Rettore with ready-made proposals which he was seldom quick-witted enough to see through and resist. These respectable conspirators had won control of the Monte di Pietà, and had installed a succession of officials who collaborated to disguise one another's peculation. The Massari would pass pledges on to one another, converting them to their own private uses. They failed to auction the more valuable objects, and the Monte never got its money back. When auctions were held, 'certain influential gentlemen' intimidated rival bidders into silence, so that the pledge could be knocked down to them at ridiculously low prices. The officials of the Monte also lent pledges freely and allowed them to be taken off the premises, including the property of churches, which they hired for masquerades and other junketing at the Carnival season before Lent. Before negotiating with the Massaro, borrowers found it necessary to produce the 'tip which is called *sotto fassa*', which had now become a 'formalized transaction (*formal mercantia*)'. Finally, confusion between the various systems of accounting and of reckoning the value of coins added to the profits made by a Massaro. For example, the coin known as the *ongaro* was rated by the city treasury at 19 lire 10 soldi; for the purpose of lending to the poor the Massaro valued the coin at 20 lire; when the borrower came to repay the loan, he found the *ongaro* again rated at only 19 lire 10 soldi. The Rettore concluded flatly that 'Circumstances have not permitted me to introduce any regulations or to root out these detestable abuses'.[28]

The corruption and nest-feathering which Nicolò Mocenigo portrayed in 1650 had its parallels in most of the other Monti di Pietà of the Venetian Republic. At the root of it, perhaps, lay the factions and in-groups which in the individual cities joined in conspiracies of silence, to conceal frauds, to falsify records, to share the assets of the Monti di Pietà among the rich. A Venetian Rettore held his post for, at the most, eighteen months to two years. The rotation of office in Venice was designed to ensure that everyone shared in office and accepted its expenses, that no provincial governor had time to build up a local following. But the result of this policy was that the Rettori—and the governors of Padua were unusually frank about this—found themselves helpless before the complexities of local intrigue. Nonetheless, there

28 *Ibid.*, report of 9 August 1650.

were plenty of cases of vigorous intervention by the Rettori, some successful prosecutions for fraud, and even some attempts to redraft the constitutions of the Monti di Pietà in order to provide more effective safeguards. Some Rettori took action against fraud as early as the 1560's or '70's. At Padua the rogues' gallery of Massari detected in embezzlement, in failing to repay or account for the funds they had handled, steadily lengthened. Pietro da Bazo in 1566; Giovanni Pizzacomino, Massaro from 1573 to 1575, and his successor Ludovico Barisone, said to have defrauded the Monte of about 17,000 ducats between them; Giacomo Capodivacca, prosecuted in 1579; Mainardo Bigolino, imprisoned in 1581–2; Borromeo di Borromei in 1599; Marco Bellacotto in 1617; Marco da Lion in 1627: these Massari were found out and sometimes effectively punished.[29] Nevertheless, the governors often experienced serious difficulty in proceeding against them, their heirs or their guarantors. They frequently, like Ludovico Barisone, took the precaution of tying up part of their estates in unbreakable entails or *fideicomissi*, or else of disguising them as part of their wives' dowries.[30] These manoeuvres effectively secured their property against legal execution, even if the Massaro himself were imprisoned, exiled or otherwise punished. In 1612, Girolamo Cornaro wrote from Verona that several Massari had in the past few years failed for sums amounting to tens of thousands of ducats. Their guarantors had frequently died or gone bankrupt themselves, 'or are defending themselves by means of *fideicomissi* and other devices'. The worst example was the Marchese Canossa, who had through acting as guarantor to his brother incurred debts of over 40,000 ducats. It was unlikely that the Monte would get a farthing of this repaid.[31]

Occasionally, however, both at Padua and at Verona, Rettori were able to claim greater success. At Padua, they prosecuted the Massaro Mainardo Bigolino, who held a doctor's degree, and who in a sycophantic but desperate petition to the Senate said that as an 'unfortunate and incautious young man' he had been seduced by his friends into lending them large sums of money without pledges and on the strength of written undertakings only. They had then defaulted and left him to take his punishment. Bigolino was condemned to lose one hand if he

---

[29] *Ibid.*, reports of Giovanni Battista Contarini, 1 May 1566; Giovanni Dandolo, 28 November 1617; Girolamo Lando, 19 October 1627; A.S.V., *Senato, Terra, filza* 76, 23 January 1578 Venetian style; *filza* 78, 25 July 1579; *filza* 79, 12 December 1579; *filza* 83, 9 November 1581; *filza* 84, 31 March and 21 April 1582; *filza* 150, 5 April 1599.

[30] A.S.V., *Senato, Terra, filza* 76, 23 January 1578 Venetian style; cf. the remarks of Ottaviano Donà, Podestà-Capitano of Treviso, in his report of 20 March 1586, *ibid.*, *filza* 97, 19 April 1586.

[31] A.S.V., *Collegio, Relazioni*, b. 50, report of 5 May 1612.

2R

failed to pay on time, but was assisted by the provision that all suits which he brought from his jail against his debtors should be judged by one or both Rettori without the possibility of further appeals or delaying tactics. This probably enabled him to pay the 800 ducats in debts which still remained to him in November 1581.[32] Turning the screw on a Massaro and his relatives by physical threats of this nature sometimes worked admirably, and silenced legalistic quibbles. About 1641, the Rettori of Verona passed a death-sentence on Angelo Alcenago, a Massaro indebted to the Monte di Pietà to the sum of 23,000 ducats. The intervention of the Venetian Avogadore di Commun saved the prisoner, but his friends and relatives had meanwhile been shocked into raising the money in the hope of getting his life spared.[33]

Perhaps the most useful general provisions made by the Rettori were those designed to expedite judicial procedure against debtors to the Monte di Pietà. Their brutality could only be justified on the grounds of administrative necessity overriding the demands of strict justice, and on the score that ordinary legal processes were being abused by the wicked. In 1591, the Venetian Senate confirmed the decision taken at Padua that if the Conservatori judged anyone to be a debtor to the Monte di Pietà, he could make no appeal unless 'he deposits in that Holy Monte a sum equivalent to the debt he has been held to owe'. If he failed to get his case judged by the Rettore within two months, then the Monte would automatically be credited with the sum deposited in its coffers.[34] The abuses to which this procedure might lend itself are obvious: but, since they would favour the Monte di Pietà at the expense of the private individual, the Venetian government was prepared to ratify the decree. Similar measures were eventually adopted at Rovigo in 1604, though here litigants were allowed as much as six months to get their cases settled.[35]

Evidence of corruption and embezzlement is not lacking: but there is little clear testimony that Monti di Pietà suffered heavily or permanently from the fraudulent conversion of their funds, in such a way that their working capital was seriously depleted and never recovered. Rovigo, however, does provide an exception to this rule. In 1564, the working capital of the Monte di Pietà stood at 11,192 ducats; but in 1608 it is probable that only 2,400–2,600 ducats remained.[36] The first

[32] A.S.V., *Senato, Terra, filza* 83, 9 November 1581; *filza* 84, 31 March and 21 April 1582.

[33] A.S.V., *Collegio, Relazioni*, b. 50, report of Alvise Morosini (?), 18 September 1641.

[34] A.S.V., *Senato, Terra, filza* 120, 27 July 1591.

[35] A.S.V., *Senato, Terra, filza* 171, 17 July 1604.

[36] See below, p. 624.

of these figures certainly includes deposits, and it is uncertain whether the second also does so. But in 1564, the capital of the Monte itself was 4,379 ducats, so that at the very least the Monte di Pietà lost 40 per cent of its capital through fraud, and the real value of its assets surely diminished much more rapidly than this. It failed altogether in its object of eliminating Jewish lending from Rovigo and the Polesine.

In 1574, the Podestà-Capitano Pietro Marcello wrote that the moneys of the Monte di Pietà had been drained into the pockets of the citizens who ran the institution and the city. They paid no interest, and had thereby driven the poor back into the hands of the Jews. Marcello had decreed that all debtors must pay up and produce arrears of interest by the end of the following August, which he deemed a suitable time for such payments—perhaps on the grounds that food prices were likely to be low.[37] However, in the next thirty years, the Monte di Pietà again deteriorated, largely through the misconduct of two Massari, Ludovico Biscaccia (or Bescazza) and Antonio Almino.[38] Biscaccia entered on office in 1593, and received the sum of 35,000 lire or about 5,800 ducats. After his death some years later, 28,000 lire were found to be missing, and by a local sentence of 27 July 1602 this sum was to be extracted from his estate. Biscaccia's heirs, however, claimed that he had in fact consigned the missing funds to his fellow-Massaro Antonio Almino. Almino suffered arrest in 1603 for another *intacco* or un-authorized raid on the funds, but he then escaped from prison to live in Ferrara, and attempts to get him arrested or extradited failed. How-ever, the Venetian authorities and the representatives of the Monte di Pietà in Rovigo pursued the matter with surprising tenacity for several years. A citizen of Rovigo, one Ludovico Delaito, petitioned the Senate in 1603, reporting irregularities and suggesting reforms. He at least did not belong to the charmed circle which had exploited the Monte di Pietà so profitably, and there was some support in Rovigo itself for Venetian intervention. Biscaccia's heirs appealed to the Venetian magistracy of the Auditori Nuovi, who then transferred the case to the supreme civil court in Venice, the Quarantia Civil Nuova. They annulled the sentence, not merely on the grounds of technical errors in procedure, but because it was fundamentally unjust. However, judicial procedure in the Venetian Republic was so cumbersome as to allow a sentence to be rescinded up to three times before it was finally broken, though litigants normally abandoned the battle after only one annul-ment. The sentence was quashed a second time, but on the third round

[37] A.S.V., *Collegio, Relazioni*, b. 46, report of 28 May 1574.
[38] For the following see A.S.V., *Senato, Terra, filza* 171, 17 July 1604; *filza* 188, 13 October 1608; *filza* 190, 26 March 1609.

representatives of the Monte di Pietà slashed cavalierly through the legal tangle by invoking the recent law which required Biscaccia's heirs to deposit the disputed sum in the Monti di Pietà before they launched their appeal. It is possible that on this occasion the Monte's defenders had picked on the wrong victims: certainly the Monte did not command support from the Venetian courts.

Embezzlement by the Massari did not account for all the depletion in the Monte di Pietà. By 1604, the needs of the commune had caused it to borrow a total of 11,534 lire, a little less than 2,000 ducats, and it had omitted to repay either the capital or the interest. Arrears of interest now amounted to 9,619 lire, and almost doubled the commune's debt. In this year, the Senate acted, and adopted the recommendations submitted in Delaito's petition and in the reports of Rettori. They introduced the procedure described above for expediting appeals. They attempted to break the ranks of the local oligarchy by prescribing that the Conservatori of the Monte should serve for periods of two years only, and that whilst half should still be chosen by the citizen Council the other half must be nominated by the Rettore. These Conservatori must on no account be related to persons who were in debt to the Monte di Pietà. The Rettore was instructed to assign the commune a date by which it must pay its debt. Again, in 1608, the statutes of the Monte di Pietà were completely redrafted, though this did not involve any radical change in the principles on which the institution ought in theory to be run.

Despite these essays in reform, the Monte di Pietà showed few signs of immediate recovery. Up to 1624 the Rettori of Rovigo were still describing it as 'ruined', 'depleted', suffering heavily from *intacchi*. Regulations demanding that office be rotated were not observed, and in 1624 it seemed that the Cassiero for the time being had held office for three years.[39] In 1625, the Podestà-Capitano Francesco Trevisan briefly described the defeat of an octogenarian citizen, Giovanni Boniffacio, in his endeavour to erect a new Monte di Pietà based on deposits. This would have borrowed at 5 per cent (a more generous rate than the 3 per cent envisaged in the new regulations of 1608), and have lent on pledge at 6 per cent. Trevisan believed that the proposal had been sabotaged by an unholy combination between the richer citizens and the Jews.[40] It is, however, possible that Boniffacio or others like him persisted in their design, since by 1637 Alvise Morosini was (with optimism uncharacteristic of the governors of Rovigo) able to

[39] A.S.V., *Collegio, Relazioni*, b. 46, reports of Pietro Gradenigo, 2 August 1612; Lorenzo Surian, 1622; Girolamo Correr, 6 March 1624.
[40] *Ibid.*, report of 5 August 1625.

report that the Monte di Pietà was in excellent order. It now had a capital of 8,000 ducats of its own, and, with the deposits of private persons added, its working capital had reached a total of 11–12,000 ducats.[41] Despite this happy conclusion—or temporary settlement—it seems clear that for at least thirty years malpractices, graft and the sordid greed of a small-town mutual protection society sadly limited the usefulness of the Monte di Pietà in Rovigo.

The reports and proceedings of the Rettori show that there were certain favourite forms of irregularity to which the Monti di Pietà were especially prone. A Massaro who felt himself unlikely to be called to account would lend vast sums upon purely nominal pledges. Giorgio Semitecolo, Podestà of Castelfranco, who courageously attacked local abuses in 1585, found that in the Monte di Pietà past Massari had lent 900 lire on a small quantity of silk, 200 lire on a broken fork, and other large sums on written bonds only.[42] In Verona in the 1640's, officials of the Monte and those employed in valuing pledges proved sensitive to bribery, and, not surprisingly, there was no incentive for the owners to redeem overvalued pledges, so that the Monte lost heavily.[43] Very widespread was the practice of 'putting back' pledges—neglecting to sell unredeemed pledges promptly as the regulations prescribed, thus tying up capital and reducing the sum available for further loans. This became doubly pernicious if the Monte di Pietà failed to exact interest on pledges it had 'put back'. In trying to remedy this abuse, the Rettori sometimes half connived at it. Pietro Gritti at Vicenza in 1571 joined the Conservatori of the Monte in asking the Senate to confirm provisions which forbade 'putting back any pledge without the disbursement of at least one-half of the capital and interest lent'.[44] If the Monti di Pietà issued longer-term loans, their turnover would inevitably be reduced. Related to this was the corrupt practice of intimidating either the officials of the Monte di Pietà or the general public in such a way as to sabotage auctions. Pledges belonging to influential and aggressive members of the community were seldom or never sold, and interest payments on them lapsed. This was a conspicuous abuse in seventeenth-century Bergamo and Brescia. In 1621, when they visited Brescia, the roving commissioners, the Sindici

---

[41] *Ibid.*, report of 11 November 1637.

[42] A.S.V., *Senato, Terra, filza* 96, 4 February 1585 Venetian style.

[43] A.S.V., *Collegio, Relazioni*, b. 50, report of Francesco Zeno, early 1640's.

[44] A.S.V., *Senato, Terra, filza* 58, 9 November 1571. Similar abuses are described at Treviso (*ibid., filza* 97, 19 April 1586; *Collegio, Relazioni*, b. 48, report of Stefano Viaro, 6 December 1595); at Asola and Brescia (*Senato, Dispacci, Provveditori da terra e da mar, filza* 270, 17 March, 5 June 1621); at Udine (*Collegio, Relazioni*, b. 49, report of Alvise Mocenigo, 3 August 1622); and at Feltre (*ibid.*, b. 41, report of Gabriele Cornaro, 23 November 1634).

Inquisitori in Terra Ferma, found it necessary to order that, if no buyers were found for unredeemed pledges auctioned by the Monte di Pietà, they must be removed to Verona or Venice to be sold under the same conditions.[45]

Neither the Massari nor the auctioneers performed their work with faultless impartiality, and the charge on the borrowers increased through the unauthorized exactions of the bribable Massari. Matters reached such a pass that it became necessary to employ middlemen to negotiate with the Massari to get reasonable terms, or to act as agents for persons unable or unwilling to join the queue of borrowers themselves. A report on the condition of Verona in 1644 refers to 'a number of petty shopkeepers called Pelagati' who accepted pledges privately, lent upon them, and then re-pledged them with the Monte.[46] Presumably, they made their profits by charging borrowers a higher rate than the Monte di Pietà itself did, and if they were operating on a small scale the difference between the rates would have to be substantial to afford them a living. The notorious brokers who disfigured the Venetian Ghetto[47] had their counterparts in the centres of Christian loan-banking, and the petty pawnshop was reappearing in the shadow of the Monte di Pietà.

Monti di Pietà did not suffer only from straightforward corruption and maladministration of this kind. Occasionally, they foundered or were reduced as a result of unwise policy. The larger Monte di Pietà in Verona developed into a personal loan bank for the great, and its undoing came when, at about the time of the War of the Mantuan Succession in the late 1620's, it accepted as pledge for loans of 130,000 ducats much jewellery and pearls from the Mantuan ruling house. At this time, the total lent annually by the Monte di Pietà was in the region of half a million ducats. The Podestà Leonardo Donà had warned the Senate in 1628, speaking of the Veronese, that:

> Their nearness to the city of Mantua, the fact that some of them own property in that state, and the favours they receive from His Highness, have attached many of them to the interests of the Mantuan court. Some are Knights of that Order, others have sons in the Duke's service, some keep up their service by visiting and vowing him obedience, and large

---

[45] A.S.V., *Senato, Dispacci, Provveditori da terra e da mar*, filza 270, orders enclosed with despatch of 4 May 1621; cf. also f. 25 of the report of the Sindici Inquisitori Leonardo Moro and Marco Giustinian, 9 August 1621, *Collegio, Relazioni*, b. 54. For Bergamo, see also the report of Bernardo Valier, 31 October 1617, *ibid.*, b. 35, and his letter in A.S.V., *Senato, Terra*, filza 226, 20 September 1617.

[46] Report of 18 October 1644 in A.S.V., *Collegio, Relazioni*, b. 50. Valier's letter, cited in the preceding note, implies that there were similar middlemen in Bergamo.

[47] See above, p. 576.

numbers have gone to congratulate this new Prince. In the present disorders, two Veronese citizens have raised companies of cuirassiers. . . .

The Veronese, therefore, made few difficulties about loans to the Mantuan court. In the 1630's, however, the Duke of Mantua failed either to redeem his pledges or to pay interest on them, and they proved unsaleable. One-third to one-quarter of the capital of the Monte di Pietà was sunk in an unrealizable asset, and by 1635 arrears of interest amounted to 50,000 ducats. There was no prospect of forcing the Duke to honour his obligations. The bottom had dropped out of the jewel market because of the impoverishment or embarrassment of the jewel-purchasing classes—if anybody gained in any sense from the great plague of 1630, it was the peasant or artisan rather than the landowner or employer. In 1641, the depreciation (*degrado*) of the jewels, and the loss of interest due upon them, was costing the Monte di Pietà 6,000 ducats a year. Worse still, the plague had coincided catastrophically with a great fire, and losses from this and other mishaps were variously estimated at 155,000, 156,000 and 162,000 ducats. Meanwhile, the destruction of population by the plague had reduced the demand for loans, and the income of the Monte di Pietà therefore became insufficient to cover interest payments to its creditors and other expenses. The fire and the affair of the jewels had reduced the capital of the Monte to 200,000 ducats, only 150,000 of which was lent annually on pledges. The only possibility lay in retrenchment, and by 1646 the Rettore Paolo Belegno believed that the Monte di Pietà had gained some relief by repaying deposits, to the extent of 40,000 ducats, to those who received the highest rates of interest. However, lending on pledges proceeded only 'sluggishly (*languidamente*)', and some 70,000 ducats were always left unused in the coffers of the Monte.[48] Imprudent lending to subjects of an alien state had depleted the resources of the Monte di Pietà, and natural disasters had reduced the demand for its services.

In its dubious practice of lending to foreigners, the Monte of Verona was not alone. Padua also did so—though perhaps only to University students;[49] and the citizens of Udine formed ties with Archducal subjects very similar to the Veronese bonds with the Mantuans. In 1620, the governor of the small town of Belluno declared that the Monte di Pietà of Udine

[48] A.S.V., *Collegio, Relazioni*, b. 54, report of the Sindici Inquisitori in Terra Ferma, Leonardo Moro and Marco Giustinian, 9 August 1621, ff. 24–5; reports of the Rettori of Verona, Leonardo Donà (6 July 1628), Nicolò Donà (21 June 1635), Lorenzo Morosini (27 November 1636), Alvise Morosini (?) (18 September 1641) and Paolo Belegno (28 July 1646).

[49] Briefly mentioned in the report of Giovanni Dandolo, 28 November 1617, A.S.V., *Collegio, Relazioni*, b. 43.

is one of the richest in the Venetian Republic, and is of the greatest service, not only to Italian peasants and small gentry (*signorotti*) who have recourse to it, but also to many great princes of Germany in their needs.[50]

However, the Udinese never apparently engaged in any speculation as disastrous as the Veronese loan on the Mantuan jewels.

Evidence about the maladministration or mishandling of the Monti di Pietà must qualify impressions of their usefulness as a social and economic organization: perhaps the majority were no more corrupt than the general run of municipal institutions, but they were certainly no better. They were not an undoubted improvement on the Jewish loan banks, which, in Rovigo (where they were allowed to survive) provided a more stable source of credit for the poor than the local Monte di Pietà. The Monti di Pietà undoubtedly reproduced on their own account most of the abuses to which the Jews were allegedly prone. Administered by persons who derived no immediate material advantage from the preservation or increase of their funds, they often fell into the hands of citizens not sufficiently disinterested to handle them uncorruptly. Constitutional devices failed to prevent the formation of oligarchies. Out of these came conspiracies to rob the Monti di Pietà, since the machinery for preventing fraud was undermined if officials held their posts indefinitely and if they were seldom compelled to hand over the funds to a successor. The system suffered if the accountants, Sindici or Conservatori belonged to the same taut little groups as the Massari they were supposed to supervise. Only external intervention, usually from a Venetian Rettore, could purge the corruption—and, given the system of rotating office which prevailed in Venice, to achieve continuity in policy was nearly impossible. A Rettore, in his brief term of office, could scarcely master the subtleties of the small-town intrigues which eddied round his palace. The achievements of Venetian provincial government were still very limited, for no integrated Venetian state had arisen, and the Rettori were still the representatives of an alien power in the cities they had come to govern.

These remarks may partly explain why the triumph of the Monti di Pietà over the Jewish loan banks was neither universal nor absolute in the Venetian dominions. Critics of the Monti di Pietà had not been entirely wrong to question the infallibility, efficiency or cast-iron virtue of these institutions. On the other hand, their faults must not be over-

[50] Report of Costantino Zorzi, 8 October 1620, A.S.V., *Collegio, Relazioni*, b. 34; cf. also the remarks of the governors of Udine, Alvise Mocenigo, 3 August 1622, and Domenico Buzzini, 7 May 1624, *ibid.*, b. 49.

stressed. At present, it is impossible to prove that—of the Monti di Pietà firmly established by the middle of the sixteenth century—more than three (those of Rovigo, Verona and Brescia) had passed through periods of severe depletion by the middle of the seventeenth. Of the rest, we know that there was some falsification of accounts and several prosecutions for fraud; that the Rettori took action against abuses, sometimes successfully and often otherwise. To assess the extent of maladministration is at present impossible, especially as it was often so skilfully concealed even from contemporaries. The undoubted fact of some corruption and misconduct must qualify all eulogies of the Monti di Pietà. What proportion of their funds found their way into the hands of the genuine and deserving poor, perhaps we shall never know. But some peculation taxed the resources of most charities and public institutions, and perhaps the average Monte di Pietà was no worse than most of these organizations. At least, in the seventeenth century, many Venetian Rettori had become aware of the problem and had begun to attack it, to save the moneys of the Monti from dissipation in the hands of the well-to-do.

*The Monti di Pietà of the Venetian Terra Ferma in the sixteenth
and early seventeenth century*

The first table which follows lists 27 Monti di Pietà known to have been active in the Venetian dominions on the Italian mainland in the sixteenth and early seventeenth century, and gives the dates at which they were founded, or by which they are known to have been in existence.

The second table presents statistical information about some of these Monti—all of it extracted from the reports or correspondence of Venetian governors or commissioners. Some of the defects of this information will be obvious at a glance—the suspicious roundness of some of the figures quoted, the likelihood that some of the Rettori were merely repeating the reports of their predecessors without troubling to bring them up to date, and so forth. Many of the statistics given by the Rettori have deliberately been omitted here, on the grounds of ambiguity. In the table, the first column shows the sum acquired by the Monte 'as its own', through outright gifts, bequests, subscriptions, etc., on which no interest was payable. The second column shows the sum deposited in the Monte by private persons or institutions, who were merely lending their capital to the Monte to be dispensed in loans to the poor. The Rettori usually gave one comprehensive figure for deposits, without distinguishing between 'gratuitous' and interest-bearing deposits, or between those made voluntarily and those made under some form of legal compulsion. Where, as at Udine and Vicenza, they did sometimes make this distinction, particulars are given in the footnotes to the table. Unfortunately, the Rettori, when they spoke of the capital of a given Monte, did not always make it clear whether they were speaking only of the capital given to it outright, or of the capital given plus the capital lent to or deposited with the Monte. Doubtful information of this kind has been omitted from the table.

The heading of 'working capital' includes all moneys which a Monte di Pietà kept in its coffers at a given time for the assistance of the poor or other clients, plus the total sum lent out at the same time on the security of pledges. In 1614, for example, the Monte di Pietà in Padua kept a total of 21,850 ducats in cash on the premises, having at the same time lent some 218,000 ducats on pledge.[1] Padua kept a deposit available for use in case of a plague epidemic, which would call for extensive poor relief: and this has been included in the figure for 'working capital'. On the other hand, the term does not include capital invested in the premises of the Monte itself, or invested in real property or other assets for the purpose of obtaining an

[1] A.S.V., *Collegio, Relazioni, busta* 43, report of Giovanni Battista Foscarini, 16 September 1614.

income. Where information about these matters is available, it is included under the heading of 'other moneys'.

The figures headed 'annual turnover' indicate the total sum which in the course of a year passed across the lending counter of a given Monte. Much of the money lent on pledge was restored to the bank, and the pledge redeemed, before a year had elapsed: so that the same sum could be lent again. In 1635, Andrea Bragadin, a governor of Vicenza, explained that the local Monte di Pietà had lent a total of 200,000 ducats in a year, and that

> the conduct of this business resembles that of merchants, who frequently reinvest in purchases the money they have obtained by sales, since it is customary for the Monte to lend one day, and the next to recover the sum disbursed, and it works continuously in this way, both lending and collecting debts, so that the sum of 200,000 ducats lent does not represent the working capital of the Monte.[2]

In Padua, the annual turnover was greater than the working capital by anything from 25 per cent to 40 per cent. On the other hand, it could occasionally be much less—in Verona, the rate of borrowing and lending in the Monte di Pietà suddenly slackened through the reduction of population by the great plague of 1630-1. Hence, in 1646, the governor Paolo Belegno asserted after his term of office in Verona that some 70,000 ducats were being left 'undisposed of' in the coffers of the Monte di Pietà.[3]

All figures are given in ducats of account, except for those relating to Bergamo, which are given in imperial lire.

MONTI DI PIETÀ FOUNDED ON THE VENETIAN MAINLAND

Place	Date	Place	Date	Place	Date
Arzignano	by 1603	Cologna	by 1599–1600	Pordenone	1601
Asola	c. 1615	Conegliano	by 1547	Rovigo	c. 1551
Asolo	by 1548	Crema	1492	Sacile	1566
Belluno	1501–3	Este	by 1614	Schio	by 1603
Bergamo	1557	Feltre	1542	Treviso	1496
Brescia		La Badia-			
(Monte		Lendenara	1552–4	Uderzo	1565
Piccolo)	1489	Moncelese	c. 1492	Udine	by 1553
(Monte		Motta	1575	Verona	
Grande)	1587	Padua	1491	(Monte	
Castelfranco	1493			Piccolo)	1490
				(Monte	
				Grande)	c. 1544
				Vicenza	1486

[2] A.S.V., *Collegio, Relazioni*, b. 51, 3 May 1635.
[3] A.S.V., *Collegio, Relazioni*, b. 50, 28 July 1646.

FINANCES OF CERTAIN MONTI DI PIETÀ ON THE VENETIAN MAINLAND

	Date	Monte's capital	Deposits	Other moneys	Working capital	Annual turnover
Belluno	1592	3,000	500		3,500[4]	
Bergamo	1575	12,199 imp. lire	17,419 imp. lire	8,217 imp. lire	37,835[5] imp. lire	
Brescia (Grande)	1645				83,470[6] ducats	
Castelfranco	1585	4,000	3,000		7,000[7]	
Feltre	1591	2,068	2,000		4,068[8]	
Moncelese	1588	c. 300	c. 1,000		c. 1,300[9]	
Padua	1554	33,500	54,000	12,400	99,900	c. 140,000
	1586	56,000				
	1606	75,500	108,500	37,670	221,670	
	1614				239,850	+300,000
	1617	72,090	106,200			
	1619	72,750	135,815			
	1625	+75,800	124,650	36,620	+237,070	
	1626					c. 258,000
	1627					c. 258,000
	1632	80,000				+300,000
	1638	80,000	150,000[10]			
Rovigo	1554	4,000	2,600			6,600
	1564	4,379	6,813			11,192
	1637	8,000	3–4,000			11–12,000[11]
Treviso	1564	11,000				
	1578	12,000				40–50,000
	1595					40,000
	1607	10–12,000				
	1609	c. 14,000				
	1612	18,000				
	1615	c. 20,000				
	1622	14,000				
	1631	c. 16,000				
	1639	c. 15,000[12]				
Udine	1599	34,000				120,000
	1615				100,000	
	1621	32,000	82,000		114,000	
	1626	40,000	71,000		111,000	
	1632	44,000				
	1635	45,000	101,000		146,000	
	1637	50,000	100,000		150,000	
	1642	50,000[13]				

[4] A.S.V., *Collegio, Relazioni*, b. 34, under date.

[5] Roncalli and Forno, *Atti di Borromeo*, I/ii, pp. 287–8, 298–9.

[6] A.S.V., *Collegio, Relazioni*, b. 37, report of Bernardino Renier, 12 April 1645.

[7] A.S.V., *Senato, Terra, filza* 93, 30 January 1584 Venetian style, letter of Giorgio Semitecolo, Podestà of Castelfranco, 10 January 1584 Venetian style.

[8] A.S.V., *Collegio, Relazioni*, b. 41, under date.

[9] A.S.V., *Senato, Terra, filza* 106, 22 March 1588.

[10] All in A.S.V., *Collegio, Relazioni*, b. 43.

[11] A.S.V., *Collegio, Relazioni*, b. 46.

[12] A.S.V., *Collegio, Relazioni*, b. 48.

[13] A.S.V., *Collegio, Relazioni*, b. 49. In 1621, the Monte di Pietà apparently paid $3\frac{1}{2}$ per cent on all its deposits; but in 1635 it held 86,000 ducats in interest-bearing deposits and 15,000 on which no interest was paid. In 1637 the corresponding figures were 80,000 and 20,000 respectively.

	Date	Monte's capital	Deposits	Other moneys	Working capital	Annual turnover
Verona (Piccolo)	1578	c. 35,000				
	1612					60,000
	1621	50,000				
Verona (Grande)	1576					+200,000
	1612					+500,000 gold ducats
	1621					c. 500,000 ducats
	1635				200,000	150,000[14]
Vicenza	1598	54,000	26,000	800 p.a. from property		
	1602	54,000	25,000	800 p.a. from property		
	1614	50,000		20,000 invested in property		c. 150,000
	1618			900 p.a. from property		
	1620	c. 80,000	c. 80,000			
	1627		200,000			
	1635				200,000[15]	

[14] A.S.V., *Collegio, Relazioni,* b. 50. For 1621, see *Senato, Dispacci, Provveditori da terra e da mar, filza* 270, f. 24, report of the Sindici Inquisitori in Terra Ferma, 9 August 1621.

[15] For 1571, A.S.V., *Senato, Terra, filza* 58, 9 November 1571; for the remainder, A.S.V., *Collegio, Relazioni,* b. 51. In 1598 and 1602, no interest was paid on deposits; but in 1627, 4 per cent was paid on some deposits.

CONCLUSION

This inquiry has tried to increase historical knowledge in two general directions: to afford greater insight into the nature of government and society in the Venetian Republic by exploring the relationship between the rich and the poor; and to throw some light on the broader question of the principles ruling poor relief in Catholic societies of early modern Europe. How far it has succeeded must be for the reader to judge. These pages offer a few tentative conclusions founded on the evidence discussed above. The book is not a history of the Venetian poor, though it is in part an account of what the richer members of society did to and for them, and of the social rôle they assigned to them. The poor were an anonymous, inarticulate group, exerting little force on Venetian affairs on their own initiative, seldom rioting very seriously. They often found spokesmen only in educated men of higher social origins who, like the Franciscans, chose to identify with them and, rightly or wrongly, to interpret their wishes and promote their interests. This is not a straightforward history of philanthropy, but rather an attempt to describe the place occupied, in society and the state, in Venice and its mainland provinces, by institutions among whose functions was the relief of the poor. Many of these institutions were not dedicated exclusively to poor relief or to charity, but discharged a variety of other functions—religious, political, economic and fiscal—determined by the needs of the societies in which they were erected.

The Scuole Grandi originally relieved the poor partly as an expression of brotherly love, and partly as one of several activities believed to procure the salvation of those who engaged in them. When their members divided into distinctive groups of rich and poor, charity bulked very large among their functions, though it never excluded the others. The organization of the Scuole Grandi helped to absorb some of the latent ambitions of social groups, the citizens and merchants, excluded from any formal part in the making of government policy through participation in the legislative assemblies of Venice (though the unacknowledged influence of government secretaries and of members of the Cancelleria must have been considerable). The Scuole, with their gorgeous processions often dedicated to the presentation and exposition of Venetian foreign policy, helped to give the people at large a closer sense of involvement in the affairs of the state. On occasion, as in the Interdict of 1606, they were used to disseminate political propaganda with a view to containing unrest. These public performances were a far cry from the humility and unworldliness of the early flagellant movements and of the brotherhoods that had developed from them. It should be said, however, that office in the Scuole seems to have become markedly less attractive by the end of the sixteenth century—partly because of the heavy expense it entailed, and partly because of the increasing burden of the fiscal obligations laid by the state upon the Scuole.

Several social institutions concerned with the poor found themselves involved in the task of financing the Venetian navy, or in providing it and the merchant marine with manpower. The Scuole Grandi, as corporations disposing of great wealth and material benefits, were compelled to use their authority over the poor and to offer them incentives to serve Venice at sea. The Republic's character as a seapower incidentally influenced much of its social policy—for the Jews were kept in Venice during the 1520's partly because a large fraction of the taxes they paid was earmarked for the Arsenal and the fleet, and therefore assumed a significance perhaps disproportionately great in the minds of many Senators and members of the Council of Ten. The function of the Jews as taxpayers, and their function as moneylenders to the poor and impecunious, as bankers bound to dispose of supplies of liquid capital, were intimately linked. The level of taxation and the level of interest charges were normally closely related, except when the government deliberately upset the balance between them as a form of economic persecution. Again, during much of the sixteenth century, the poor law seems to have been enforced in a manner which threw heavy stress on supplying the galleys with vagabond labour to supplement the efforts of convicts from the jails, and also on equipping merchant vessels with apprentices or cabin boys forcibly enlisted from the ranks of beggar children. However, by the turn of the century, there may have been rather less tendency to use the sea as the cure for all evils, as a drastic form of character training for the poor, ignorant and undisciplined. Even the Monte di Pietà in Padua was, by the early seventeenth century, contributing to the recruitment of the Republic's armed forces—of soldiers, rather than of sailors.

During the period reviewed here, the social and economic functions of the Jews and of the Monti di Pietà changed very substantially, and were not confined to the relief of the poor. The Jews had always lent to persons on several social levels, and not merely to those who were poor in the most literal sense. After 1573, the Venetian state threw far less emphasis—except in emergencies—on the Jews' function as taxpayers

627

contributing directly to the treasury. They were commanded, instead, to tax themselves in order to provide a service mainly designed for the Venetian poor, though not successfully confined ιo them: a service from which the Jews themselves could hope to extract little or no financial profit. The state cultivated the Levantine and Ponentine communities in Venice itself, both on account of the services they could render to Venetian commerce with parts of the Ottoman Empire, and because the profits of this trade could be taxed by Jewish agents for the benefit of the Venetian loan banks. Apart from their services as second-hand dealers, the Jews on the mainland, at least in Padua and to some extent Verona, offered valuable competition to Christian guildsmen by breaking their monopoly of the textile trades and by forcing them to lower their prices. At all times, the position of the Jews within the Venetian Republic depended on the prevailing balance between two sentiments in the minds of the policymakers—on the one hand, contempt and distrust of the Godkilling nation which persistently refused to acknowledge the truth, but which must still be preserved—somewhere—in a condition of servility and apartness; on the other, a shrewd and realistic sense of the economic and social utility of the Jews, and of the difficulty of adequately replacing them. Both these sentiments, in their different ways, contributed to making the Jews into lenders to the poor: forcing them to engage in an activity at once despised and indispensable, essential and uncreative.

The Monti di Pietà also changed their shape and modified several of their original ideals. At first they aimed specifically at serving the poor. But in order to increase their resources and to serve as a more complete replacement for the Jews they chose to act as banks paying interest on deposits and to offer loans of undefined extent, not only to the poor, but also to persons of higher condition. They survived and expanded partly, perhaps, because they offered a safe investment at a time when other opportunities were restricted—although in theory the acceptance of interest on moneys deposited with a Monte di Pietà could only be justified on the grounds that the investor was acting in a spirit of charity and had chosen to neglect other, more profitable opportunities. The Monti di Pietà probably came to act, not only as charitable institutions, but also as public banks forbidden to engage in commercial or other speculation—though more research would be required to establish whether the Monti of the Venetian mainland in fact abstained from all such activities. The corruption and dishonesty of the Massari was certainly a grave hazard—but was evidently not serious enough to destroy general confidence in the Monti in most major centres. At least in Padua, the Monte di Pietà extended its services by operating as a bank prepared to lend to the commune at times of serious disaster which called for extensive poor relief, and especially in seasons of famine or pestilence. Certainly in Padua, and perhaps elsewhere, the Council of the Monte di Pietà served some of the same ends as the chapters and benches of the Scuole Grandi in Venice. It offered, to persons excluded from participation in the communal councils, opportunities for political activity, competition and intrigue: together with some real influence over municipal finances.

In many respects, the social institutions of Venice contrasted with those of her chief provincial towns, some of which had developed before the fifteenth century as capitals of independent signories, whilst others had formed part of different states. The Venetians were the sovereign people, supplying governors to the great provincial centres, but (from sheer lack of sufficient manpower among other things) allowing them a high degree of autonomy in managing their own local affairs and communal institutions. The Venetian government did not issue social legislation for the whole Terra Ferma, though it might occasionally make general recommendations. Rather, it allowed individual cities and ecclesiastical authorities to initiate proposals about such matters as the reorganization of hospitals, the expulsion or retention of the Jews, or the foundation of Monti di Pietà. It was content to ratify local decisions and to arbitrate in case of disputes, acting on the advice of its own Rettori and on petition from the communal council. The Rettori often tried to check local corruption in the management of charitable institutions, but the brevity of their terms of office made effective interference difficult.

Nevertheless, the organization of poor relief tended to resolve itself into certain broadly similar patterns, so that the mainland cities were not completely diverse and individualistic in their arrangements. State-wide legislation was not chiefly responsible for this situation: most important was the existence of the standardized, exportable institution, whose statutes could easily be transplanted from one town to another and adapted to local conditions. Travelling evangelists, Franciscans or Jesuits, a Bernardino of Feltre, a Michele of Acqui or a Benedetto Palmio, helped to publicize these establishments. So did the occasional travelling organizer like Girolamo Miani, who was not a fashionable preacher in the same sense as those just mentioned. Rome contributed to the process, though it did not do so because the Papacy legislated for the whole of Italy. The Curia provided a meeting-point for career priests from all over the peninsula, who exchanged ideas and subsequently carried them back to their home towns, as Thiene did to Vicenza or Bartolomeo Stella to Brescia; or, like Giberti, introduced

629

2s

them into the dioceses to which they were subsequently appointed. Rome, too, was the site of some of the early Jesuit experiments, such as the houses for the reform of prostitutes and for the education of their children. The Papacy often responded to, rather than created, opinion; like the Venetian government, it confirmed and ratified proposed arrangements, on receiving applications from particular princes, states or communes. It seems to have had little to do with confirming agreements with Jews in the Venetian Republic (once the Signory had obtained reassurance from Pius II's legate Bessarion, Venice was prepared to accept full responsibility for these contracts). But the Papacy did, as at Vicenza and Bergamo, occasionally approve local decisions about the administration of Monti di Pietà.

In several respects, the dominating city of Venice proved to be more conservative than its subject provinces on the Italian mainland. It had, perhaps, been just as receptive to the flagellant movements of the thirteenth century, but its authorities eventually chose to reject the Monte di Pietà and at last adopted a highly individual solution to the problem of providing cheap credit for the poor. Venice could not equal Perugia's record for pioneering new movements, though she soon came into contact with most of them: the Compagnie del Divino Amore, the Theatines, the Capuchins, the Jesuits, the early Paulines or Barnabites. Girolamo Miani was one of the few native Venetians to start a wide-ranging charitable movement. In Venice, the Scuole di Battuti probably assumed a far greater social importance than their equivalents in most mainland cities, though these probably ran on similar principles and subscribed to the same religious ideals. The Venetians did not centralize the organization of their hospitals in the same way as the subject towns of Brescia and Bergamo, and they had no overwhelmingly large general almonry like the Misericordia of Bergamo. They did, however, establish the magistracies of the Provveditori alla Sanità and (years later) of the Provveditori sopra gli Ospedali e Luoghi Pii, and assign them the task of supervising and co-ordinating certain forms of poor relief. Always, however, there were important institutions like the Scuole which were not under the jurisdiction of these boards of commissioners. On the other hand, the establishments of the Incurabili, of the Convertite, of the Zitelle and of the Soccorso penetrated into Venice as they did into its Italian dominions.

In any analysis of poor relief in any early modern European society, it is natural to try to answer certain standard questions, at least tentatively. There must be some discussion of the motives from which the relief of the poor was undertaken, of how far poor relief was designed to procure social improvement, and of the extent to which it was designed to procure spiritual benefits both for the almsgiver and for the recipient of charity. One needs to form an opinion of how far poor relief was administered discriminately, with proper attention to the needs of the recipient and of the society of which both giver and receiver formed part. How did the methods of poor relief change during the period under review? How far was poor relief in the hands of ecclesiastics, and to what extent was it the concern of laymen? What was the relationship between state action and private initiative, and in what sense (if any) is it possible to speak of a social policy?

The Venetians and their subjects relieved the poor from a wide variety of motives, some explicitly declared, others implied. Much poor relief was, in a very simple sense, 'charitable': it originated in the desire to express the love of God through the love of one's neighbour, and to make contact with Christ through one of the least of his brothers. This motive usually combined with a certain sense of spiritual self-interest, arising from the charitable man's personal desire to procure his own salvation. Venetian charity was often 'spiritual' charity as well as material, revealing anxiety to save both one's own soul and the soul of the recipient by encouraging him to desist from sin or by imparting to him some form of Christian knowledge. The Scuole Grandi existed to do everything believed to contribute to the salvation of those who did it; to correct faults, and prevent the commission of such sins as blasphemy, wrath and adultery; and to express brotherly love, especially between members of the same spiritual fraternity. An aggressive, crusading concern for the souls of those whose poverty made them especially prone to sin and ignorance was deeply characteristic of movements associated with the Counter Reformation. The exhortations of Benedetto Palmio assured his audience of the great spiritual benefits they were procuring for themselves by their dedication to this kind of evangelical social work. Concern for one's own soul and solicitude for the souls of others were not, and were never believed to be, mutually exclusive. Occasionally, public authorities performed acts of charity—as the Venetians founded the hospital of Gesù Cristo di Sant'Antonio—out of a desire to acquire merit for a whole community, and thereby to invite God to favour and prosper it in war or in other trials. The expulsion of the Jews—which demanded that other arrangements be made for providing cheap credit to the poor—was conceived as a similarly pious act. The Venetians and their subjects also performed acts of charity out of a professed desire to preserve the community from the contamination of alien faiths (especially Judaism) and from the evil effects of ignorance of spiritual truth.

On the other hand, some poor relief was clearly inspired by the determination to preserve public order and decency: not only to save the social order from the danger of actual sedition, but also to preserve respectable citizens from smaller annoyances—from violent tramps and importunate beggars in public places and in churches. The state willingly recognized its obligation to preserve its subjects from diseases associated with poverty, vagrancy and immorality. In Venice, the Provveditori alla Sanità assumed the chief responsibility for the enforcement of the poor law, and this in itself provides strong evidence of the connexion between systematic poor relief and the fear of disease. Epidemics and famines, as in Venice in 1528 and 1576, caused the state to levy general poor-rates. Hence, at certain times, the poor were relieved, not by voluntary acts of mercy or charity, but by compulsory payments levied by public authorities. Another motive was municipal pride—the desire to save the streets and public places from disfigurement by the presence of the abjectly poor and diseased; the anxiety not to seem backward or negligent in comparison with other cities. No doubt some individuals, too, performed acts of charity from a desire to compete with their fellows, to cut a figure in the world, and to win the honour which Venetian society—through the Procurators of St Mark's and the Guardians of the Scuole Grandi—undoubtedly accorded to the charitable man. The practice of charity carried with it power, influence and respect. Perhaps to many men and women who did not closely examine their own motives the doing of acts of charity was largely a matter of habit, or of conforming to social usage. It may be that to noblewomen and society ladies good works provided a welcome means of occupying their endless leisure, and an opportunity to do something valuable.

One essential form of poor relief lay in the provision of cheap personal loan services of which the poor (among others) could take advantage. The Jewish bankers who sometimes provided these services were not required to be charitable towards Christians. By accepting interest on their loans they were in a sense performing a hostile act towards the devotees of an alien faith who surrounded them. They did not rely for support on the gifts, bequests or subscriptions of Christians—though before 1565 they could evidently employ moneys deposited with them by Christian creditors. When Jewish banks ceased to be self-supporting their funds were raised by taxation levied by and on the Jews. Before that time, the Jews had been earning their living in one of the few ways left open, and equipping themselves to pay the taxes required of them by their host country as a condition of residence. The state or commune which contracted with the Jews was performing a service to its subjects by making available to them the services rendered by the Jews, at rates cheaper than those demanded by Christians. But, since (at least before 1573) the Venetian state got so much from the Jews in return, it was hardly peforming a charitable act in the strict sense of the word.

On the other hand, the Monti di Pictà were, as their name clearly implies, regarded as charitable establishments. It was true that the poor did not obtain an outright gift of money from the Monte, and that they were required to pay for the services of the officials who obliged them. But they did enjoy, gratuitously, a benefit—that is, the use of money— which would never normally have been granted to them without payment by a person or organization whose motives were other than charitable. The theory was always that the poor were not paying their 5 per cent for the use of money, but to reward those who were working on their behalf, keeping the books, valuing and storing pledges, and so forth. Even the persons who deposited money at interest in the Monti di Pietà were, in theory, acting from a charitable motive: because they had chosen to forego the higher rewards which could have been obtained from other forms of investment.

The machinery for the relief of the poor in the Venetian Republic in the sixteenth and early seventeenth century was formed by the blending together of old and new institutions, without a clean break with the past. The history of the Scuole Grandi testifies to the survival and the continued popularity of a form of organization whose origins lay in the thirteenth century—though of course it had developed very considerably since its beginnings. The Scuola di San Rocco, founded as late as 1478, prospered and acquired great wealth during the sixteenth century, attracting generous legacies. One of the preoccupations of sixteenth-century reformers was to revive ancient, decayed foundations, to make the best use of them possible, and where necessary to adapt them to present-day needs. But there is ample evidence of increasing concern with the problem of the poor, and of a somewhat different approach to it, beginning towards the middle of the fifteenth century—if no earlier. The Observant Franciscans started their campaign for the protection of poor persons' welfare, for the improvement of morality, and for the maintenance of public decency. In many parts of central and northern Italy, there was a movement towards the more efficient and rational organization of poor relief, involving the centralization of hospitals and a higher degree of public supervision over charitable foundations. Franciscan preaching contributed to a new invention, the Monte di Pietà, a highly effective weapon in a general attack upon usury and particularly on the economic power wielded by Jews over Christians. Much of this work continued along similar lines in the sixteenth century and during the Counter Reformation, in response to

633

the increasingly severe challenges of disease, famine and renewed population pressure. The sixteenth century saw the acceptance and the development of proposals—such as the Monti di Pietà—which had at first been regarded as dubious by many sincere critics.

If the first turning-point had occurred in the mid-fifteenth century, a second followed during the Italian wars, and especially during the 1520's. Further intellectual stimuli, which sought to convert charity into a way of life rather than a series of isolated acts, combined with the stimuli of disease and famine—to which the wars contributed. Syphilis spread, typhus appeared in epidemic form, outbreaks of plague recurred. War and famine broke up many of the normal securities based on the family, the parish and the village, and increased the numbers of refugees, vagabonds and orphans. War caused the dispersal and the redistribution of old-established Jewish communities in the Venetian Republic, and the Venetians themselves made their controversial decision to allow the Jews to settle permanently in Venice itself. With the foundation of the Ghetto, of the Incurabili, of hospitals for orphans in Venice itself, and with the passage of the poor law of 1529, much of Venice's new social machinery was erected. Later, it was further extended, and the principles now formulated were further applied.

The expansion of population in the second and third quarters of the sixteenth century, even though it contributed to economic growth, still created an unstable situation—especially through the increasing liability of the Venetians and their subjects to outbreaks of famine. From the middle 1540's onwards, the enforcement of the poor law was one of several measures designed to deal with these circumstances. So too, perhaps, was the extension of Monti di Pietà through new foundations and through the acceptance of interest-bearing deposits which increased their capital. At the same time, government policy forced the Jews to lower their interest rates and indirectly compelled many Jews to emigrate. None of these phenomena can be explained in exclusively economic terms: but population pressure certainly contributed to them. If population pressure provided incentives to state action and private charity, so did those non-economic forces—such as disease and foul weather—which offered to bring it under control. The plague of 1576 called for a very high degree of resolute state action. During the 1590's, the assaults of the weather, together with the effects of population pressure in some of the countries from which Venice had normally imported food, contributed to some further advances, and especially to the foundation of the hospital of the Mendicanti.

The new forms of poor relief contrasted in several respects with the methods employed by older institutions such as the Scuole Grandi. In general, the new movements adopted a more aggressive, militant and evangelical approach. They showed a greater concern to use charity to promote general moral improvement and disciplined behaviour. The tendency of the Scuole Grandi had been rather to use all charity— towards the close of the fifteenth century—to encourage punctiliousness in outward devotional acts, in attending processions, funerals and so forth. The Scuole Grandi dealt chiefly with the respectable, resident poor, with natives of Venice or with people long domiciled in the city. Their procedures for the correction of sin were not designed to produce positive improvement on the part of their members so much as to prevent them from lapsing or deteriorating. The new movements undoubtedly dealt to some extent with respectable people—by definition, the societies for the Poveri Vergognosi catered for persons whose upbringing or natural modesty made them shrink from the shame of publicly seeking alms. But beyond this was a much broader concern with social outcasts—with syphilitic patients (the new lepers of the sixteenth century), with beggars, prostitutes and prisoners. Charity was offered to them on condition that they made some effort to repent and improve—certainly not on the grounds favoured by some of the Mendicants in the Netherlands and in Spain, when they argued that a truly merciful giver would not inquire into the morals of the recipient. Sometimes, with state aid, the new movements forced the poor to take advantage of institutions provided for them, such as the Incurabili or Mendicanti, or forcibly apprenticed them to the mariner's trade. Other institutions—such as the Convertite or Soccorso—were open only to volunteers. The new charity concentrated more heavily on youth— though the dowry trusts of the Scuole Grandi had always shown an appreciation of the needs of reputable young women. The new charity showed a preoccupation with education at an elementary or technical level—with instilling a modicum of Christian knowledge, with teaching a trade, with communicating the principles of submissive and respectful conduct. The new movements emphasized different kinds of religious activity—they stressed, both for givers and receivers, the use of the sacraments of confession and communion, rather than merely attendance at Mass, acts of austerity, or participation in public processions and displays of relics. There was less ostentation on the part of those who dispensed the charity—the societies of the Poveri Vergognosi adopted highly secretive procedures. The structure of the confraternity changed, and its members focused their attention on outsiders, rather than on their own brothers. Activities such as moneylending were conducted on a more moralistic basis, for the officials of the Monti

635

di Pietà were supposed to inquire much more closely into the condition of the borrower, the origins of his pledge, and the use to which he proposed to put any loan he received. The financial structure of the new institutions, at least in Venice, differed from that of the old. They showed a greater tendency to keep their assets liquid, rather than to invest them in property or other safe securities: though this was probably not entirely the result of personal choices, and was very likely dictated by their different position with respect to the state's mortmain laws.

The new institutions contrasted rather than conflicted with the old, and their aims were complementary rather than opposing. The new fraternities owed much in their organization to the Scuole developed from the thirteenth century onwards, although they modified the structure quite considerably and concentrated on rather different ends. Borromeo attempted in the second half of the sixteenth century to revive the practice of self-flagellation and to resuscitate the Scuole dei Disciplinati in his province. The procurators of the Incurabili, in 1524, tried to include the leading members of the Scuole Grandi in their projected Monte di Pietà. The harshest known criticisms of the Scuole Grandi came from Alessandro Caravia, who, with his Erasmian if not Protestant leanings, was scarcely a typical figure of the Catholic reformation. Only on exceptional occasions, like the crisis of the Interdict, did the Scuole Grandi clearly take the opposite side to the new religious orders associated with much of the new charity.

Evidence from the Venetian Republic leaves little room for doubt that at least from the mid-fifteenth century onwards subjects of this particular Catholic state believed in employing the moneys available for poor relief in a highly discriminate fashion: so as to relieve the poor in the most effective manner possible, both for their own sakes and for the general good of society. Almsgiving was not generally regarded as an act deriving its value solely from the spiritual benefits it conferred on the almsgiver. Undoubtedly he did, according to Catholic theology, benefit his own soul, but he was often exhorted to think of the souls of others. The highest professed aim of charity in the second half of the sixteenth century was to procure the spiritual good of the poor through acquainting them with spiritual truth and with the use of the sacraments, and in that sense the object of charity was other-worldly, rather than purely 'secular' or 'social'. But the means to this end was the determination to build a disciplined, stable and moral society.

Neither the Venetians nor their subjects showed any intention of tolerating a parasitic class of professional poor or one which traded on the belief of the almsgiver that good works—even if done to the undeserving—contributed to the salvation of those who did them. The existence of the Scuole, even before the mid-fifteenth century, guaranteed that a high proportion of the poor obtained relief from the officers of societies to which they belonged, and hence from persons with some reason to know their needs. The Scuole did not devote all their resources to straightforward almsgiving: much of their charity was devoted to making marriage economically possible for young women whose claims had been examined by boards of trustees. One cannot truthfully conceive of Catholic poor relief in general in terms of beggar hordes creeping round from one monastery gate to another to receive, at the hands of uncritical monks, distributions of money or bread, with no questions asked. Certainly, in Verona in the 1530's and in Bergamo in the 1570's steps were taken to curb this type of indiscriminate almsgiving, and to redirect the funds on which it depended. In Venice and on the mainland public and private initiative strove to co-ordinate charitable work either by introducing a high degree of centralization or of central supervision, or by founding a series of specialized institutions which discharged complementary functions. There ought, in theory, to be one particularly appropriate institution to which a pauper could be directed, and this ought to prevent him from trying to benefit from several. In Venice and elsewhere, systematic campaigns developed to punish professional beggars, to anticipate the needs of the genuine house-poor so as to keep them off the streets, to affirm the principle of local responsibility, and to deal with abject poverty through institutions and through furnishing opportunities to work. The general tendency, particularly marked among the newer institutions, was to encourage systematic inquiry into the needs, character and behaviour of the poor, and to establish an order of priorities on economic and moralistic grounds: without, however, eliminating the possibility of extending charity to repentant sinners, or of forcing it in a semi-penal fashion on the godless, disorderly or ignorant.

There is no reason to attribute these characteristics of Venetian poor relief either to the indirect influence of the Protestant Reformation or to the independent action of the sixteenth-century state, which had become more conscious of its own powers and of the demands of social expediency. Since some of these movements became clearly visible in the course of the fifteenth century, chronology opposes any such interpretation. Politicians, aldermen, churchmen and religious reformers often subscribed to very similar ideals, and state or communal policy was open to influence from persons who were loyal and devout members of the Catholic Church. In the Venetian Republic there was no obvious dichotomy, over questions of poor relief, between Church and

State: ecclesiastics and lay churchmen were just as interested in the establishment of a disciplined and ordered society as were magistrates and town councils. There is no sign of an attack on public policy towards the poor like the one launched by the Mendicant orders in the Netherlands and Spain. During the sixteenth century, Catholic and Protestant societies often responded to a common economic challenge on similar lines, partly because they possessed a common heritage: in principles first formulated by the Fathers of the Church and later embodied in the canon law. Some of these asserted the need to administer poor relief in a highly discriminating fashion where resources were insufficient to provide for everyone. During the sixteenth century, the general problem of poverty did become more acute, especially through the growth of population, and the need for discrimination became increasingly urgent. Institutional forms certainly differed substantially between one country and another. There was nothing in Elizabethan England exactly corresponding to a Scuola dei Battuti, a Monte di Pietà, or a Jewish loan bank: though a Venetian would have been familiar with some of the principles behind the English poor law. But general attitudes to the poor were often determined by a rather similar mixture of pity and fear, of genuine humanity and brutal paternalism, and by a similar determination to eliminate criminals and social parasites—whether a given society had remained Catholic, or whether it had severed its allegiance to Rome.

Clearly, to a very large extent, charity in Venice and elsewhere in the Republic was in the hands, not of individuals, but of corporations, societies or institutions whose officers were supposed to act according to very clearly formulated rules. One cannot, of course, form any idea of what proportion of all charity passed through these institutions: institutional charity keeps records, and some of these survive; usually casual almsgiving leaves none. An extensive survey of wills, similar to Professor Jordan's analysis of English philanthropy, might establish how far testators relied on private persons as trustees or executors, and how far they applied to public bodies. But there is much charity which never gets into wills. Nevertheless, it is possible to see, in Venice, the importance of boards of public trustees prepared to undertake the administration of a wide variety of charitable commissions. The Procurators of St Mark's and the officers of the Scuole Grandi were public trustees in that they were subject to close surveillance by the state and recruited from the most prominent members of the two highest estates within Venetian society. Almost certainly, the Misericordia played a similar part in Bergamo. During the sixteenth century, a number of other organizations—the new general hospitals, the society for the

Poveri Vergognosi—acquired a special status, and testators were strongly encouraged through the notaries to make bequests to them. It may be that after the mid-sixteenth century public policy aimed, less at encouraging new foundations, than at directing the wealth of private testators towards a few large established institutions. In the Venetian Republic, philanthropy was obviously institutionalized to a fairly high degree: societies, councils, boards and committees abounded.

It was quite common for charities to be founded on the initiative of voluntary societies which offered to subscribe to, or to organize, institutions for the benefit of the whole community. Direct state or communal initiative was comparatively rare, except in such matters as contracting with Jewish moneylenders, and except in the emergencies created at intervals during the sixteenth century by famines or epidemics. But the Venetian government or the individual communes and Rettori in the provinces found many reasons to intervene in the affairs of charitable organizations. Some of these concerns were private in the sense that they were based on voluntary associations of private citizens, and in the sense that no public official or ecclesiastical dignitary enjoyed any automatic right to participate in them. But all charities were engaged in an activity which strongly affected the common welfare and even the security of the state, both from sedition and from diseases. The state or commune could not be indifferent to them. In Venice the Council of Ten regulated all Scuole partly from a general determination to keep watch on all forms of assembly, in the interests of public safety, and of preventing conspiracies against the established regime. Since the bigger charitable societies acquired wide influence and authority over the poor, it was vital that they should be in the hands of persons with good reason to be loyal to the Venetian state. No institution or society should be allowed to acquire excessive influence—hence, perhaps, the suppression of the project for a Monte di Pietà in Venice in 1524. In general, too, the state recognized its duty not only to protect the property of its subjects but also to guarantee their right to dispose of it after death as they wished. For this reason, also, it came to supervise charitable foundations increasingly closely in the course of the sixteenth century. The system which prevailed in Venice itself, and possibly elsewhere in the Republic, can perhaps be described as based on 'charities administered by voluntary associations under lay management, and under increasingly close public surveillance and protection, their resources being supplemented in emergencies by direct state action'.

One activity—the provision of a cheap loan service—called from the start for an exceptionally high level of public initiative or at least public regulation. Unlike other forms of poor relief, this entailed a serious

639

risk of infringing the canon laws which a Catholic state was supposed to respect and uphold, although there was much room for interpreting them diversely. Only a prince, a government or a commune could accept the responsibility for deciding, in the first instance, how best to save subjects from the necessity of committing sins: especially as, in the opinion of many people, both contracts with Jewish bankers and (in the early stages) the foundations of Monti di Pietà were in themselves dubious actions. The Jews were peculiarly situated—as a tolerated but officially despised minority of hardened unbelievers, alleged to be peculiarly treacherous towards Christians, but acknowledged to be potentially useful. Their status made it vital for a Catholic state or commune to regulate their activities exceptionally closely and to lay down very specifically the conditions on which they were entitled to dwell in its midst. As the state or commune had once watched over the Jews, even so it came to control the institutions designed to replace them, or at least to reduce their economic power over Christians. Hence, Monti di Pietà were as a rule either administered directly by communal councils, or by special councils of the Monte on which officers of public organizations and communal institutions were heavily represented. From the twelfth and thirteenth centuries onwards, lending at interest to the poor or impecunious was an activity so fraught with danger, and yet so inescapable a part of social life, that it demanded a high degree of public control.

It is impossible to give any very convincing answer to the question: how far was poor relief controlled by the Church during the period reviewed by this book? Only a very extensive survey of the social activities of monasteries and parish churches could solve this problem. It is, however, worth saying at this point that, in Venice at least, the state, through the enforcement of the poor law, assumed jurisdiction over parochial poor relief, which was not an activity independent of the state. Some regular clergy, especially Mendicants identifying themselves with the poor, received charity as much as they dispensed or inspired it. It may be—though this is only a very tentative suggestion—that the social utility of nunneries did not lie so much in any alms they may have dispensed as in their occasional willingness to provide shelter to poor girls whom they admitted to their communities. Convents of Convertite were founded specifically for this purpose.

Much philanthropy was in the hands of lay organizations and publicly controlled institutions. The Scuole Grandi were, ultimately, the product of a popular movement which had started independently of official promptings from churchmen—though prelates and friars walked in the processions of the flagellants in 1260. On the other hand, many societies and institutions—including the first centralized hospitals and Monti di Pietà on the mainland, and houses like that of the Zitelle in Venice—were inspired by the eloquence of travelling preachers, especially of Franciscans or Jesuits, and often owed much to the initiative of the local bishop acting in concert with the communal authorities. Sometimes a bishop—like Valier at Verona—tendered important advice on the management of a local charity, and after the passage of the Tridentine decrees there was at least a danger that provincial bishops might claim rights of supervision over all charities and confraternities. However, episcopal initiative generally proved to be far stronger in the subject provinces of Lombardy and the Veneto than in Venice itself, where the Patriarch was less of an independent authority. Moreover, Venetian policy aimed at excluding clerics from control over the finances and property of charitable institutions—to prevent excessive wealth from passing under clerical jurisdiction; to avoid disputes over taxation—for corporations like the Scuole, if not hospitals or Monti di Pietà, were of great importance to the fisc; and to prevent the export of wealth from the Venetian state to the papal Curia or to mother houses abroad. Clergymen were often members of charitable fraternities, and were needed to act as chaplains, celebrate Masses, bury the dead and administer spiritual consolation—especially in the hospitals and Scuole. Circles of devout laymen engaged in good works formed round highly respected confessors or congregations of priests, like the Theatines, Paulines and Jesuits in Venice. But the functions of the clergy ought, at least in theory, to be advisory and auxiliary rather than managerial: they ought to be inspirers rather than directors. Almost certainly, the government could uphold this principle rather more successfully in Venice itself than in its mainland provinces.

In the Venetian Republic, the aim behind most poor relief was the preservation of the existing social and political order, of a disciplined and moral society, as a means to securing the salvation of the greatest possible number—both of rich and of poor. The efficiency of poor relief in Venice and its dominions may have contributed to the legendary stability of the Venetian government in the sixteenth and early seventeenth century. Government policy encouraged systematic and honest poor relief: it did not attempt to level, to redistribute wealth compulsorily, or to increase social mobility—except, in a sense, at the very bottom of the social scale. Here, it did aim at the total elimination of unlicensed begging (in the mid-sixteenth century), and, at the end of the century, at the total elimination of all begging save by the blind. It did seek to upgrade beggars, especially beggar children, to the level of sailors, respectable artisans or domestic servants: to encourage them to become useful members of society. Begging could be uprooted, but poverty and inequality would go on.

Such was the experience of Venice and its Italian dominions. Certainly it was not in all respects unique, for the Republic was exposed to many currents of opinion and many economic phenomena which also affected other Catholic states in early modern Europe. The history of social institutions in the Venetian Republic may provide a sounding-board on which the general validity of assumptions about Catholic societies in early modern Europe can be tested. But, above all, the history of these organizations is the history of the Venetian Republic. What of the experience of other countries?

> 'History has many cunning passages, contrived corridors
> And issues, deceives with whispering ambitions,
> Guides us by vanities',

and many more of its by-ways must be explored before its vanity and deception are even partly overcome.

NOTE ON THE ARCHIVES OF VENICE

I. *Archives of the chief legislative councils*

(a) *The Senate*

Of supreme importance to this study is the series *Senato, Terra,* divided into Registers, containing fair copies of the proposals put to the vote in the Senate, and Files (*filze*), which contain rough drafts of these resolutions and frequently preserve the written information submitted to the Collegio and the Senate to enable them to arrive at a decision. This often consists of a petition formally addressed to the Doge and Signoria (otherwise the Pien Collegio), and of reports and opinions on it drawn up by the magistrates most closely concerned with the matters involved. Verbal remarks made in the course of discussions in the Collegio and Senate are not minuted, unless they resulted in some form of proposal being put forward. However, the voluminous *Diarii* of Marino Sanuto, extending over the first third of the sixteenth century, frequently provide information about senatorial debates: e.g. the debate on the Jews in 1519–20, extensively described above at pp. 488–98. I have examined all registers in the series *Senato, Terra,* from the mid-1530's (the point at which Sanuto's *Diarii* ends) to 1620, referring from them to the files where appropriate for further information. Before the mid-1530's, I have referred occasionally to the records of the Senate in order to supplement information contained in Sanuto. Sanuto's accounts of the resolutions of the Senate, when checked against the original, have proved to be accurate. The subject-matter of *Senato, Terra,* is extremely varied, and it is the chief achival source used here for matters relating to hospitals and Monti di Pietà in Venice and on the mainland, and for the agreements concluded between the Venetian government and the Jews. However, some agreements of the early sixteenth century are preserved either in the series *Senato, Deliberazioni (Secreta),* or in the archives of the Council of Ten. Parallel to *Senato, Terra* is the series *Senato, Mar,* similarly organized in registers and files, to which I have referred chiefly in matters concerning the recruitment of galley crews for the reserve fleet, to which the Scuole Grandi contributed. Where *Senato, Terra,* deals with the internal affairs of Venice and the mainland, and with matters concerning the land forces of the Republic, *Senato, Mar,* records deliberations affecting the maritime provinces and colonies, Venetian interests in the Levant, and the Venetian navy.

(b) *The Council of Ten*

The series *Consiglio dei Dieci, Parti Miste,* in registers and files, continues to the end of 1524, and I have occasionally referred to this collection. In search of information about the Scuole of Venice, I have consulted all the

643

Registri Comuni of the Council of Ten between the years 1530 and 1625, referring where appropriate to the files which (as in the Senate's archive) supplement the registers. The Jewish Capitoli of 1513, 1528, 1533 and 1537 are preserved in the records of the Ten—as are the constitutions of the proposed Monte di Pietà, suppressed in 1524.

On one occasion I have referred to the separate Notatorio recording the decisions of the Heads or Capi of the Council of Ten, who were chosen in rotation from among its ordinary members. They dealt, among much else, with the licensing of books.

(c) *The Maggior Consiglio*
I have examined the comparatively small collection of registers recording the deliberations of the Great Council between the mid-1530's and 1620.

(d) *The Collegio*
There are a few references to the Notatorio on which the deliberations of the Collegio were commemorated.

II. *Information supplied to the Senate by Venetian governors and by representatives abroad*

The reports of Rettori, of Capitani and Podestà in the chief cities of the Venetian mainland, which usually include information about their charitable institutions, are assembled in the series *Collegio. V (Secreta), Relazioni*, where for the most part they are arranged according to the city concerned, in chronological order. Two very elaborate surveys of the provinces of Bergamo (in 1596) and Brescia (in 1610), both compiled by the Capitano Giovanni Da Lezze, are preserved as *buste* 63–4 of the series *Sindici Inquisitori in Terraferma*.

There are occasional references to the correspondence of ambassadors in Rome in the 1540's (*Archivio Proprio Roma, fascicolo* 6) and in Germany in the 1590's—*Senato (Secreta), Dispacci Germania, filze* 17–18; also to the reports made by the commission of Sindici Inquisitori in Terra Ferma in 1620–1 (*Senato, Provveditori da terra e da mar, filza* 270).

III. *Archives of Venetian magistracies*

(a) *Inquisitori et Revisori sopra le Scuole Grandi*
This magistracy was established as a sub-commission of the Council of Ten in 1622, and was responsible for the good administration of the Scuole Grandi. Its Capitulary, which defines its competence, probably constitutes the fullest collection of legislation on the Scuole, though it needs to be supplemented by the collection in the *Compilazione delle Leggi* (see below) and by the records of the Scuole themselves.

(b) *Collegio alla Milizia da Mar*

The Collegio alla Milizia da Mar was responsible for naval recruiting and for raising galley crews to man the reserve fleet. Like the series *Senato, Mar*, the archives of this magistracy contain copies of the budgets submitted by the Scuole Grandi in a spirit of protest against the excessive fiscal burdens laid upon them. I have examined:

Milizia da Mar, fascicolo 706: *Conti et altro delle Scole Grandi debitrici per conto tansa da galliotti*, marked 1594, though the papers in it, not always dated, evidently belong to the first quarter of the seventeenth century.

fascicolo 707: *Carattade diverse de galeotti fatte in diversi tempi per l'armar delle cinquanta galere. In essecution delle deliberationi dell'Eccellentissimo Senato 1595 et 1602*

fascicolo 723: *Suppliche dell'Arti e per liberta de traghetti della Dominante e fuori, ricordi, denoncie, deposizioni per le Scole Grandi per l'imposizioni de galeoti e notte de morti che possedevano liberta dall'anno 1604 sino 1621*

fascicolo 755: *Processi per galeotti 1540–1719*

(c) *Dieci Savii sopra le Decime in Rialto*

The Dieci Savii formed a fiscal board responsible for the assessment of the tithe or Decima levied by the Venetian state on income from real property, and were also charged with ensuring that any such property bequeathed to religious institutions or to the clergy was sold after the statutory period had elapsed. Its Capitularies provide a compact source for mortmain legislation. From the assessments of the Decima for 1581, contained in this archive, it has proved possible to discover the extent of the real property owned by the Scuole in that year.

(d) *Provveditori alla Sanità*

This magistracy, which became a permanent foundation in 1486, was charged with the care of public health in general, with the restraint of vagrancy, with the enforcement of the poor law, and with the control of prostitution. The Capitolari are the registers defining the powers of the magistracy, recording both legislation of the Senate and important decisions of the magistrates themselves which involved questions of principle and might establish precedents. The Notatorii record the day-to-day decisions of the magistrates and much of their judicial activity. Most useful for the purposes of this book are Notatori II–VI, vols. 726–30 in the archive of the magistracy, covering the years 1522–63. The later Notatori are far less informative than their predecessors, and are chiefly concerned with minutiae relating to the appointment of minor officials.

(e) *Provveditori sopra gli Ospedali e Luoghi Pii*

The volume in this archive, *Atti e Terminazioni 1561–1575, busta* 17/21, records the efforts of this board to reform abuses in certain of the smaller hospitals of Venice.

2T

(f) *Ufficiali al Cattaver*

Volumes 242–6 and vol. 258 in the archives of this magistracy register the decisions of the Ufficiali on various routine matters relating to everyday life in the Ghetto between 1564 and 1618, and chiefly to the affairs of the German–Jewish community residing mainly in the Ghetto Nuovo.

(g) *Santo Uffizio*

The inquiries of the Inquisition in Venice into the beliefs of Alessandro Caravia are recorded in A.S.V., *Santo Uffizio, busta* 13.

IV. *Venetian Legislation*

The *Compilazione delle Leggi*, compiled during the eighteenth century, is a collection of official copies of decrees issued by the Councils and magistracies, arranged according to subject-matter. *Busta* 309 contains state legislation on the poor, and *busta* 344 legislation on the Scuole.

V. *Archives of Hospitals and Scuole*

Ospedali e Luoghi Pii, busta 910, contains various papers relating to the hospital of Santi Giovanni e Paolo, in the middle and late sixteenth and in the early seventeenth century.

The *Scuole Grandi*: the forms of useful material which these archives preserve may be classified roughly as follows:

(a) The Mariegole. These documents consist of the foundation statutes of the Scuola with later additions, or of a list of brothers who swore to observe them, or of both these things. I have examined:

A.S.V., *Scuola Grande di Santa Maria della Carità*, vols. 233, 233 *bis.*, 234, 236. *Scuola Grande di S. Giovanni Evangelista*, vol. 7 and vol. 3 (Latin and Italian statutes of the fourteenth century); vols. 5 and 6 (lists of Guardians and of brothers of the fourteenth and fifteenth centuries, with a note on the origins of the Scuola). Other Mariegole covering the late fourteenth and fifteenth centuries are preserved in the Sala Diplomatica Regina Margherita, LXXVI–22.

A.S.V., *Scuola Grande di Santa Maria della Valverde o della Misericordia*, vol. 2: the statutes—beginning in 1261—of a Scuola dedicated to the Virgin Mary and to St Francis, which may have been the immediate ancestor of the Scuola Grande di Santa Maria della Misericordia, founded in 1308. For the fourteenth-century statutes of the Scuola Grande della Misericordia, see Sala Diplomatica Regina Margherita, LXXVI–3 and LXXVI–11.

A.S.V., *Scuola Grande di S. Marco*, vols. 4 and 6: these volumes contain lists of brothers only. I have not discovered the original statutes, but some idea of them can be gained from vol. 8, a *Summario generale di tutte le leggi, constitutioni e terminationi della veneranda Scola di San Marco*, compiled in 1681 by Giacomo Angeli, a former Guardian Grande.

The Mariegola of the Scuola Grande di San Rocco remains in the possession of the present Archconfraternity of San Rocco, on the premises of the Scuola itself. I am indebted to the Cancelliere, Dr Alessandro Mazzucato, for permission to examine this and other papers in the archive.

(b) Minute books recording the decisions of the Banca and Zonta, and of the Chapter-General of the Scuola. These are known as Libri delle Parti or Registri delle Terminazioni in the archives of the Scuola di San Rocco, and as Notatorii in those of San Marco, San Giovanni Evangelista and Santa Maria della Carità. They form the backbone of each archive. I have examined:

A.S.V., *Scuola Grande di San Marco*, vols. 18–21.

A.S.V., *Scuola Grande di San Rocco, seconda consegna*, vols. 44–7.

A.S.R., *Registri delle Terminazioni*, vols. 2–4 (vol. 1 is merely a copy of original material contained in the Archivio di Stato).

A.S.V., *Scuola Grande di San Rocco, seconda consegna*, vol. 48, *Notatorio* no. 1 (1596–1720), includes scraps of information about the finances of the Scuola and its efforts to furnish the state with galley crews at the turn of the sixteenth and in the early seventeenth century.

A.S.V., *Scuola Grande di San Rocco, seconda consegna*, vol. 7, *Catalogo delle leggi pubbliche e parti di Scola*, contains notes of some resolutions of the 1480's which do not appear either on the Mariegola or on the earliest minute book (*seconda consegna*, vol. 44).

(c) Copies of wills which named the Scuola as trustees or beneficiaries, or both. The whole text of the will was almost invariably copied for the Scuola's use. In Part I of this book, I have analysed wills contained in:

The *Libro de Testamenti*, in A.S.V., *Scuola Grande di San Rocco, prima consegna, busta* 438.

The *Catastichi dei Testamenti, ibid., buste* 64–9.

(d) The financial records of the Scuola di San Rocco, especially the records of the administration of trusts, from which I have worked extensively. They contain much valuable incidental information about wages and the movement of rent.

Records belonging to the Scuola itself and to the minor trusts it administered include:

A.S.V., *Scuola Grande di San Rocco, seconda consegna*, vol. 387 (*Libro di Dare ed Avere*): a copy of the original accounts of the Scuola, which do not appear to survive, made in the late seventeenth or early eighteenth century.

Ibid., seconda consegna, vol. 705, *Compendio delle spese che furono fatte dalla Veneranda Scola di San Rocco per conto dell'impositione de galeotti dell'anno 1587 18 ottobre*.

The two receipt books running from 1487–1564 and from 1564–1623, *ibid., seconda consegna, busta* 423.

Records belonging to the major trusts administered by the Scuola include:

The *giornali*, or daybooks, of the trust founded by Maffeo Donà (*prima consegna*, vols. 606–9), together with a *Sommario di tutte le dispositioni e spese fatte dalla Veneranda Scola di S. Rocco per conto della Commissaria del quondam N.H. Maffio Dona fu de Bernardo (1527–1743)*, ibid., *prima consegna*, vol. 22; and a *Quaderno affittuali Commissaria Donà, 1557–1582*, ibid., *seconda consegna*, vol. 21.

The *giornali* of the trust founded by Nicolò Moro, *ibid., prima consegna*, vols. 545–7, with a *Bilancio della Commissaria Moro, ibid., seconda consegna, pacco* X, *fascicolo* 650/III.

The *giornali* of the Zucca trust, *ibid., prima consegna*, vols. 586–90, with vol. 657, a *Registro della Commissaria Zucca: Bilancio 1557–1742.*

The *giornali* of the Dalla Vecchia trust, *ibid., prima consegna*, vols. 570–572.

The trust founded by Costantin de Todero Marcora has left two registers covering the periods 1564–91 and 1591–1617, *ibid., seconda consegna, pacco* 716.

NOTE ON OTHER MANUSCRIPT SOURCES

Other Manuscript Sources

(a) *In the library of the Museo Civico Correr, Venice*
Gradenigo MSS. no. 194: Miscellaneous information about the Scuole, including lists of Guardiani Grandi.
Cicogna MSS., *busta* 3063, *fascicolo* 10: nineteenth-century lists of the Guardiani Grandi of the Scuole di San Giovanni Evangelista and of the Misericordia, with the occupations of some of them.
Cicogna MSS., no. 859: *Mariegola della Scuola di San Teodoro*: surviving fragments of a list of officers and of their occupations, for the years 1547 and 1550–62.
MSS. P.D. (Provenienze Diverse) c. 951, *fascicolo* 45: *Informatione per la supplica della Scola di S. Marco per diminuir l'imposizione per i galeotti* (c. 1590).
Ibid., *fascicolo* 60: *Riscossioni fattesi nel corso di molti anni della capa depositi de'galeotti* (1636).
MSS. P.D., *busta* 506 c., *fascicolo* 16: *Scuole di devozione e di beneficenza*, containing, at ff. 1–5, a list of religious associations existing in Venice in 1732.
Cicogna MSS. no. 1547: *Monumenti della peste di Venezia del 1575, raccolti da Cornelio Morello.*
Cicogna MSS. no. 2583: 'Variorum ad Venetam ecclesiam atque ipsius Veneti cleri spectantia', vol. II.
Cicogna MSS. no. 2853: *Cronaca Agostini*, vol. II (1462–1570).
Cicogna MSS. *busta* 2987/2988, *fascicolo* 19, *Ospitali e Case date da abitare per carita* (a list of charitable institutions in the city of Venice in the middle and late sixteenth century).
Cicogna MSS., *busta* 2999, *fascicolo* 22: text of an oration by Baldassare Bonifaccio, *La Nova Accademia de'Nobili Veneti* (1635).
Cicogna MSS., *busta* 3118, *fascicolo* 6: *Constitutioni et ordini della Compagnia della Carita del Croceffisso per li carcerati di Venetia.*
Cicogna MSS. no. 3690: *Notizie istoriche della Pia Casa di Santa Maria del Soccorso*, a collection of documents compiled in 1761 by Angelo Malipiero, a governor of the Casa del Soccorso.

(b) *In the Biblioteca Nazionale Marciana, Venice*
MSS. Italiani, Classe VII.
no. 153 (8812): *Compendio di me Francesco da Molin de Missier Marco delle cose, che reputero degne di venerne particolar memoria, et che*

sucederanno in mio tempo si della Republica Venetiana e di Venetia mia Patria come anco della special mia persona.
no. 134 (8035): *Cronaca Agustini over Savina.*
no. 1818 (9436): Gian Carlo Sivos, *Delle vite dei Dosi di Venetia, Libro Terzo.*
no. 122 (8863): Gian Carlo Sivos, *Libro quarto delli Dosi di Venetia.*
no. 90 (8029), ff. 218–21: Zuanne Foscarini, *Notta di Gentil'huomini li quali hanno preso per moglie cittadine, o altre persone inferiori dall'anno 1600 fino il giorno presente come in essa appar.*

(c) *In the British Museum*
Additional MSS. 5471: *Relatione universa delle cose di Venetia fatta da Don Alonso della Cueva ambasadore di Spagna hoggi Cardinale.*

(d) *In the Public Record Office, London*
S.P. 99/3: some official correspondence of Sir Henry Wotton, English Ambassador to the Venetian Republic, at the time of the Interdict of 1606–1607.

ABBREVIATIONS

A.S.R.   Archivio Privato della Scuola Grande di San Rocco, Venice

A.S.V.   Archivio di Stato, Venice

B.M.V.   Biblioteca Nazionale Marciana, Venice

B.R. Bullarium Romanum: i.e. *Bullarium diplomatum et privilegiorum sanctorum Romanorum pontificum Taurinensis editio locupletior facta* (24 vols., Aosta, 1857–72)

C.S.P.V. *Calendar of state papers and manuscripts relating to English affairs, existing in the archives and collections of Venice, and in other libraries of Northern Italy,* ed. Rawdon Brown and others (London, 1864 onwards)

D.M.S. *I Diarii di Marino Sanuto,* ed. Rinaldo Fulin and others (58 vols., Venice, 1879–1903)

H.C. *Hierarchia Catholica medii et recentioris aevi,* ed. Conrad Eubel and others (Munich and elsewhere, 1913 onwards)

Mansi, *Concilia.* J. D. Mansi, *Sacrorum Conciliorum nova et amplissima collectio* (56 vols., Florence and elsewhere, 1759 onwards)

M.C.V. Biblioteca del Museo Civico Correr, Venice

M.G.H., Ss. *Monumenta Germaniae Historica, Scriptores*

M.H.S.J. *Monumenta Historica Societatis Jesu*

Muratori, R.I.S. L. A. Muratori, *Rerum Italicarum Scriptores* (original edition, 25 vols., Milan, 1723–51; modern edition, Città di Castello and elsewhere, 1900 onwards)

P.R.O. Public Record Office, London

BIBLIOGRAPHY

Abaco, Domenico dall'. *Stato di Padova e suo territorio nel 1552–53*, ed. E. A. Cicogna (Venice, 1850).

Acta Ecclesiae Mediolanensis (Milan, 1583).

Alberi, Eugenio, ed. *Relazioni degli ambasciatori veneti al Senato*, series II, volume v (Florence, 1858); series III, volume i (Florence, 1840).

Alberigo, Giuseppe. 'Studi e problemi relativi all'applicazione del Concilio di Trento in Italia (1945–58)', *Rivista Storica Italiana*, LXX (1958).

Alberigo, Giuseppe. *I vescovi italiani al Concilio di Trento (1545–7)* (Florence, 1959).

Alberigo, Giuseppe. 'Contributi alla storia delle confraternite dei Disciplinati e della spiritualità laicale nei secoli XV e XVI', in the volume *Movimento dei Disciplinati*, cited below.

Alpago-Novello, Luigi. 'La vita e le opere di Luigi Lollino, vescovo di Belluno (1596–1625)', *Archivio Veneto*, 5th series, XIV–XV (1933–4).

Annales Foroiulienses, ed. W. Arndt, in M.G.H., Ss., XIX, ed. G. H. Pertz (Hanover, 1866).

Annales Placentini Gibellini, ed. G. H. Pertz, *ibid.*

Annales Sanctae Iustinae Patavinae, ed. Philippe Jaffé, *ibid.*

Ardu, Emilio. 'Frater Raynerius Faxanus de Perusio', in the volume *Movimento dei Disciplinati*, cited below.

Aretino, Pietro. *Il secondo libro delle lettere*, ed. Fausto Nicolini (Bari, 1916).

Arnold, Denis. 'Music at the Scuola di San Rocco', *Music and Letters*, XL (1959).

Arnold, Denis. 'Music at a Venetian confraternity in the Renaissance', *Acta Musicologica*, XXXVII.

Arnold, Denis. 'Instruments and instrumental teaching in the early Italian conservatoires', *The Galpin Society Journal*, XVII.

Arnold, Denis. 'Orphans and ladies: the Venetian conservatoires (1680–1790)', *Proceedings of the Royal Musical Association*, 59th session (1962–1963).

Ashley, W. J. *An introduction to English economic history and theory*, II (London, 1893).

Aspetti e cause della decadenza economica veneziana nel secolo XVII: Atti del Convegno 27 giugno—2 luglio 1957, Venezia, Isola di San Giorgio Maggiore (Venice–Rome, 1961).

Aymard, Maurice. *Venise, Raguse et le commerce du blé pendant la seconde moitié du XVIe siècle* (Paris, 1966).

Bacon, Francis. Essay, 'Of Riches'.

Bailo, Luigi. *L'istituzione del Monte di Pietà in Treviso, 1496* (Treviso, 1885).

Ballerini, Pietro. *De jure divino et naturali circa usuram* (2 vols., Bologna, 1747).

Barbieri, Gino. *Il Beato Bernardino da Feltre nella storia sociale del Rinascimento* (Milan, 1962).

Barbour, Violet. *Capitalism in Amsterdam in the seventeenth century* (Baltimore, Maryland, 1950).

Bardi, Girolamo. *Delle cose notabili della città di Venetia* (Venice, 1606).

Barkan, O. L. 'Essai sur les données statistiques des registres de recensement dans l'Empire Ottoman aux XVe et XVIe siècles', *Journal of the Economic and Social History of the Orient*, I (1958).

Baron, Hans. 'Religion and politics in the German imperial cities during the Reformation', *English Historical Review*, LII (1937).

Baron, S. W. 'The Jewish factor in medieval civilization', *Proceedings of the American Academy for Jewish Research*, XII (1942).

Baron, S. W. *The Jewish community: its history and structure to the American Revolution* (3 vols., Philadelphia, 1948).

Baron, S. W. *A social and religious history of the Jews* (8 vols. and Index, New York, 1952–60).

Bascapè, G. C. 'L'assistenza e la beneficenza a Milano dall'alto medioevo alla fine della dinastia sforzesca', in Fondazione G. Treccani degli Alfieri, *Storia di Milano*, VIII (Milan, 1957).

Becker, M. B. 'Church and state in Florence on the eve of the Renaissance (1343–82)', *Speculum*, XXXVII (1962).

Beloch, K. J. 'La popolazione di Venezia nei secoli XVI e XVII', *Nuovo Archivio Veneto, nuova serie*, III (1902).

Beloch, K. J. *Bevölkerungsgeschichte Italiens*, I (Berlin–Leipzig, 1937).

Belotti, Bortolo. *Storia di Bergamo e dei Bergamaschi* (3 vols., Milan, 1940).

Beltrami, Daniele. *Storia della popolazione di Venezia dalla fine del secolo XVI alla caduta della Repubblica* (Padua, 1954).

Beltrami, Daniele. *Saggio di storia dell'agricultura nella Repubblica di Venezia durante l'età moderna* (Venice–Rome, 1955).

Beltrami, Daniele. 'Un ricordo del Priuli intorno al problema dell'ammortamento dei depositi in Zecca del 1574', in *Studi in onore di Armando Sapori* (2 vols., Milan, 1957).

Beltrami, Daniele. *La penetrazione economica dei Veneziani in Terraferma: forze di lavoro e proprietà fondiarie nelle campagne venete dei secoli XVII e XVIII* (Venice–Rome, 1961).

Bembo, Pierluigi. *Delle istituzioni di beneficenza nella città e provincia di Venezia* (Venice, 1859).

Bembo, Pietro. *Historiae Venetae*, in *Istorici delle cose veneziane*, II (Venice, 1718).

Beneyto, Juan. *Fortuna de Venecia: historia de una fama política* (Madrid, 1947).

Bennett, R. F. *The early Dominicans* (Cambridge, 1937).

Ben-Zvi, Itzhak. 'Eretz Yisrael under Ottoman rule, 1517–1917', in Louis Finkelstein, ed. *The Jews: their history, culture and religion* (2 vols., London, 1961).

Besta, Enrico. *Il Senato Veneziano* (Venice, 1899).

Besta, Fabio. *Bilanci generali della Repubblica di Venezia* (Milan, 1912).

Biéler, André. *La pensée économique et sociale de Calvin* (Geneva, 1959).

Bloom, H. I. *The economic activities of the Jews of Amsterdam* (Williamsport, Pennsylvania, 1937).

Blumenkranz, Bernard. 'Les juifs dans le commerce maritime de Venise, 1592–1609', *Revue des études juives, série iii*, vol. II (1961).

Boccalini, Traiano. *Ragguagli di Parnaso, con la Pietra del Paragone Politico*, ed. G. Rua and Luigi Firpo (3 vols., Bari, 1910, 1912, 1948).

Bodin, Jean. *Six books of the Commonwealth*, ed. M. J. Tooley (Oxford, 1955).

Boehmer, Heinrich. *Ignatius von Loyola*, ed. Hans Leube (Stuttgart, 1941).

Bonenfant, Paul. 'Les origines et le caractère de la réforme de la bienfaisance publique aux Pays-Bas sous le règne de Charles-Quint', *Revue belge de philologie et d'histoire*, V–VI (1926–7).

Borgherini-Scarabellin, Maria. *La vita privata a Padova nel secolo XVII* (Venice, 1917).

Botero, Giovanni. *Relatione della Republica Venetiana* (Venice, 1605).

Botero, Giovanni. *The greatness of cities*, reprint of the English translation by Robert Peterson, 1606 (London, 1956).

Braudel, Fernand, with Romano, Ruggiero. *Navires et marchandises à l'entrée du Port de Livourne (1547–1611)* (Paris, 1951).

Braudel, Fernand. 'La vita economica di Venezia nel secolo XVI', *La civiltà veneziana del Rinascimento* (Florence, 1958).

Braudel, Fernand, with Jeannin, Pierre, Meuvret, Jean, and Romano, Ruggiero. 'Le déclin de Venise au XVIIème siècle', in the volume *Aspetti e cause*, cited above.

Braudel, Fernand. *La Méditerranée et le monde méditerranéen à l'époque de Philippe II* (2nd, enlarged, edition, 2 vols., Paris, 1966).

Bremner, R. H. 'Modern attitudes towards charity and relief', *Comparative studies in society and history*, I (1958–9).

Brown, Horatio F. *The Venetian printing press* (London, 1891).

Brucker, G. A. *Florentine politics and society, 1343–78* (Princeton, 1962).

Brulez, Wilfrid. 'La navigation flamande vers la Méditerranée à la fin du XVIe siècle', *Revue belge de philologie et d'histoire*, XXXVI (1958).

Brulez, Wilfrid. *Marchands flamands à Venise, I (1568–1605)* (Brussels, 1965).

Brunetti, Mario. 'Un critico della Scuola di San Rocco nel '500', in the volume *Scuola Grande di S. Rocco, Venezia, nel VIo centenario dalla morte del patrone* (Venice, 1927).

Brunetti, Mario. 'Il diario di Leonardo Donà, Procuratore di San Marco de Citra (1591–1605)', *Archivio Veneto*, 5th series, XXI (1937).

Brunetti, Mario. 'Tre ambasciate annonarie veneziane', *Archivio Veneto*, 5th series, LVIII (1956).

Buoninsegni, Thomaso. *Trattato de'traffichi giusti et ordinarii*, Italian translation by Vitale Zuccoli (Venice, 1588).

Canale, Cristoforo. *Della milizia marittima libri quattro*, ed. Mario Nani Mocenigo (Venice, 1930).

Canalis, A., and Sepolcri, P. 'Prescrizioni mediche ufficiali e altri provvedimenti di governo in Venezia nella peste del 1575–6', *Annali della Sanità Pubblica*, XIX (1958).

Capitolare del Maggior Consiglio (Venice, 1740).

Capitoli della veneranda congregazione dell'hospitale di Santo Lazaro et Mendicanti della Città di Venetia (Venice, 1619).

Capitoli et ordini per il buon governo della Pia Casa del Soccorso di Venetia (Venice, 1701).

Capitoli et ordini per il buon governo del Pio Hospitale de Poveri Derelitti appresso SS. Giovanni e Paolo (Venice, 1704).

Capitoli et ordini per il buon governo della Congregatione del Monasterio di Santa Maria Maddalena delle Convertite della Giudecca (Venice, 1719).

Cappelletti, Giuseppe. *I Gesuiti e la Repubblica di Venezia* (Venice, 1873).

Caravia, Alessandro. *Il Sogno dil Caravia* (Venice, 1541).

Caravia, Alessandro. *Calate fantastiche che canta Naspo Bizaro da Veniesia, Castelan, sotto i balconi de Cate Bionda Biriota, per cavarse la bizaria del cervello e'l martelo del cuor* (Venice, 1565).

Cardano, Girolamo. *De methodo medendi*, revised edition in his *Opera Omnia*, VII (Lyons, 1663).

Cardano, Girolamo. *The book of my life* (*De vita propria liber*), transl. J. Stoner (London, 1931).

Carpentier, Elisabeth. *Une ville devant la peste: Orvieto et la peste noire de 1348* (Paris, 1962).

Carpi, Daniele. 'Alcune notizie sugli ebrei a Vicenza (secoli XIV–XVIII)', *Archivio Veneto*, 5th series, LXVIII (1961).

Cassuto, Umberto. *Gli ebrei a Firenze nell'età del Rinascimento* (Florence, 1918).

Cattaneo, Enrico. 'Influenze veronesi nella legislazione di San Carlo Borromeo', in *Problemi di vita religiosa in Italia nel Cinquecento: Atti del Convegno di Storia della Chiesa in Italia* (Padua, 1960).

Cavriolo, Elia. *Dell'istorie della città di Brescia libri XIV* (Venice, 1744).

Cecchetti, Bartolomeo. *La Repubblica di Venezia e la Corte di Roma nei rapporti della religione* (2 vols., Venice, 1874).

Cessi, Roberto, ed. *Deliberazioni del Maggior Consiglio di Venezia*, II (Bologna, 1931).

Chill, Emmanuel. 'Religion and mendicity in seventeenth-century France', *International Review of Social History*, VII (1962).

Chinazzo, Daniele di. *Cronica de la guerra da Veniciani a Zenovesi*, ed. Vittorio Lazzarini (Venice, 1958).

Chronicon Marchiae Tarvisinae et Lombardiae, ed. L. A. Botteghi in Muratori, R.I.S., VIII/ii (Città di Castello, 1916).

Ciardini, Marino. *I banchieri ebrei in Firenze nel secolo XV e il Monte di Pietà fondato da Girolamo Savonarola* (Borgo San Lorenzo, 1907).

Cicogna, E. A. *Inscrizioni veneziane* (6 vols., Venice, 1824–53).

Cipolla, C. M. 'Une crise ignorée: comment s'est perdue la propriété ecclésiastique dans l'Italie du Nord entre le XIe et le XVIe siècle', *Annales: Économies, Sociétés, Civilisations*, II (1947).

Cipolla, C. M. 'The economic decline of Italy', English translation of revised version in Pullan, ed. *Crisis and change*, cited below.

Ciscato, Antonio. *Gli ebrei in Padova (1300–1800)* (Padua, 1901).

Cistellini, Antonio. 'La "Confraternita della Carità" di Salò (1542)', *Rivista di Storia della Chiesa in Italia*, I (1947).

Cistellini, Antonio. *Figure della riforma pretridentina* (Brescia, 1948).

Clay, R. M. *The hospitals of mediaeval England* (London, 1909).

Clough, C. H. Review of Ventura, *Nobiltà e popolo*, cited below, in *Studi Veneziani*, VIII (1966).

Cognasso, Francesco. 'Istituzioni comunali e signorili di Milano sotto i Visconti', in G. Treccani degli Alfieri, *Storia di Milano*, VI (Milan, 1955).

Cohn, Norman. *The pursuit of the Millennium* (London, 1957).

Coniglio, Giuseppe. Article 'Monte di Pietà' in *Enciclopedia Cattolica*, VIII.

Coniglio, Giuseppe. *Il Viceregno di Napoli nel secolo XVII* (Rome, 1955).

Constitutioni et regole della Casa delle Citelle di Venetia eretta e fondata sotto il titolo della Presentatione della Madonna (Venice, 1701).

Contarini, Gasparo. *De magistratibus et republica Venetorum libri quinque* (Basel, 1547).

Contarini, Gasparo. *The Commonwealth and Government of Venice*, transl. Lewes Lewkenor (London, 1599).

Contarini, Gasparo. *De officio episcopi*, in his *Opera* (Paris, 1571).

Contarini, Nicolò. *Historie Venetiane*, extracts published in Cozzi, *Il Doge Nicolò Contarini*, cited below.

Contento, Aldo. 'Il censimento della popolazione sotto la Repubblica Veneta', *Nuovo Archivio Veneto*, XIX–XX (1900).

Cornet, Enrico. *Paolo V e la Republica Veneta: giornale dal 22 ottobre 1605—9 giugno 1607* (Vienna, 1859).

Corte, Girolamo Dalla. *Istorie della città di Verona* (3 vols., Venice, 1744).

Corti, Ugo. 'La francazione del debito pubblico della Repubblica di Venezia proposta da Gian Francesco Priuli', *Nuovo Archivio Veneto*, VII (1894).

Coryat, Thomas. *Coryat's Crudities* (reprint of the edition of 1611, 2 vols., Glasgow, 1905).

Coyecque, Ernest. 'L'assistance publique à Paris au milieu du XVIe siècle', *Bulletin de la Société de l'Histoire de Paris et de l'île de France*, XV (1888).

Cozzi, Gaetano. *Il Doge Nicolò Contarini: ricerche sul patriziato veneziano agli inizi del Seicento* (Venice–Rome, 1958).

Cozzi, Gaetano. 'Paolo Sarpi tra il cattolico Philippe Canaye de Fresnes e il calvinista Isaac Casaubon', *Bollettino dell'Istituto di Storia della Società e dello Stato Veneziano*, I (1959).

Cozzi, Gaetano. 'Una vicenda della Venezia barocca: Marco Trevisan e la sua "eroica amicizia" ', *ibid.*, II (1960).

Cozzi, Gaetano. 'Federico Contarini: un antiquario veneziano tra Rinascimento e Controriforma', *ibid.*, III (1961).

Cracco, Giorgio. *Società e stato nel Medioevo Veneziano (secoli XII–XIV)* (Florence, 1967).

Crawfurd, Raymond. 'Contribution from the history of medicine to the problem of the transmission of typhus', *Proceedings of the Royal Society of Medicine*, VI: *Section of the History of Medicine* (1913).

Creighton, Charles. *A history of epidemics in Britain* (new edition, with additional material by D. E. C. Eversley, E. Ashworth Underhill and Lynda Ovenall, 2 vols., London, 1965).

Cristiani, L. *L'Église à l'époque du Concile de Trente* (Paris, 1948).

Davide M . . . da Portogruaro, *Storia dei Cappuccini Veneti* (2 vols., Venice–Mestre, 1941–57).

Davies, C. S. L. 'Slavery and Protector Somerset: the Vagrancy Act of 1547', *Economic History Review*, XIX (1966).

Davis, J. C. *The decline of the Venetian nobility as a ruling class* (Baltimore, Maryland, 1962).

Davis, N. Z. 'Poor relief, humanism and heresy—the case of Lyon', *Studies in Medieval and Renaissance History*, V (1968).

Davis, Ralph. 'Influences de l'Angleterre sur le déclin de Venise au XVIIe siècle', *Aspetti e cause*, cited above.

Davis, Ralph. 'England and the Mediterranean, 1570–1670', in *Essays in the economic and social history of Tudor England in honour of R. H. Tawney*, ed. F. J. Fisher (Cambridge, 1961).

Delumeau, Jean. 'Les dettes à Rome au XVIe siècle', *Revue d'histoire moderne et contemporaine*, IV (1957).

Delumeau, Jean. *Vie économique et sociale de Rome dans la seconde moitié du XVIe siècle* (2 vols., Paris, 1957–9).

Depping, G. B. *Les juifs dans le Moyen Âge: essai historique sur leur état civil, commercial et littéraire* (Paris, 1834).

Dittrich, Franz. *Gasparo Contarini, 1483–1542* (Braunsberg, 1885).

Documenti per la storia della beneficenza in Venezia (Venice, 1879).

Donazzolo, Pietro, and Saibante, Mario. 'Lo sviluppo demografico di Verona e della sua provincia dalla fine del secolo XV ai giorni nostri', *Metron*, VI (1926).

Doucet, Roger. *Les institutions de la France au XVIe siècle*, II (Paris, 1948).

Dunbar, C. F. 'The Bank of Venice', *Quarterly Journal of Economics*, VI (1892).

Ehses, Stephanus, ed. *Concilii Tridentini Acta*, Parts II, V and VI (Freiburg-im-Breisgau, 1911, 1919, 1924).

Elliott, J. H. 'The decline of Spain', *Past and Present*, no. 20 (November, 1961).

Elliott, J. H. *Imperial Spain, 1469–1716* (London, 1963).

Elton, G. R. 'An early Tudor poor law', *Economic History Review*, VI (1953–4).

Elton, G. R. Review of Jordan, *Philanthropy in England*, cited below, in *The Historical Journal*, III (1960).

Emminghaus, Albert. *Poor relief in different parts of Europe* (London, 1873).

Enno van Gelder, H. A. *The two Reformations in the sixteenth century: a study of the religious aspects and consequences of Renaissance and Humanism* (The Hague, 1964).

Erasmus, Desiderius. *Enchiridion militis Christiani*, reprint of English translation (London, 1905).

Erasmus, Desiderius. *Opus Epistolarum*, ed. P. S. and H. M. Allen (12 vols., Oxford, 1906–58).

Fantozzi, Antonio. 'Documenta Perusina de S. Bernardino Senensi', *Archivum Franciscanum Historicum*, XV (1922).

Favre, Pierre. *Fabri Monumenta*, ed. in M.H.S.J. (Madrid, 1914).

Felloni, Giuseppe. 'Per la storia della popolazione di Genova nei secoli XVI e XVII', *Archivio Storico Italiano*, CX (1952).

Ferrari, Ciro. *L'Ufficio della Sanità in Padova nella prima metà del secolo XVII* (Venice, 1910).

Ferrari, Giannino. 'La legislazione veneziana sui beni comunali', *Nuovo Archivio Veneto, nuova serie*, XXXVI (1918).

Ferro, Marco. *Dizionario del diritto comune e veneto*, 2nd edition (Venice, 1845).

Fink, Z. S. 'Venice and English political thought in the seventeenth century', *Modern Philology*, XXXVIII (1940–1).

Fink, Z. S. *The classical republicans: an essay in the recovery of a pattern of thought in seventeenth-century England* (Evanston, Illinois, 1945).

Fiumi, Enrico. *Storia economica e sociale di San Gimignano* (Florence, 1961).

Fortis, D. 'Gli ebrei di Verona: cenni storici', *L'Educatore Israelita*, XI–XII (1863–4).

Fosseyeux, Marcel. 'La taxe des pauvres au XVIe siècle', *Revue d'histoire de l'Église de France*, XX (1934).

Fracastoro, Girolamo. *De contagione et contagiosis morbis et eorum curatione* (Lyons, 1550).

Francastel, Galienne. 'Une peinture anti-hérétique à Venise?', *Annales: Économies, Sociétés, Civilisations*, XX (1965).

Franco, Veronica. *Lettere: dall'unica edizione del MDLXXX*, ed. Benedetto Croce (Naples, 1949).

Friedberg, Emil, ed. *Corpus Iuris Canonici*, Part II, *Decretalium Collectiones* (Leipzig, 1881).

Gaeta, Franco. 'Alcune considerazioni sul mito di Venezia', *Bibliothèque d'humanisme et Renaissance: travaux et documents*, XXIII (1961).

Gallicciolli, G. B. *Storie e memorie venete profane ed ecclesiastiche* (8 vols., Venice, 1795).

Gallo, Rodolfo. 'Una famiglia patrizia: i Pisani ed i palazzi di Santo Stefano e di Stra', *Archivio Veneto*, 5th series, XXXIV–XXXV (1944).

Gallo, Rodolfo. 'La Scuola Grande di San Teodoro di Venezia', *Atti dell'Istituto Veneto di Scienze, Lettere ed Arti*, CXX (Classe di scienze morali e lettere), 1961–2.

Garrani, Giuseppe. *Il carattere bancario e l'evoluzione strutturale dei primigenii Monti di Pietà: riflessi della tecnica bancaria antica su quella moderna* (Milan, 1957).

Gascon, René. 'Un siècle du commerce des épices à Lyon: fin XVe–fin XVIe siècles', *Annales: Économies, Sociétés, Civilisations*, XV (1960).

Génicot, Léopold. 'Crisis: from the Middle Ages to modern times', *Cambridge Economic History of Europe*, II: *The agrarian life of the Middle Ages*, second edition, ed. M. M. Postan (Cambridge, 1966).

Geremek, Bronislaw. 'La popolazione marginale tra il Medioevo e l'èra moderna', *Studi Storici*, IX (1968).

Ghinato, Alberto. 'Un propagatore dei Monti di Pietà del '400: Padre Fortunato Coppoli da Perugia, O.F.M.', *Rivista di Storia della Chiesa in Italia*, X (1956).

Ghinato, Alberto. 'Ebrei e predicatori francescani in Verona nel secolo XV', *Archivum Franciscanum Historicum*, L (1957).

Giannotti, Donato. *Libro de la Republica de Vinitiani* (Rome, 1542).

Gianturco, Elio. 'Bodin's conception of the Venetian constitution and his critical rift with Fabio Albergati', *Revue de littérature comparée*, XVIII (1938).

Giberti, Gian Matteo. *Opera* (Ostiglia, 1740), ed. Pietro Ballerini.

Gilbert, Felix. 'Florentine political assumptions in the period of Savonarola and Soderini', *Journal of the Warburg and Courtauld Institutes*, XX (1957).

Gilbert, Felix. 'The date of the composition of Contarini's and Giannotti's books on Venice', *Studies in the Renaissance*, XIV (1967).

Gilbert, Felix. 'The Venetian constitution in Florentine political thought', in *Florentine studies: politics and society in Renaissance Florence*, ed. Nicolai Rubinstein (London, 1968).

Graf, Arturo. 'Una cortigiana fra mille: Veronica Franco', in his *Attraverso il Cinquecento* (Turin, 1888).

Guiraud, Jean. *Histoire de l'Inquisition au Moyen Âge* (2 vols., Paris, 1938).

Hale, J. R. *England and the Italian Renaissance* (London, 1963).

Helleiner, K. F. 'The population of Europe from the Black Death to the eve of the vital revolution', *Cambridge Economic History of Europe*, IV: *The economy of expanding Europe in the sixteenth and seventeenth centuries*, ed. E. E. Rich and C. H. Wilson (Cambridge, 1967).

Herlihy, David. *Medieval and Renaissance Pistoia: the social history of an Italian town, 1200–1430* (New Haven–London, 1967).

Hill, Sir George. *A history of Cyprus*, III (Cambridge, 1948).

Hirst, L. F. *The conquest of plague: a study of the evolution of epidemiology* (Oxford, 1953).

Hník, F. M. *The philanthropic motive in Christianity*, transl. M. and R. Weatherall (Oxford, 1938).

Holzapfel, Heribert. *Die Anfänge der Montes Pietatis (1462–1515)* (Munich, 1903).

Hyde, J. K. *Padua in the age of Dante* (Manchester, 1966).

Imbert, Jean. *Les hôpitaux en droit canonique (du décret de Gratien à la sécularisation de l'administration de l'Hôtel-Dieu de Paris en 1505)* (Paris, 1947).

Imbert, Jean. 'Les prescriptions hospitalières du Concile de Trent et leur diffusion en France', *Revue d'histoire de l'Église de France*, XLII (1956).

Ive, Antonio. 'Banques juives et Monts-de-Piété en Istrie: les *Capitoli* des juifs de Pirane', *Revue des Études Juives*, II (1881).

James, F. G. 'Charity endowments as sources of local credit in seventeenth- and eighteenth-century England', *Journal of Economic History*, VIII (1948).

Jarrett, Bede. Article 'Third Orders', *Catholic Encyclopedia*, XIV (New York, 1912).

Jedin, Hubert. *A history of the Council of Trent*, transl. Ernest Graf, I (Edinburgh, 1957).

Jedin, Hubert. 'Zwei Konzilsdekrete über die Hospitaeler', *Atti del Primo Congresso Italiano di Storia Ospitaliera* (Reggio Emilia, 1957).

Jiménez Salas, Maria. *Historia de la asistencia social en España en la Edad Moderna* (Madrid, 1958).

Johnston Abraham, J. 'The early history of syphilis', *The British Journal of Surgery*, XXXII (1944–5).

Jones, P. J. 'Medieval agrarian society in its prime: Italy', *Cambridge Economic History of Europe*, II: *The agrarian life of the Middle Ages*, second edition, ed. M. M. Postan (Cambridge, 1966).

Jordan, Édouard. *Les origines de la domination angevine en Italie* (Paris, 1909).

Jordan, W. K. *Philanthropy in England, 1480–1660* (London, 1959).

Kamen, Henry. *The Spanish Inquisition* (London, 1965).

Kaufmann, David. 'Contribution à l'histoire des juifs de Corfu', *Revue des études juives*, XXXII–XXXIII (1896).

Kellenbenz, Hermann. 'Autour de 1600: le commerce du poivre des Fugger et le marché international du poivre', *Annales: Économies, Sociétés, Civilisations*, XI (1956).

Kellenbenz, Hermann, 'Le déclin de Venise et les relations économiques de Venise avec les marchés au nord des Alpes', in *Aspetti e cause*, cited above.

Kiriaki, A. S. De. *La beneficenza elemosiniera a Venezia nel passato e nei nostri tempi* (Venice, 1897).

Kiriaki, A. S. De, and others. *La beneficenza veneziana* (Venice, 1900).

Kisch, Guido. *The Jews in medieval Germany: a study of their legal and social status* (Chicago, 1949).

Klassen, P. J. *The economics of Anabaptism, 1525–60* (The Hague, 1964).

Koenigsberger, H. G. *The government of Sicily under Philip II of Spain* (London, 1951).

Lainez, Diego. *Lainii Monumenta*, ed. in M.H.S.J. (8 vols., Madrid, 1912–1917).

Lane, F. C. *Venetian ships and shipbuilders of the Renaissance* (Baltimore, Maryland, 1934).

Lane, F. C. 'The rope factory and hemp trade in the fifteenth and sixteenth centuries', in *Venice and history: the collected papers of Frederic C. Lane* (Baltimore, Maryland, 1966).

Lane, F. C. 'Venetian shipping during the commercial revolution', *ibid.*

Lane, F. C. 'Venetian bankers, 1496–1533', *ibid.*

Lane, F. C. 'The Mediterranean spice trade: its revival in the sixteenth century', *ibid.*

Lane, F. C. 'The funded debt of the Venetian Republic, 1262–1482', *ibid.*

Lane, F. C. 'The merchant marine of the Venetian Republic', *ibid.*

Lane, F. C. 'Investment and usury in medieval Venice', *ibid.*

Lane, F. C. 'Medieval political ideas and the Venetian constitution', *ibid.*

Lapeyre, Henri. 'Banque et crédit en Italie du XVIème au XVIIIème siècle', *Revue d'histoire moderne et contemporaine*, VIII (1961).

La Piana, George. 'The Church and the Jews', *Historia Judaica*, XI (1949).

Lattes, M. 'Documents et notices sur l'histoire politique et littéraire des juifs en Italie', *Revue des Études Juives*, V (1882).

Lazzarini, Vittorio. 'Le offerte per la guerra di Chioggia e un falsario del Quattrocento', *Nuovo Archivio Veneto, nuova serie,* IV (1902).

Lazzarini, Vittorio. 'Beni carraresi e proprietari veneziani', *Studi in onore di Gino Luzzatto*, I (Milan, 1949).

Lea, H. C. *A history of the Inquisition of the Middle Ages* (3 vols., New York, 1888).

Lecce, Michele. 'Le condizioni zootecnico-agricole del territorio veronese nella prima metà del '500', *Economia e Storia*, V (1958).

Lecce, Michele. 'I beni terrieri di un antico istituto ospitaliero veronese (secoli XII–XVIII)', *Studi in onore di Amintore Fanfani*, III (Milan, 1962).

Leff, Gordon. *Heresy in the later Middle Ages: the relation of heterodoxy to dissent, c. 1250–c. 1450* (2 vols., Manchester, 1967).

661

Leggi e memorie venete sulla prostituzione (Venice. For Lord Orford. 1870–1872).

Leonard, E. M. *The early history of English poor relief* (Cambridge, 1900).

Lewkenor, Lewes. *Divers observations upon the Venetian Commonwealth*, appended to his translation of Contarini, *Commonwealth*, cited above.

Liebeschütz, H. 'The crusading movement and Jewry', *Journal of Jewish Studies*, X (1959).

Loevinson, E. 'La concession de banques de prêts aux juifs par les papes des seizième et dix-septième siècles: contribution à l'histoire des finances d'Italie', *Revue des études juives*, XCII–XCV (1932–3).

Logan, O. M. T. *Studies in the religious life of Venice in the sixteenth and early seventeenth centuries: the Venetian clergy and religious orders, 1520–1630*, Ph.D. thesis, University of Cambridge, 1967.

Lombardini, Gabriele. *Pane e denaro a Bassano: prezzi del grano e politica dell'approvigionamento dei cereali tra il 1501 e il 1799* (Venice, 1963).

Loyola, Ignatius. *Monumenta Ignatiana*, ed. in M.H.S.J. (4 series, Madrid, 1903–   ).

Luther, Martin. *Reformation writings of Martin Luther*, ed. B. L. Woolf (2 vols., London, 1954–6).

Luzzatto, Gino. 'Les banques publiques de Venise—siècles XVIe–XVIIIe', in J. G. van Dillen, ed. *History of the principal public banks* (The Hague, 1934).

Luzzatto, Gino. 'Le vicende del Porto di Venezia dal primo Medio Evo allo scoppio della guerra 1914–18', in his *Studi di storia economica veneziana* (Padua, 1954).

Luzzatto, Gino. 'Tasso d'interesse e usura a Venezia nei secoli XIII–XV', in *Miscellanea in onore di Roberto Cessi*, I (Rome, 1958).

Luzzatto, Gino. *Storia economica di Venezia dall' XI al XVI secolo* (Venice, 1961).

Luzzatto, Simone. *Discorso circa il stato de gl'Hebrei, et in particolar dimoranti nell'inclita citta di Venetia* (Venice, 1638).

MacArthur, W. P. 'Old-time typhus in Britain', *Transactions of the Royal Society of Tropical Medicine and Hygiene*, XX (1926–7).

Macchi, Mauro. *Istoria del Consiglio dei Dieci* (2 vols., Turin, 1848–9).

McLaughlin, T. P. 'The teaching of the canonists on usury (XII, XIII and XIV centuries)', *Mediaeval Studies*, I–II (1939–40).

Magalhães-Godinho, Vetorino, 'Le repli vénitien et la route du Cap, 1496–1533', *Éventail de l'histoire vivante: hommage à Lucien Febvre*, II (Paris, 1953).

Magnocavallo, A. 'Proposto di riforma bancaria del banchiere veneziano Angelo Sanudo (secolo XVI)', *Atti del Congresso Internazionale di Scienze Storiche*, IX (Rome, 1904).

Majarelli, Stanislao, and Nicolini, Ugolino. *Il Monte dei Poveri di Perugia: periodo delle origini (1462–74)* (Perugia, 1962).

Major, R. H. *Classic descriptions of disease with biographical sketches of their authors* (London, 1945).

Mâle, Emile. *L'art religieux de la fin du XVIe siècle, du XVIIe siècle et du XVIIIe siècle* (Paris, 1951).

Malipiero, Domenico. *Annali veneti dall'anno 1457 al 1500*, ed. Agostino Sagredo in *Archivio Storico Italiano*, VII (1843–4).

Manselli, Raoul. 'L'anno 1260 fu anno gioachimitico?' in the volume *Movimento dei Disciplinati*, cited below.

Mantese, Giovanni. 'Nota d'archivio sull'attuazione dei decreti tridentini a Vicenza', *Rivista della Storia della Chiesa in Italia*, XIV (1960).

Mantese, Giovanni. *Memorie storiche della Chiesa Vicentina*, III/2 (Vicenza, 1964).

Martini, Angelo. 'Tentativi di riforma a Padova prima del Concilio di Trento', *Rivista della Storia della Chiesa in Italia*, III (1949).

Martini, Angelo. 'Di chi fu ospite S. Ignazio a Venezia?', *Archivum Historicum Societatis Iesu*, XVIII (1949).

Mary Monica. *Angela Merici and her teaching idea (1474–1540)* (New York, 1927).

Mathews, Shailer. 'The Protestant churches and charity', in Ellsworth Faris and others, *Intelligent philanthropy* (Chicago, 1930).

Mattei, Pietro. *Cenni storici sui banchi di pegno e i Monti di Pietà: il Monte di Pietà a Padova* (Padua, 1953).

Maulde La Clavière, René de. *Saint Cajetan*, transl. C. H. Ely (London, 1902).

Mazzatinti, G. 'La lezenda de Fra Rainero Faxano', *Bollettino della Società Umbra di Storia Patria*, II (1896).

Medina, Juan. *De la orden que en algunos pueblos de Espana se ha puesto en la limosna: para rimedio de los verdaderos pobres* (Salamanca, 1545).

Meersseman, G. G. 'Disciplinati e penitenti nel Duecento', in the volume *Movimento dei Disciplinati*, cited below.

Milano, Attilio. 'Considerazioni sulla lotta dei Monti di Pietà contro il prestito ebraico', *Scritti in memoria di Sally Mayer: saggi sull'ebraismo italiano* (Jerusalem, 1956).

Milano, Attilio. *Storia degli ebrei in Italia* (Turin, 1963).

Mirkovich, N. 'Ragusa and the Portuguese spice trade', *Slavonic and East European Review*, XXI (1943).

Mohler, Ludwig. *Kardinal Bessarion als Theologe, Humanist und Staatsmann*, III (Paderborn, 1942).

Molmenti, P. G. *La storia di Venezia nella vita privata dalle origini alla caduta della Repubblica*, II (Bergamo, 1925).

Monti, G. M. *Le confraternite medievali dell'alta e media Italia* (2 vols., Venice, 1927).

Monticolo, Giovanni. *I Capitolari delle Arti veneziane sottoposte alla Giustizia e poi alla Giustizia Vecchia dalle origini al MCCCXXX*, II (Rome, 1905).

663

Monumenta Historica Societatis Iesu: Epistolae Mixtae (5 vols., Madrid, 1898–1901).

Monumenta Historica Societatis Iesu: Fontes Narrativi de S. Ignatio de Loyola et de Societatis Iesu initiis (Rome, 1943–   ).

Monumenta Historica Societatis Iesu: Litterae Quadrimestres (vols. I–V, Madrid, 1894–1925; vol. VII, Rome, 1932).

Mooney, Canice. 'The writings of Father Luke Wadding, O.F.M.', *Franciscan Studies*, XVIII (1958).

Moorman, John. *A history of the Franciscan Order from its origins to the year 1517* (Oxford, 1968).

Morey, J. 'Les juifs en Franche-Comté au XIVe siècle', *Revue des études juives*, VII (1883).

Morghen, Raffaello. 'Ranieri Fasani e il movimento dei Disciplinati del 1260', in the volume *Movimento dei Disciplinati*, cited below.

Morigia, Paolo. *Historia delle antichità di Milano* (Venice, 1592).

Moro, Jacopo. *Il Monte di Pietà di Padova, 1469–1923* (Padua, 1923).

Morosini, Andrea. *Historiae Venetae*, in *Istorici delle cose veneziane*, VI (Venice, 1719).

Moryson, Fynes. *Shakespeare's Europe*, ed. Charles Hughes (London, 1903).

Moryson, Fynes. *Itinerary* (4 vols., Glasgow, 1907—reprint of the original edition of 1617).

Mosto, Andrea Da. *L'Archivio di Stato di Venezia* (2 vols., Rome, 1937–1940).

Movimento dei Disciplinati nel settimo centenario dal suo inizio (Perugia—1260), Appendice 9 to *Bollettino della Deputazione di Storia Patria per l'Umbria* (Spoleto, 1962).

Nani Mocenigo, Mario. *Storia della marina veneziana da Lepanto alla caduta della Repubblica* (Rome, 1935).

Nasalli-Rocca, Emilio. 'Gli ospedali italiani di San Lazzaro o dei lebbrosi', *Zeitschrift der Savigny-Stiftung für Rechtsgeschichte, kanonische Abteilung*, XXVII (1938).

Nelson, B. N. 'The usurer and the merchant prince: Italian businessmen and the ecclesiastical law of restitution, 1100–1550', *Journal of Economic History*, VII (1947), Supplement VII.

Nelson, B. N. *The idea of usury: from tribal brotherhood to universal otherhood* (Princeton, 1949).

Nicoletti, Giuseppe. *Illustrazione della Chiesa e Scuola di S. Rocco in Venezia* (Venice, 1885).

Nitti, F. S. 'Poor relief in Italy', *The Economic Review*, II (1892).

Nolf, J. *La réforme de la bienfaisance à Ypres au XVIe siècle* (Ghent, 1915).

Noonan, J. T., Jr. *The scholastic analysis of usury* (Cambridge, Massachusetts, 1957).

Odoricus Raynaldus. *Annales ecclesiastici ab anno MCXCVIII*, IX, ed. J. D Mansi (Lucca, 1752).

Ordini et Capitoli della Compagnia dell'Oratorio il quale è nell'Hospitale de gli Incurabili in Venetia, circa il governo delle Schole de Putti che sono in detta Città: nelle quali s'insegna la dottrina christiana a' figlioli il giorno della Festa doppo il disnare. Raccolti dal Reverendo Padre Don Giovan Paolo da Como, Preposito delli Reverendi Padri Clerici Regolari di San Nicola (Venice, 1568).

Origo, Iris. *The world of San Bernardino* (London, 1964).

Paleotti, Gabriele. *Acta Concilii Tridentini annis 1562 et 1563 originalia,* ed. in Sebastian Merkle, *Concilii Tridentini Diaria,* III/1 (Freiburg-im-Breisgau, 1931).

Pane, Luigi Dal. 'La politica annonaria di Venezia', *Giornale degli economisti e annali di economia, nuova serie,* V (1946).

Papadopoli-Aldobrandini, Nicolò. *Le monete di Venezia descritte ed illustrate,* II (Venice, 1907).

Parkes, James. *The Jew in the medieval community: a study of his political and economic situation* (London, 1938).

Parsons, Anscar. 'Bernardine of Feltre and the *Montes Pietatis*', *Franciscan Studies,* new series, I (1941).

Parsons, Anscar. 'The economic significance of the *Montes Pietatis*', *Franciscan Studies,* new series, I (1941).

Partner, Peter. 'Florence and the Papacy, 1300–75', in *Europe in the later Middle Ages,* ed. John Hale, Roger Highfield and Beryl Smalley (London, 1965).

Paschini, Pio. *San Gaetano Thiene, Gian Pietro Carafa, e le origini dei Chierici Regolari Teatini* (Rome, 1926).

Paschini, Pio. 'Le Compagnie del Divino Amore e la beneficenza pubblica nei primi decenni del Cinquecento', in his *Tre ricerche sulla storia della Chiesa nel Cinquecento* (Rome, 1945).

Paschini, Pio. *Venezia e l'Inquisizione Romana da Giulio III a Pio IV* (Padua, 1959).

Pasero, Carlo, ed. *Relazioni di rettori veneti a Brescia durante il secolo XVI* (Toscolano, 1939).

Pasero, Carlo. 'Dati statistici e notizie intorno al movimento della popolazione bresciana durante il dominio veneto (1426–1797)', *Archivio Storico Lombardo,* 9th series, vols. I–II, *anno* 88 (1963).

Pastor, Ludwig von. *The history of the Popes from the close of the Middle Ages,* ed. and transl. F. I. Antrobus, Ralph Kerr, Ernest Graf and E. F. Peeler (40 vols., London, 1891–1953).

Pecchioli, Renzo. 'Il "mito" di Venezia e la crisi fiorentina intorno al 1500', *Studi Storici,* III (1962).

Pilot, Antonio. 'Del protestantesimo a Venezia e delle poesie religiose di Celio Magno', *L'Ateneo Veneto, anno* XXIII, vol. I (1909).

Pino-Branca, A. 'Il comune di Padova sotto la Dominante nel secolo XV (rapporti amministrativi e finanziari)', *Atti del Reale Istituto Veneto di*

Scienze, Lettere ed Arti, XCIII (1933–4), XCVI (1936–7), XCVII (1937–1938).

Pirri, Pietro. *L'Interdetto di Venezia del 1606 e i Gesuiti* (Rome, 1959).

Polanco, J. A. De. *Vita Ignatii Loiolae et rerum Societatis Jesu historia* (6 vols., Madrid, 1894–8).

Polanco, J. A. De. *Polanci complementa*, ed. in M.H.S.J. (2 vols., Madrid, 1916–17).

Poliakov, Léon. 'La communauté juive à Rome aux XVIe et XVIIe siècles', *Annales: Économies, Sociétés, Civilisations*, XII (1957).

Poliakov, Léon. *Histoire de l'antisémitisme*, II (Paris, 1961).

Poliakov, Léon. *Les banquiers juifs et le Saint-Siège du XIIIe au XVIIe siècle* (Paris, 1967).

Pommier, Édouard. 'La société vénitienne et la Réforme protestante au XVIe siècle', *Bollettino dell'Istituto di Storia della Società e dello Stato Veneziano*, I (1959).

Porgès, N. 'Élie Capsali et sa chronique de Venise', *Revue des études juives*, LXXVII–LXXIX (1923–4).

Porto, Luigi Da. *Lettere storiche dall'anno 1509 al 1528*, ed. Bartolomeo Bressan (Florence, 1857).

Premoli, O. M. *Storia dei Barnabiti nel Cinquecento* (Rome, 1913).

Priuli, Girolamo. *I Diarii*, vol. I, ed. Arturo Segre (Città di Castello, 1912), vol. IV, ed. Roberto Cessi (Bologna, 1938).

Pullan, Brian. 'Poverty, charity and the reason of state: some Venetian examples', *Bollettino dell'Istituto di Storia della Società e dello Stato Veneziano*, II (1960).

Pullan, Brian. 'The famine in Venice and the new poor law, 1527–9', *ibid.*, V–VI (1963–4).

Pullan, Brian. 'Wage-earners and the Venetian economy, 1550–1630', *Economic History Review*, XVI (1964).

Pullan, Brian. 'Service to the Venetian state: aspects of myth and reality in the early seventeenth century', *Studi Secenteschi*, V (1964).

Pullan, Brian, ed. *Crisis and change in the Venetian economy* (London, 1968).

Querini, Antonio. *Relatio rationum Serenissimae Reipublicae Venetae, difficultatibus Pauli V Pontificis oppositarum*, in Melchior Goldast, *Monarchia Romani Imperii, sive de jurisdictione imperiali*, III (Frankfurt, 1668).

Rabinowitz, L. *The social life of the Jews of northern France in the XII–XIV centuries as reflected in the rabbinical literature of the period* (London, 1938).

Ranke, Leopold von. *The history of the Popes during the last four centuries*, transl. Foster, revised by G. R. Dennis (3 vols., London, 1908).

Raulich, Italo. 'Una relazione del Marchese di Bedmar sui Veneziani', *Nuovo Archivio Veneto*, XVI (1898).

Renaudet, Auguste. *Érasme en Italie* (Geneva, 1954).

Révah, I. S. 'Les Marranes', *Revue des études juives*, 3rd series, vol. I (1959).

Révah, I. S. 'Pour l'histoire des Marranes à Anvers', *Revue des études juives*, 4th series, vol. II (1963).

Richards, R. D. *The early history of banking in England* (London, 1929).

Rodenwaldt, Ernst. *Pest in Venedig, 1575–1577. Ein Beitrag zur Frage der Infektkette bei den Pestepidemien West-Europas* (*Sitzungsberichte der Heidelberger Akademie der Wissenschaften, Mathematisch-naturwissenschaftliche Klasse*, Heidelberg, 1953).

Rodolico, Niccolò. *I Ciompi: una pagina di storia del proletariato operaio* (Florence, 1945).

Rodriguez, Simon. *De origine et progressu Societatis Iesu*, in M.H.S.J., *Epistolae patrum Paschasii Broeti, Claudii Jaji, Joannis Codurii et Simonis Rodericii* (Madrid, 1903).

Romanin, Samuele. *Storia documentata di Venezia* (reprint, 10 vols., Venice, 1912–21).

Romano, Ruggiero. 'La marine marchande vénitienne au XVIe siècle', in *Les sources de l'histoire maritime en Europe, du Moyen Age au XVIIIe siècle: Actes du Quatrième Colloque International d'Histoire Maritime*, ed. Michel Mollat (Paris, 1962).

Romano, Ruggiero. 'Economic aspects of the construction of warships in Venice in the sixteenth century', English version in Pullan, ed. *Crisis and change*, cited above.

Roncalli, A. G., and Forno, Pietro. *Gli atti della visita apostolica di San Carlo Borromeo a Bergamo, 1575* (2 vols. in 5, Florence, 1936–57).

Roover, Florence Edler De. 'Restitution in Renaissance Florence', *Studi in onore di Armando Sapori*, II (Milan, 1957).

Roscher, Wilhelm. 'The status of the Jews in the Middle Ages considered from the standpoint of commercial policy', *Historia Judaica*, VI (1944).

Rossi, Vittorio. 'Un anneddoto della storia della Riforma a Venezia', in *Scritti varii di erudizione e di critica in onore di Rodolfo Renier* (Turin, 1912).

Roth, Cecil. *The last Florentine Republic, 1527–1530* (London, 1925).

Roth, Cecil. *The history of the Jews of Venice* (Philadelphia, 1930).

Roth, Cecil. 'Les Marranes à Venise', *Revue des études juives*, LXXXIX (1930).

Roth, Cecil. *A history of the Marranos* (Philadelphia, 1932).

Roth, Cecil. 'Immanuel Aboab's proselytization of the Marranos', *Jewish Quarterly Review*, new series, XXXII (1932–3).

Roth, Cecil. *The ritual murder libel and the Jew: the report by Cardinal Lorenzo Ganganelli (Pope Clement XIV)* (London, 1934).

Roth, Cecil. 'The mediaeval conception of the Jew: a new interpretation', in *Essays and studies in memory of Linda R. Miller* (New York, 1938).

Roth, Cecil. *History of the Jews of Italy* (Philadelphia, 1946).

Roth, Cecil. *The House of Nasi: Doña Gracia* (Philadelphia, 1947).

667

Roth, Cecil. *The House of Nasi: the Duke of Naxos* (Philadelphia, 1948).

Roth, Cecil. 'La ricondotta degli ebrei ponentini, Venezia, 1647', *Studi in onore di Gino Luzzatto*, II (Milan, 1950).

Rowntree, B. Seebohm. *Poverty: a study of town life* (new edition, London, 1922).

Rubinstein, Nicolai. 'I primi anni del Consiglio Maggiore di Firenze', *Archivio Storico Italiano*, CXII (1954).

Rubinstein, Nicolai. 'Politics and constitution in Florence at the end of the fifteenth century', in *Italian Renaissance Studies: a tribute to the late Cecilia M. Ady*, ed. E. F. Jacob (London, 1960).

Ryan, J. A. Article 'Charity', *The Catholic Encyclopedia*, III (New York, 1908).

Sacchini, Francesco, *Historiae Societatis Iesu*, Part II (Antwerp, 1620).

Salimbene de Adam, *Chronica*, ed. Oswald Holder-Egger in M.G.H., Ss., XXXII (Hanover–Leipzig, 1905–13).

Salter, F. R. *Some early tracts on poor relief* (London, 1926).

Salter, F. R. 'The Jews in fifteenth-century Florence and Savonarola's establishment of a *Mons Pietatis*', *Cambridge Historical Journal*, V (1936).

Sansovino, Francesco, and Martinioni, Giustiniano. *Venetia, città nobilissima et singolare* (Venice, 1663).

Sanuto, Marino. *Vita de' Duchi di Venezia*, in Muratori, R.I.S., XXII (Milan, 1733).

Sanuto, Marino. *I Diarii*, ed. Rinaldo Fulin and others, 58 vols. (Venice, 1879–1903).

Sapori, Armando. 'La beneficenza delle compagnie mercantili del Trecento', in his *Studi di storia economica medievale* (2nd edition, Florence, 1946).

Sapori, Armando. 'L'interesse del denaro a Firenze nel Trecento (dal testamento di un usuraio)', *ibid.*

Sapori, Armando. 'I precedenti della previdenza sociale nel medioevo', *ibid.*

Sardella, Pierre. 'L'épanouissement industriel de Venise au XVIe siècle', *Annales; Économies, Sociétés, Civilisations*, II (1947).

Sardella, Pierre. *Nouvelles et spéculations à Venise au début du XVIe siècle* (Paris, 1948).

Sarpi, Paolo. *Discorso della origine, forma, leggi ed uso dell'Ufficio della Inquisizione nella città e dominio di Venezia*, in his *Opera* (Helmstat, 1761–8), vol. IV.

Sarpi, Paolo. *Istoria dell'Interdetto (e altri scritti editi e inediti)*, ed. M. D. Busnelli and Giulio Gambarin (3 vols., Bari, 1940).

Schapiro, J. S. *Social reform and the Reformation* (New York, 1909).

Schiavi, L. A. 'Gli ebrei in Venezia e nelle sue colonie', *Nuova Antologia*, 3rd series, XLVIII (1893).

Schwarzfuchs, Simon. 'Les marchands juifs dans la Méditerranée orientale au XVIème siècle', *Annales: Économies, Sociétés, Civilisations*, XII (1957).

Sella, Domenico. *Commerci e industrie a Venezia nel secolo XVII* (Venice-Rome, 1961).

Sella, Domenico. 'The rise and fall of the Venetian woollen industry', revised English version in Pullan, ed. *Crisis and change*, cited above.

Sella, Domenico. 'Crisis and transformation in Venetian trade', revised English version in Pullan, ed. *Crisis and change*, cited above.

Seneca, Federico. *Il Doge Leonardo Donà: la sua vita e la sua preparazione politica prima del Dogado* (Padua, 1959).

Sevesi, Paolo. 'Il Beato Michele Carcano di Milano, O.F.M.', *Archivum Franciscanum Historicum*, III–IV (1910–11).

Sevesi, Paolo. 'Beato Michele Carcano, O.F.M. Obs., 1427–1484 (Documenti inediti)', *Archivum Franciscanum Historicum*, XXXIII–XXXIV (1940–1).

Sheedy, A. T. *Bartolus on social conditions in the fourteenth century* (New York, 1942).

Sherley-Price, L. D., ed. *St Francis of Assisi: his life and writings as recorded by his contemporaries* (London, 1959).

Simonsfeld, Henry. *Der Fondaco dei Tedeschi in Venedig und die deutsch-venetianischen Handelsbeziehungen*, 2 vols. (Stuttgart, 1887).

Smith, Logan Pearsall. *The life and letters of Sir Henry Wotton* (2 vols., Oxford, 1907).

Soldo, Cristoforo Da. *Memorie delle guerre contra la Signoria di Venezia dall'anno 1437 fino al 1468*, in Muratori, R.I.S., XXI (Milan, 1732).

Soranzo, Giovanni. 'Rapporti di San Carlo Borromeo con la Repubblica Veneta', *Archivio Veneto*, 5th series, XXVII (1940).

Soto, Domingo. *Deliberacion en la causa de los pobres* (Salamanca, 1545).

Squitinio della liberta veneta, nel quale si adducono anche le ragioni dell'Impero Romano sopra la citta e Signoria di Venetia (Mirandola, 1612).

Stein, Siegfried. 'The development of the Jewish law on interest from the Biblical period to the expulsion of the Jews from England', *Historia Judaica*, XVII (1955).

Stella, Aldo. 'La crise economica veneziana nella seconda metà del secolo XVI', *Archivio Veneto*, 5th series, LVIII–LIX (1956).

Stella, Aldo. 'La proprietà ecclesiastica nella Repubblica di Venezia dal secolo XV al XVII (lineamenti di una ricerca economico-politica)', *Nuova Rivista Storica*, XLII (1958).

Stella, Aldo. 'La regolazione delle pubbliche entrate e la crisi politica veneziana del 1582', *Miscellanea in onore di Roberto Cessi*, II (Rome, 1958).

Strack, H. L. *The Jew and human sacrifice (human blood and Jewish ritual): an historical and social inquiry*, transl. H. Blanchamp (London, 1909).

Strauss, Gerald. 'Protestant dogma and city government: the case of Nuremberg', *Past and Present*, no. 36 (April 1967).

Strauss, Gerald. *Nuremberg in the sixteenth century* (New York, 1966).

Tacchi Venturi, Pietro. 'La prova dell'indifferenza e del servizio negli ospedali nel tirocinio ignaziano', *Archivum Historicum Societatis Jesu*, I (1932).

Tacchi Venturi, Pietro. *Storia della Compagnia di Gesù in Italia* (2 vols. in 4, Rome, 1950–1).

Tadić, Jorjo. 'Le port de Raguse et sa flotte au XVIe siècle', in *Le navire et l'économie maritime du Moyen Âge au XVIIIe siècle, principalement en Méditerranée: Travaux du Deuxième Colloque d'Histoire Maritime*, ed. Michel Mollat (Paris, 1958).

Tadić, Jorjo. 'Le commerce en Dalmatie et à Raguse et la décadence économique de Venise au XVIIème siècle', in the volume *Aspetti e cause*, cited above.

Tartagni, Alessandro, of Imola. *Consilia* (7 vols., Frankfurt-on-Main, 1575).

Tassini, Giuseppe. *Veronica Franco* (Venice, 1888).

Tassini, Giuseppe. *Curiosità veneziane, ovvero Origini delle denominazioni stradali* (new edition, ed. Lino Moretti, Venice, no date).

Tenenti, Alberto. *Naufrages, corsaires et assurances maritime à Venise, 1592–1609* (Paris, 1959).

Tenenti, Alberto. *Cristoforo Da Canal: la marine vénitienne avant Lépante* (Paris, 1962).

Tenenti, Alberto. *Piracy and the decline of Venice, 1580–1615*, transl. Janet and Brian Pullan (London, 1967).

Tentorio, Marco. 'I Somaschi', in Mario Escobar, *Ordini e congregazioni religiosi* (2 vols., Turin, 1951–2), vol. I.

Thiene, Gaetano. *Le lettere di San Gaetano da Thiene*, ed. Francesco Andreu (Vatican City, 1954).

Thomas Aquinas. *Summa Theologica*, in *Opera omnia iussu impensaque Leonis XIII Pontificis Maximi edita*, XI (Rome, 1903).

Thomson, J. A. F. 'Piety and charity in late medieval London', *Journal of Ecclesiastical History*, XVI (1965).

Tierney, Brian. 'The Decretists and the "deserving poor"', *Comparative Studies in Society and History*, I (1958–9).

Tierney, Brian. *Medieval poor law: a sketch of canonical theory and its application in England* (Berkeley–Los Angeles, 1959).

Tortora, Agostino. *Vita Hieronymi Aemiliani*, in *Acta Sanctorum*, February, II (Antwerp, 1658).

Trachtenberg, Joshua. *The Devil and the Jews: the medieval conception of the Jews and its relation to modern antisemitism* (New Haven, Connecticut, 1943).

Troeltsch, Ernst. *The social teaching of the Christian churches*, transl. Olive Wyon (2 vols., London–New York, 1931).

Trugenberger, A. E. *San Bernardino da Siena: considerazioni sullo sviluppo dell'etica economica cristiana nel primo Rinascimento* (Bern, 1951).

Tucci, Ugo. *Lettres d'un marchand vénitien: Andrea Berengo (1553–6)* (Paris, 1957).

Tucci, Ugo. 'Mercanti veneziani in India alla fine del secolo XVI', *Studi in onore di Armando Sapori*, II (Milan, 1957).

Ughelli, Ferdinando. *Italia Sacra* (5 vols., Venice, 1717–22).

Varchi, Benedetto. *Storia fiorentina: nella quale principalmente si contengono l'ultime revoluzioni della Repubblica Fiorentina e lo stabilimento del principato nella Casa de' Medici* (Cologne, 1721).

Ventura, Angelo. *Nobiltà e popolo nella società veneta del '400 e '500* (Bari, 1964).

Villavicencio, Lorenzo de. *De oeconomia sacra circa pauperum curam* (Antwerp, 1564).

Vives, Ludovico. *Il modo del sovvenire a poveri* (Venice, 1545).

Volpe, Gioacchino. *Movimenti religiosi e sette ereticali nella società medievale italiana (secoli XI–XIV)* (Florence, 1961: reprint of the original edition of 1922).

Wadding, Luke. *Annales Minorum, seu trium ordinum a S. Francisco institutorum*, XIV–XV (Rome, 1735–6).

Webb, Beatrice and Sidney. *English poor law history*, Part I: *The old poor law* (new edition, with an introduction by W. A. Robson, London, 1963).

Weber, Max. *The Protestant ethic and the spirit of capitalism*, transl. Talcott Parsons (London–New York, 1930).

Winckelmann, Otto. 'Die Armenordnungen von Nurnburg (1522), Kitzingen (1523), Regensburg (1523) und Ypern (1525)', *Archiv für Reformationsgeschichte*, X (1912–13).

Woolf, S. J. 'Venice and the Terraferma: problems of the change from commercial to landed activities', reprinted in Pullan, ed. *Crisis and change*, cited above.

Zanelli, Agostino. *Delle condizioni interne di Brescia dal 1426 al 1644 e del moto della borghesia contro la nobiltà del 1644* (Brescia, 1898).

Zanelli, Agostino. 'Predicatori a Brescia nel Quattrocento', *Archivio Storico Lombardo*, 3rd series, vol. XV, *anno* XXVIII (1901).

Zanelli, Agostino. 'Pietro del Monte', *Archivio Storico Lombardo*, 4th series, vol. VIII, *anno* XXXIV (1907).

Zech, Francis-Xavier. *Rigor moderatus doctrinae pontificiae circa usuras, Dissertatio II* (Ingolstadt, 1749).

Zenoni, Luigi. *Per la storia della cultura in Venezia dal 1500 al 1797: l'Accademia dei Nobili in Giudecca* (Venice, 1916).

Zini, P. F. *Boni pastoris exemplum*, in Giberti, *Opera*, cited above.

Zinsser, Hans. *Rats, lice and history* (London, 1935).

671

INDEX OF PERSONS

673

2x

INDEX OF SUBJECTS, PLACES AND INSTITUTIONS